A BRIEF HISTORY OF THE WESTERN WORLD

WESTERN WORLD

Sixth Edition

A BRIEF HISTORY OF THE
WESTERN WORLD

Sixth Edition

THOMAS H. GREER

Michigan State University

GAVIN LEWIS

John Jay College,
City University of New York

HARCOURT BRACE JOVANOVICH COLLEGE PUBLISHERS

Fort Worth   Philadelphia   San Diego   New York   Orlando   Austin   San Antonio
Toronto   Montreal   London   Sydney   Tokyo

For Margarette and Nadia

Acquisitions Editor: Drake Bush
Manuscript Editor: Jon Preimesberger
Production Editor: Michael Kleist
Designer: Lori J. Mc Thomas
Art Editor: Avery Hallowell
Production Manager: Mary Kay Yearin

Cover: Canaletto, (detail) *La Riva verso la Zecca* (*The Left Bank of the Zecca* [Venice]), Rome Collection © Art Resource.

Maps by J. P. Tremblay, Robert Yochum, and Maryland Cartographics, Inc.

ISBN: 0-15-505552-6
Library of Congress Catalog Number: 91-71016
Printed in the United States of America

Picture credits on pages A-15–A-16 constitute a continuation of the copyright page.

Those who cannot remember the past are condemned to repeat it.

GEORGE SANTAYANA
1863–1952

Preface
to the Sixth Edition

What is the nature of the Western world? How has it shaped the men and women who are its heirs? Many of today's young people, in search of their own identity, are asking such questions. The search is not new; it traces back to the ancient Greeks. Inscribed on the temple of Apollo at Delphi were the words of the god: *Know yourself.* And one way to self-knowledge is to learn of the past experiences of humans like ourselves. As William Shakespeare observed, *What's past is prologue.*

Our aim in this book is to present a clear, concise account of truly meaningful human experiences — relevant to the society in which we live. Following this aim, we have focused on the outstanding institutions, ideas, and creative works that have formed (and expressed) Western civilization. This book is designed also as a guide and companion for further and deeper explorations of the human past. These can best be accomplished, we believe, by reading original sources and worthy interpretative works. To this end, we have prepared a selection of books for "Recommended Further Reading" that can be found at the back of this book (pp. A-1 through A-15).

Throughout the book we have sought to illuminate the narrative by means of various visual features. These include *maps* of the places and areas under discussion; *time charts* showing the chronological relationships of notable individuals, events, and works of art; and *time lines* showing the sequence and duration of particular historical periods. (The duration of these periods is indicated by the length of the respective line segments; the shaded portion normally corresponds to the period under discussion on the same or nearby pages.) In addition, we have provided an illustration of each work of art described in the book.

Other special aids for the student include the identification of *important historical terms.* These are marked by an asterisk (*) placed before selected entries in the index; the *meaning* of each term is explained on the pages shown for that entry. And throughout the book we have provided numerous *cross-references* to help point out the *interconnections* of ideas and events that occur in various times and places.

A distinguishing feature of this Sixth Edition is the participation by Gavin Lewis, who has joined Thomas H. Greer as coauthor of the work. The general content of the book continues to follow the plan of previous editions. However, we have added information on a number of topics, in response to recent scholarly findings and the developing interests of teachers and students.

These expanded topics are concentrated around three themes of major importance to understanding the course of Western civilization. In dealing with ancient and early medieval times, we have stressed the importance of interaction between civilized and barbarian peoples in the spread of civilization. Increased attention is given to the early development of the barbarian peoples of Europe, the continuous evolution from the later Roman Empire to the barbarian-ruled kingdoms of the West, and the role of the ninth- and tenth-century invasions in the formation of Europe.

In addition, we have enlarged our treatment of *eastern* Europe. New material is presented on the expansion of the Slavs and their relations with Byzantium, the divergent courses of eastern and western Europe in the Middle Ages, and the rise of eastern European multinational monarchies in the early modern period.

We have also enlarged our account of social, economic, and technical developments occurring at key periods in the history of civilization. Thus, technical innovations and the invention of writing in ancient Mesopotamia, agricultural advances and new devices and machinery in the Middle Ages, and the worldwide spread of the Industrial Revolution in the nineteenth and twentieth centuries are all presented more fully.

In the final chapters of this edition we have given close attention to the stupendous happenings of the past few years: the collapse of communism in eastern Europe, the multiple crises in the Soviet Union, the ending of the Cold War, the reunification of Germany, and the continuing upheaval in the Middle East — including the Persian Gulf War.

We hope that our readers will find a measure of excitement, challenge, and pleasure in this book!

THOMAS H. GREER

GAVIN LEWIS

CONTENTS

PART TWO
MEDIEVAL CIVILIZATION

PART THREE
THE COMING OF MODERN TIMES

PART FOUR

THE MODERN WORLD

MAPS

A Brief History of the
Western World
Sixth Edition

1-1 Marcus Aurelius sacrificing, from the Arch of Marcus Aurelius, late second century A.D. Rome.

PART ONE

THE ANCIENT WORLD

	POLITICAL, SOCIAL, AND ECONOMIC DEVELOPMENTS	RELIGION, SCIENCE, AND PHILOSOPHY	HISTORY AND LITERATURE	ART AND ARCHITECTURE
B.C. 3000	Earliest civilization in Mesopotamia and Egypt Beginning of spread of Indo-European peoples	Creation and Flood myths (Sumer) Belief in immortality (Egypt)	Invention of writing Gilgamesh epic poetry	First temples and palaces Early megalithic monuments (Europe) Pyramids of Gizeh (Egypt)
2500	Minoan (Cretan) civilization begins	Beginning of mathematical sciences Foundations of medical science		Ziggurat of Ur (Sumer)
2000	First appearance of Indo-European-influenced tribal groups in Europe Babylonian kingdom Law code of Hammurapi Achaean migrations into Greece	Abraham		Palace of Knossos (Crete) Stonehenge (England)
1500	Mycenaean civilization	Moses and the Hebrew Covenant	Development of alphabet (Phoenicia)	Temple of Karnak (Egypt)
1200	Dorian invasions of Greece Trojan War (legendary) "Dark Ages" of Greece (1200–800)			

1000	Hebrew kingdoms (1000–600)	David Solomon		
800	"Homeric Age" of Greece Greek city-states founded Greek colonization of the Mediterranean and Black seas Rome founded Assyrian empire	Amos First Olympic games honoring Zeus Zoroaster (Persia)	Homer and Greek epics Lyric poetry begins	
600	Solon of Athens "Babylonian Captivity" of the Jews Persian Empire	Thales of Miletus Growth of mystery cults (Greece)	Sappho of Lesbos Greek drama emerges	Greek archaic style of sculpture Palace of Persepolis (Persia)
500	Roman Republic established Twelve Tablets of law (Rome) Persian Wars in Greece: Darius, Xerxes Athenian supremacy and empire Pericles Peloponnesian War Plague of Athens	Parmenides of Elea Heraclitus of Ephesus Hippocrates of Cos Protagoras and Sophists Aristippus of Cyrene Socrates	Aeschylus Herodotus Sophocles Aristophanes Euripides Thucydides	Classical style: Phidias Parthenon Erechtheum (Porch of Maidens) Myron
400	Philip of Macedon Alexander the Great	Plato Aristotle		Praxiteles
300	Hellenistic kingdoms Urbanization	Epicurus, Zeno (Stoicism) Cyrenaic school (hedonists)		Hellenistic style

	POLITICAL, SOCIAL, AND ECONOMIC DEVELOPMENTS	RELIGION, SCIENCE, AND PHILOSOPHY	HISTORY AND LITERATURE	ART AND ARCHITECTURE
250 B.C.	Punic wars (Rome against Carthage)			
200	Reforms of the Gracchi in Rome		Plautus Terence Polybius	
100	Civil wars in Italy			
	Rome completes conquest of the Mediterranean world Julius Caesar's conquest of Gaul Overthrow of the Roman Republic Augustus and the foundations of the Roman Empire Pax Romana (27 B.C.–A.D. 180)	Cicero Lucretius Livy	Vergil Horace Ovid	
A.D.	Tiberius Nero	Birth of Christ Peter and Paul	Plutarch, Suetonius Tacitus Juvenal Seneca	Colosseum Trajan's Forum Pantheon
100	Trajan Hadrian Epidemics in Italy begin	Ptolemy Galen Marcus Aurelius		

	Art and Architecture	Religion	Political and Other Events
200	Pont du Gard Baths of Diocletian	Rivalry of Mithraism and Christianity Last great persecution of the Christians Anthony (hermit monk)	Period of "barracks emperors" Attacks by Germanic tribal confederacies Diocletian: Reconstitution of the empire
300		Toleration decreed for Christians Council of Nicaea Christianity becomes official Roman faith Pagan religions outlawed	Constantine Constantinople founded Theodosius
400		Jerome and Vulgate Augustine Recognition of papacy in the West	Beginning of Germanic takeover of the Western Roman Empire Sack of Rome by Visigoths Sack of Rome by Vandals End of Western Roman Empire
500	Sant' Apollinare basilica	Benedict and his monastic rule	Roman law codified by Eastern emperor Justinian Bubonic plague

CHAPTER
1

The Birth of Civilization in the Middle East

Western civilization is rooted in the past of Greece, Rome, and Europe. By the word "civilization" we mean a *developed* form of human culture* based on city life, written language and law, division of labor, and advanced arts and sciences. The *first* civilization arose in the Middle East nearly three thousand years before the creative age of Greece and Rome. But civilization, whether of East or West, is a very recent turn in the long road of evolution. Human beings roamed the earth for several million years before the coming of civilization, and civilization remains but a thin veneer on a much older cultural foundation.

THE PREHISTORIC ERA

Viewed in relation to more ancient life forms (fish, reptiles, insects) and in relation to the age of the planet, humans are latecomers. Though the age of the earth (about four billion years) is beyond comprehension, the human-to-earth time *relationship* can be grasped through a drastic reduction in the time scale. If we reduce the age of the earth to the period of our familiar twenty-four-hour day, the time that elapsed prior to the appearance of humans is twenty-three hours and fifty-eight minutes. And of the two remaining minutes, representing the time of humans on earth, the period of *civilization* is less than the *last half-second!*

Seen as a recent arrival (with a brief past and an uncertain future), and as one of millions of biological types that have inhabited the earth, the human animal is in a sense an insignificant creature. But in another sense humans have

---

*By "culture" we mean here the sum total of the social habits, beliefs, arts, and institutions of *any* group of people.

already demonstrated a striking importance — certainly uniqueness — by the fact that they are the first earthly beings to have moved beyond the patterns of instinct and repetitive behavior. They are also the first to achieve at least a dim idea of self-identity in relationship to the universe — and to exert a substantial degree of control over their environment.

In all of nature, it appears that only humans possess the means (their brains) to frame and ponder a "philosophical" question such as this one: Why was civilization *so long* in coming on this planet — some billions of years? An answer takes form as we peer back through those thousands of centuries. We see that civilization was neither a *chance* happening nor a happening of "nature"; it was, rather, an extraordinary *creation* by one species. After developing physically and completing a series of successful responses to the environment, human beings were at last able to take the first important steps toward civilization.

A key step was the invention of writing. Because written language led quickly to "historical records," it established a clear dividing line between "historic" and "prehistoric" epochs. Drawing upon nonwritten evidence from geology, paleontology, anthropology, and archeology, we will first look briefly at the long prehistoric period — from the first appearance of human beings to the dawn of civilization.

The Origins and "Ages" of Human Beings

To discover the origins of humans, we must first identify them as a biological type. In the current scientific scheme of classification, their type is designated (in Latin) as *Homo sapiens sapiens*, "thinking thinking human being." *H. s. sapiens* (the abbreviated form) is so called because it is the most advanced and the only surviving subspecies of the species *Homo sapiens*, "thinking human being," and the genus *Homo*. Excavations of fossils (remains of organisms) at a number of locations indicate that *H. s. sapiens* goes back only about thirty thousand years. But archeologists tell us that related subspecies of *Homo sapiens* first appeared about one hundred thousand years ago, and that the first hominids (humanlike creatures) appeared about two million years ago. They differed from *Homo sapiens* chiefly in the size of their skulls, which limits the size of the brain. The brain of today's species is nearly twice as large as that of the earliest species (and four times that of our closest biological relations, the great apes). This larger brain, which accounts for superior intelligence, is the reason why classifiers agreed upon the term *sapiens* (thinking) to distinguish modern *Homo* from preceding species.

Classification and comparison among advanced biological types may be based on criteria other than brain size. One of those criteria is the use of *tools*, a product of intelligence. Though certain other animals (notably, apes) can and do make limited use of simple implements, humans clearly surpass them in

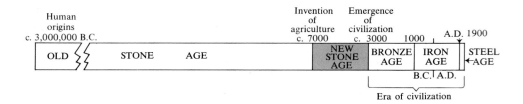

conceiving, fashioning, and employing tools. Since humans are comparatively weak physically, this toolmaking ability proved critical in the struggle for survival against competing, tougher creatures. Small in size (except for their brains), humans have used tools as extensions of their mental and physical being — as ever more powerful levers for subduing competitors and for constructing worlds of the human imagination.

Given the significance of tools as technology — and all that technology has come to mean for human growth and power — it is fitting that the past "ages" of human beings have been identified and classified according to the development of tools. Thus, the earliest (and longest) prehistoric period is called the Old Stone (Paleolithic) Age. This era reaches back to the beginnings of early human types, whose bones have been discovered in various excavations, along with the first chipped stones (tools). A standard method of dating such remains is by investigating the geological stratum (earth layer) in which they are found.

Though humans made improvements during the passing thousands of years, the basic tools remained chipped stone, bone, and ivory — developed in that order. After 10,000 B.C.* humans began to invent tools that were more and more highly specialized and found means of making them stronger and sharper. By 7000 B.C. these advances had gone so far that modern archeologists refer to the next era as the *New* Stone (Neolithic) Age. In parts of the Middle East this era was followed in turn by a Bronze Age (about 3000–1000 B.C.) and an Iron Age (after 1000 B.C.). Each of these periods has been named after the material that was most commonly used for making tools.

Archeological evidence now indicates that the earliest humanlike species originated in East Africa (in Tanzania). A later species, designated *Homo erectus*, appeared about three hundred thousand years ago; variations have been found in Europe and Asia as well as Africa. At some point — exactly where and when is unknown — *Homo erectus* evolved into a new and more advanced human species, *Homo sapiens*. Several different subspecies of *Homo*

---

*The Christian scheme of dating events or periods is based on the number of years *before* or *after* the birth of Jesus Christ. Thus, 10,000 B.C. (*Before* Christ) means 10,000 years *before* his birth. The initials A.D. (from the Latin *Anno Domini*, "in the year of the Lord") mean *after* the year of Christ's birth. The Christian calendar is standard for the Western world, but different systems of counting years prevail in other parts of the globe. Muslim countries, for example, date events from the year of Muhammad's departure (Hegira) from Mecca, A.D. 622 (p. 190). The Jewish time system starts with their year for the Creation (calculated from Biblical sources).

sapiens are known to have existed, one of the most widespread of which was *H. s. neanderthalensis*, first discovered in the Neander Valley of Germany. This type, found at numerous sites in Europe and western Asia, predominated from about 100,000 B.C. until becoming extinct around 30,000 B.C. The reason for its disappearance is unknown, as is the reason for the extinction of all earlier human species. (A possible explanation is malnutrition and diseases caused by parasitic microorganisms.)

Homo sapiens sapiens, the sole surviving form of the human species, made its first known appearance at about the same time as *H. s. neanderthalensis* was dying out, and in the same geographical areas. It seems to have arrived in these areas as an immigrant, perhaps from Africa where so many other types of human being evolved. Its evolutionary origins and precise relationship to *neanderthalensis* remain a mystery, though it is generally agreed that they were both subspecies of *Homo sapiens*. The advantage of the new subspecies over the older one seems to have lain not so much in brain size as in behavior and social organization.

H. s. sapiens inherited the cultural accomplishments of preceding species. This type knew how to use fire, a skill that had appeared many centuries earlier. It also became increasingly sophisticated in making and using tools; it was this ability, no doubt, that permitted *H. s. sapiens* to survive, in the face of a hostile environment, after all other human species had succumbed. Like the types that came before, these humans lived for thousands of years as migratory (wandering) hunters, fishers, and gatherers of edible plants, wholly dependent for food and shelter on whatever the land and water offered. For purposes of hunting and protection, they usually combined into small groups of perhaps twenty to thirty. (The "pack," rather than the single family, was probably the basic social unit of most early hunter societies.) These groups fashioned shelters where they could — caves or crude huts, with room for storing their tools and provisions.

Most important, perhaps, is that *H. s. sapiens* possessed the capacity for *language*. We have no way of determining precisely when and how this unique means of communication came into use. But it proved extremely helpful to humans in hunting, fighting, and other cooperative enterprises. Language also aided in the creation of abstract ideas — such as the concepts of guardian spirits, magic, and life after death (religion). Along with these creations came the development of forms of aesthetic expression (art) as shown in prehistoric cave paintings (*Fig. 1-2*).

From its original homeland, *H. s. sapiens* spread gradually outward. Its appearance in Europe and western Asia about 30,000 B.C. was probably part of this outward movement. By 25,000 B.C., following earlier human types, it had penetrated to Australia; a few thousand years later, making use of a "land bridge" that at that time connected the eastern tip of Asia with Alaska, it had pioneered the human colonization of the Americas. At the latest, by 20,000 B.C. *H. s. sapiens* had spread throughout the world.

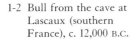

1-2 Bull from the cave at Lascaux (southern France), c. 12,000 B.C.

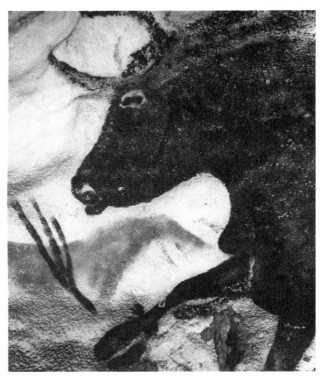

At some point in its development — once again, how and when are quite uncertain — *H. s. sapiens* came to be divided into a number of *races*, each with its own set of physiological characteristics. Among these were the color of the skin and the shape of various facial features, which form the basis of the present-day distinctions among whites, blacks, Orientals, and other races. Each of these races, in turn, consists of many subraces that share (more or less) the characteristics by which the group is popularly identified. By comparison with the variation that exists within many other species, the racial variations among human beings are small. Races are not even subspecies within a species, but mere varieties of a subspecies, *H. s. sapiens*. This fact provides a biological basis for the centuries-old religious and philosophical concept of the "brotherhood of man" (one community of *all* human beings).

The New Stone Age: The Agricultural Revolution

As we have seen, accelerated toolmaking skills brought such a change in techniques that archeologists have named the period after 7000 B.C. the New Stone (Neolithic) Age. These advances in toolmaking led to fundamental alterations in human social organization and way of life. The term New Stone Age tells us that we have come to a different era, succeeding the much longer

Old Stone (Paleolithic) Age. As a descriptive term, however, it fails to suggest the radically different character of human affairs after 7000 B.C. For during the next two or three thousand years substantial portions of the human species shifted from migratory hunter-gatherer patterns of existence to forms of settled agrarian life. This giant step, which involved the *domestication* of plants and animals, led to the founding of agricultural villages (such as Jericho, in Palestine) and the growth of more highly organized community relations. As a result of this "Agricultural Revolution," humans no longer lived in the "wild"; they became food-*makers* instead of food-*finders*.

This change in the manner of providing nourishment brought greater security and stability to individuals and groups. It increased the supply of food (and other commodities) from what nature offered to what humans, with nature's help, could produce. One major consequence was a steep rise in actual and potential *population*. Total numbers of humans on earth, probably no more than four million at the close of the Old Stone Age, have grown to more than four *billion* today.

The Agricultural Revolution, which began in the Middle East, was preceded and conditioned by important geologic and climatic changes. The earth's most recent ice sheet, which had covered much of Europe after 70,000 B.C., began to melt and withdraw northward around 10,000 B.C. By 8000 B.C. the glaciers (which are still melting) had pulled back more or less to their modern limits. Europe was left cold and rainy; North Africa, formerly cooled and watered by glacial influence, began to dry up. The most favored areas lay in the Mediterranean latitudes, which include the Middle East (p. 12). In locations with fertile soil and a good water supply, the inhabitants had an opportunity to cultivate crops. Similar opportunities had existed countless times before. But only now did humans possess that combination of mental capacity, tools, and will that permitted them to make a successful response.

We can only imagine how farming began. Seed grains — wheat and barley — flourished naturally in the grasslands above the river valleys of the Middle East. Food-gatherers (probably the women) no doubt observed that seeds that had fallen on the ground would sometimes sprout into plants. The idea must have followed that seeds could be collected and sown and the resulting plants nurtured and harvested. But the process demanded a great deal of effort and patience. Crude hoes were fashioned to break the soil for seeding; flint-edged sickles were made for cutting the grain. Months of watching and waiting were required between sowing and reaping, and bad weather could wipe out the fruits of hard labor.

Closely associated with crop cultivation was the domestication (taming and breeding) of animals. The keeping of herds was sometimes an independent occupation, but more often it accompanied farming. Wild dogs were the first animals to be tamed by humans, probably by hunting groups using them as protectors and pets. With the Agricultural Revolution, however, sheep, goats, pigs, and cattle became more important. Animals were raised for food

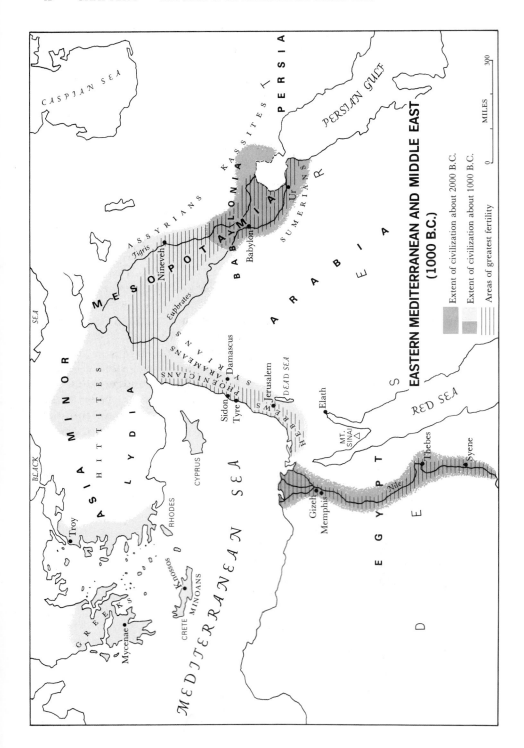

EASTERN MEDITERRANEAN AND MIDDLE EAST (1000 B.C.)

Extent of civilization about 2000 B.C.

Extent of civilization about 1000 B.C.

Areas of greatest fertility

and for their wool, skins, and milk; some time later they were also trained to perform work. The wild camel and ass were used as pack animals, and cattle were trained to pull simple plows. (The horse, which originated in central Asia, did not come into use in the Middle East until after 2000 B.C. — p. 46.)

Looking after the crops and animals required more or less permanent settlements. The first agricultural villages, constructed about 6000 B.C., consisted typically of sunbaked-brick huts, with a few special-purpose buildings such as granaries. The huts contained many articles unknown to earlier hunting societies. Fired-clay pottery appeared for the first time, used mainly as vessels for cooking and storing food. (Stewing meats and vegetables not only added variety to prehistoric menus, it also destroyed parasitic microbes that might be present in uncooked foods.) The skills of spinning and weaving developed for the making of numerous types of cloth. Such practical enterprises stimulated *artistic* expression, whose character and quality are preserved in the pottery of the New Stone Age (*Fig. 1-3*).

The social and intellectual consequences of the Agricultural Revolution were far-reaching. The typical village, with two or three hundred inhabitants, required greater control and organization than the earlier hunting packs of twenty to thirty persons. Authority no doubt continued to rest in the hands of male elders, who elected a chief to lead them. The farmlands, which were usually considered common property, were worked cooperatively. Since individual and community survival depended on closely coordinated efforts, a premium was placed on consensus and conformity. In such a society there was little room for dissent and individualism. Ideas or actions that interfered with community patterns were viewed as "wrong" (immoral) and were punished accordingly. Thus, the foundations of both "ethics" and "law" were laid in those early agrarian societies.

1-3 Prehistoric jar, Egypt,
c. 4000 B.C.

Religious beliefs and rituals were closely associated with food production. As hunters, humans had displayed a respect for animal spirits in their daily pursuit of game. As farmers, they worshiped the spirit of the earth — the fruitful "Great Mother" who brought forth the harvest. Worship of the Great Mother expanded quickly, and priests came into being to seek her favor. Countless other spirits and deities were revered by farmers and herders. Of particular importance were sky objects, especially the sun and the moon. The moon had a special value, for it enabled people to keep track of the passing days. The revolutions and phases of the moon provide a visible, simple, and regular calendar; and a calendar is indispensable for the accurate timing of plantings and harvests.

Over many centuries the Agricultural Revolution and the changes that went with it spread outward from the region of their origin. The Neolithic peoples of Europe adapted wheat and barley to the cooler and wetter conditions of that continent; in Africa and tropical Asia where the crops of the Middle East would not grow, villagers domesticated local plants such as yams or rice. By 3500 B.C. farming had spread to much of the Eastern hemisphere. Roughly one thousand years later, entirely separate agricultural revolutions, based on crops such as corn and potatoes, brought settled village life to the humans of the Western hemisphere as well.

In this way, the small agricultural community, with its farms, established routines, and watchful priests, became the typical way of life of the human race throughout much of the world. In spite of countless changes in farming methods, customs and traditions, and religious beliefs, this way of life persisted for thousands of years down to the time of the Industrial Revolution (pp. 511–12), and it is still to be found in many parts of the world at the present day.

The Neolithic villages also prepared humans for their next cultural leap: the rise of the first true *civilizations* (p. 6). This was not a simultaneous worldwide development. On the contrary, throughout human history it has only rarely happened that a prehistoric society of farmers and villagers has evolved into an advanced civilization. For this to happen seems to require a stimulating combination of advantages and difficulties, which are only encountered at certain times and places. There must be favorable conditions of soil and climate that make primitive farming unusually productive, thereby enabling farmers to produce the wealth necessary for advanced civilization; but there must also be difficulties and problems in exploiting these conditions, which force prehistoric peoples to develop new technical and cultural abilities.

The best-known "cradles of civilization" of this kind are the river valleys of the Middle East about 3500 B.C., where the earliest known civilizations arose; those of northern India and northern China about a thousand years later; and the plains, forests, and mountain valleys of Central America and the Andes toward 500 B.C. Later we shall be dealing with the civilizations of Asia and those of the Western hemisphere, at the time when the Europeans came into contact with them (pp. 296, 297–98, 542–43). For the moment, we are concerned with the civilizations that evolved in the Middle East, from which the Western civilization of later times is directly descended: those of Mesopotamia and Egypt.

THE EARLIEST CITIES: MESOPOTAMIA

The civilizations of Mesopotamia and Egypt emerged at about the same time (from roughly 3500 B.C. onward), seemingly independent of each other. They lasted down to the beginning of the Christian era, leaving a massive inheritance of cultural achievement, technical and scientific knowledge, and religious belief that has influenced many subsequent civilizations down to the present day. For many centuries, all direct knowledge of ancient Mesopotamia and Egypt was lost, until in recent times archeologists dug up their cities, and scholars deciphered their writing systems and languages. As a result, recorded history now goes back almost to the beginnings of these earliest known civilizations. In the case of Mesopotamia, it is even possible to reconstruct how civilization arose out of the earlier village life of the region.

The scene of this momentous development was a vast plain stretching between two great rivers of the Middle East, the Tigris and the Euphrates. These "twin" waterways follow generally parallel courses for about six hundred miles from their headwaters in present-day Turkey, until they finally enter the Persian Gulf (p. 12). The area bounded by them forms the heartland of the modern states of Syria and Iraq, but in ancient times the Greeks aptly named it Mesopotamia, "the land between the rivers."

About 3500 B.C., several thousand years after the beginning of the Agricultural Revolution, Mesopotamia and the region surrounding it already had many prosperous villages. But the *leap to civilization* began in a much more restricted area: the southernmost portion of Mesopotamia, where the twin rivers ran close to each other before entering the Gulf. This was an unattractive district: the land was flat, marshy, and open to disastrous floods. Rainfall was slight, and the summers were hot and humid. To live here at all, the local farmers relied on irrigation. Seasonal river floodings deposited the water and its rich silt (earth materials containing plant nutrients) that had washed down from distant hillsides; the villagers diverted the waters onto their fields and palm groves, which were the most productive of the entire Middle East. But because of the sheer size of the rivers, there were not many places where the waters were controllable enough for irrigation to be practicable, so that villages and patches of cultivation were actually fewer and farther between than elsewhere in Mesopotamia.

Just as the Agricultural Revolution had been conditioned by major continental climatic changes, so the rise of civilization in southern Mesopotamia seems to have been made possible by a minor local one. Sometime after 3500

B.C., the weather became slightly colder and drier. With less water flowing through them, the twin rivers, especially the Euphrates, became easier to harness for irrigation. The effects were dramatic. In two or three centuries around 3000 B.C., the population of this area expanded *tenfold*. Many new villages were founded; some older villages grew into small towns; and a few of the towns grew still further. They became the first true *cities* in the history of the world, with populations estimated as high as forty thousand. With growing population and wealth came technical innovation, cultural development, and more complex social organization.

Eventually, as the landscape continued to dry out and water actually became scarce, the wealth and population ceased to grow. But the waters never retreated so far as to make city life impossible. Instead, the cities responded to the new problems with new solutions. They built large-scale, centrally controlled water conservation and irrigation systems. Intensive warfare also began among them, for control of scarcer resources. Governments developed that were powerful enough to plan and organize these things. Nurtured by a favorable environment and then toughened by harsher conditions, there grew up in southern Mesopotamia a new kind of society, so much more advanced than the older one that today it counts as one of the world's first true civilizations.

Sumer (3500–2400 B.C.)

The ancient name of the southern portion of Mesopotamia where the new civilization arose was Sumer, and the people who created it are therefore known as the Sumerians. They seem to have arrived in southern Mesopotamia sometime after 3500 B.C., conquering or absorbing the earlier inhabitants. We have no evidence regarding their origins, but it is possible that they came from somewhere in central Asia; very likely, they were attracted to their new homeland by its growing wealth and fertility, as the environment there began to change. They settled in and ruled over the communities of the region, including its growing cities, each of which became the seat of government for a surrounding area of villages and countryside. The ruins of many of these cities have been excavated in recent times, with especially spectacular discoveries of buildings and works of art at the city of Ur on the Euphrates River. For over one thousand years the Sumerians controlled the southern parts of Mesopotamia, and for long periods much of the north as well. They shaped the basic ideas and institutions — political, economic, social, religious, and artistic — that would become the models for civilization throughout Mesopotamia and, later, Europe.

As the population of Sumer grew there was a heightened need for social direction, regulation, and discipline. At first, this was exercised mainly by a specialized *priesthood*. The power of the priests originally came from their status as servants of the gods and goddesses — the personified forces of nature (p. 19) on whom the Sumerians believed that the survival of their communities depended. As these communities became more prosperous and powerful, they devoted much of their new resources to the service of the gods and goddesses, thereby greatly increasing the power and wealth of the priests and priestesses. These, for their part, were far from confining themselves to matters of ritual and belief. They also directed the building of unprecedentedly large temples to house the gods and goddesses, employed craftsmen to furnish the temples with costly and beautiful works of art, managed vast properties, introduced technical innovations, and were responsible for the *invention of writing*. In Sumer, the priesthood led the process of social, technical, and cultural innovation out of which civilization emerged.

In time, however, as the waters retreated and resources grew scarcer, there arose another group of leaders, whose power was originally based on military might rather than religious belief. In a drier landscape, the cities of Sumer became increasingly tempting to roving gangs of bandits and wandering peoples, and the Sumerians fought among themselves over rival land claims and the division of waters. (This latter issue has persisted to the present day. Dam-building by Turkey on the upper reaches of the Euphrates has reduced the flow of water to Syria and Iraq, thereby provoking tensions with those countries; and Iraq's recent war with Iran originated in conflicts over control of the lower waters.) In Sumerian times, as the competition for resources grew more intense, so did warfare among the cities or with foreign peoples. In each city, soldiers and armies appeared. Military chieftains, arising as defenders of their communities, won power and rewards. By 2500 B.C. these military leaders had come to be called "kings," with power not only in war but in the peacetime governance of the cities (now properly called, in a political sense, city-*states*). Their relationship with the priests seems to have been one of both partnership and competition. Like the priests, the kings claimed that they ruled under the direction of the gods; and to make sure of divine support, they built temples and took a leading part in temple rituals. At "divine command," they also taxed the people and built impressive palaces for themselves. In varying forms, *palace* and *temple* have continued to be the dual houses of social power in virtually every civilization since Sumer.

Priests, kings, and the artisans and soldiers whom they employed all depended for their food on the cultivators of the soil — who made up about ninety percent of the population. The farmland surrounding most cities was divided into one section worked for the temple priests, another for the king, and the remainder for large private landowners. Most people were tenant farmers who worked on one of these sections and received a share of the crop for their labors — the rest went for the upkeep of the other groups, or into vast temple storehouses that the community as a whole could draw on in time of famine or siege. The farmers were prosperous enough to purchase pottery, textiles, and tools manufactured by skilled artisans; some became craftsmen themselves, employed in temples and palaces to produce tools, weapons, works of art, and other articles for use by the priests and rulers. Others turned to commerce, shipping surplus produce beyond the city in exchange for commodities (such as metals, timber, and stone) that the city lacked. Finally, some people — mostly farmers — who had fallen into heavy debt sold themselves (or their children) as payment for debt and labored as artisans or domestic servants for fixed periods of time. They shared this early, limited form of slavery with captives of war.

With its priests and kings, soldiers and craftsmen, merchants and farmers, Sumer developed one of the main features that distinguished civilized from primitive societies: the *division of labor* and *specialization of social functions*. Out of this, in turn, there developed a system of *ranks* of prestige, authority, and power. At the top, acting in the name of the city's chief god or goddess, were the king, the high priests, and their principal officers and agents. Next in order were the private men of wealth — great landowners and merchants. Then came the largest group by far — the commoners, consisting mainly of farmers (peasants) and a smaller number of free craftsmen. At the very bottom were the slaves, who were regarded as the property of their masters. Sumerian *women* originally enjoyed nearly equal rights with men of the same social rank, but as time passed women lost some of these rights.

In addition to making these advances in social and political organizations, the Sumerians were among the most innovative peoples in history. They were the first known users of ox-drawn plows, which broke up the ground faster than the previously used stone-bladed hoes and made agriculture more productive; and of wheeled wagons, which were a far more efficient form of transportation than the backs of people or animals. They were the first to make systematic use of metal tools and weapons (especially of bronze — p. 26), which were more effective than those made of stone. Above all, it was the Sumerians who invented one of the world's first systems of writing.*

For such a momentous invention, the origins of Sumerian writing were surprisingly humdrum. Nearly all of the earliest known written documents of Sumer (dating from about 3100 B.C. onward) are accounting records, providing information on supplies delivered to temple storehouses or consumed by temple officials. Thus, it seems that writing was developed in response to the increased prosperity of Sumer and the increased need for direction and control — both of them things that the wealthy and powerful Sumerian priesthood would have been particularly well aware of.

Even before the rise of civilization, Neolithic villagers had used a simple record-keeping system based on clay counters with pictograms (drawings of objects, such as sheep or bales of cloth that they wanted to keep track of) scratched into them. In the Sumerian temples, which had much more property to keep track of and consequently a greater need for detailed records, this system of counters developed into something much more sophisticated. The pictograms were simplified so that they could be more easily and quickly

---

*The Egyptian writing system, which dates from about the same period as that of Sumer, is discussed on p. 32.

"drawn." Eventually, each symbol became no longer a picture but simply a series of wedge-shaped marks; hence Sumerian writing is known as "cuneiform" (from *cuneus*, Latin for "wedge"). Some of the symbols came to be used as ideograms (symbols for *ideas*, such as "life"); in time, others were adapted to become phonograms, which stood for the sounds of words or syllables. Just as important, the new symbols were no longer written singly, each on its own small counter. Instead, any desired combination of symbols was scratched with a sharpened piece of reed, or stylus, into a larger piece of moistened clay, known as a tablet. The tablet was then dried to form a permanent record of complicated transactions involving any number of items.

But as a result of all these improvements, the system had outgrown its original purpose. By 2600 B.C. a writer could produce a *visual* statement not just of business dealings, but of anything that was spoken. In addition to keeping accounts, writing could now express any human thought or feeling.

By present-day standards, cuneiform writing was clumsy and hard to learn. Writing was practiced only by professional scribes who had to master hundreds of symbols (characters) and the delicate skill of imprinting them on moist clay. But so valuable was the practice of writing, for keeping records and preserving ideas in religion, law, and literature, that other peoples of the Middle East later borrowed the cuneiform symbols and adapted them to their own languages. For thousands of years, cuneiform writing remained the main vehicle of communication throughout much of the Middle East, and it was not until after the beginning of the Christian era that it finally fell out of use.

Written laws, which are essential to the very concept of civilization, were among the fruits of the invention of writing. They first appeared as statements of the customary rules and practices of early Sumerian society. Judicial officers, usually members of the privileged priestly class, may have felt little need for written guides as they interpreted traditional rules and decided on penalties in the cases brought before them. But the commoners no doubt insisted on the protection afforded by written statements of those rules; to use a modern phrase, they sought "a government of *laws*, not men." By 2500 B.C. most city-states had begun to assemble summaries, or *codes*, of accumulated law.

Law and life in Sumer were geared to an intensely religious view of the universe and humanity. Civic order, maintained by human authority, was viewed as part of universal order, upheld by divine power. The Sumerians believed not in a single all-powerful god, like the God of the Jewish, Christian, and Muslim faiths, but in hundreds of deities. This type of religion, which is called *polytheism* (belief in many gods), as distinguished from *monotheism* (belief in one god), was inherited by the Sumerians from their more primitive ancestors. It probably originated in the belief, which seems to date back to the earliest times of the human species, that powerful living beings, both friendly and hostile, caused the workings of nature. In addition, Sumerian religion had two other characteristics, which probably originated with the rise of civilization, and were passed on to subsequent peoples. It was *anthropomorphic*, regarding the deities as *humanlike* in character and appearance; and among its deities, a dozen or so great gods and goddesses were considered to excel all the others in power and holiness.

Many of the Sumerian deities are described in surviving religious writings. The highest among them was the god of heaven (or sky), named An. Important also were Enki, the god of the waters, and Inanna, goddess of fertility. These and other leading gods and goddesses were believed to be concerned chiefly with their own affairs; the role of humans was to serve and amuse them. They had homes (temples) in particular cities. There they were served by priests who sought their favor through prayer, sacrifices, and rituals. The will of the gods could be revealed and interpreted (by means of divination) through signs (omens) that appeared in dreams, the entrails of animals, and the stars. It was in Sumer that such "mystical" arts, including astrology, made their appearance.

Humans could expect neither immortality nor rewards and punishments after death. Rather, the Sumerians believed that the spirits of the dead descended to a dark underworld, where they eventually passed into nothingness. (This view of the afterlife was a forerunner of the ancient Greek *Hades* and the Hebrew *Sheol* — pp. 64, 141.) And so the Sumerians generally made no effort to prepare the bodies of the dead for a voyage beyond the grave. The only true life for humans was life on earth, and that life was brief, hard, and uncertain; this view was in some measure a product of the unpleasant physical environment of Mesopotamia. The gloom of daily existence was reinforced by religious myths of the Creation and the Flood, each showing humanity at the mercy of divine powers.

Though passive "acceptance" was no doubt the main popular mood, the surviving literature of the Sumerians reveals a many-sided humanity. Fables, legends, psalms, and proverbs were passed down mainly by word of mouth. The most impressive literary creations of these people, recited by bards and minstrels and recorded on clay tablets, are their epic poems. This form of expression, dealing with heroes and their ambitions and struggles, is common to many societies. Most of the Sumerian epic poems concern the career of an early king, Gilgamesh. Though Gilgamesh was probably a real person, in epic poetry he becomes a semidivine character, who embodies the values and aspirations of the people of Sumer. He fights for his city-state, slays hostile humans and animals, and displays bravery and cunning and a sense of fairness and mercy. A principal theme of the epics — his quest for immortality — ends in failure, as it does for all people. The epics of Gilgamesh, along with the religious myths of the Sumerians, provided a rich cultural inheritance for later civilizations in the Middle East. Through direct contact with Mesopotamia and indirectly through the Syrians and Hebrews, the Greeks and Romans shared that inheritance.

In addition to their pioneering contributions to writing, law, religion, and literature, the Sumerians established the foundations of mathematics, science, and engineering. These latter developments were direct responses to their practical needs in cultivation, irrigation, and commerce. The Sumerians created the basic processes of arithmetic: multiplication, division, and the square and cube root. In counting and measuring, they used a sixty-base system as well as the ten-base (decimal) system. They divided the hour, for example, into sixty minutes and the minute into sixty seconds — a method of time-keeping that we still use. In their system of weights and measures, the smallest unit was the *shekel*. Sixty shekels equaled a *mina* (about one pound), and sixty minas equaled one *talent*. These units of measure (later applied also to coinage) were widely used throughout the ancient world. In geometry, the Sumerians marked out a circle of three hundred sixty degrees, devised the formula for computing the hypotenuse of a right triangle, and worked out the method for calculating the area of a rectangle.

A lunar (moon) calendar provided for a month equal to the period of one lunar revolution, about twenty-nine days. Since twelve "months" do not quite equal a solar (sun) year, an extra month had to be added every few years to keep the calendar in harmony with the solar year. The seven days of the week were named for heavenly bodies (Sun Day, Moon Day, and so forth), and the most prominent sky objects were charted by official astronomers. These trained observers also charted the twelve divisions (signs) of the zodiac, which are still familiar to the followers of astrology.

The Sumerians accomplished little in the field of medicine, for they remained ignorant of the physical basis of disease. They believed that sickness was caused by spirits entering the body. The physician, accordingly, prescribed magical charms (or bitter-tasting drinks) to exorcise the culprits. Surgery was sometimes employed, but progress was retarded by severe penalties imposed on the surgeon in event of failure.

Architecture and the arts served both everyday purposes and religious and political needs. The construction of simple mud-brick (adobe) houses and walls was not a very difficult problem, but the raising of mighty temples to gain the favor of the gods, or palaces to display the power of kings, was a challenge that brought forth some spectacular monuments. We know of these only through fragmentary remains, because the Tigris-Euphrates region contains no durable stone. Even the most ambitious structures, such as hundred-room palaces for kings, were built of mud brick, which is neither a beautiful nor a durable material. The builders used as basic forms the self-supporting *arch*, the tunnel-shaped *vault*, and the *dome*, but they did not exploit those forms as the Romans were to do many centuries later (pp. 120–22).

We know from remains and records that temples were the most distinguished structures. The principal temple of a Sumerian city was invariably built at the center of the city, with structures for priests and temple craftsmen surrounding it. Typically, it consisted of an enclosure placed atop a manmade "mountain," a kind of step-pyramid called a *ziggurat* (*Fig. 1-4*). The first level of the ziggurat at Ur was a solid mud-brick mass some fifty feet high and two hundred by three hundred feet at its base. It supported two ascending set-back levels, the higher one serving as a pedestal for the shrine (house) of the deity. (A structure of this type was probably the model for the Biblical Tower of Babel,

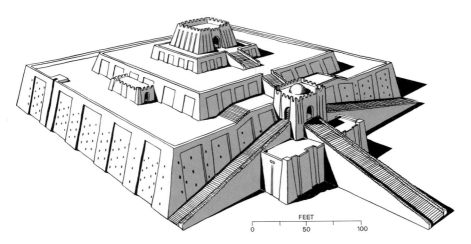

1-4 Reconstruction of the Ziggurat at Ur.

with its "top in the heavens" — Genesis 11:1–9.) The religious significance of the ziggurat to the Sumerians has been variously interpreted. Mountains have often been associated with divine powers; the hundred-step ramps suggest a sacrificial climb before the worshiper approaches the deity, or perhaps the descent of the deity from heaven to be present among the people; and the sheer mass of the monument symbolizes the power and rank of the god in comparison with ordinary mortals. This general type of mountain-temple has reappeared throughout the world over long stretches of time and place, notably in Mexico, Yucatán, and India. It evidently corresponds to a deep-seated religious attitude of human beings at a certain stage of cultural development; it is an architectural response to the presence of "a power beyond the powers of this world."

The Sumerian temples were dominated by statues, which the faithful believed embodied divine personalities. The sculptors displayed extraordinary skill in creating highly stylized humanlike forms; deities, high priests, and kings were their main subjects. In all of the statues the most prominent feature is the eyes; the pupils are magnified enormously, reflecting, perhaps, the dominance of eye function in human perception and communication (*Fig. 1-5*). Because durable stone was hard to come by in Mesopotamia, sculptors often used sandstone or clay, adding shells, alabaster, and semiprecious stones for dramatic effect. Other artisans crafted exquisite jewelry and metalwork, chiefly for use in the temples and palaces.

Babylonia (2400–1200 B.C.)

One of the most remarkable features of Sumerian civilization is that it served as a base for all later cultural growth in the Middle East (including that of the Hebrews). It absorbed numerous infiltrations and conquests by peoples from outside Mesopotamia, but the patterns of work, class structure, law and government, religious and literary traditions, and art forms persisted pretty much unbroken. For more than three thousand years, from the earliest city-states until the last days of the Persian Empire (330 B.C.), the institutions established at Sumer provided a groundwork of civilization — from the Persian Gulf westward to the Mediterranean and Black seas.

The early Sumerian city-states were frequently at war, but no one of them managed to keep down the others. After 2400 B.C. that balance was destroyed by conquerors from an area just north of Sumer, called Akkad. These conquerors spoke a Semitic language (one of the major linguistic branches) that was common to the inhabitants of the Arabian peninsula (p. 12). They had migrated over a period of centuries from Arabia into the Akkad region. At last, about 2350 B.C., one of their military chieftains, Sargon, began to attack the Sumerian cities. His ruthless campaigns won for him not only Sumer but also the rest of the Mesopotamian region. Sargon was history's first great military conqueror. His empire fell within a century, however, to be followed by a long period of struggles for control over the Tigris-Euphrates valley. It was not until about 1900 B.C. that order and security were once again restored. This was the accomplishment of the Amorites, another tribe of Semitic nomads, who had settled near the city-state of Babylon, on the midcourse of the Euphrates River.

1-5 Head of Sumerian statue from Abu Temple, Tell Asmar, c. 2700–2600 B.C.

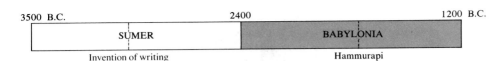

The Amorite kings of Babylon forced into submission the cities of Sumer to the south. The greatest king of their line was Hammurapi, who completed the conquest of all Mesopotamia by 1700 B.C. A Semitic tongue, Akkadian, now became the language of the new empire of Babylonia, and the Sumerian language was afterward used only by priests and scholars. Now the Creation myth was revised, and Marduk, patron god of the city of Babylon, was portrayed as the Maker of all things. He soon became the foremost deity of Mesopotamia and was commonly called *Ba'al* (Lord). (In a still later revision of the Creation myth — in Genesis — Hebrew writers would identify the Lord and Maker with Yahweh, the patron god of Israel.)

Hammurapi was the most impressive ruler in the history of Babylonia, and under his long reign the arts and sciences advanced and commerce prospered. He developed an efficient civil service, permitting effective administrative control over his far-reaching empire. The fundamentals of Sumerian culture remained intact; only minor cultural shifts are reflected in the Code of Hammurapi, the best-known collection of laws of the ancient world. We know that Sumerian law codes existed several centuries earlier, but only Hammurapi's code has been recovered in its original form (*Fig. 1-6*). The code is engraved (in cuneiform writing) on a seven-foot-tall black stone pillar; a single relief sculpture at the top shows the Babylonian god of justice, Shamash, holding the symbols of divine authority while dictating the laws to King Hammurapi. (The scene reminds us of the later Biblical account of the Hebrew god, Yahweh, dictating the Commandments to Moses on Mount Sinai.)

The intention of the sculpture is clear: the rules engraved on the black stone represent the will of the god coming through the person of a divinely sent king. In form and content, they resemble the rules that make up the Mosaic code — which was also engraved on stone (Exodus, chapters 19–31). Actually, the laws of Hammurapi are a summation of legal concepts and practices that had grown out of centuries of human experience in the Tigris-Euphrates valley. The chief importance of the code is that it provided a *uniform* standard of law, in place of differing interpretations, for the whole empire of Babylonia.

Hammurapi's code is divided into nearly three hundred clauses, or "case laws," dealing with the administration of justice, social classes, property, trade and commerce, assaults, wages, and marriage and the family. Marriages, we find, were arranged by parents, the marriage contract specifying the price of the bride and the amount of her dowry. Husbands could divorce their wives freely and were complete masters of their unmarried children. A wife, however, could seek separation only on charges of cruelty or neglect, and if the

1-6 Pillar of Hammurapi (upper part), Susa, c. 1760 B.C.

court found her to be at fault she was subject to death by drowning! A sterile wife could find a concubine (female companion) for her husband to bear him a child; the concubine and her offspring were accepted as legitimate members of the family. Though women were barred, legally, from engaging in business, records show that some did so and that some held property in their own name.

Punishments for criminal acts were quite different from modern practices. Neither imprisonment nor forced labor was imposed; penalties took the form, rather, of physical acts against the person judged guilty. The supporting principle was "retaliation in kind" (Latin, *lex talionis*); as passed on to the Hebrews, it was expressed as "eye for eye, tooth for tooth . . ." (Exodus 21:23–25). Mutilation was common for a variety of offenses, depending on the nature of the crime. A son who struck his father might have his hand cut off; a snooper or a spy might have an eye put out. Capital offenses (such as murder, treason, vandalism, disorder, theft) were punished in a number of ways — to "fit the crime." These ways included drowning, burning, hanging, crucifying, and impaling. Some of King Hammurapi's forms of punishment persisted through ancient times and survived in Europe until the eighteenth century. They have also influenced Islamic law, down to the present times.

The Babylonians built upon the achievements of the Sumerians in several fields of technology. One advance was in the making of metal tools. As we have seen (p. 8), after about 3000 B.C. the New Stone Age was followed by the Bronze Age. Primitive people had learned to use the loose pieces of copper they found lying on the ground. By hammering the metal, either cold or heated, they managed to create a variety of useful articles. The supply of surface copper was limited, however, and tools made from copper are rather soft. A breakthrough came when they discovered that they could extract metal from ores and that they could then alloy (blend) one of those metals — tin — with copper to make a much stronger metal — bronze. The processes of extracting and alloying metals from ores require extremely high temperatures, and heat-resistant ovens, or kilns, were gradually improved until the arts of smelting and casting (metallurgy) were established. Bronze proved to be an excellent alloy for implements and weapons as well as for sculpture. By 1700 B.C. the working of bronze had reached a high stage of development in the Middle East. Bronze remained the king of metals until the general adoption (by about 1000 B.C.) of techniques for smelting iron and for producing iron tools and weapons.

The high state of technology, law, and economy achieved by the Babylonian empire did not spare it from falling apart soon after the death of Hammurapi. Less civilized peoples to the north and east were attracted, as they had been previously, by the wealth of the Tigris-Euphrates valley. One of these peoples, the Kassites, conquered most of Babylonia about 1600 B.C. Their language did not belong to the Semitic or any other known group.

The Kassites controlled Mesopotamia until 1200 B.C. After their fall the region broke into a number of small states, with no single ruler comparable in stature to Hammurapi. To the north and west of Babylonia were the Hittites, conquerors of Asia Minor (modern Turkey), who spoke a language belonging to the Indo-European group (p. 47). The Hittites had brought iron, the horse, and the war chariot (p. 46) to the Middle East, and for a time they controlled lands as far south as Egypt. The Phoenicians, a Semitic-speaking people, established themselves on the seacoast, in the area today called Lebanon (p. 12). As seafarers, they would play a leading role in the wider spread of Mesopotamian culture by sending out colonists and traders far across the Mediterranean Sea. Still more important, the Phoenicians invented a written *alphabet* in the fourteenth century B.C., from which the principal ancient and modern alphabets have been derived.

South of Phoenicia was another community of Semites, the Hebrews, who had migrated from Mesopotamia to the land of Canaan (Palestine) around 1900

B.C. In the temporary absence of great-power dominance in the Middle East, the Hebrews (Jews)* built a unified state during the tenth century B.C. under the hero-kings David and Solomon. Their state soon fell apart, but the Jews themselves, who would move out later to all parts of the Mediterranean world, carried elements of Mesopotamian culture with them, as well as their own unique way of life. Their vital religious and literary contributions will be discussed in Chapter 4.

LAND OF THE PHARAOHS: EGYPT

The valley of the Nile River, like the twin valleys of Mesopotamia, was a center of early civilization. Its people were of mixed stock, having entered the area from Arabia (to the east), Nubia (to the south), Libya (to the west), and Palestine and Syria (to the north). Racially, the ancient Egyptians were of both Caucasoid (light-skinned) and Negroid (dark-skinned) origin. They spoke an African (Hamitic) tongue, which was modified in time by Semitic influences.

During the New Stone Age the people of the Nile had moved toward civilization in response to the same influences that gave rise to the cities of Sumer, some nine hundred miles to the east (pp. 15–16). But the speed and course of development in the two civilizations were quite different. For some two thousand years Egypt remained a unified, conservative, and rather insulated society. Compared with Mesopotamia, Egypt experienced few internal or external disturbances; it enjoyed a continuity and stability that gave its inhabitants a sense of permanence, even perfection, in their institutions and way of life. That sense was embodied and reflected in Egypt's economy, government, literature, and art. Thus, the culture of the Nile contrasts in some critical respects with that of the Tigris-Euphrates; Western peoples are heirs to both.

The Nile and the "Two Lands"

The Nile played a role in Egypt similar to that of the rivers of Mesopotamia. The cycle of labor and of life itself depended on its annual flooding and receding. The mighty Nile, the longest river in the world, rises in central Africa and winds northward for thousands of miles before descending into the torrid Egyptian desert. From that point it continues as a single navigable stream for some five hundred miles until it flows, about a hundred miles from the Mediterranean Sea, into a fan-shaped pattern of waterways, or *delta* (p. 12). The country is thus divided into two distinct geographical sections, called in ancient times the "Two Lands": Upper Egypt (the Valley) and Lower Egypt

---

*The terms "Hebrews" and "Jews" are sometimes used interchangeably; both derive from the languages of ancient Israel. Most commonly, however, Hebrews refers to the Israelites of earliest times, while Jews refers to the generations since about 500 B.C.

(the Delta). Lower Egypt is a triangular area of rich soil (deposited by the Nile); Upper Egypt is long and narrow, averaging no more than twelve miles in width. Beyond those areas of fertile land, Egypt was (and is) a barren wasteland.

The river god (Hapi) seemed benevolent and generous to the residents of the Two Lands, for the Nile delivered its riches on a regular schedule. Unlike the unpredictable and often angry Euphrates, the Nile was reliable and controllable. Perhaps because of that difference, the ancient Egyptians held a brighter, more optimistic view of life. Whereas the Sumerians felt they were subject to the whims of the deities (sometimes expressed in rampaging floods), the people of the Nile believed that the divine order was working *for* humanity. That belief, in turn, may explain why the Egyptians were so determined to extend their lives indefinitely (immortality), while the Sumerians resigned themselves to nothingness beyond the grave (p. 20).

The Egyptian rulers drew their strength from the "gift of the Nile," from the natural (desert) defenses of the country, and from the ready acceptance of their authority by the people. Unlike Mesopotamia, where the rise of independent city-states worked against the formation of larger political units, Egypt witnessed an early consolidation of its agricultural districts ("nomes") into the two kingdoms of Upper Egypt and Lower Egypt. A king of Upper Egypt completed the unification of the country, around 3100 B.C., by his conquest of Lower Egypt. There he built a new capital, south of the Delta and close to the boundary between the Two Lands; he called it Memphis, and it remained the center of royal administration for the next nine hundred years.

Government by a God-King (3100–1200 B.C.)

From the beginning, every king of Egypt proclaimed himself a *god*. During his lifetime he was represented as Horus, the falcon-headed ruler of the sky. When he died he was identified with Osiris, god of the underworld. (In order to keep the divinity of his heirs pure, the king often married his sister or some other female relative.) All of Egypt and its inhabitants belonged to him as personal property — a gift from the gods. And so he exercised absolute (*unlimited*) authority over the country, with no one questioning his right to do so. Because he was a god, he was immortal, and in the early centuries of Egypt it was believed that only close associates of the king could gain everlasting life.

These convictions about the king (later called the pharaoh) greatly simplified the problem of administering the country. In Egypt there were no power struggles among rival social classes and city-states, as there were in Mesopotamia. The economy, the military, and the priesthood were closely supervised by the household staff of the king. This smooth control was vital to a society whose prosperity required unified direction, cooperation, and stability. The king, of course, could and did delegate many of his functions to others.

His chief deputy (vizier) directed most royal affairs; his high priests regulated religious matters.

The royal administrators and priests made up a kind of aristocracy (nobility) between the monarch and the commoner (peasant) class. Minor officials, soldiers, artisans, and laborers were drawn from the commoner class, but most commoners toiled as sharecroppers on the pharaoh's land. (Slaves, captured in wars, formed a small underclass.) No distinct business class emerged, as it did in Mesopotamia; foreign trading expeditions, mining, and similar large enterprises were conducted by select companies of the royal household. All exchanges and payments were in *kind* (goods). As a consequence, no cities of commerce arose in Egypt; the urban centers remained essentially administrative capitals or extensive temple compounds. In most places and levels of society, women held a subordinate position. Harems (of concubines), dancing girls, and female musicians were accepted members of the royal and noble households. Monogamous marriage (*one* wife) was the rule, however; and though the husband was the master, the wife was generally admired and respected. Women appear to have enjoyed considerable freedom of movement and were permitted to own property.

If durability is a measure of the success of political and social systems, ancient Egypt was extraordinarily successful. The absolutist god-kingship (theocracy) directed a unified government and way of life in the valley of the Nile for most of two thousand years — longer than any other system known to recorded history. The Egyptian *idea* of kingship was, indeed, the most complete idea of *personal human power* ever imagined. It placed absolute and total authority, both divine and worldly, in a single person who was believed to be immortal and infallible. No wonder the Egyptians revered authority and strained to carry out the pharaoh's will. No wonder, too, that there was little social criticism or dissent, and little innovation or experiment.

However, there were periods of slippage and change — even in the changeless valley of the Nile. The "Old Kingdom," founded about 3100 B.C., fell into serious difficulties by 2200 B.C. A series of weak pharaohs allowed power to pass to local administrators and temple priests, who came to regard their positions as hereditary. For more than a century Egypt remained in turmoil as the pharaohs tried to regain their divine powers. This was at last achieved, about 2050 B.C., by a new dynasty (family line of rulers). These rulers transferred the royal capital upriver, from Memphis (near the Delta) to their home city of Thebes. From Thebes, succeeding pharaohs brought prosperity to Egypt throughout the period known as the "Middle Kingdom."

After about 1800 B.C., however, a renewal of internal conflict and foreign invasion brought the Middle Kingdom to an end. Royal control was not reestablished until about 1600 B.C., when another dynasty brought the nation into its imperial era, called the "New Kingdom" (1600–1200 B.C.). This concluding period of Egypt's greatness saw the invaders expelled and Egyptian armies sent

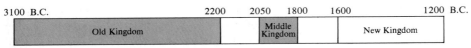

into Nubia, Palestine, and Syria. It was a time of aggressive warfare, military glory, and more open contact with the world beyond the Nile. The New Kingdom, in turn, eventually failed because of a final weakening of royal authority, abuses of priestly power, and fresh invasions.

Despite the ebb and flow of the nation's fortunes, the core institutions of Egypt remained essentially unchanged until the onset of irreversible decline (about 1200 B.C.). This was especially true of the centuries between 3100 and 1800 B.C., the time span of the Old and Middle Kingdoms. Over this very long period the whole of Egypt shared in a single civilization.

Religion and Law

Religion was the base of the pharaoh's authority. It provided an acceptable explanation of the Creation, the nature of the world, ethical principles, and life after death. Egyptian religion was by no means a simple set of beliefs: traditions merge with and overlap other traditions; legends about the gods sometimes differ; symbols and rituals are often unclear in meaning. But these difficulties apparently did not bother the Egyptians. They took their religion as they found it, untroubled by the questions raised by modern skeptics, rationalists, and theologians.

Like the Mesopotamians, the Egyptians believed in the existence of numerous divine forces and beings (polytheism). Many of their deities, tracing back to the Stone Age, were originally conceived in the forms of animals; during historic times the divine images often bore animal heads or bodies. The pharaoh himself, as the sky-god Horus, is usually represented with the head of a falcon, but sometimes, as in the Great Sphinx, he has a human head on a lion's body (*Fig. 1-7*). Other important deities included the sun-god, Re, and the ram-headed Amon, who came to be joined with Re as "king of the gods." Much of the time, labor, and wealth of Egypt were devoted to sacred services. Priests engaged in elaborate rituals and urged the faithful to pray and sacrifice to the temples and their divine inhabitants.

The gods of Egypt did not demand virtuous behavior of the people. They had created the universal order and continued to regulate it benevolently; humans were expected, in return, simply to perform specified services. Ethical ideas, however, gradually crept into the religious teachings. The major gods, especially Re, came to be associated with the ideals of truth and justice. By the time of the Middle Kingdom, about 1800 B.C., a rising interest in Osiris, god of the underworld, provided additional motivation for living a righteous life. As

1-7 Great Sphinx, c. 2500 B.C., and Great Pyramid of Khufu, c. 2600 B.C., at Gizeh, Egypt.

the old myths were expanded, Egyptians came to believe that the soul of a deceased person had to stand before Osiris for judgment. The soul recited its good deeds and denied doing anything evil (cheating, adultery, lying). The heart (character) of the person was then weighed in a balance to measure the soul's truthfulness. If the soul passed this test, it was admitted to everlasting life in a garden paradise; otherwise, it was cast into the crocodile jaws of a monster.

This Egyptian idea of rewards and punishments after death and the expectation of immortality itself were original contributions to the religious beliefs of the world. They were passed on to later civilizations and clearly influenced their ideas about a life after death. Scholars have discovered Egyptian views about the next world mainly by studying funeral texts and paintings in tombs. The findings are not always certain or consistent, but these points are clear: the people of the Nile were strongly attached to life; they were convinced that each person possesses a supernatural "double," or soul (*ka*), that persists after the body dies; and they thought that preserving the body (mummification) and providing it with comforts in the tomb would aid the soul during its life to come.

Though the Egyptians had a strong desire for social order and harmony, they developed no system of law comparable to that of Mesopotamia. This is understandable when we recall that all law, right, and justice flowed from only one source: the pharaoh. Law was whatever he, or his administrators, *said* it was. Hence, no class, no section of the country, demanded a written code of law for its protection. Royal decrees and court decisions were recorded, but the principal guides for judges were custom and the will of the ruler.

The law, furthermore, was not seen as an instrument of change or "progress," as it is in some modern societies. Egypt was self-satisfied, conservative, static; therefore, the law did not serve as a social tool. Although the king's officials regularly boasted of their even-handed administration of justice, there is little evidence to support that claim. Court procedures as we know them did not exist. One account of the trial of a man accused of treason suggests how the judges behaved: "They examined his crimes; they found him guilty; they caused his sentence to come upon him." Forms of punishment included beatings and mutilations; more serious crimes brought forced labor or execution.

Literature, Science, and Art

Writing, the indispensable tool of civilization, probably started in Egypt around 3000 B.C. It developed independently of Sumerian writing (pp. 18–19), but the *idea* may have been borrowed from Sumer. At first simplified drawings of objects (pictograms) were used. Other types of symbols were then added to the drawings to represent the *sounds* of syllables or consonants. The characters remained essentially pictorial, and were used mainly for ritual purposes; hence they came to be known as "hieroglyphs" (sacred carvings). The hieroglyphs were also viewed as an art form and were freely used to ornament the walls and columns of temples and palaces (*Figs. 1-8, 1-9*).

From the hieroglyphs there soon developed a system of characters that could be much more easily and quickly written, the "hieratic" (priestly) script. In spite of its name, the hieratic script was used not only by priests but for general literary and administrative purposes; eventually, an even simpler system, the "demotic" (popular) script, came into use. Thus, writing was as much part of the everyday life of civilization in Egypt as it was in Mesopotamia.

Most Egyptian writing, especially the hieratic and demotic, was done not on buildings or stones but on *papyrus*. (It is from this Greek word that our word "paper" derives.) The Egyptian technique of preparing writing scrolls from the stems of the water-grown papyrus plant was a major cultural breakthrough. The Mesopotamians had never advanced beyond using clay or stone as materials to write on. The advantages of papyrus in cost and convenience were soon recognized everywhere, and papyrus scrolls (rolls) became the "books" of the ancient world.

The easy availability of writing materials no doubt encouraged the Egyptians to create a national literature. Much of it served religious purposes, as, for

1-8 Obelisk at Luxor Temple of Amon, c. 1500 B.C.

example, tales about the gods and phrase books to aid the passage of the soul to the afterworld. But virtually all forms of literature arose: philosophical essays, books of "wise sayings," manuals for personal conduct, tales of adventure, romances, texts on medicine and magic, poems, and songs. The Egyptians, strangely, produced no heroic masterpiece to equal the Sumerian epics of Gilgamesh (p. 20), but they excelled in the scope and quantity of their literary creations.

The Egyptians showed no interest in mathematical theory and lagged behind the Mesopotamians in dealing with practical problems. They had no tables for multiplication, division, squares, or square roots. Surviving geometry texts explain how they computed the areas of fields, the volumes of various shapes, and the properties of pyramids. In counting, they used a ten-base (decimal) system, with an awkward style of notation (numbering). A major Egyptian contribution, however, was the invention of a solar calendar of 365 days. They divided the year into twelve equal months of thirty days, adding five "free" days at the end. They divided each month into three "weeks" of ten days each, and each day into twenty-four hours. They also invented sundials, of the kind still seen today, for telling the hours of the day. Although they charted the heavens and recorded the daily rising of certain stars, they seem to have had no interest in a general science of the skies (astronomy).

1-9 Temple to Amon at Karnak, c. 1300 B.C.

Medical science was a different matter; some writers declare that the Egyptians were the *founders* of scientific medicine. They developed systematic procedures for handling cases of illness, wrote books about diseases, and established medical libraries and schools. The attention given to medicine was a response, in part, to a condition of chronic and widespread disease in the steaming Nile Valley. Peasants wading in warm, shallow pools were susceptible to waterborne parasites, especially the blood fluke. The debilitating illness carried by the flukes, now known as schistosomiasis, infected those peasants as it has infected millions of their descendants down to the present day.

The ancients understood nothing of germs or infections. The "demonic" theory of sickness that prevailed in Mesopotamia (p. 21) prevailed also in Egypt. But alongside the magic formulas and priestly exorcists were some healing drugs and trained physicians and surgeons. One reason for the superiority of their medical techniques, no doubt, was the anatomical knowledge (unique in the ancient world) derived from the Egyptian practice of mummification. Prior to embalming with special preservatives, the body of the deceased was opened and the internal organs (except the heart) were removed.

The final resting place for a king's body (and the bodies of other prominent personages) was a stone tomb. The best-known tombs are the giant royal pyramids—the structures that come most readily to mind when we think of Egypt. These masterpieces of practical engineering (and social discipline) sum up, in many ways, the character of that ancient civilization. They were built to last forever by a people who believed that they and their ways would go on forever. The four-sided, pointed design of a pyramid was the most stable and resistant structural form they could conceive; limestone was the most durable material within reach. The art of the Egyptians was, indeed, "art for eternity."

The largest of the pyramids was built by order of King Khufu, who ruled about 2650 B.C. Located at Gizeh (near modern Cairo), the Great Pyramid measures 476 feet in height and 760 feet on each side of its base (*Fig. 1-7*). This mountain of stone consists of some 2,300,000 cut blocks, each one weighing about two and a half tons! The sides of the pyramid were originally coated with polished marble, but that was stripped away long ago by thieves (who also robbed the royal tomb within). Close by is the Great Sphinx, another type of monument, carved soon afterward for another king (Khafre). The enormous head of this man-beast, cut from the cliff of the valley wall, rises sixty-six feet from its base.

The passion for permanence, symmetry, and colossal size was exhibited in many Egyptian works of architecture and sculpture. One form of particular interest is the *obelisk*, a slim, four-sided stone shaft that tapers upward to a pyramidal cap. The obelisk was sacred to the sun-god, Re, but many obelisks were raised to honor other deities and rulers as well (*Fig. 1-8*). Several of these ancient monuments have been transported from Egypt to the West, and modern copies stand in cities around the world. Travelers today can see obelisks not only in the valley of the Nile but in Rome, Paris, London, and Buenos Aires. The copy most familiar to Americans is the Washington Monument, erected in the nineteenth century to honor the first president.

Religious shrines (with their special rituals) were the primary architectural concern of Egyptian priests and worshipers. Temple buildings were usually supported by the "post-and-lintel" method, that is, horizontal beams (lintels) held up by columns (posts). This method had been known to Mesopotamian architects, but it was not practical for their structures, which were made of brick. (They had to use solid walls or self-supporting brick arches to hold up the roofs of their buildings.) The method was very suitable, however, for *stone* structures; and Egyptian builders, unlike the Mesopotamians, had easy access to immense supplies of stone.

The temple of Amon at Karnak (near Thebes) was begun about 1530 B.C. and completed about 1300 B.C. (*Fig. 1-9*). The largest religious building ever constructed, it covered a ground area of 1,220 feet by 340 feet (about ten acres)—and enclosed a space large enough to contain four of the huge Gothic cathedrals that were built more than twenty-five hundred years later in Europe. The roof of the main hall rested on 134 columns, each made of elaborately carved stone drums; the central (nave) columns are 70 feet in height and 12 feet in diameter. As the builders intended, the gigantic proportions of Karnak overwhelm its viewers and make them feel insignificant.

1-10 King Menkaure and his wife,
     c. 2500 B.C.

Sculptors and painters worked under the direction of architects to fulfill the aims of each kind of building. They did much of their work for the interiors of royal and noble tombs. Representations of the deceased were believed to contribute to the welfare of the soul of the dead; therefore, stone statues of the individual (and members of the household) were usually placed within the tomb. The walls of the tomb were painted with scenes of Egyptian life related to the career of the deceased. Though lifelike, these representations were seldom *naturalistic* (the way persons and objects normally look to the eye). Sculptured portraits, for example, had to be made according to set rules. Rather rigid postures were required, and the figures were placed so as to be viewed from the front ("frontalism"). Usually the left foot was placed forward; wigs and beards were treated in a standard stylized manner. Yet the human quality of these statues comes through the somewhat stilted forms (*Fig. 1-10*).

This humanistic quality is evident also in the tomb *paintings*, from which we have learned many details about Egyptian civilization. There was no attempt to provide perspective, or depth, in these pictures; artists were free to arrange their compositions as they thought best within the assigned space. Thus, some scenes might be laid out on a line parallel to the base line of the picture frame, some (in the same picture) on a line perpendicular to the base line. Also, individual figures might be drawn to different scales, though the *king* was always shown as the largest person in a given frame.

A governing principle of Egyptian painting was that a representation must reflect established knowledge of the object and must be shown from the angle that best reveals that knowledge. For example, the face is always shown in profile, except for the eye, which is shown as it appears frontally. Shoulders and torso are viewed from the front, legs and feet in profile (*Fig. 1-11*). Strict rules of this sort tend to keep artistic expression in a static mold, and that was just what the rulers of Egypt desired for their static ("perfected") society. In the long run, such rules lead to a dead end for both art and culture. Nonetheless, the Egyptian painters, within their rules, developed techniques of line, design, and color that were extraordinarily effective. The artistic creations of the Egyptians, including jewelry, metal, and glass, became admired models for the ancient world — both East and West.

1-11 *Offering Bearers*, from Tomb of Sebekhotep, Thebes, c. 1500–1300 B.C. Tempera on mud plaster.

THE FIRST UNIVERSAL EMPIRES: ASSYRIA AND PERSIA

The brilliant civilization of Egypt developed independently from the civilization of Mesopotamia. The creative forces of both cultures appear to have run their course by about 1200 B.C. As we have seen, the New Kingdom in Egypt had fallen into a fatal decline by that time (pp. 29–30); and the Kassite kingdom in Mesopotamia, heir to Sumer and Babylonia, was soon to end (p. 26). But the final, dramatic phase of the ancient Middle East was now about to open — the merging of the various cultural streams of the region into *one*. This merger was not to be realized, however, through peaceful dialogue and common consent. Rather, it was forcibly imposed by the first "universal" empires.

The use of armed force was by no means new to the Middle East. The Sumerian city-states had fought among themselves; the conqueror Hammurapi, and then the Kassites, had seized control of Mesopotamia; and the Egyptians had repelled invaders and established military control for a time in Palestine and Syria. But the new conquerors had grander ambitions than any of their predecessors. They sought to draw under their sole control all the world that was within their reach. This achievement would bring to the Middle East a *cosmopolitan* (mixed) culture, enormous problems of administration, and the deeper question of how to hold together a far-flung collection of diverse peoples.

In producing the Agricultural Revolution of the New Stone Age, humans had responded successfully to the challenge of providing reliable supplies of food and shelter (p. 11). Later, they created the first civilizations. Could they now unite those groups in a manner that would secure peace and the benefits of economic and cultural exchange? The Assyrians were the first of many peoples who have tried to meet this ultimate challenge to human survival.

Assyria (900–600 B.C.)

The Assyrians lived for centuries along the middle and upper reaches of the Tigris River (p. 12). They were a small kingdom of Semitic-speaking people who entered this region from Arabia as early as 3000 B.C. Their location exposed them to frequent attacks by nomadic tribes from the north and east; though they were essentially farmers, herders, and traders, they grew into tough soldiers as they defended their lands. Survival, rather than conquest, was their main concern during most of their history. But the weakening of the great power centers in the Middle East after 1200 B.C. presented Assyria with an opportunity to turn to the offensive. Assyrian leaders saw that rich profits were to be reaped from controlling the trade routes between western Asia and the Mediterranean. And, as they gradually accomplished this aim, they began to conceive of the larger object of a universal empire. As one of their rulers would declare, "I am the legitimate king of the world . . . of all four rims of the earth . . . king of kings."

Like most subsequent empires, the Assyrian empire was not built in a day. The Kassites (p. 26), who had ruled Babylonia from 1600 to 1200 B.C., were driven out by the Chaldeans, a new group of Semitic invaders from Arabia. The Assyrians, living to the north of Babylonia, soon came into conflict with the Chaldeans. In a series of wars after 900 B.C., the Assyrians gained supremacy; and in the eighth century the king of Assyria added the crown of Babylon to his possessions.

Meanwhile, the Assyrians had also struck out to the north and west and had taken over the southern portion of Asia Minor, as well as Syria, Phoenicia, and part of Palestine. The empire reached its greatest extent in the seventh century B.C., when the rest of Palestine and most of Egypt fell under its control. During the turbulent period of conquests, insurrections, and frontier wars, the Assyrians faced the endless task of holding a widespread empire together. Drained of their strength at last, they were overcome by a rebellion of their old enemies, the Chaldeans, aided by the Medes (p. 41) attacking from the east. In 612 B.C. their high-walled capital at Nineveh, on the Tigris, was broken into and burned; most of their army and royal family were wiped out; and the Assyrian nation sank into obscurity, never to rise again.

The terrible vengeance brought down upon the Assyrians by their conquerors was in large measure a response to the nature of their rule. The basis of Assyrian power, from its beginning, was armed force and terror. Assyria was the first truly military state. All adult males were subject to military service, commanders were rewarded with the best lands and highest honors, and war was glorified and pursued as the principal business of the kingdom. The Assyrians, with their passion for war, became the most advanced people of their time in the arts of weaponry and military tactics. They were among the first to use iron swords, helmets, and shields; their chariots, manned by bowmen, constituted a fearsome shock force; their engineers devised battering rams and siege engines to break down the stoutest defense.

As the nation's manpower was reduced by its wars, the imperial masters relied increasingly on drafted or hired troops drawn from subject peoples. A fatal weakness in the Assyrians' system was that they were too small a nation to enforce their rule over the vast reaches of their conquests. To compensate, they pursued a policy of deliberate *terror*. By building a reputation for brutality against those who resisted them, they could win the submission of their victims with the least expenditure of soldiers.

The Assyrians discovered, as have numerous conquerors after them, that in the long run terror proves self-defeating. They used and boasted of inhuman practices; skinning and mutilating bodies, torturing, impaling, burning alive, and displaying stacks of human skulls. Their behavior was excessive even by the standards of ancient warfare, and Assyrian palace art still proclaims their acts of violence in superb and explicit wall reliefs (*Figs. 1-12, 1-13*). The "propaganda of the deed" was no doubt an effective source of power; it made the

1-12 An alabaster relief showing an Assyrian king on a hunt.

Assyrians the most feared people of the ancient world. But they themselves were at last destroyed by the storm of hatred they had raised.

And yet, whatever their methods and motives, the Assyrian kings succeeded in bringing together the largest collection of peoples ever united up to that time. This achievement vastly improved communication throughout the Middle East, stimulated commerce and the growth of cities, and gave fresh vigor to technology, literature, and the arts. The Assyrians themselves, heirs to the ancient Babylonian civilization, made few original contributions except in military affairs and the art of administration. Theirs was the first truly *imperial* government. Conquered lands were usually organized as provinces, with Assyrian nobles appointed as governors by the great king. Some of the "tribute states" were permitted, in return for regular payments, to keep their own rulers, under the watchful eyes of Assyrian officials. Systematic intelligence and administrative reports flowed from all corners of the empire to the capital at Nineveh. The successes and failures of the Assyrian system provided valuable lessons to the next builders of empire—the Persians.

Persia (550–330 B.C.)

After the fall of Assyria, the peoples of the Middle East returned again to their separate ways. The Chaldeans, having liberated Babylonia, stimulated a rebirth of industry and the arts. Their vigorous King Nebuchadrezzar II (the Old Testament's Nebuchadnezzar) renovated his capital city of Babylon and reached out to subjugate the kingdom of Judah, in Palestine, in 597 B.C. (This

1-13 Assyrian relief sculpture showing storming of a city and executions of victims.

Jewish kingdom had retained limited self-rule as a tributary state under the Assyrians.) Nebuchadrezzar is hatefully remembered by the Jews for having destroyed the temple of Jerusalem and for having deported the leading citizens to Babylon (an act referred to by Jews as the "Babylonian Captivity"). The deportation was a control measure that the Assyrians had used earlier in order to subdue rebellious subjects. But the power of the Chaldeans' "New Babylonia" was short-lived; like the rule of the Medes in the upper region of Mesopotamia, it shortly fell to the Persians.

Medes and Persians were among a number of Indo-European tribes that had entered the areas of Media and Persia many centuries before (p. 47). After the Medes had helped the Chaldeans crush the Assyrians, the Persian King Cyrus (the Great) moved to take over all the surrounding lands. He defeated the king of the Medes in 550 B.C. and made their capital at Ecbatana his own. In so doing, Cyrus also sought the support of the Medes for his further ambitions; by treating them generously, he won their sympathy and aid. Thus, in this very first step, Cyrus showed that he meant to reject the Assyrian way of taking power. Rather than terrorizing his opponents he sought to win them over by reasonable and decent treatment.

The Persian conquests, dramatically swift, were aided not only by Cyrus's method and style but by the fact that the people of the Middle East had learned from Assyria's accomplishments the advantages of unification. Most of them, except for the princes and lords who clung to their petty privileges, were ready for a political reality to match the economic and cultural reality of the time. This desire revealed itself in the quick acceptance of Persian rule. Within twenty years after his victory over the Medes, Cyrus was in control of the Middle East from the Indus Valley to the Mediterranean. Four years later (525 B.C.) his son Cambyses added Egypt and Libya to the new universal state, making it larger by far than any previous empire (p. 42).

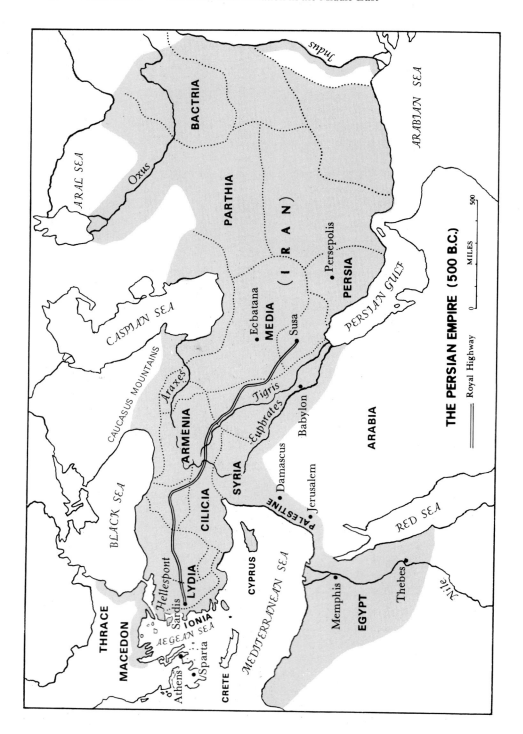

THE PERSIAN EMPIRE (500 B.C.)

══════ Royal Highway

900 B.C.		612	550		330 B.C.
ASSYRIAN EMPIRE		Chaldean "New Babylonia"	PERSIAN EMPIRE		
		Nebuchad-rezzar II (604-562)	Cyrus the Great and Darius (558-486)		Alexander the Great (356-323)

This second attempt at political unification resembled the Assyrian effort in many ways. Governmental form was essentially the same; the style of monarchy practiced for centuries in Mesopotamia and Egypt found its final embodiment in the Persian absolute ruler. He was, again, the "Great King," the "king of kings," identified with divine will and justice. He sat upon a gold and blue throne in a huge palace, dressed in purple cloth and laden with jewels. In his presence, ordinary mortals were required to lie, face down, before him; his royal word, like that of the ancient pharaohs, was an unquestioned command. This Persian image of divine kingship became the model for other individuals of grand ambition who would follow Cyrus. Among them were Darius, who succeeded him, Alexander the Great, Caesar, Diocletian, and the Eastern Roman (Byzantine) emperors.

Standing ready to carry out the commands of the throne were the Persian army and civil servants. The military forces were similar in organization and weapons to those of the Assyrians; tough Persian troops constituted the backbone of the heavily armed infantry. But large supporting forces were drawn from the conquered populations, including Syrians, Phoenicians, Egyptians, and Greeks. Because of the moderate nature of Persian rule, these forces were generally loyal. Once established, the empire seldom engaged in offensive wars, and insurrections by the conquered peoples were few. In consequence, the state did not develop a militaristic character. The monarchs preferred to spend their energies and resources for public buildings, roads, and services, rather than for military campaigns. Unlike the Assyrian rulers, they advertised their peaceful accomplishments, not their bloody battles.

For administrative purposes the realm was divided into some twenty provinces (satrapies). The king placed a nobleman (usually a Persian) as governor (satrap) in charge of each province; the satrap ruled with a light hand, however, under the guiding principles of restraint and tolerance. Taxes and military supplies were rigorously collected, but local customs, language, and religion were left alone. As a further measure of administrative control, the monarchs also appointed royal inspectors, the "king's eyes," who supervised the work of the satraps and reported directly to the royal palace.

The Persians were outsiders who had thrust themselves into the mature culture of the Middle East, and they added little to the basic arts of civilization. Their primary role was to unify the varied peoples of the area, maintain an environment favorable to constructive pursuits, and protect the frontiers from attack by barbarians.

One original contribution sprang from the teachings of a Persian religious reformer, Zoroaster, who had been born in the seventh century B.C. King Darius was a convert to this new faith, and it became ultimately the state religion of Persia. Zoroaster rejected the polytheism common to earlier Middle Eastern beliefs and taught of one almighty god of goodness and light (Ahura Mazda). This early monotheism, with its ideas of rewards and punishments in an everlasting life after death, had an influence on the religious beliefs of the whole region. (The influence of Zoroastrianism on Judaism and Christianity, in particular, will be discussed in Chapter 4.)

Babylonian astronomers continued, with Persian encouragement, to advance their knowledge of the heavens; one result was their learning how to calculate and predict eclipses of the moon. Persian art and architecture were chiefly adaptations of earlier styles and techniques. The most magnificent example, the royal palace at Persepolis, was a successful combination of building and sculptural elements from Assyria, Babylonia, Egypt, and Greece. The Persians helped to make Aramaic, a Semitic tongue, the common language of commerce for the Middle East. This was good for trade, as was the Persian development of *coinage*. Prior to this time, payment for goods was generally made in *kind* (goods) or with bars of precious metal. Coins, to make payment easier, had been invented by the Lydians of Asia Minor in the seventh century B.C.; their Persian conquerors adopted the use of coins and carried it to all parts of their domain.

The Persian Empire lasted for two centuries until it fell in its turn — for some of the same reasons that later empires, like that of Rome, also fell. It had to contend with human aggressiveness and corruption, as well as the immense difficulty of managing large numbers of diverse peoples. It was weakened by internal conflicts among the Persians themselves, and declining loyalty to their own king. At last (330 B.C.), the Greek, Alexander the Great, brought down the failing empire in a brilliant military campaign (p. 90).

All the same, the Persian Empire set the standard for a successful world state. The civilized Middle East of Persia's time had grown into an economic and cultural unit, and the empire's subjects showed a longing for unity, peace, and the freedom of movement and ideas that unity permits. The Persian Empire satisfied that longing, while permitting its subject peoples to maintain their own identities. United yet diverse, enriched by many different cultural traditions that had grown up over the centuries, the Persian Empire was the culmination of three thousand years of civilization in the Middle East.

THE EUROPEAN BARBARIANS

Throughout the three thousand years from early Sumer and Egypt to the Persian Empire, civilized peoples amounted to only a small proportion of the human species as a whole. During this period, civilizations also arose in India,

China, and the Western hemisphere (p. 14). Elsewhere, however, most humans still lived the life of farming and herding (without cities, written records, or fixed structures of government) that had emerged from the Agricultural Revolution (pp. 13–14). In particular, the territory of what we today call Europe was inhabited by such peoples, whom the sophisticated rulers, priests, and scribes of the Middle East no doubt thought of as "barbarians," if they bothered to think about them at all. Yet it was out of the *encounter* between the European barbarians* and the great civilizations of the Middle East that Western civilization was born.

For many centuries, the way of life of these barbarians remained only distantly affected by the rise of civilization in the Middle East. Even so, they made a great many advances of their own. In western Europe well before 3000 B.C., there were peoples who were sufficiently skilled and well organized to build circles and rows of huge upright boulders, and earthen tombs and fortifications, that were large and durable enough to survive to the present day. In southeastern Europe about the same time, there were barbarians so technically skilled that they were able to develop the basic methods of metalworking independently of the Middle East.

Perhaps the most notable single achievement of the European barbarians was the building of the great open-air monument — probably a temple — of Stonehenge in the west of England. Stonehenge was constructed over several hundred years down to 1550 B.C. by a prosperous people of farmers and traders that inhabited the region. In its final form the temple consisted of about 160 massive boulders, weighing up to fifty tons, all of which had to be dragged many miles to the site. Forty of the largest boulders were "trimmed" with stone tools to form neatly rectangular structural components; these were set upright with others placed horizontally on top of them as cross-pieces (similar to the post-and-lintel construction of Egyptian temples — p. 35). Together with the other boulders, they were arranged in four circular or horseshoe-shaped groups one inside the other, all carefully aligned to the movements of the sun and moon. The whole vast structure, much of which is still standing today (*Fig. 1-14*) is testimony to the level of wealth, organization, and skills attainable by the peoples of barbarian Europe.

Both the barbarian villagers of Europe and the civilized city-dwellers of the Middle East were frequently the victims of a *third* group of peoples. These were the migratory herders or *nomads* who inhabited the steppes (prairie grasslands) that stretched for thousands of miles from eastern Europe almost to the

---

*"Barbarian" is a Greek word, which originally designated all non-Greek individuals or nations, whether civilized or not. Today the word is often used contemptuously, to refer to people believed to be less intelligent, refined, or humane than oneself. By scholars, however, the word is used simply to denote peoples who have advanced beyond hunting and gathering (p. 9), but lack the characteristics of civilization defined on p. 6. Throughout this book, the word is used in this neutral sense.

1-14 Stonehenge: view from the south.

Pacific Ocean. The nomadic way of life was no throwback to the times before the Agricultural Revolution. It was an innovation that arose from 4000 B.C. onward as farming peoples moved onto the steppes and found that the grassy plains were best exploited by herding large numbers of animals. Among the animals that these settlers herded was one that was native to the steppes, the horse. By 3800 B.C. the steppe peoples were keeping the horse for its meat and hide; by 2000 B.C. they were harnessing it to wheeled vehicles; and by 1200 B.C. — having bred it to be larger and stronger than before — they had learned to ride it. As the "partnership" of man and horse grew closer, the steppe peoples concentrated more and more on herding. On light chariots, and later on horseback, they could follow larger herds farther across the grasslands, in search of grazing and water; and over the generations, they gave up settled village life altogether.

Their partnership with the horse also made the steppe peoples a serious menace to the inhabitants of surrounding regions. The powerful animal gave speed and weight to the attack of the warrior on the battlefield; and there were few settled peoples, barbarian or civilized, who could stand up to the charge of the nomadic charioteers (p. 24) and horsemen. Over the centuries right down to quite recent times, the names of nomadic invaders — such as the Huns, Avars, Hungarians, Turks, and Mongols — have left a fearsome echo in the history of their victims (pp. 137, 138, 187, 203, 207–8, 212, 267, 283–85). But the nomads also played a peaceful role, changing the ways of life of the peoples they conquered, and enabling trade, inventions, and cultural influences to travel vast distances — notably from the civilizations of the Far East to Europe.

The nomads who had the most far-reaching influence on Europe were a prehistoric people or group of peoples, known today as the Indo-Europeans. Probably originating in the steppes of present-day southern Russia, they spread outward from their homeland over many centuries between 4000 and 1000 B.C., as raiders, conquerors, and rulers. Some of them moved south into the civilized Middle East, and eastward as far as India (p. 296); those who moved into these lands, such as the Hittites, Medes, and Persians (pp. 26, 41), usually adapted to the ways of the civilizations they encountered. Other Indo-European peoples moved westward into Europe, and by 1000 B.C. they had occupied most of the region. Everywhere they moved, the Indo-Europeans brought great changes, above all in the languages of the peoples they encountered. Throughout vast areas of Europe and Asia, the inhabitants abandoned their original tongues and came to speak that of the Indo-Europeans, as their descendants still do at the present day. Languages as different as English and Bengali, or Russian and Spanish, are all derived from dialects spoken by the prehistoric Indo-Europeans.

On the barbarians of Europe, the impact of the Indo-European nomads was especially deep. From 2000 B.C. onward, under the influence of the newcomers, the settled peoples of the region began to form themselves into new ethnic groups, each made up of many different tribes. The way of life of these tribes was a mixture of their traditional patterns and the new Indo-European influences. On the one hand, they did not become nomads — which would have been impossible in the forests, mountains, and swamps of Europe — but continued to live the settled village life of their ancestors. On the other hand, in place of their earlier tongues, they now spoke languages of Indo-European origin; and in other ways, too, their way of life and social organization underwent important changes.

In addition to the deities of earth and fertility, and the dominant mother-goddesses (p. 14) that many European peoples had traditionally worshiped, they now also turned to gods of fatherhood, thunder, and war. They developed *elites* of warriors — often charioteers and horsemen — whose lives centered around strength and courage, comradeship and loyalty, contests and battle. They came to regard warfare not only as necessary, profitable, and pleasing to the gods, but also as honorable and noble — that is, as enhancing the value of the warrior as a human being. To a greater extent than with their ancestors, warfare became for the European barbarians a way of life.

One by one, over a period of three thousand years from 2000 B.C. right down to 1000 A.D., these barbarian warrior peoples came into contact with civilization. Sometimes they lived without conflict in the neighborhood of civilized peoples, trading with them, learning from them, and thereby acquiring the wealth and skills of civilization. Sometimes the barbarians were conquered by powerful civilized states, which then imposed their versions of civilization on their victims. Sometimes it was the barbarians who were the conquerors, for they were organized for war, and they fought with the same weapons as their civilized opponents. Even when victorious, the barbarians did not seek to destroy civilization; they wanted to enjoy its fruits, and in time, they usually adopted the ways of the civilized peoples they conquered.

Thus whatever the nature of the contacts between barbarian and civilized peoples in Europe, the results were always the same. One by one, the barbarian peoples of Europe became civilized; the chieftains and warriors of one era became the leaders and defenders of civilization in the next, often making their own contribution to the civilization they had acquired; and eventually, all the peoples of Europe entered the orbit of civilization.

This happened, in turn, to the Latin tribes of Italy (p. 93), the Celtic peoples of western Europe (pp. 94, 110, 181), the Germanic nations of northern Europe (pp. 127–29, 130–31, 136–39, 177–79, 208), and the Slavs of the east (pp. 186–89, 212–14). But the first such barbarian warrior people to make contact with civilization on European soil were the Greeks. As a result of their encounter with the civilized peoples of the Middle East from 2000 B.C. onward, the Greeks became the *founders* of Western civilization.

CHAPTER

2

The Greek Beginnings of Western Civilization

The Greeks, as the founders of Western civilization, drew freely upon the older civilizations of the Middle East. Especially through their contacts (chiefly commercial) with the Persian Empire, they absorbed much of the cultural heritage of both Mesopotamia and Egypt. As we saw in Chapter 1, that heritage included techniques for writing, forms of literature, styles of art and architecture, elements of mathematics and medicine, and methods of conducting trade. (The Greeks knew, but generally rejected, the Persian model of the "universal" empire governed by a divinely appointed ruler.) But Greek civilization drew on another cultural heritage as well—that of ancient Aegean civilization, which preceded the arrival of the Greeks.

THE AEGEAN BACKGROUND

Between 3000 and 2000 B.C. a distinct civilization—known to us as Minoan (from Minos, a legendary king)—arose under Middle Eastern influence on the island of Crete. The ruins of elegant palaces, especially at Knossos (where the palace was equipped with baths and plumbing), indicate a rich, refined civilization. That civilization rested on control of the surrounding seas and on widespread, thriving trade. Its artistic remains suggest a peaceful, pleasure-loving society, in which women played a prominent role—a society devoted to spectacular games and the worship of a fertility goddess.

By 1600 B.C. versions of this civilized way of life were flourishing along the coast and on the islands of the Aegean Sea (p. 50). These civilized societies, the first to appear on the continent of Europe, are known as Mycenaean after the name of the earliest mainland site to be discovered in modern times. The Mycenaean settlements, in contrast to the Minoan sites, were fortified with massive walls, and their inhabitants carried on both trade and warfare. For a time they struggled with the Cretans for control over the commerce of the

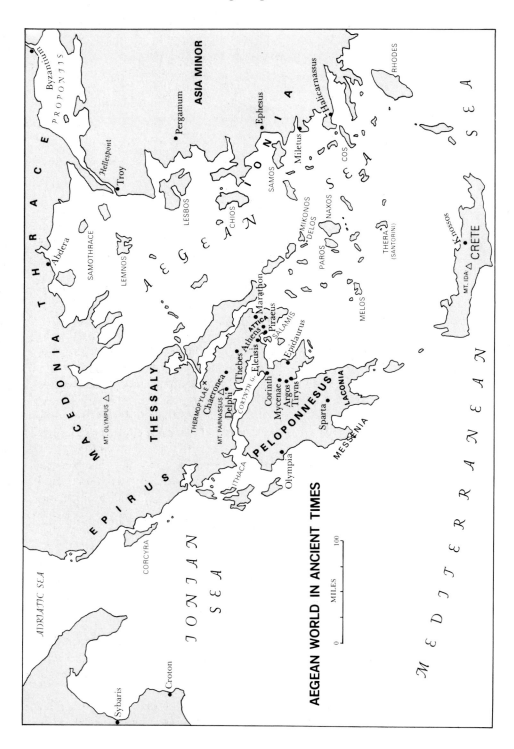

AEGEAN WORLD IN ANCIENT TIMES

c. 3500 B.C.   c. 800 B.C.

MESOPOTAMIAN CIVILIZATIONS		
EGYPTIAN CIVILIZATION		
MINOAN CIVILIZATION	MYCENAEAN CIVILIZATION	GREEK DARK AGES
c. 3000	c.1600	c. 1150

eastern Mediterranean Sea; the rivalry ended after the mysterious destruction of the Minoan towns around 1400 B.C., perhaps as a result of a decisive Mycenaean victory. (Some historians once held the view that the towns were demolished by a tidal wave following the explosion of a volcano on the island of Thera [Santorini], some seventy miles north of Crete. However, recent excavations indicate that the explosion occurred some two hundred years before the destruction of the Minoan towns.) Whatever the cause of the destruction, precise knowledge of Minoan civilization was lost until archeological investigations began at Knossos about A.D. 1900.

It was after the collapse of Minoan civilization that the Greeks, the people who were to lay the foundations of Western civilization, began to assert themselves. Apparently of mixed Nordic and Alpine stocks, speaking an Indo-European language (p. 47), they had begun to wander southward with their flocks after 2000 B.C. from the region of the lower Danube River. The earliest of them, called Achaeans, played some role in both the Minoan and the Mycenaean societies, though the details are unclear. But after 1200 B.C. fresh waves of more warlike Greeks overran the Aegean world; around 1150 they sacked "golden" Mycenae. Shortly before this event, according to tradition, an expedition of allied Greek forces had besieged and captured the flourishing city of Troy, on the northwestern coast of Asia Minor (p. 50).

The destruction of Mycenae, Troy, and many other towns marked the eclipse of civilization in the Aegean area for nearly four centuries — a period known as the "Dark Ages" of Greek history (1150–800 B.C.). The latest conquerors had come down from the north as a barbarian folk. Their society was geared to the family, the clan, the tribe, and the village; their economy was simple and largely self-sufficient; they had neither a written law nor any developed structure of government.

During the Greek Dark Ages a mingling of populations occurred that would produce the Greek of "classical" antiquity. Starting with the remnants of Minoan and Mycenaean achievement, joining them with their own simpler ways, and adding elements drawn from contact with the civilized East, the Greeks succeeded in creating their own distinctive culture. By the eighth century B.C. it extended from the Greek mainland to the Aegean islands and the western coast of Asia Minor. This is the culture we sometimes call "Homeric." (The poet Homer is believed to have lived in the eighth century.)

The country the Greeks had invaded and settled they named Hellas, after their mythical forefather, Hellen. It consisted of a mountainous mainland —

with narrow valleys, few rivers and plains, many bays and harbors — and hundreds of rocky islands strewn across the Aegean Sea. This arm of the Mediterranean was, in fact, the geographical center of the Greek world, bounded on the west and north by the European land mass, on the east by the coast of Asia Minor, and on the south by the island of Crete, which lies like a breakwater between the Aegean and the Mediterranean. Though the climate was mild, Hellas was poor in natural resources. As the Greek tribes settled on the conquered land, they turned to herding and farming; barley, grapes, and olives were the main crops. But the rocky soil provided most farmers with only a meager livelihood, and some of them, during the long summers, supplemented their income by trade — which often meant piracy.

Geographical variety and the surrounding sea encouraged movement and enterprise among the Greeks. Unlike the Mesopotamians and Egyptians, who usually clung to their river highways, the Greeks became a daring and venturesome people. This expansive character resulted in part from the pressure of population on their skimpy food supply. Despite efforts to hold down population, chiefly by infanticide (infant exposure to the elements), Greek settlements often grew beyond supportable numbers (especially after 800 B.C.). When that happened, the "city fathers" usually sent out expeditions to find a suitable spot for the founding of a "daughter" settlement (colony). From the Black Sea westward to the coast of Spain, the Mediterranean's shores came to be dotted with Greek colonies.

And yet, despite their wide dispersion, the Hellenes (as the Greeks called themselves) maintained a sense of "oneness." As early as 776 B.C., according to tradition, they celebrated the first Olympic games. The contests were part of a Pan-Hellenic gathering (that is, for all Greeks) in honor of the god Zeus. This celebration at Olympia, in the Peloponnesus (p. 50), was held every fourth year thereafter and served as one of the binding forces in Hellenic life.

THE CITY-STATE

Soon after the first Olympic celebration, the social and political unit known as the city-state began to emerge out of the simple family and clan organization of earlier times. This development was not unique to Greece. The early centers of civilization in the Middle East had also been temple-states or city-states before they were merged into larger political units. The major Greek city-states, however, remained independent during their most creative period; it is impossible to separate the idea of the city-state from Greek civilization itself.

The mature Greek city-state, or *polis* (source of our words "metropolis" and "political"), was more than just a government, a trading center, or a place to live. It ranged in extent from a few square miles to an area about the size of Rhode Island (in the case of Athens and Sparta). When possible, the city proper was built around a protecting hill, with a fortress crowning the summit, or *acropolis* (*Fig. 2-1*). The surrounding countryside, the mountains, and the sea

2-1 The Acropolis of Athens.

nourished the city with agriculture and commerce. The population (of both town and country) ordinarily numbered only a few thousand, though the largest, Athens, may have reached two hundred fifty thousand. Each city-state regarded itself as a *sovereign* (independent) unit of government; it was *the* government, the *sole* law for all of its inhabitants.

Yet the law was not something that was forced upon the citizens; they did not view it as an "interference" in their private lives. Although various types of government evolved over centuries, from kingship to democracy, the Greeks generally saw the city-state as a *community* enterprise. (Slaves and other noncitizens were not considered full participants in this community.) The source of the citizens' spirit, which existed even in such large city-states as Athens, lay in the origins of the community. Each was believed to have been founded and developed by a family or a clan—a kinship group—and most of its citizens could trace their ancestry back to common forefathers. In other words, they could think of themselves as distantly related members of one big family. They saw no more reason for conflict between the individual and the state than between the individual and the family. The "good life" for the individual was a life of active participation in civic affairs.

The city-state was also the citizens' "church." Although Greeks everywhere believed in the same pantheon (group of gods), they paid special reverence to the particular god or goddess who was associated with their own city. Local legend almost invariably held that the founder of the community was divine or semidivine and that a certain deity gave favor and protection to the city. The goddess Athena, for example, was the patron (guardian) of Athens, and all Athenians were therefore united in a special faith and ritual. The temple priests, moreover, did not form a class apart from the state; rather, they were state officials.

Finally, the city was the citizens' school, recreation center, and club. There was no classroom education for adults; instead, the citizens exchanged and discussed ideas daily as they talked in the marketplace, gymnasium, or assembly, and at civic festivals. These, rather than the home, served as the main social centers (which explains in part why the citizens paid far more attention to public architecture than to private dwellings, as we will see later).

It is not surprising that Greeks cherished their city-state, with its harmonious design for living. True, it was in a sense a narrow and artificial unit, poorly suited to an expanding world of trade and politics. When a colony was settled abroad by citizens from a "mother" city, the new settlement became a separate, independent state. And when one city conquered another, it extended its control but not its citizenship. In the end, these tiny states destroyed one another through endless rivalry, jealousy, and war — for each had its own armed force as well as its own law. By failing to join together in larger political units, they exposed themselves to foreign conquest. But Greek citizens were unwilling to accept any reduction in the independence of their city-state. They valued it even more highly than Westerners value the nation-state today; for to them it was not only the object of patriotic fervor but an extension of themselves and their family, a place of livelihood, learning, and pleasure — and a thing divine.

Although the Greek city-states had many features in common, each was individual in character and had its own personality. Athens brought forth in the course of a century more enduring creations of the human mind and spirit than any city before or since. Yet Athens was by no means the only center of creativity; there were, for example, Miletus and Ephesus in Asia Minor and Thebes, Argos, and Corinth on the mainland. But the power that contended with Athens for supremacy in Greece was Sparta. Though both were city-states, their particular institutions and ways of life were strikingly different. Before examining the remarkable achievements of Athens, we will look at its polar opposite in the Greek world.

Sparta: The Military Ideal

The Spartans were the chief descendants of the warlike Greeks who had conquered the southern mainland (p. 51). The land surrounding Sparta, known as Laconia, forms part of the Peloponnesus, a hand-shaped peninsula attached to the mainland by the Isthmus of Corinth (p. 50).

The Spartans, in the eighth century B.C., were a ruling minority (less than ten thousand adult males). Possessing poor lands of their own in Laconia, they pushed westward into the broad and fertile plains of Messenia. There, they subjugated the inhabitants, who outnumbered them about ten to one.

The conquerors became prisoners of their own success. Instead of extending political rights to the defeated people, they forced them to become semi-slaves (serfs), bound to the land by the state and compelled to work it for the citizen landholders. This situation required the Spartans to place themselves under a rigid system of life — one which would enable them, through the use of *terror*, to hold down a population much larger than their own. This demanded cultivation of their physical strength and endurance (for soldiering), strictest discipline, and a continuous watch (spying) upon every individual. The Spartans rarely wavered, over several centuries, from their self-imposed way of life. The very name "Spartan" became a byword for courage, stamina, sternness, and determination.

The Spartans' failure to move on through the stages of political growth experienced by other Greek communities was due largely to their fear of change. Because their control over conquered people was often threatened, they hesitated to tamper with any of the institutions on which that power rested. They kept their dual kings, for example, long after kings had disappeared elsewhere in Greece — though they did limit the royal powers. While the kings continued to command in battle, policy decisions were taken over by a council of elders. This consisted of the kings, along with some thirty other men chosen for life (by the citizens) from among the leading families. The elders had to be at least sixty years of age. And the five officials called ephors (overseers), who held executive authority in the city, were usually old men, too (elected annually). Thus, the Spartan government was actually an *oligarchy* (rule by the *few*). In most of the other Greek cities the popular assembly, which was open to all adult male citizens, became a genuine lawmaking body. But in Sparta the members of the Assembly were not even permitted to debate. Instead, the council of elders drew up all proposals and then presented them to the Assembly for approval or disapproval only — and this was given not by vote but by a shout.

The Spartans tried to seal off their city from outside influences. Compared with other Greek cities, Sparta had little contact with foreigners; it discouraged trade, and showed visitors little hospitality. Its citizens feared that "subversive" ideas might upset the delicate internal balance, and they resorted to secret police and physical isolation to keep ideas out. (The Spartans were not the first — or the last — to fear the power of ideas.) But they were not motivated by fear alone; most Spartans *wanted* to preserve intact their system of government, their way of life, their ideal of virtue (personal excellence).

Spartan men were required by law to serve as professional soldiers; all other occupations were closed to them. Property was fairly evenly divided among them, and any tendency to luxury was frowned on as a sign of softness. Their farms, as noted, were worked by the conquered people (called "helots") while a middle class of aliens (noncitizens) was permitted to conduct such little business as there was.

The Spartan army was the most respected in Greece. The core of its fighting power consisted of units of heavily armed infantry, with about four hundred men in each. The individual soldier wore a helmet and protective armor and fought with a round bronze shield, long spear, and short iron sword. This type of warrior, called the "hoplite," was the backbone of military forces everywhere in Greece. Lighter-armed troops, and cavalry, sometimes covered the flanks of hoplite formations.

One of the most curious features of the Spartan social system was the family life (or lack of it) among the ruling class. The men, when they were not out fighting, lived in barracks until they reached the age of thirty. They might then have some home life with their wives and children (they were permitted to marry after age twenty), but they still had to take their chief meal each day at a soldiers' mess. Infants who showed any sign of weakness were abandoned to die of exposure — a common Greek practice. Boys were taken by the state at the age of seven; they were taught manly behavior and reading and writing, and were started on a lifelong routine of physical toughening and military instruction. Bachelors were punished, and the state encouraged the mating of the best human specimens. All this regimentation, this denial of personal choice and decision, was directed toward one main goal: the maintenance of military supremacy.

Girls were also required to participate in drills and exercises, which were designed to develop them into healthy, childbearing women. Partly for this reason, and partly because for most of their lives they lived apart from their husbands, Spartan women were active and energetic, and were considered scandalously "liberated" by other Greeks. But they fully shared the militaristic ideal of their menfolk. The story was told of the Spartan mother whose parting words to her son, as she sent him off to battle, were that she expected him to return to her either *with* his shield (that is, as a victor) or *on* it (as a corpse).

Although the Spartans paid a high price for security, their system did what they wanted it to do. For centuries Sparta dominated the Peloponnesus, and in the desperate struggle with democratic Athens (during the Peloponnesian War) the Spartans came through weakened but victorious. Their way of life had its compensations, too: the men spent their days exercising, hunting, fishing, fighting, drinking, and eating; the women and girls had few housekeeping chores; and the boys spent their time in physical contests, war games, and outdoor living. For their helots, on the other hand, the Spartan system was brutal, toilsome, and dehumanizing.

Athens: The Glory of Greece

To the Athenians, the Spartan style of life was not worth living. One of their favorite quips was that the life led by the Spartans explained their willingness to face death. The Athenians sought a more balanced life. While they grudgingly admired the Spartans' physical toughness, they insisted that people had other potentialities that were equally or more important. The Spartans had a reputation for action rather than speech; the English term "laconic," which means "sparing of words," is derived from "Laconia," the Spartan homeland. The Athenians, on the other hand, loved to talk, though they could also act. From Athens flowed the daring inventiveness, the glorious literature, the stunning creations of mind and hand that have so enriched our heritage. Athens, rather than Sparta, is nearer to our image of Greek culture — though one reason may be that the Athenians wrote most of Greek history.

The contrasts between the two cities are endless. Sparta was agricultural and landlocked; Athens carried on a prosperous commerce and had direct access to the sea. Sparta had the more powerful army; Athens' chief strength was its navy. Sparta sought cultural isolation; Athens welcomed foreign ideas and visitors. Sparta had been founded on conquests; Athens was the product of a gradual and less violent development.

The Athenian homeland lay about a hundred miles northeast of Sparta, in the central portion of ancient Greece where the peninsula of Attica juts into the Aegean Sea (p. 50). Here a band of Greeks had settled sometime after 2000 B.C. (the date is uncertain). We know that by about 800 B.C. the neighboring communities of Attica had merged into the Athenian city-state. This slow and comparatively easy development led to a stable social condition that was not charged with the tensions existing in Sparta. While war and discipline were common to both states, the inhabitants of Athens enjoyed relatively greater freedom and leisure. In this situation Athenian culture came to full flower in the fifth century B.C.

The turning points in the life of Athens and the rest of Greece were two, both military. The first was the Persian Wars, in which Athens led the Greek city-states to victory over the mighty oriental empire. This exhilarating success was followed by the Age of Pericles (460–430 B.C.), a period of highest confidence, power, and achievement in Athens. That period, in turn, was cut short by the second turning point, the Peloponnesian War, between Athens and Sparta. But let us now view Athens at its best. The signal that set Athens on the path to glory was the Persian attack.

Persia (Iran) lies to the east of the Tigris-Euphrates valley, one of the birthplaces of civilization. In the sixth century B.C., its rulers had succeeded in overrunning Mesopotamia, Syria, Egypt, and Asia Minor and had welded together the largest empire known up to that time (p. 41). The "Great King," Darius I, determined (about 494 B.C.) to extend his control into Greece, for the Athenian upstarts had recently aided a rebellion against him by the Greek cities of Asia Minor. Darius (and later, his son, Xerxes I) sent several expeditions by land and sea against the mainland Greeks; he lost the first decisive battle at Marathon in 490 B.C. (The original "marathon" was run by the messenger of victory, who sped the twenty-six miles to Athens to break the news.) Ten years later, in a sea battle near Athens (off the island of Salamis), the Athenian navy smashed the Persian fleet.

Sparta, which shared with Athens the leadership of the Greek defense, also contributed to the defeat of Persia. The Spartans' suicidal stand at Thermopylae (480 B.C.) remains a symbol of heroism, and soon after Thermopylae the Spartans routed a Persian army in the pivotal land battle of Plataea. But in the course of the long war Athens made the greater sacrifices; and by 445 B.C., when final peace was made with Persia, Athens was the controlling power of the Aegean Sea. (Most significant, in the longer historical view, was the Athenian achievement of stemming the Eastern tide, thus preserving the Greek roots of Western civilization.)

The courageous and resourceful little state had demonstrated surprising capacity in fighting the Persian forces. The Athenians had twice fled their homes and watched the enemy burn their city to the ground. With their victory came a new-felt power. How had they, so few in number and so limited in wealth, turned back the power of the Great King, with his millions of slavish subjects? To the Athenians, flushed with confidence and pride, there could be only one answer: they and their free institutions were *superior*. As they rebuilt the temples of their Acropolis more magnificently than ever before, they worked with a sense of mission and assurance. The structures they erected (including the Parthenon) show their genius. And the same spirit inspired the sculpture, drama, and philosophy of these remarkable years. True, the Golden Age of Athens had been for centuries in gestation, but it was the crisis successfully met, the quickened pulse, the thrill of triumph that brought it to splendid birth.

Pericles, whose name is synonymous with the Golden Age, was the leader of Athens after the victory over Persia. It was largely through his initiative and guidance that the ambitious public-works program on the Acropolis was carried through. A man of wealth and learning, Pericles nevertheless identified himself with the "popular" faction in politics. By virtue of his personal influence and his long tenure in important elective offices, he acted as the city's guiding force during the thirty-year period of Athenian supremacy in Greece. His death in 429 B.C., soon after the start of the Peloponnesian War (p. 87), signaled the end of the Golden Age.

Before the time of Pericles, Athens had passed from monarchy through several stages of political growth. But through all these stages — including, for a period, rule by tyrants — there was one clear trend: the extension of political power to all adult male *citizens*. (Citizenship was a matter of birth; the status of a father normally determined that of his children.) Most notable among the early "lawgivers" was the wise and respected aristocrat, Solon. After 600 B.C., at a time of severe economic and political crisis (loss of farms through debt, and demands of poor citizens for a share of political power), Solon had been appointed to arbitrate the crisis and reform the laws. He acted first to cancel existing debts and prohibit enslavement for nonpayment of debts in the future. Then he altered the constitution by granting voting powers to the poorer classes while confirming for the aristocrats the sole right to hold public office.

(The aristocrats were descendants, usually rich, of the "best" founding families of Athens.) Though Solon's reforms did not permanently solve the persisting problems of the city, they were crucial steps on the path toward majority rule.

Around 500 B.C., another aristocratic statesman, Cleisthenes, led the way to complete *democracy*. (Democracy means the right of *all citizens* to political participation, and their acceptance of decisions made by a *majority*.) Ultimate power in Athens now rested in the Assembly of adult male citizens. All major decisions were made there: for peace or war, for sending forth expeditions, for spending public money, and for the general control of public affairs. Meetings were held about once a week, and the number of citizens present was usually less than five thousand. Although many more were eligible to attend, men who lived in the country districts of Attica were often unable to come to town. At first the Assembly met in the marketplace (agora) of Athens, later on the slopes of a nearby hill (Pnyx). Although it could draw up laws on its own, ordinarily it discussed proposals put before it by a committee of the Council of Five Hundred. The latter body was chosen annually by lot to draft the laws and to supervise their administration.

Debates in the Assembly were often spirited. Naturally, those with a talent for public speaking enjoyed a great advantage over their fellows. The members of the Assembly, highly critical and not always polite, might express their disagreement with an argument by jeering or whistling. But a shrewd and skillful orator like Pericles could win and hold the favor of the Assembly. And, once he had done so, he became the most powerful man in Athens, for the decisions of the Assembly were final. Voting was usually by a show of hands, and a simple majority determined the outcome.

The Athenian citizens insisted on *direct* democracy (personal participation), not only in making laws but in administering them. There were up to a thousand public officials in Athens — tax-collectors, building inspectors, and the like — and all but a few of them were chosen annually by *lot*. (Those chosen must have volunteered to serve and were subject to examination for fitness by the courts.) Since these officials were paid for their services, poor men as well as rich could afford to hold office. Here was a system of "rule and be ruled," the full application of a deep faith in the political capacity of every male citizen.

The Athenians did not, however, trust to lot in selecting their *chief* executive officers. These were the Ten Generals (*Strategoi*), who were chosen each year by vote of the male citizens. They commanded both the army and the navy, managed the war department, and had extensive control over the treasury. The Ten Generals chose their own chairman; the popular Pericles was elected general by the people and chairman by the board for sixteen years in succession.

The laws of Athens, then, were made and administered by the male citizens. The first important *code* of Athenian laws was published by the statesman Draco in 621 B.C. It was a collection of customary legal procedures and punishments, applying mainly to homicides. This code was amended and expanded over time by Solon and Cleisthenes, and by Assembly legislation.

And who interpreted the laws and passed judgment upon alleged violators? Again, it was the citizens themselves. Athenian courts differed from American courts in several respects. They were much larger in size, usually about five hundred members. The reasons for this were to make bribery or coercion difficult and to guarantee a broad cross section of citizen judgment. The court for each trial was chosen by lot from a long list of names. There was no officer, like a judge, to decide questions of law; the Athenian court was *judge* and *jury* combined. By majority vote, it ruled on all issues of procedure, legal interpretation, guilt or innocence, and type of punishment. There were no lawyers, either. Every citizen argued his own case — another reason why the ability to speak effectively was so valued in Athens.

The Athenians practiced what they preached about political democracy. In fact, they *invented* democracy (as well as the word itself). Civic and political participation was part of the Athenian way of life for all adult male citizens. We have no statistical records, but estimates suggest that during the Age of Pericles the number of adult male citizens was only about forty thousand out of a total citizen population (including children) of perhaps one hundred thousand. Beneath the citizens in status were resident aliens, chiefly artisans and tradespeople, who may have numbered fifty thousand. At the bottom of the social structure were the slaves, who were perhaps equal in number to the citizen class. Thus, the estimated forty thousand male citizens controlled the government of a state of possibly two hundred and fifty thousand inhabitants. And yet, even though female citizens, aliens, and slaves were excluded, there were doubtless more individuals *actively participating* in government in Athens than in any other city of comparable population before or since.

Slaves were found in all the city-states, as they were throughout the ancient world. They were chiefly non-Greeks, usually descended from captives of war. The Athenians (including the philosopher Aristotle) justified slavery by arguing that Greeks were superior to non-Greeks and that it is good and right for superiors to rule inferiors. Slaves, Aristotle declared, were necessary "instruments" for the use of their superiors. By taking over the dull and heavy tasks, they freed their masters for greater leisure and cultural attainments. Most of the slaves in Athens were household servants; some worked in the fields; some were craftsmen; about ten thousand of them worked in the silver and lead mines of Attica. The mine workers were driven cruelly, but the others seem to have been treated humanely. Slaves were legally the property of their owners, and they worked and lived pretty much as their masters chose. A few were permitted to rise to positions of considerable importance in Athens, and many were set free as a reward for faithful service. At any rate, there were no slave revolts such as those that occurred in Sparta and in most other places where slavery has existed. The orator Demosthenes claimed that Athenian slaves enjoyed greater freedom than the citizens of many other lands, and he was probably right. A favorite taunt by the Spartans (in a way, a compliment) was that on the streets of Athens one could not tell a citizen from a slave. As a matter of fact, the Athenians did not stress social and economic differences. The majority of citizens were people of limited means: small farmers, artisans, or merchants.

But the Athenian economy was diversified and balanced; its chief products were wine and olive oil. (Olive oil was an important commodity in the ancient world, where animal fats were scarce. It took the place of butter and soap and served as a lubricant and as a fuel for lamps.) By the fifth century Athens had become well known also as a manufacturing center. Free men and slaves, working in small shops, produced excellent metal weapons, pottery, and hand-wrought articles of silver, lead, and marble. Most of these were sold abroad in return for grain, meat, fruit, textiles, and lumber. Many citizens made their living by building or sailing ships, for Athens was a leading maritime power. Wages and profits were generally low, but so was the cost of living.

And the Athenians had simple needs. Wraparound garments and a single pair of sandals made up the typical wardrobe. They took but one main meal each day, consisting normally of grains, fruits, vegetables, and fish. Wine was consumed daily; meats were reserved for holidays. Recreation was free at the civic festivals, which included athletic contests, dances, and dramatic performances. What most Athenian males sought was not great wealth but leisure: time for talk, for exercise and games in the public gymnasium, and for engaging in the affairs of their city. Living standards did vary, of course, and there was always some feeling of hostility between rich and poor — hostility softened, however, by common devotion to the community and by the fact that the wealthy paid for festivals, dramatic shows, and ships for the navy. (The state received additional revenue through court fines, customs duties, an annual tax on aliens, and certain sales taxes — including one on prostitution.)

Women did not enjoy the general freedom of Athens; they were regarded as inferior, by nature, to men. In fact, Athenian women had fewer rights than those of Sparta or Egypt. Poor women sometimes worked in trades outside the home: as weavers, innkeepers, and vendors in the marketplaces. (In the countryside, they helped in the fields.) Well-off female citizens, however, seldom went into the street except to attend religious celebrations; banquets and entertainments were usually for men only. Women had but limited property rights, and marriages and divorces were negotiated by their male relatives. Though mutual respect and affection were normal between spouses, marriage was viewed primarily as a practical partnership for producing heirs and keeping house.

The sexual liberty of the husband was taken for granted. In addition to his wife, he had access to his household slaves as well as the public prostitutes (noncitizens). And if he found his wife boring, and could afford to do so, the husband might take up with more engaging female companions (*hetaerae*). These women, usually noncitizens from Asia Minor, were schooled in the arts of conversation and entertainment. The most famous of them was the intelligent and charming Aspasia, the consort and mistress of Pericles.

In addition, well-off Athenian men, like all other upper-class Greeks including the Spartans, could without dishonor form homosexual relationships, so long as these were of a particular sort. Perhaps because of their relatively restricted family life, the Greeks found it normal and even praiseworthy for adult men to fall in love and have sexual relationships with teenage boys. Sooner or later, when the boy grew up, a relationship of this kind was supposed to turn into ordinary friendship, and homosexuality between "consenting adults" was generally frowned on. Within these limits, male homosexuality played an important part in the sexual and emotional life of the Greeks.

The Athenians lavished great care upon their children, especially their sons. Though the girls received little formal training, most boys were instructed in private schools or, individually, by tutors. They were taught to exercise, to play games, and to compete in sports. They were also instructed in reading, writing, and speaking, as well as the popular legends, music, and the poems of Homer. After reaching eighteen years of age, the young men were assigned to special companies for two years of military and civic training. But the city itself was the principal school for young and old. Talking in the marketplace, the Assembly, and the courts; listening to music and dramas; visiting the temples; and participating in athletic contests — in these ways the male citizen could approach the classical ideal of "a sound mind in a sound body."

The City-State Way of Life

In Athens we find the full flowering of Greek genius, but there were scores of other city-states in which the way of life was similar. And, though Greek civilization expressed itself through these independent city-states, we should not lose sight of the "oneness" of their culture. Each city paid special respect to its favorite gods, but all sacrificed to the same chief deities, just as they shared common shrines and oracles and celebrated such all-Greek festivals as the Olympic games. All claimed a common forefather, Hellen, and all had a common inheritance in the heroes and history of Homer.

The same language bound these freedom-loving peoples together and set them apart, in their own view, from outsiders. Those who did not speak Greek they called barbarians (*barbaroi*) (p. 45). This was not necessarily a term of discredit or blame, for the Greeks applied it to refined and sophisticated Persians as well as to primitive and untamed tribes. It meant simply that those outsiders could not speak Greek, from which it followed that they could not think Greek, hence know or live the Greek way.

What was this Greek way? How did it differ from the Eastern way? The cardinal distinction lay in the Greek view of the *individual*. In the ancient cultures of the Middle East ordinary people were of small account. The ruler of Egypt, the pharaoh, owned and regulated the land and its inhabitants through divine right. Guided by priests and working through an army of agents and bureaucrats, he ordered the pattern of existence for everyone. The idea of personal liberty had little meaning to the mass of his subjects, and no one in authority regarded them as capable of governing themselves (pp. 28–29).

But Greek citizens would be slaves to no person and to no state. They believed in law and in an orderly society protected by the gods, but they generally insisted upon a substantial measure of freedom and political participation (for adult males). The city-state was more than a means of government; it was in itself a way of life — the only "good life." And, the Hellenes believed, all free and intelligent Greeks were capable of enjoying this good life. They did not take the view, characteristic of the East, that individuals must resign themselves to a fate altogether beyond their control. In a limited way, the Greeks were optimistic about the world and about what a man could do on his own — if he did not presume too far. During the Golden Age, at least, they showed tremendous zest for living. The struggle, the contest, the game — even when lost — seemed exciting and challenging. Above all, out of the fertile and stimulating environment of the city-state came the renowned achievements of the Greeks, in religion and philosophy, in literature, architecture, and sculpture, that have formed part of the heritage of Western civilization ever since.

GREEK RELIGION

While the Greeks' view of life was reflected in their politics, it was expressed most fully in their religion, philosophy, and art. Greek religion by the Age of Pericles (fifth century B.C.) had become a well-developed institution of the state. It ordered the daily lives of citizens, inasmuch as the community undertook no important act without giving thought to the gods, but there was no authoritative body of dogma, no "Word of God," and no special *class* of priests. Prayers, rites, and festivals were rooted in customs that traced back to the misty beginnings of Greek history and were preserved in the works of early poets. The greatest of these poets, Homer (p. 74), drew portraits of the gods and told colorful tales about them. Another poet, Hesiod, wrote more directly about the ancestry of the gods and the creation of the universe. These works and those of several lesser writers were generally accepted by the Greeks as highly respected accounts of the divine scheme of things.

Gods and Goddesses

From earlier civilizations, the Greeks inherited the basic ideas of polytheistic and anthropomorphic religion (p. 19). They believed that the natural world and human affairs were controlled by hundreds of living beings, similar to humans in appearance and character except for their immortality; among these, a few were thought to be superior in power and majesty. While far from being the first to personify the forces of nature and fortune in this way, the Greek poets and artists surpassed all others in their appealing imagery. The creations of their mind and spirit survive gracefully and lustily in Greek sculpture, painting, and mythology.

The gods lived close by — the great ones on top of Mount Olympus, the highest peak of Hellas (p. 50). There, behind a veil of clouds, Zeus, father of the gods, presided over his divine family. The Olympian deities were usually perfect and beautiful in shape, but they displayed human frailties and emotions. They knew ambition, pride, and jealousy, and they took an active interest in affairs on earth. Though they were not all-powerful, they merited the respect of mortals, who took pains to win their favor by sacrifices, honors, and prayers. Human and divine beings alike, moreover, were thought to be subject to the mysterious and irresistible force of *Moira* (Fate).

Zeus (Jupiter),* whose special zone was the sky, shared overlordship of the world with two of his brothers: Poseidon (Neptune) ruled the sea, and Hades, or Pluto (Dis), ruled the underworld. The underworld was a dark, forbidding place where spirits of the departed lingered for an uncertain period. There was, generally, no expectation of immortality for humans and no system of rewards and punishments after death. But the gods could inflict their power for good or ill on a person during life. Many a Greek who had offended Zeus had been struck by his thunderbolt, and every sailor knew the fury of the sea when Poseidon was angered. In this fashion the elements of nature were personified and interpreted by the Greeks.

As Zeus embodied the patriarchal (fatherly) principle, his wife Hera (Juno) embodied the matriarchal (motherly) principle. She was regarded as the protector of womanhood and marriage. But she was also something of a shrew, and Zeus found comfort in extramarital romance — which resulted in numerous divine offspring. His favorite daughter was Athena (Minerva), a spirited virgin noted for her wisdom, armed and martial in bearing, the consoler of maidens, and the protector of Athens. The Athenians raised many monuments in her honor; the most perfect was the temple of the Parthenon (Virgin), which still crowns the Acropolis of Athens.

The legends of the love affairs of Zeus and of other gods and goddesses had doubtless grown up as a way of explaining the special character of individual deities and their relationships to one another. But the Greek poets gave extraordinary color and vigor to these legends. They told, for example, how Leto, one of the companions of Zeus, had presented him with a splendid pair of twins — the handsome Apollo and his sister, Artemis (Diana). Apollo, later associated with the sun, was widely worshiped as the god of poetry, music, art,

---

*The names of deities in parentheses are those of the Roman gods and goddesses later identified with the Greek Olympians.

and manly grace. Artemis, associated with the moon, was the goddess of wild nature, a hunter, and the model of athletic girlhood.

A female of quite another type was Aphrodite (Venus), goddess of beauty and love. Aphrodite tried her charms on many men and gods, among them the bluff and powerful Ares (Mars). But the god of war, "the curse of men," preferred the thrill of killing to the pleasures of lovemaking. More companionable was the fleet Hermes (Mercury), messenger of the gods and patron of athletes. He had the lithe form of a perfect runner, and he glided on winged sandals over land and sea. Dionysos (Bacchus) was a son of Zeus by a mortal woman (Semele). It was, in part, this mixed parentage that made him so popular and beloved among the Greeks. Many legends were mingled in Dionysos: he was the god of wine and indulgence; he was also associated with the fertility principle in nature, with the suffering of death, and with the joy of rebirth. It is not surprising that "mystery" cults (worship groups), promising personal immortality, grew up in connection with Dionysos.

Priests, Oracles, and Mystery Cults

The Greeks had no churches — neither organizations nor buildings — as we think of them. And, because they had no rigid teachings, people could believe what they pleased so long as they did not openly deny or insult the official deities. (Such acts were forbidden because they might bring down divine punishment, not only upon the offending individual, but upon the whole community.) The temple, the chief place of worship, was designed as a "home" for the personal use of the god it honored. A statue of the god was normally placed in the interior, which was seldom entered by the public. An appointed priest was responsible for the care and protection of the statue and the sacred temple area.

Ceremonies in honor of the god were usually performed in front of the temple, where the worshipers presented the priest with gifts — pottery, garments, whatever might be pleasing to the god or goddess. They also offered up prayers and animal sacrifices to win divine favor and assistance. After a sheep or pig had been roasted and the aroma had reached the nostrils of the god, the priest and the worshipers ate the meat in a common sacred meal. (The only food and drink taken by the gods themselves were the divinely perfect "ambrosia" and "nectar," believed to nourish their immortality.)

Some priests and priestesses claimed that they had the power to see into the future, by interpreting certain "signs" (omens) or by verbal communication with the gods. The Greeks took special interest in these seers (oracles) and paid them high honor and respect. The most famous oracles in all Greece were the priestesses of Apollo who lived at Delphi (p. 50). Politicians, generals, heads of families — the mighty and the lowly — went or sent to Delphi for advice on such matters as whether or not to undertake a military campaign or what they must do to end a plague. A priestess would fall into a trance, relay the question to Apollo, and then utter the answer received from him. The utterance was usually unclear and had to be interpreted for the questioner by a priest. The Delphic oracles won a high reputation for accuracy, partly because the advice and predictions were in such vague, ambiguous terms that they could be made to fit almost any later event.

The official religion thus offered mortals a glimpse of the divine will. It also explained the mysteries of nature and provided a means of gaining the favor and help of superhuman forces. What it did not provide was consolation to those who lost the game or suffered misfortune. Nor did it hold any promise of life other than the one on earth; only the gods enjoyed eternal life. As if to balance these shortcomings, various cults grew up alongside the official religious beliefs and practices. Because their rituals were usually known only to the initiated, these came to be called *mystery* (secret) cults.

Dionysos, the central figure of worship in most of these cults, was associated with seasonal death and rebirth (winter and spring). His followers believed that they could identify themselves with the god, and thus share his rebirth, by means of ritualistic experiences; these included undergoing severe physical tests, becoming intoxicated with wine or drugs, eating a sacred meal, and witnessing a dramatic representation of the god's death and resurrection. At the end of such ordeals the worshiper sensed a mystic union with the god and assurance of everlasting life. The mystery religions supplemented, rather than replaced, the official religion, and probably only a minority of the citizens underwent the initiation rites.

Other Greeks were more interested in the relation of religion to morality. The gods of Homer had shown slight concern for customary moral standards, but by the time of the Golden Age they had become more closely identified with ideas of right and wrong. Zeus was regarded as the upholder of justice, especially of the sanctity of oaths. Human crimes were frowned upon by most of the Olympians, and divine punishment would surely fall on the murderer, perjurer, or arrogant individual. Even so, the official religion, with its accounts of strange and questionable acts performed by the gods themselves, did not fully satisfy the moralists. Greek dramatists and philosophers ("serious" thinkers) began to challenge the traditional beliefs, insisting that religion should include a definite *moral* order. Failing to find it in the Greek legends, they either rejected the gods or made them subordinate to a "higher power" of justice.

THE FOUNDERS OF WESTERN PHILOSOPHY

The earliest Greek philosophers (sixth century B.C.) began by criticizing the popular nature-myths. They found it hard to believe that earthquakes were caused by the stamping of Poseidon or that lightning was a bolt from Zeus. They made the intellectual leap from a primitive view of nature to a *reasoned*, analytic view.

Pioneers of Rational Thought

One of the questions they sought to answer concerns the composition of the physical universe: What are the elements from which all *material* things are made? Around 600 B.C., Thales of Miletus (in Asia Minor) theorized that water is the basic element. This was a logical notion, since water seems to be present, in various forms, throughout the world of space and matter. It fills the sea, rivers, and springs; it falls from the sky; it is found in the flesh and organs of animal bodies. And, under varying conditions of temperature and pressure, it changes from a liquid to a solid or a vapor. Thales was no doubt aware that his theory did not explain all the varied appearances of matter; but he and other Greek thinkers were convinced that nature, in its unseen being, is far simpler than it appears to be.

Though later philosophers rejected Thales' belief that everything can be reduced to water, they agreed that he was on the right track. Some believed the prime substance to be air or fire; others concluded that there are four basic elements: earth, air, fire, and water. But during the fifth century B.C. Democritus of Abdera (in Thrace) developed the theory that all physical things are formed by combinations of tiny particles, so small that they are both invisible and indivisible. He called them *atoms*. Democritus' atoms are identical in substance but differ in shape, thus making possible the great variety of objects in the world. They are infinite in number, everlasting, and in constant motion. They account, said Democritus, for everything that has been or ever will be. Democritus offered no concrete evidence to prove the existence of atoms, but the fact that he could arrive at this remarkable idea demonstrates the far-reaching achievement of Greek reasoning.

Rational thought was also applied to diseases. In the fifth century B.C., Hippocrates of Cos (an island in the Aegean) openly challenged traditional supernatural explanations of illness. He insisted that *natural* causes be looked for and that natural means be used to treat disease. He was one of the first physicians to stress the influence of the *environment* (climate, air, and water) on health. His most notorious theory, however, was that of "humors." The human body, Hippocrates believed, contains four humors (fluids): blood, phlegm, yellow bile, and black bile. When these are in proper balance, the individual enjoys normal health. But when the balance becomes disturbed, the physician must use his skill to restore it. This unproved theory was widely accepted in the West until the eighteenth century — and sometimes brought suffering or death (from bloodletting). Hippocrates is credited also with having initiated the first code of ethical behavior for physicians — and with it, the "Hippocratic oath," by which doctors pledge to use their knowledge solely for healing and human benefit.

Turning to more abstract and universal matters, the philosopher Parmenides of Elea (in southern Italy) tackled the controversial issue of permanence versus change in the world. He convinced himself that everything in the universe must be eternal and unchangeable. Change requires motion, he reasoned, and motion requires empty space. But empty space equals nonexistence, which by definition does not exist. Therefore, he concluded, motion and change are impossible. Parmenides readily admitted that some things *appear* to move and change; but this must be an illusion of the senses, he said, because it is contradicted by logic. And *logic*, the Greek philosophers thought, is the most reliable test of truth.

Logic did not always lead to the same answers, however. While Parmenides satisfied himself that matter was unchanging and permanent, another Greek reached the opposite conclusion. Heraclitus of Ephesus (in Asia Minor) insisted that the universe, instead of standing still, is in continuous motion. He declared that a person cannot step into the same river twice — in fact, the river is changing even as one steps into it. This doctrine proved most disturbing, for if everything is constantly changing (including ourselves), how can we gain true knowledge of anything? By the time our mind has been informed, the object of our attention is no longer what it was!

The Sophists

Discomforting suggestions such as these led many Greeks to abandon the effort to find absolute or final truth. During the fifth century B.C., serious thinkers began to turn from baffling questions about physical matter, permanence, and change to the more immediate and engaging problems of *human life*. A group of professional teachers, called Sophists because they claimed to make their pupils wise (*sophos*), played a leading part in this shift. Most of them, as teachers, had visited various cities of the Mediterranean area in order to earn their living. Hence, when they settled in Athens, as many did, they held more cosmopolitan views about the world than did ordinary Athenian citizens. Prominent among the Sophists was Protagoras. He is famous for having declared, "Man is the measure of all things, of what is and of what is not." Completely skeptical (doubting) of general truths, even about the gods, he insisted that truth is different for *each individual*. What was true (or right) for a Spartan might well be false (or wrong) for an Athenian. Furthermore, as Heraclitus had suggested, our bodies and minds are changing every moment, and our perceptions and ideas change with them.

The Sophists thus rejected the established view that there existed a common, "objective" reality that all persons can grasp in the same way. They concluded, therefore, that it is pointless to look for *absolute* truth about either nature or morals. Because truth is *relative* to each individual, it is important only to know what one finds agreeable and useful, such as the arts of persuasion or how to achieve "success." And one leading Sophist, Aristippus of Cyrene (in North Africa) equated success with *pleasure*. He and his followers (the Cyrenaic school) were convinced that the only sensible goal for each individual is personal enjoyment. They were not the first humans to "discover" such an idea, but they may have been the first to justify it with *reasoned* arguments. As they claimed *hēdonē* (pleasure) to be the "highest good," they and people of like mind are often called "hedonists."

Pleasures arise from many varieties of experience, Aristippus observed, and can be either bodily or mental. Which sort should be sought after? He answered that no pleasure is by *nature* superior to others; its relative value depends only upon its *intensity*. Individuals should therefore seek bodily pleasures in preference to mental ones, since they are usually the more intense. But Aristippus made it clear that one cannot achieve a high sum of pleasures if one stumbles blindly from one sensation to another. The successful hedonist is not a slave to pleasure but, rather, *commands* it — through a strategy of judging and selecting, and adapting to circumstances.

The Sophist teachings that equated morality with success or pleasure and contradicted traditional beliefs about truth, standards, and duty were radical for the times. As news of these teachings circulated in Athens and elsewhere in Greece, the more conservative citizens became shocked and alarmed. Such ideas smacked of blasphemy (disrespect for the gods) and threatened to subvert the laws and moral code of the state. Protagoras protested that his theories did not call for the denial of authority (anarchy) and cautioned his pupils, "When in Athens do as the Athenians." Social order, he agreed, requires reasonable conformity to the laws of the community, whether or not they are absolutely true or right. But the conservative elders were not reassured. It was upsetting to them to think that one person's ideas are as "true" as another's. And the laws of gods and mortals, they argued, cannot be properly respected and upheld unless the citizens believe them to be true and just — in an *absolute* sense.

Socrates and Plato

The greatest teacher of the fifth century was Socrates, who met the Sophist view of how to get on in life with the full force of his intellect and will. He was not a defender of the Olympian religion or of traditional morality; he was convinced, rather, of the existence of a higher truth. Socrates did not claim to know this truth but spoke of himself only as a seeker after knowledge. Because of his skeptical approach and his primary interest in *human* affairs, Socrates was often mistaken for one of the Sophists. He believed that knowledge must proceed from doubting, and he was forever posing questions and testing the answers people gave him. The Athenians resented having to justify their ways and ideas to Socrates, and he became increasingly unpopular. But he persisted in his arguments and discussions, for, he felt, "The unexamined life is not worth living."

Socrates believed that a technique of careful questioning can lead to the discovery and elimination of false opinions, which often pass for "truth." He cross-examined his associates on their definitions of justice, right, and beauty, moving them constantly toward answers that seemed more and more certain.

This "Socratic method," sometimes called the "dialectical method," is simply a procedure for reaching toward truth by means of a *dialogue* or directed discussion. Socrates did not believe it necessary to observe and collect data in order to find absolute knowledge; he had a deep conviction that truth is implanted in the mind but becomes hidden by erroneous sense impressions. The function of the philosopher is to *recover* the truth that lies buried in the mind.

Socrates' theory of knowledge is closely related to his idea of the soul (the seat of the mind). Almost all we know about his idea of the soul, as well as his other views, comes to us through the writings of his brilliant pupil, Plato. In the dialogue of the *Phaedo*, Plato describes the final hours of his great teacher. Condemned to death by an Athenian jury on charges of corrupting the youth and doubting the gods, Socrates faces his fate cheerfully. He does so because he believes the soul is immortal, though during life it is hindered by the troubles and "foolishness" of the body. Death brings release for the soul and the opportunity to see the truth more clearly than before. And for Socrates the real aim of life is to know the truth, rather than to seek the satisfactions of the body. His devotion to the search for truth persisted unto death.

It is difficult to say where the ideas of Socrates end and those of Plato begin. Plato wrote masterly literary works in the form of dialogues in which Socrates usually appears as the chief speaker. It seems clear that Plato took up the main thoughts of his teacher and carried them through a full and positive development. It is even possible that Socrates would have challenged some of the conclusions reached by his pupil. Plato, after traveling widely through the Mediterranean lands, founded a school at Athens (385 B.C.). The Academy, as it was called, became the most influential intellectual center of the ancient world. It endured after its founder's death for over nine hundred years, and it served as a model for similar schools in other cities.

Plato continued the Socratic attack on the Sophist theory of relative truth. He refused to admit that the world consists of nothing more than imperfect nature in a constant state of flux. Turning back to the controversies of earlier Greek thinkers, who had been concerned with the "stuff" of the universe and with the question of permanence and change, Plato felt that the imperfect *surface* of things conceals a perfect, absolute, and eternal order. With daring imagination, he constructed a picture of the universe that satisfied the demands of his intelligence and his conservative temperament.

In his famous "Doctrine of Ideas," Plato conceded that the *physical* world is just what Heraclitus and the Sophists suggested: imperfect, changeable, and different in appearance to every individual. But the physical world is superficial, possibly only an illusion of our senses; above and beyond it, Plato asserted, is the "real" world of *spirit*. This consists of perfect Ideas (Forms) authored by "God," which exist unchanged through all the ages. There are, for example, the Ideas of Man, Horse, Tree, Beauty, the State, Justice, and the highest of all Ideas — Goodness. These exist independent of individuals and can be known to them only through the mind (soul). The physical objects that the senses report are at best imperfect reflections or copies of the master Ideas; hence, though they may offer clues to the Ideas, they have no value in themselves. Philosophers should turn away from these sensory impressions and focus upon the discovery and contemplation of the perfect, the eternal, the real. It is in the Ideas (Forms) that they will discover *absolute* truths and standards.

Plato and thinkers of similar outlook have found this conception sublimely illuminating and satisfying. It is a possible explanation of the universe, though not a convincing one for persons who place faith primarily in their senses. Many arguments can be marshaled to support it, and centuries later Plato's view was to prove adaptable to the teachings of Christianity (p. 145). For the Christians, also, subordinated physical things and urged believers to think upon the world of spirit — the "other" world of divine order and perfection.

Affairs on earth, according to Plato, are best guided by absolute principles as interpreted by true philosophers. Partly to provide a model society and government (state), he wrote the best known of his dialogues, the *Republic*. The book is rich with suggestions on education, literature, and the arts, but its major influence has been on social and political thought. Plato believed that human institutions should aim, not at complete individual freedom and equality, but at social justice and order. Justice, to Plato, meant *harmony of function* within each individual and among the individual members of a state. (An aristocrat by birth and inclination, Plato admired Spartan institutions and had contempt for democratic ways.) Reflecting his view of the state as an *organic* unity, he argued that the foot should not try to become the head — nor the head the stomach. Every part of the human body and every member of the body politic should do the job it was designed to perform. Only then can friction, envy, and inefficiency — the chief sources of human and social sickness — be eliminated.

To reach this objective, Plato felt, the state must be structured according to natural capacities. The bulk of its citizens would make up the class of Workers (producers), who would be sorted into various occupations according to their aptitudes. Above them would be the Guardian class, which would be trained in the arts of war. From this disciplined class would be chosen, with the greatest care, the rulers of the state (Plato's "philosopher-kings"). While the Workers would be permitted to live "naturally," procreating and raising families, the Guardians would follow a most austere and regulated life. Matings among them would be arranged by the state, to ensure the production of superior offspring. Any infant showing a physical defect would be left to die of exposure, and normal infants would be taken from their mothers and placed in a community nursery. Parents would not be permitted to know their own children, nor would they be allowed to possess personal property. Such extreme measures are necessary, thought Plato, if rulers are to become truly selfless and dedicated to the welfare of the *whole community*.

The education of the Guardians, the same for males and females, was to be closely controlled. Only the "right" kind of music, art, and poetry would be taught, so that pupils would receive the desired moral indoctrination. Men and women chosen from this class to be the rulers would have additional training in philosophy and would serve a period of political apprenticeship before taking their place as directors of the state. The Republic of Plato remains to this day an example for believers in aristocracy, planned society, equality for women, and state control over education and the arts. It was the first of a series of *utopias*, or model states, that have offered radical solutions for the problems of human society.

Aristotle

Plato's own pupil, Aristotle, combined the brilliant imagination of his master, who had made mind the sole reality, with a sense of the reality of the physical world. Born in Stagira (in Thrace), Aristotle made his way early to Plato's Academy in Athens; years later he founded a school of his own there — the Lyceum (335 B.C.). Far more than his teacher, Aristotle was interested in the evidence of the senses. He was, in fact, the greatest collector and classifier in antiquity. His interests ranged from biology to poetry and from politics to ethics.

Aristotle accepted Plato's general notion of the existence of Ideas (Forms), but he held that physical matter also is a part of reality and not to be despised. Matter, he thought, constitutes the "stuff" of reality, though its shapes and purposes come from the Forms that Plato had set forth. By logical thinking, people can gain knowledge of the purposes of things and of their interrelations, knowledge that will give meaning and guidance to their lives and bring them at the same time closer to God — whom Aristotle conceived as pure spirit and the source of the Forms. To Aristotle, logic is the indispensable key to truth and happiness. For this reason, he worked out precise and systematic rules for logical thinking, rules that have been respected by philosophers for centuries.

In his study of society and government, Aristotle began by examining existing constitutions and states. In his classic work, the *Politics*, he analyzed and evaluated the major types of political organization. He did not draw from these a model organization suitable for all cities; rather, he recognized that there are differences in local conditions and classes of inhabitants. Aristotle identified three basic types of government: rule by *one* (monarchy), the *few* (aristocracy), and the *many* (democracy). Each of these types, if devoted to the general welfare, he considered legitimate, but any one of them becomes a "perversion" when the rulers pursue their *own* interest alone. (The worst government of all, he thought, is a perversion of rule by the *many*.) Under whatever constitution, Aristotle favored a strong role for the "middle class" of citizens. The more numerous poor, he stated, lack experience in directing others; the very rich are not used to obeying. The middle class knows what it is both to command and to obey and may be counted on to avoid political extremes.

The same spirit of moderation — "nothing in excess" — marks Aristotle's comments on what constitutes the "good life." In accordance with his theory that all things have a purpose, he taught that every organ and creature should function according to its *design*. The function of the eye is to see; the function of the ear is to hear; the function of a human is to *live* like a human. This last one calls for a harmonious balance of faculties (abilities) of both body and mind. But, since the mind is the crowning and unique part, it is clear that individuals should be governed by *reason* rather than by their appetites and emotions. Further, Aristotle insisted, it is not enough just to be a human; the "good life" must be *nobly* lived, with every action aimed at *excellence*.

But what makes an action excellent (virtuous)? Aristotle admitted that this is a difficult question, which cannot be answered by any exact rule. Excellence is more than a matter of knowledge or science; it is an *art* that each individual must develop through practice. He advised that, in general, excellence in a particular activity lies somewhere between extremes. In battle, a warrior should exhibit neither a lack of nerve (cowardice) nor an excess (foolhardiness). Rather, he should strike a happy medium (courage). A work of sculpture or architecture should be judged by asking whether it might be improved, either by taking something away or by adding something to it. If it cannot, the work is "just right" — excellent.

Aristotle warned that his advice did not apply to things that are good or bad in themselves. Truth and beauty, for example, should be sought in the highest degree, while murder, theft, and lying are evil in any degree. But in most activities each person should find, through trial and self-criticism, the desired mean (midpoint) between extremes. This has come to be called the Golden Mean. It does not signify a pale average, or mediocre standard; rather, it calls for the *best* performance of mind and body working together in harmony.

GREEK LITERATURE

Aristotle did not invent the Greek ideals of excellence, but he did reflect and express them. Everywhere around him, especially in literature and art, he observed the products of Greek genius. Western drama, prose, history, and poetry are Greek in origin; painting, sculpture, and architecture, too, have drawn heavily from Hellenic models. The Greeks believed that each art form enjoyed the patronage (support) of a minor goddess, or Muse, sprung from Zeus himself. Notable among the Muses were: Calliope (epic poetry), Euterpe (lyric poetry and music), Melpomene (tragedy), Thalia (comedy), Terpsichore (dance), and Clio (history).

Epic and Lyric Poetry

The Greeks recognized and made use of various types of poetry suited to different moods and purposes, but their earliest and greatest was the epic. Almost every people has at least one major epic: the Sumerian *Gilgamesh*

(p. 20), the English *Beowulf*, the French *Song of Roland*. An epic is the story of great deeds and heroes. It is a narrative in poetic form, usually recited to the accompaniment of a stringed instrument. With the passing of time it becomes a legend, common to all the nation and stirring patriotic feelings.

The father of the Greek epic, and of all Western literature, is Homer. He composed his poems for *oral* presentation, but they were written down by him or others afterward. (The Greek form of *writing* was developing in Homer's time — modeled upon the Phoenician alphabetic system — p. 26). Homer's *Iliad* and *Odyssey* came to be known and recited by nearly every Greek of the Golden Age. Respected as fountains of wisdom, they provided later Greek writers with countless plots, themes, and characters. No one knows exactly who Homer was, though his authorship of the two epics is firmly established by tradition. It is believed that he lived in one of the Greek cities on the coast of Asia Minor, perhaps about 800 B.C. He gave final form to tales that had been in circulation for several centuries before him. The general setting of his poems is the Trojan War, a struggle between early Greeks and the defenders of Troy (Ilium), which purportedly took place in the twelfth century B.C. (p. 51).

Later writers gave a full account of the legendary war and its aftermath in a collection of poems called the Epic Cycle. In the *Iliad* Homer concentrates on the decisive point of the struggle, during the tenth (and last) year of the war: the wrath of Achilles and its consequences for the Greeks and Trojans. Homer's sequel, the *Odyssey*, skips the overthrow and destruction of Troy and tells a story of high adventure, the return of the Greek war heroes to their homes. The central figure is the wily and brave Odysseus (in Latin, Ulysses), king of Ithaca.

The *Iliad* is much more than a bloody tale of war. It shows the Greek zest for living, desire for glory, and high sense of personal honor. In brief, it tells of the angry quarrel between King Agamemnon, leader of the Greek expedition against Troy, and Prince Achilles, the mightiest warrior of the Greeks. Achilles sulks and refuses to fight because Agamemnon has deprived him of a beautiful slave, his prize in battle. Neither man will give in. The Trojans, led by the powerful Hector, take heart upon learning that Achilles has quit the field. Only after his dearest friend, Patroclus, is slain and dishonored does Achilles return to the battle, to seek vengeance and to avert disaster. With the help of the goddess Athena, the Greek hero succeeds in killing Hector. The loss of their leader seals the fate of the Trojans.

Exploiting the richness and precision of the Greek language, Homer presents the human traits of courage, pride, envy, sacrifice, and love with striking realism. But the gods, too, are very much a part — if not the leading part — of the epic. Homer thus sketched, in the story of Achilles, a typical Greek view of mortals and gods, morals and fate. That view was to be restated, many times over, in classical literature, drama, and art.

The Greeks created lyric poetry as well as epic poetry. It is called *lyric* because it was normally sung to the playing of a lyre (a plucked, harp-type instrument). The distinguishing mark of this poetry is its *personal* nature. Instead of recounting the deeds of others, as in epic poetry, lyric poets express their own thoughts and feelings about life, love, patriotism — even the consolations and pleasures of wine.

Solon, the Athenian lawgiver (p. 58), was as famous for his poetry as for his statesmanship. One of his verses is a proud defense of his record in politics. Referring to Athenians he had released from slavery, he wrote: "These I set free; and I did this by strength of hand, welding right law with force to make a single whole. So have I done, and carried through all that I pledged."

But Solon's favorite subject was individual happiness: how it is won and lost. Foreshadowing later Greek dramatists, he advised his listeners "to call no man happy until the day of his death." Every life is uncertain, takes unexpected turns, and must be judged in its *entirety*. Solon cautioned especially against the pursuit of material wealth as a way to happiness and warned that the gods will punish those who acquire wealth unjustly.

Sappho of Lesbos, the first female poet of record, lived in the time of Solon (sixth century B.C.), but she expressed herself in a more private and passionate manner than did Solon. Though most of her lyrics have been lost, the surviving fragments display a spontaneous and graceful style. She sang mainly of romantic love — frequently of beautiful youths preparing for their wedding. Her language is remarkable for its moving imagery (figures of speech); for example, Sappho describes her jealous passion while watching an adored young woman sharing intimacies with a young man: "To watch has made my heart a pounding hammer in my breast. . . . My silent tongue is broken, and a quick and subtle flame runs up beneath my skin. . . . I drip cold sweat, and a trembling chases all through me. I am greener than the pale grass and it seems to me that I am close to death."

Though Sappho loved both women and men, her most erotic feelings appear to have been aroused by the beautiful girls who formed her circle of companions. This did not seem abnormal to the ancient Greeks, any more than did the accepted form of male homosexuality (p. 62). Later generations, however, would sometimes use the word "Lesbian" in referring to women of Sappho's sexual temperament. (The poetess and her companions lived on the Aegean island of Lesbos.)

Drama: Tragedy and Comedy

Though Aristotle admired poetry, he regarded *tragic drama* as a higher form of art. In addition to being read or sung, Greek drama was acted out. It was "theater," involving dancing, pageantry, and spectacle. Further, it was more concentrated than poetry; its tighter structure gave it superior unity and impact. Classic tragedy remains an unsurpassed means for placing human affairs under close and sympathetic inspection. It enables the audience, with a sense of detachment, to see the common destiny of themselves and others.

Greek tragedy grew out of ancient religious ceremonials. It began in the sixth century B.C. as part of the annual spring festival in honor of the god Dionysos. On those occasions it was customary for a choral group to sing hymns about the gods and heroes of Greek legend. As the chorus sang, it danced in dignified fashion around a circular plot of ground, called the orchestra (derived from the Greek word for dance). Drama was born when the leader of the chorus was permitted to step out from the group and carry on a kind of conversation (in song) with the chorus.

By the beginning of the fifth century B.C. the choral dramas might have several individual characters, though no more than three actors plus the chorus took part at any one time. Thus, the ancient, repetitive ceremonial became a medium for expressing *new* ideas. Gradually the connection with Dionysos faded away, and writers of tragedy were allowed to choose whatever serious themes suited their purpose. The religious origins were not forgotten, however, and tragedy remained moral in purpose and character.

Comedy, the other form of Greek drama, grew from a different side of the Dionysiac tradition. Dionysos personified the annual death and rebirth of plant life, but he was also known as a god of fertility, joy, and mirth. The rites in his honor (both spring and winter) included not only somber dances and chants but raucous processions and frenzied revels. It was out of these joyful celebrations that Athenian comedy was born. The earliest comedies were crude slapstick performances, but gradually they became clever and biting satires. Aristophanes, the chief writer of comedy whose works have come down to us, used his plays to make fun of local politicians, poets, and philosophers with whom he disagreed. Ridicule was his weapon of criticism. A good example is *The Clouds* (423 B.C.), a hilarious satire on the supposed teachings of the Sophists (pp. 68–69). Another example is the frank *Lysistrata* (412 B.C.), a feminist antiwar comedy. Its plot revolves around a sex strike by the wives on both sides of a war between Athens and Sparta. Their warrior-husbands at last give in: they agree to stop fighting in return for an end to the strike.

The comedies and tragedies were presented during the Dionysiac festival season in open-air amphitheaters. The theater of Athens was located on a slope of the Acropolis. Rows of seats, arranged in a semicircle, descended from the top of the hill to the orchestra. (The best-preserved Greek theater, at Epidauros, is shown in *Fig. 2-2*.) Beyond the orchestra, across the open end of the theater, stood a *skēnē*, or actors' building; in front of it was a porch, or platform, from which the speakers usually recited their lines.

The Greek actors (all men) wore masks that identified their roles and were shaped to help them project their voices. The performances were colorful, with grand speeches, music, graceful dancing and singing, and rich costumes and headdresses. The effect was more that of opera than of modern stage-acting. The author himself wrote the music as well as the text and also trained the cast.

During the standard three-day festival of Dionysos, dramatic performances began each morning and lasted until nightfall. There was no curtain or

2-2 Amphitheater at Epidauros, Greece.

lighting, and very little scenery. Usually, three playwrights competed on successive days, and a prize of great honor was awarded to the one who was judged best.

Three of the greatest playwrights of Western history were Greek. They all lived in one century, the fifth century B.C., and in one city, Athens. Aeschylus, Sophocles, and Euripides wrote nearly three hundred plays, although only about thirty have survived. The earliest tragic dramatist was Aeschylus, whose plays transform suffering and death into inspiration and the will to live. That, in fact, is the measure of true tragedy. A play that merely presents pain and grief with a sense of despair or baseness may be "dramatic" and "pathetic," but it is not "tragic." The Greek play, and its successors in the tragic spirit, generally show a hero of high rank, a great struggle, and intense suffering. But justice triumphs in the end, and there is reason beneath the suffering. One leaves Aeschylus with the feeling that individuals pay for their crimes — that the gods and the moral law are hard — but that one can face fate bravely and nobly.

In the Orestes trilogy — *Agamemnon*, the *Libation Bearers*, and the *Eumenides* — Aeschylus' central theme is the family crimes of the royal house of Atreus. The plot, well known in Greek legend, revolves around the murder of King Agamemnon by his wife when he returns from the Trojan War. Wife, son, and daughter are involved in the crimes that follow; all of them can justify their acts, but all are nonetheless guilty. To Aeschylus, these crimes and the sufferings they bring are divine punishment for violations of the moral order. In the final play of the trilogy, Athena herself intervenes to protect the murderer Orestes, son of Agamemnon, and to stop the terrible cycle of crime and punishment. Primitive revenge is transformed into the justice of the city-state, and Orestes is restored to respectability.

Because Sophocles reflected the Greek ideal of "nothing in excess," he has been called the "most Greek" of the three playwrights. He focused upon the consequences of *exaggerated pride*. In the tragedy *Oedipus the King*, Oedipus thinks he can avoid his fate, which has been foretold by the Delphic oracle of Apollo. A man of good intention, he tries to escape from the shocking prophecy that he will kill his father and marry his mother. But in the end the truth of his moral crimes, which he has committed unknowingly, is brought to light by his own insistent searching. He realizes at last the folly of his conceit and savagely blinds himself as punishment for the foulness of his deeds.

Euripides, the youngest of the great Greek tragedians, probably had the deepest insight into human character. He has been called "poet of the world's grief." Euripides was also considered something of a radical, for he challenged the traditional religious and moral values of his time. He opposed slavery and showed the "other side" of war. Greek epic poetry had glorified the exploits of the mighty warriors of the Trojan War, but in Euripides' *The Trojan Women* the battle ends with a broken-hearted old woman sitting on the ground holding a dead child in her arms. Euripides was keenly sensitive to injustice, whether of the gods or of mortals, and he pleaded for greater tolerance, equality, and decency.

History

The Greeks rank high in historical writing as well as in dramatic literature. The "father of history," Herodotus, was born in 485 B.C. in Halicarnassus, a Greek city on the shore of Asia Minor. A great traveler, he visited various parts of the Persian Empire — Mesopotamia, Syria, and Egypt. He also toured Greek colonies from the Black Sea to southern Italy. Having lived through the time of the Persian Wars, which ended in the triumph of Athens and its allies (pp. 57–58), he decided to set down a record of that struggle and of the events that led up to it.

Herodotus called his work the *Historia*, which means, in Greek, "investigation." Until his time, the legends of poetry had been accepted as true accounts of the past. He set out to separate fact from legend, to write an account based on direct observation and evidence. The sources he used, to be sure, were not all reliable, but he usually warned his readers when he was passing along doubtful information. The major portion of the *Historia* is a survey of Herodotus' world: political and military affairs, social customs, religious beliefs, and leading personalities. We owe much of our knowledge of the early history of Greece and the Persian Empire to Herodotus. In the final portion of his work he tells the story of the Persian Wars in a manner sympathetic to both Persians and Greeks, though presenting it as a dramatic contest between slavery and freedom.

A generation later the Athenian Thucydides lifted the writing of history to a much higher critical level (though at some sacrifice of literary charm). In the first "scientific" history, he wrote about the long and cruel war between Athens and Sparta that had broken out soon after their joint victory over Persia (pp. 87–88). An exiled general of Athens, he had traveled widely to gather information during the war.

His subject is far more limited than that of Herodotus, but his account has greater unity and depth. And he excluded all suggestion of *supernatural* interference: history, he insisted, is made by *human beings*. Thucydides was convinced that human nature could be understood through careful study of the past and that the knowledge so gained could be useful as a guide to understanding the *future*. He presented his facts from both sides, showing the reader the causes, motives, and consequences of the war. But his work is more than military history; it deals with the still-relevant questions of imperialism, democracy, and the whole range of social relations.

ARCHITECTURE AND SCULPTURE

The words of Thucydides, Aeschylus, Plato, and Homer tell us a great deal about the Greeks, but they cannot tell us the whole story. For there are many creations of the human spirit that display themselves *visually*. The most conspicuous of the visual arts — and another glory of ancient Greece — is architecture.

As we have seen, the Greeks regarded community activities as more important than private affairs; hence, they put their best efforts into *public* structures. The temple, which represented a strong bond between religious and patriotic feelings, was their supreme architectural achievement. But they constructed other types of public buildings as well: there were the open marketplaces, enclosed on four sides by a covered colonnade; the outdoor amphitheaters (*Fig. 2-2*) for dramatic festivals; and open-air gymnasiums, racecourses, and stadiums. The Greeks seemed least interested in private dwellings, which were small, simple, and built of light materials. Plumbing and sanitary facilities were primitive or nonexistent.

Up to the sixth century B.C. even the most important buildings were usually made of wood. Gradually, however, limestone and marble took the place of timber in public structures. This was a natural development, because the country's forests were thinning out while there were ample supplies of stone. The Greeks used the "post-and-lintel" method for supporting the roofs of their buildings, meaning simply that the horizontal members (beams or lintels) rested on vertical posts or columns. A series of columns placed at close intervals could thus support a roof of considerable weight. The effectiveness of this building method had been demonstrated centuries earlier by Egyptian architects (p. 35).

Temple Building: The Parthenon

The Greek temple represents the perfection of *post-and-lintel* construction and of the refinements of the stone *column*. The early buildings had a rather heavy appearance, as in the sixth-century temple at Paestum, Italy (*Fig. 2-3*). Gradually, however, the proportions of the temple, and of the columns especially, were modified. The finest result of this development was the Parthenon of Athens (*Fig. 2-4*). In this shrine for Athena a perfect balance of architectural elements was achieved. The supporting columns give a feeling of the structure's strength, grace, and ease.

The exterior columns of the Parthenon, which form a continuous colonnade on all four sides of the temple, are of the Doric "order." This was the earlier of the two basic styles, Doric and Ionic, that the Greeks developed. The differences lie in the *base, shaft*, and *capital* of the columns and in the *entablature* (horizontal structures) that they support. The Greeks later developed a third "order," called Corinthian; it was similar to the Ionic except for the column capitals, which were decorated with stylized leaves of the acanthus plant.

2-3 Temple of Hera at Paestum, Italy.

2-4 The Parthenon, Athens.

The floor plan of the Parthenon is simple. It divides the interior into two rectangular enclosures. The principal enclosure (cella) originally contained a statue of the goddess and has but one entrance, facing east. The smaller cella, whose entrance faces west, contained the treasury of Athens. The roof of the building was gabled (slanted) and supported by a wooden framework. It was closed at each end by a triangular slab of marble, called the *pediment*.

The Parthenon was designed about 450 B.C. by the architect Ictinos, as part of Pericles' plan for rebuilding the Acropolis after the Persians had destroyed the earlier sacred structures there. Though ravaged by time and war, it still embodies the Greek ideal of the Golden Mean. It is not a huge structure (one hundred by two hundred thirty feet), but it was perfectly suited to its purpose and position. The pediments and portions of the entablature were decorated with sculpture, and pastel paints were applied to add warmth and interest. The paints have long since faded, but the weathered marble now provides attractive color of its own.

The wonder of the Parthenon comes, in part, from the painstaking details of its design. Subtle curves, rather than straight lines, avoid any impression of stiffness. Each of the supporting columns, for example, consists of many marble drums so carefully placed above one another that each column appears to be a *single* piece. The diameter of the column diminishes gradually as it rises to its capital, in a slightly curving line (*entasis*). The Greek builders had discovered that a perfectly straight profile makes a column look too rigid. They had also found that by adjusting the spacing between columns they could improve the visual effect of the entire structure. Hence, in the Parthenon the space between each corner column and the column next to it is *less* than the space between other columns, and this gives a feeling of extra support at the points of extra stress. The fact that the builders went to such pains to satisfy the demands not only of engineering but of esthetics as well is testimony to their desire for excellence.

Images of Gods and Men

Little has survived of Greek painting other than the charming miniatures on pottery vases. But the Greeks' passion for beauty, interest in human forms, and their striving for the ideal are clearly reflected in their *sculpture*. Only a few originals — and those in mutilated condition — have come down to us, but hundreds of copies of Greek statues, produced in Roman times by Greek artisans, still survive. The Greek originals, or what we know of them, have served through the centuries as models for Western sculptors.

Early Greek statues reveal an Egyptian influence. The Egyptians sought solidity and permanence in their figures; they did not aim to reproduce natural appearances (pp. 36–37). This same purpose is apparent in the many statues of young men, probably victorious athletes, that have been unearthed in Greece (*Fig. 2-5*). But the Greeks grew dissatisfied with this kind of representation and turned steadily toward greater naturalism, movement, and grace in their figures. Classical sculpture found its most perfect expression during the fifth century B.C., at the time of the building of the Parthenon. The statues carved in that period were chiefly of gods and goddesses; like the deities themselves, they resembled mortals — not actual individuals, but *idealized* men and women.

Phidias, the most highly respected sculptor of Athens in the Age of Pericles, was put in charge of the Parthenon sculptures. It was he who carved from wood the gigantic statue of Athena (some thirty-five feet tall) that was placed in the main cella. Although the original was lost long ago, ancient descriptions tell us that it was richly decorated with ivory, gold, and jewels. Phidias also planned and supervised the carvings of the marble pediments and the marble frieze (band) that ran around the outside of the cella walls. Fragments of this sculpture are still in existence, most of them in the British Museum in London. These fragments (*Fig. 2-6*) show that the frieze was sculptured not "in the round" but "in relief." They form parts of a carved procession of young women and men, some on horseback, moving toward a platform on which various deities are seated. The sense of ease and motion, the splendid proportion and form, are evident even in these fragments.

Better known is the *Discus-thrower* by Myron, another sculptor of the time of Phidias (*Fig. 2-7*). The original bronze casting has been lost, but the figure was so much admired that many marble copies were made. In this statue, Myron chose to portray the athlete at the moment before he made his supreme effort, so that he would appear dynamically poised and in full self-control. The

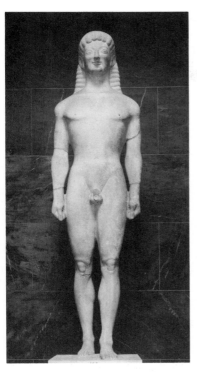

2-5 *Youth from Tenea*, c. 600 B.C. Glyptothek, Munich.

2-6 *Horsemen in Procession*. From western frieze of Parthenon.

2-7 *Discus-thrower*.
After Myron.
Terme Museum, Rome.

2-8 Praxiteles. *Hermes
with the Infant Dionysos*.
Museum, Olympia.

statue is not an accurate picture of a real discus-thrower; rather, it is an ideal representation of the male figure — a masterpiece of line and form.

After about 400 B.C. Greek sculptors tended toward greater delicacy and gracefulness, producing by our standards of perception a more effeminate impression. The leading developer of this style was Praxiteles. Only one of his original statues has survived — *Hermes with the Infant Dionysos* (*Fig. 2-8*). Although this figure lacks the masculine power of the *Discus-thrower*, it is a fine expression of ease, smoothness, and relaxation. The famous *Aphrodite of Melos*, also known as the *Venus de Milo* (*Fig. 2-9*), is thought to be a copy of an original from the time of Praxiteles (fourth century B.C.). After its discovery and exhibition in the early nineteenth century, this Venus was held up as a model of female form in the West.

Along with the trend toward greater delicacy there developed an interest in portraiture, emotional expression, and representation of ordinary people —

2-9 *Venus de Milo* (copy). Louvre, Paris.

street vendors, dancers, and common soldiers. The sculptors of the fifth century had carved only deities and heroes. They had also avoided showing facial expression and, generally, any indication of pain or suffering. But with the passing of centuries exact likenesses became popular, and more and more statues showed intense emotion. Probably the most famous example of works of the latter kind is the marble group known as *Laocoön and His Sons* (about 50 B.C.). This group shows a Trojan priest and his young sons being crushed by two deadly serpents (*Fig. 2-10*). (According to legend, the goddess Athena had

2-10 *Laocoön and His Sons*. Vatican Museum, Rome.

aided the Greeks during their siege of Troy (pp. 51, 74). When the Greeks schemed to take the city by hiding soldiers inside a giant wooden horse — offered as a gift — Laocoön warned his fellow Trojans not to allow the horse to pass through the city's gates. Angered by this interference with her plans, Athena sent the serpents from the sea to strangle the priest and his sons.)

THE DECLINE OF THE GREEK CITY-STATES

Art during and after the fourth century B.C. reflected an attitude toward life that was considerably different from the attitude of Greeks during the Age of Pericles (fifth century B.C.). The change was an outgrowth of the Peloponnesian War and its aftermath. The Persian Wars had brought confidence and glory; the Peloponnesian War left disillusionment and decay. Most of the Greek city-states were caught up in the conflict, but the principal antagonists were Athens and Sparta. The Athenians called it the "Peloponnesian" war because their chief enemies were Sparta and its allied cities of the Peloponnesus (p. 50) — the "Peloponnesian League." There had been earlier conflicts between Sparta and Athens, but the long struggle that opened in 431 B.C. and lasted until 404 B.C. ended with the final defeat of Athens.

The Peloponnesian War

The underlying cause of the Peloponnesian War, and of the endless wars that preceded and followed it, was built into the Greek city-state system. Each city had its own military forces and asserted its complete independence of any higher authority. When differences developed that could not be settled by agreement, either party might resort to war. Some cities managed to subdue their neighbors temporarily by force of arms, but the defeated communities refused to be absorbed and waited patiently for a chance to regain their independence. Hence, the Greek world was in a constant state of war. The cities refrained from fighting one another only when it was necessary to join together against a *foreign* foe. It was through such a general alliance that they had, with difficulty, met the Persian threat in the first half of the fifth century B.C. (pp. 57–58).

Soon after Athens became the accepted leader in 478 B.C., it moved to solidify its influence in the Greek world. Athens sponsored formation of the "Delian League," which consisted of most of the Greek cities on the Aegean coasts and islands. (The League was named, by modern historians, after the island of Delos, sacred to Apollo, where the alliance was founded.) Members agreed to contribute money annually for the construction of warships, which were placed under Athenian command. The city thus gained control of several hundred vessels with their crews — ships of sail and oar. The most formidable type was the swift and maneuverable *trireme*, which carried three banks of rowers on each side of the hull and had a ram projecting from its bow. In battle the trireme sank enemy vessels by ramming them, or hooked up alongside and put soldiers aboard.

After the Persian threat had passed (445 B.C.), the League members announced that they would make no more payments. But Athens threatened to use force should they cease sending money. What had been contributions for the common defense against Persia were thereby transformed into tribute to Athens.

All Greece was aroused by the Athenians' behavior. The smaller cities appealed to the Spartans (who headed the Peloponnesian League) to put a check on Athens. At last the Spartans decided to support their ally, Corinth, which had become involved in a naval war with Athens. The Athenians, with their league of allies (forced and voluntary), took up the challenge.

In the course of the war (431–404 B.C.) the Athenians at first, under the guidance of Pericles, showed caution and sound strategy. Their most serious reversal was not by arms, but by disease. A terrible plague struck the city in 430 B.C. Though the exact nature of this infection remains uncertain, it is known to have come by sea from Egypt to the Athenian port of Piraeus. The plague was brief but deadly, killing thousands of inhabitants, including a fourth of the army. Pericles himself was a victim.

The plague came without warning and turned the optimism of the Athenians into gloom. As public confidence slipped, control of the city passed into the hands of willful and reckless politicians. While the Spartans on several occasions offered terms of compromise and "peace without victory," these Athenian leaders spurned their offers and held out for a clear-cut triumph. But such hopes were shattered by the annihilation of an expedition against Syracuse (in far-off Sicily), an ally of Sparta. Even after that setback (413 B.C.) Athens won some battles at sea, but its fate appeared sealed when Sparta secured financial aid from Persia, the traditional enemy of Greece. Now the Spartans were able to equip a powerful fleet, which succeeded at last in overcoming the proud navy of Athens. Stripped of the protection of their warships, the Athenian citizens were starved into surrender (404 B.C.). They gave up all their outlying possessions, pulled down their defensive walls, and became forced allies of Sparta.

But Athens was not alone in defeat. The victors as well as the vanquished were weakened by the loss of men and resources. Greek civilization in its traditional form never fully recovered from the ruinous struggle, even though Athens retained its cultural leadership for another century. The pattern of Greek life, best exemplified by Athens in the Age of Pericles, could not be restored. Sparta for a while, then Thebes, tried unsuccessfully to exert leadership and maintain order. But it was only a matter of time until the quarreling Greek cities were to fall before foreign powers (first Macedonia, then Rome) and to surrender for good their cherished independence. When the city-state lost its old meaning, the core of Greek life itself crumbled, for the city had been the focus of the citizens' loyalty, pride, and love. Henceforth, they tended to turn inward, to regard politics and civic affairs as things apart from themselves and their families.

The average citizen lost faith not only in the city-state but in its religious and moral principles. Athena had failed to save the city of her name from disaster and humiliation. The Olympian gods may have defended the Greeks against the Persians, but they had not preserved them from self-destruction. And the citizens who survived found little solace — no promise of a better world to come — in their traditional religion. Many of them turned to more personal and hopeful faiths.

Disillusionment spread in other directions as well. The search for truth, the appeal to reason, and the counsel of moderation had not brought the anticipated satisfactions and happiness. Democracy itself came in for a share of blame, because the leaders of democratic Athens were held chiefly responsible for bringing on and prolonging the disastrous war. Sparta and its allies, on the other hand, had favored oligarchy (p. 55). The military triumph of the Peloponnesians strengthened aristocratic attitudes and weakened the democratic cause in most parts of Greece. And, in every city where democratic and oligarchic factions still vied for power, the struggle was intensified by bitter memories of social division and civic betrayal during the war.

Even though the city-state declined as a unit of *sovereign power*, the city itself remained for many centuries the basic building block of *government* and *community life*. In the age of the Hellenistic states (pp. 91–92), new cities, founded by Greek emigrants, sprang up throughout Egypt and the Middle East. The greatest empire of ancient times was built up by a city-state, Rome; and the Roman Empire was governed as a kind of federation of cities (p. 110).

The Rise of Macedonia

Meanwhile, to the north of the weakened city-states, a new power was rising. Macedonia (p. 50) was a backwater of Greek civilization, several centuries behind Athens in its cultural development. But Philip, who became king of Macedonia in 359 B.C., admired the Greeks and longed to associate himself with them. A shrewd man of broad vision, he determined to gain control of the weak and divided city-states and to lead the Greeks and the Macedonians in a united force against the weakening empire of Persia. First, he consolidated his own position in Macedonia, strengthened his army, and made careful plans for infiltrating and conquering Greece.

Philip's agents worked to prevent the city-states from joining forces against him. One eloquent Athenian, Demosthenes, recognized the peril and repeatedly warned his fellow citizens. But the traditional reluctance of the city-states to work together, combined with their failure to take the new menace seriously, played into Philip's hands. At last he was ready to move. Through diplomacy and military pressure Philip thrust into northern and central Greece. The Athenians, aroused at last, formed an alliance with the Thebans

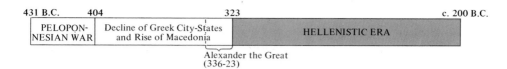

431 B.C.	404		323	c. 200 B.C.
PELOPON- NESIAN WAR	Decline of Greek City-States and Rise of Macedonia		HELLENISTIC ERA	

Alexander the Great
(336-23)

in an attempt to stop him. It was too late. At the Battle of Chaeronea (338 B.C.) the Macedonians won a decisive victory. What remained of Greek independence was left for Philip to decide.

The Macedonian king used his new-won power wisely. After advancing into the Peloponnesus, he established himself as the president of a league of Greek states. He treated the Greek cities considerately and let them manage their own affairs except in the conduct of foreign policy. Philip, now at the head of a powerful alliance, vowed to avenge the insults and injuries inflicted upon Greek temples and sanctuaries by the invading Persians more than a century before (p. 58). But, as he stood at the very brink of fulfillment, Philip was assassinated in 336 B.C. His son, Alexander III, only twenty years old, succeeded him. This inexperienced youth must have seemed unprepared for the task of carrying out his father's grand design.

ALEXANDER THE GREAT AND THE WIDER SPREAD OF GREEK CULTURE

Those who knew the young Alexander — men like his one-time teacher, Aristotle — were not surprised by his display of authority and determination. After dealing with disturbances in Macedonia and Greece that had broken out after his father's death, he crossed into Asia Minor (334 B.C.) to launch the campaign that would make him one of the greatest conquerors in history. True, the Persian Empire had declined in military power, but Alexander's daring and generalship proved successful beyond anyone's expectations. His small but well-disciplined army, consisting of about thirty-five thousand Greeks and Macedonians, broke the power of the Persian king within four years. Asia Minor, Syria, Egypt, and Mesopotamia fell before him (p. 12). Pushing on through Persia to the frontiers of India (p. 42), he was checked only by the grumbling and protests of his own men. (The soldiers' reluctance was fortunate, because India held a number of diseases against which the Greeks had little immunity.) At the age of thirty-three, Alexander died of a fever (probably cholera) in the city of Babylon, which he had chosen for his imperial capital.

Alexander's Dream of "One World"

Alexander left no son to inherit his throne. But he had established certain principles of government for his new world-state — a successor to the universal empires of Assyria and Persia (pp. 38–44). He hoped that his conquests would lead to an ultimate *fusion* of East and West and put an end to the struggle that had begun nearly two centuries earlier with the first clash between Persians and Greeks. Though he believed in the superiority of Greek culture, Alexander had no intention of destroying the culture of the East. Rather, he had hoped to fuse the best features of each civilization into a new culture. To achieve this end, he founded cities in the regions he conquered and sent Greeks or Macedonians to colonize them. Their military garrisons would serve to maintain order in the surrounding countryside, and the cities themselves would serve as cultural "melting pots." He made Greek the official language and distributed Greek books and works of art throughout his empire; he hoped by these means to spread Hellenic ideas and standards, at least as a veneer, over the oriental pattern of life. He encouraged intermarriage and led the way himself by marrying an eastern princess (Roxana). But even with an expanding Greek population, there were not enough Greeks to go around. The hoped-for fusion of cultures never became more than an imperfect mixture, and the ways of the East persisted as in the past.

Alexander's "one world" was divided after his death among his top generals. After a series of conflicts, three major states emerged from Alexander's conquests and survived until the Romans took over the eastern Mediterranean. These states were based, respectively, on Macedonia, Egypt, and the remains of the Persian Empire in western Asia.

Although Alexander's dream was never fulfilled, it had a profound effect on the development of the West. The culture of Greece, formerly limited to the Aegean area, was spread throughout the entire Middle East. Because Athens and the other centers of Hellenic culture were to be overrun again and again by invaders, most Greek works of art and literature might have been lost forever had it not been for Alexander's conquests. The Greek legacy was passed on to the West not by the city-states of Hellas, but by the libraries and museums of the Alexandrian world.

The Hellenistic States

The mixed culture that emerged in the Middle East was markedly different from the culture that had flourished in Athens in the Age of Pericles. To describe this mixture of Greek ways with Eastern ways, historians have invented the term "Hellenistic." The term suggests that the culture was "Greekish" — not wholly Greek. And the political forms of the Hellenistic world were actually more Eastern than Greek. After Alexander, the independent city-state became virtually extinct, and having lost their independence, the cities now became parts of a greater whole. Now people were thinking in terms of a much larger unit of power — the great state, or empire — and of loyalty to a personal ruler, not to a community. Democracy, as practiced in Greek cities of the preceding century, was put down by the new order of things. Absolute rule by divinely sent monarchs, a concept upheld by the traditions of the East (pp. 28–29, 43–44), was accepted as the only effective means of governing large areas.

Alexander's vision of a unified world-state and culture lived after him and served as a model for later conquerors and statesmen of the West — for Caesar, Charlemagne, and Napoleon.

The economy of the Hellenistic age was also markedly different from that of earlier times. The new and more extensive political units encouraged large-scale production and trade. The Greeks had carried on a far-flung commerce, ranging from the Black Sea to Gibraltar, but now the gates were opened eastward — as far as India. The vast new market stimulated enterprise: huge fortunes were made, banking and finance were expanded, and a kind of capitalism took shape. The heads of the great states had a keen interest in business affairs. They promoted commerce by aiding navigation and transport and made up their expenses by taxing the enterprises. The Ptolemies, rulers of Egypt, also set up hundreds of state-owned factories and shops for the direct support of their families.

Although wages and general living standards remained low, the growth of industry and trade created many new jobs in the cities. As a result, thousands of peasants moved from the countryside into the urban centers of the Middle East. The typical Greek city-state had been a community of perhaps five or ten thousand citizens, but the *metropolis* (great city) now became the central unit of social organization. Many such cities grew up around the centers Alexander had tried to establish. The largest and most renowned was Alexandria, which he had founded at the mouth of the Nile River, in Egypt. Its population may have approached one million by the time of Christ, and it rivaled imperial Rome in size and magnificence. Alexandria was the economic and cultural hub of the eastern Mediterranean; for centuries its marvelous library and museums were centers of scholarship and scientific study.

When the Romans conquered the Hellenistic states (in the second and first centuries B.C.), they recognized the richness and sophistication of these cities. Here they found the culture — the philosophy, science, literature, and art — that they were to absorb and pass on to western Europe. The Hellenistic world submitted to the Romans and paid tribute to them, but it was otherwise little affected by the conquest. It remained a distinct cultural section of the Roman Empire; and after the empire began to crumble (fourth century A.D.) the Hellenistic portion continued for centuries as an area of prosperity and advanced civilization.

CHAPTER

3

The Roman Triumph and Fall

The Greeks were the most brilliant *originators* of Western civilization; the Romans were its best *organizers* and *preservers*. By force of arms and statesmanship, the Romans linked the proud cultures of the Hellenistic East with the less advanced cultures of the western Mediterranean. Taking Alexander's dream as their inheritance, they made the idea of "one world" a reality.

THE RISE OF ROME

The question of why Rome "fell" has challenged scholars for centuries. An even more fascinating question is how Rome *rose* from the status of a small Italian city-state to become the master of its world. Athens and Sparta had failed to maintain power in the limited area of the Aegean Sea, and Alexander's conquests had fallen to pieces soon after his death. But Rome built an enduring order of astonishing size, given the technology of the time. How did the Romans surpass all that had gone before them?

Italy and Its Peoples

While the Greeks (p. 51) were moving down into the Aegean area, tribes speaking another Indo-European dialect (p. 47) made their way from the north into central Italy. There they mingled with earlier inhabitants to form the Latin people. Some of them settled near the mouth of the Tiber River (p. 95), building a cluster of huts on low-lying hills along the river — the famed "Seven Hills." These settlements joined together to form a city-state around 750 B.C. By 500 B.C. Rome had grown to be the chief power of Latium, an area reaching some one hundred miles southward.

The natural resources of the Italian peninsula, though not rich, are superior to those of Greece. Most of the land is mountainous, with the Apennines

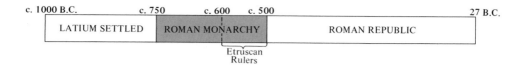

forming a spiny barrier from the Po Valley in the north to the very toe of the Italian boot. But there were extensive pasturelands and fields, and the peoples who settled this country were self-sufficient from their very beginnings.

Rome itself was strategically situated on the peninsula. Lying fourteen miles from the sea, the city was fairly easy to defend; it was even better adapted to offense, for it controlled the principal routes of travel. The Italian peninsula itself was to serve later as a superb base for Rome's far-ranging conquests. Astride the Mediterranean, it commanded east and west, north and south.

The Romans did not have the peninsula to themselves, however (p. 95). Early in the fifth century B.C. barbarian Gauls invaded the Po Valley; later, around 390 B.C., they raided southward and burned the city of Rome. (The Gauls were a branch of the Celtic tribes, yet another barbarian group speaking an Indo-European language — p. 47. By 500 B.C. the Celts, who were fierce warrior-horsemen, seized and occupied much of present-day Germany, Britain, Ireland, and France.) More important to the Romans were the Etruscans and the Greeks, both latecomers to Italy. The Etruscans, whose background is mysterious, apparently arrived about the ninth century B.C. After gaining control of the north-central portion of the country in the seventh century B.C., they struck out in all directions.

They conquered Latium, and for a time Etruscan kings ruled Rome itself. Around 500 B.C. the Etruscans were ejected from Rome by an uprising. Their power was short-lived, because they failed to conciliate or assimilate the people they conquered. But they carried with them a superior, urban culture that was readily absorbed by the Romans. From the Etruscans the Romans learned a great deal about war, politics, religion, and agriculture, and they adopted such specific features as a street plan for cities, the insignia of authority (fasces), the triumphal procession, gladiatorial combats, and the masonry arch.

The Romans also borrowed freely from the Greeks. As early as the eighth century B.C. the city-states of Hellas had begun to plant colonies in southern Italy, where the heel of the Italian boot lies only fifty miles from the Greek coast. So extensive was this colonization that the Romans, like the Greeks before them, came to call southern Italy and Sicily "Greater Greece" (*Magna Graecia*). Among the earliest settlements were Cumae, Paestum, Naples, Tarentum, and Syracuse (in Sicily). From Cumae the Latins first learned the alphabet and something of the Olympian gods. And in dealing with the Greek colonies they came into direct contact with the civilized life of the Greek city-state. The Romans, realizing that this civilization was more advanced than their own, gradually absorbed Greek ideas and arts into their culture.

CELTS
(GAULS)

CELTS (GAULS)

Mediolanium (Milan)

CISALPINE GAUL

Placentia
Genua
Parma
AEMILIAN WAY
Bononia
Ravenna
Rubicon

ETRUSCANS

Arretium
Clusium

Narnia

CASSIAN WAY
FLAMINIAN WAY
Tiber

ADRIATIC SEA

SABINES
AEQUIANS

Alba   Corfinium

ROMANS

CORSICA

Rome
Ostia

LATIN WAY
APPIAN WAY
VOLSCIANS

SAMNITES

LATIUM

APPIAN WAY

APULIA

Barium

Brundisium

Tarentum

SARDINIA

Cumae
Naples
Pompeii
MT. VESUVIUS
Paestum

LUCANIANS

Heraclea

TYRRHENIAN SEA

MAGNA   GRAECIA

Croton

Messana

Locri

Rhegium

MT. ETNA

Carthage

SICILY

GREEKS   Syracuse

MEDITERRANEAN SEA

AFRICA

ROME IN ITALY

Roman territory about 325 B.C.

Territory controlled by Rome at the start
of the second Punic War, 218 B.C.

Key Roman Military roads

0   MILES   150

The Government of the Early Republic

Under the cultural influence of the Etruscans and the Greeks, the Romans acquired the skills that enabled them to build their unique political institutions. For several centuries they were governed by kings whose authority resembled that of the rulers of Homeric Greece. The king served as high priest of the state religion, military commander, supreme judge, and chief executive. He was advised by a council of elders (Senate) composed of the heads of the leading families (the patricians). When a king died, his successor was chosen by the Senate from among its own members, subject to approval by an assembly of all male citizens old enough to serve in the army.

Around 500 B.C., when the Etruscans were expelled and the monarchy was abolished, military and executive power was transferred to two chief magistrates (consuls), elected annually by another body of male citizens, the Assembly of Centuries. The Romans created this *plural* executive to guard against tyranny, and they empowered each consul to veto any lawmaking proposed by the other. This was not an unprecedented arrangement, for the conservative Spartans had always placed power in two kings (p. 55). But the Romans extended this practice by electing two or more men (*collegae*, or colleagues) to every important office of the republic (*res publica*, or commonwealth). Those who shared a given office were usually given separate duties, but on important matters of common concern they were required to act in *concert*. This principle of joint responsibility in administration proved a two-edged sword. It guarded against hasty action and undue concentration of power, but it sometimes led to costly delays, or even paralysis. To correct this weakness, the republic permitted the appointment of a "dictator" in time of emergency. The dictator was chosen by the consuls with the advice of the Senate, and his term was limited to six months.

The evolution of government under the republic reflected the serious social struggle that was taking place among the Romans. On the one side were the upper-class citizens, the patricians (aristocrats), who belonged to the oldest and noblest Roman families and who alone could perform the religious rituals on which the safety of all depended. These families could be traced back, through the male line, to the earliest leaders of the community — to the military chieftains and the wealthy owners of land and flocks. On the other side were the common citizens, the plebeians, whose origins are not entirely clear. They appear to have been subject to the patricians, in varying degree, from the very beginning. Some may have been descendants of the earlier native population that had been suppressed by invaders in the dim past. Some had fallen into dependency because of debts, while others no doubt had come as fugitives and immigrants from surrounding cities.

By 500 B.C. the line between these classes had become sharply drawn. The patricians, though they made up only a tiny fraction of the total citizenry, dominated Roman politics. The several citizen assemblies, which included the plebeians, held the powers of approving laws and electing public officials, but their voting procedures were usually arranged to favor the patricians. Further, magistrates could be named only from the upper class, and they were expected to act under senatorial advice. The Senate consisted of a fixed number (about three hundred) of the heads of patrician families; senators were appointed for life by the consuls.

The plebeians, who felt that they were being treated as second-class citizens, were determined to win equal rights. They resorted to various means of putting pressure on the patricians — including acts of passive resistance and threats to secede and start a rival settlement. Since they managed, however, to stay within the bounds of law and order, the republic was not subverted.

Among the chief complaints of the plebeians was that they lacked legal protection. Before the fifth century B.C. there had been no written code of law to which an accused person could turn for guidance or defense. The sacred traditional laws were interpreted by judges, who were, of course, patricians. Understandably, the plebeians protested that they were not receiving equal treatment in the courts. About 450 B.C., in response to their demand, the laws of Rome were set down in writing. The new code was engraved on twelve tablets (wooden or bronze) and mounted in the chief public square (Forum) for all to see. These Twelve Tablets defined private and public rights and penalties and served as the foundation for the elaborate system of Roman law that grew up in the centuries to come.

The plebeians also demanded admission to the major public offices (magistracies), especially the consulship. Although the patricians firmly resisted this demand, they did agree to let the plebeians elect officials of their own, called tribunes. Immune from interference when in the pursuit of their duties, the tribunes had power to protect any citizen who they thought was being wronged by a patrician magistrate. Later, the tribunes acquired the further right to initiate laws in the Assembly of Tribes (where plebeians had a majority of the votes).

This compromise, like others that gradually admitted the plebeians to greater power, was characteristic of the Roman approach to politics. Instead of abolishing or radically altering an old institution, the Romans preferred to install a counterweight. This habit exasperates modern political scientists who try to analyze precisely how the republic worked, but the Romans themselves were little disturbed by the complex checks and balances, the contradictions between political form and reality, and the unplanned growth of offices. They had a lingering affection for traditional ways, and their system showed a flexibility and resilience often lacking in more logical political structures.

By 250 B.C. the plebeians had won the main objectives in their contest with the patricians: eligibility for *all* public offices, the right to marry into the patrician class, and admission to the Senate itself. These changes did not bring about democracy, however. Control of the republic still rested in the hands of the Senate, which was now an oligarchy of wealth. After the third century B.C.

senators were appointed from the list of ex-magistrates; and running for the public offices, which paid no salary, was expensive. To seek the votes of the plebeians, candidates had to spend large sums for displays and popular entertainments. In addition, they often carried on a long-standing Roman practice of supporting *clients* (dependents); these were normally plebeians, "protected" and paid by their rich *patrons* for personal services and campaigning. Due to such heavy costs, only the rich could afford to become members of the Senate.

Those who did make it sat in the seats of the mighty, for the Senate was a permanent body of enormous prestige and influence. The consuls, tribunes, praetors (judges), pontiffs (priests), and other magistrates were elected by the citizen assemblies for one-year terms. But all turned to the Senate for guidance and looked forward to the day when they, too, would "join the club."

In conducting the endless wars that Rome waged during these centuries, the Senate earned a reputation as a "council of kings." The senators possessed tested political experience and wisdom, and they demonstrated a patience, canniness, and will that carried Rome to victory over a succession of powerful foes. They set long-range policies and made immediate decisions on pressing matters. They appointed and instructed the military leaders of the republic, received foreign ambassadors, and concluded treaties. They supervised finances and investigated high crimes. The powers of the Senate grew not so much by law as by general consent. The magistrates and citizen assemblies continued to perform their duties, but the Senate was the balance wheel in the complicated machinery of the state. Until the final century of the republic (150 B.C.–50 B.C.), it governed firmly and effectively.

Roman Expansion

The Romans were, above all, a military people — patriotic farmer-soldiers. The first campaigns that we know much about were essentially defensive — against the Etruscans, Gauls, Greeks, and competing Italic tribes. Then, as the Romans secured their position at home, they began to reach out for territories and allies. Along the way they encountered ever more enemies, for across each new frontier stood a new danger. The Romans, of course, lost as well as won battles, but they invariably won the war.

In addition to the toughness of its soldier-citizens and the shrewdness of its Senate, Rome had a superior military organization. Its manpower was based on conscription ("draft") — all male citizens could be called up for duty. At first they served without compensation, usually for short periods. Later, the state began to pay them, in order to permit longer campaigns and better training. A professional force ultimately replaced this citizen army.

The Roman army was made up of legions, whose organization and tactics were an innovation in the Mediterranean world. Each legion consisted of some four thousand infantrymen organized in maneuverable units of about one hundred men (centuries). The soldiers and the rugged centurions who led them carried light armor, helmet, and a shield. For weapons they had a short sword, lance, and a javelin. But what most distinguished the Roman army was its iron discipline. Penalties for cowardice or neglect of duty were severe and cruel; on the other hand, there were generous rewards and promotions for the brave and the victorious.

The Romans applied this same incentive-deterrent system to the peoples they conquered in war. They avoided the mistake of treating all their vanquished foes alike, for they found it more profitable to convert their former enemies into friends and allies than to make them permanent slaves. The rule of conquest, booty, and massacre that had usually prevailed in the ancient world was supplanted by an improved formula: in exchange for "cooperation," the Romans offered protection and self-rule. Those who remained loyal and contributed the most aid were given the highest privileges; those who wavered or deserted were punished or annihilated. (Understandably, peoples who preferred their independence to these alternatives saw the Romans simply as destroyers of liberty.)

The new conquerors refrained from interfering with local laws, religion, or customs, insisting only that the defeated communities submit to Rome's direction of external relations and provide troops for the Roman forces. They tightened their control over the Italian peninsula by creating a network of colonies in which the settlers enjoyed political rights almost equal to those of Roman citizens. These colonies served both as garrisons and as working models of Roman civic organization. Gradually, other forms of participating citizenship were offered to the inhabitants of Italy. Thus Rome, unlike the exclusive Greek city-states (pp. 52–54), became an expanding, *absorptive* political entity.

Roman methods of conquest and administration were shrewd, flexible, and judicious. They paid handsome dividends, for by 250 B.C. all of Italy south of the Po Valley was in Roman hands. The City of the Seven Hills had compounded its resources until they included the peninsula and most of its peoples. The conquered, too, began to appreciate the advantages of Roman rule. In place of bloody anarchy, the victors brought peace, order, roads, and prosperity. It was this principle of two-way benefit that the Romans would extend, step by step, to the whole Mediterranean world. The army was the foundation of Roman power, but the conquered domains were cemented to Rome by *mutual* interest and service.

No sooner had the Romans secured their position on the peninsula than they were challenged by a power beyond the sea. That power was Carthage, a rich empire with its capital on the north coast of Africa (p. 95). The city had been founded about 700 B.C. by colonists from Phoenicia (modern Lebanon), a trading folk of Semitic origin who had built up a thriving commercial civilization (p. 26). Organized as an oligarchic republic similar in form to Rome, Carthage spread its influence across North Africa, southern Spain, Sardinia, Corsica, and Sicily (p. 95). It was the Carthaginians' interest in Sicily, lying between Africa and Italy, that brought them into conflict with the Romans. The Greek city-states of Sicily had for centuries been struggling with Carthage for control of the island, and the Romans had inherited the struggle when they took over responsibility for protecting their Greek allies. Thus began the fateful Punic Wars (264 B.C.–146 B.C.), which lifted Rome into the position of a "world" power. (The term "Punic" derives from *Poeni*, the Latin name for the Phoenicians, the settlers of Carthage.)

After some opening skirmishes between Rome and Carthage, it became clear that more was at stake than the harbors and hills of Sicily. These two proud and aggressive antagonists were fighting for command of the whole western Mediterranean. The struggle was waged on land and sea, in three vicious rounds, but Rome's system of alliances proved strong enough to meet the test. The loyalty of the Romans' allies and the perseverance of their own forces enabled them to triumph. In a final act of vengeance, the victorious Roman general leveled the city of Carthage to the ground and sold the survivors into slavery.

The former possessions of Carthage became the first Roman *provinces* (Sicily, Spain, Africa). These administrative units did not enjoy the status of Rome's allies in Italy; instead, they were ruled as conquered lands by senatorial appointees (proconsuls). They paid tribute to the Roman state and provided opportunities for influential Roman citizens to build up private fortunes. (It was not until the time of Augustus, after 27 B.C., that the provinces began to share the benefits of Roman order. See pp. 107–8.)

The conquerors found their new wealth and power very much to their liking. Even before the defeat of Carthage, venturesome Romans were looking eastward for new areas to exploit. The prospect in that direction was promising, for the Hellenistic world was in turmoil.

Rome's first involvement was in Greece, and it grew out of a special invitation. Around 200 B.C. ambassadors from various Greek city-states appealed to Rome for aid in resisting the king of Macedonia, who had been allied with Carthage. Moved by admiration for Hellenic culture, as well as by greed, the Romans replied by sending an army. Their professed aim was to secure the liberties of the proud and quarrelsome Greek cities and then withdraw. But they soon became entangled in the politics and conflicts of the East. In the course of endless maneuvering and fighting, the Romans carved one province after another out of the Hellenistic kingdoms, until, by the time of Christ, they were supreme in the eastern Mediterranean. From Gibraltar to Jerusalem fell the shadow of mighty Rome.

THE OVERTHROW OF THE REPUBLIC

Rome's triumphs abroad had a profound effect on society at home. In former days, the farmer-soldier had been the backbone of the state. But the social and economic revolution that followed the Punic Wars and Rome's adventures in the East changed all that.

The Impact of War and Conquest

During one phase of the Punic Wars, a Carthaginian general, Hannibal, had marched up and down the Italian peninsula for years. Thousands of Roman farmers had been slain and their fields laid to waste. And then, after Hannibal's defeat, new calls were made on the farmer-soldiers to serve in Greece and Asia. Many never came back; those who did often found their farms spoiled by neglect. Some farmers remained stubbornly on their land, but most gave up and drifted into the cities, especially Rome. Many of these became clients of the well-to-do (p. 98) and began to look to the politicians for security and entertainment ("bread and circuses").

While small independent farmers were disappearing, a new social class was rising to prominence in Italy. It consisted of war profiteers of various sorts — contractors to the armed forces and dealers in booty. They used their wealth to buy up ruined farms, restock them, and turn them to new purposes. Small plots on which independent farmers had raised grain were often merged into large tracts (*latifundia*) for use as vineyards, olive groves, or pasturelands for livestock. The new owners, who operated their holdings as capitalistic enterprises, had little interest in the displaced farmers either as tenants or as hired hands. Most of the labor was now performed by gangs of slaves, who had become plentiful and cheap as a result of Rome's conquests overseas. Ecological consequences of this agrarian transformation were severely damaging to Italy: exhaustion of soils and destruction of forests.

By 150 B.C. the social composition of Rome and the peninsula as a whole had undergone a drastic alteration. Rome was now the largest slave-holding society in the ancient world; slaves made up nearly one-third of the population of Italy. They labored mainly on the latifundia, where they generally were treated little better than beasts of burden. In the cities slaves were better off, working as household servants or in various commercial occupations (including prostitution). The master had a right to a slave's earnings, but he sometimes permitted the slave to withhold a portion. By this means some slaves saved enough money to purchase their freedom and, with it, Roman citizenship. Thereafter they were called "freedmen" or "freedwomen" and normally kept their place in the labor force.

Within the body of citizens the number of small farmers continued to fall. At the same time the class of capitalists and landowners mounted in importance, while the urban mob (*proletariat*) steadily swelled in size. The senatorial class, which had guided Rome through its long wars, still held the highest rank and power — though its war-connected prosperity would soon corrupt its character.

From the earliest days of the republic, the noble families of Rome had valued honesty, simple living, and strict moral conduct. But few could resist the lure of the riches that now poured into Rome from across the seas. Senators were required by law to hold most of their property in land and were forbidden to engage in business. Many of them, however, found ways of sharing in the new opportunities for profit — especially those who secured appointments as provincial administrators. Gradually the old republican virtues were eroded by the temptations of wealth. Plain living and discipline gave way to indulgence and moral decay, while the gulf between the rich and the poor widened dangerously.

The failure of virtue at the top was in time communicated to the rank and file of the population. Patriotism and respect for law and order declined among civilians, and to the soldiers discipline and bravery now seemed less important than the chance for promotion and spoils. Polybius, a Greek scholar who wrote around 150 B.C., had foreseen this general decline. Carried to Italy as a hostage after a Roman campaign in the East, he had been freed by his captors to write a history of their conquests. He wrote a fair-minded account, in which he analyzed the factors underlying Roman success. But he warned that the fruits of victory would lead to the breakdown of the republic.

One result of the deterioration was a worsening of Rome's relations with its provinces and its Italian allies. Until the Punic Wars, Rome had enjoyed a reputation for fair treatment of conquered foes. Now, during the final century of the republic, its allies complained of unfair dealings, and the provincials cried out against Roman plunder.

Thus began the republic's time of troubles. Some Roman moralists held that the growing influence of Greek attitudes and ideas was responsible for Rome's plight. But this influence was probably of minor significance. The fact is that the Romans had become subject to powerful new forces within themselves; their change in moral outlook was a direct consequence of their rise to imperial fortune.

The republic paid for this fortune with its life, for the new wealth and corruption upset the political balance of Roman society. Had the Senate been able to meet the problems that came crowding in on Rome, its position could have remained secure. But the senators, absorbed in seeking personal gain and privilege, proved unequal to the broader challenges of their times. Meanwhile, *new* leaders, contemptuous of ancient traditions, were seeking to enlarge their own influence. In so doing they ran into fierce opposition from the entrenched senatorial class, and civil strife was the result. As one legal procedure after another was violated, the life of the republic became a raw contest for personal power. It became clear, at last, that the old political arrangements were hopelessly obsolete; only a major *revolution* could save Rome from collapse.

The first sign of political breakdown had appeared in the latter part of the second century B.C. Tiberius and Gaius Gracchus (the Gracchi), sons of a patrician family, thought that a partial solution to Rome's troubles would be to resettle many of the city's poor on small farms and to provide a subsidy of grain for those who remained in Rome. Such a program, they hoped, would raise the number of independent farmers and reduce the gap between rich and poor.

Though unable to win Senate support for these measures, the Gracchi proposed them directly to the Assembly of Tribes. Tiberius, who was elected tribune of the people in 133 B.C., initiated the reform effort. But his term as tribune, limited by custom to one year, allowed him insufficient time to carry through his long-range program. Moreover, the Senate attacked him as a dangerous troublemaker. Tiberius decided to break custom and stand for reelection as a tribune; in so doing he gave his opponents an excuse to instigate and condone his murder, along with hundreds of his supporters. His younger brother, Gaius, carried forward the reform crusade; he, too, fell under attack by the Senate and met a violent death (121 B.C.).

The Gracchi were compassionate and well-meaning, but their proposed reforms were a futile attempt to turn back the clock of Roman history. And even if they had succeeded they would have corrected only part of the republic's difficulties. Actually, their defiance of custom set in motion a chain of events that would destroy respect for legality, lead to the rise of standing armies and class war, and end, at last, in the overturn of the republic.

The Turn to Monarchy: Julius Caesar

The agent of the final overturn was Julius Caesar. From an old patrician family, he had entered the city's politics as a young man. His early ambitions were doubtless for personal fame and power, but as he grew in maturity and experience he also came to identify Rome's key problems both at home and abroad. In the class struggles he sided with the poorer citizens and used his influence with them to advance his own cause. By 59 B.C., when he was first elected consul, he had begun to plan far-reaching schemes for his future. His main chance came soon afterward, when he won an appointment as proconsul in the Roman province of Gaul (p. 95). Now he had a military command, which was indispensable to the building of personal influence. For eight years he led his troops in Gaul, expanding Roman authority from the Alps northward and westward, and reducing the inhabitants to obedience. His brilliant campaigns reached the Rhine River and the Atlantic Ocean, with forays into Britain and Germany. In 50 B.C. the victor had built a powerful army personally devoted to him; he was ready to challenge the Senate and its backers.

When Caesar was recalled from Gaul by the senators, he decided to return with part of his army. This was contrary to law. As he crossed the river Rubicon, the southern boundary of Gaul, he declared fatefully, "The die is cast." A rival general, Pompey, was hastily commissioned to defend the Senate, but his forces were no match for Caesar's veterans. Forced to flee from Italy, Pompey was later defeated by Caesar in Greece. After subduing opponents in various other provinces, Caesar returned to Rome in triumph in 46 B.C. The Senate, which had once branded him an outlaw, now hailed him as the "father of his country."

Caesar moved swiftly to consolidate his position and launch a program of reform. Publicly he rejected the offer of a royal crown, but by indirect means he gathered to himself the authority of a king. He secured the republican office of consul, then that of dictator (for ten years). He had himself appointed to the office of tribune, censor, and *pontifex maximus* (chief priest of the state religion). He altered the functions of most of the republican institutions, though he was careful to preserve their form. A citizen assembly, for example, continued to exist, but under Caesar it did little more than endorse his proposals. He showed respect to the Senate but treated it as a mere advisory body.

Caesar used his new powers to attack the grave problems facing Rome. He revived the agrarian program of the Gracchi by resettling war veterans on farmlands in Italy and the provinces. He extended Roman citizenship to portions of Gaul and Spain, appointed provincials to the Senate, and tried to make Romans more conscious of the world beyond Italy. By reducing the barriers between the city and the provinces, he initiated the historic union of Rome and its dominions in a single commonwealth.

Romans at home and abroad applauded the deeds of Caesar. He gave them splendid public buildings and roads, and he introduced reforms into every department of administration. The Senate, now enlarged by his own appointees, paid him noble compliments, and its members vowed to risk death in defense of his person. But there remained a stubborn core of older senators who were disturbed by Caesar's successes. Their personal prestige and privilege had been reduced, and they saw Caesar as a destroyer of the republic. Their concern deepened further when, in 44 B.C., he secured a vote from the Senate making him dictator for *life*.

Caesar himself grew ever more arrogant in manner. He permitted a religious cult to be established in his honor, and he wore the purple robe of the ancient kings. These acts were in defiance of republican tradition, and the diehard senators found them intolerable. At last, some sixty of his enemies entered into a conspiracy to assassinate him when he visited the Senate House on the Ides of March (March 15), 44 B.C. In spite of urgent warnings, Caesar appeared, unarmed and unguarded, according to his custom. The conspirators, crying "Tyrant!," struck him down with their daggers.

The murder of Caesar did not restore the republic. It served only to disrupt political reconstruction and to throw Rome again into civil disorder. Cassius and Brutus, the leaders of the senatorial plot, spoke of themselves as liberators; but the populace and the army, urged on by Caesar's fellow consul, Mark Antony, turned against them. Antony was soon joined by the youthful Octavian, Caesar's grandnephew and adopted heir. The senatorial forces were defeated in battle, and Octavian and Antony for a short while held the Roman world between them. Antony, captivated by the Egyptian queen Cleopatra, ruled the eastern half from Alexandria; Octavian ruled the West. Their partnership soon turned to hostility, however, and, after a decisive naval engagement near Actium (in Greece) in 31 B.C., Octavian emerged as sole master.

THE IMPERIAL FOUNDATIONS

Octavian completed the reforms and reconstruction begun by Caesar. Familiar with civil strife from an early age, he matured rapidly into a shrewd and subtle statesman. Once in sole command, Octavian set about advancing the new order at home and abroad. Soon after his triumph at Actium, the Senate conferred upon the young man the title of "augustus" (revered), which had formerly been reserved for the gods. The main lines of the "Augustan settlement" had emerged by 27 B.C., the year generally accepted as the beginning of the Roman Empire.

Note that the word "empire" can be used in two senses. It can mean the control by one state over others; in this sense, the Roman Republic exercised imperial power as early as 250 B.C. (by which time it had established mastery of the Italian peninsula). In the second sense, the word "empire" means a form of *internal* government in which supreme authority is held by a single ruler. After Caesar's overthrow of the republic, Rome became an empire in *both* senses. Augustus developed and refined the new political arrangements, which worked satisfactorily until A.D. 180. After that, when the government fell into less able hands, the Roman Empire entered a period of civil war and near anarchy (pp. 130, 131).

The Augustan Political Settlement

Though Augustus completed the founding of the Roman Empire (in *fact*), he took pains to *deny* it. He recognized that affection for the republic persisted, especially in high places, and he chose to utilize that sentiment rather than resist it. He also knew that Rome and its subjects were eager for peace — for an end to the violent conflicts of rival factions. He could have ruled, as others had before, by military force alone. Instead, having used ruthless means to secure power, he chose to direct that power toward making a peaceful world of "law and justice." The Roman citizens, for their part, recalling the fate of Caesar and the shameful disorders that followed his death, felt that the time had come for tolerance and compromise, rather than defiance and conspiracy.

After celebrating his military triumphs in traditional style, Augustus announced that his aim was to restore peace and the republic. He refused the offer of kingly honors and referred to himself simply as "princeps" (first citizen). By arrangement with the Senate in 27 B.C., Augustus accepted election or appointment to the principal republican offices (including consul, censor, and pontifex maximus). In return, he permitted the Senate to supervise Italy and the city of Rome and to administer certain provinces. He kept for himself control of the major provinces and continued as commander in chief (*imperator*) of the armed forces. Every soldier swore obedience to Augustus personally and looked to him for pay and maintenance.

Augustus kept all his arrangements flexible, but no one doubted where the real authority lay. By cloaking his authority in traditional trappings he gained

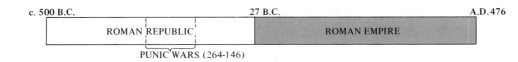

the backing of conservatives, thereby strengthening his power and reducing the danger of assassination. His prudence brought genuine harmony to Rome. After removing hostile members from the Senate, Augustus consulted it frequently and treated it generously. The citizen assembly, meanwhile, faded into oblivion. In contrast to the royal manner affected by Caesar, Augustus wore the toga (robe) and insignia of a consul and lived like any other wealthy patrician. Although he was essentially an innovator bent on creating a new world order, in his own time Augustus was known as a divine *restorer* and *preserver* of the republican tradition.

Augustus strove for peace throughout the empire as well as for harmony at home. He halted the continual advancement of Rome's frontiers, the lengthening of lines of military supply, and the mounting burden of arms expenditure. Up to this time, no one had given serious thought to fixing the boundaries of the empire. Augustus marked defense lines that could readily be held and then sent out adequate forces to man them. He wanted the army to serve no longer as a means of personal adventure and gain; he limited its role to keeping the Roman Peace (*Pax Romana*).

Reforms and Reconstruction

After his victory over Mark Antony, Augustus found himself in command of some sixty legions (about three hundred thousand men). These soldiers were professional volunteers recruited chiefly from the lower classes of society. They had fought for one commander after another during the death struggles of the republic and had developed a taste for spoils and political influence. In short, they were a potential danger to peace and order. Augustus quickly cut the troop strength in half. He provided pensions for the discharged men and kept the rest on a volunteer basis, with fixed rates of pay and long terms of service. In addition to the regular legions, which he stationed on the frontiers, Augustus created a select corps (the Praetorian Guard) to protect himself and the city of Rome.

One of Augustus' aims was to bring just administration to the empire's far-flung territories. During the days of the republic, as we have seen, the provinces had suffered under grasping governors and dishonest officials, who amassed private fortunes at the expense of the people they governed. Caesar had made a start at correcting this abuse; Augustus began a whole series of carefully planned reforms.

First, in appointing governors for the imperial provinces Augustus chose men of demonstrated ability and loyalty and paid them ample salaries. Second, he entrusted imperial administration more and more to career civil servants, rather than to political appointees. Third, in order to make tax assessments fairer Augustus ordered a census of the provinces at regular intervals. (This census is referred to in the Gospel of Luke [2:1]: "In those days a decree went out from Caesar Augustus that all the world should be enrolled.") And he sent inspectors to make sure that the tax-collectors were behaving honestly.

During the course of numerous personal tours of the provinces, Augustus showed his respect for local institutions and encouraged provincial leaders to fulfill their responsibilities. Control over the affairs of the empire as a whole he kept in Rome, but control over local affairs he left to the individual provinces. Finally, he strengthened the economy of the empire by driving pirates from the sea, building new roads, and extending the postal service.

It is hardly surprising that Augustus was respected in Rome and worshiped in the provinces. In the East especially, people were soon looking upon him as a divine being. Tradition had long accustomed them to worship demigods and god-kings, such as the Egyptian pharaohs (pp. 28–30) and the Greek Alexander; Augustus was quickly given a place among the countless deities of the Hellenistic world. Temples were built in his honor, and worship groups sprang up throughout the Eastern provinces. Augustus approved of these and promoted their spread to the Western provinces. Emperor-worship (more strictly, the worship of the emperor's *genius*, or spirit) was thus established as part of the state religion. Whatever Augustus himself may have thought about his divinity, he realized that this strong religious feeling would foster loyalty and unity throughout the empire. Reverence for the emperor later became a symbol of civil respect and obedience everywhere, and those who refused to bow before the imperial statues were suspected of treason.

Augustus also tried to restore the ancient Roman virtues, which had been corrupted by the spoils of conquest. Through personal example he strove to guide the Romans back to the virtuous paths of the old republic. He had stricter laws passed on personal behavior and adultery and divorce, and he encouraged poets to praise high-mindedness, noble conduct, and love of country. In these efforts, however, Augustus was less successful than in his other undertakings.

THE APPROACH TO ONE WORLD: PAX ROMANA

The very success of the reforms introduced by Augustus raised in people's minds a worrisome question: Who would take his place when he died? The simplest solution would have been for Augustus to establish a family line based on hereditary succession. But it had been the suspicion that Caesar was plotting just such a scheme that had led to his assassination. Augustus denied any such ambitions, insisting that his sole aim was to restore the republic. This meant that legally and constitutionally he held his immense powers simply as a gift of the Senate.

The lack of a definite arrangement for orderly succession was a serious flaw in the Augustan settlement. The problem grew out of the contradiction between the *fact* of monarchy under Augustus and the *form* of the republic through which it operated. Theoretically, when the princeps died, power would go back to the Senate until that body named his successor; during that interval the door might well be opened to civil war. Augustus was able to provide only for his immediate heir. He brought his stepson, Tiberius, into the government and appointed him to a series of important public offices. He trusted that the Senate, after his death, would respect his intention and proclaim Tiberius as his successor. When Augustus died in A.D. 14, the Senate declared Tiberius the new princeps, and he assumed full authority without challenge.

Most of the emperors who succeeded Tiberius during the first century A.D. were chosen in a similar manner. The rulers of the second century, in contrast, preferred to pick successors from outside their own families, presumably on the basis of merit alone. Each of these men, by "adoption and designation," became a junior colleague of the ruler during his lifetime and took full charge when he died. The custom was never put into *law*, however, and the choices of later emperors (of the third and fourth centuries) were often ignored after their deaths. Perhaps no single factor contributed more to the ultimate downfall of the Roman Empire than the absence of a sound and accepted *rule of succession*.

And yet the administration of the empire continued to run smoothly for nearly two centuries after Augustus. Even when the capital at Rome was torn by plots and violence, life in the provinces remained relatively calm. The governing structure that Augustus had built proved remarkably stable, and a growing class of civil servants, in partnership with local agencies of self-government, tended to the daily business of the empire.

The Empire: Extent and Composition

The empire reached its greatest extent during the second century A.D. (p. 109). Actually, the area under continuous control was limited by the natural frontiers Augustus had chosen: the African desert in the south, the Atlantic Ocean in the west, and the Rhine-Danube line in the north. In the east, where there were no natural barriers, the Roman frontier between the Black Sea and the Arabian desert shifted back and forth for centuries. Most of Asia Minor, however, and Syria and Palestine were kept under Roman control. The chief antagonist in the East was the kingdom of Parthia (later, Persia), which, though a stubborn foe, was only a minor state compared with the empire itself. The Romans had trading links with India and Ceylon, but the only other great power of which the Romans were aware was China, then under the Han dynasty (pp. 542–43). And China was a distant land, known to the Romans only through the reports of middlemen in the overland silk trade.

From west to east the empire measured nearly three thousand miles; from north to south, nearly two thousand. (Total land area was about half that of the continental United States.) Its population was perhaps fifty million, and during

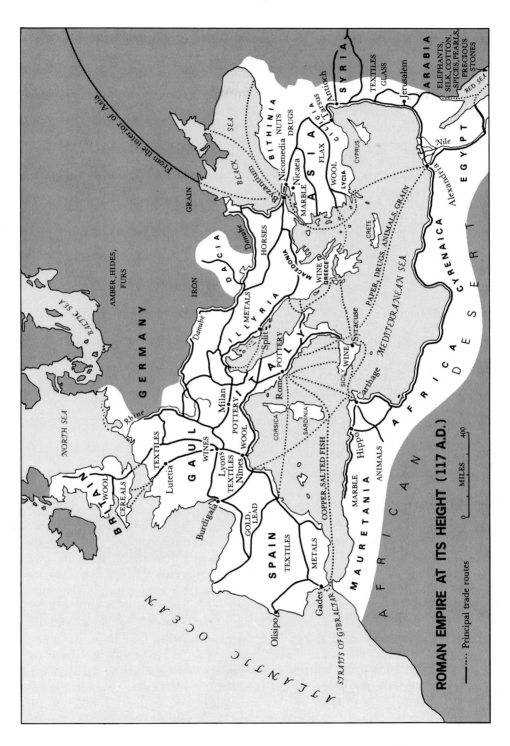

ROMAN EMPIRE AT ITS HEIGHT (117 A.D.)

------ Principal trade routes

0   100   200   300   400
MILES

its most prosperous period (around A.D. 100) the number may have risen to seventy million. The peoples of the empire fell into three broad cultural groups, each having many dialects, religions, and ways of life. The Eastern group, which was least affected culturally by the Romans, consisted of Egyptians, Jews, and Syrians. These Easterners had learned long ago how to adjust to foreign domination, and they persisted in their traditional ways. The second group, the Hellenic, including the Aegean Sea area and southern Italy, was influenced only slightly by Rome. The third cultural group occupied the largest geographical area: the Western, or "Romanized," section of the empire. Here the stamp of Rome was unmistakable. From Italy northward to the Rhine and Danube rivers, the once-barbarian lands were gradually civilized by Roman armies, governors, and colonists. This section included Spain and North Africa as well as distant Britain.

Cities of the Empire

Although the empire was administered through some *forty* provinces, the basic unit of government and of social and economic life was the city (*municipium*). In fact, the Roman Empire has been called a league of cities. It was more than that, of course, but the imperial structure rested upon a foundation of city-states. Rome itself was the city-state triumphant, and its patterns of social organization were imitated everywhere. Where cities existed in conquered territories, the Romans strengthened them as centers from which to control the surrounding districts; where there were no cities, the Romans created new ones in the image of Rome. In contrast to the self-destroying independence of ancient Athens or Sparta, there was an even balance between municipal self-government and centralized power under the early empire.

The cities of the empire were bound together by a network of sea lanes and highways, with Rome, the magnificent capital, at the center. During the prosperous second century, nearly a million people lived there. *Roma Aeterna* ("eternal Rome") was stamped on the imperial coins, and the city has, indeed, stood through the centuries as a timeless glory of Western civilization. Augustus is said to have found Rome a city of brick and to have left it a city of marble. And the emperors who followed him lavished gifts upon the capital, building temples, forums, arenas, monuments, public baths, and palaces to honor themselves and to please the populace. There were, in addition, the elegant private estates of the wealthy, both in the city and in its suburbs. True, not everyone lived in villas; the poor lived in wretched tenements. But Rome gave a stunning impression of affluence and grandeur.

Only a few cities approached Rome in size. Whether large or small, the cities of the empire were alike in their social and political organization. In each city a *senate* managed local affairs, and in each there was a rigid structure of social classes. In the oriental and Greek cities, the old patterns of society persisted. But the cities of the West — in Italy, Gaul, Spain, and Africa — strove to copy Rome. Each had its forum and senate house, its baths, arena, and temples.

The excellent water supply and underground sewage systems explain the comparatively good health of the imperial population until late in the second century. The remains of these admirably planned cities are still to be seen, notably at Pompeii and Herculaneum (Italy), Segovia (Spain), and Nîmes (France).

The Meaning of the Roman Peace

During the second century the empire was favored by a line of able rulers who succeeded one another by the rule of "adoption and designation." The great Spaniard Trajan, who became emperor in A.D. 98, was the first; he had been picked by a wise predecessor, Nerva. His selection reflected the widening base of political participation, for he was the first non-Italian to sit on the imperial throne. Trajan, in turn, exercised sound judgment in selecting Hadrian (another Spaniard) as his junior colleague and ruler-elect. Hadrian was followed by the wise Antoninus and the philosopher-statesman Marcus Aurelius. These conscientious, intelligent men demonstrated the full merits of the Roman imperial system when it was directed by able rulers.

What was the Roman world like in the period from Trajan to Marcus Aurelius? For one thing, it was a peaceful world. From the dawn of history the Mediterranean lands (as well as Europe) had been convulsed by wars, violence, and robbery; the Pax Romana brought comparative political and social stability within its boundaries. Now people could live with less fear. Productive forces — agriculture, industry, and commerce — could advance without disturbance, and the empire cleared the broadest area of trade known until that time. The flow of people, goods, and ideas was stimulated by the extension of Roman citizenship — first to Spain and Gaul and then to the East. Later, in 212, the Emperor Caracalla decreed that Roman citizenship be given to *all* freeborn inhabitants of the empire. Protection under a universal and fair system of law became the birthright of every free person.

The Romans built an empire, but they permitted all the races and nations that lived within it to participate in its administration. Provincials could become judges, senators, generals, emperors. There were no barriers of color or religion, and interracial marriage was widespread and legal. Rome thus became the fulfillment of the idea of universal empire, previously conceived and partially achieved by the Assyrians, the Persians, and Alexander the Great (pp. 90–92). It is no small wonder that ancient tribal and local loyalties were transcended by a new sense of belonging to the *human family*. The Greek biographer Plutarch, writing in the second century, remarked, "I am a citizen, not of Athens or of Greece, but of the world."

ROMAN CHARACTER AND THOUGHT

Unless we dismiss the Romans' achievement as a mere accident of history, we must conclude that it was in some measure the product of their *character*. What was the "inner" nature of those remarkable conquerors and governors?

Religion, Family Life, and Morality

The Romans, from earliest times, accepted the existence of powers outside themselves that had to be treated with respect. They regarded themselves neither as completely free agents nor as pawns of supernatural forces. In their primitive period, they had viewed the world as teeming with spirits (*numina*), each with a special function. There were protective spirits of the hearth, the cupboard, the house; other spirits were active in the fields, in the woods, and on battlegrounds. The Romans sought the help of these forces by certain rites, prayers, and sacrifices; the head of the family (*paterfamilias*) usually acted as priest. Home and family (which meant all members of a household, including slaves) were a more intimate part of life in Rome than in Greece. The father was responsible for the education and devotions of his children and, in theory at least, was absolute master of his household. He alone (as in Greece) decided the fate of new-born infants. Those showing physical defects were ordered abandoned; sons were more likely than daughters to be chosen for rearing. (Significantly, daughters were not given *personal* names, as were sons; they were called, simply, by their *family* names.) If spared at birth, girls were expected to marry in their early teens and to bear children soon afterward. As wives they had to accept the same "double standard" with respect to extramarital sexual relations as did the wives of Greece (p. 62). But Roman women did enjoy greater social respect, freedom, and legal rights; they could, for example, own property outright and were often consulted by their husbands about important family matters.

The role of women and the character of family living evolved with Rome's growing wealth. The simply "country" life of the early republic gave way to more costly and varied styles of living — and to greater personal independence. By the time of Augustus, upper-class wives had become frequent targets of moralists and satirists (all male) because of their "libertarian" behavior. They also shared increasingly the lavish feasts and entertainments of the large cities.

Though Roman women possessed, legally, no *political* rights, some in the imperial family wielded awesome power "behind the scenes." Livia, Augustus' third wife, plotted to ensure that Tiberius, her son by a previous marriage, would become Augustus' successor (p. 108); it was even thought that she may have poisoned Augustus to clear the way. Later in the first century A.D., three of the most influential persons in the court of the Emperor Nero were his mother Agrippina, his wife Octavia, and his mistress Poppaea. In contrast to the political impotence of most Roman women, these women demonstrated that neither gender nor law necessarily weakens the will to power.

Religious ideas also underwent changes during the centuries of Roman expansion. When the Italic peoples first began to associate with the Greeks of southern Italy (after 300 B.C.), they encountered a more developed religion than their own. Their beliefs gradually came to reflect the anthropomorphism of Greek religion (p. 63), and their major deities took on distinctive person alities. Educated Romans, in particular, began to identify their sky spirit, Jupiter, with the Greek lord of the sky, Zeus; their Juno with Hera; Venus with Aphrodite; Mars with Ares; and so on. In addition, they worshiped *personifications* of valued qualities and "powers," usually represented as goddesses; among these were Fortuna (Luck), Salus (Health), Felicitas (Success), Victoria (Victory), and Pax (Peace).

The Romans' ideas about their gods remained within the bounds of their old-fashioned values. They could not accept as proper, for instance, the rather scandalous image of the gods and goddesses portrayed by Homer. For the Roman character was traditionally marked by moral strictness. And what the Romans held to be moral was, generally, what *had been done* — what was recorded about Rome's heroic farmer-soldiers. Even during the late republic and the empire, when Roman morality sadly declined, this conviction did not wholly disappear. Certainly the noblest and truest Romans embodied the "high old virtues" of the early republic.

The moral quality most valued by the Romans was *virtus*. This meant, literally, "manliness," but it carried the special sense of bravery in battle. This quality was considered of such importance that the term came to suggest, in time, the character of moral goodness as a whole; hence, the broader meaning of our modern word "virtue." Manliness was tempered by *pietas*, a disciplined acceptance of the authority of higher powers, both human and divine. Also valued was *gravitas*, a sense of responsibility and seriousness; every matter at hand, however small, had to be weighed with care. The best Romans might be good-humored and easy in manner, but they were rarely lightminded or impulsive. A related quality was *simplicitas*, the ability to look at things clearly and directly.

Literature as Moralistic Expression

Roman literature reflects these qualities of mind and action. It is less imaginative than Greek literature; and though it includes examples of sensual and emotional writing, a substantial portion is sober and moralistic in tone.

Among the first Roman writers was Livius Andronicus, a poet of Greek origin who wrote in the third century B.C. It was Livius who translated Homer's *Odyssey* into Latin. Roman poets were soon writing epics and dramas of their own; during the second century B.C., for instance, Plautus and Terence authored comedies that are still performed today. The republican age produced two more memorable poets during the first century B.C.: one was the philosopher Lucretius, whom we will speak of again (p. 115); the other was Catullus, a writer of sensitive and passionate lyrics.

The greatest prose writer of the first century B.C. was Cicero. A distinguished figure in public life during the last troubled days of the republic, he was best known for his speeches in the law court and the Senate. In addition, he wrote long philosophic essays on the art of government, justice, and theology in which he provided digests of the best Hellenistic thought. These essays gave Romans a literature of philosophy that they had lacked before and made Greek thought available to future generations.

Historical writing in Rome, though lively, was less reliable than that of the best Greek historians (pp. 78–79). Livy's *History of Rome*, for example, is hardly an objective inquiry; it is moralistic in character, drawing chiefly from previous histories and well-known legends about ancient heroes. Most famous is the legend of Romulus and Remus, twin sons of the war-god Mars. They were abandoned near the Tiber River (p. 93), but were saved and suckled by a she-wolf. The twins, when grown to manhood, quarreled over which one of them would found and govern a new city on the banks of the river. According to Livy, Romulus slew his brother, started the city, and gave it his name (Rome).

Three outstanding poets adorned the reign of Augustus (27 B.C.–A.D. 14): Vergil, Horace, and Ovid. Vergil was the eloquent spokesman of the Romans' spiritual tradition and of their love for the soil. He was also the prophet of Rome's mission and destiny. At a time when the old republican order was lying in ruins, his desire, like Livy's, was to promote a regeneration of patriotic values. Although the spirit of Vergil's masterpiece, the *Aeneid*, is Roman, he took Homer's epic form as his model, and the adventures of his hero, Aeneas, parallel those of Odysseus after the fall of Troy (p. 74). Guided by the gods, Aeneas wanders to Italy, where he and his companions become the "fathers" of the "Roman race."

The lyric poems of Horace (the *Odes*) range over a variety of moods: trivial, moralizing, and romantic. His patriotic verses consistently reflect the spirit of the Augustan revival and sing of the destiny of Rome. Ovid's erotic poems, published under such titles as *Loves* and *The Art of Love*, deal in a playful, witty, adult manner with the life of the senses. In an age when official policy was committed to the restoration of morality, these poems seemed highly immoral. It was partly for this reason that Augustus banished Ovid to a remote town on the west coast of the Black Sea.

Though the literature of the century after Augustus' death is usually judged inferior to that of the preceding century, it was not lacking in distinction. The philosopher Seneca was known for his epigrams (cleverly turned phrases), and his polished letters are considered the forerunners of the essay form in Western literature (p. 348). He also wrote melodramas based on the Greek myths. Catering to the Roman taste for plottings and violence, Seneca emphasized passion and horror in his plays.

Biographical writing was of higher quality and proved popular with the upper classes. The Greek Plutarch, a man of cosmopolitan tastes, wrote *Parallel Lives*, some fifty short biographies of Greek and Roman statesmen and generals. Appearing about A.D. 110, these served to remind his readers of the glory of ancient Greece and to compare the talents of the best Greek and Roman leaders. Suetonius, who lived about the same time as Plutarch, wrote short biographies (*Lives of the Caesars*) of the Roman rulers, from Julius Caesar to

Domitian (who died in A.D. 96). Unlike Plutarch, Suetonius refrained from making interpretations, confining himself to personal details and anecdotes, many of them of a scandalous nature.

The scandals of the empire brought blistering attacks from the satiric poet Juvenal (who wrote after A.D. 100). In his verse we find once more that continuing trait in Roman literature, a longing for the *past* and its ideals. Juvenal, in his satires on the moral lows of "high" society, the "wickedness" of women, and the indignities of life in the great metropolis, pointed again and again to the "good old days" of *early* Rome.

Roman Epicureanism and Stoicism

The Romans borrowed freely from Greek philosophy as well as from Greek literature. But it was not the thought of Plato or Aristotle that attracted them. Rather, they were drawn to the more individualistic philosophies of the Hellenistic period. One of these was Epicureanism, which enjoyed a vogue among educated Romans. Epicurus, who had taught in Athens around 300 B.C., concentrated not on cosmic problems, but on ways of achieving individual happiness. (In this aim, he followed the lead of the earlier Greek Sophists, pp. 68–69.) The chief promoter of his teachings in the West was the Roman poet Lucretius (first century B.C.), who articulated them in his eloquent *De Rerum Natura (On the Nature of Things)*. This poem is also a hymn to Epicurus himself, whom Lucretius praises for having liberated the human mind from superstitious fears.

Epicurus had presented a "scientific" and *materialist* view of the universe. Setting aside mythological explanations, he accepted the principle of Democritus of Abdera (p. 67), which reduces all matter to atoms. To Epicurus, all forms of existence are temporary combinations of minute, imperishable particles; death and dissolution occur when the atoms separate. Only the laws of motion and chance determine the shape and character of things, and there is no governing "purpose" on earth or in the heavens.

In such a universe, Epicurus believed, the only logical aim for the individual is to strive for *personal happiness*. The individual is powerless to change the material world and has no obligation to try. As a guide in the search for happiness, Epicurus formulated this basic equation: happiness equals pleasure *minus* pain. He suggested that the major way to secure happiness is by decreasing the pain factor, rather than by increasing the pleasure factor of the equation. Though he conceded the existence of bodily aches, Epicurus taught that fear, the "ache of mind and heart," is the deepest source of human pain; and fear feeds on ignorance and superstition.

Religious teachings, Epicurus had charged, were aimed at frightening simple-minded believers with tales of darkness, terror, and punishment. Priests and magicians played on the fear of death, a fear that is natural to everyone, in order to serve their own purposes. Epicurus was no atheist; he did not deny the existence of the gods (whom he thought of as made of atoms). But, he insisted, the gods live far from humans and have no concern for them. Prayer is useless, for one cannot expect help from the gods. Yet there is some consolation in believing, as Epicurus did, that the gods do no *harm*.

To dispel the dread of death, Epicurus insisted that death is *nothing* — simply a *separation* of atoms: "Death, usually regarded as the greatest of calamities, is actually nothing to us; while we are, death is not, and when death is here, we are not." Epicurus' statement may reduce the fear of death, but it offers little emotional reassurance.

The pursuit of pleasure — the other factor in Epicurus' "happiness equation" — is an art more difficult than the avoidance of fear. Epicurus warned that bodily pleasures are usually self-defeating, for they stimulate appetites that act as fresh sources of pain (until they have been satisfied). Such pleasures as eating and drinking, which arise from the satisfaction of hungers, Epicurus classified as "dynamic" (restless) pleasures. Rather than feed these appetites, he thought it wiser to *discipline* them and to reduce their influence on behavior.

Epicurus urged the cultivation of the "passive" (quiet) pleasures, those agreeable experiences that do not arise from the satisfaction of hungers. These include the pleasures of literature, recollection and meditation, personal friendship, and the enjoyment of nature. He shunned the pursuit of wealth or public office, for it often brings disappointment, trouble, and pain. Epicurus valued, above all, calmness, poise, and serenity of mind. (It is ironic that his name has become linked with pleasures of the appetites and that a connoisseur of fine food and drink has come to be known as an "epicure." One who enjoys such bodily pleasures is closer in spirit to the Sophist teacher, Aristippus, discussed on p. 69.)

Epicureanism as a way of life has appealed only to the few, mainly because it demands solitary courage, intellectual resourcefulness, self-control, and refined taste. The great majority of Romans — those who visited the arenas and the banquet tables — preferred the coarser thrills to the gentle pleasures recommended by Epicurus and Lucretius. Nevertheless, Epicureanism attracted some leisured devotees in the Roman world, and its ethical teachings served, indirectly, as a moderating influence on the times.

The most influential of the philosophies Roman intellectuals imported from the East was Stoicism. One reason, no doubt, is that its ethical code paralleled the traditional Roman virtues. We might almost say that the Romans had practiced Stoicism before hearing of it. The term itself derives from the porch (stoa) in Athens where Zeno, the founder of Stoicism, had taught (about 300 B.C.). Zeno, like Epicurus, had a materialist view of the universe. But passive matter, he held, contains within itself an active principle known variously as "divine fire," "providence," "reason," and "God." The universe is not *chaos*; rather, it functions according to a plan of goodness. Although people cannot control what is beyond themselves, they are masters of their own beings: they can hold themselves ignorant, can rebel against nature, or can live in harmony with it.

Harmony and happiness, declared the Stoics, are achieved by striving for *virtue*, rather than pleasure. Virtue, according to their definition, consists of understanding nature through reason, accepting by self-discipline God's purpose, and living in accordance with duty, truth, and natural law (justice). They regarded all persons as inherently equal, because all share, in common with God, the spark of reason. Consequently, they challenged the ancient practice of slavery and taught that all individuals should tolerate, forgive, and love one another as brothers and sisters. The ideal Stoic is self-sufficient, dutiful, compassionate, and calm.

Because Stoicism spoke to those of all classes and stations in society, it had universal appeal. While Epicureanism found most of its followers among members of the upper classes, Stoicism appealed to the thoughtful of all ranks. These included Cicero, the noble lawyer and senator; Seneca, the writer and adviser to the Emperor Nero; and Epictetus, once a learned slave in Nero's court. But the Roman who most closely *lived* a Stoic life was an emperor — Marcus Aurelius. The last of the "good emperors" of the second century (p. 108), he embodied Plato's dream that kings should be philosophers, or philosophers kings (p. 71). Day by day he set down his inmost thoughts in a little book, called *Meditations* (*Thoughts to Himself*). The work of God (providence), wrote Marcus Aurelius, is in its *totality* good. But specific events may seem harmful to the individual who is immediately affected by them. In order to live in wisdom and harmony, individuals must learn to accept such events as necessary to the total good. Then personal suffering will actually give them a sense of participation in the greater works of providence. No matter what their lot, they will bless God and conduct themselves calmly.

Stoicism, as formulated by Marcus Aurelius, was quite in accord with the ancient Roman virtues. "Let it be your hourly care," he advised, "to do stoutly what the hand finds to do, as becomes a man and a Roman, with carefulness, unaffected dignity, humanity, freedom, and justice. . . . Perform every action as though it were the last of your life, without lightmindedness, without swerving through force of passion from the dictates of reason." Every man, whether emperor or slave, must do his duty as it falls to him. Thus, nature's plan is served, and the individual's life is blended with that of the universe.

To the weary burdened with care, Marcus Aurelius said, "Trouble not yourself by pondering life in its entirety." The individual should live *one day* at a time, leaving the past to itself and entrusting the future to providence. One should strive to avoid "distractions" — elegant clothing, stylish homes, the opinions of others — and concentrate on one's *own* mind and character.

Stoicism made a significant mark on Roman times and influenced the future; it offered a noble standard of conduct and in its ethics anticipated Christianity. Perhaps the most direct influence, however, was on Roman legal thought, in which the Stoic idea of "natural law" — law identical with reason and God — was of high importance.

Science and Medicine

In literature and philosophy, we have seen that the Romans were essentially preservers and carriers of Hellenistic culture (p. 92). The same is true in the "sciences." While Athens remained the leading center for philosophical studies, Alexandria (in Egypt) continued as the hub of scientific and medical works. It was there, in the second century A.D., that the Greek astronomer and geographer, Claudius Ptolemy, compiled his marvelous *Almagest*. (The title means "the greatest" work.) Bringing together the accumulated learning of the Greeks about the earth and the heavenly bodies, Ptolemy set forth a "model" of the universe that was generally accepted in the West until the scientific revolution of the seventeenth century (pp. 410–15). Of equal influence was a series of books written about the same time by a Greek physician, Galen of Pergamum (in Asia Minor). Galen stressed the importance of personal hygiene to health, and his views on anatomy and physiology were accepted until the emergence of scientific biology in the seventeenth century (p. 418).

ROMAN LAW

The Romans were content to leave many areas of thought and artistic expression to others — especially the Greeks. But they were vigorous originators in the field of law, and their most enduring contribution to Western institutions lay in legal theory and practice.

The Evolution of Roman Law

In the later republic the Romans gradually developed the idea that the law of the state should reflect what is *right* according to *universal reason*. Hence, they used the word *justitia*, which is related to *justus*, or "right." According to Cicero's definition, "Law is the just distinction between right and wrong, made conformable to most ancient nature." As we have seen (p. 97), the "customary" laws that the patrician judges had been observing were recorded in the Twelve Tablets during the fifth century B.C. That early code remained the basis of Roman law for centuries. Although it provided for harsh penalties, the judges gradually modified them through interpretation. The rulings of the courts thus conformed ever more closely to *justitia*.

After 366 B.C. a special magistrate, called a *praetor*, was elected annually to administer justice to the citizens of Rome. He was expected to follow the code of the Twelve Tablets but was given some freedom in interpreting it. Each praetor, at the start of his term, was required to announce his own interpretation of the law. Through this interpretative decree and through his daily decisions, he adapted the original tablets to the cases before him. By 246 B.C. another praetor had been established, to deal with disputes between Roman citizens and foreigners under Roman jurisdiction. This official had a still wider basis for interpretations, for he could draw on the various foreign laws, as well as on Roman law, in arriving at fair decisions and settlements. Thus, there grew up, in the days of the republic, two distinct bodies of law: the law of citizens, or *jus civile*, and the law of "peoples," or *jus gentium*. (In the conquered provinces, native laws and procedures continued to apply in cases that did not involve Roman citizens.)

Because the law of "peoples" drew from broader sources than the law of citizens did, the Roman praetor for citizens tended to be guided more and more in his own decisions by the *jus gentium*. By the first century A.D. the basic provisions of the two bodies of law had been brought close together; after 212, when all free inhabitants of the empire were declared Roman citizens, the dual system disappeared. From that time on — in theory, at least, and usually in practice — one system of law prevailed throughout the empire.

Under the empire, the ancient statutes of the republic were further expanded by the decrees and interpretations of rulers and by the opinions and commentaries of legal experts. The praetors themselves were not always professional lawyers, and even during the first century B.C. they had established the custom of consulting men who were "skilled in the law" (*jurisprudentes*). The emperors regularly appointed outstanding legal scholars to advise magistrates on specific cases. Since the Romans had profound respect for the law, and for experts in law, the commentaries carried considerable authority. The judicial traditions of the West owe much to the clarifying and humanizing influence of these fair-minded and dedicated scholars.

The Idea of "Natural Law"

Most of the jurists were well-educated men who felt at home with Stoic philosophy. They observed that the laws of nations had many elements in common and that the laws themselves were gradually fusing into the single law of the empire. This similarity in legal ideas among the peoples of the empire coincided nicely with the Stoic belief that there was one law in nature, the law of reason. From this the jurists inferred the reality of "natural law" and concluded that human rules could and should conform to this "higher law." Thus, the Roman experience, supported by Hellenistic philosophy, gave rise to the doctrine of natural law, or *jus naturale*.

This doctrine, which has deeply influenced legal theory in the West, is the basis of the idea of law and human rights contained in the Declaration of Independence. Cicero, in the *Laws*, observed, "Law and equity have not been established by opinion, but by nature." The regulations of states that do not conform to reason, he declared, are not truly *laws* and do not deserve obedience. Clearly, this doctrine is a two-edged sword: it gives added authority to those laws that citizens regard as *right*; but in the case of laws they believe to be *wrong*, it opens the door to disobedience (and rebellion).

Codification of the Laws

Over the centuries, several emperors tried to bring a degree of order into the mounting accumulation of laws, interpretations, principles, and procedures. But it was not until the sixth century (after the division of the Roman Empire) that a complete codification was carried through, under the Emperor Justinian (p. 184). Justinian's *Corpus Juris Civilis* (*Body of Civil Law*) consists of several parts: the *Digest*, a summary of judicial opinions and commentaries; the *Code*, a collection of statutes from Hadrian to Justinian; the *Novels*, a collection of statutes enacted after the publication of the *Code*; and the *Institutes*, a brief discussion of legal principles, designed for law students. Justinian's great codification became the foundation for the legal systems that were later developed throughout Europe. Hundreds of millions of people today live under systems that are modeled, in whole or in part, upon Roman law as found in the *Corpus*.

ARCHITECTURE AND ENGINEERING

The Romans built their state, their law, and their public structures for eternity, and there is no more impressive proof of their sense of power and permanence than their architecture. After centuries of erosion and vandalism, the ruins of hundreds of Roman buildings still stand on three continents — from the shores of the eastern Mediterranean to the Scottish border. Although the architects of Rome borrowed and adapted techniques from a wide variety of styles, the primary influences were Etruscan and Hellenistic. The Romans built on a larger scale than the Greeks, however; while the typical Greek city-state had to provide public structures for only a few thousand citizens, the population of Rome numbered hundreds of thousands. The Romans, moreover, developed a taste for grandeur, elegance, and display, and they expressed this taste freely in their architecture.

Construction materials were readily available: the Italian peninsula had plenty of timber and stone, as well as good clays (for brick) and lava and sandy earth (for concrete). Other materials, such as decorative marble, were often imported. Brick and concrete faced with stucco or marble veneer were the materials most commonly used in Rome itself.

Architectural Forms and Aims

Although the Romans made some use of the post-and-lintel method of construction (p. 80), their preference in large buildings was for the *arch*, *vault*, and *dome* — first used in ancient Sumer (p. 21). They realized that an arch formed of bricks, stones, or poured concrete could carry a far heavier load than a stone beam supported at either end by a post or column. And they discovered

3-1 Pont du Gard.

that a series of arches placed side by side could carry a bridge or an aqueduct across a deep valley (*Fig. 3-1*).

The vault is actually an extension of the arch. The typical tunnel, or barrel, vault is an arch extended in depth to produce a tunnel-shaped enclosure of the desired width and length (*Fig. 3-2a*). Because this type of vault admits light only at the two ends, however, it is of limited usefulness in public structures. To overcome this difficulty, Roman architects devised the *cross-vault* plan, which permits light to enter from the sides as well. It consists of one or more short vaults intersecting the main vault at right angles (*Fig. 3-2b*). This kind of structure can be carried to a substantial height and can be made to enclose a huge space with no need for supporting members between floor and ceiling.

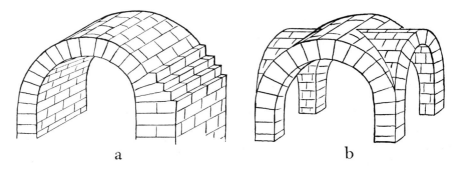

a   b

3-2 Roman vaulting systems: (a) barrel vault; (b) cross vault.

Another architectural form used by the Romans to provide an uncluttered enclosure was the dome, which is simply a hemisphere resting on a cylindrical wall or on a circle of supporting arches (*Fig. 3-4*). A large dome was built up of a series of progressively smaller horizontal rings of brick, stone, or concrete. When completed, the parts formed a single unit firmly set in place.

The Romans were especially clever in designing structures to serve the practical needs of the population. To provide their cities with water for public baths and ornamental fountains and also to ensure a good supply of drinking water, they built great aqueducts leading down from distant mountain springs. Much of the way, the water descended through pipes or channels in the mountains or hills, but across a valley or a plain it flowed through a channel carried by an aqueduct. Since the Romans had no mechanical pumps, the aqueduct had to be engineered so that the water flowed steadily by force of gravity alone. The famous Pont du Gard (*Fig. 3-1*) is part of a Roman aqueduct that once carried water across the Gard River and valley to the provincial city of Nîmes, in southern France. The upper level of arches supported a covered water channel nine hundred feet in length. The entire structure, one hundred eighty feet high, was built of stone blocks fitted together without mortar.

Roman engineers also reduced the spread of disease from marshy areas, especially south of the capital. Mosquitoes, the carriers of malaria, breed easily in wetlands. By means of extensive drainage works, the Romans — without understanding the mechanism of the disease — hit at the source of malaria. As a result, this illness was kept within bounds in Italy — while elsewhere, notably in Greece, malaria continued to take a heavy toll of victims.

Perhaps the most impressive practical achievement of the Romans was their wide-ranging network of roads. Their military expansion demanded a swift and reliable means of overland movement. Over the centuries, they built or improved some fifty thousand miles of roads, reaching out from Rome to the farthest corners of the empire. While they were constructed by a variety of methods, the typical roadbed was about fifteen feet wide and five feet deep. Broken stone and gravel were packed down to form a foundation, which was then surfaced with thick blocks of hard stone. Sections of these remarkably durable highways are still in use.

The army had priority in the use of the strategically planned system of roads, but they were open to public travel and served as the basis for a postal system operated by the state. The roads were regularly patrolled, and guidebooks were issued to travelers. On the major arteries there was a stable every ten miles and a hostel every thirty miles. No road system comparable to the Roman highways was to be undertaken again until the twentieth century.

In domestic architecture the wealthy Romans found their model in the dwellings of the ancient Etruscans. The basic plan of the Roman villa, with its central court (atrium) partly open to the sky, was Etruscan in origin. Such homes were extremely comfortable and luxurious, as we can tell from the remains of the splendid houses at Pompeii, located near Naples. (An eruption of Mt. Vesuvius in A.D. 79 buried the city in layers of lava and ashes, thus preserving it virtually intact.) Excavations have revealed the well-designed homes, with their fountains, sculptures, wall paintings, mosaics, and metalware. The great mass of the urban populations, however, lived in crowded apartment buildings. Examples of these have been uncovered at Ostia, a port and suburb of Rome.

Civic Architecture and Monuments

It is in the public buildings, however, that we find the grandest and most enduring monuments of Roman architecture. In the major cities of the empire there was always a public square — a forum — that served as a civic center. The Roman Forum, for example, was a marketplace in the early days of the republic, but it was gradually transformed into an impressive meeting place with handsome statues, temples, and halls of government. Overlooking the Forum was the sacred Capitoline Hill topped by the temple of Jupiter, while across the Forum, on the Palatine Hill, stood the palaces of the emperors.

Several emperors constructed their own forums in Rome as memorials to themselves. One of these, the Forum of Trajan, was built early in the second century A.D. on a spacious site near the Capitoline Hill. Symmetrically laid out, it included a large area for shops, an imposing hall (*basilica*), a library, and a temple dedicated to the deified emperor. Dominating all the rest was the towering marble Column of Trajan, with a spiral band of sculptured relief (three feet high and six hundred fifty feet long) retelling the emperor's conquests.

Most of the public meeting halls in Rome and the other cities of the empire were built in the style of the basilica. This was a rectangular building constructed either on the cross-vault principle or with a roof supported by columns in the Greek manner. In either case, there was a wide central aisle (nave) running the length of the building, with narrower side aisles. By lifting the roof of the center aisle higher than the roof of the side aisles, the architects were able to admit light through a series of "clearstory" windows. A semicircular area, called an *apse*, was joined to one end; sometimes there was an apse at each end. Covered by a half-dome, the apse was frequently walled off from the central hall and used as a chamber for courts of law. In the fourth century, when the Christians were finally permitted to build public houses of worship, they adapted the basilica to their own needs. The congregation *stood* in the open rectangular area, and the apse was used to house the altar and sacred objects. This plan of church architecture persisted for centuries (*Fig. 3-3*).

Religious shrines did not occupy the prominent place in Roman architecture that they did in Greek (p. 80). The usual Roman temple resembled the Greek, but it followed more precisely an Etruscan plan. Though columns were used to support the roof, the Roman temple stood on a higher base (*podium*) than the Greek and faced in only one direction. The most impressive of all

3-3 The nave of Sant' Apollinare in Classe, Ravenna, Italy.

Roman temples, however, has a design unlike that of earlier structures. It is the Pantheon in Rome (*Fig. 3-4*), a temple dedicated to all the gods (*pantes theoi*). The present building is actually a reconstruction ordered by the Emperor Hadrian about A.D. 120 to replace the original temple, which had been destroyed by fire. It was converted into a Christian church (St. Mary of the Rotunda) in the seventh century and has been used continuously since then as a place of worship. (This conversion explains its protection, across the centuries, by the Christian authorities in Rome; the basic structure remains intact, the best-preserved building of pagan antiquity.)

The Pantheon consists of a round central hall, or *rotunda*, capped by a vast concrete dome. To carry the great weight of the dome, the rotunda wall was built twenty feet thick. The height of the dome and its diameter are identical (one hundred forty feet), assuring geometrical balance; and the dome is pierced by an eye (*oculus*) thirty feet across, which serves as the source of light. Originally, it is believed, statues of the seven "planetary" deities stood in the seven niches cut into the wall. There is a single doorway, which is approached through a Greek-style porch. From the outside, the Pantheon has a squat, heavy appearance. But the interior gives a dramatic impression of space and buoyancy. The Pantheon has served as the *first* of a noble line of domed structures, including St. Peter's in Rome, St Paul's in London, and the Capitol in Washington, D.C.

The civilization of the empire, as we have seen, was mainly urban, and elaborate structures were erected to satisfy the recreational needs of city people. Particularly popular were the public bathhouses (*thermae*), which were equipped with steam rooms and small pools filled with hot, lukewarm, or cold

3-4 (*Above*) The Pantheon,
exterior. (*Left*) The
Pantheon, interior.
Painting by Giovanni
Paolo Panini,
eighteenth century.

water. The emperors also courted popular favor by donating magnificent pleasure palaces that housed not only baths but large indoor and outdoor swimming pools, gymnasiums, gardens, libraries, galleries, theaters, lounges, and bars. Because these recreational centers were especially attractive to the lower classes and to idlers, their reputation in polite society was not altogether respectable.

The best-preserved pleasure palace in Rome is the complex of buildings known as the Baths of Diocletian, built in the late third century. Its main hall, which once enclosed a huge swimming pool, is constructed on the cross-vault principle. It is three hundred feet long, ninety feet wide, and ninety feet high. In the sixteenth century, Michelangelo converted this great room into the central section of a Christian church, St. Mary of the Angels. The church is still standing, along with a series of huge tunnel vaults and half-domes that formed portions of the original baths. It is estimated that the baths could accommodate three thousand bathers in lavish surroundings of gilt and marble.

One of the most popular pastimes of the Romans was watching the chariot races of the circus and the gory combats of the arena. As the *theater* symbolized the cultural tastes of the ancient Greeks, the *arena* best symbolized the cultural tastes of the Romans. Although every city of the empire had places for mass entertainment, the most famous arena was the Colosseum of Rome (*Fig. 3-5*). This huge structure, which covers about six acres and seated more than fifty thousand spectators, was the largest of its kind. The crowds made their way to their seats through some eighty entry vaults, and the stairways were arranged so that the stadium could be emptied in minutes.

A variety of materials was used in the construction of the Colosseum. Key areas of stress, such as archways and vaults, are generally of brick; other sections are of concrete and broken stone. The outer facing is divided into three stories topped by a high wall of stone blocks. Between the arches of each story, and above them in the high wall, stand Greek-style half-columns. Sockets set inside the high wall once held great poles, on which protective awnings could be mounted. A coating of marble originally covered the exterior of the Colosseum, but the marble (and other building material) was carried off, over the centuries, for use in other structures.

Underneath the arena floor, which was made of wood covered with sand, lay a maze of corridors, chambers, and cells, where animals and humans (mainly slaves or criminals) awaited their turn at combat. These contests were usually fought to the death, but the crowd's appetite for violence was hard to satisfy. "Roman holidays," about one hundred a year, were lengthy affairs, lasting from early morning till dark. Wealthy donors seeking popularity usually paid the bills, including the cost of food and refreshments.

To impress the citizens and the thousands of visitors who flocked to Rome, the emperors ordered monuments built in their own honor — triumphal arches, columns, and statues (*Fig. 1-1*, p. xii). These are still to be found in abundance in the Eternal City, as well as in the provinces. Like the mighty

3-5 The Colosseum. Engraving by Giovanni Piranesi.

Column of Trajan, they carry a sense of pride, power, and permanence. To the Roman rulers, works of sculpture were also viewed as a medium of propaganda. They might relate the events of a military campaign, or present, simply, the unaffected portrait of a man. Figures of gods and goddesses were based on Greek models, and the same idealized style might be used to represent the rulers themselves (*Fig. 3-6*). Most Roman portraits, however, are extremely lifelike (*Fig. 3-7*). In the National Museum of Naples there is a superb collection of original busts of emperors, each bearing the mark of individual personality.

THE END OF ROME AND THE BEGINNING OF EUROPE

The great age of the Pax Romana ended with the death of Marcus Aurelius in A.D. 180. The third century was a time of revolts and civil wars and fierce barbarian attacks, which almost destroyed the empire. In the fourth century there was a recovery, largely thanks to the reforms brought by the emperors Diocletian and Constantine. But the reformed empire was very different from that of Augustus. The social structure was highly regimented, the rulers held power by divine right, and in place of the pagan gods, the empire eventually adopted the new religion of Christianity. Within the changing empire, a new civilization was coming into being.

From the late fourth century, the pace of change quickened. It proved impossible to hold together the whole vast fabric of the empire. First its administration was divided between East and West; then, in the fifth century, the

3-6 Equestrian statue of Marcus Aurelius, c. A.D. 165. Bronze, more than life-size. Capitoline Hill, Rome.

western portion succumbed to Germanic invaders. The "fall" of the Roman Empire was perhaps the most dramatic event in the long and turbulent history of the relations between ancient civilized states and the barbarian peoples of Europe (pp. 47–48). But it was far from spelling the end of the civilization that

3-7 Portrait of a Roman, c. 80 B.C.
Palazzo Torlonia, Rome.

the Greeks had founded, and the Romans organized and preserved. The eastern half of the empire continued to survive as a powerful civilized state, Greek in culture and Christian in religion (pp. 183–89). In the West, the Latin-speaking culture of Rome, as well as the empire's recently acquired Christianity, were accepted by the new Germanic rulers. Instead of dying, the civilization of Greece and Rome began to change, and to spread among many still-barbarian peoples, until it became the European civilization of the Middle Ages.

The Problems of the Empire

The weakening of the Roman Empire was a gradual process marked by temporary periods of recovery. For much of the time, the average citizen had no sense of sudden catastrophe; despite the many ills of the empire, life went on much the same. Scholars have written hundreds of volumes on the problems that the empire faced; their evidence suggests that several weakening forces were at work.

The economic weakness of the western portion of the empire was one of these factors. For Italy, the centuries of the late republic and the early empire were a period of gradual economic decline. Since the Punic Wars of the second century B.C. (p. 100), Italy had been able to live off the profits of conquest. But as Augustus and his successors lifted the burdens of tribute from the provinces (pp. 106–7), Rome and Italy gradually lost their favored position. Tax rates had to be raised in Italy, leading to gradual impoverishment of taxpayers, which the government tried to make up for by boosting taxes still further.

In other areas of the West, such as Spain and Gaul, much the same thing happened. Following upon the Roman conquest of each province, there was a period of prosperity, as cities were founded, agriculture flourished, and commerce developed. Even so, the western provinces had fewer people, cities, and economic resources than those of the East. Over the years the army, the civil officials, and the tax-collectors grew ever more demanding; without the wealth to meet these demands, the western provinces grew gradually poorer.

Besides these economic problems, the empire continued to suffer from its inability to ensure stable and effective *leadership*. As we have seen, the gravest weakness of the imperial system was the lack of a sound and certain means of selecting new rulers. During the second century, the method of "adoption and designation" was used with good results (p. 108). But Marcus Aurelius chose to name his own offspring, the worthless Commodus, as his successor. Commodus was murdered after twelve years of irresponsible rule, and rival generals then fought one another to take over the imperial office. Even successful and capable emperors were beholden to the soldiers of the armies that won them the supreme power: the resulting gifts and pay raises increased the burden on the empire's resources.

These difficulties, in turn, made it harder for the empire to deal with a third major problem: the still-unconquered barbarian peoples who lived to the north of its European frontiers. These were the Germanic peoples, who spoke closely related Indo-European languages, and who had much the same way of life as other Indo-European barbarians such as the Celts — or, for that matter, the Greeks and Romans before they became civilized (pp. 47–48). They were farmers, livestock breeders, and warriors, living a settled life in villages, but liable to move around in search of new land, or as a result of defeat in war or natural disasters. Neighboring villages formed more or less permanent tribes, each of which could field at most a few thousand warriors.

Before historic times, the Germanic tribes had lived in Scandinavia and northern Germany, but by the time of Caesar they had spread into the broad area between the Baltic and North seas and the Rhine-Danube frontier. In the third century A.D. they moved into eastern Europe as well. The Romans applied the name of one of the tribes, the *Germani*, to the tribes in general and spoke of their homelands as *Germania* (Germany) — a considerably larger area than the present-day country of that name (p. 109).

As soon as the Romans, for their part, reached north of the Alps, they came into close contact with the Germanic tribes. These contacts were just as often friendly as hostile, for the tribes had no feelings of solidarity among themselves and no deliberate intention of destroying the empire. Many Germans joined the supporting forces of the Roman army, and some enlisted in the legions themselves. It became a common practice for the Romans to permit — or sometimes even compel — fairly large groups to settle within the frontier, as a buffer against further encroachments.

Over the centuries, contact with Rome brought changes among the Germanic tribes. Whether as enemies or as soldiers of Rome, the Germanic warriors learned the empire's methods of fighting and adopted its weapons. Trade, booty, and Roman subsidies to friendly tribes brought wealth to Germany, and fostered the growth of an elite of powerful chieftains and warriors. Warfare among the tribes became more profitable, fiercer, and broader in scale. From late in the second century A.D., the tribes began to form larger confederacies. Individual warriors or tribes would join or leave these alliances depending on the fortunes of war, but on the whole they lasted through the following centuries. With new and better weapons and the ability to field armies as large as twenty thousand warriors, the tribal confederacies had formidable war-making capacity, both against each other and against Rome. Ironically, the more advanced the Germanic barbarians became under Roman influence, the more dangerous they were to the empire.

About the middle of the third century, the combination of diminishing resources, political divisions, and growing barbarian strength brought about a crisis that almost destroyed the empire. The economic situation was made even worse by a decline in population. This came about mainly from repeated outbreaks of disease, spread through much of the empire by Roman troops that had campaigned in Syria. Political collapse set in, as provincial armies battled to advance their favorite candidates and the imperial succession was determined by the clash of legions. (Because of this fact, the middle of the third century is often referred to by historians as the period of the "barracks emperors.") Surprisingly, many of the emperors so chosen proved to be forceful and competent leaders. This did not save them from violent death, and their terms of office were generally short.

Profiting from the civil wars, barbarian tribal confederacies devastated the empire from Gaul to the Black Sea. Even territories far from the frontiers, such as Spain, Greece, and Italy itself, were looted by barbarian war-bands, while the civilized but hostile Persians ravaged the provinces of the Middle East. The entire empire seemed on the brink of falling apart.

Reconstitution of the Empire by Diocletian and Constantine

At last, in A.D. 284, a ruler came to power who in origin was simply another "barracks emperor," but who had the shrewdness and good fortune to avoid sudden death, and the vision and determination to rescue the failing empire. Diocletian is often credited with undertakings that were begun before his time, and many of his innovations were carried to completion by his successor, Constantine. Nonetheless, he was the principal agent in shoring up the crumbling foundations of the empire.

In many ways Diocletian was a typical third-century man. Born in Illyria (modern Yugoslavia), the son of a freed slave, he enlisted in the ranks, worked

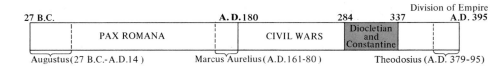

his way up, and was at last proclaimed emperor by his troops. Rivals contested his claim to the throne, but he subdued them all. Though he himself had gained power by illegitimate means, Diocletian set out to restore legitimacy to the empire. After a reign of some twenty years, he retired voluntarily to a palatial estate at Split, in his native Illyria (p. 109).

It is true that Augustus, at the very outset, had relied on his personal power in launching the empire. Yet he had also made effective use of the ancient republican institutions (especially the Senate) and the Italian citizen class. Moreover, he could count on the cities of the empire to carry much of the burden of local administration. But Diocletian found that most of these sources of support had been undermined by the calamities of the third century. And so he was obliged to utilize and strengthen the only means left to him: the army, the imperial bureaucracy, and his personal authority. Consequently, the "late empire" took on a centralized, regimented, and militarized character.

Diocletian's first major step was to overhaul the civil administration. The empire was now too big, he decided, for one man to administer; so he divided it in two. In theory, Diocletian was still monarch of the entire empire. But he moved his capital to Nicomedia, taking direct charge of the eastern portion, and in 286 he appointed a fellow general, Maximian, as joint ruler to govern the western portion from Milan. (Milan was closer than Rome to the threatened frontiers.) After 293 the two *augusti*, as they were called, were each assisted by a junior colleague (a *caesar*), who was assigned to rule a specified subportion (*prefecture*). Thus began the separation of East and West, which became complete and permanent in 395.

Diocletian reduced the size of the individual provinces (and increased their number) and placed them under closer supervision. The one hundred twenty provinces were grouped into twelve units called *dioceses*: the dioceses were in turn grouped into four prefectures, each ruled by one of the augusti or caesars. This arrangement of ascending ranks of authority (*hierarchy*) ensured stricter control from the top and reduced the possibility of provincial revolts, which had plagued the third century.

In his reform of the military establishment, Diocletian stripped the provincial governors of their former command of troops. Armed forces stationed in the provinces were decreased, and powerful mobile armies were concentrated near each of the imperial capitals. More and more of the soldiers were recruited from among the barbarians, and in time many of them rose to positions of high command. Since the barbarians still had little or no sense of collective identity, and those who were promoted generally identified themselves wholeheartedly with Rome, this did not damage the army's reliability. Thus, Diocletian succeeded in restoring authority and order within the empire and on the frontiers.

Diocletian was less effective in his economic measures. He ordered a new survey of the empire's population and wealth, revised taxes, and improved the coinage of money, but neither the ruler nor his advisers knew enough about economics to deal with the deeper problems. A tough old soldier, Diocletian knew how to face up to barbarian invaders. But what to do about unemployment, lack of capital investment, and rising prices? (Even today, the answers remain uncertain.) In a heroic attempt to check inflation, he issued an "edict of maximum prices," which froze the price level of all basic commodities. This, however, only worsened the difficulties of producers and traders. The death penality, which he decreed for violations, was rarely imposed, but the threat had a depressing and stagnating effect. Eventually, all efforts to enforce the edict collapsed, and prices continued to soar.

Thousands of those who were still trying to carry on business grew discouraged in the face of mounting difficulties and simply gave up. Some became roving bandits; others made their way to the large cities, already suffering from food and housing shortages. Alarmed by this trend, which threatened to reduce production still further, Diocletian took a desperate measure. He ordered that critical occupations be made *hereditary* and that all persons remain at their jobs. This sweeping decree destroyed the mobility of the labor force, weakened what was left of individual incentive, and made workers virtual slaves to their jobs. Strict enforcement proved impossible, though substantial efforts were made to put the order into effect. This measure did not solve the basic economic problems, but it did hold back the descent into complete economic collapse.

From the beginning of his reign, Diocletian realized that he had to strengthen the respect and obedience of all his subjects if he was to hold the empire together and win acceptance of his reform decrees. Following the trend of centuries, he transformed the imperial office into a *sacred monarchy*. The affected simplicity of Augustus was replaced by undisguised absolutism. The title of "princeps," preferred by Augustus, gave way to "dominus" (lord). The few persons admitted to the presence of the emperor no longer offered the republican salute (a raised, outstretched arm); they were required to lie flat on the floor before his sacred person.

At Nicomedia, Diocletian built a two-thousand-room palace of oriental splendor, set in a vast park. From the ancient Persian monarchs he copied regalia (kingly garments and emblems) dating back to the Great King, Darius (p. 43). On state occasions the emperor sat on an immense throne beneath a canopy of Persian blue and the glittering emblem of the sun. He wore a magnificent costume, gold fingernails, and a crown of pearls. Visitors, after being screened by the secret police, were brought to the throne room through a maze of chambers, doorways, and corridors. This arrangement served not only to protect the emperor from assassination but to overwhelm his visitors with a sense of mystery and majesty.

Diocletian's successor, Constantine, and the rulers who followed him recognized the effectiveness of these devices. The tradition of seclusion, secrecy, and elaborate display persisted in the Eastern empire until the fall of its capital in 1453 — and afterward in the principality of Moscow, the self-proclaimed "third Rome" (pp. 405–6). In the West, also, the oriental court-model was later studied by those who would wield absolute authority. Examples of its influence are the splendid court of the Renaissance papacy at Rome and the court of the French monarchy in the eighteenth century at Versailles (pp. 390–91).

Diocletian succeeded in reestablishing imperial authority. But, like his predecessors, he failed to solve the troublesome succession issue. He had planned an orderly procedure, with the junior rulers becoming augusti as the senior rulers retired or died. But, later, when one of the augusti died, a struggle broke out among various claimants to power. After years of dreary fighting, one of them — Constantine I — emerged as sole victor. By 324 he had disposed of all rivals, and for a brief period there was again one empire and one emperor.

Constantine carried forward most of Diocletian's reforms. His major departure was in the empire's policy toward Christians — a departure for which Christian historians have styled him "the Great." (The rise of the Christian Church is discussed in the next chapter.) Diocletian had persecuted the Christians, in the belief that they were undermining his efforts to save the empire. His suspicions are understandable, for the Christians met together in what appeared to be secret societies, they opposed military service, and they refused to recognize the emperor as divine (pp. 150–51). Diocletian persecuted them not because of their strange beliefs (he supported the idea of religious toleration), but because of their seeming *disloyalty to the state*.

Constantine, however, observed that persecution had failed to crush the determined and well-organized sect. Instead, martyrdom seemed only to nourish its growth. At last, in 313, Constantine gave his personal support to Christianity and ordered complete freedom of worship throughout the territories under his control (Edict of Milan).

Although he continued to tolerate other faiths after 313, the emperor showed his preference for Christianity. When he founded his new capital on the Bosporus (New Rome, later called Constantinople), he made it a Christian city from the start. His religious policy may be seen as a completion of the Pax Romana. A world of one law and one citizenship called logically, perhaps, for one *faith*. The pagan cults survived for another century or more, but most citizens followed the emperor's example.

Constantine exercised shrewd statesmanship in taking the Christian Church into partnership. To him, it was always a *junior* partner, however, for the emperor remained supreme. And the long line of Eastern emperors who succeeded him at Constantinople continued to place the Church under the imperial will.

If Constantine and his successors hoped that the binding power of a single faith would hold the empire together, they were to be disappointed. At about the same time that Christianity ceased to be despised and persecuted, it also lost its unity. In the fourth century, the Church was rent by bitter doctrinal disputes. In the West these were settled by the end of the century, but in the East, they lasted beyond the year 600 (p. 160). The Christian emperors had to spend a great deal of time trying to settle these disputes. When, as often happened, they failed to impose their views, they thereby lost authority and prestige. In this way, the acceptance of Christianity introduced a new source of discord into the empire.

In addition, the adoption of Christianity could not solve the empire's other problems: rivalries and warfare among emperors and would-be emperors, the economic decline of the West, and the rising threat of barbarian invasions. In 381 the Emperor Theodosius I ("the Great") made Christianity the sole legal religion. But he was the last to rule a united empire: before he died in 395, he made a permanent division. Theodosius split the empire along the lines established earlier by Diocletian, naming one of his sons emperor of the West (at Milan, and later Ravenna) and the other emperor of the East (at Constantinople).

Worst of all, Christianity did not alter the overriding fact that like most highly centralized, regulated, and militarized states, the empire of Diocletian and Constantine was squandering its most precious asset: the willingness of the citizens to bear the burden of keeping it going. Particularly in the West, high taxation and rising prices were as destructive and demoralizing in the long run as the most savage barbarian attacks. Already in the third century, the prosperous cities of the early empire had been reduced to heavily fortified outposts, whose citizens had lost all real self-government. With the triumph of Christianity, the cities began to find a new source of civic leadership in the persons of the bishops (pp. 153–54). But rather than bolstering the authority of the government, the bishops often had to act as substitutes for it. They occupied themselves with matters of social welfare to which the government paid no attention, and with protecting the citizens, in the name of Christian mercy, from excessive government demands.

Meanwhile the country dwellers, bankrupt by the endless demands of the tax-collectors, came under the domination of a tiny elite of landowners — those who were wealthy enough to carry the burden of taxes or influential enough to gain tax exemptions. The debt-ridden peasants sold out to these wealthy men and became sharecroppers or laborers — giving up part of their harvest, or doing farmwork in return for continuing to occupy their holdings. Though they were not human property like the slaves who worked alongside them (p. 101), the peasants became bound to their landlords by ties of personal obedience and subjection. The landowners usually dealt with the government on behalf of their peasants. They often shielded them from the tax-collectors as best they could, if only in order to exploit the peasants more effectively themselves.

In spite of their power and wealth, there were limits to the sacrifices that the landowners were willing to make for the emperors. Many emperors — and often the most shrewd and successful ones — kept the landowners out of the most important government positions. The high army commands went to barbarian generals, and the leading administrative positions to the ruler's trusted personal advisers. The landowners had to be content with local positions — especially that of *count*, an official in charge of a city and its surrounding territory — in the regions where they were influential. In addition, new positions of local leadership and responsibility were now open to them as bishops; and many members of wealthy families served the Church with the same self-sacrificing sense of duty that leading citizens had formerly brought to the service of the empire.

In this way, landowners and bishops came to form a kind of interlocking elite over much of the Western empire. They were strongly attached to the ideal of Rome, and far from disloyal to the emperors; but in practical politics, what counted most for them was not the empire as a whole, but their local power and local responsibilities. Increasingly, it was to this elite, not to the army, the bureaucracy, or the emperor, that ordinary citizens in the West looked for help and protection, and to whom they acknowledged a duty of loyalty and obedience.

Thus, in reaction against the overmighty state of Diocletian and Constantine, some of the features of later European society (of the Middle Ages) were already beginning to appear — notably the power of landowners over peasants and the institution of *serfdom* (pp. 221–22), and the deep involvement of the Church in matters of worldly government (pp. 217–18).

Germanic Invasions of the West

Thanks to the reforms of Diocletian and Constantine, the empire held off barbarian attacks for most of the fourth century. During this time, there was plenty of brutal and exhausting warfare between the Romans and their barbarian neighbors, but in many ways they were becoming increasingly alike. Leading Romans began to take up barbarian ways: even the emperors, when not dressed for court ceremonial, now wore the cloak, tunic, and pants of Germanic chieftains, instead of the traditional Roman toga. For their part, the Germanic chieftains, when chosen as such by their warriors, would be raised on the back of a shield to receive the warriors' acclamation — a custom that they had picked up from the Roman legions, who saluted a newly chosen emperor in this way. Many of the tribal confederacies living nearest to the empire even became Christian, though they usually adopted the unorthodox, Arian version of the new religion that Rome itself had rejected (pp. 139–40). The historical stage was being set for a "merger" between Rome and the barbarians. When it came, the merger was a vast and long drawn-out process, involving the entire western half of the empire and taking more than a century to accomplish. At some times, and in some regions, it took the form of bloody conquest; at other times and in other regions, it resembled a peaceful takeover.

The Germanic barbarians began to move in on the empire not because of any deliberate plan of conquest, but as a result of the appearance of yet another barbarian group, which threatened both Germans and Romans alike. In 370, a great horde of nomadic horsemen, the Huns, swept out of Asia and into Europe. Their movement was the outcome of warfare and shifts in power among the nomadic peoples (pp. 45–47) that had begun as far away as the frontiers of China; the effect on the peoples of Europe was devastating. For three-quarters of a century the Huns dominated much of central and eastern Europe. They subjected and destroyed some Germanic tribal confederacies in this region, and caused others to flee.

Among those who fled were the Visigoths, a tribal confederacy that lived on the lower Danube River, and which in 376 begged to be admitted to Roman territory. Their plea was granted, but the starving tribespeople were ruthlessly oppressed by corrupt Roman officials and provision merchants. Finally the Visigoths took up arms; at the battle of Adrianople their horsemen won a crushing victory over the imperial foot soldiers, killing the emperor Valens. His successor, Theodosius I, decided to make the best of the situation. First of all, he gave the Visigoths a substantial grant of land in the Eastern empire, and then he used them as allies against a rebellious army commander in the West.

After the death of Theodosius and the division of the empire in 395, the Visigothic leader Alaric began to exploit the weakness of Theodosius's successors to gain yet more land and power within the empire. He did so sometimes by playing off the Eastern against the Western emperor, sometimes by helping both against their foes, and sometimes by warfare or blackmail against them. Sensing the greater weakness of the West, Alaric finally concentrated his efforts there, and in 408 led the Visigoths into Italy.

Meanwhile, the West was being penetrated from another direction. In 406 and 407, taking advantage of the Western emperor's problems with the Visigoths, several other Germanic tribal confederacies crossed the frontier on the Rhine River. By 410, they had spread far and wide into Gaul and Spain. In that year, too, the Visigoths, angered by what Alaric saw as the Western emperor's unreasonable refusal to grant them land and Roman civil and military titles, captured and sacked the city of Rome itself. This was a disaster that, perhaps for the first time, made the empire's citizens seriously doubt its permanence.

During the fifth century, the story of these opening moves in the barbarian takeover was repeated, with variations, over and over again. The leaders of the tribal confederacies were not deliberately trying to destroy the empire, but rather to extract concessions from its rulers. Depending on circumstances, they would fight the Romans or each other, make deals with emperors or local Roman commanders, or even set up puppet emperors of their own to get whatever particular advantages they wanted. The last emperor in the West, Romulus Augustulus, was such a puppet emperor. His name, ironically, combined that of the legendary founder of the city of Rome with a diminutive version of the name of the founder of the empire. He was deposed in 476 when his Germanic master had no further use for him.

As for the Romans, they simply no longer felt their old sense of urgency to expel the barbarians. Instead, rival emperors or would-be emperors would often seek the help of the invading tribal confederacies in wars against each other. The Eastern emperors did not hesitate to rid their territories of barbarian armies by persuading them to move to the West. Even when the Romans defeated some barbarian group, the victors would not force the invaders to leave the empire, but rather settled them down within its frontiers.

Partly, the Romans were making the best of a deteriorating situation. The western portion of the empire, in particular, no longer had the resources with which to defend itself. But also, the Romans generally no longer felt strongly the need to defend the empire. The ordinary citizens were crushed by the tax burdens imposed by Diocletian and Constantine; the wealthy landowners, while clinging to Roman culture, thought more of their local power and position than of the empire as a whole; for the bishops, the Church, not the empire, was their main concern. To all these, the empire seemed hardly worth saving — particularly since the barbarian chieftains were found to be "men one could do business with."

In the whole period of the Germanic takeover, there was perhaps only one occasion when it seemed a matter of vital importance to repel barbarian invaders. In 451, at the battle of Châlons, Romans and Germans fought side by side to hold off an invasion of Gaul by the Huns under their famous and terrible ruler Attila. This victory marked the beginning of the end of the Hunnish menace that had given the original impetus to the Germanic takeover. Within two years, Attila was dead and his people began to retreat back into Asia and disperse. But if anything, the defeat of the Huns made the Germanic takeover itself more acceptable to the Romans.

By the early sixth century, the Western empire had been carved up into a number of territories, each dominated by one or other Germanic tribal confederacy. Africa belonged to the Vandals; the Ostrogoths now held Italy, while the Visigoths had moved on to occupy Spain; the Franks were supreme in most of Gaul; the Angles and Saxons had sailed across the North Sea to conquer Britain. Most of the Germanic rulers had won some kind of recognition and official titles from the emperors in Constantinople, and hence they were in theory the emperor's subordinates. In practice, however, they all acted independently, and they all bore the Germanic title of "king," signifying leadership in war and, among those tribes that were still pagan, the favor of the gods.

The Germanic kings assigned portions of the lands they occupied to their followers: leading warriors gained vast properties, while the mass of tribal fighters were given small freehold homesteads. In most of the regions they took over, the Germanic settlers were a small minority of the population, with their own status, customs, and laws, which at least to start with were different from those of the Romans among whom they lived. (Britain, where the Angles and Saxons assimilated or drove out the local population, was an exception.)

Yet the Romans were not treated as a mere conquered people. Roman government and institutions continued to function in the service of the Germanic kings. Roman culture survived: the conquering chieftains revered it, and even if they were illiterate themselves (which was not always the case), their sons and daughters became educated people of Latin culture. Roman landowners kept their inherited power and status, and although they had to give up a great deal of land for the benefit of the Germanic settlers, they remained exceedingly wealthy. Thus over the centuries, the Germanic invaders were absorbed into the mass of the Roman population; but their laws, customs, and traditions significantly influenced the emerging European society of the early Middle Ages (pp. 177–79).

In general, the new Germanic kingdoms failed to reverse the trend of impoverishment and decay that had begun in the later centuries of the empire. City life continued to fade, violence and destructive warfare remained constant hazards, and the power and influence of landowners and bishops continued to grow at the expense of government authority. Amid the decay, however, much of Roman culture and civilization remained intact, and new institutions were developing that would form the basis of European civilization for many centuries to come.

Of these institutions, the single most important was the Christian Church. Under Germanic rule, the Church not only survived but prospered. Still-pagan conquerors, notably the Franks, were baptized into the orthodox form of Christianity that prevailed in the Roman West. Those, such as the Visigoths, who were already unorthodox (Arian) Christians (p. 140), clung to their version of the faith for several generations, and this was the main source of conflict between them and their Roman subjects. But in this conflict, it was the rulers who yielded, conforming to the Roman version of the faith. Thus by A.D. 600, though the Roman Empire had fallen, the Christian Church was more or less united in its beliefs, and had emerged as the principal binding force among the diverse peoples and kingdoms of the West.

4

A Conquering New Faith: Christianity

The Church as an institution matured during the declining years of the Roman Empire, but the *origins* of Christianity were older than the empire itself. A product of centuries of human experience in the ancient Middle East, Christianity arose in Palestine — then spread throughout the Roman world of many different peoples. By the time of the Emperor Constantine (313) it had become a truly universal faith. And when the empire fell in the West (fifth century) the Church remained as a base for the revival and continuance of civilization.

SOURCES OF CHRISTIANITY

Christianity had first appeared as a sect among the Jews. The disciples of Jesus embraced him as the Christ, the Messiah (anointed one), for whom the tribes of Israel had been waiting for centuries. Indeed, for some years the pagan Romans made no distinction between Jews and Christians.

Judaism

In order to understand Christianity itself, one must be aware of its close relationship with Judaism (the historic religion and culture of the Jews). Though other faiths and philosophies influenced Christianity, its foundations were essentially Jewish. Jesus,* of course, was born a Jew, as were his twelve disciples. His very words, as found in his teachings, reflect the traditions of Jewish rabbis (religious leaders). The elements common to both Jews and Christians are so familiar that they are sometimes overlooked: the faith in one almighty God; the story of Creation; Adam and Eve and their disobedience; the Ten Commandments; ethical teachings stressing righteousness and love;

---

*"Jesus" is the Latin name for the Hebrew "Joshua."

			Assyrian Conquest	Roman Conquest
c. 2000 B.C.	c. 1300	c. 1000 c. 900	722	63 B.C.
HEBREW NOMADIC TRIBES	Hebrew Conquest of Palestine	United Kingdom	Division into Israel and Judah	Subjection by Successive Conquests

Abraham   Moses   Kings Saul, David, and Solomon

and the expectation of a savior, the Messiah. The Hebrew (Jewish)* holy books make up the Old Testament of the Christians and are accepted by them as the word of God. The chief *differences* between the faiths are these: Christians claim that Jesus *is* the Messiah, while Jews deny it; and Christians believe in eternal life after death, while Jews have no common belief about a hereafter. (The *ancient* Hebrews, generally, thought that deceased persons exist briefly in a dark underworld called Sheol.)

To uncover the beginnings of Judaism, one must go back about two thousand years before the birth of Christ, to the time traditionally associated with the patriarch Abraham, legendary "father" of the Jews. His people were a migratory Semitic tribe. Though their origins in Arabia and Mesopotamia are obscure (pp. 23, 26–27), we know that by 1200 B.C. some of them had settled in the hilly country west of the river Jordan known as Canaan (Palestine). The history of these determined and resilient people was marked by deep troubles. Caught between the power centers of Egypt and Mesopotamia, they refused to be assimilated and yet were too small in number to preserve their political independence.

A decisive event, according to tradition and Scripture, was the liberation of a community of Hebrews who had crossed into Egypt and fallen into servitude. Some time in the thirteenth century B.C. they were led across the Red Sea by the prophet Moses, who had been called to his liberation mission by the Hebrew deity, Yahweh (sometimes called Jehovah). On the slopes of Mount Sinai, south of Palestine, Moses then received the Law from on high and renewed Yahweh's earlier Covenant (agreement) with Abraham. In this Covenant, Yahweh promised the Hebrews protection and favor as his Chosen People in return for their pledge of exclusive allegiance and obedience.

Their subsequent history is one of temporary victory in the promised land of Palestine, followed by centuries of struggle to preserve their identity; recurrent persecutions; internal divisions; and a persisting sense of frustation as the Chosen People. When they despaired of overcoming their enemies through their own efforts, their inspired prophets preached that ultimate success yet would come through a divinely sent savior, the Messiah. This unyielding faith in their destiny in the face of setbacks and humiliations produced one of the most extraordinary chapters of history. Countless tribes and peoples in various parts of the world have emerged, been assimilated, and disappeared — the Trojans, the Assyrians, and the Visigoths, to name only a few. But the Jews have kept their special culture intact for some four thousand years. (This habit of

*For usage of the terms "Hebrews" and "Jews," see footnote, p. 27.

perseverance, passed on to the Christians, undoubtedly helped the Christians, in turn, to survive their own ordeal of persecution.)

What was the source of the Jews' extraordinary will? It is true that for a brief but splendid period around 1000 B.C. the Jews, under the reigns of David and Solomon, tasted military triumph and worldly power of their own. On Mount Zion, in the heart of Jerusalem, they raised a magnificent temple and palace. Thus, Zion became a symbol of both holiness and glory in Jewish hearts and minds. But other peoples have experienced grandeur and have then slipped into oblivion. What was it that gave the Jews their determination to persist?

There appears to be only one answer: their unique religious experience. At first, when they were still a nomadic people, they thought of Yahweh as a fierce and jealous god who would support them against hostile tribes and gods. When they moved into Palestine, the local deities of the region began to compete with Yahweh for their allegiance. Some of the Jews succumbed to this temptation, but most remained faithful to Yahweh. After the eighth century B.C., when Assyria and then Babylonia conquered and dispersed the Jews, many of the faithful concluded that the gods of foreigners — gods like the Assyrian Assur — were stronger than Yahweh. Once again, however, the more devout Jews refused to forsake their god. But they had to answer this question: If their god was all-powerful, and if they were his Chosen People, why had he abandoned them to their enemies?

For generations the prophets had been warning the Jews that they were straying from righteous living and were neglecting their loyalty to Yahweh, but many had failed to listen. The devout Jews now interpreted their troubles as confirmation of both the prophets and their god. This explanation found its boldest expression in the writings of the second half of the Book of Isaiah (written about 540 B.C.). The disaster that had fallen on the nation, Isaiah asserted, was not an occasion for despair but, instead, proof of divine power. The Jews had not been overcome by foreign gods; rather, they were being punished by the one and almighty God for violating his commandments. The Assyrians — in fact, all peoples and all nations — were simply his instruments. Once the Jews had turned their hearts back to God, had cleansed themselves of sin, and had returned to the path of virtue, they would be restored to power and granted victory over their enemies (Isaiah 45:8–25).

Thus, under the guidance of their prophets, the Jews were the first people to arrive at a clearly defined, exclusive belief in one God. Their *monotheism* proved to be a precious heritage, for it is a kind of faith that is especially strong in times of trouble. A polytheist, who believes in the existence of many gods, is likely to interpret disaster as a sign that his own gods are weak, indifferent, or unfriendly. But, for one who firmly believes that only one God exists and that he directs the universe according to his own good and secret purposes, *nothing* can happen, logically, that will contradict the believer's faith and take away its comforts.

There is one disturbing thought connected with this line of reasoning. If disaster strikes (as it had struck the Jews), and if the *deity* cannot be blamed, then the fault must lie with the people themselves. This conclusion gave the Jews a deepened consciousness of *sin* and its consequences — and a stronger feeling of individual moral responsibility, which was passed on to the Christians. The Jews were at the same time uplifted by a sense of historical mission. Surrounded by "unenlightened" Gentiles (nonbelievers), they saw themselves as unique witnesses to the *one* true God.

Hebrew literature provided a further source of strength. The best of it is included in the Holy Scriptures, which, unlike the literary works of most cultures, were read by all classes of Jews. The Hebrew Scriptures consist of three parts: the Torah (the story of the Creation and the Law), the prophetic books (Jewish history and ethics), and the Writings (proverbs, psalms, and moralistic narratives). Thus, in every Jewish home there was a source of poetic beauty and a revered document embodying the nation's history and purpose. The Scriptures have a message for all peoples, but to the Jews that message is especially personal.

Persian Religious Ideas and Practices

Other oriental religions also had some effect on Christianity, though their influence is less obvious than that of Judaism. In fact, some of the ideas from these religions seem to have come to Christianity by way of Jewish thought. During the sixth-century exile (the so-called Babylonian Captivity) following the conquests of Palestine by Assyria and Babylonia, many Jews lived in daily contact with Mesopotamian culture (pp. 40–41). When Cyrus the Persian conquered Babylonia in 538 B.C., he permitted those Jews who desired to do so to return to Palestine. He imposed his rule upon their country, however, as he did on the rest of the Middle East; thus, for the next two centuries (ca. 500–300 B.C.) Jews everywhere came under Persian influence. It was during this time that Persian religious ideas made their mark on Jewish thought.

The greatest figure in Persian religion is Zoroaster, who lived in the seventh century B.C. Zoroaster transformed the ancient beliefs and superstitions of his people into a noble and inspiring faith in one God, the author of good and evil. His followers turned this faith into a *dualism* that taught that the world was the scene of *two* rival forces: Ahura Mazda, god of goodness and light, and Angra Mainyu, demon of evil and darkness. At the end of time Ahura Mazda would triumph, Angra Mainyu would be made harmless, and all of humanity would be raised to enjoy eternal bliss. All this had been *revealed* and written down in the Avesta, the Persian holy books.

There is a striking similarity between Zoroastrian teachings and later Christian ideas about evil (personified in Satan) and eschatology ("things to come"). At the approach of the last days a Savior would appear, miraculously born, to prepare the way for the final Judgment. Moreover, Zoroastrianism was an ethical religion, which praised truthfulness, love, and the "Golden Rule" and condemned pride, lust, and avarice. Whether a person's soul went to heaven or hell upon death was determined by conduct during life. All people, however, would ultimately be saved by Mazda's goodness; unlike Christian damnation, the Persian hell was not forever.

With the sweep of Persian conquest in the sixth century B.C., the missionary religion of Zoroaster, much altered since his time, was carried to all the peoples of the Middle East (p. 44). For several centuries it worked its influence in those lands. Alexander the Great, after defeating the Persians in 330 B.C. (pp. 90–91) tried to undermine the religion by destroying copies of the Zoroastrian holy books. But he could not destroy the faith; and when Persia revived, during the period of the late Roman Empire, the religion of Zoroaster regained its position as the state religion of Persia.

Zoroastrianism, mingling with Greek and oriental polytheism, won followers throughout the Roman world. An especially popular offshoot was Mithraism, carried westward from Asia Minor after the first century B.C. by soldiers and merchants. It flourished in the empire, particularly among the Roman legions, until Constantine threw his support to Christianity in 313 (p. 134).

The divine Mithra was believed to be a lieutenant of Ahura Mazda, but he attracted worshipers in his own right. According to legend, he was born of a rock and was first attended by shepherds. (Long before Christ, December 25 was celebrated as the date of his birth.) Mithra was also associated with the sun, and his followers marked Sunday as his day of worship. They called it the "Lord's Day," for Mithra was known to them as Lord. Only men were admitted to this faith, and initiates had to undergo secret and terrifying rituals designed to instruct them and to test their will. Among the milder ceremonies were baptism in holy water and the partaking of a sacred meal of bread and wine. After passing through successive ordeals, converts were "born again" in Mithra. This experience charged them with new hope, for, though Mithra had ascended to heaven, he had promised to return and guide his loyal followers to their reward in paradise (a Persian word).

In the competition for souls during the troubled third century (p. 131), Christianity found a strong rival in Mithraism. The ancient gods of the Greeks and Romans had lost their attraction, but "mystery" (secret) religions like Mithraism had a powerful appeal in those trying times. People were casting about for a message of hope and consolation, for a promise of better things — if not in this life, then in the next. They were particularly responsive to the tales of *miracles* that clustered around such deities as the Persian Mithra, the Phrygian Cybele, and the Egyptian Isis and Osiris.

All these mystery religions grew out of ancient vegetation myths; all told of a god who had died and was resurrected, as the cold death of winter is followed by the warm life of spring. And all taught that the individual worshiper, through initiation and ritual, might win eternal life. These religions interacted with Christianity for several centuries and influenced its development.

Greek Philosophical Thought

Greek philosophy, too, had an effect on Christianity, especially as the new faith began to expand beyond Palestine into more thoroughly Hellenized lands. Plato's Academy, founded in the fourth century B.C., continued to train scholars far into the Christian era, and the impact of Plato's thought on Christianity was immense. Plato had been the first to elaborate the concept of an eternal "soul" distinct from the body (pp. 70–71). In his "Doctrine of Ideas" he spoke of an eternal spiritual order of perfection, presided over by the Idea of Goodness (God). He considered the human body a source of distraction and evil, a view that reinforced the *ascetic* strain in Christainity (pp. 165–66).

Stoicism also exerted a strong influence on Christianity. Belief in a cosmos ruled by providence, emphasis on universal love and on the virtues of justice, compassion, and restraint — all were central to its teachings (pp. 116–18). Stoicism was widespread among the educated classes of the Roman Empire, and its numerous parallels with Christianity helped to prepare the way for the new faith.

THE LIFE AND TEACHINGS OF JESUS

After we have sifted through all the historical influences, however, we must recognize Christianity as a religion with its own integrity and power. Jesus is not a vague mythological figure (like Mithra) but a person who lived and taught in Roman times. And it is his life, character, and message that stamp the Christian faith with its unique meaning.

What is known of Jesus' career is contained in the four New Testament "Gospels": Matthew, Mark, Luke, and John. Scholars are not certain as to the actual authorship and dates of composition of these books, but they were obviously written by true believers. In explaining the relationships of the Gospels to one another, scholars generally agree that Mark (and possibly another, undiscovered book) was used as a source by Matthew and Luke. John's account, which was written later (at the close of the first century), reflects a more developed theology, with emphasis on the divine nature of Jesus and his affirmations of immortality.

The "Nature" of Jesus

But there are gaps even in this composite biography. The Gospels focus on the birth of Jesus, the brief years of his ministry, and his death and reported resurrection; the disciples felt no need to set down all the details of his life, for to them the gospel (literally, "good news") required no "historical" proof. Faithful converts would later accept him as the Christ (Messiah), the true God in human form (incarnate). They would believe that his sacrifice on the Cross *atoned* for the sins of humanity and that his resurrection promised life eternal to all who loved and followed him. Thus, the Cross would become the dominant symbol of Christianity.

An objective scholar looking for the historical Jesus will not find an answer as simply and clearly as does the believer. To begin with, because the Gospels were written by close disciples of Jesus, the story is colored by their personal relationship to him. Moreover, though the Gospels agree in general outline, they differ in their accounts of Jesus' personality and identity. Did he, for example, represent himself as God (or the "Son of God")? Some Gospel passages (notably, Matt. 16:15–17 and John 17:1) appear to say this, but at least one passage indicates that Jesus did *not* identify himself with God: "Why do you call me good? No one is good but God alone" (Mark 10:18).* Perhaps, some scholars suggest, Jesus' claims to divinity were introduced into the Gospels only after converts had accepted him as divine.

The nature of the historical Jesus, then, is shrouded in doubt. Was he "Son of God," "son of man," inspired teacher, religious reformer, humanitarian idealist — or, as his Jewish critics insisted, a "false prophet"? A final answer, acceptable to *all*, cannot be drawn from the available sources.

The Sermon on the Mount

The ethical teachings of Jesus are most clearly summarized in the Sermon on the Mount (Matt. 5–7). In his account the disciple Matthew brought together the best-remembered sayings, stories, and moral advice of his master. What manner of life is most pleasing to God? What virtues does he value most highly? Jesus answered these questions directly and precisely, in the context of his own place and time. During the years of his ministry, he was challenged by various Jewish sects and tried to answer their teachings. He opposed, for example, the Pharisees, who stressed Jewish exclusiveness and strict observance of the rites, regulations, and holidays prescribed by the Jewish Law. And he criticized fellow Jews who had given over their lives to the pursuit of power and wealth. So he spoke not as an aloof divinity, but directly to the people with whom he came in contact.

Blessed are the meek, he declared, the merciful, the peacemakers, and the pure in heart. In other words, he was telling his listeners to turn away from the warrior ideal exemplified by Achilles, Alexander, and Caesar, since righteousness and love are more precious in God's sight than worldly success and honor. Moreover, Jesus assured his listeners that there was no conflict between his teaching and that of the Hebrew prophets of old, that he came not to destroy "but to fulfill." His moral demands, indeed, were based on the traditional ethics of Judaism, but he carried them beyond ordinary human reach. Obeying the Law and the Commandments was not enough. In the new testament that Jesus taught, one must love not only the Lord but one's *enemies*; one must refrain not only from adultery but from lustful *thoughts*; one must not only give up the search for material goods but *give away* all possessions; one must not merely resist evil but "turn the other cheek."

---

*Quotations from Scriptures in this text are from the Revised Standard Version.

This code of conduct makes extreme demands on the human spirit. Did Jesus actually expect men and women to live up to it? To this question, too, there is no clear-cut answer. A few Christians have taken his instructions literally, straining to measure up to Jesus' "unnatural" standards; this may be accomplished, they believe, by a "transformation" of the whole person. Others have discounted the code as idealistic, beyond the grasp of most people in the real world. The view generally taken by the Church is that Jesus' teachings form an ideal toward which all should strive but which none can attain. Therefore, all will fall short — yet all may be saved by repentance (sorrowful regret) and God's mercy.

When Jesus himself was seized on charges of posing as king of the Jews, his very disciples failed him. Judas betrayed him, Peter denied him, the others abandoned him in terror and despair. Thus, even the devoted twelve fell short of their master's expectations. But the faithful did not founder on the rock of Calvary. According to the Gospels, the crucified Christ rose from the tomb and showed himself several times to his disciples before ascending to heaven. His reappearance renewed the faith of his followers and gave them the will to obey his last instruction as recorded in the Scriptures: "Go ye into all the world, and preach the gospel to the whole creation" (Mark 16:15).

THE EARLY CHURCH AND ITS EXPANSION

The Acts of the Apostles, which tells the story of the early Church, reveals that the disciples were at first dismayed by Jesus' command to set forth as missionaries. How could they, a handful of despised and humiliated men, succeed in such a task? They were simple and uneducated Jews, with little knowledge of foreign lands or languages. So they waited patiently, mindful of Jesus' promise: "But you shall receive power when the Holy Spirit has come upon you" (Acts 1:8).

Missionary Beginnings: Pentecost

According to Scripture, the missionary work started at Pentecost (fifty days after the Resurrection). The book of Acts relates that the Holy Spirit descended upon the disciples like "the rush of a mighty wind" (2:2). The Spirit gave them the gifts of wisdom, languages, and healing, thus distinguishing them from other men and preparing them for their task. But the mission was not easy. Three thousand, the Scriptures say, were baptized in the faith of Pentecost. These first converts, however, were all Jews, and soon the apostles were faced with a thorny question: Could they share food with Gentiles (nonbelievers), contrary to Jewish law, and baptize them directly in Christ? Or must Gentiles first become Jews (subject to circumcision, dietary rules, and special rituals)? Peter, the first disciple of Jesus, leaned toward the latter view. But a vision taught him his error, and he began to baptize Gentiles as well as Jews. The issue was finally settled by a council of apostles and elders at

Jerusalem in A.D. 44, which decided that Gentile converts were not to be bound by the Jewish Law.

Peter continued to hold that those who had been born to the Law should hold to it, but the trend was steadily away from the observance of the Law by Christians. Easter, for example, displaced the Jewish Passover, which commemorates the deliverance of the ancient Hebrews from Egyptian bondage. This event was the high point of Jewish history as told in the Torah; but in the Christian view it was eclipsed by the Resurrection, which promised salvation to *all*. Thus, Easter became the climactic day of the Christian year. Similarly, the Jewish Sabbath (seventh day) gave way to Sunday as a day of rest and worship, for it was on the "first day of the week" that Christ arose from the dead.

The Apostle Paul

Paul, the "apostle to the Gentiles," led the way in making clear the differences between Christianity and Judaism. He declared that the Gospel had superseded the Law — even for Jews. No one can be saved by the Law, Paul taught; the Law can only bring people to an understanding of their dependence upon Christ. A Christian of passionate conviction (though he had never met Jesus), Paul undertook the religious conquest of the non-Jewish world.

Of all the apostles, Paul was perhaps the best qualified for this mission. He was not one of the original twelve, not even a native of Palestine, but a Jew born in the city of Tarsus, in Asia Minor. He claimed Roman citizenship and apparently came from a well-to-do, educated family. Trained in both Hebrew and Greek, he was familiar with the religions and philosophies of the Hellenistic world, and, as a member of the orthodox sect of Pharisees, he shared the prophetic hope that the God of the Jews would one day be accepted by all humankind. Yet he knew at first hand how reluctant the Gentiles were to accept the burden of the Jewish Law.

While studying at Jerusalem, Paul witnessed the first Christian martyrdom. Stephen, one of the early converts, was preaching against dependence on the Law, and he condemned the Jews who stubbornly refused to accept Christ. The crowd charged Stephen and stoned him to death. Paul, then full of zeal for the Law, approved the killing and looked for other Christians to bring before the Jewish court. While engaged in this undertaking, on the road to Damascus, in Syria, Paul was suddenly converted. The book of Acts tells us that he was blinded by a great light and heard the voice of Jesus asking why Paul persecuted him. After three days Paul's eyesight was restored, and God announced that he had become a "chosen vessel" to bear the name of Christ to the Gentiles.

The Epistles of Paul, in the New Testament, reflect the enthusiasm and skill he brought to his missionary task. He had become convinced that Christ represented the fulfillment of historical Judaism — but a Judaism made pure and universal. With the barrier of the Law taken away, and with the "good news" of the Cross, the true religion could now be carried to the Gentile world.

Though Paul was not one of Jesus' companions and, indeed, at first appeared as an enemy, he is ranked by the Church as a leading apostle, second only to Peter. This recognition speaks eloquently of his accomplishments. An enthusiastic and able organizer, he made hard journeys by land and sea and founded numerous congregations in Asia Minor and Greece. His task was made easier by the existence of the Pax Romana and the imperial roads and by the fact that the Greek language was universally spoken in the eastern parts of the empire. Still, these means would have been worthless had it not been for his fearless devotion to the cause of Christ.

In the course of his missionary work, Paul became of necessity an interpreter of the new faith, for Jesus had left few stated doctrines. When Paul carried the gospel to the curious Greeks, he was met by all kinds of questions — many of which are recorded in his Epistles, or Letters. He answered the questions humbly, explaining that he spoke only as the Lord gave him power.

The First Epistle to the Corinthians illustrates the manner in which Paul developed his interpretations. The congregation at Corinth had asked him numerous questions: Is virginity more seemly to God than marriage? Are women by nature subordinate to men? In what *kind* of body will believers be raised from the dead? In his patient answers to these and countless other questions, Paul set forth doctrines that would carry down through the centuries. Among them was his support for the tradition of male supremacy in both worldly and spiritual matters, and his acceptance of the practice of slavery: "Wives, be subject to your husbands, as to the Lord. . . . Slaves, be obedient to those who are your earthly masters. . . ." (Ephesians 5:22; 6:5). According to his teachings, however, the gospel *transcends* all worldly relationships; *all* individuals are *equal* in the eyes of Christ.

Paul was convinced that, in order to move Christianity from being a sect among Jews to being a *universal* faith, Jewish observances and rites would have to be discarded. In winning souls for Christ, he was admittedly "all things to all men" (1 Cor. 9:19–23). He demanded no particular style of life, no legalistic rules of conduct. It was enough that individuals simply have faith in Christ as their Savior.

Paul thus laid the foundation for the belief that salvation depends exclusively on *faith*, rather than following the Law or doing "good works." This belief was to raise a problem for Christian ethics and discipline, because one may well ask, "Why, then, bother to obey the rules and teachings of the Church?" Paul's answer would be that good works will flow naturally from faith, but it is *faith*, not works, that saves one. The Church, traditionally, has been fearful of the consequences of this interpretation when carried to the extreme, and theologians have had serious difficulties in explaining the relationship between faith and works.

Paul's position led him unavoidably to another problem: How do individuals *receive* faith? Do they earn it through their own efforts, or is it a gift freely granted by God, for his own secret reasons? Paul believed that faith was a gift of God, a conviction that was confirmed by his own experience. Why had Paul, a stony-hearted enemy of Christ, been chosen by the Lord to see the light of conversion? The only answer, Paul felt, lay in God's secret will. As Paul expressed it in his Epistle to the Romans, "So then he has mercy upon whomever he wills, and he hardens the heart of whomever he wills" (9:18). This view, variously referred to as the doctrine of "predestination" or of "election," was to become a source of controversy within the Church. Augustine (in the fifth century) and Calvin (in the sixteenth) (pp. 163, 365) are among those who have pursued Paul's line of thought most vigorously, but the idea that some human souls are excluded from all hope of salvation has proven unacceptable to many Christians.

Paul did not labor alone in his efforts to bring Christianity to the Gentiles. Tradition holds that Peter reached Rome and founded the congregation there. Other missionaries were busy in Egypt, Syria, and Asia Minor. The leading apostolic churches (those founded by apostles) were at Jerusalem, Alexandria, Damascus, Antioch, and Rome. By the end of the first century there were more than fifty Christian congregations, and during the next hundred years the gospel was carried to every province of the Roman Empire.

Persecution of the Christians

But the early Church was met everywhere by popular and official hostility. It is often difficult for modern Christians to understand why the followers of Jesus, with their teachings of love and peace, should have been persecuted. Yet for some three hundred years, beginning with the crucifixion of Jesus himself, the faithful were distrusted by Jews and Gentiles alike. Stephen was stoned to death by the Jews; Paul was beheaded by the Romans; and most of the original twelve apostles (and countless Christians who followed them) met violent deaths.

The long roll of martyrs was partly the product of rumors and misunderstandings regarding the new religion. Since the Christians spoke out against established institutions — such as the Jewish Law and the Roman practice of emperor-worship — they were widely thought to be contemptuous of the whole existing order. They often refused to associate with pagans, and they condemned such popular amusements as those of the public baths and combat arenas. The respected Roman historian Tacitus concluded that they felt "hatred for the human race."

Many of the accusations made against the Christians — such as cannibalism and incest — sprang from prejudice and ignorance. Other charges, however, arose from the actual nature of the Church. Christianity was truly a *revolutionary* movement that aimed to turn Roman life upside down. Understandably, people of conservative leanings considered the missionaries "subversive" — unpatriotic, fanatical, and atheistic (toward the pagan gods). Moreover, the Christians often took on an air of spiritual superiority and exclusiveness. It is little wonder that the resentment of other citizens sometimes flared into violence.

The attitude of the Roman government was somewhat different. Ordinarily, Roman officials refrained from interference in local affairs and practiced religious toleration throughout the empire. The imperial government outlawed Christianity as early as the first century, however, on the grounds that it was a secret group dangerous to the state. But enforcement of the ban was lax and irregular; persecution usually occurred only when the populace became aroused against the Christians, or when the emperor needed a scapegoat to divert attention from his other problems.

The government continued to look upon Christians with disapproval, however. They refused to burn incense before the emperor's statue, would not serve in the army, and seemed lacking in public spirit. Worse, they often caused trouble by criticizing rival faiths and seeking to convert all nations. Consequently, the more conscientious rulers concluded that the Christians, by their efforts to subvert established institutions, had forfeited their right to toleration. Accordingly, these rulers sought to compel Christians to renounce their faith — or at least to pledge allegiance to the emperor. When the faithful refused to take the required "loyalty oath," they were sentenced to death.

Practices of the Early Congregations

Persecution did not check the spread of the gospel. There was a yearning, especially among the common people, for the "good news" the Christians brought. Most of the early converts were of the poorer classes — men and women who had found a home in Christ. They were predominantly city-dwellers; the conservative peasants (*pagani*) held stubbornly to the ancient beliefs. Moreover, some of the converts, looking forward to the expected Second Coming of Christ, sold what little they possessed and gave the money to their congregation. This urge toward *community property* began to fade during the second century, however, when it appeared that the Savior's return would not be as speedy as was first thought.

Because the Christians found the doors of Jewish synagogues closed to them, and since the government forbade them to build temples of their own, they usually met in private homes or halls. There, accepting one another as brothers and sisters, they prayed, sang psalms, and took part in simple rituals. Though the ceremonies were not at first uniform, two were performed by every congregation. One was baptism, the purifying rite of Christian initiation; the other was the partaking of bread and wine, in keeping with the Gospel story of Jesus' last supper with his disciples (Mark 14:17–25). This second ritual came to be known in the Greek service as the Eucharist and in the Latin service as the Mass. (In Protestant services it is commonly called Holy Communion or the Lord's Supper.)

THE GROWTH OF CHRISTIAN ORGANIZATION AND DOCTRINE

From such beginnings, the Church had developed an elaborate system and structure by the time of the Emperor Constantine (fourth century). The Mass remained the central ceremony, but a host of companion rites and practices grew up. The developing liturgy — that is, the forms of worship — reflected the influence of Judaic tradition and of the Greek and oriental mystery religions. Incense, bells, and ritual garments came into use, along with holy water, oil, candles, and prayer beads. And gradually the religious calendar, with its cycle of fasts and feast days, was worked out. From birth to death the Church provided the faithful with guidance through a ceaseless round of services and observances. In short, the *idea* of Christianity took solid form as an *institution*.

The Rise of the Priesthood and the Emergence of Bishops

It would have been impossible to accomplish all this without strong leadership and organization. In the beginning, little formal structure was necessary; but as the gospel spread throughout the Roman world a need arose for supervision and direction. Moreover, *unity* among the scattered congregations served as a defense against persecution. The first step toward formal organization was the emergence of a body of church officers set apart from the ordinary members of the congregation. So long as the congregations were small and the Second Coming was still believed to be near at hand, all the members probably shared in the management of local affairs. But as the congregations grew larger, and as ritual became more complex, it was natural to develop a specialization of talents and responsibilities. Those who were assigned special functions came to be known as the "clergy"; the rest of the congregation was called the "laity."

Differences in degrees of authority were also recognized. Though the early groups viewed all their members as equal in authority, they gave special status to the original twelve apostles. The twelve were reported to have been filled with the Holy Spirit at Pentecost, thereby gaining special powers of wisdom and healing. These powers, it was believed, could be passed on to others by the solemn act of the "laying on of hands." According to the Book of Acts, Matthias had been chosen to take the apostolic place of the betrayer Judas (1:26), and Paul had received the power of the Spirit at the hands of the disciple Ananias (9:17).

The theory of *ordination* (admission to the Christian ministry) that grew out of these traditions justified the special role and authority of the priesthood. The priests, through the "laying on of hands," were believed to have received the power to perform the miraculous rites of the Church. This theory strengthened the clergy's authority over the laity and ensured, at the same time, that unauthorized persons would not be able to assume roles of leadership.

At first the priests and lesser officials were elected (or approved) by their congregations; but as time passed the clergy grew more and more independent of the laity. They sensed a need for closer association among themselves and for superior levels of authority. They believed that by these means they could better hold the scattered congregations together against external attacks and internal divisions. And so there grew up over the years a system of rising ranks and jurisdictions — the *hierarchy* (sacred rule) of the Church.

Before the end of the second century, each city in which there was a Christian congregation had a chief priest who was recognized as its overseer, or bishop. He was selected by the priests of his community, aided by the laity, and he held his position for life. Responsibility and authority in local affairs went increasingly to the bishop. He was ordained to the office by other bishops, and the theory gradually developed that the bishops together constituted the *successors* of the original apostles. (The church of each bishop, by tradition, was believed to have been founded by an apostle or by the companion of an apostle.) The bishops alone possessed the power to ordain others. They taught that priests, deacons, and lesser clerics received, through the bishops, a *portion* of apostolic authority, but that only the bishops possessed it in full. This explanation of the authority of bishops came to be known as the doctrine of "apostolic succession."

Because control of the Christian communities in the second and third centuries rested largely in the hands of the bishops (*episkopoi*), the system is referred to as the *episcopal* form of church government. This form still holds in the Roman Catholic Church, the Greek Orthodox Church, and the Anglican (Episcopal) churches. It was not seriously challenged until the time of the Reformation, when most Protestant leaders (like John Calvin) adopted the *presbyterian* system. This system puts control in the hands of assemblies of ministers and elders (presbyteries) elected by the congregation (p. 369).

A third-century bishop was a busy man. He oversaw the preaching of the gospel, the performance of religious rites, the care of the sick and poor, the management of church property, and the improvement of Christian morals. He spoke for the faithful in dealings with civil authorities and represented them at larger religious gatherings. His area of jurisdiction, known as a *diocese*, normally included the city in which his church was located and the surrounding district. The diocese was divided into *parishes*, each with its local congregation and priest (pastor). Because both clergy and laity were required to obey the bishop, he held full control over the Christian community.

In coordinating their religious activities, the bishops turned to the model of Roman imperial administration. As Diocletian grouped several provinces into a civil diocese, the bishops (reversing the terms) grouped several dioceses into a *province*. Over this larger jurisdiction reigned the bishop of the chief city in the province. Since a great city was known as a "metropolis," this bishop took on the higher title of "metropolitan" (later, archbishop).

By the time of Constantine there were five leading metropolitans: the bishops of Jerusalem, Alexandria, Antioch, Constantinople, and Rome. Their importance led to their being designated as "patriarchs," a title and rank above that of the other metropolitans. Thus, from the parish priest upward there were four distinct levels in the Christian hierarchy, just as there were in the hierarchy of the late empire (p. 132). Both church and state achieved, at about the same time, closely supervised and authoritarian systems of control.

Roman Supremacy: The Pope

The final step in the organization of the Church was the establishment of a "monarchy" (control by *one* person). The theory of apostolic succession ensured a framework of legitimate authority, which could settle differences and enforce discipline at the local level; the bishops exercised control within their dioceses by assuming the right to *excommunicate* — that is, to exclude individuals from church fellowship and services. But when issues arose that divided the bishops themselves, serious troubles ensued.

A question had come up, for instance, around the year 150, regarding the correct day for celebrating Easter. The Gospels were contradictory on this point; the churches of the East observed one day, the churches of the West another. It seemed odd, if not unholy, for one group of Christians to be feasting while another was fasting. Later in the second century, Victor, Bishop of Rome, decided to settle the question by excommunicating the Eastern churches, on the grounds that the authority of the Roman bishop was superior to that of all others. In any event, the Eastern churches accepted Victor's date for Easter, and the excommunication was lifted.

Thus, unity of practice was achieved through the acceptance of a higher *authority*. And many church leaders felt that the only way to solve the countless other issues, of a more serious nature, that divided the Church was to recognize a final authority at the top of the hierarchy. Each of the five patriarchs believed that the top position rightly belonged to him. Alexandria, Jerusalem, Antioch, and Constantinople offered impressive arguments, but Rome seemed to have the strongest claim. The Roman bishop had several decisive advantages: the Eternal City still enjoyed great prestige among the communities of the empire; Rome was the scene of the missionary work and martyrdom of the two leading apostles, Peter and Paul; and, according to tradition, the Roman diocese had been founded by Christ's *first* disciple, Peter.

Roman bishops made the most of this Petrine tradition. They interpreted a passage in the Gospel of Matthew (16:18–19) to mean that Christ had founded his Church upon Peter and had entrusted to him alone the "keys of the kingdom of heaven." This, they insisted, made Peter supreme among the apostles. And, since each bishop of Rome was the direct successor to Peter, the bishop of Rome was clearly supreme among the bishops of the world.

The rival patriarchs rejected Rome's assertion of supremacy, pointing out that such a sweeping claim could hardly be justified by a brief passage appearing in only one of the Gospels. They argued, further, that during the early days of the Church all important decisions were made by a council in Jerusalem, a council in which Peter had participated but had not ruled. Paul had made no references to Peter as the supreme head, and Peter had made no such claim for himself.

Nevertheless, the position and dignity of Rome and its association with both Peter and Paul won for it a place of *primacy* in the Christian world. The patriarchs of the East conceded that the successors to Peter had a right to sit at the "head of the table," so to speak, as *first* among *equals*; but ultimate power, they contended, resided only in *general councils* of bishops, such as the Council of Nicaea (p. 159). The Roman bishop, however, was not satisfied with this; he continued to insist on his *supremacy*, on being recognized as *absolute monarch*, the "Vicar (Deputy) of Christ" on earth.

In the West, where there was no rival, Rome achieved that supremacy. By the fifth century the Roman bishop had begun to reserve to himself the title of *papa* (pope). This word, meaning "father," had formerly been used to refer to any bishop or priest, but henceforth it was used only for the bishop of Rome, in the broader sense of "Father of the Church." And from this usage arose the term "papacy" to refer to the office of the pope.

Following the Muslim conquest of Alexandria, Antioch, and Jerusalem in the seventh century (p. 191), the pope and the patriarch of Constantinople were left as the two most powerful bishops, heading the *Latin* and *Greek* churches respectively. In spite of many rivalries and disagreements, Rome and Constantinople for several centuries thereafter accepted each other as fellow members of a single all-embracing Christian Church. From the eleventh century onward, however, the popes and their western European supporters grew strong enough to try to impose their views on Constantinople by force. They failed, but the attempt led to permanent bitterness and division. In 1054, papal representatives in Constantinople formally excommunicated the patriarch, whereupon the document of excommunication was solemnly burnt by the Greeks, and the patriarch excommunicated the pope's representatives in their turn. In 1204, crusaders from the West captured Constantinople and appointed a new patriarch loyal to the pope, whom most of the Greek Church refused to recognize (p. 270). From that time on, a state of *schism* (formal separation, with each side considering itself the only true Christian Church) came about. Though the

excommunications of 1054 were lifted by both sides in 1965, the schism between the Latin (or Roman Catholic) and the Greek (or Orthodox) churches
still persists today.

The Canon of Scriptures

The administrative authority given to the Church hierarchy was paralleled
by the development of Biblical authority. At last, in the fourth century, the
canon (that is, the authorized list) of Scriptures was established. Previously a
great many "holy" books and epistles had been in circulation, but the bishops
agreed that if the unity of the Church was to be preserved these writings would
have to be screened for certification. How were they to decide which had been
inspired by God and which had not? Some of the bishops objected to accepting
the Hebrew Scriptures, but these writings were so well established by tradition
that it was finally decided to accept them. The Greek translation of the
Hebrew writings (the Septuagint) was taken as the canon for what Christians
now call the Old Testament.

For other writings (the New Testament) there was no such guide in tradition, so the bishops resorted to *authority*. They decided that only writings by
apostles or their companions, clearly inspired by the Holy Spirit, would be
admitted. Although this rule at once eliminated many disputed books of uncertain origin, it did not work automatically. For example, when a certain
gospel attributed to Peter was found to favor a doctrine offensive to the
bishops, they simply declared that Peter could not have been its author. On the
other hand, books and epistles that struck the bishops as "right" in doctrine
were readily attributed to an apostle — and thereby included in the canon.

This practice may seem to violate modern rules of critical scholarship, but
it was in keeping with ancient tradition. The Jews had made Moses the author
of all the sacred books on law, David the author of the psalms, and Solomon
the author of the books of wisdom. And so, in the final analysis, it was the
judgment of the bishops that determined whether a particular writing was
admitted into the canon.

The bishops did not reach final agreement on the canon until near the end
of the fourth century, when the pope proclaimed that Jerome's Latin translation (p. 168) was the standard text for the Church. In the West, where Latin
was the *common* language, Jerome's version became known as the Vulgate
(*vulgatus*, meaning common). It remains to this day the "authentic" Bible for
Roman Catholics — though Church scholars have continued to examine other
documents for elucidation of its meaning.

Doctrinal Differences: Orthodoxy and Heresy

Even with its priestly hierarchy and canon of Scriptures, the Church was
frequently split by serious disputes over doctrine. These ranged over a broad
area: the liturgy, sacred rites, rules of Christian conduct, and the complex field

of Christian theology — that is, explanations of God, the Creation, sin, and salvation. For centuries, the existence of conflicting positions disturbed the leaders of the Church. If there is to be one Church, there must be one doctrine; if truth is single and absolute, then differing views must be *false*. Committed to these assumptions, the Church Fathers could not rest while heresy stirred.

"Heresy" may be defined as any belief that deviates (departs) from the "true," or "orthodox," doctrine as taught on the authority of the Church. All deviations disturbed the Church, some more deeply than others. One of the earliest, most persistent, and most radical of the heresies was Gnosticism (from the Greek *gnosis*, or knowledge). The Gnostics were a religious-philosophical group with origins distinct from those of Christianity. Many of them, however, found their way into the Church, where they formed factions and held to secret teachings that made use of certain Christian ideas. Had their influence proceeded unchecked, they might have revolutionized Christian doctrine.

Gnostic thought was a curious blend of Greek and Middle Eastern thought. It revolved around a *dualistic* conception of the universe, similar to that which runs through Platonic thought (pp. 70–71). According to the Gnostic view, the universe is divided between spirit and matter. Spirit is the only true good; matter came into existence as a kind of casting off from spirit when the physical world, including human bodies, was created. The body (as Socrates had taught) imprisons the soul and is the source of evil; the true aim of life is to gain knowledge by which the soul may liberate itself and join with the *universal spirit*. But, said the Gnostics, this knowledge cannot be attained through reason; it comes only as *mystical* insight, which the initiate achieves after passing through secret rites. Similar notions had appeared in Persian thought, particularly in the dualism that followed Zoroaster's teaching (p. 143).

Gnostics who had become Christians interpreted Christ as the Savior who would emancipate humankind from the prison of the flesh (sin). Moreover, because Christ is all-good, he could not have had a body; hence, the Incarnation, Jesus' life as a man, and his human suffering were only *appearances*. They could not have occurred, logically, for goodness consists of pure spirit.

This view clearly ran counter to basic Christian doctrines, and it alarmed the Church leaders. During the second and third centuries, the bishops struck hard at such unauthorized teachings. When the Gnostics declared that their wisdom had come to them through "chosen" persons, the bishops replied that no one but the apostles and their successors could speak for the Church. The ordained bishops stood firm, and at last the Gnostics were suppressed as heretics. In varying forms, however, the central idea of this heresy continued to plague the Church. It cropped up in the fourth century as Manicheism, and again in the thirteenth as the Albigensian heresy (pp. 239–40).

The persistence of such deviations arises from the fact that the orthodox Christian position itself rests on a delicate balance between spirit and matter, soul and body. This position holds that both exist and that both are essentially good, for both are the handiwork of a perfect God. Yet there is a clear tendency in the Scriptures, in the preachings of Jesus and Paul, to place spirit *above* matter, although *how far* above is not made clear. Given this lead, some Christians have tended to praise the soul as the true home of God and to put down the body as the "devil's workshop." Those who follow this line to the extreme show contempt for *all* worldly things, including food and drink, sexual activity, and care of the body. A practical outlet for this impulse, within the limits of Church control, is *monasticism* (pp. 164–71).

No sooner had the Gnostic threat been suppressed than a heresy of a different sort erupted: the Donatist heresy, named after Donatus, Bishop of Carthage (in Africa). This heresy threatened the organization and functioning of the Church, rather than its basic doctrines. It gave rise to a particularly bitter feud, partly because North Africans still held traces of the resentment Rome had generated by its destruction of Carthage centuries before (p. 100). Consequently, many Africans supported Donatus out of "local" loyalty. (Not infrequently in history, movements of this sort have sprung from a *combination* of religious and political protests.)

The religious issue was simple: Are the rites and ordinations performed by a priest valid if the priest is a sinner or not in good standing in the Church? During the persecutions under Diocletian, some African bishops had given up their holy books at the demand of the Roman authorities, thereby saving their own lives. Their surrender was regarded as an act of treason to the Church, and, although the bishop of Rome reinstated the offenders after they had shown due repentance, many members of the African Church refused to accept them. Worse, Donatus and his followers insisted that all the rites performed by the bishops after their sinful acts were *invalid*. Thrown into question were ordinations of priests (p. 153), marriages, baptisms — all the sacred rites of the Church. Here was a challenge that could not be ignored.

In 313 a council of bishops at Arles (in southern France) considered the question and decided against the Donatists. They declared that priests who had surrendered to persecution might be restored and that their ritual acts were in no way affected by personal guilt or nonguilt: "Once a priest, always a priest." The power given through ordination was indelible and could not be erased. This reasoning is logical, and, for practical reasons, it appears to be the only position the Church could have taken. If the council had ruled that a priest must be a state of goodness (grace) in order to discharge his duties, the validity of any ceremony he performed would be open to question. The decision at Arles sealed the powers given by ordination and set at rest the doubts of the faithful. The Donatists, however, stubbornly refused to accept the ruling, and the heresy smoldered until the seventh century, when the Islamic tide rolled over North Africa (p. 191).

The Council of Nicaea and the Trinitarian Creed

The doctrinal dispute that came nearest to splitting the Church was over the "nature" of Jesus and his relationship to God. We have already seen that the

Gnostics believed Jesus to be pure spirit and denied his human nature. In direct opposition to that view was the idea that Jesus was *only* a man, although a man of superior moral stature, who had been adopted by God for his divine purposes. Between these extremes were countless other points of view, most of which *subordinated* the Son in some manner to the Father. All the variety and subtlety of Hebrew and Greek tradition were brought into play in this crucial theological debate. For how could Christians worship as one body unless they agreed on the nature of the godhead?

The argument was still raging three centuries after the birth of Christ. By the early fourth century, however, opinions had been reduced to two main views. One was set forth notably by Athanasius, Bishop of Alexandria, and the other by Arius, a learned priest of the same city. Athanasius held that Father and Son were two equal persons but *one substance*. Arius insisted that, because Christ had been "begotten," there must have been a time when he did not exist. Because he was not co-eternal with the Father, he could not be co-equal.

When the Emperor Constantine learned of this religious division, he was deeply distressed. After accepting Christianity in 313, he had given the Church legal status (p. 134), fully expecting that it would serve as a unifying force in the empire. But now he found it, instead, a source of discord. Most of the East leaned to Arius; the West supported Athanasius. How could Constantine heal the spirit and restore Christian unity?

He knew that the dissension could not be bridged by means of reason, for logical arguments were being spun out endlessly by both sides. Realizing that, as in matters of discipline, the final resort would have to be to *authority*, he summoned the leaders of the Church to a meeting at Nicaea (in Asia Minor) in 325. This was the first general (worldwide) council of the Church, and more than three hundred bishops attended. On the question put before them, the majority sided with Athanasius. A formal *creed* (statement of belief), expressing his view, was drawn up in a carefully worded document that excluded all forms of "subordinationism." The statement also stressed the nature of Christ as *both* man and God, thus striking at Gnostic teachings.

This Creed of Nicaea, as amended at the Council of Constantinople (381), remains the orthodox view. It declares that the Son is of one being, or essence, with the Father. It rejects the view that there was a time "when he was not" or that he is of "another substance or essence." The creed also includes the Holy Spirit, thus completing the concept of the godhead as a Trinity: one *substance* in three equal but distinct *persons*.

The Council of Nicaea did not immediately succeed, however, in restoring unity on the issue of the Trinity. When Arius and several other priests at Nicaea refused to sign the creed, Constantine banished them. The power of the state, formerly employed against Christians, was henceforth used to support orthodoxy against heresy. Ten years later, an Eastern council at Tyre (in modern Lebanon) reversed the decisions of Nicaea and exiled Athanasius instead of Arius. Constantine's successors held differing opinions on the issue, and for some forty years the banishing or recalling of bishops turned on the whims of

Pentecost c. A.D. 33		Constantine 313	Theodosius 381
Christian Missionary Work and Persecution of Christians in Roman Empire		Legal Toleration	Official State Religion

the emperors. Athanasius was banished six times in all. Finally, a new emperor, Theodosius I, reunited the empire and summoned a second general council. This meeting, held at Constantinople in 381, reaffirmed the Nicaean decision and put an end to the exhausting debate.

The divisions within the Church, nevertheless, persisted stubbornly. Rejected within the Roman Empire, Arian missionaries took their faith outside its frontiers, to the Germanic barbarians who eventually took over the empire's western provinces (pp. 136–39). It was only toward the year 600 that most of the barbarian conquerors finally converted to the beliefs of their Roman subjects, and that Christians throughout the West finally achieved unity of faith.

In the East, on the other hand, that unity was never attained. In the fifth century, new differences arose over the *exact relationship* in Christ of the divine to the human, which pitted the bishop of Constantinople (supported, in this case, by Rome) against Alexandria, Antioch, and Jerusalem. After changing sides several times, the Eastern emperors finally backed the view of Rome and Constantinople, which has remained Christian orthodoxy ever since. By force and persecution, the emperors tried to convert the "heretics" of Egypt and the Middle East to what was now the orthodox view. In doing so, the emperors aroused such fury and hatred among their subjects that in the seventh century, when the Muslims conquered the region (p. 191), they were welcomed by most of the people as liberators. To this day, the issue of the exact nature of Christ divides most of the remaining Christian populations of Egypt and the Middle East from all other Christians, whether Roman Catholic, Greek Orthodox, or Protestant. At the time these disputes took place, they were an important factor in swinging the balance of power within organized Christianity from the divided East to the united West.

THE WORLDLY VICTORY OF THE CHURCH

The early leaders of the Church guided Christianity through the critical period of the first three centuries and made possible its ultimate triumph. Had it not been for their devotion to unity, all the efforts to establish doctrine and organization might well have led to nothing. From each persecution and heresy the Church emerged stronger and wiser than before.

The Conquest of the State

The rise of Christianity was aided by the shortcomings of rival faiths and the trouble that fell upon the empire. In fact, the Church made its great leap forward during the third century, when Roman rule was suffering from an endless struggle over the succession to imperial power (pp. 130–31). The new emperors raised up by the troops were usually too busy looking out for their own safety to be much concerned about the Christians. At the same time, many Romans of the middle and upper classes had grown weary of civil strife and had begun to look with sympathy and respect upon the outlawed faith. Membership in the Church, once restricted to the poorer people, now cut across society. The number of converts mounted swiftly; by the time of Constantine, probably ten percent of the population was pledged to the Cross.

The last persecutions, which took place at the beginning of the fourth century, were failures. Many martyrs earned their reward, but public opinion had shifted from contempt to compassion for the Christians. It was clear that the Church could not be broken. At last, when Constantine came to power and was won over, people began to accept the fact that the Cross had conquered the crown and had actually enlisted it as an ally against the pagan rear guard. In 381 Theodosius I legalized the victory by making Christianity the religion of the state and forbidding pagan rites. Now the tables were turned. Mobs began attacking pagan temples, smashing idols and attacking worshipers. By the end of the fourth century, pagans (and Christian heretics) were being sentenced to death. The Church, which had once protested to emperors for their intolerance of Christianity, now joined with the state to stamp out rival faiths.

An exception was the Jewish faith. Since the time of Theodosius, Christians have pursued an uneven and ambivalent policy toward the Jews. On the one hand, they have tolerated Jews as the bearers of the religious tradition that provided the historic foundation for Christianity; on the other hand, they have often chastised Jews for rejecting Christ. During Roman times most Jews migrated from their home in Palestine to various parts of the empire. (This movement was a continuation of the historic Jewish dispersion, or Diaspora, that resulted from successive occupations, repressions, and ejections by foreign conquerors.) The exiles usually congregated in large cities, where they established themselves in commercial enterprises.

Theodosius and succeeding emperors took the view that the Jews could be considered neither pagans nor heretics in the Christian sense; they were seen as a special group whose national and religious character made them incapable of assimilation into Gentile society. Theodosius ordered that their religious practices be tolerated and that they be protected against attacks by Christian mobs. Soon afterward, however, steps were taken to limit the contacts and influence of Jews. They were forbidden to seek converts or to build new temples; intermarriage between Jews and Christians were severely punished; and Jews were excluded from government service.

The worldly triumph of the Church was due to a combination of forces. In a time when old beliefs had grown stale, Christianity emerged as an appealing faith. It put trust in one God of justice and mercy, taught compassion and love, and promised life everlasting in a better world. Though this religion was unique, it contained elements that had been made familiar by Judaism, the mystery religions, and Greek philosophy. Hence, the ideas of Christianity were easier to explain and to accept than if they had been totally strange. Its ritual satisfied the emotions; its theology challenged the intellect.

The teaching and practice of charity — especially, caring for the sick — also advanced the acceptance of Christianity. Christians were the only group in the ancient world to provide anything resembling public hospitals. This service became especially important after 200 A.D., when the empire was ravaged by epidemics (p. 131). In a time of widespread death the Church offered comfort to the sick of this world while promising eternal life after death to all who embraced Christ. Speaking of a particularly devastating plague, the bishop of Carthage explained in 251: "This mortality is a disaster to the Jews and pagans and enemies of Christ; to the servants of God it is a happy departure. . . . The just are called to refreshment; the unjust are carried off to punishment. . . ."

The Church, finally, benefited from the limitations and weaknesses of its competitors. Most of them were local or ethnic in outlook, while Christianity, a *missionary* faith, aimed at *universality*. The pagan religions lacked organization and enthusiasm; the Christians were well disciplined, aggressive, and uncompromising. Their stubborn faith in ultimate victory strengthened them through the dark and bloody years of their persecution.

Augustine: The Philosopher of Christian Victory

Augustine, one of the Fathers of the Church, symbolizes the Christian triumph. His own life, with its pagan beginnings and ultimate acceptance of Christ, parallels the larger struggle within the empire. Born of a Christian mother and a pagan father, Augustine was attracted at one time or another by the leading philosophies of his day, and he watched the steady progress of Christianity until at last it became the established religion under Theodosius. About 387 Augustine was himself converted and rose swiftly to a position of importance in the Church. A man of extraordinary intellectual power, he influenced succeeding generations even more than his own, for his ideas have helped shape the theology, morals, politics, and philosophy of the Western world. A prolific writer, he set down his major thoughts in his *Confessions* and *The City of God*.

Augustine grew up in a small town in North Africa. He was sent for schooling to cosmopolitan Carthage, a Roman city built on the ancient Phoenician (Punic) site. There he plunged into the study of classical literature and the arts of logic and argumentation, which were to serve him later as an advocate of Christian doctrine. During those same years he indulged his taste for pleasure and went deeply into pagan thought. When at last he felt the pull of Christianity, he discovered that he could not make his way to God by himself; the *Confessions* tells the story of his inner struggle.

Augustine's youthful association with Manicheism (a dualistic philosophy of Persian origin) gave him a lifelong bias toward dualism (p. 157), which influenced his interpretations of his personal history and of world history. He saw the struggle within himself between *two sides* of his character: his love of worldly things versus his love of the Lord. Ultimately, by God's grace, the higher love won out, and the tortured young man was baptized a Christian. Thanking the Lord for this gift, Augustine confessed, "For so completely did thou convert me to Thyself that I desired neither wife nor any hope of this world, but set my feet on the rule of faith." He became a priest and, later, bishop of Hippo, in North Africa (p. 109).

From his personal experiences Augustine concluded that bodily appetites (as well as false philosophies) distract people from the contemplation of God. He denounced as sinful, therefore, even the simplest of physical pleasures, and he thought that all individuals bear an enormous burden of sin. Their only hope for salvation is to pray for God's help in bringing them to repentance and self-denial. Augustine himself gave up family and possessions and lived like a monk. The power of his intellect, will, and example thus came down on the side of Christian asceticism (pp. 165–66).

His own experience also led him to embrace Paul's doctrine of "predestination"—that the Lord chooses those who are to be saved (p. 150). The original sin of Adam, wrote Augustine, condemned all men to eternal punishment—but "the undeserved grace of God saved *some* therefrom." Thus, Paul was chosen from among the Pharisees and Augustine from the Manicheans to become servants of God. Neither felt he had earned grace through his own behavior, and so both gave full credit to the Lord's *mercy*.

Augustine expanded this idea of the "elect" and the "nonelect" into a comprehensive, and profoundly simple, philosophy of world history. Following his inclination to view matters in a dualistic way, he declared that all of humanity—the dead, the living, and the unborn—is divided into *two* communities. The first is moved by love of self, the second by love of God. These conflicting loves, he argued, are more important than the superficial attachments to race, nation, and class. He called one community the "Earthly City" and the other the "Heavenly City" (the City of God). Though the members of these two communities are intermixed in the present world, they have separate *fates*. The first will suffer everlasting punishment with the devil, and the second will live eternally with God. History, Augustine wrote, is a drama planned by the Lord and centered upon a continuing struggle between the two "cities."

It was in this light that he explained the sacking of Rome by the barbarian Visigoths in 410 (p. 137). That calamity, occurring only a generation after Theodosius had made Christianity the state religion, shocked and disheartened many Christians, and surviving pagans whispered that it was a punishment sent by their gods. Augustine indignantly denied their claim and began to write his monumental book, *The City of God*, which put the fall of Rome into a larger perspective. With immense labor he listed the earlier reverses and disasters of Rome, thus "proving" that the city's troubles were not the result of its having embraced Christianity. If Rome was being punished again, it was because of its ancient crimes: paganism, conquests, enslavements, and the persecution of Christians.

Augustine assured the faithful that the sack of Rome was, in truth, a spectacular confirmation of basic Christian teachings: it demonstrated that even the most powerful of earthly cities must sooner or later crumble and fall. The only *true* Eternal City is the City of God, and the whole earthly show of history is a passing thing. To some, Augustine's interpretation implied that they should simply stand by and let events take their course ("God's will be done!"). But he reminded them that the empire, whatever its past sins, was now a *Christian* state and a protector of order; he therefore urged all its citizens to resist the barbarians who were bringing plunder and anarchy.

But, some critics objected, are not fighting and killing contrary to the commandments of God? Augustine, interpreting Scripture, answered that God's law against killing applies only to *personal* behavior. A war declared by officials of the state can be morally "right," and in a "just war" killing is permissible. Augustine's idea of the "just war" carried with it an inescapable implication: if one side is just, then its enemy must be unjust. He thus laid the foundation for Christian approval of wars and the "good"-versus-"evil" idea about disputes between nations.

Along with his explanation of history, the bishop of Hippo offered this view of the future beyond history: while sinners endure unending torment, the "elect" (the saints) will enjoy the perpetual presence of the Lord. Augustine's picture of heaven was based on his reading of the Scriptures, but it also reflected his personal feelings about human nature. He believed that the citizens of heaven are furnished (as Paul had written) with "incorruptible" bodies. These are not unruly, as mortal bodies are, but behave according to the commands of the will. As a special gift, God also rewards the saints (in heaven) with the *inability to sin*. Thus, they come to know true freedom — the freedom enjoyed by God himself, who cannot sin. Augustine's concept of the hereafter and his philosophy of history guided Christian thinking for centuries to follow. More immediately, his example and teachings lent support to an emerging institution of the Church — monasticism.

EARLY CHRISTIAN MONASTICISM

The way of life followed by a monk or a nun often strikes the modern mind as odd and *unnatural*. Yet monasticism has been a recognized way of life in Western culture for centuries, answering the needs of a sizable minority of people. Today there are some two hundred religious orders in the Roman Catholic Church alone, with a membership of nearly a million and a half men and women.

The words "monasticism" and "monk" derive from the Greek *monachos*, meaning "one alone." The basic motivation of the monastic is to escape from society, to pray and contemplate in solitude, and so to come nearer the desired spiritual goal. The urge is older and broader than Christianity; there were "holy" hermits in ancient Egypt and Greece and ascetic communities in Palestine. The Dead Sea Scrolls (unearthed in 1947) describe the rules of discipline in the Qumran community near Jerusalem before the time of Christ. In other parts of the world—especially the Far East—the monkish life has attracted millions of individuals over the centuries.

The Ascetic Ideal

There is no simple explanation for the appeal of monastic life. The walls of a monastery (or convent) have always offered a haven to those who wish, for whatever reason, to remove themselves from the world. They may be prompted by disgust, fear, failure, or the urge to repent. Sometimes a severe personal tragedy will induce an individual to retreat to a monastery, and others are attracted by the security it affords. None of these reasons, however, was central to the rise of Christian monasticism. Its primary motive was the desire to lead a "purer" life, as understood through faith. This desire, in turn, sprang from two forces: love for God and fear of damnation.

The holy life, in the Christian view, is not easily attained. It requires, above all, self-discipline—strict control over the natural self and its appetites. The very term "ascetic" is derived from the Greek word for the *exercise* practiced by a trained athlete. Just as the discus-thrower must discipline his muscles, so the "perfect" Christian must gain control over his or her entire body and mind. Only then will that individual be free from sinful thoughts and acts—free to follow Christ's commands and, perhaps, to know the ecstasy of heavenly visions.

No mortal can expect to match Jesus in purity of life, but some have experienced a keen urge to perfection. Not content to abide by the minimum requirements of Church and Scripture, they have preferred a harder road—to suffer, even as Christ suffered. They have adopted a more rigorous code than they could observe in worldly surroundings and have voluntarily withdrawn from human contacts in order to gain, in solitude, mastery over the flesh.

Why have some Christians thought of perfection in such "unnatural" terms? In most cases, they have taken their lead from the example of Christ. Jesus was no monk, but his teachings had a decidedly ascetic quality. As we have seen, his ethical teachings called for a degree of selflessness that few humans have been able to achieve: "If you would be perfect, go, sell what you possess and give to the poor, and you will have treasure in heaven; and come, follow me" (Matt. 19:21). Added to this original emphasis was the influence of Paul. He distinguished two standards of Christian conduct, the permissible and the heroic, and set the second above the first. While conceding, for instance, that it is "better to marry than to be aflame with passion" (1 Cor. 7:9), he ranked virginity above the married state. "It is well," Paul advised, "for a man not to touch a woman" (7:1). Finally, the impact of Gnostic views, which identified the body with evil (p. 157), reinforced the ascetic tendency in Christianity.

The Hermit Monks: Anthony

In the early days of Christianity, a man who aspired to the ascetic ideal simply abandoned civilization. In Egypt, where Christian monasticism was exceedingly popular during the third century, this was an easy matter, for the empty desert was close at hand. There, exposed to the burning heat and sand, the hermit could punish his body and strengthen his will. One of the most celebrated hermit monks was Anthony, whose biography by Bishop Athanasius was widely read throughout the empire. The son of an aristocratic family of Alexandria, Anthony became a devout Christian (about 270). After selling all his possessions, he headed for the desert and spent the rest of his life subjecting his body to increasingly severe discipline. So famous did he become that thousands sought him out, hoping for cures and advice from this "holy man." To preserve his privacy, he was forced to move deeper and deeper into the desert.

Anthony's hardest struggle was with sexual desire. His biographer reported that the devil would appear to him at night in the "form and deportment of a woman." But Anthony stubbornly resisted, and at last he cried out so fiercely that the devil "fled in terror." Other monks, too, were bedeviled by the sexual urge, which, more than any other, symbolized to them the disturbing appetites of the body. Monastic chronicles are full of anecdotes about the monks' torments of desire and their efforts to dispel them. One way was to keep from looking at a woman. But, as Anthony discovered, this did not shield the mind from provocative fantasies. A surer way was to keep the body weak, bruised, and exhausted — a solution that also enabled the monk to display his contempt for the flesh.

Anthony was a model Christian hermit, fasting constantly and wearing a prickly hair shirt beneath his leather outer garment. He never washed his body and was at pains to keep even his feet out of water. His solitary life of prayer and contemplation was frequently rewarded, we are told, by divine visions. This way of life must have agreed with Anthony, or else he was of very hardy stock: at the age of one hundred, writes Athanasius, the hermit fell ill and died in his desert cell.

Stirred by the example of Anthony and other world-renouncing hermits, a multitude of Christians throughout Egypt and the East began to abandon the cities and take up a solitary life. Though most were sincere, there were many faddists among them. The behavior of a few was quite alarming. We are told of men grazing in the fields like animals, rolling naked in thorn bushes, and living in snake-infested swamps. One of the most famous of all the hermits was Simeon Stylites of Syria, who built a sixty-foot pillar, climbed to the top, and squatted there for thirty years until he died.

The Church could hardly ignore such excesses, even though they were not typical. The bishops (as well as some in the monastic movement) decided that it was unwholesome for men to live in solitude and that the ascetic impulse, though good in itself, must be tamed. Solitary life should be combined with community living. And so in time the first monasteries, for men only, were founded. Here each monk had a private cell for devotions, but during certain hours of the day he joined his fellow monks for common meals and labor.

Regulated Communities: Basil, Jerome

The earliest religious "houses" were organized in the fourth century. One of these was founded by Pachomius, a desert hermit, who built a crude compound on an island in the Nile River. A former soldier, Pachomius laid the place out like an army camp and imposed a strict schedule and discipline on his Christian "recruits." The regulations came to be known as the "Rule" of Pachomius and were later adopted and modified by Basil, a bishop of Asia Minor. The Basilian Rule became the basis of monasticism in the East and has remained so to the present day.

The ascetic impulse spread westward across the Mediterranean world, spurred by the changing relationship between Christianity and the empire. Constantine's recognition of Christianity was followed by Theodosius' decision to make Christianity the empire's official religion. By making it safe to practice the faith, these measures brought into it large numbers of converts who lacked the sincerity and conviction of the earlier Christians. In other words, as the Church advanced into the world it became more worldly. Even the clergy began to fall to corruption and ambition as the doors to wealth and power opened before them.

Christians who wished to imitate Christ and the holy martyrs were upset and repelled by the growing worldliness of the Church; after the fourth century, many of them chose monasticism as a substitute for martyrdom and as a refuge from the distractions of worldly affairs. The Latin Fathers gave warm support to this ascetic trend. Augustine established a monastic community in North Africa and practiced rigid self-discipline himself. The scholarly Jerome, who lived in the same period, gave up a comfortable life in Rome to become a hermit.

The earlier hermits had shown contempt for all books other than the Scriptures. Anthony, for instance, was an uneducated man who believed that all a devout Christian needed was a sound mind and the inspiration of the Spirit. His attitude was in keeping with the teachings of Jesus, which might be characterized as anti-intellectual. And Paul, like Jesus, had put faith and love above reason and learning. Jerome, however, could not bear to leave his library at home, and so he carried it with him to the Holy Land. But his passion for the classics at last filled him with anxiety, and he decided that he must be either a "Ciceronian" or a Christian. He determined therefore to give up his attachment to pagan literature. Yet as soon as he stopped studying he was tormented by visions of Roman dancing girls. Like Anthony, he tried to beat down his lustful thoughts by starving and mortifying his body. Nothing helped until he hit upon the idea of learning Hebrew. Because Hebrew was the language of the Scriptures, he believed that this study would be pleasing to the Lord. Furthermore, it required such mental concentration that his tantalizing visions began to fade.

Eventually Jerome was able to look at women without desire. When he was called to Rome on Church business (382), he took the opportunity to spread the gospel of asceticism among the noble ladies of the city and persuaded many of them to turn their lives to Christian purity. "Marriage fills the earth," he counseled: "virginity fills heaven." On his return to Palestine, he founded, in partnership with a rich widow named Paula, several monastic communities in Bethlehem — some for men and some for women.

Jerome's most famous literary work, completed about 400, was a translation of the Bible into Latin from the Hebrew and Greek sources. Jerome decided to set the monks and nuns to work on scholarly projects also. His success in turning the energy of monasticism to productive literary enterprise established an important precedent. During the Middle Ages monasteries helped safeguard the cultural heritage of the West by preserving and copying manuscripts and by providing elementary schooling for the clergy.

Benedict and His Rule

The most influential founder of European monasticism was Benedict of Nursia. The son of a noble Italian family, he began early in life to follow Anthony's example. Sickened by the vice he saw in Rome, he fled to the nearby hills and imposed on himself a rule of physical self-punishment and spiritual dedication. So famous did the austere hermit become that he attracted other young men who wished to share his way of life. Convinced at last that asceticism was better practiced in groups, he left his solitary cave and established several small communities for his disciples.

The monastery at Monte Cassino (*Fig. 4-1*), which Benedict founded about 529, served as the center of his work. It has been rebuilt many times (most recently, after the Second World War), and it still stands on a towering hill overlooking the town of Cassino, between Rome and Naples. There Benedict drew up a set of regulations to govern the lives of his monks. This Benedictine Rule reflected the ideals of love, humanity, and piety that inspired the life of its

4-1 The monastery at Monte Cassino (before the Second World War).

author. It struck a balance between solitary meditation and group activities. The Rule proved so successful that it became the model constitution for all other religious orders in the West, and within a few centuries nearly forty thousand monasteries and nunneries were governed by it. Since then, many millions of lives have been subject to its daily regulation.

Any free man or woman was eligible to commit his or her life to the Rule. After spending a probationary (testing) year to ensure that they were equal to its rigors, they took three perpetual vows: chastity, poverty, and obedience. In addition they pledged "stability," which meant that they had to remain on the monastery grounds unless given permission to leave. The monk or nun thus surrendered sexual gratification, private property, and personal freedom for the chance of living a life more pleasing to God and of gaining salvation through discipline.

Benedict felt that control by *one* person made for the greatest serenity and harmony within the monastic community. Consequently, he granted authority over the monks to a "superior" known as an abbot. The abbot was chosen by the monks to serve for life, and Benedict advised the utmost care in his selection. He also gave the abbot advice on how to govern. The abbot, said Benedict, ought "rather to be of help than to command"; he should "exalt mercy over judgment . . . and strive rather to be loved than feared." He should always be aware of his own imperfection and should keep himself from becoming troubled and anxious; if he grows jealous or suspicious, he will have no rest. He should use moderation in assigning labor to his monks: "He shall so temper all things that there may be both what the strong desire, and the weak do not shrink from" (*Rule*, LXIV).

On all matters of importance, Benedict urged, the abbot should consult the assembled brothers and weigh their advice seriously: "Do all things with counsel, and you shall not thereafter repent" (*Rule*, III). At the same time, he warned the abbot against shutting his eyes to the vices of the monks. In dealing with a rebellious monk, the abbot should first correct him and, next, exclude him from association with his brothers. If these steps, supported by prayer, did not cause the offender to obey, the abbot was authorized to use the lash and, as a last resort, expel him from the monastery: "Remove evil from you, lest one diseased sheep contaminate the whole flock" (*Rule*, XXVIII).

Though Benedict left the abbot some measure of discretion, he set down in detail the standard monastic routine. The most important activity of all was the saying of Divine Office (obligatory daily prayers); seven times a day the toll of bells called the monks to their knees. During meals they were to observe the rule of silence while one of them read aloud from the Scriptures. Certain hours of the day they were to spend alone in their private cells reading and meditating. To Benedict, the monastery was a "school for the service of the Lord."

Since each monastery depended on its own resources, the monks had to spend much of their time growing and preparing food and providing for their other material needs. From four to eight hours a day were set aside for manual labor, which, Benedict thought, would provide a wholesome balance to their intellectual and spiritual activities. The monks cleared new land for cultivation; aided the sick, orphans, and widows; learned the arts of agriculture; and preserved ancient handicrafts in their workshops. Their services to Western civilization during the Middle Ages were immense, for they also served as missionaries, preserved and copied ancient writings, and carried on scholarly tasks after the example of Jerome.

Yet direct service to God remained the primary aim of the Benedictine houses and of the religious orders that arose later. The monastics devoted their lives to prayer and charity, providing a model for Christians outside the cloister. To some degree their example moderated the brutality and coarseness of a turbulent time. They also exercised a corrective influence on the more worldly priests and bishops of the Church. During the fifth and sixth centuries, when the moral level of the clergy outside the monasteries declined sharply, the superior conduct of the monks led to their being recognized as a distinct branch of the Church. Because they lived under a special rule (*regula*), they came to be called the "regular" clergy. Clerics who were free to move about in the world (*saeculum*) came to be known as the "secular" clergy.

By the sixth century the very existence of the Church depended heavily upon the regular branch. Acting as the conscience of the secular clergy, its members began to regard themselves, in moments of suspended humility, as a spiritual elite. Some of the most vigorous and devoted leaders of the Church came up through the Rule — men like Gregory the Great, who became bishop of Rome in 590 and was a molder of the medieval papacy. After the collapse of imperial power, the survival of Western civilization itself rested largely on the three organized forces within Christianity: the papacy, the secular clergy, and the monastic orders. Ironically, it fell to the Church, whose primary mission was to open the way to the *next* world, to safeguard the civilization of *this* world.

5-1 Chartres Cathedral, France, façade.

PART TWO

MEDIEVAL CIVILIZATION

	POLITICAL, SOCIAL, AND ECONOMIC DEVELOPMENTS	RELIGION, SCIENCE, AND PHILOSOPHY	HISTORY AND LITERATURE	ART AND ARCHITECTURE
500	Kingdom of the Franks established by Clovis Justinian's temporary reconquest of the western Mediterranean **Bubonic plague** Slavs spread through eastern Europe (550–900)	Benedict and his monastic rule		Hagia Sophia
600	Islamic conquest of Middle East and Mediterranean world Rise of Carolingian Dynasty	Muhammad and the Koran The Hegira		
700	Charles Martel and repulse of the Muslims in France	Donation of Pepin ("States of the Church")		
800	Charlemagne crowned "Roman Emperor" by Pope Leo III Division of Islamic conquests **Breakup of Charlemagne's empire** Invasions of western Europe by Vikings (Norsemen), Muslims, and Hungarians			Palace at Aachen
900	Emergence of feudal and manorial systems Partial recovery of central authority in France and Germany	Monastic reform movements: Cluny		

	Art & Architecture	Literature	Religion & Philosophy	Social & Political
1000	Romanesque style of architecture	Growth of vernacular literature	Ecclesiastical reform: Hildebrand (Gregory VII) College of Cardinals created Cistercian order	Revival of trade Norman conquest of England Rise of towns and guilds
1100	St. Trophîme Cathedral (Arles) Gothic style	Chivalric romances: Chrétien de Troyes Goliardic poetry	Widespread persecution of Jews Rise of universities Impact of Muslim scholars: Averroës	The crusades (1096–1204)
1200	Chartres Cathedral	*Song of Roland* Omar Khayyám (Persia)	Final separation of Greek and Latin churches Papacy at height of power: Innocent III Franciscans and Dominicans (friars) Grosseteste Thomas Aquinas Scholastic philosophy dominant Papal Inquisition Roger Bacon	Magna Carta Mongol invasions of eastern Europe Emergence of capitalism Growth of banking Origins of Parliament
1300		Dante Chaucer Christine de Pisan	Decline of papal power: Boniface VIII	

CHAPTER

5

The Creation of Europe: Political and Social Foundations

The passing of Greece and Rome brings us to a new phase of Western history. Geographically, the focus shifts from the lands surrounding the Mediterranean Sea to western and central Europe — that favored region jutting into the Atlantic from the Eurasian land mass. The main territories of this region straddled the former frontier of the Roman Empire, including both civilized and formerly barbarian lands. Gaul, Britain, Italy, and Germany formed the core of what was to become a distinctly European civilization.

In the seventh century, the surviving eastern half of the Roman Empire split into two parts: Byzantium and Islam. Byzantium (heir to the Eastern Roman Empire) included Greece, much of southeastern Europe, and Asia Minor, while the tide of Islam rolled across the rest of the Middle East and the southern rim of the Mediterranean, then north through Spain to the Pyrenees Mountains. Thus, the "one world" of the Pax Romana was broken into three separate areas (p. 180).

Later in this chapter we will look briefly at Byzantium and Islam, for both of these areas were still connected with the West and contributed much to its development. But our attention will center on western and central Europe, for it was here that Western civilization was reconstructed, to emerge one thousand years later as a *worldwide* force. The budding European culture was not just a duplication of the old Greco-Roman culture, though many of the same ingredients were present. Rather, it emerged as a *new* compound of classical, Christian, and Germanic elements.

The Church was the principal agency of the rebuilding of the West, and it set the tone of European civilization for many centuries. The ascetic, "other-worldly" view of Christianity displaced the more down-to-earth attitude of the ancient Greeks and Romans. This shift, which had set in during the twilight of the empire, became irreversible once Constantine accepted the Cross in 313 (p. 134), and the ascetic ideal persisted in Europe for a thousand years.

For most of the same thousand years, the worldly affairs of Europe were dominated by an elite whose power came principally from the fact that they were owners of *land* and leaders of *warriors*. This elite originated partly among the wealthy landowners of the later Roman Empire, and partly among the warrior aristocracies of barbarian peoples (pp. 47, 131, 135, 138–39, 178, 188). Political and military power were shared among the members of this elite. Its most prominent leaders, the kings of the various European states, could not govern effectively without the cooperation of the rest of the elite, who came to be known as the *nobles*.

If one considers the "modern" period of Western history — with its worldwide expansion of European civilization, materialistic emphasis, and gradual loss of power by kings and nobles — to have begun about 1500, then the period between it and the ancient world is fittingly called the *Middle Ages*, or the *medieval* world. (Both terms apply only to the unfolding of Western civilization and are meaningful only in relation to the history of Europe.)

EUROPE IN THE EARLY MIDDLE AGES

After the fall of the Roman Empire in the West, conditions of life remained at a low ebb there for several centuries. The social and economic trends that had begun under the empire — the decline in population, the loss of vitality of the cities, and the growth of great landed estates — continued under barbarian rule. The *urban* civilization of Rome gave way to a *rural* culture, and this culture was kept in a chronic state of turmoil by a number of disturbing influences. The most important of these were the wars of the Eastern emperor Justinian together with disastrous epidemic diseases in the sixth century (p. 184); the rise of Islam and the accompanying warfare with the Arabs from the seventh century onward (pp. 189–91); and destructive invasions, at frequent intervals down to the tenth century, by new barbarian groups (pp. 186–89, 207–8). Education, literature, and the arts retreated to the monasteries (pp. 170–71); in the world outside, even the greatest rulers were illiterate. Hence the period from 500 to 1000 in western Europe is often called the "Dark Ages."

Yet the groundwork of civilization survived. The Muslims were held off, barbarians were either repulsed or absorbed, and by 1000 A.D., civilization had actually spread northward and eastward to occupy most of the territory of present-day Europe. Under the stress of turmoil and invasion, new social institutions grew up (pp. 214–23), which matured into a more or less effective system of government; eventually, economic prosperity and urban life revived as well (pp. 223–29). On these foundations the West achieved stability and moved into a brilliant era of creativity.

The Germanic Barbarians

We have already discussed the Roman and Christian ingredients of medieval civilization (Chapters 3 and 4). Now let us look at the new element — the

Germanic. The Germanic barbarians, together with their eastern counterparts, the Slavs (pp. 186–89), were the last major wave of northern barbarians to move into the lands of the south. With the spread of civilization to the northernmost tribes of these barbarian groups about 1000, the long history of interaction between civilized and barbarian European peoples (pp. 47–48) finally came to an end.

By the fifth century A.D., when the Germans took over the western provinces of the Roman Empire, long exposure to Roman influence had made their way of life more advanced and sophisticated than that of earlier times (pp. 136–39). Nevertheless, some of their older traditions persisted, and influenced various features of the emerging civilization of Europe.

The Germans, when first reported on by Roman writers about 100 B.C.–100 A.D., lived in tribal societies based on farming, hunting, herding, and warfare. They had also developed a social structure embracing several different groups. Although most of the Germans were ordinary farmers and, when necessary, warriors as well, each tribe also had a *nobility* based on *birth*. In addition, there were some individuals who were "bound" to do labor for others in payment for debt; and there were slaves who had been captured in battle.

The Germans also had their characteristic political and military institutions. Within the tribe, each village held a monthly *assembly*, open to all free males, which served as both a council and a court of justice. (There were no written laws until after the Germans moved into the empire.) The principal tribal military unit was the *comitatus* or war-band, a group of elite warriors who pledged themselves to follow a tribal chieftain and defend him with their lives. The chieftain, in turn, supported the warriors and gave them a share in the spoils.

Over several centuries of close contact with the Romans, some of these institutions persisted — especially those that were more warlike and "aristocratic." The war-bands, in particular, were well adapted to provide leadership for the larger tribal confederacies that developed around 200 (pp. 130–31). Thriving on warfare, wealthy from Roman pillage or Roman subsidies, and eager to spend their wealth on the luxurious trappings of the upper-class Roman way of life, the members of the war-bands became an elite that stood somewhat apart from the average Germanic warrior-tribesmen.

When the tribal confederacies took over the Western Roman Empire in the fifth century, the chieftains shared newly acquired land with the members of their war-bands, who became owners of vast properties. They took up Roman ways, and often intermarried with Roman aristocrats. The Germanic warriors eventually lost their separate identity; but at the same time, they changed the way of life of the relatively *un*military Roman landowners. The members of the new European elite were both landowners and warriors, whose power came partly from their control of economic resources, and partly from their skill in warfare and military leadership. Consisting as it did of warriors, the elite was generally unruly, and given to feuding and private warfare; but it was also held together by the warrior virtues of honor, comradeship, and loyalty.

The more "democratic" element in early Germanic institutions, notably the regular tribal assemblies, did not long survive the move into the Roman Empire. Even among the tribes that did not move into the empire, the spread of Christian and Roman civilization enhanced the power of chieftains and their favored warriors at the expense of tribal assemblies. All the same, a tradition of popular participation in government lingered on, especially in the field of law and justice. In many western European countries in the early Middle Ages, groups of ordinary freemen would be summoned and sworn to reveal their collective knowledge of the truth, in such matters as identifying the originator of a blood feud, establishing ownership of property, or accusing wrongdoers. In England this practice continued and evolved right through the Middle Ages. Eventually (from the thirteenth century onward) the practice also grew up of summoning groups of freemen not to *reveal* what they knew, but to *render a verdict* on the truth of testimony given by others. The result was the development of the modern jury system as it is known in England and the United States.

What information we have about the religion of the Germanic tribes indicates that, like that of other ancient peoples, it was *polytheistic*, including a pantheon of anthropomorphic deities, some of whom were considered especially powerful and holy (pp. 19–20). Although the tribes abandoned their pagan deities after adopting Christianity, many traditions persisted in Germanic folklore and symbolism. Thus in the English language, the names of Tiu, the Germanic war god; Woden, who was thought to take a special interest in the affairs of the human race; Thor, the thunder god; and Frigg, the fertility goddess, are still honored in the names of days of the week: Tuesday, Wednesday, Thursday, and Friday. Even the climactic day of the Christian calendar received its name, in most northern lands, from Eastre, the ancient German goddess of spring.

Perhaps the most important consequence of the Germanic takeover was that in the long run, it led to the disappearance of the already crumbling frontier between civilized and barbarian Europe. In Germany, the Low Countries, and the Scandinavian lands further north, there remained many Germanic peoples who had not moved into the Roman Empire. These barbarians now began to look southward in their turn, for trade, conquest, Roman culture, and Christianity. The more or less civilized Germanic rulers of former Roman lands, for their part, were less cautious than the Romans had been about expanding their power north and east of the Rhine and Danube rivers. Thus, by a strange and momentous twist of fate, the fall of the Roman Empire actually led to the spread of Roman and Christian civilization beyond its frontiers.

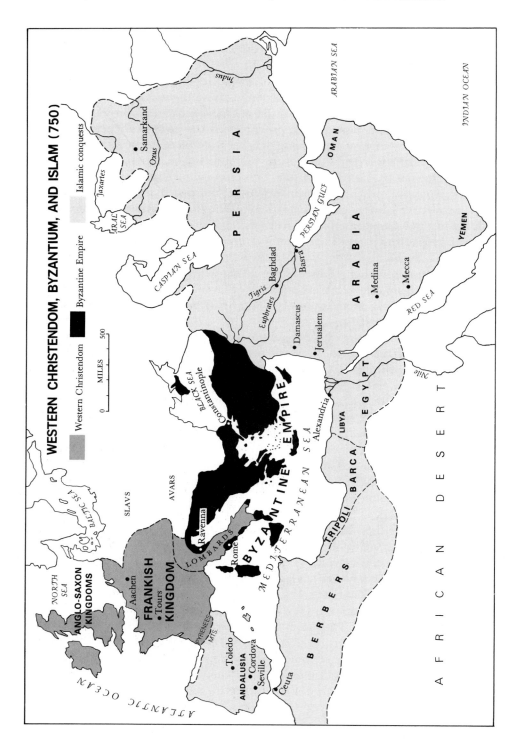

43 A.D.		c. 400		c. 900	1066
	ROMAN BRITAIN		SEPARATE ANGLO-SAXON KINGDOMS	UNITED ANGLO-SAXON KINGDOM	

The Kingdom of the Franks

Most of the half-dozen or so barbarian-ruled kingdoms that emerged from the fifth-century invasions had a relatively short life. In the following two hundred years, they fell victim to Byzantine efforts at reconquest (p. 184), to the power of Islam (p. 191), or to each other. In the end, only two Germanic nations succeeded in building permanent states on former Roman territory: the Anglo-Saxons and the Franks. It was these two nations, together with the non-Germanic Irish, that played the leading role in preserving Roman and Christian civilization and spreading it beyond the former frontiers of the Western empire.

From the area which is now Denmark, the Anglo-Saxons sailed over the North Sea and invaded Britain during the fifth century — after the Romans had withdrawn their protection from that distant province. The Anglo-Saxons overran the native Britons, who were quarreling among themselves, and established several kingdoms of their own. (Scotland and Wales alone retained their independence.) Within the Anglo-Saxon kingdoms, local Germanic dialects and customs took firm root. From these, the English language and some of the laws and institutions of English government would evolve over many centuries. Though pagan when they first settled, most of the Anglo-Saxons became Christian during the seventh century, partly as a result of missionary efforts sponsored by the papacy from 595 onward, and partly under the influence of two neighboring, already Christian nations: the Irish and the Franks.

Ireland was the first territory outside the frontiers of Rome to which Christian civilization spread when the the empire collapsed. A remnant of the Celtic peoples who centuries earlier had dominated much of western Europe (p. 94), the Irish had never been conquered by Rome. In the turmoil of the fifth century, the missionary and (later) saint Patrick brought Christianity to the island. (Patrick was a native Briton, who had been captured by Irish raiders.) Following this, Christian monasteries came to dominate the tribal life of the country. Under their influence, a unique Irish civilization grew up, based on the Christian faith, Roman literature, and the heritage of Irish barbarian culture. This civilization, in turn, came to influence much of western Europe during the early Middle Ages.

The most powerful state to arise in the West was that of the Franks, who were to give their name to modern France. When the big invasions began in the fifth century, the Franks were joined together in a loose tribal confederacy that controlled an extensive area along the lower Rhine River. One of their chieftains, Clovis, welded the confederacy into a *unified* force and then (in 486) started campaigns against neighboring Germanic kingdoms and against the Romans in Gaul.

The victorious Clovis and his successors pushed south to the Pyrenees Mountains and eastward from the Rhine. Unlike the other barbarian tribes, the Franks never abandoned their base on the lower Rhine; as a result, their forces were never cut off, surrounded, and absorbed. The eastward thrust was particularly significant, for it closed a large gap (between the Alps and the North Sea) through which repeated barbarian invasions had come. In addition, it brought under Frankish rule many Germanic tribes that still lived east of the Rhine. As the Franks became Christian and adopted Roman ways, so also did some of their subject tribes. In this way, the spread of Christian and Roman civilization beyond the empire's former frontiers began on the mainland of western Europe.

Clovis now began to build a stable system for governing his territories. He shared the conquered land with his principal warriors, as Germanic custom required, but made sure that the lion's share went to himself and his descendants. Instead of overthrowing the existing Roman elite of landowners, counts, and bishops (pp. 135–36), he let them keep much of their property and their positions in church and state; he then made use of their services in governing his kingdom. Clovis's power over his conquered territories was further strengthened by his early conversion to orthodox Christianity (unlike other barbarian rulers who had become Arian Christians (pp. 159–60), which helped gain him the support of powerful Romans. The bishops encouraged Clovis to regard himself as the preserver of both Christian and Roman traditions. Thus, though the level of public protection and administration declined considerably, a certain continuity of order was maintained. The alliance between the Church and the Franks provided the West with a new base of power to replace the shattered authority of Rome.

When Clovis died, however, much of what he had done to restore stability was destroyed. Following Germanic custom, he divided his kingdom among his four sons, treating political authority as though it were private property. This practice was to plague the Frankish kingdom throughout its life, since the sons usually quarreled over their shares and gave the leading nobles of the kingdom a chance to play off one brother against another.

This group of leading men developed out of the gradual merging of Clovis's followers and the old elite of Roman Gaul. As landowners, they had since late Roman times possessed power not only as landlords, but also as rulers and protectors of the peasants; as warriors, they had their own followers who would fight for them and owed them loyalty and obedience. The kings needed the cooperation of these powerful leaders so as to govern effectively. In order to win their support, the kings had to give them government positions, royal lands, and the right to control these lands without royal interference. In addition, the kings, who as Catholic rulers had authority over Church appointments, also had to give wealthy and powerful positions as bishops to men from this same leading group.

As a result, a vicious circle set in. The rulers' lands, revenues, and control over the government and Church gradually dwindled; this forced them to depend still more on the leading nobles, and to concede them still more land and power. By the end of the seventh century, the Frankish kings were mere puppets of their chief officials, the "mayors of the palace." The mayors were themselves usually the heads of powerful factions among the nobles; but since these factions feuded ferociously with each other, and since there was usually more than one *rival* mayor, each associated with one or other rival king, even the power of the mayors was insecure. In consequence, the authority of the central government became increasingly weakened, with each family of nobles acting as a power unto itself.

Compared with the Roman Empire in its most glorious days, the Frankish kingdom, and the many small kingdoms of England and Ireland, were feeble political structures, yet their role in the building of European civilization was important. For all their feuding, bloodthirstiness, and greed, the kings and nobles of the Franks, the Anglo-Saxons, and the Irish were professed Christian believers and respecters of Roman tradition. They invested an extremely large proportion of their resources in monasteries that harbored learning, culture, and religion. The Franks passed these practices on to the neighboring Germanic nations to the east and north, often with the help of Anglo-Saxon and Irish missionaries.

Even in politics and government, the Frankish kingdom in particular was of more importance than its history of conflict and disintegration might suggest. Within the kingdom, the main elements of the "feudal state," with its decentralized authority and its constant interplay of monarch, powerful nobles, and leading churchmen, were already coming into existence. In later centuries these elements would be refined and formalized, and made to operate more effectively (pp. 214–18). The feudal state would remain the predominant form of government throughout the rest of the Middle Ages and beyond — until the seventeenth- and eighteenth-century revolutions of liberalism and nationalism finally swept it away (Chapter 11).

THE RIVAL CULTURE OF BYZANTIUM

While the Franks, with the help of the Church, were seeking to restore order in the West, the emperors at Constantinople continued to claim authority over East and West alike. (The Greek name for the ancient site of Constantinople was Byzantium, and this name has been used by Western writers to refer to the empire, church, and culture of which Constantinople was the capital.) Byzantium could not make good its claims to authority over the West, but it remained powerful in the eastern Mediterranean. The strength of the Eastern empire rested on foundations that had been laid by Diocletian and Constantine. Centralized control was assured through an absolute monarchy sustained in oriental splendor at the grand court of Constantinople. The emperor commanded a professional bureaucracy and well-trained armies and navies. Moreover, his productive realm provided him with sufficient revenues to support administration and defense. He was supported, too, by the powerful Greek Church (p. 155), of which he was the formal head.

Justinian

Several Byzantine emperors tried to recapture portions of the West. In the sixth century a grand, if somewhat foolish, effort was made by the energetic Justinian. This man of extraordinary talent and determination, who came to the throne in 527, took seriously his role of God-appointed despot and determined to strengthen and expand his empire. One act of enduring value was his codification of Roman law, known as the *Corpus Juris Civilis* (p. 120). The emperor also took firm command of the Greek Church, appointing its presiding bishop, or patriarch (p. 154), deciding theological disputes, and enforcing clerical discipline. The Greek and Latin branches of Christianity were drifting apart in their relations to the state as well as to each other. While the Roman popes, in response to the decline of civil authority in Italy, became more and more independent of the state, the patriarchs at Constantinople fell under the domination of the Byzantine emperors. Both the emperors and the patriarchs rejected the claim of the popes to supremacy in religious matters.

Justinian's driving desire was to reconquer the imperial territories in the West (p. 138). At severe cost in men and resources he succeeded in wresting Italy and northwest Africa from their German masters. His armies and navies also won the western Mediterranean islands, including Sicily, and gained a foothold in Spain. The Mediterranean world became once more the province of the "Romans." The popes, though threatened by Justinian's claim as protector of Italy, managed to preserve their independence, and after Justinian's death in 565 the peninsula slipped from Byzantine control.

Justinian's fleets and garrisons had been spread too thin, and the lengthened frontiers of empire invited attack at many points. In addition, beginning in 542, the resources of Byzantium had been sapped by waves of bubonic plague. Since this rat-borne disease had not previously penetrated the Mediterranean world, the population was especially vulnerable to it. The plague first reached Egypt from Ethiopia or India. From there it spread throughout the Mediterranean area and to much of western Europe. The toll was staggering, equaling that of the later Black Death (p. 280). For centuries afterward, the Byzantine empire, and all of the Mediterranean area, suffered from the frightful consequences of this plague.

The Persians, renewing their ancient feud with Rome, launched a vicious assault on Justinian's successors. The onslaught was eventually checked, and the Persians were driven from Syria and Egypt (630). But the imperial troops were so exhausted that those lands fell easy prey to the Arabs a short while later.

Meanwhile, the withdrawal of Byzantine forces from the West (to meet the Persian threat) exposed the empire's European territories to new invasions. In the sixth century, most of northern Italy was conquered by yet another Germanic nation, the Lombards; early in the seventh century, nearly all the empire's possessions in southeastern Europe were overrun by non-Germanic invaders, the Slavs (pp. 186–89). In time, Byzantium was able to assert its power over these Slavic invaders, but the Lombards dominated northern Italy for two hundred years until conquered in their turn by the Franks (pp. 200–201, 206). Byzantium managed to hold a few coastal areas of northern Italy, together with southern Italy and Sicily, and thereby preserved some direct contact with the West.

Byzantium's Historic Role

In spite of Justinian's ill-advised strategic policy, he did manage to strengthen the internal administration of his empire. And his successors, though harassed on every side, succeeded in keeping the machinery of government running. This was fortunate for Europe, since Byzantium guarded the continent against attack from the East. Another key to imperial strength was the superb defensive position of the capital itself, which was surrounded by water on three sides. Though Byzantium slowly yielded its Asiatic provinces to invaders from the East, it held the invasion door to Europe until 1453. Persians, Arabs, and Turks were brought to a halt before the gates of Constantinople.

Byzantium also served as the custodian of classical culture when the Western world was being ravaged by barbarism. The rich literature of ancient Greece was conserved in archives and libraries, and Byzantine scholars enriched their heritage by adding their own commentaries and summations. Greek learning continued to serve as the foundation of education in the empire. Though Justinian, in his role as Christian ruler, closed the philosophical schools of Athens, a great Christian university grew up in Constantinople.

Some critics have charged that the Byzantines were so busy with conserving the culture they had inherited that they devoted little energy to creating a culture of their own. Even so, their accomplishments were impressive — particularly in the decorative arts and architecture. Byzantine craftsmen produced superb objects in gold, silver, and enamel of exquisite color and design. Visitors from the West were dazzled by the magnificence of the "city of cities."

Justinian himself had launched an ambitious building program for the capital. The principal monument, to the glory of God (and the pride of the emperor), was the mighty church of Hagia Sophia (Holy Wisdom). An elaborately planned structure, it employs domes and half-domes to create a vast interior space. The most striking feature is the main dome, over one hundred feet in diameter and one hundred eighty feet in height. It does not rest, as does the dome of the Pantheon (p. 124), upon a cylindrical wall. Instead, it rests on four giant arches, which mark off a central square beneath the dome. The

5-2 Hagia Sophia,
     Istanbul, interior.

arches carry the downward thrust to four corner stone *piers*, which are reinforced by massive stone supports on the outside. Arched windows piercing the
base perimeter of the dome crown the interior with a halo of light (*Fig. 5-2*).

Built in only six years' time, under the urging of the impatient emperor,
Hagia Sophia is one of the world's architectural wonders. It combines the
building principles of the Romans with the decorative splendor of the Persians.
The columns of the interior are of richly colored marbles taken from various
parts of the Mediterranean world. The vaultings are covered by multicolored
mosaics, which have survived the whitewash of later Muslim conquerors. This
temple inspires, in its own fashion, the sense of marvel and holy mystery that
the cathedrals of Europe were to achieve centuries later and has served as a
model for thousands of churches and mosques in Middle Eastern lands.

Byzantium and the Slavs

Besides its own artistic achievements and its role in the preservation and
defense of Greek and Christian civilization, Byzantium was also the main
force behind the spread of these traditions throughout *eastern Europe*. This was
chiefly the result of Byzantium's relations with the barbarians who came to
dominate the East, just as the Germanic barbarians dominated the West:
namely, the Slavs.

The Slavs, like so many other European barbarian peoples, were a group of tribes with a language and customs of Indo-European origin (p. 47). They first came to the knowledge of the Romans, as a people living somewhere to the east of the Germans, during the second century A.D.; by the time of the fall of the empire in the West, the Slavs are known to have inhabited an area stretching from the east of present-day Poland to the northern coastlands of the Black Sea. This was a fertile region of forest and grassland, and originally the Slavs seem to have been farmers, living a simple tribal life and worshiping gods and goddesses of weather and fertility.

From about the third century onward, however, the Slavs began to advance in wealth, organization, and finally in power. To begin with, this was not the result of direct contact with civilization, as in the case of the Germans (p. 131). Rather, it was the effect of contact with other barbarian peoples, more sophisticated and warlike than themselves. To the west of the Slavs lived the Germans; to the east stretched the vast Asiatic grasslands, the home of many nomadic (wandering and stock-rearing) peoples (pp. 45–47). More than once the Slavs were conquered and subjected by these neighbors, but they did not lose their identity. Instead, they served their various overlords in peace, fought under them in war, followed them on campaigns of conquest all over eastern Europe, and finally inherited their dominion.

In the sixth and seventh centuries, in the course of one such series of conquests under foreign leadership, the Slavs moved south from their homeland, crossed the Danube River, and broke the defenses of Byzantium. They took over most of the empire's provinces in southeastern Europe, including for a time even Greece itself. In the same period, other Slavic tribes moved north and west, until they reached the Baltic Sea and threatened the eastern frontier of the Frankish kingdom. More slowly and peacefully, yet other Slavs settled the vast forest region that stretched for hundreds of miles northeast of their homeland. By 900, the Slavs had occupied almost all of eastern and central Europe.

Whereas the Germanic tribes had been absorbed and lost their identity nearly everywhere they migrated, in eastern Europe it was the Slavs who assimilated or drove out the earlier peoples of the region. They also absorbed or overthrew the Asiatic and Germanic overlords under whose command they had spread so widely — notably the Avars, Bulgars, and Norsemen (pp. 203, 208, 281) — and established many Slav-ruled states. As a result, most of the peoples of eastern Europe are still ethnically and linguistically Slavic at the present day.

From the point of view of Byzantium, the expansion of the Slavs was both a terrible threat and a magnificent opportunity. On the one hand, the Slavs were numerous and warlike enough that, in combination with the empire's other enemies, they could destroy the empire. On the other hand, unlike the highly civilized Persians and the devoutly Muslim Arabs, the Slavs were barbarians and pagans. As with so many other pagan barbarian conquerors, the very success of the Slavs had uprooted them from their traditional way of life. Migration and war had fostered among them the growth of a wealthy and powerful elite of chieftains and warriors, and this elite was now in direct contact with Byzantine civilization.

For the Slavs, as for other barbarian invaders of the early Middle Ages (p. 213), contact with civilization was often divisive. Some among the Slav warriors feared the changes that this contact might bring: the abandonment of their traditional gods and goddesses; the transformation of their chieftains into Byzantine-style despots; perhaps even subjection to Byzantium itself. But others — usually including the chieftains themselves — welcomed the influence of Byzantium. Like the Germans before them (pp. 137, 138), the chieftains of the Slavs had no desire to destroy the civilized state they threatened. Rather, they wanted to enjoy its luxuries, win acceptance and recognition from it, build up their power with the aid of its bishops and administrators, and ultimately to participate in its way of life. With utmost exertion, the armies and navies of Byzantium could never banish the Slav threat; but the Christian religion and the Greek heritage might at least bring them under the empire's spiritual and cultural sway.

In the ninth and tenth centuries, the Byzantine emperors and leading clergymen of the Greek Church deliberately set about the task of bringing Christianity and Greek culture to the Slavs. So eager were the Byzantines to make their message acceptable that they even allowed the Slavs to worship in their own language, rather than in Greek.* (The Latin Church, on the other hand, usually insisted that whatever the languages spoken by newly converted peoples, the Mass [p. 152] must always be celebrated in Latin.) To make Christian worship and the absorption of Byzantine civilization still easier for the Slavs, Byzantine monks also adapted the Greek alphabet to the sounds of the Slav language. The result was the Cyrillic alphabet (named for the missionary Cyril, one of the leaders in the project of converting the Slavs); it has remained the standard script in Russia and several other Slav countries ever since.

These Byzantine gifts of religion, culture, and literacy were usually combined with others that were just as appealing: military alliances, commercial treaties, and prestigious imperial titles for the Slav chieftains. In the long run the combination proved irresistible. One by one, the chieftains invited Byzantine missionaries to their lands, or came in person to Constantinople to be baptized. The opposition of pagan warriors faded away, or was brutally crushed. More serious competition came from the Latin Church, which was able to attract the westernmost Slav tribes into its orbit (pp. 212–13). Elsewhere it was Byzantium that triumphed. By 1000, most of the Slavs, together with the Greeks and other eastern European peoples, formed a community of peoples

---

*At this time, the Slavs all spoke one and the same language, with minor local variations. The various Slavic languages of the present day — Russian, Polish, Czech, and others — developed later in the Middle Ages out of this common ancestral tongue.

on much the same level of civilization as those of western Europe — but one that looked to Constantinople instead of to Rome.

What held this community together was not, as in the West, the inheritance of Roman civilization, the Latin Church, and obedience to the pope. Instead, the peoples of eastern Europe were held together by the inheritance of Greek civilization, the Greek Church, and reverence for the Byzantine emperor (or in some cases his actual overlordship). Thus, there appeared in the East a variant of European civilization that was noticeably different from the Western variant. The cultural divergence between the two areas that grew up in the early Middle Ages still persists today.

The Arabs, as well as the Slavs, were to learn from the Byzantines. When they swept out of Arabia, as we will shortly see, they were a generally illiterate people. In a less direct way, Byzantium also contributed to the education of western Europe. All through the Middle Ages, there was constant interchange between East and West — by way of clergy, warriors, pilgrims, traders, and scholars. Though there was more antagonism than affection between the two, both were heirs of Hellenism. And it was Byzantium that *guarded* their common cultural endowment.

THE BOOK AND SWORD OF ISLAM

About A.D. 400 a period of mass migrations and head-on collisions set in throughout Eurasia: Germans, Slavs, Huns — and countless others were caught up in a restless stirring. Tribal wanderings had been going on for centuries, of course, but the Roman world was not affected by them until the Rhine-Danube defenses cracked open (p. 139). Then, as one tribe after another passed through, they left living space into which others pushed. The break in the Roman wall thus served as a stimulus to movements in areas as far distant as central Asia.

The Arabs and Muhammad

Two centuries later a second invasion into the Mediterranean world came from a different direction. The weakening of Byzantine defenses resulting from Justinian's military adventures (p. 184) opened the way to an invasion from Arabia. Semitic-speaking tribes, from as far back as 3000 B.C., had from time to time moved from Arabia to more fertile zones of the Middle East (pp. 23, 38). But in the seventh century A.D. the peninsula became, for the first time, a major pivot of history as yet another group set out to create a new, universal empire. The Arabs (or Saracens, as the Romans called them) brought a crusading faith and succeeded in building a brilliant and distinctive culture. Their religion and their culture are known by the name of *Islam*.

At the opening of the seventh century most of the Arabs were nomadic tribesmen. Because they conquered and adapted to an advanced civilization, there is a parallel between their role in the Mediterranean world and that of the Germans in western Europe. There are significant differences, however. For the Arabs, instead of being converted by the Christians they conquered, were fired with a religious zeal of their own and sought to impose what they considered to be a superior spiritual truth upon the peoples they overcame. (Islam, like Christianity, is one of the few *missionary* religions in world history.)

The founder of the faith was Muhammad (the Prophet), a man who was destined to transform the lives of millions. Born about 570 in Mecca, a trading center near the western coast of Arabia, he apparently grew up with no formal education. He did, however, learn something of the teachings of Judaism and Christianity, which had sifted down from Palestine and Syria. When he was about forty years old, he turned from his life as a merchant to become a religious hermit. Spending days in lonely meditation, he began to experience visions that he believed to be direct revelations from God (Allah). In one of these visions the Archangel Gabriel directed him to carry these messages to his people, and from that time on he abandoned all other activities.

Most Arabs, however, were polytheists who worshiped idols and nature spirits, and Muhammad soon found himself a prophet "without honor in his own country." His insistence that "there is no God but Allah, and Muhammad is his Prophet," proved offensive to them. He became especially unpopular in the city of Mecca, where a building known as the Kaaba housed idols and a Black Stone considered holy by the Arabs. When he denounced this shrine, he was branded a blasphemer and a disturber of the peace. Faced with this opposition, Muhammad left Mecca in 622, "shaking its dust from his feet," and fled northward to Yathrib (later renamed Medina, "City of the Prophet"). There he was able to preach freely, and his band of disciples began to grow — and to follow his example of seeking to convert others. The year of his flight (Hegira) is regarded as the beginning of the Muslim era — year *One* according to the Muslim calendar.

Muhammad's purpose was to wipe out primitive superstitions, put an end to tribal feuds, and unite the Arabs under a *single* pure faith. This could be done only if the Arabs would surrender to the will of Allah as revealed by the Prophet. The Arabic word for submission is *islam*, and the word for one who has submitted is *muslim*. These are the terms used to identify, respectively, the faith and the believer.

Though Muhammad viewed himself as a spiritual leader, he became a political and military chieftain as well. His disciples responded to his words without question; and he was persuaded through revelation that he should use force, if necessary, against unbelievers. Soon he was leading his followers on raids against desert caravans, an activity that turned out to be highly profitable. He justified these hijackings by declaring that the unbelievers deserved no better, thus giving rise to the Muslim concept of "holy war" (*jihad*). The proud Meccans were at length compelled to yield, and the Prophet returned to Mecca in triumph. He ordered that all the idols in the city be destroyed, but he preserved the Black Stone as a symbol of the new faith. Attracted by his mili-

tant methods and by his visions of bringing the whole world under Islam, the desert tribes began to flock to his leadership. By the time of his death, in 632, he had extended his personal control over a large portion of Arabia.

The Saracen Empire

Once the pattern of expansion had been established, the movement spread with lightning speed. Muhammad, though many times married, had left no son to inherit his mantle, so his disciples chose a successor (*caliph*) from among his close relatives. Family connection with Muhammad was accepted from the beginning as a mark of political legitimacy. Under the first two caliphs, Abu Bakr and Omar, the Arabs carried their holy war to the neighboring peoples of the Middle East. Within a decade their hard-riding horsemen had conquered Persia and had taken Egypt, Syria, and Mesopotamia from the Byzantine Empire. Though outnumbered in almost every battle, the crusaders for Islam succeeded in routing their opponents. At the end of two generations, their empire (*caliphate*) stretched from India in the East, across North Africa, to Gibraltar in the West (p. 180). By 720 they had taken Spain from the Christianized Visigoths and were sending raiding parties across the Pyrenees into France. Near Tours, in 732, they were stopped by Frankish warriors under Charles Martel (p. 178).

How can we explain these amazing conquests? They were due, in part, to the faith that sparked the Arabs. Every Muslim warrior knew that he would share in a rich booty if his side was victorious, and he believed that if he fell in battle his soul would fly straight to paradise. But there are other reasons as well. The effects of the bubonic plagues of the preceding century have already been mentioned (p. 184). Byzantium and Persia, the only substantial powers in the area, had weakened each other militarily by years of bitter warfare and could offer no effective resistance. Further, many of the peoples of the Middle East and Africa were discontented under their old rulers and welcomed the Saracens as liberators. Syrians and Egyptians, for example, tended to look with satisfaction on the overthrow of Greek and Roman control that reached back a thousand years, to the time of Alexander the Great (pp. 90–91). They also resented the heavy Byzantine taxation and the continuing persecution of Christian heretics.

Though determined to drive out paganism and eager to convert all peoples to their faith, the Saracens offered toleration to Jews and Christians (upon payment of a special tax). Within a few generations, however, most Christians in the conquered territories embraced Islam. There were legal and social advantages in becoming Muslims, and the religion appealed to many Christians. The conversion was to prove lasting; except for Spain, the lands that fell to the Arabs are still the lands of the mosque.

Islam and Christianity

What were the teachings of this new faith? Muhammad never claimed divinity for himself, though his followers would no doubt have accepted him as divine. A radical monotheist, he insisted only that he was the last and greatest of Allah's prophets. He set his revelations in the context of Judaism and Christianity, identifying Allah with Yahweh (Jehovah) and accepting the line of Jewish prophets, from Abraham through Jesus. Instead of claiming that he was introducing a *new* religion, he insisted that his work was the fulfillment of the old. His position with respect to Judeo-Christianity was similar to that of Jesus with respect to Judaism. His message, as recorded in the Koran (Book), might be viewed in this light as a *sequel* to the Old and New Testament.

Some Christian theologians of the Middle Ages agreed with the Prophet's explanation of his relation to Christianity. While denouncing him as an instrument of Satan, they classified Islam as a heresy or schism, rather than as a new religion. The learned Dante (p. 264) put Muhammad in one of the lower circles of his Inferno, among the creators of *division*. (Muhammad's punishment, symbolic of his alleged crime, was to have his torso repeatedly axed down the middle.)

The central spiritual appeal of Islam is its stress on the *oneness* of God. Most of the Koran is given over to describing and praising Allah, who alone is the supreme reality, all-knowing and all-powerful. The true believer must submit unreservedly to Allah's will as expressed through the Prophet. This could be done simply and without doubting; unlike Christianity, Islam raised no questions concerning the nature and persons of the godhead (pp. 158–60).

Similarly, there were no arguments over what made up the sacred canon (authorized holy books). Muhammad's revelations were memorized by his disciples and written down in final form shortly after his death; this original Koran, in Arabic, remains the only authorized version. Shorter than the New Testament, it is a poetic book, which thousands have *memorized*. Though today Muslims are outnumbered by Christians two to one, the Koran is undoubtedly the most-read book in the world. It serves not only as a record of divine inspiration, but as a guide to morality, legislation, and science — and as a text from which young Muslims learn their Arabic. In some Muslim countries the Koran is the *supreme law* of the land; the legal code (*Sharia*) is based upon it and is applied, notably, in Iran today.

Islamic Social and Ethical Ideas

Muhammad's ethical teachings are in the Judeo-Christian tradition, and the Koran repeats many of the proverbs and stories of the Bible. Because the Prophet had a practical mind, the model life that he described is within the reach of the faithful. While stressing love, kindness, and compassion, he did not insist on self-denial beyond the powers of most people. He saw no particular virtue, for instance, in sexual abstinence. He did, however, try to moderate the traditional Arab practice of *polygamy*. Repugnant to Christian doctrine (though not to all Christians), polygamy had arisen chiefly from the imbalance in the number of men and women among the Arabs, whose tribal feuds resulted in a chronic shortage of men. One means of providing security for the surplus females was to permit each male to take *several* wives. The practice had eventually led to sexual promiscuity, however, and the Prophet declared that a man should have no more than four wives at a time. (The quota did not apply to Muhammad himself, who was exempted by a special revelation.) No limit was set on the number of concubines a man might have. Though women possessed some property rights, Muslim society was (and is) a "man's world."

A conservative reformer, Muhammad did not condemn profit-making so long as the profit was reasonable and honest. Once a merchant himself, he did not feel that business dealings are intrinsically displeasing to Allah. Islam thus did not give rise to the tension between commerce and religion that has troubled the conscience of the West.

A characteristic of Islam that appealed to many is the absence of a formal priesthood. Every Muslim stands as an equal before Allah — though, in practice, religious scholars and "holy men" (*mullahs* and *ayatollahs*) enjoy special respect and authority. There are no saints mediating between humans and God (as in Catholic Christianity — p. 234); and because there are no priests, there are no mysterious rites that only priests can perform. To increase the worshiper's concentration on Allah, statues and images are banned from Muslim art. The place of worship — the mosque — is devoid of anything that resembles an idol.

All this contrasted sharply with the Greek Church, with its apostolic succession (p. 153), its distinctions between laity and clergy, and its elaborate rituals. Dedicated Muslims felt that their faith was spiritually purer and more democratic than Christianity. They scorned the Byzantines as people addicted to wrangling over doctrine, content to worship three or more divine figures, and cloaked in pagan superstition.

Obligations of the Faithful

The religious duties of Muslims, known as the "Five Pillars of Faith," are clearly stated in the Koran. The first is the familiar profession of belief, "There is no god but Allah, and Muhammad is his Prophet." By accepting and repeating these words, the convert is initiated into the faith.

Daily prayer — at dawn, midday, midafternoon, sunset, and nightfall — is the second duty. At the appointed hours, from atop slender minarets (towers) the muezzins (criers) call upon the faithful to bow down. The posture of the body and its positioning (turned toward Mecca) are described, and the prayer must be said in Arabic. The prayer itself, which is not unlike the Christian Lord's Prayer, usually includes the short opening verse of the Koran, praising Allah and asking for guidance along the "straight path." This formula is repeated many times each day. The only public religious service is the midday prayer on Fridays, which must be attended by all adult males (and is closed to females). Inside the mosque, standing in self-ordered rows, the congregation prays aloud in unison; then the leader, a layman, delivers a brief sermon. After the service normal everyday activities may be resumed.

The third duty is giving to the poor. At first, almsgiving was practiced as an individual act of charity, but it gradually developed into a standard payment. In the Islamic states, the money was collected through regular taxation and was used to help the needy and to build and maintain the mosques. The usual amount was one-fortieth of the individual's income.

Fasting, the fourth pillar of faith, ordinarily is confined to *Ramadan*, the ninth month of the Muslim lunar (moon) calendar. It was during Ramadan that Allah gave the Koran to the Archangel Gabriel for revelation to Muhammad. For thirty days no food or drink may be taken between sunrise and sunset. Fasting, which was not practiced by the Arabs before Muhammad, was adopted from Jewish and Christian custom.

Finally, every Muslim who can afford it must make a pilgrimage to the Holy City of Mecca at some time during his or her life. Over the centuries, this practice has had a unifying effect on the different peoples that embrace Islam. Rich and poor, black and white, Easterner and Westerner — all come together in the Holy City. Although the majority of Muslims are unable to fulfill this obligation, many millions do make the journey. In the early stages of Muslim history, a *sixth* duty was required of all able-bodied men: participation in the *jihad* (holy war). It was this requirement that sparked the first explosive conquests of the Arabs. Each caliph believed it his obligation to expand the frontiers of Islam and thus reduce the infidel "territory of war."

The Pillars of Faith are only the *minimum* requirements of Islam. In all things true believers must seek to do the will of Allah as revealed in the Koran. They must also believe that God has *predestined* the ultimate fate of all humankind, to be revealed in the Last Judgment. Muhammad left vivid descriptions of hell and heaven. Unbelievers will burn eternally in a great pool of fire; believers who die in sin will also suffer there for a time but will finally be released. In the end, *all* Muslims (male and female) — who have accepted Allah — will enjoy the pleasures of paradise. Muhammad, drawing from Persian sources, pictured paradise in sensual terms as an oasis of delight, with sparkling beverages, luscious fruits, and dark-eyed beauties.

Religious and Political Divisions

In spite of the comparative simplicity of Muhammad's teachings, they were open to conflicting interpretations as the years passed. The major disagreements arose over the principle of succession to the caliphate, religious doctrines, and the proper way of life for Muslims.

Because Islam had no authoritative priesthood for dealing with internal differences, a large number of rival sects evolved. The main division was between the Sunnites and the Shiites, a division that still disturbs the Muslim world. The Sunnites were associated with the Ommiad dynasty, which seized the caliphate in 661 and moved the capital of Islam from Medina to Damascus, in Syria. They accepted as valid certain traditions (Sunna) that had grown up outside the Koran. The Shiites, on the other hand, held strictly to the Koran and insisted that only descendants of the Prophet could become caliphs. The Abbassid family, of the Shiite sect, gained power in 750 and moved the capital again, this time to the new city of Baghdad (p. 180), in the modern state of Iraq.

After the eighth century the Saracen empire began to break up. The ousted Ommiad family established itself in Spain and broke off political connections with Baghdad. Similarly, a descendant of Fatima (Muhammad's daughter) later declared himself an independent caliph in control of Egypt, Syria, and Morocco. Provinces in Arabia and India also fell away, until by 1000 the Abbassid ruler controlled only the area surrounding Baghdad.

The Muslim Legacy to the West

Despite all these political divisions, Muslim civilization reached its height in the ninth and tenth centuries. The Arabs, who themselves were culturally backward, brought little of their own to this development. But the unifying faith, the common language (Arabic), and the relative stability they provided served to bring about a revival in the Middle Eastern world. The Islamic achievements of this period are a blend of various traditions, especially Hellenic, Syrian, and Persian.

Striking advances were made in agriculture and commerce. Trade routes were made secure, and merchants traveled from Spain to China and the East Indies. Arab rulers supported studies of geography and navigation, and encouraged popular education and universities. There is hardly a branch of learning that was not advanced by the Muslims. Despite a religious ban on the dissection of human bodies (similar to that of the Christian Church), they took notable steps in the science and art of medicine. Scholars translated into Arabic the writings of such ancient Greek physicians as Hippocrates and Galen (pp. 67, 118). Muslim doctors wrote useful books of their own: best known is the *Canon* of Avicenna (ibn-Sina), a summary of the medical knowledge of his time (eleventh century).

In other fields of learning, perhaps the most valuable Muslim contribution was the introduction from India of what we now call Arabic numerals — an innovation that freed mathematicians from the awkward Roman system. One way of suggesting the range of Muslim influence is to mention some of the thousands of Arabic words that survive in our vocabulary: zero, algebra, alcohol, chemistry, zenith, nadir, admiral, arsenal, traffic, check, bazaar.

Muslim literature mirrored a broad sweep of attractive subjects: desert life, bustling cities and bazaars, the mosques, fierce warrior horsemen, and mysterious veiled women. The literary *forms* included prose for history, philosophy, and religion; fantastic and romantic stories; and colorful poetry. Among the stories the *Arabian Nights* has become the one most widely read in the West: an enchanting collection drawn from many times and places of the Islamic world. (Its best-remembered characters, no doubt, are Sinbad the Sailor, Alladin, and Ali Baba.)

Popular also are the charming verses of the Persian Omar Khayyám, a mathematician and astronomer of the twelfth century — as well as a poet. His *Rubáiyát*, composed of a thousand quatrains (four-line verses), expresses a scientific-determinist point of view. Omar has few illusions about the universe or humanity. In memorable figures of speech, he accepts, yet protests both Fate and Death — noting sadly and wishfully:

> Alas, that Spring should vanish with the rose!
> That youth's sweet-scented manuscript should close!
>   The nightingale that in the branches sang
> Ah, whence, and whither flown again, who knows?

> •   •   •   •   •

> Ah, love, could you and I with Fate conspire
> To grasp this sorry scheme of things entire,
>   Would we not scatter it to bits — and then
> Re-mold it nearer to the heart's desire?

To Omar, one's life was part of a *caravan* traveling from nothingness to nothingness. Therefore, he concluded, we should . . .

> Make the most of what we yet may spend,
> Before we, too, into the dust descend . . .

In other words, one should plunge into the pleasures of the *present*. The poet urges his beloved:

> Come, fill the cup, and in the fire of Spring
> The winter garment of repentance fling:
>   The Bird of Time has but a little way
> To fly — and lo! The Bird is on the wing.*

Omar's philosophy connects, across centuries and cultures, with the ideas of two philosophers of ancient Greece: the *materialist* Epicurus and the *hedonist* Aristippus (pp. 69, 115–16).

A further contribution of the Muslims was the preservation of literary and scientific writings of the ancient Greeks. This was achieved through translating those works into Arabic and carrying them to all parts of the Islamic world. Great centers of learning sprang up, notably at Cairo (Egypt), Toledo (Spain),

*From the *Rubáiyát of Omar Khayyám*, translated into English by Edward Fitzgerald (1st ed., 1859). Stanzas 7, 23, 72, 73.

and Palermo (Sicily), where scholars studied Aristotle and Plato and tried to relate their writings to Muhammad's religious teachings. Gradually, European scholars made their way to Spain and Sicily to study the scientific and philosophic works of the Greeks. As the Muslim tide receded from those areas after 1000, the Christians of the West seized on the rich intellectual deposit and made it their own. Europe recovered through Arabic translations many of the treasures of Greek learning that had been lost for centuries.

Western artisans and builders were also impressed by what they discovered in Muslim countries. In the tenth century, when most of Christian Europe was busy trying to fend off attacks from every quarter, Muslim Spain was enjoying unequaled prosperity. Its capital, Cordova, the largest city of Europe after Constantinople, boasted magnificent mosques and palaces, public baths, colleges, libraries, and private homes. Cordovan leather, textiles, and armor were famous everywhere. Scholars, poets, and musicians were generously patronized by the rulers.

Muslim architecture, a blend of Persian and Mediterranean styles, was distinguished by its graceful variations of the Roman dome and arch — typically pointed or in the shape of a horseshoe. Walls were richly decorated with marble, precious stones, and glazed tiles. Since Muhammad had forbidden the representation of human or animal figures, painting and carving consisted mainly of geometrical and floral designs (arabesques). Spanish architecture still reflects this Muslim influence.

The triumph of the Islamic style, however, is to be found not in Spain but in India, in the seventeenth-century mausoleum (tomb) at Agra (*Fig. 5-3*).

5-3 Taj Mahal.

Built by a wealthy ruler to honor his favorite wife, the Taj Mahal stands as one of the supreme works of architecture of the world.

After the Christian crusades (to be discussed in Chapter 6) and the later Mongol invasions of the Middle East, Muslim culture fell into a decline from which it never recovered. But until the thirteenth century it was in most respects superior to that of Europe. Though there was fierce hostility between Christendom and Islam, the developing civilization of the West gained much of value from the Muslims.

THE EMERGENCE OF MEDIEVAL CIVILIZATION

Now that we have considered briefly the cultures of Byzantium and Islam, we return to western Europe. The Franks, it will be recalled, were the only Germanic tribal group to establish a lasting state on the continent. By 700, however, the Frankish kings had become powerless. The leaders of competing factions among the nobles had taken away their authority and struggled for the only offices of real power, those of "mayor of the palace" in each of the territories of the divided kingdom (p. 183).

The Rise of the Carolingian Dynasty

What finally put an end to this situation was the triumph of one particular family in the continual struggles for power among the nobles. From the name of the family's most famous member, Charles the Great (Charlemagne — p. 201), the family is usually known as the Carolingians (*Carolus* being the Latin for Charles). This name applies also to the period when they were dominant, the eighth and ninth centuries.

Well before Charlemagne's time, late in the seventh century, the Carolingians were able to unite the several offices of mayor of the palace in the person of the head of their family. They thereby restored unity to the Frankish kingdom, and established a hereditary claim on the office. In 714, the "mayoralty" descended to Charles Martel ("the Hammer"), grandfather of Charlemagne. In bitter fighting, Charles was able to crush the opposition of rival claimants, and secure firm control of the kingdom. With the legal ruler (the king) pushed ever more into the background, the actual ruler turned to the grim task of reconstruction.

In 732 Charles Martel faced a historic challenge, when the Saracens swept north from Spain and made raids into the Frankish kingdom (p. 191). They found the richest booty in the treasuries of churches and monasteries, and were riding toward the abbey of St. Martin of Tours, the richest in the country. Charles Martel commanded a defense force that consisted of foot soldiers supported by a small number of mounted knights. The Saracen horsemen had superior mobility and striking power, but Charles maneuvered them into launching an attack on a fort surrounded by implanted wooden stakes. The raiders, badly hurt by a shower of arrows and javelins, decided to pull back to Spain.

Charles was hailed as a hero, the savior of the West. But he knew that more attacks were coming and that he must convert his entire army into a mounted force in order to withstand them. (The power of cavalry had been sharply increased by the introduction of the saddle *stirrup* in the eighth century; this permitted the rider to put the weight and power of his horse behind his long-sword or lance.) Charles knew, too, that the thousands of horses and armed riders he needed could be assembled only at great expense. Because wealth existed mainly in the form of land, he began to look about for available property.

The Church caught his eye at once. Bishoprics and monasteries, as a result of generous gifts and legacies, now held from a third to a half of all the land in the realm. Charles Martel tried to persuade church officials to part with some of their holdings, so that he could assign them to noblemen in exchange for their service as warriors. Though the clergy knew that they would suffer if the Saracen raids continued, they rejected his appeal. Charles then took matters into his own hands: he seized many church properties and distributed them as military grants (benefices) to certain noble warriors. In return, each warrior bound himself to supply a body of armed cavalry when called upon. Thus was laid the basis of the "feudal compact" (p. 215), in which the use of land was exchanged for military equipment and service.

Within a century the Frankish army had been converted into a force of mounted warriors—*chevaliers* (horsemen in French, and in English, knights). Infantry largely disappeared, and for the next five centuries the cavalry was to be the "queen of battles." So long as physical defense depended on the service of an armored cavalry, and so long as land remained the principal source of wealth, landholding would be closely associated with the knights.

The Alliance of the Franks and the Papacy

Charles Martel's son, Pepin, decided that the time had come for the *actual* power in the kingdom to be recognized as the *legal* power. For nearly three-quarters of a century the Carolingian family had assumed responsibility for the defense and administration of the kingdom; the Frankish monarchy had become a mere shadow. But it was not a simple matter to take the crown from the descendants of Clovis. Though they were only figureheads, they were respected as the rightful possessors of the kingship and all the powerful men of the kingdom — bishops, nobles, and mayors of the palace — had sworn loyalty to them.

Pepin, anxious to avoid another civil upheaval, tried to win the Frankish bishops over to his side before deposing the reigning monarch. But the bishops were still angry over Charles Martel's seizure of church lands and had no intention of supporting his son. Pepin then went over their heads and appealed directly to Rome. The pope, for his own reasons, approved the deposition in 751.

Pepin was shortly thereafter crowned and anointed (holy oil placed on him) by a clergyman who was close to both himself and the pope: the monk, missionary, and (later) saint Archbishop Boniface of Fulda. This was the first time in the history of the Frankish kingdom that a king inaugurated his reign with a solemn religious ceremony conducted by a leading clergyman (representing the pope). The ceremony was deliberately patterned after the consecration of the Israelite kings at God's command, as described in the Old Testament. Against the hereditary legitimacy of the descendants of Clovis, Pepin now claimed a special holiness and authority from God. It was not long before clerical coronation and anointing became the normal ceremony of inaugurating kings throughout Europe. The idea behind the ceremony, that the power of kings came from God, strengthened royal power for many centuries to come, though in the Middle Ages the popes always stressed that this divine authority was *conferred* by the *Church* (pp. 205–6, 408).

Later it was Pepin's turn to do the pope a favor. Almost two centuries before, in 568, the Lombards had invaded Italy, defeated the Byzantine forces stationed there, and threatened the independence of the papacy. They were restrained for a while, but during the eighth century it began to appear that they would extend their control over all of Italy, depriving the popes of their power in Rome and in nearby territories. Because the Byzantine rulers still claimed Italy, the pope, Stephen II, might have appealed to Constantinople for aid. But the rivalry between the Latin and Greek churches (p. 155) had strained relations between East and West; moreover, the Eastern emperor had military problems of his own. So Stephen turned to Pepin for protection. Stephen journeyed to the Frankish court in 754, reanointed the king, and won promises of military help.

Two years later, Pepin fulfilled his obligation to the papacy by crossing the Alps, defeating the Lombards, and transferring a strip of territory across central Italy to the governing authority of the pope. Thus, by the so-called Donation of Pepin, the States of the Church came into being as a sovereign political entity. They remained so for over a thousand years — until the unification of Italy in 1870 (p. 498).

At about the same time as Pepin's gift, the papacy justified its right to govern this territory with a far bolder claim. It asserted that the Emperor Constantine, when he moved to Byzantium, had bequeathed *all* of the West to Pope Sylvester and his successors. As proof of this claim the papal court produced a signed document. The Donation of Constantine, as this paper came to be known, also declared the pope to be the superior of all other bishops and of the *emperor* himself. In the fifteenth century the document was shown to be a forgery (p. 325), but in the meantime it served to advance the ambitions of the papacy.

For centuries the Donation of Constantine and other false documents were accepted as part of canon (church) law. In the long run, they would prove harmful to the Church, for the papacy could not make good its claims to worldly supremacy. And in seeking such power, the medieval popes often neglected their spiritual mission. The Donation of Pepin, however, was genuine and had immediate results: it sealed the alliance between the Frankish state and the papacy, the two strongest forces in the West. The outcome of this alliance was the empire of Charles the Great.

Charlemagne

Charles, Pepin's son and Charles Martel's grandson, stands as one of the towering figures of history. Through the force of his personality and the challenges of a long reign (forty-six years), he contributed mightily to the evolution of Europe. After centuries of near chaos, he restored some measure of unity to Western Christendom and advanced its frontiers. Charles personified the merging of Germanic, Roman, and Christian elements.

Tall and blue-eyed, Charles was proud of his German heritage. His given name was Karl, and, though he knew Latin, he preferred to speak in his native Frankish tongue. The French language and nation were yet to emerge, and the name "Charlemagne" (French) did not appear until more than a century later. Nevertheless, he is usually referred to in French and English histories as Charles or Charlemagne (Charles the Great).

As a champion of the Church, Charlemagne pushed the boundaries of Christianity eastward by military force. He admired the Roman ideals of universality, law, and justice, and sought to make them realities in Europe. During his lifetime he created a kind of reincarnation of Roman power in the West, but because conditions were not favorable to its survival, his empire faded soon after his death. Even so, he revived the idea of a strong central state and laid the foundation for many European political institutions.

Charlemagne was almost constantly at war. Ruthless and cruel in battle, he fought, not primarily for spoils, but for what he considered to be the higher goals of Christianity and universal order. When advised by the pope that the Lombards were again threatening papal territory, he led his armies into Italy in 774 and broke the Lombard power. Now he called himself king of the Lombards as well as king of the Franks and extended his authority over most of Italy (p. 202).

His hardest campaigns, which lasted some thirty years, were against the Saxons. These tough warriors, some of whom had crossed the North Sea to Britain in the fifth century, occupied the region north and east of the Frankish boundaries (as far as the Elbe River — p. 202). The only Germanic tribe as yet unconquered by the Franks, they clung stubbornly to their primitive heathenism. Charlemagne, encouraged by the Church, was determined to

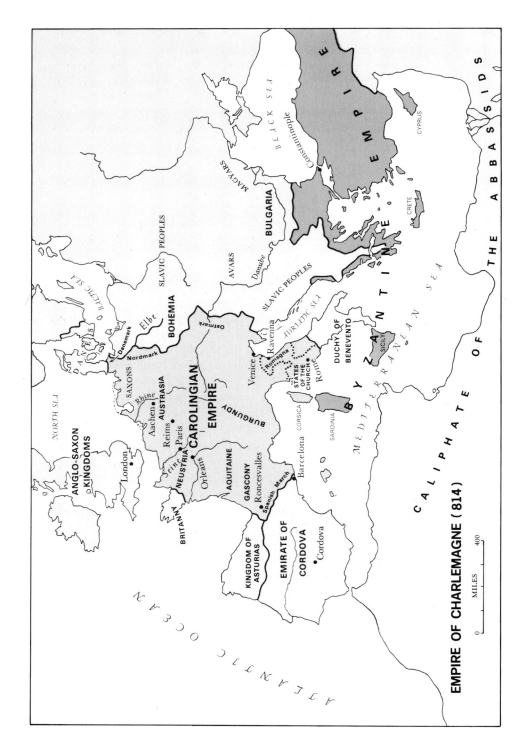

EMPIRE OF CHARLEMAGNE (814)

transform the Saxons into loyal Christian subjects. He succeeded, but only after laying waste to Saxony, massacring countless captives, and relocating thousands of families in other parts of his empire. At last the Saxons accepted Christianity, and the Frankish clergy moved in to establish bishoprics and monasteries.

With the conquest of Saxony, Charlemagne's power extended to the borders of the heathen Danes (p. 202). Instead of invading their territory, however, he created a military zone, called a march, or *mark*, along the frontier. This barrier between Christianity and heathenism stood for more than a century. In the eleventh century, after the Danish king had been converted, the kingdom came to be known as Denmark (*Danemark*).

Other European states developed from military zones along other stretches of the Frankish borders. The North March (*Nordmark*), set up on the eastern frontier of Saxony as a defense against the Slavs, was to become the duchy of Brandenburg (later, Prussia). Charlemagne colonized still another area, the East March (*Ostmark*), from which the duchy of Austria was to emerge.

Charlemagne reconquered the East March from the Avars, a nation of Asiatic nomads (pp. 45–47) who since the sixth century had controlled much of central and eastern Europe — like the Huns before them (pp. 137–38). As with the Huns, the defeat of the Avars caused most of them to retreat and disperse; but they left behind Slavic tribes who had accompanied them on their campaigns of conquest (p. 187). All along its eastern frontier, from the North March to the East March, Charlemagne's empire now confronted Slavic peoples, whether as enemies to be conquered or as neighbors to be influenced and converted (pp. 210–13).

South of the Pyrenees Mountains, Charlemagne erected the Spanish March as a wall against the Muslims. From this foothold Christianity gradually expanded into the kingdoms of Aragon and Castile. The setting up of the Spanish March had literary as well as political consequences. Returning from a raid below the Pyrenees, Charlemagne's rear guard was ambushed in the pass of Roncesvalles by the mountain-dwelling Basques in 778. Commanded by Roland, nephew of the king, the Frankish warriors fought bravely but were finally wiped out. Their heroism passed into legend and ballad, finally emerging as the epic *Song of Roland* (p. 262).

Charlemagne concerned himself with domestic matters as well as with military campaigns. Recognizing the Church as the only institution that was accepted by all his subjects, he worked to strengthen its leadership and extend its activities. Though a devout and submissive Christian in private life, he believed that as *king* he must act as head of the Church. Viewing the religious structure as part of his royal administration, he appointed bishops, issued reform orders to the clergy, and assumed, in general, the same attitude the Byzantine emperors took toward the Greek Church (p. 184). He treated bishops and abbots as agents of his government and saw to it that they received copies of all his imperial decrees.

Aside from Church law and imperial decrees, Charlemagne issued no uniform legal code for his sprawling territories, leaving the various peoples — Franks, Lombards, Saxons, Romans — to govern themselves according to their own laws. This attitude was typical of Charlemagne's administration: he chose for the most part to accept existing institutions as he found them. One regular feature of his government, inherited from earlier kings and late Roman rulers, was the role played by his counts (pp. 136, 180). Each *count* represented the crown in a given region, called a *county*. He presided over a court that met once a month, collected fines, and, in time of war, assembled the knights of his county for military action. Sometimes, for purposes of defense, several counties were grouped into a larger unit headed by a *duke* (leader). Both counts and dukes were selected from the local landed nobility. Their counties and duchies eventually became the historic provinces of France (Brittany, Champagne, Flanders, Burgundy, Gascony, Poitou, and so forth).

As a check on the honesty and efficiency of these officials, the king appointed royal inspectors, who visited all his territories once a year. Traveling in pairs (a nobleman and a clergyman), they investigated the performance of the counts and dukes and reported their findings to Charlemagne. By acting vigorously in response to this intelligence, he succeeded in holding together his far-flung empire.

Because there was no general system of taxation, the king had to draw most of his revenue from the crown lands, which he kept as his own. He held thousands of estates, most of them concentrated between the Seine and Rhine rivers (p. 202). Understandably, he was keenly interested in the efficiency with which his properties were managed, and he prepared detailed instructions for the guidance of his royal stewards (estate managers).

Charlemagne made his capital at Aachen, which was surrounded by productive crown lands in the heart of the ancient Frankish territories. His palace chapel at Aachen, which still stands, was the first important stone building to be erected north of the Alps after the fall of Rome (*Fig. 5-4*). This fact in itself indicates the slow recovery of the West. The chapel was modeled on the church of San Vitale in Ravenna, a Byzantine outpost on Italy's east coast. San Vitale, in turn, was built in the same general style as the grand Hagia Sophia (*Fig. 5-2*). The king was so impressed when he first saw San Vitale — a rich church, glistening with mosaics — that he directed his builders to duplicate the plan in his own capital. Thus, the art of Constantinople found its way to Aachen and the Frankish heartland.

By importing artisans and artists from Italy, Charlemagne stimulated the development of the arts in northern Europe. He was concerned, as well, over the low level of education and scholarship in his realm and issued a decree instructing bishops and abbots to improve the training of the clergy. In Aachen itself, around 780, he set up a palace school that would become a center of intellectual activity. The school came under the guidance of a monk named Alcuin, who was the leading scholar of his day. Charlemagne had called him from the cathedral school of York, the finest in England.

5-4 Palace chapel at Aachen, Germany, interior.

Alcuin trained a staff of expert scribes (copyists), who brought back the monastic tradition of reproducing ancient manuscripts. This was, perhaps, his principal contribution to Western culture; most of the ancient Latin literary works that we possess have come down to us from Carolingian copies, carefully preserved in monastic libraries. Alcuin also established a course of studies, based on that of the monastic and cathedral schools, for selected young men of the Frankish nobility. The faculty of the school at Aachen was made up of distinguished scholars drawn from all over Europe. Many of their pupils became outstanding teachers themselves in other intellectual centers of Germany and France. Though Charlemagne's empire barely survived him, the "Carolingian renaissance" of the arts and scholarship provided a lasting impetus to the cultural development of Europe.

The Restoration of the "Roman Empire"

The most dramatic event of Charlemagne's rule — one that captured the imagination of Europe — was his coronation as "Charles Augustus, Emperor of the Romans." The event took place on Christmas Day, 800, while the Frankish king was attending Mass in St. Peter's Basilica in Rome. Apparently he had not planned the coronation beforehand; his biographer, Einhard, reports that Pope Leo III, without warning, placed the crown on his head and pronounced him emperor.

The pope had his own reasons for taking this historic step. Now that he could no longer call on the Byzantine (Eastern) emperor for help, he needed a strong protector in Italy. Pepin and Charlemagne had defended the papacy from the Lombards in years past, but the pope was eager to win a guarantee for the future. Further, there was the possibility that the Franks themselves might prove dangerous. By taking the initiative in 800, the pope succeeded in defining the relationship between the restored (Western) empire and the Church. By setting himself up as a *donor*, he secured the *superior* position: Charlemagne received the crown from the hand of the pope, thereby putting the emperor under obligation to the papacy. The action also gave force to the later claim that the papacy had a right to *withdraw* what it had given. Later popes, making this claim, would unseat emperors.

Though Charlemagne may have been surprised by the circumstances of his crowning, there is no evidence that he was displeased. From the time of Clovis's conversion to Christianity in the fifth century (p. 134), there had been close ties between the Franks and the papacy. Together, they had worked to spread the faith and to reestablish order in the West. By Charlemagne's time the Frankish state had become extensive enough and substantial enough to qualify as a successor to the Roman Empire. The pope now recognized and blessed the Frankish king as *augustus*, and the new emperor pledged himself to defend and champion the Church.

The restoration of the empire in the West demonstrates the historical force of an idea. Through four centuries of struggle and near anarchy, the *idea* of universal law and order had lived on. At the first sign of its becoming a reality, the "restoration" was proclaimed — even though an "Emperor of the Romans" had been sitting in Constantinople since the fourth century. (The pope may have chosen to act when he did because at that moment a woman, Irene, was reigning over Byzantium. Because, in the Roman tradition, females were considered ineligible to rule, the pope elevated Charlemagne to a "vacant" throne.)

In any case, his empire incorporated the three major elements of medieval civilization: the *Roman* idea of universality and order, the *Christian* religion, and *Frankish* military power. In extent it was substantially less than even the western half of ancient Rome; missing were North Africa, Sicily, Spain, and Britain. On the other hand, territories east of the Rhine that had never been controlled by Rome were part of Charlemagne's rule.

There were other significant differences between the two empires. In Charlemagne's territories there was no single citizenship, no unified law, no professional civil service. There were few cities, since few had survived, and the roads had fallen into disrepair. Christianity, which had become the state religion in the closing years of the old Roman Empire, was the main unifying force in the new, and yet the agencies of the Church could not make up for the absence of firm political institutions. Charlemagne's empire was held together chiefly by the strength of his personality. Soon after his death in 814 the empire fell apart — leaving but a *fiction* of unity and an *ideal*.

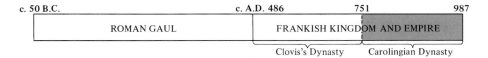

The Dissolution of Charlemagne's Empire

The ninth century was a time of unprecedented struggle in western Europe. The promise of order and stability held out by Charlemagne faded in the dusk of renewed civil wars and invasions. Yet in a sense this was a return to "normal" conditions. The turbulent centuries from 500 to 1000 were marked in both Europe and Asia by grand breakups, mass migrations, and clashes of faiths. For a time Charlemagne had checked the forces of chaos in the West. After his death, however, those forces rose again, and under his successors the Carolingian empire dissolved. Yet out of the conditions that accompanied the collapse emerged the peculiar institutions of medieval Europe that would govern Western life and thought until the fifteenth century.

The troubles of the ninth century sprang in part from the inner weaknesses of the Frankish kingdom and in part from external forces. Charlemagne was succeeded (814) by his only surviving son, Louis the Pious. Louis was a good emperor, but he lacked the determination of his father. Though he tried to hand on the bulk of his territories to his eldest son, Lothar, this led to warfare with his younger sons, who were determined to get equal shares in accordance with Frankish custom (p. 182). Finally, after Louis's death, his sons arrived at a settlement that marked an important early stage in the development of the countries of western Europe. By the Treaty of Verdun (843), Lothar was named emperor-elect and given the middle portion of the empire; this included Italy and territory north of the Alps that came to be called after him, Lotharingia (Lorraine). The second son, Louis, received the portion of the empire east of the Rhine, which would become Germany. Charles, the youngest son, inherited the western third, which would become France.

But France and Germany were centuries away from true national statehood, and the Treaty of Verdun did not prevent continued fighting among the sons of Louis the Pious and among their descendants. Within a short time the middle kingdom (Lotharingia) disappeared altogether; most of its territory was ultimately taken over by the rulers of the eastern portion.

The disintegration of Charlemagne's empire was speeded up by ferocious attacks from outside. One arm of invasion came from the Mediterranean, where Muslim raiders from North Africa had established themselves in Sicily and Sardinia. They preyed on shipping, struck at the coastal towns of Italy and southern France, and made off with everything they could carry. In 846 they captured Rome itself and pillaged the surrounding countryside. In desperation, Pope Leo IV built a wall around the heart of Rome. The rest of the city, however, lay open to the Muslims when they returned some years later.

On the eastern frontier, there appeared yet another nation of Asiatic nomads (pp. 45–47), the Magyars or Hungarians, who sought to dominate central and eastern Europe as the Huns and Avars had before them (pp. 137–38, 203). The Hungarians occupied the plain of Pannonia (present-day Hungary), and sent plundering expeditions throughout Germany, sometimes striking as far as the Netherlands and southern France. For much of the tenth century, they kept central Europe in turmoil.

By far the strongest blows against Europe came from the Norsemen or Vikings ("men of the North" or "pirates" in their own language), the fierce barbarian warriors of Scandinavia. The Norsemen were a branch of the Germanic peoples, whose more southerly tribes had been responsible for the breakup of the Roman Empire in the fifth century (pp. 130–31, 136–39). In Roman times, the Norsemen had already traded actively with the civilized lands to the south; now, with the northward spread of Christianity and Roman culture, they found themselves on the fringe of the civilized world (p. 203). As a result, they in turn became more advanced. By the ninth century, though still pagan and mostly illiterate, they had become a formidable nation of seafarers, traders, and warriors. Moreover, their numbers had grown, so that there were too many of them for the scanty harvests of their northern homeland to support. Consequently, they struck out on what proved to be the last great barbarian invasion of civilized Europe.

From 800 on, the long, high-prowed vessels of the Norsemen began to appear all along the coastline of Europe. The warriors who leaped ashore demanded tribute from the inhabitants and carried off what they could. From the coasts, they moved up the rivers and carried their raids deep into the interior. Finally, the Viking raids turned into regular campaigns of conquest, in which they seized and settled whole territories.

No part of northern Europe was safe from the Norse attacks. Their western tribes, the Norwegians, mainly sailed the "outer passage," and took over much of Scotland and Ireland; by 1000, their westward urge had taken them across the Atlantic, to Iceland, Greenland, and "Vinland" (North America). The southernmost Norse tribes, the Danes, generally followed the "middle passage" to the coastlands of the North Sea and the Channel: England, France, and the Netherlands. The Anglo-Saxons were forced to surrender a large portion of England (the Danelaw) to the invaders. The Frankish monarchy, similarly, was compelled to yield a substantial area along the Channel: it was called after the Norsemen, the duchy of Normandy. The Norsemen of the east, the Swedes, took the "eastern passage" across the Baltic Sea, and thence by river hundreds of miles south to the Black Sea. They won power over the Slavic tribes that had settled this vast region of eastern Europe (pp. 187, 213); and in 860, their longboats attacked Constantinople.

Throughout the territory of Charlemagne's empire, the struggles among his descendants, as well as barbarian and Muslim attacks, made violence and danger more than ever a normal condition of life. Everywhere, people turned from the distant and helpless central government to whomever was near enough and strong enough to offer them some protection. Free peasants bound themselves and their descendants to labor on the lands of local warriors as *serfs*

(p. 221–22). Lesser warriors agreed to serve greater ones in war and peace as their *vassals* (p. 215), and in turn received from the greater warriors secure possession of land. Everywhere, effective power came to be exercised by the strongest warrior nobles, who could gain the allegiance of the largest number of lesser warriors to swell their armies. They could then use their armies to assert control of the most important resources: land, the labor of peasants, and the goods and treasure obtainable by trade or pillage.

As well as gaining dominance over those below them, the leading warrior nobles also increased their power at the expense of those above them, the rulers of the various Carolingian kingdoms. Partly by grants from Carolingian rivals who sought their support, and partly by simple seizure from feeble rulers, the leading nobles took over royal lands, collected royal revenues, and exercised royal judicial functions. And they treated all these new resources and powers, as well as the rights they acquired over lesser warriors and peasants, as family property. The *hereditary possessor* of such a property was known as a *lord*. The leading lords also took over such former royal offices as *duke* and *count* (p. 204), and converted these into hereditary titles.

There was nothing that the Carolingian monarchs could do to end their dependence on these powerful warriors. In both the eastern and the western Frankish kingdoms, the succession to the kingly office itself came to be determined through *election* by the great lords. When the direct descendants of Charlemagne finally died out — in the eastern kingdom in 911, and in the western kingdom in 987 — the great lords chose new (and powerless) kings from among *themselves*.

Europe Takes Shape

The dissolution of Charlemagne's empire did not mean the end of civilization in Europe. On the contrary, as in the case of the fall of Rome in the fifth century, the collapse of the empire and barbarian invasions actually led to the wider spread of civilization.

Government itself did not simply disintegrate, but rather developed into new and in the long run more effective forms. The great lords had a strong interest in keeping the powers and possessions that they had acquired in the best condition for themselves and their descendants. They therefore began to depart from the Germanic custom — previously followed by nobles as well as kings — of dividing their properties among their children. Instead, during the eleventh century the custom grew up of handing the bulk of the property on to the eldest son. This was known as the right of "primogeniture" (from the Latin for *firstborn*). As a result, "dynasties" of great lords emerged that were able to control fairly stable blocks of territory over several generations. Sooner or later, any individual "dynasty" would usually fall victim to defeat in war, or failure to produce male heirs. As a group, however, the great lords came to constitute a class of regional potentates, presiding effectively over a chaotic but dynamic warrior society. They defended their possessions against Norsemen,

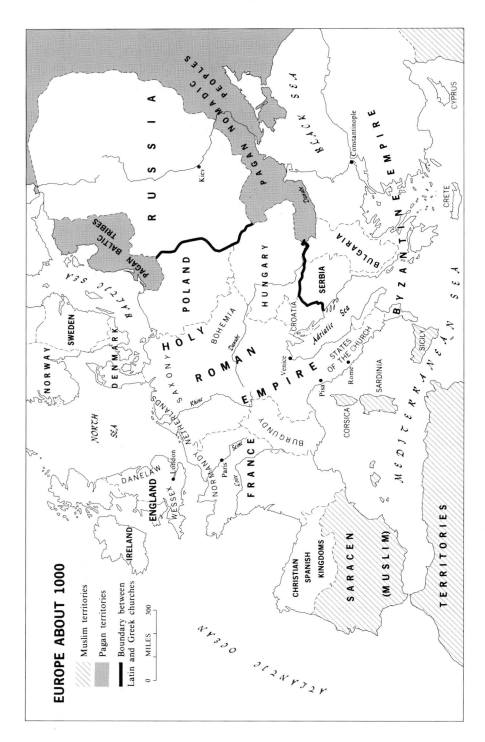

EUROPE ABOUT 1000

Muslim territories

Pagan territories

Boundary between
Latin and Greek churches

0   MILES   300

Hungarians, and Saracens; they undertook counteroffensives, such as the reconquest of Spain or the crusades (pp. 210, 265–70); and they fought continually against each other.

But these lords did more than wage wars. They generously endowed monasteries and supported movements of reform and reorganization in the Church (p. 236). They pushed the peasants on their lands to carve new farms and villages out of the wilderness that at that time covered much of Europe; and they even took a hand in founding towns as centers of trade and industry (though these mostly outgrew their control). The role of these leading nobles in the building of medieval European civilization was an important one.

As for the central authority of kings, though much diminished for a time, it never entirely disappeared and eventually revived. In the *western* Frankish kingdom — now coming to be known by the modern name of France — the new king who replaced the last Carolingian in 987 was Hugh Capet, count of Paris. Though Hugh wielded little power outside the area of northern France that he controlled as count, he did at least manage to hand on the kingship — whole and undivided, like the rest of his possessions — to his son. The great lords, for a while, followed the practice of electing the eldest son of Hugh Capet's family line to the kingship; and eventually, his descendants managed to dispense with the need for election altogether. Having thereby won "independence" from the other great lords, the Capetians would lead the way, by the thirteenth century, to the establishment of a *strong hereditary monarchy* and *state* in France.

Elsewhere in western and central Europe, the revival of central authority was much swifter. In fact, the very same Norse and Hungarian attacks that helped demolish the power of the Carolingians also led to the appearance of new forms of central government, so as to defend whole countries against these barbarians.

Already in ninth-century England, King Alfred of the southern kingdom of Wessex led all the Anglo-Saxons in resistance to the Danes. Even though he had to concede the Danelaw to the invaders (p. 208), it remained under his overlordship; and his tenth-century successors were able to recover the lost territory and build for the first time a united English state.

In the *eastern* Frankish kingdom, feeling the need for strong leadership against the Hungarians, the great lords finally permitted the most powerful family among them, the dukes of Saxony, to fill the office of king. The ablest of that family, Otto I, defeated the Hungarians decisively in 955, ending their raids into Germany. Otto next joined his kingly title to a higher and broader one. He reclaimed the "Roman" imperial title, which had fallen into disuse, and was crowned emperor by Pope John XII at Rome in 962. Actually, Otto's holdings included only Germany and the northern and central portions of Italy; and the empire he founded came to be known as the "Holy Roman Empire of the German Nation," or Holy Roman Empire (p. 210). Though its rulers always had to be elected by the great lords, they remained powerful down to the later Middle Ages, and kept alive the universal political ideal of Augustus and Charlemagne. From the fourteenth century onward the Holy Roman Empire grew progressively feebler, but it lasted well into modern times. It was finally abolished in 1806, but the heartland of its territory was soon thereafter reunited to form a very different entity: the modern national state of Germany (pp. 314–17, 399–400, 469, 496–99).

Even where the barbarian invaders were able to take over parts of western Europe, this did not put an end to effective government, or to civilization as such. As so often before, barbarian conquerors ended by adopting the civilization of the areas they conquered.

In the principal western European territories seized by the Vikings — the Danelaw and Normandy — the Norse settlers agreed to become Christian in return for recognition of their conquests by the English and French kings. In England, Danes and Anglo-Saxons became so mixed in language and customs that within a few generations they were hard to tell apart; in Normandy, the sons and daughters of the invaders already spoke French. From England and France, and under the influence of the adjoining Holy Roman Empire, Christianity and Roman civilization spread back to the Norse homelands, so that by 1000, Norway, Denmark, and Sweden were on the way to becoming Christian kingdoms.

Among the Norse conquerors, the Normans in particular went on to make an important contribution to the development of civilization in the West. In 1066 Duke William of Normandy conquered the Anglo-Saxon kingdom of England, coming not as a barbarian invader but with his banners blessed by the pope, as a claimant to the country's Christian kingship. Building on the institutions of the Anglo-Saxon kingdom, the Norman kings made innovations in the fields of administration and justice that have influenced the laws and government of England, and of countries inheriting English traditions, down to the present.

Meanwhile, other Normans acting independently of their dukes wrested Sicily from Muslim control, and together with warriors from other parts of France, they gave fresh vigor to Christian efforts at the reconquest of Spain (p. 265). In this way, the descendants of barbarian conquerors became Christian warriors, helping their adopted civilization take the offensive against the forces of Islam.

In central Europe, barbarian conquerors were absorbed in much the same way as in the West. After their defeat by Otto I in 955, the Hungarians still held a region extending from the frontiers of the Holy Roman Empire to those of Byzantium (p. 210). Instead of retreating and dispersing as earlier defeated nomads had done, the Hungarians held on to the territory they had conquered, and won acceptance from the Holy Roman Empire by adopting its Latin Christianity and culture. Further north, the chieftains of two groups of Slavic tribes that in earlier centuries had seized much of central Europe (p. 187), the

Czechs (living in Bohemia) and the Poles, now also adopted Latin Christianity so as to win the friendship of the powerful Western empire.

With many of these barbarian peoples, the process of adopting civilization was far from peaceful. Among the Norsemen and Hungarians, as among the Slavs (p. 188), at least some of the leading warriors opposed the change. They clung to traditional pagan belief, which told them that their warrior way of life was pleasing to the gods; they rightly suspected that their rulers would swell from mere chieftains into kings who would demand obedience in peace as well as war; and they feared (usually with less reason) that submission to the Latin Church would bring subjection to the Church's worldly partner, the Holy Roman Empire.

Throughout Scandinavia, and in Poland and Hungary as well, the coming of Christianity led to rebellion and civil war; and the triumph of the new religion was military as well as spiritual. But the upshot was that the ninth- and tenth-century invasions ended in a further spread of Christian and Roman civilization: north to Scandinavia, south to much of Spain, and eastward to Hungary and Poland.

Still further east lay the region of barbarian peoples, mostly of Slavic origin, whose contacts with civilization came mainly through Byzantium (pp. 186–89). In Byzantium, too, under stress of external attack, central power grew stronger. The emperors reorganized their administrative and military system from the seventh century onward, and over several centuries of continual warfare, in spite of many setbacks, they gained territory from both the Arabs and the Slavs. By 1000, some of the Slavic tribes that had taken over southeastern Europe (p. 187) were under Byzantium's rule, and most of the others were subject to its religious and cultural influence.

Byzantium's greatest success was with the Slavs of northeastern Europe, between the Baltic and the Black seas. These Slavs came to be known by the name of the particular group of Swedish Vikings who conquered them in the ninth century (p. 208): the "Rus," or Russians. The Swedish conquerors formed their territories into a powerful state, which they ruled from the important commercial center of Kiev, in the south of their dominions (p. 210). Like the Norse conquerors of Normandy, those of Russia quickly adopted the language and customs (in this case Slavic) of their subjects; but they did not lose their Viking appetite for trade and warfare.

The main trading partner of the Russians, and the frequent victim of their raids, was Byzantium. However, the Russian rulers also admired the empire's way of life, and respected its ancient glory. Finally, in 988, Prince Vladimir of Kiev made a bargain with Byzantium: in return for the exceptional honor of marriage to the emperor's own sister, he threw down the pagan idols of Kiev and was baptized into the Greek Church. Thus, Russia became the easternmost of the states that shared in the religious and cultural heritage of Byzantium.

In this way, the turmoil of the ninth and tenth centuries produced a surprising result: by 1000, three thousand years of interaction — in which Europe had been both the meeting place and the arena of conflict between civilized and barbarian peoples — had all but come to an end (pp. 47–48). In the regions immediately south and east of the Baltic Sea there still lived pagan tribes of Slavic and other ethnic origins. But they were neither powerful nor numerous enough to present a serious threat to civilization, and in the following centuries they would mostly fall victim to their Christian neighbors. Apart from these remnants of the traditional barbarian way of life, all of Europe had come within the orbit of civilization, and this civilization had already developed distinctive features that have characterized it ever since. The Christian religion and the inheritance of Greece and Rome, in spite of all divergences between Rome and Byzantium, gave European civilization its basic unity. Numerous different ethnic groups and independent states supplied the vigor of diversity and competition, as well as the destructive urge to conflict and domination.

It is time now to turn to the political, social, and economic institutions on which this new civilization was built, especially those that had emerged in western Europe; for it was these institutions that would govern Western life and thought until the fifteenth century, and exert a continuing influence well into modern times.

FEUDALISM

Today the ancient Greek city-state and the Roman "world"-state are closer to modern experience and easier to understand than the feudal state of the Middle Ages. Feudalism was not a tidy, unified system spelled out in any decree or constitution. As a matter of fact, it was hardly a "system" in the usual meaning, and the word "feudalism" itself was never used in the medieval period. It was coined by historians centuries afterward to indicate a general set of political relationships that was common during the Middle Ages. These relationships showed marked variations in time and place and were a curious mixture of fact and theory. Nevertheless, the "system" did afford some measure of security and justice to millions of Europeans for more than *five hundred* years. Feudal relationships similar to those of medieval Europe have grown up in like circumstances in other parts of the world — in China, Japan, and India, for example — following the collapse of *centralized* government.

By the eleventh century there were three principal feudal states in Europe: the Holy Roman Empire, revived by Otto the Great; the kingdom of France, ruled by the Capetian monarchs; and the kingdom of England, put together by William the Conqueror, a Norman. In each of these, the monarch claimed *sovereign* (supreme) power over the whole state, even though his actual power was limited by the extent of his personal landholdings (the "royal domain"). As we have seen (pp. 208–9), most of the land was held by dukes, counts, archbishops, abbots, and warrior nobles of lesser degree, who owed certain obligations to the king as their overlord. Except for these obligations, they governed their territories without royal interference.

The barons (a general term for great lords holding property directly from the king) were unable to exercise their control by themselves. In order to gain military aid and to administer his duchy, county, or bishopric (diocese), the holder found it necessary to distribute part of his estate to other warriors. These warriors, in return, became bound to the barons in more or less the same way in which the barons were bound to the king. But all relationships were personal and variable, based upon *local custom*. What existed, in fact, was a host of miniature governments, loosely associated for mutual defense and self-interest.

The Feudal Compact

At first the feudal relationship was extremely vague, consisting essentially of an unwritten agreement that was subject to a wide range of interpretations. By the eleventh century, however, the feudal compact, or contract, had evolved into a fairly standard arrangement governing an exchange of *property* for *personal service*. The king or the duke — whoever granted property to another — stood in the position of "lord"; the recipient of the property was his "vassal." Property in the Middle Ages nearly always meant real estate, for land was the main source of wealth. A piece of land granted by a lord to a vassal was called a "fief" (Latin, *feudum*), and the vassal was entitled to the income from it so long as he fulfilled his *feudal* duties.

The fief carried with it certain *political* responsibilities as well as economic benefits. The vassal was expected to protect the inhabitants of his fief, collect revenues, and dispense justice. Thus, under feudalism political authority was linked to landholding. Since only professional warriors could provide physical protection and undertake the obligations of fief-holding, political and economic power rested in the hands of a military aristocracy (the *nobility*).

Each vassal, in return for the benefits of his fief, owed important obligations to his lord. Chief among these was *military service*. Every vassal was expected to serve his lord in person, and the holder of a large fief was required, in addition, to furnish a body of armed men. In this way the kings and the barons, who found it impracticable to pay for "standing armies," were able to raise fighting forces when needed. At first the vassal's obligation to fight when called on by his lord was unlimited, but gradually it was set by custom at about forty days' service each year.

The holder of a fief was obliged also to serve on the lord's *court*, which was usually held once a month. This court heard disputes among the lord's vassals, often over land and interpretations of feudal rights. It also heard *criminal* charges. The lord presided in all cases, and his vassals acted as judges. It then became the lord's duty to enforce their decision, but should the losing party refuse to accept it, armed conflict could result.

Medieval court procedures were simple, and often harsh, by modern standards. They rested on *custom*, growing out of ancient Germanic practices. One practice, for example, was the testing of accused persons by "ordeal." When evidence was lacking, the court might require individuals to walk barefoot over hot coals, or thrust their arms into boiling water, or risk personal injury in some other way. It was believed that God would save them from harm if they were innocent and telling the truth. But bodily damage from such a test was seen as proof of *guilt*, and the court then imposed the customary penalty for the alleged crime. Not until the thirteenth century did the Church withdraw its support of trial by ordeal. By that time the more humane procedures of ancient Roman law were being revived.

Under the feudal compact a vassal was required to make certain payments to his lord. After receiving his fief he normally paid its first year's income to the lord. This was called "relief," a sort of transfer or inheritance tax. He also owed his lord "hospitality." For a given number of days each year the lord and his family and attendants could demand food, lodging, and entertainment from the vassal. On certain special occasions — the *knighting* of the lord's eldest son or the *marriage* of his eldest daughter — the vassal was required to make another payment. Finally, if the lord was captured in battle his vassal was obliged to pay *ransom* for his release.

All these duties were indeed burdensome. Yet we should remember that the vassal enjoyed the security of his fief and the military protection of his lord. If anyone threatened the vassal's land or person, he had a right to call upon the lord for help. In those violent and dangerous centuries, the feudal compact served as a necessary alliance for the defense of life and property.

Homage and Knighthood

The granting of a fief, with all its requirements, was formalized by the vassal's swearing a pledge of personal loyalty to his lord. This was called the act of *homage*. Usually the vassal knelt down, put his hands between those of his lord, and offered himself as the lord's man (*homo*). The lord accepted the vassal's homage, told him to rise, and embraced him. Next, it was customary for the vassal to make a Christian vow of fealty (faithfulness) in addition. The lord, in exchange for the declaration of vassalage, customarily presented his vassal with a clod of earth or some other symbolic object to serve as the "investiture," by which he invested ("clothed") the vassal with the right to govern and use the fief.

The feudal contract remained in effect so long as lord and vassal honored their mutual obligations or until one of them died. By the custom of primogeniture (p. 209), the eldest son of each came to enjoy the right of succession to his father's position with respect to a fief. But whenever a lord or a vassal died, new pledges of homage and new acts of investiture were necessary.

Only professional warriors (by now called knights) could become vassals and fief-holders. Before a young man could qualify for knighthood, he had to serve an apprenticeship as squire to his father or some other fighting man and then undergo severe tests of courage and military skill. Once he had passed these tests, he was ready for the knighthood ceremony.

There is no record of such ceremonies before the eleventh century, and the early ones noted seem to have been simple affairs. Within a century or so, however, knighthood took on more of an aura of romance and idealism. The ritual of knighting was the initiation of a young man into a professional caste, marked by the presentation of a sword to him by a qualified knight.

This ceremony soon developed spiritual and religious overtones. By the middle of the twelfth century the knight's sword was usually placed upon an altar before the presentation, implying that the knight was obliged to protect the Church. By the thirteenth century the ritual was normally performed in a church or a cathedral, rather than in a manor house or a castle. The initiate spent a night of vigil and prayer before the day of the ceremony, emerging from the ritual as a "soldier of Christ." The earlier, more worldly view of the knight and his role did not disappear, however, and the behavior of the warriors seldom measured up to the ideals of the Church. Yet the transformation of the knighting ceremony into a religious ritual tended to improve the conduct of Europe's military aristocracy.

When a vassal died and left an heir who was not a qualified knight, special arrangements had to be made. If the heir was a son who had not yet attained his majority, the lord would normally serve as guardian until the youth could qualify as a knight and become his vassal. If the sole heir was a daughter, the lord would serve as guardian until he found her a knightly husband. Then her husband, through the act of homage, would receive the fief as the lord's new vassal. Such marriages were one of the chief means of expanding individual and family power during the feudal age. When a vassal died leaving no heir, the fief reverted to the lord, who could keep it for himself or grant it to a new vassal on the same terms.

The Feudalization of the Church

Not all the land of western Europe was held in fief during the Middle Ages. Certain properties were owned outright, with no obligation of vassalage. But most of the usable land, including that held by the Church, was bound up in the feudal pattern. Church lands were held as fiefs by archbishops, bishops, and abbots who had sworn fealty to counts, dukes, princes, and kings. But how, one may ask, could clergymen perform military duties and *kill* on the field of battle? They were not trained knights, and Church law forbade the shedding of blood by the clergy.

The higher clergy were usually the sons of noblemen and familiar with the ways of war. During the ninth and tenth centuries, in fact, they often ignored the Church prohibition and engaged in personal combat. Archbishop Turpin, in the epic *Song of Roland* (p. 262), wields his sword against the infidel and dies a hero's death along with Charlemagne's lay vassals. However, with the reform movement of the eleventh century (to be discussed in the next chapter) clerical vassals were directed to satisfy their military obligations by assigning portions of their properties as fiefs to *warrior nobles*. These warriors pledged, as vassals, to perform the required military services. This arrangement illustrates how, by a series of adaptions to circumstance, feudalism developed as a workable system of government for western Europe. Lay and spiritual lords became closely associated at all levels of authority.

MANORIALISM

In medieval society, the *clergy*, as guardians of people's souls, were regarded as the "first estate" (class). The *nobility*, as protectors of life and property, were ranked as members of the "second estate." All other persons fell into the "third estate" and were considered *commoners*. Though they made up about ninety percent of the population of Europe, these commoners had little political voice and even less social prestige. It is to their life, work, and forms of community that we now turn.

The Manorial Estate

Because land was the basis of wealth in medieval Europe, most of the people were farmers, or peasants. Normally, however, they did not work on individual, privately owned farms. For the principal unit of agricultural production was the manorial estate, or manor. A great fief was usually subdivided into hundreds of these estates, which were also the basic social units of the Middle Ages.

To the peasants who worked on a particular estate, the limits of the manor were the limits of their world. Ordinarily they were not allowed to leave the manor at all, and only rarely did they go beyond the nearest town or fair. In some areas peasants enjoyed the right of *pilgrimage*, once each year, to Christian shrines (pp. 234, 264). But travel, even when permitted, was seldom undertaken because of its perils. Roads were poor, hostels few, and banditry widespread. Manorial estates ranged in size from about three hundred acres to, perhaps, three thousand. The average estate was probably about a thousand acres, supporting some two or three hundred people. The estate had to be large enough to support its manorial community and to enable its lord to fulfill his feudal obligations, but it could not be so large as to be unmanageable as a farming unit.

The productive heart of the manor consisted of the arable (plowable) fields, and more than half the estate was normally used for crops. Technical innovations (especially between the seventh and tenth centuries) significantly boosted crop yields in western Europe; these innovations included the heavy metal plow, the horse collar, and nailed iron horseshoes. The latter two inventions enabled horses to replace the slower oxen as the principal work animals. Another innovation, which particularly affected the northern half of Europe, was the three-field system of cultivation. The arable fields of the manor were usually divided into three planting areas. In a given farming year, beginning in the fall, one of these areas would be planted, another in the spring, and the third left fallow (unseeded). In the following year the fallow area would be planted in the fall, the previous fall area in the spring, and the previous spring section left unseeded; and in the third year, the three areas would be rotated yet again. Thus, each year two-thirds of the arable lands were in use while one-third was lying fallow. This simple *conservation* measure helped to maintain the fertility of the soil, as did the use of animal manures.

A unique feature of medieval land cultivation was the "strip" system. A peasant who held land or who was bound to work certain land did not have a compact area assigned to him. Instead, he held long, narrow strips in each of the three planting areas (*Fig. 5-5*). Although the origins of this system are uncertain, several reasons for its widespread use have been suggested. First, the system permitted the farmers to work in *each* of the planting areas, thus allowing their continuous employment. Second, because work animals were scarce and small (by modern standards), plowing and harvesting had to be done on a *cooperative* basis; the large, unfenced "open fields," where the strips lay side by side, were easier to work in this manner than smaller fields enclosed by fences or hedges. The strip system also made it possible to distribute fairly the good and poor areas of land among the peasants. Finally, it guarded against disastrous loss to any one farm family. If crop failure struck one area of the estate, the peasant suffering loss there would have strips elsewhere to help carry him through.

The shape of the strips was apparently governed by the techniques of cultivation. One long furrow could be plowed more efficiently than several short ones. The typical strip was a rod wide (about seventeen feet), allowing ample turning space for a team of oxen or horses, and forty rods long (a *furlong*, or one-eighth of a mile). A unit of these dimensions could be plowed comfortably in a morning or an afternoon, which meant that the workday could be conveniently planned. The lord of the manor, according to his privilege, usually retained a special plot of land for his exclusive use (the "close"). This, together with his strips in the open fields, was known as the lord's "demesne." Other strips were set aside for the benefit of the resident priest ("God's acre").

In addition to the arable lands, supporting areas were essential for the estate. There was a common forest or *woodland* where the peasants were permitted to gather fuel, a *meadow* to provide hay for the work animals, and a *pasture* where the sheep and cattle grazed. A water source (usually a *stream* or a pond) was indispensable, as well as an area for dumping waste. Only a small section of the estate was occupied by the village itself, while the lord's residence (a manor house or a castle) was usually located on a commanding site some

5-5 Plan of a manor.

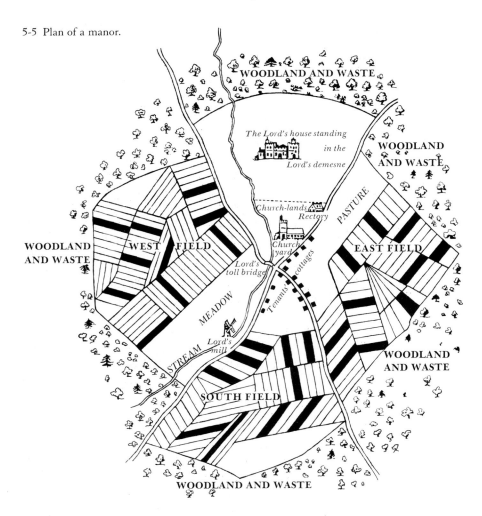

distance from the flimsy cottages of the peasants. The barns and outbuildings of the manor, in fact, were likely to be more substantial than the thatch-roofed, mud-walled homes of the village. Around these windowless cottages the villagers kept small vegetable gardens and raised a few hens, pigs, or goats to supplement their diet. The food grown in the open fields consisted chiefly of staples: wheat, rye, oats, barley, peas, or beans. The common beverage was homemade beer or wine.

Every village had a church and a priest's house. In addition, the lord usually provided (for a fee) a grinding mill, a bake oven, and a wine press to serve the villagers. Some of the peasants became specialists in manual arts such as metalworking (blacksmithing) and shoemaking. Until the later Middle Ages the manor produced little surplus for *exchange*, depending on home manufactures for almost all its needs.

The People of the Manor

The records of village life prior to the thirteenth century are meager. But we do know that in those mute centuries the basic habits of work, law, worship, and play evolved into established custom. And we have abundant evidence that village life as it existed in the thirteenth century persisted with little change for the following five hundred years. The rise of trade and the growth of cities, the emergence of national states, the struggles between religious factions — all seem to have had slight effect on the basic patterns and rhythms of rural life. One of the striking facts about medieval life, in contrast to modern times, was the general lack of *privacy*. Homes were tiny, consisting usually of *one* room. Adults, children, and animals often spent the night under the same roof. Such "togetherness" may explain, in part, the appeal of monastic orders in the Middle Ages: they offered the security and privacy of a convent cell (pp. 168–71).

The lord of the manor was presumably guided by the rules of God and by custom; in any case, his word was law. Whether a simple knight or a noble of high degree, he was often away from home for long periods of time. He was a warrior as well as a landlord and had his feudal obligations to fulfill. When he was not performing those duties, his favorite pastime was hunting. He typically took little direct interest in farming and left the management of his lands and local justice to his overseers (*stewards* or *bailiffs*). The lord's wife spent most of her days in the manor house supervising the servants, household operations, and entertainment of guests. (The food at her disposal was more plentiful and varied than that available to commoners.) If she was a lady of high rank, she might also act as a partner in the conduct of her husband's political and administrative affairs.

From his own farms and payments by the peasants in kind (crops), the lord normally took about half the total produce of the estate. This may appear excessive, but we must remember that as a mounted knight he had to feed his personal aides as well as the members of his own family. In addition, he was obliged to make certain payments in kind to his overlord. Finally, he maintained a *reserve* of grain in his barns, so that in years of crop failure he would be able to provide the peasants with food. He could not allow them to starve, for, aside from humane considerations, they represented his labor force. Nevertheless, *famine* was always a threat — and sometimes a reality — throughout the Middle Ages.

Most of the peasants were *serfs* (Latin, *servi*), whose special status and ties to the soil were inherited. The origins of serfdom can be traced back to the western provinces of the Roman Empire in the third and fourth centuries (pp. 135–36); by 1000 it had spread beyond the empire's former frontiers, and was normal throughout most of Europe. During the turbulent times of the early Middle Ages, whole communities of farmers had placed themselves under some powerful warrior for protection (p. 208). And it was always possible, even later, for peasants to commit themselves and all of their descendants to perpetual servitude, in return for a piece of land to cultivate. In addition, in territories that had once belonged to the Roman Empire many serfs were descended from earlier generations of slaves who had worked on the estates of great landowners (p. 101); in their case, serfdom represented an improvement in status. Nevertheless, a serf was legally unfree. The lord could free a serf when he chose, but otherwise serfs were held to their obligations.

The status of serfs was hardly enviable. They were bound to work on their assigned strips of land and to turn over to the lord a fixed share of their crop. They also had to cultivate and harvest the lord's lands and the strips set aside for the parish priest. In addition, they could be called on to build roads, clear forests, and do other work whenever the lord demanded. The serfs' children were likewise bound to the manor; no members of their families could leave the estate or marry without the consent of the lord. A serf's eldest son normally inherited the rights and duties of his father.

Peasants whose ancestors had managed to avoid serfdom had the status of *freemen*. This did not necessarily mean that they were better off; some, in fact, lived on the edge of starvation. If the freeman farmed land, he did so as a farm *tenant*, paying rent to the lord in the form of a share of his crop. The lord could evict a freeman whenever he saw fit, whereas a serf could not legally be separated from his land.

Free or not, the peasants of a manorial village shared a hard and isolated life. Husbands and fathers exercised primary rights in their households, but men, women, and children alike toiled together in the fields. Illiterate and uneducated, they knew little of the outside world, save for news and gossip brought by the lord, the priest, or traveling peddlers and clerics. The course of their lives was shaped by the pattern of labor, the seasons, the cycle of religious holidays, and the round of births, marriages, and deaths.

In spite of the harsh life to which it condemned the peasants, manorialism was a highly successful form of economic and social organization. The three-field system was more productive than earlier farming methods. More secure than freemen, and with far greater property rights than slaves, the serfs had an incentive to found families and increase the amount of land they farmed. The lords had a strong interest in helping the serfs to do these things, for the amount of labor and resources at the lords' command would increase as a result. Partly for these reasons, the emergence of manorialism by 1000 was followed by three centuries of agricultural boom. Throughout Europe, the serfs cut down forests, drained swamps, and brought grasslands under the plow. Thousands of new villages sprang up, and by 1300 the population of Europe had risen from roughly forty million to about one hundred million.

This *internal colonization*, as it is called, was spurred on by the lords, who founded new manors on uncultivated land and moved serfs into them. But to get the cooperation of the serfs, the lords had to offer them concessions, such as larger holdings, smaller crop deliveries, and fewer hours of work. So profitable was it for the lords to bring new land under cultivation that they did not hesitate to offer these concessions, and of course the serfs were eager to accept them. In time, the lords even found it preferable to abolish servile obligations altogether and turn their serfs into free tenants, paying rent in produce or cash. (The lords, however, usually retained manorial powers of government and justice, and ultimate ownership of the land.) In western Europe this eventually led, by the end of the Middle Ages, to the almost complete disappearance of serfdom (pp. 288–89). Already by 1300, the peasants had gained considerably in prosperity and freedom.

In addition, European society as a whole had become much wealthier, and also more complex and diverse. As the population swelled and peasants and lords both prospered, so commerce and industry also began to grow, and the number of people who made a living by these activities increased. Alongside the manor, the typical community of peasants and lords, there appeared another type of community, formed by merchants and craftsmen: the town.

THE RISE OF TRADE AND TOWNS

While the manor remained the principal unit of European society until the eighteenth century, the seeds of "modern" civilization were being nourished as early as the eleventh. With the reopening of trade routes and the appearance of new marketing centers came the emergence of the towns that were destined to convert Europe from a *rural* to an *urban* society. The lords and peasants who remained on the manorial estates played a limited role in the growth of these towns. An expanded cast of characters gradually appeared there, consisting of merchants, bankers, lawyers, artisans, and unskilled laborers. In the thirteenth century these groups made up but a fraction of Europe's population (less than ten percent), but their numbers were destined to grow until, by the twentieth century, they would be a majority (p. 512).

Origins

There was little resemblance or connection between the city-states of the ancient world and the new communities of western Europe. Athens, for example, was founded by warrior landholders under the patronage of a goddess. The Greek *polis*, or the Roman *civitas*, was seen as a sacred and sovereign community, whose leading members lived in town but held properties in the surrounding farmland (pp. 52–54). It was loyally supported by the citizens of both town and country as a *kinship* unit. Medieval towns, by contrast, were largely isolated from rural society. They developed with the revival of trade, and their immediate aims were narrowly materialistic. Their founders were generally not warriors, nobles, or kings but landless commoners, most of whom came originally from manorial villages. The townspeople had to struggle for many generations to win from the landed aristocracy a degree of self-government for their communities.

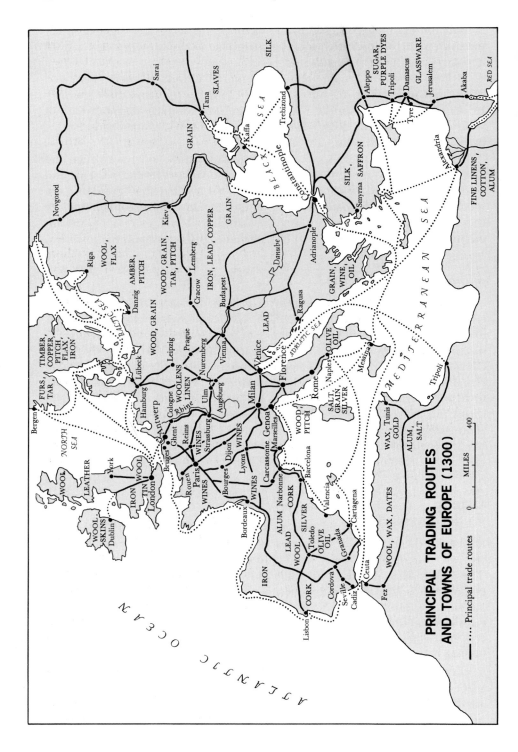

PRINCIPAL TRADING ROUTES AND TOWNS OF EUROPE (1300)

..... Principal trade routes

The stimulus for the revival of trade came from the Mediterranean world. Byzantium and Islam were vigorous commercial societies and manufactured elegant articles for export. Their merchandise was brought to western Europe by overland routes through Spain or, more commonly, through Venice and other port cities of Italy (p. 224). Constantinople was the main source of luxury goods, which found a growing market among European aristocrats. Those who could afford them sought spices (pepper, ginger, and cinnamon) to relieve the monotony of medieval cooking; silks and satins; precious jewels; statues, rugs, and tapestries. It was the desire of the well-to-do for such luxuries that set in motion the wheels of commerce in Europe and thus led to the rise of towns.

Gold and silver had largely disappeared in the West, and the Europeans had to sell goods in order to pay for their imports. Their commodities included woolens and linens, horses, weapons and armor, timber, and furs. From all parts of Europe caravans carried these items across the Alps, chiefly to Milan. There they were taken over by merchants from the Italian port cities for shipment to the East. Northern Italy thus became the focus of the reviving commerce between West and East.

This trade first became important in the eleventh century and expanded rapidly during the twelfth and thirteenth centuries. It was closely connected with the rise in population and production in the countryside. With more land being cultivated by improved methods, the owners of manors and even better-off peasants had more to spend on the luxuries that the towns had to offer. Likewise, with some assurance that crops could be marketed in the towns, peasants and lords had an additional incentive for increasing farm output. Church lords and nobles, instead of consuming all the food and supplies that the peasants produced for them, sold some of the produce in the towns, in return for cash; or instead of receiving their income in goods and services, they freed their serfs and charged them rents to be paid in money. Gold and silver were being mined and coined again and were passing into circulation with the speed-up in trade. Money, little used in the early Middle Ages, was now seen as the key to new comforts and delights.

The wool and textile industries provided the bulk of European exports. These industries centered in the Low Countries, where conditions were favorable to sheep-raising. In time this region gained fame also for its manufacture of woolen cloth, and Flemish producers finally had to turn to outside sources of raw wool to satisfy their needs. English farmers and landlords met this demand by converting more of their holdings into pastureland. After the thirteenth century, both in England and on the continent, there was a growing cash market for wool. A single peasant, with only a few sheep, might thus become a participant in the trading revolution.

Along with the trading revolution and connected with it there took place what is sometimes called the "industrial revolution" of the Middle Ages. Though this was far smaller in scope than the Industrial Revolution of the eighteenth and nineteenth centuries (pp. 501–5), it displayed some of the same features: an increase in production, often based on the use of labor-saving machinery, and a continuing spurt of technical inventiveness.

This spirit of technical progress was shared by all classes of society. Feudal lords from the tenth century onward were forward-looking enough to equip their manors with water-mills, thereby both easing the labor of peasants in grinding grain, and also finding a new source of profits for themselves (p. 220). (Later in the Middle Ages, water-powered machinery was adapted by inventive craftsmen to speed up the production of woolen textiles, paper, and finally gunpowder.) Cistercian monks of the twelfth century (p. 237) who retreated to the wilderness in search of God also called in prospectors to search for iron ore — and blacksmiths who could work it — thereby playing a pioneer role in the growth of the iron industry. And the lives of fourteenth-century townspeople came to be regulated by one of the most influential of medieval innovations, the mechanical clock. High in a tower of town hall or cathedral, it was visible to all as its hands moved in step with the movement of the sun itself; and all could hear its tones as — with no human intervention — it struck the changing hours of the day. Automatic operation and exact precision of measurement, two typical features of modern technology and science, were significantly advanced by the clockmakers of the Middle Ages.

The Location and Appearance of Towns

The medieval towns were essentially trading posts where local produce could be sold and foreign merchandise purchased. Traveling merchants, moving along familiar land and water routes, carried imported goods from northern Italy to such trading sites as the junction of highways, the confluence of rivers, or the capital of a duchy or a kingdom (p. 224). Ancient Roman cities that happened to be well located reawakened as bustling towns. The community surrounding a cathedral (that is, the headquarters of a bishop or an archbishop) might also become an important trading center.

Physical protection for the merchants was, of course, a necessity. They usually set up their shops in the shadow of a castle or a fortified settlement — then raised walls around their "new" town, linking it to the old. The English word "town" derives from the Anglo-Saxon *tun* (enclosure). And the widely used suffix "borough" (French *bourg*, German *burg*) originally meant a fortified community. As a town grew outward from its center, successive walls were constructed to afford continuing protection. The remains of these walls may still be seen in many of the old cities of Europe, notably Carcassonne in France (*Fig. 5-6*), Avila (Spain), and Rothenburg (Germany).

Understandably, space was at a premium in these towns. Streets and passageways were kept as narrow as possible, so that a maximum number of buildings could be erected. And the buildings themselves had as many stories as safety would permit. Even so, housing was painfully cramped — tighter, sometimes, than the space in peasants' cottages. There was very little town planning, and sanitation was notoriously poor. From the very earliest times

5-6 Walled town of Carcassonne, France, as restored.

European cities faced problems of congestion, traffic jams, infectious diseases, and slums.

Nevertheless, there was a certain order in most medieval towns. By the thirteenth century a typical pattern appeared. The town was usually dominated by the towers or spires of its main church. Next in importance were the town hall and the buildings of the various trading and industrial organizations (the guilds). The heart of the town was the central marketplace and shops. At first most of these were the places of traders, but artisans of all kinds (weavers, smiths, bakers) soon found they could sell their services in town, and they set up workshops there. Thus, towns became centers of industry as well as trade.

The new towns presented an avenue of escape to men and women who were seeking release from the drudgery and routine of the manorial village. This was especially true for serfs who longed to cast off their inferior status. They could, if they grew desperate enough, run away from the manor and lose themselves in a distant town. According to the custom of the period, they were legally *free* if the lord failed to recapture them within a "year and a day." (Later in the Middle Ages serfs could gain their freedom by making a cash payment to their lord.)

A New Social Element: The Bourgeois

Yet life in town was by no means a guarantee of absolute freedom, for the towns had a social structure of their own — though one not quite so rigid as that of the manor (pp. 221–22). At the top were the leading merchants and moneylenders and the heads of the guilds. Beneath them were skilled artisans and clerks, and at the bottom were apprentices and unskilled laborers.

The members of the highest group dominated civic affairs and came to be known by the end of the Middle Ages as the *bourgeois* (townspeople). They constituted a new social element in European society, which gained in wealth and power as the centuries passed. Even so, the bourgeois were regarded as *commoners*, legally and socially inferior to the clergy and the nobility. Later, they came to be referred to also as the *middle* class: *between* the nobility and the mass of commoners.

Because the whole pattern of life in the towns was different from that of the feudal estate, a new plan for government had to be made for the new communities. The townspeople sought special *charters* that would free them from the customary obligations of the feudal relationship and would permit them to establish appropriate rules of their own. These charters, granted by the king, nobleman, or bishop holding authority over the area, recognized the citizens of the town as constituting a political body, or *corporation*, with legal privileges and powers. In return for these privileges, and in place of feudal services, the corporation made regular payments of money to the grantor. The form of government differed from one town to another, but in most places control rested in the hands of a governing *council* and an official called a *mayor* or *burgomaster*. Though voting rights (for adult males only) were often quite liberal, it was uncommon for any but the leading bourgeois families to hold important offices.

Economic Theory and Control: The Guilds

The governing council imposed strict political control on the community. Legally, the citizens of a town were free individuals, but the idea of *collective* responsibility and regulation was accepted in town and countryside alike. Economic activities in the town were kept under close supervision. Authority over trade and industry was delegated to special corporations, called *guilds*, which acted in accordance with these general principles: production and sale of goods were *common* ventures limited to members of the guild; standards of business practice and quality of merchandising must be upheld; and the price of every commodity should be set at a "just" figure, corresponding to the amount and type of labor that produced it.

The principal organization in most towns was the *merchant* guild, which established rules governing the marketplaces. These rules controlled the times and places at which goods could be sold, the standard weights and measures, and the grades and prices of the commodities sold. At first the merchant guild included most of the tradespeople in a given town. With growing specialization, however, one group after another split off from the parent unit to form independent *craft* guilds: weavers, dyers, tailors, carpenters, masons, silversmiths, bakers, barbers, and the like. The number of separate craft guilds differed from place to place; by the thirteenth century there might have been as many as thirty or forty such guilds in a single town.

The primary function of a craft guild was to supervise the production of goods and the training of artisans. Craftsmen were classified as masters, journeymen, or apprentices. Only the masters had the right to operate workshops and train others; they alone were voting members of the guild and directed its policies, and their coveted status was won by other craftsmen only after long experience and proof of excellence. Before the masters certified a journeyman to their rank, they customarily required him to submit an example of his workmanship. This effort, the finest he was capable of, was called his "masterpiece." Journeymen were licensed artisans who had served an apprenticeship. They were employed by the masters and were usually paid at a fixed rate per day (French, *journée*). Before becoming a journeyman, an individual was obliged to work for a specified period of time, ranging from two to seven years, as an apprentice (learner) in the shop of a master. In return for their labor, apprentices received only food and lodging. Though women of the towns were permitted to perform some skilled and unskilled services, they were generally excluded from guild membership.

The guilds were primarily economic units, but they also performed personal and social functions. If a member fell sick, was put in jail, or got into some other kind of trouble, he could count on help from the guild brotherhood. The guilds provided proper ceremonies on the occasions of births, marriages, and funerals; they conducted social affairs; and they celebrated church festivals as a body. Each one, moreover, honored a particular Christian saint (p. 234) who was associated by tradition with a given craft. (St. Joseph, for example, was honored by the carpenters.) The guilds often dedicated altars or chapels in the town church to their special saints. In all their varied activities they embodied the *corporate* and *community* spirit so characteristic of medieval society.

6

The Flowering
of Medieval Culture

During the eleventh century, as the disturbances of earlier centuries passed, the political and economic institutions of western Europe took on strength and stability. The order that emerged was to endure for some five hundred years. Feudalism and manorialism, the towns and the guilds, furnished a foundation on which Western society could build a rich and distinctive culture.

THE MEDIEVAL CHURCH

In the preceding chapter we concentrated on the material side of life in the Middle Ages. But medieval men and women were more concerned with what lies *beyond* this world; they looked toward life eternal. And because the central role of the Church was to guide souls to everlasting salvation, the Church was regarded as the *primary* institution in society.

So widespread was the Christian faith, and so confident the expectation of a better life after death, that the era is often called the Age of Faith. Never before had the Church been so dominant in the affairs of Westerners, nor has it been so since. Though priests and bishops looked toward eternity, they paid close attention to what happened on earth. For what people did in the "here and now" could bear upon their fate in the hereafter. Consequently, the clergy felt they had a duty to examine the heart and deeds of every Christian and to ensure that human institutions reflected the will of God.

The Sacraments

The extraordinary power of the medieval Church rested solidly on the trust of the people. The rich left it generous gifts, and bishops and abbots thereby acquired vast properties in land, serfs, animals, and buildings. The Church had deeper and broader sources of strength, however — among them, the direct and intimate relationship with every inhabitant of the "Christian commonwealth." For the Church was believed to be the sole door to *salvation*; a bishop, by his authority to open or close that door (by excommunication — p. 154), possessed an immense influence.

The sacraments (defined as instruments of God's grace, or divine aid) were in the keeping of the clergy. A general theory of the sacraments, as well as an explanation of each of the rites, had appeared by the eleventh century. It ran as follows: Adam and Eve's Original Sin against God's will has stained all human beings with guilt. Although this guilt can be washed away through the rite of baptism, men and women, by their sinful nature, continue to fall into disobedience. Only through divine aid (grace) can they be strengthened and forgiven. And the Lord in his goodness has created the sacraments as the means of dispensing that grace. Priests alone can administer the sacraments, for priests acquire miraculous power when they receive, through a bishop, the rite of *ordination*. By this rite they acquire a portion of the powers originally given by the Holy Spirit to the twelve apostles.

Seven sacraments, counting *ordination* itself, were recognized. Through *baptism* the individual was initiated into church membership and cleansed of the stain and penalty of past sin. The second sacrament was *confirmation*. Whereas baptism was customarily administered to infants, this rite was administered (by a bishop) only after individuals had received religious instruction and had expressed their willingness to live as Christians. Through it, they were confirmed in their acceptance of Christ and were strengthened in faith by the Holy Spirit. Because ordination, baptism, and confirmation each left a special mark upon the soul that was believed to be indelible, these sacraments were administered only once during a person's lifetime.

The other four sacraments could be repeated. Foremost among them was the *Eucharist* (*Mass*), which was believed to provide food for the soul. The Church taught that at a certain moment in the rite the bread and wine were transformed (*transubstantiated*) into the body and blood of the Savior. The recipient, sharing in the strength of Christ himself, would thus be aided in doing good and resisting evil. Christians were required to take the Eucharist at least once each year. But the Eucharist was beneficial only if received worthily — that is, only if the individual was in a "state of grace," forgiven for past sins. To prepare for the Eucharist, the individual took the sacrament of *penance*, which consisted of the following steps: inward repentance (sorrowful regret) for misdeeds, oral confession, and acceptance of a penalty. The person was then pardoned by the priest. When Christians appeared to be on the point of death, they were given the sacrament of *extreme unction* (last rites), which granted them final forgiveness for the sins of their lifetime.

The seventh sacrament was *matrimony*, the joining together of husband and wife. The clergy compared the matrimonial bond to the union between Christ and the Church and held it to be unbreakable so long as the two partners lived. Should one of them die, the survivor could take another spouse by repeating the matrimonial rite. This sacrament and that of ordination were not essential to the individual's salvation. But the other five were compulsory, and the clergy taught that only through them could a Christian reach heaven.

Christian Devotional Life

The sacraments were central to the spiritual life of medieval men and women. They were part of many religious observances that followed the calendar and the clock. These included all the formal worship services (liturgy) of the clergy and the laity; the most important of these services was the Mass. Though Masses were performed every day, the main service was on Sunday, when attendance was required of all Christians. In the larger churches this became an elaborate performance, with the chief priest and his assistants wearing rich and colorful robes. The appeal to the senses was heightened by the use of music, incense, and gold and silver vessels. These sights and sounds combined to create an atmosphere of mystery and awe.

The experience of the Mass strengthened human associations in the Age of Faith. Clergy and laity were joined in a common drama as men and women of all social classes participated together under one roof. They were taught that the sacrament was a mystic union — a holy communion — between Christ and themselves. No other ritual has symbolized more completely the intimate association between human and divine beings.

In addition to conducting worship services, the clergy had the further obligation of saying daily prayers, called the "Divine Office." They used an authorized book of prayers (breviary) that marked the ones to be recited at seven specified times each day (the canonical hours). Prayers consisted, for the most part, of praise and thanksgiving to God, together with pleas for guidance and aid. The Divine Office also served as a continuing reminder to the clergy that they should dedicate their whole lives to praising the Lord and fulfilling his will. The laity believed that the offering of prayers by the clergy brought benefits to the entire society of Christians.

Around these official devotions were countless informal practices, which made up the "popular religion" of the times. These special devotions, or cults, grew out of the beliefs, fears, and hopes of the common people. While such practices were sometimes regulated by the priesthood, they were often outside the bounds of official doctrine, as we shall see.

The cult of the Crucifixion, for example, was not the result of priestly teaching. It grew out of a deep and spontaneous sympathy for Jesus as a *man*. In earlier centuries theologians had tended to stress the role of Jesus as *God*. His life, death, and resurrection were seen as part of a grand design by which the Lord overcame the devil and opened the way to salvation. The Crucifixion, in this view, was an act of divine majesty — above the fears and pains of ordinary human beings. Early Christian art usually portrayed the Savior as the risen Christ sitting in royal dignity upon the heavenly throne. Sometime after the year 1000, a new view of his life on earth began to gain attention. It emphasized Jesus' *human* experiences — his struggles, humiliations, and physical sufferings. Both theologians and the common people drew fresh meaning from the Passion (Suffering) of their Lord, recognizing in his agony their own anguish and miseries. Artists increasingly showed the dying Christ hanging heavily from the Cross. Gradually the crucifix, which aroused in pious hearts the deepest feelings of compassion and love, became the most popular devotional object (*Fig. 6-1*).

Interpretations of the gospel were influenced by this more human view of Jesus. The changes are reflected most clearly in Christian sculpture and painting: the infant Jesus in early portraits appears as a kingly figure, but during the Middle Ages he was made to look like any infant held in the arms of a loving mother. And Mary herself was presented in a way ever more tender and human.

The cult of the Virgin was exceedingly popular in the Middle Ages. The monasteries played a leading role in developing it, but ordinary people responded warmly to the appeal of Mary. Aside from her role as the mother of God, she personified the Christian ideals of womanhood, love, and sympathy. During an upsurge of religious fervor in the thirteenth century, many of the

6-1 Giotto. *Crucifix*.
Santa Croce, Florence.

great new cathedrals were dedicated to "Notre Dame" (Our Lady, Mary). A rich literature and a host of legends came into being that told of the countless miracles of the Virgin. She was pictured as loyal and forgiving toward all who honored her and ready to give earthly benefits and heavenly rewards to those who prayed to her. From time to time the higher clergy grew concerned over the intensity of this Marian cult. There was always the risk that honoring the Virgin might compete with worship of God. The bishops nonetheless encouraged the cult as part of general reverence for the saints.

Mary ranked highest among the saints, but there were hundreds of lesser figures who also attracted prayer and devotions. It is difficult to understand all this except in terms of the strong *will to believe* among medieval people. Faith in marvels, omens (signs), and supernatural appearances was nearly universal; devils and demons were thought to lurk everywhere; and miraculous cures and resurrections of the dead were reported almost daily. These wonders, many of which were credited to the saints, fired the imagination of the ignorant and educated alike.

The saints were the heroes of the Middle Ages, as the epic warriors had been the heroes of classical Greece (pp. 73–74). They included the twelve apostles and the early martyrs, as well as a host of later men and women. Their individual fame as preachers, hermits, and workers of miracles became established by tradition; it was not until the thirteenth century that the popes assumed the exclusive right to identify them formally as saints (canonization). The bishops, from early times, required Christians to show the saints the special honor of *veneration* (deep reverence). Though it was taught that veneration should not become *worship* (which was reserved for God), medieval Christians directed a large share of their devotions to the saints. These included pilgrimages to the shrines associated with them (pp. 218, 264).

The Church taught that saints have the power to perform miracles after their death as well as during their life on earth. In heaven, because of their privileged position, they can win divine aid for mortals by interceding (pleading) with God. Moreover, some of their power was thought to stay on earth in their physical remains (relics). Hence, immense value was placed on the bones, teeth, and intimate possessions of departed saints. No church or monastery was without its collection of relics — its "spiritual endowment." To this day the treasuries of many European churches are rich with golden reliquaries (containers) and their precious contents.

Hardly any act was undertaken in the Middle Ages without first calling upon the saints. Oaths and treaties were sworn on saintly remains; townspeople carried them in religious processions; before setting out on a dangerous journey or campaign, men prayed to a saint and touched the saint's relics; knights often inserted holy bits in the hilts of their swords. The skulls, bones, and hairs of saints were the most common relics, but some stranger items were preserved as well: the sweat, tears, and umbilical cord of Jesus; St. Joseph's breath, and the Virgin's milk. Fragments of the "true" Cross seemed to be

everywhere — enough, it was said later, to build a ship. Several heads of John
the Baptist were claimed, as were the whole skeletons of many lesser saints.
The genuineness of these relics was not questioned by the faithful, and their
number, for the whole of Europe, ran into the millions. At last, by the close of
the Middle Ages, some devout Christians began to express doubts of their
authenticity.

Monastic Reform Movements: Cluny and the Friars

In addition to providing spiritual guidance, the medieval Church served
society in numerous other ways. The "secular" clergy (p. 170) acted as coun-
selors and administrators for rulers; bishops and archbishops functioned as
vassals of kings and emperors. Different sorts of services were carried on by the
"regular" clergy, who lived in the great monastic houses. After the founding of
Monte Cassino in 529, monasteries began to appear all over western Europe,
most of them independent houses pledged to the Benedictine Rule (pp. 168–
71). Although their primary function was to serve as a refuge for ascetics seeking to devote themselves to God, the monks answered the needs of the times by
taking on other important functions as well.

The regular clergy preserved and copied manuscripts (p. 205) and provided elementary schooling for youths planning to enter the clergy, thus keeping literacy and learning alive. At the same time they preserved in their workshops the useful arts of weaving, pottery-making, and metalworking, and in
the fields they developed more efficient tools and techniques of farming. Over
the centuries the religious houses became large landholders, and, though the
monks themselves were bound by vows of poverty, the corporate (collective)
wealth of the monasteries rose steadily.

As a result of this growing wealth the monastic establishments became
more and more involved in the affairs of the world. The head of a monastery — the abbot — held the monastery's property as a fief from some overlord,
and he had the usual military, financial, and political responsibilities of a vassal.
He met his obligations, in part, by granting some of the monastery's lands to
knights, who, as vassals of the abbot, performed the required military duties.
From the ninth to the twelfth century military units from monastic fiefs were
important components of feudal armies.

The kings and the feudal barons frequently chose their administrators
from among members of the regular clergy (as well as the secular). At a time
when few people could read, the regulars furnished a valuable supply of civil
officials. Because the monasteries from which they came were well rewarded
for these services, the houses became richer and richer, and the monks became
more deeply involved in secular affairs. These developments improved the
stability of the government and the economy, but they tended to interfere with
the ascetic way of life once so characteristic of the regular clergy. By the tenth
century some Church leaders had become alarmed by the growing divergence
between monastic ideals and practices.

Wealth brought the ways of the world into the religious orders themselves. Some abbots lived as elegantly as great nobles, and ordinary monks enjoyed the produce of the prospering estates. Plenty of food and wine led to a broader pursuit of pleasure. Obedience to monastic rules weakened, the vow of chastity was taken less seriously, and physical labor grew less attractive. The monks tended, at the same time, to neglect the arts of reading and writing.

Standards of learning and conduct fell to an even lower level among the secular clergy. The appointment of bishops and archbishops was generally controlled by powerful nobles, who often sold these offices (positions) to the highest bidder. Some of these "successors of the apostles" were more active in politics than in spiritual matters. Many parish priests also fell short of their responsibilities; some were unable to read; some, contrary to Church law, had wives and families. The popes, as the monarchs of the Church, might have tried to correct these abuses, but they were as open as other bishops to the influences of the times. They, too, sought to extend their wealth and power, and some of them owed their very office to the efforts of local nobles or the Holy Roman emperor (pp. 211–12).

Distressed by the widespread corruption within the Church, a few conscientious rulers, bishops, and abbots started a program of reform. The most far-reaching of these efforts was undertaken in the Burgundian monastery of Cluny, founded in 910 by the Duke of Aquitaine. In order to protect themselves from local interference, the Cluniac monks placed themselves under the direct authority of the pope. The first abbot, Berno, set out to revive the strictness of the Benedictine Rule. From Cluny the move for reform spread to all parts of the clergy.

Though Cluny aimed at restoration of the Church as a whole, it focused upon monastic organization. Formerly each Benedictine house had been independent; now the abbots of Cluny proceeded to found "daughter" houses subject to the "mother" house. Their purpose was to protect individual houses from falling under local political influences. Within a century there were some three hundred Cluniac houses spread across western Europe, but only the mother house was called a *monastery*. The daughter houses were called *priories*, and the priors (subabbots) who governed them were appointed by the Great Abbot of Cluny.

Heads of the older Benedictine houses also came under the influence of the reform spirit; bishops, too, and the papacy itself were caught up in this revival of Christian purpose and discipline. The Cluniac movement was a striking success. Monastic life was restored to something like its original rigor; simony (the selling of Church services or offices) was exposed and reduced; and the rule of priestly celibacy (prohibition against marriage) was more strictly enforced. Part of Cluny's success can be attributed to a series of extraordinary abbots. Moreover, because its monks came chiefly from noble families, Cluny took on an aristocratic style and enjoyed generous support and gifts from the landed classes. In the end, Cluny's very success brought about its decline as a model of reform. By the twelfth century, surrounded by mounting wealth and influence, the monks of Cluny slipped into the ways of material ease.

Repeating the Cluniac pattern, a new order now appeared. It, too, ran its reform course and then slackened. This order arose in a barren area of Burgundy (southeastern France), with the founding of an abbey at Citeaux (Latin, Cistercium) in 1098. Its daughter houses expanded spectacularly under the leadership of the saintly and charismatic Bernard of Clairvaux, who was to promote the Second Crusade in 1146 (p. 269). The Cistercians, as they were called, wore white robes to distinguish themselves from the black of the Benedictines. There was acute rivalry between the two orders, with the Cistercians at first deploring the riches of Cluny. But the white robes, too, became soiled by economic success, gifts, and worldly power. Within a century of the abbey's founding the Cistercians had fallen to the comforts of wealth.

A third reform effort followed a similar course. Early in the thirteenth century a young Italian, Francis of Assisi, felt himself called to live his life in imitation of Christ. The son of a wealthy merchant, Francis gave up his home, his fine clothing, and the security of his family to travel about in voluntary poverty — supported by begging alone. Soon he was joined by companions of like mind, forming a company of twelve. Rejecting the routine of monks in some remote cloister, they chose, instead, to work among the needy of the towns. In the expanding centers of trade the Franciscans preached and served the poor, stressing the ideal of Christian love and brotherhood.

Francis was reluctant to found an order, for he believed that formal organization tends to hold down individual freedom of action. He also feared the effect of wealth — even collective wealth — on the ideal of holy poverty. The papacy, however, was worried about what Francis and his followers would do if they were permitted to carry on their activities without supervision by the Church. Consequently, the papacy authorized Francis to establish an *order* under his direct control. Soon the brothers (friars) of the new order, who had previously lived by begging, began to accept gifts of property and buildings. Within a century the Franciscans became another wealthy religious order, and their devotion of poverty and simplicity gave way to increasing concern for material things.

The Franciscans originally had little use for books or education. Francis himself was a *mystic* — one who seeks God's truth through *inner inspiration* and *revelation*. He and his fellow mystics, who had substantial influence in the Middle Ages, were doubtful of book learning and human reason. Of a contrary view was the Spaniard Dominic, a contemporary of Francis. Dominic was an intellectual who saw God's truth as a *reasoned* ideology, and the order of friars he founded was devoted chiefly to scholarship, teaching, and preaching. Alarmed by the spread of heretical doctrines in his time, Dominic believed he could best serve the Lord by guiding the thoughts and education of Christians. Francis appealed mainly to people's *hearts*; Dominic appealed more to their *minds*. Both the gray friars (the Franciscans) and the black (the Dominicans) became familiar figures on the streets and highways of Europe.

The Papal Monarchy

The most significant reforms of the medieval Church were associated with the papacy itself. For centuries the feudal nobles of Italy had competed with one another for control of the office. In the tenth century, after the east Frankish king Otto became Holy Roman emperor, he passed over the Italians and set German bishops on the throne of St. Peter. Conscientious leaders of the Church, spurred by the Cluniac reform, tried to lift the papacy out of the arena of imperial politics to a position of independence. In a very real sense, the effort to cleanse the Church as a whole depended on the success of this endeavor.

The Italian Hildebrand was the chief promoter of papal independence. As archdeacon of Rome, a key office in the Church's administration, he proved himself a shrewd planner and tactician. In 1059, with one masterful stroke, he brought into being a new system for the election of popes — the College of Cardinals. Prior to that time popes had been elected, theoretically, by the entire clergy of the Roman diocese, subject to the approval of the city's populace. This arrangement had lent itself readily to interference by local nobles and foreign monarchs.

Hildebrand corrected the situation by restricting the papal electors to the *cardinal* clergy — a small number of the ranking priests of Rome. The cardinals were appointed by the pope, and when one pope died they met in seclusion to name his successor. Because they usually chose from their own membership, the body automatically furnished select candidates for the papal office. In subsequent centuries the College of Cardinals was expanded to include leaders of the Church throughout the world (though Italians have almost always constituted a majority). Except for rare occasions when foreign military forces were present in Rome or when the Church suffered from division, the electoral system has functioned remarkably well. It has brought to the highest office of the Roman Catholic Church a succession of individuals whose leadership ability, on the average, has surpassed that of most lines of hereditary rulers.

In 1073 the cardinals chose Hildebrand as pope (Gregory VII). Conditioned by his earlier training at Cluny, he applied himself to a sweeping reform of the Church. One of his main objectives was to strengthen the papacy, to make it a monarchy in fact as well as in theory. Under his guidance, the central administration of the papacy came to be handled through a number of bureaus, departments, and assemblies — called, collectively, the papal *curia* (councils). The officers in charge of these agencies were usually chosen from among the cardinals and formed, in effect, a kind of "cabinet" for the pope.

Beyond Rome, papal authority reached into every diocese of Western Christendom. According to the doctrine of apostolic succession (p. 152), the bishops constituted the core of the Church. But all were subordinate to the supreme bishop, the successor to Peter: the pope. He kept in touch with them through continual correspondence — the papal letters run to thousands of volumes. Bishops (and archbishops) were also required to make regular visits to Rome, which often involved arduous travel. In order to boost his influence outside Italy, Gregory initiated the practice of sending forth papal *legates* (ambassadors). These deputies of the pope came to be assigned more or less permanently to the capitals of Europe. Each legate conducted inquiries and oversaw the Church organization in the territory where he resided.

In addition to the income from their extensive properties in Italy, the popes received large revenues from all over Europe, including such special levies as "Peter's pence," an annual tax on Christian families in England. The popes also collected a substantial sum from every newly appointed prelate (high-ranking cleric). Countless other payments flowed to Rome: fees for appeals from bishops' courts, for dispensations (exemptions) from canon law, and for papal *indulgences*. The latter were certificates, issued through agents of the pope, that supposedly reduced the penalties (now and after death) due to sin. All these revenues were used for various purposes — administrative and political as well as religious, charitable, and artistic.

Papal influence over medieval society was reinforced by sweeping disciplinary power. The pope (and the bishops) could *excommunicate* Christians and thus deprive them of the benefit of the sacraments. Since the sacraments were considered essential to salvation, excommunication was regarded as a fearful penalty. The threat or use of excommunication usually brought obedience from clergy, noblemen, and commoners alike — even from kings and emperors.

If excommunication did not bring a ruler to his knees, the pope could resort to the *interdict*. This was an order closing the churches and suspending the sacraments for an entire area. A ruler, no matter what his own religious convictions, could scarcely ignore the interdict. For his subjects, fearing that their souls were in danger, would press the ruler to yield so that the churches might be reopened. Moreover, should the ruler continue his defiance, the pope could declare the ruler *deposed* and release his subjects from obedience to him.

The disciplinary power of the pope had certain limits of effectiveness, however. A person who had been excommunicated could beg forgiveness; if he or she showed evidence of genuine repentance, the pope was virtually obliged to lift his order. And extreme measures like the interdict often boomeranged. If a ruler who was in dispute with the pope had the sympathy and support of his people, the interdict might cause them to rally to the ruler's side.

Nevertheless, through the channels and agencies of the Church the papacy could exert a powerful influence on popular thought and behavior. By means of proclamations, letters, and speeches, for example, the pope could spread his ideas and exert active leadership. At his command were the bishops, the religious orders, and the church schools — all of which were in contact with the people. The sacrament of penance, with its oral confession, kept the priesthood in touch with the inmost thoughts and feelings of men and women. And the bishops, especially, were on the alert to spot signs of heresy and to stamp out heresy wherever they found it.

Their efforts were reinforced in the thirteenth century by special courts of inquiry set up by the papacy. These courts, known as the Inquisition, were eventually introduced to many areas of Europe, but the earliest was the one established in the south of France after heresy and revolt had gripped that region. The main disturbance there was called the "Albigensian heresy," after the cathedral town of Albi, where it started. At the request of Pope Innocent III (p. 242), French nobles from the north cruelly suppressed the rebellion by 1226. But heresy smoldered even after this "crusade" against the Albigensians was over. To snuff out the remaining embers, Innocent's successor, Pope Gregory IX, established the Inquisition as a permanent court for finding and trying heretics.

The pope's Grand Inquisitor was placed at Carcassonne, in the south of France. He sent deputies, drawn chiefly from the new Dominican order (p. 237), to the towns and cities of the area. In the public square of each place the deputies would announce their mission, then call for people to testify regarding suspected heretics. In pursuing their inquiries, the deputies resorted to torture to wring confessions from uncooperative suspects, and they denied accused persons legal counsel and the right to call or confront witnesses. Proceedings were usually conducted in secret. Lucky prisoners would confess early, repent, and forfeit only their property. Those who proved stubborn, or who lapsed again into heresy after repenting, were excommunicated and turned over to the civil authorities for more severe punishment.

Canon law (Church law) forbade the clergy to take life, but the civil authorities felt no such inhibition. And, because heresy was often associated with popular discontent or rebellion, the civil authorities regarded it as equivalent to *treason* and therefore set the penalty of death for convicted heretics. If a responsible official failed to apply that penalty, he was himself liable to excommunication and punishment. The most common means of execution was burning at the stake — a means that gave heretics a chance to make a final repentance as the flames reached higher and higher. They might then have time to beg for God's forgiveness and the salvation of their souls. But in no case would the fire be quenched; the body of a "confirmed" heretic was already forfeit.

The procedures and penalties of the Inquisition appear cruel and inhumane to modern minds. In the view of medieval churchmen, however, the end (rooting out heresy) justified the means. Even the "Angelic Doctor" of the Church, Thomas Aquinas (p. 359), held that extreme punishments were necessary to protect souls from the contamination of false beliefs. His was no doubt an honest argument. But the Inquisition was also open to the foulest abuses. To level the accusation of heresy became a convenient way of injuring or getting rid of personal enemies, and the accusers were never identified by the court. Despite the justifications advanced by its defenders, the Inquisition was generally abandoned after the seventeenth century.

The Struggle for Supremacy over the State

Gregory VII, as we have seen, worked to strengthen the control of Rome over the Church and to free it from secular interference and corruption. To the extent that he accomplished these goals, he fulfilled the aims of the pervasive

		Accession of Pope Gregory VII	Death of Pope Boniface VIII	
529	910	1073	1303	1417
Spread of Benedictine Monastic Houses		Cluniac Reform Movement	Pope and Emperor Struggle for Supremacy	Avignon Papacy and Great Schism

Cluniac reform movement. But Gregory aspired to go much further. Cluny had concentrated on the reform of the clergy and had tended to accept the secular world as it was; Gregory sought to alter the balance between church and state. Where Cluny aimed to set the Church *apart* from the state, Gregory desired to place it *over* the state. He would thus give to the Church — and to its monarch, the pope — the responsibility and the power to purify the *whole* of Christian society.

Before Gregory's time Christian teaching had given to civil monarchs a *sacred* character as well as secular authority. Their powers were approved by God; they defended the Church and were blessed by it. The Emperor Charlemagne, who was held up as a model, had appointed bishops and abbots to their offices and had employed clergymen as administrators and as teachers in his palace school. Mutual support between the nobility and the clergy existed at all levels of feudal government. It was this relationship that Gregory and his successors sought to change.

By various historical arguments and documents, including the falsified Donation of Constantine (pp. 200–201), Gregory claimed to be the overlord of the rulers of western Europe. He declared, for example, that the Holy Roman emperor, Henry IV, was his vassal, on the ground that Charlemagne, Henry's predecessor, owed his crown to Pope Leo III (p. 206). He objected particularly to Henry's control over the election of German bishops, who were important fief-holders and vassals of the emperor. Henry was exercising a traditional right when he influenced their selection and invested (clothed) them with their symbols of office. Gregory insisted, however, that bishops were *spiritual* officers and could be invested with ring and staff, the symbols of their religious authority, only by the pope. What he sought, of course, was papal control over the elections themselves. This *investiture* issue set off a prolonged conflict between Rome and the European monarchs, but it was only one aspect of the papal bid for supremacy.

Gregory employed every means at his command to bring Henry down. He plotted with the emperor's enemies in Germany, subjected him to excommunication and deposition (1076), and turned to the Normans in southern Italy for military assistance against Henry's forces. After his excommunication, Henry outmaneuvered his adversary by crossing the Alps in winter and appearing as a penitent before Gregory at the palace of Canossa (in northern Italy). Standing barefoot in the snow, he begged the pope to forgive him for his offenses and restore him to communion with the Church. Acting in his priestly role, Gregory granted the request; but the contest shortly resumed, and the pope once again excommunicated Henry. In the long run, Gregory lacked sufficient armed power to transform occasional triumphs into lasting victory. Though he aggravated civil war and destruction in Germany — and in Italy as well — he failed to win control over the Holy Roman Empire. The investiture argument itself was settled later by compromise: Henry's successor agreed in 1122 to give to the pope the investiture of religious symbols, but he retained the emperor's traditional influence over the selection of German bishops.

Gregory's successors carried on his struggle. During the reign of Innocent III the papacy reached its height of prestige and power. Its strength was shown by the humbling of King John of England, who, after a bitter dispute with Innocent over the election of the archbishop of Canterbury, was forced to submit. John was deposed; afterward, he was granted the realm of England *as a fief from Rome*, but only after pledging homage to the pope (1213).

Papal claims were carried even further by the aggressive Boniface VIII. He met his master, however, in King Philip (the Fair) of France. Philip, who was waging war against England, levied a tax on church properties in 1296. This bold move, contrary to existing law, was answered by Boniface with angry denunciations. The violent dispute reached its climax a few years later when Boniface issued a papal *bull* (pronouncement) titled *Unam sanctam*, which included the most extreme claims of Gregory and Innocent. Boniface declared that *all* secular rulers were subject to the pope and that the pope could be judged by God alone. He concluded, daringly, "We declare, state, define, and pronounce that it is altogether necessary to salvation for every human creature to be subject to the Roman pontiff." Yet Boniface's words did not prevail over Philip's deeds. Philip, realizing that no peaceful solution could be reached with Boniface, sent a military force across the Alps to seize the aged pontiff. Roughly treated and humiliated by the French soldiers, Boniface died of shock soon afterward (1303).

These events set the stage for a rapid decline of the papacy. The popes had overreached themselves in their pursuit of worldly power, and their absorption in politics had caused them to neglect the spiritual affairs of the Church as a whole. The fourteenth and fifteenth centuries would see the unhappy consequences of papal extremism.

CHRISTIAN ART

Despite the later decline of the papacy, the Church was a powerful creative force throughout the Middle Ages. Nowhere is this force displayed more clearly than in the arts. Faith in God and hope for salvation held a central place in the hearts of medieval men and women, and the artisans of the age dedicated their efforts to creating works for the Church.

For several centuries after the Germanic invasions of the West, the unsettled conditions of society had proved unfavorable for the arts in general and for architecture in particular. Until the tenth century most new buildings north of the Alps were built of timber; the first stone structure of importance was Charlemagne's chapel at Aachen, completed around 800 (*Fig. 5-4*, p. 205). With the return of stability and security in the eleventh century, architecture began to revive. Increasing wealth and technical progress enabled European civilization to produce the first truly European style; and like so many burgeoning civilizations before it, that of Europe invested its newfound wealth and skills above all in the construction of magnificent religious buildings. But whereas the civilizations of the past had built great temples, the Europeans now built great churches.

Christian churches differed widely from pagan temples, not only as regards the god they glorified, but also in terms of the purpose they served. A pagan temple was the "home" of a god or goddess, which the ordinary worshiper might never enter (pp. 21, 65); all that mattered was that by means of the temple, the divine being could be made to live among and protect the community that built it. But the Christian God dwelt "in a house not made with hands." It was not God, but his worshipers who needed a building — one that would bring them close to him. Hence the church was intended to communicate to believers something of the nature of God and the universe he ruled. Paintings and sculptures taught these lessons to the mass of illiterate believers. The educated, too, were meant to perceive in the church, with its ordered structure centered upon the altar, an image of the universe ruled by God. It was this theory that was responsible for the overwhelming impression that the great churches of the Middle Ages still create today: an impression of orderly and logical perfection, and yet also of mystical and inexpressible holiness.

The Romanesque Style

The first European style, known as the Romanesque, predominated from about 1000 to 1200, and found expression in painting and sculpture as well as architecture. The term "Romanesque" is somewhat misleading, for this first European style was based only partially on Roman examples. The relationship is most apparent in architecture, where the round arch and the vault served as basic structural elements. But the builders of the Middle Ages used these elements in a manner quite different from the ancient Romans. Moreover, they adhered to no *unified* style; instead, different styles developed from region to region. Byzantine, oriental, and barbarian influences were also evident in the Romanesque.

The monastic reform movement that originated at Cluny provided an impulse for widespread building activity during the eleventh and twelfth centuries. Though secular structures of various kinds were erected, the most important building of this period was of monastery churches. And these churches reflect a surprising variety of styles, notably the styles of Normandy, Burgundy, Provence, and Lombardy.

Wealthy as the monasteries were in corporate property, the individual members were committed to the ideal of poverty. This ascetic goal, along with the missionary zeal of the monks, impressed itself upon the architectural spirit of the times. Religious houses and churches were built of thick stone walls with narrow openings. The effect, from the outside, was forbidding; inside, one felt withdrawn and protected from the world. Although the architectural designs were well planned and aesthetically satisfying, little attempt was made to give the buildings any elegance or sensuous appeal.

The earliest Christian churches (of the fourth century) had been modeled on the Roman basilica, a lofty hall in which legal or financial business was transacted. The typical basilica had a rectangular floor plan divided longitudinally into a central aisle (nave) and two or more side aisles. At one end of the building there was customarily a small semicircular extension (the apse) covered by a half-dome. Here the Romans sometimes built a platform for the chair (cathedra) of the presiding official.

Although at first the bishops simply adapted the basilica to the needs of their congregations (*Fig. 3-3*, p. 124), developments in worship services during the Middle Ages led to a shift to the cruciform (cross-shaped) plan (*Fig. 6-2*). The nave and the side aisles were kept, but the apse was enlarged, and chapels were built into its perimeter. A transept, or crossarm, was introduced

6-2 St. Sernin, Toulouse,
     France, ground plan.

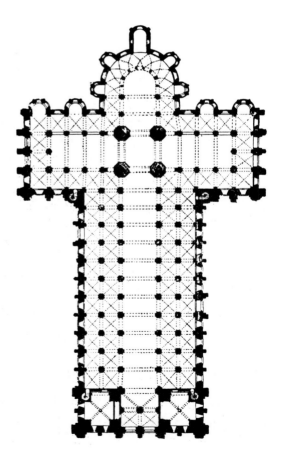

at right angles to the nave, with entrances at either end. This new plan provided more space for the clergy participating in the Mass, for members of the choir, and for worshipers making private devotions. It became, with numerous variations, the favored plan for large churches all over the West.

Aside from its functional merit, the cruciform plan had obvious symbolic meaning. When the faithful entered the church, they were "returning to the Cross." The façade (front) of the building usually had *three* main portals, symbolizing the *Trinity*. Whenever possible, the cross was positioned so that the nave ran from west to east, with the altar at the eastern end. Thus the worshipers faced more or less in the direction of Jerusalem.

Elements of ancient architectural forms may be seen in the rounded doorways and windows of Romanesque churches and in the arches and tunnel vaults used to support the roof. The roofs of earlier churches had generally rested on a framework of timber; the Romanesque architect, seeking greater permanency, chose stone. But how could the massive weight of a stone ceiling be held up? One way was to bridge the nave by means of a tunnel (barrel) vault (*Fig. 6-3*). Such a vault placed severe stress on the stonework below, which usually had to be supported by half-vaults built over the side aisles. It also

6-3 St. Etienne, Nevers, France.

followed that the size of windows was strictly limited, for large openings would have made the walls dangerously weak. Hence, scant daylight found its way into the nave.

To admit more light, medieval architects often divided the nave into a series of rectangular spaces, or "bays." The stone ceiling over each bay was formed by a Roman-type cross vault (*Fig. 3-2b*, p. 121). This type of construction permitted larger openings in the "clearstory" portion of the nave — that is, the part rising above the side-aisle roofs.

The round dome, which also goes back to Roman times, was frequently used by Romanesque builders. More characteristic of the Romanesque style, however, was a *new* architectural feature: the *tower*. The earliest known towers in western Europe date from the fifth century A.D. and were used chiefly for hanging bells; the bell tower thereafter became closely associated with church architecture. In Italy, the graceful campanile (bell tower) stood by itself a few feet away from the church; elsewhere in Europe the tower was an integral part of the main building. It was sometimes built over the "crossing," where the nave and the transept cross, but more commonly a tower or a pair of towers formed part of the front of the building. Though of all shapes and sizes, they generally followed a pattern for a given reason. In some areas, for example, they were capped by a soaring *spire*. Church towers remain to this day a symbol of Western Christianity.

Sculpture, an art on which the Greeks and Romans lavished their genius, had fallen into decline with the triumph of Christianity in the fourth century. The Church at first linked sculpture with the pagan worship of idols, and this put a temporary end to life-size works in western Europe. Artistic activity during the Dark Ages was limited mainly to small-scale carving and manuscript illumination (decoration). With the beginning of the Romanesque period, around 1000, full-size painting and sculpture were revived. The renewed interest in these art forms was prompted by the accelerated pace of church building; in fact, painting and sculpture remained subordinate to architecture until the close of the Middle Ages. Sculpture was used almost exclusively for religious purposes: the glorification of God and the instruction of the faithful. Overcoming the barrier of illiteracy, each medieval church was virtually a "Bible in stone."

Nowhere is the atmospheric contrast between the medieval world and the ancient world more sharply displayed than in sculpture (*Fig. 6-4*). The "idealistic" style of the Greeks and the "naturalistic" style of the Romans (pp. 82, 127) are both absent. Few ancient statues were available to the sculptors of the eleventh and twelfth centuries; they took as their models the illustrated figures of medieval manuscripts, the only art form that continued uninterrupted throughout the medieval era. These miniature figures were crudely drawn, with little regard for anatomical accuracy. Their purpose was to fulfill a design of line and color and to "support" a story or a moral.

The strange animal figures that appear often in Romanesque sculpture came directly from the northern barbarian tradition. Numerous books were

6-4 St. Trophîme at Arles, France, tympanum.

available describing hundreds of imaginary beasts, and sculptors copied them in stone. Romanesque churches were studded with frightening monsters and demons, which looked all too real, no doubt, to the congregation.

Romanesque sculptors mingled the natural and the supernatural, the earthly and the unearthly. Hence, the real may look unreal and the unreal real. To ensure that the idea or story they were illustrating would be correctly interpreted, sculptors relied heavily on symbols. Although they might show St. Peter in a number of poses, they always *identified* him by giving him a set of *keys*. Matthew was consistently shown as an *angel*, Mark as a *lion* (*Fig. 6-4*). Having identified a figure with its traditional symbol, the artist could then treat it in an *individual* manner.

This freedom presented an opportunity for creativity quite unknown in classical art. Romanesque sculptors, though often showing inferior technique, were not bound to exacting artistic rules or to naturalistic representation. This also permitted them greater liberties in overall *composition* — a freedom shared by painters and other artisans of the period.

The Gothic Style

One of the features of Western civilization that distinguish it from the Eastern is its *dynamic* quality. Styles of art in the East have lasted thousands of years, but in the West constant change has been the rule. The Romanesque style marked a break with the past, but in less than two centuries it had begun

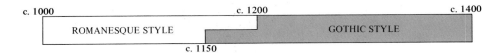

to give way to yet another style. Out of the Romanesque, in response to changing social, spiritual, and technical forces, came the later style of the Middle Ages — the Gothic. This style showed itself first in architecture, around 1150, reached its prime by 1300, and declined in vitality with the closing of the Middle Ages.

The term "Gothic" was applied to the style only in later centuries, by individuals who had come under the spell of a *classical* revival. They abhorred the disruption of the classical tradition and looked upon the medieval period as a Germanic (Gothic) interlude. We can see now that they failed to recognize medieval culture as a unique blend of German, Roman, and Christian elements. This culture reached its full development around 1300, and the Gothic style was its grandest expression.

While the Romanesque style had flourished in the monasteries, the Gothic style flourished in the towns. There the bishops and their cathedrals became the centers of attention and the *ascetic* spirit was now overshadowed by a more *worldly* one. Insecurity was giving way to a new confidence: Gothic cathedrals were built to the glory of God, but they reflected the *pride of humans*.

Yet the Christian faith remained the leading force in Western society, and the Gothic cathedrals also represented a new way of giving expression to religious belief. The educated clergy of the twelfth century wanted to build churches that would be a true image of the universe as they believed it to be: a vast structure, designed by its creator to be perfectly harmonious in every detail, and glowing with *light* that flowed from God himself. Only a building of this kind, they thought, would truly lead the worshipers to the knowledge and love of God.

Judged by this standard, existing Romanesque churches were inadequate. Their thick walls often gave a feeling of confinement, their massive arches seemed ill-proportioned, and their relatively small windows did not provide a rich illumination. But any attempt to alter this pattern raised difficult technical questions. How could architects increase the spaciousness and height of a building, reduce the thickness of the supporting walls and arches, and enlarge the area of the windows? They found their answer in "rib" vaulting.

In the twelfth century Romanesque builders had developed a better system than cross-vaulting (p. 246) for supporting a heavy roof. They marked off each rectangular bay by four (vertical) stone pillars. From the top of each pillar they connected ribs of arching stone to the tops of the other three; then they filled in the ceiling areas between these ribs with light brick. Thus they constructed a *framework* of *stone* (*Fig. 6-5*) on which they could rest the roof of the nave. The weight of the gabled roof (which was generally tiled on its outer surface) was carried to the ground through this stone framework. Consequently, no force was exerted on the areas *between* the pillars.

6-5 Amiens Cathedral, France, vault.

Gothic architects developed the full potential of the new method. This revolutionary plan of construction enabled them to lift roofs to soaring heights and to make the walls of the clearstory into softly glowing sheets of stained glass. They could discard the idea of a building as a stone mass enclosing static space and think of it, instead, as a web of stone with space and light flowing freely through it. Among the refinements they advanced to carry out their idea were the *pointed arch* and the *flying buttress*.

The graceful pointed arch, which resembles a pair of hands touching in prayer, is a hallmark of the Gothic style. Although the builders no doubt appreciated its spiritual and aesthetic quality, they also had practical reasons for using it. It accentuated the vertical lines of their structures and lifted the vaults to greater heights than could be achieved with the round arch. With the pointed arch, the direction of thrust is more *down*ward than *out*ward, decreasing the danger that the supporting pillars will collapse. Moreover, the pointed arch is far more adaptable to rib vaulting, for the steepness of its curving ribs can be fitted to varying distances between the pillars, whereas the round arch follows a fixed curve.

To make the soaring vaults safer, French architects added external buttresses (props) of masonry. They could not place these buttresses directly against the pillars of the nave, because the side aisles, with their separate, lower roofs, stood in the way. So they erected massive pillars at intervals *outside* the side aisles. They rose almost to the level of the nave ceiling and were *connected* to the pillars of the nave by stone ribs, or spokes. (An early example of this may be seen at Chartres, *Fig. 6-6.*) Since the ribs appear to be suspended over the side aisles, they are commonly called "flying" buttresses. Though they support the stone framework at critical points, they interfere only slightly with the flow of light through the great clearstory windows.

The Gothic cathedral, pointing to heaven, stood high above the houses huddled in the town (*Fig. 6-7*), symbolizing the commanding position of the Church in the lives of medieval men and women. As travelers approached a cathedral town, the first sight they saw on the horizon was the spire, or spires, reaching hundreds of feet into the sky (*Fig. 5-1*, p. 172). Then the whole of the

6-6 Chartres Cathedral, buttresses, nave exterior from south.

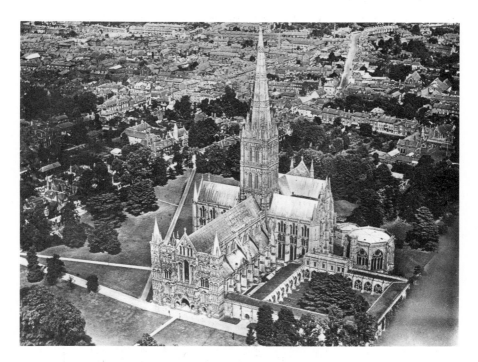

6-7 Salisbury Cathedral, England.

cathedral would gradually come into view. If the travelers were pilgrims, they would approach the west façade and reverently prepare to enter.

Set into the façade were stone sculptures representing figures from the Bible. Gothic artists were more naturalistic in style than Romanesque artists. Although the figures could still be identified by certain symbols, they looked more lifelike than the Romanesque (*Fig. 6-8*). The artisans of this period relied less on copybook drawings and looked more to live models. Their technique and general craftsmanship rose steadily in excellence.

Inside the cathedral, the emphasis was on space, light, and color (*Fig. 6-9*). Here one forgets the calculation and engineering wisdom that made possible the complicated thrust and counterthrust of arches, vaults, and buttresses. One is absorbed by the vastness, rhythm, and splendor of the interior. Stained glass is the special glory of the Gothic. By daylight, the upper levels of the interior glow with luminous blues, reds, greens, and golds. The windows, of varying shape and size, consist of mosaics of colored glass. The glass pieces are held together by lead strips and bars creating geometrical designs. The function of the windows, like that of the sculpture, is to illustrate Biblical events, but the figures are often absorbed into the broader patterns of line and color. Thus, in its immensity, its harmonious beauty, and its glowing illumination, the building conveys something of the image of the universe and its creator that inspired the builders.

6-8 Reims Cathedral,
France, Annunciation
and Visitation, central
portal, west facade.

6-9 Amiens Cathedral, nave looking east.

THOUGHT AND EDUCATION

Medieval education, as well as the arts, was dominated by the Church. At no other time in Western history have the channels of communication and education been so completely in the hands of one institution. The members of the clergy, who made up the only literate and educated class of society, staffed virtually all the schools, libraries, and centers of higher learning. Almost all manuscripts and books (*Fig. 6-10*) were produced in the monastic scriptorium, or copy room, and the principal means of oral communication was the pulpit. Every idea expressed inside or outside the Church was subject to the scrutiny and judgment of the higher clergy.

The result of this intellectual supervision was not so repressive as one might suspect. The feudalistic and local character of the times counterbalanced what was, in theory, the monolithic force of the Church. The methods of long-distance communication were primitive, and the Church itself was split into

6-10 Manuscript page of a fourteenth-century book of religious services, the *Pontifical of Metz*.

many authorities, orders, and factions. Although basically only a Catholic point of view could be professed in western Europe, a wide range of intellectual inquiry and debate was still possible.

During the troubled centuries immediately after the fall of Rome, there had been a real danger that learning and scholarship would vanish from Europe. The monasteries then arose as the conservers of precious manuscripts, and they provided at least the rudiments of education to the clergy, the only class of society that was thought to have need for it. Around 800 Charlemagne gave strong support to the revival of interest in intellectual matters (pp. 204–5). Though advance was slow, it may be said that by 1200 Western civilization had reached the general level of learning of ancient times and had begun to match that of the Muslims. The monasteries still provided elementary education, and cathedral schools were beginning to respond to a growing desire for education in the towns. But the most significant development was the rise of the universities.

The Rise of Universities

The earliest steps toward higher education were taken in southern Europe. Formal medical instruction started at Salerno (Italy) before the twelfth century, and training in the law began about the same time at Bologna. The universities founded at these centers were professional in nature. They were stimulated by Muslim learning in Sicily and by the demand for physicians and lawyers to serve Italian princes and merchants. The word *universitas* was simply the Latin word for a body or corporation, such as a guild. When a number of teachers (or students) in a given place joined together as a legally chartered body, a *university* came into existence.

The university movement spread northward from Italy to Montpellier and Paris. It was in Paris during the thirteenth century that Europe's foremost institution of learning was established. Its faculty was made up of professors drawn from the cathedral school and from local monastic schools, along with lay lecturers in law and medicine. Paris was the first university to offer the four major curriculums that have become identified in the West with the idea of a university. Whereas Salerno and Bologna limited themselves initially to professional training in medicine and law, Paris offered instruction in all the recognized fields of knowledge. The university was divided into four faculties: medicine, law, theology, and liberal arts. The last two earned for Paris its high reputation. From Paris, which served as the model in the north, the movement spread to England, Germany, and the rest of western Europe (p. 258). By 1500 the total number of universities, many of which are still in existence, exceeded eighty.

Each university operated under the protection of a charter granted by a ranking official of the Church or the state (usually the pope or a king). Thus, the universities were freed, for the most part, from the jurisdiction of local courts and local clergy. One justification for this exempted status was that teachers and students came from all over Europe, making the universities truly international. Moreover, most students held minor clerical rank and therefore could claim immunity from civil authority ("benefit of clergy"). In the Middle Ages the word "clerk" (cleric) usually meant "scholar."

The organization of a university controlled by teachers paralleled that of a craft guild (pp. 228–29). The guild *masters* (professors) had the sole right to award qualifying certificates, or "degrees." The *apprentices* (students), upon earning the appropriate degree, were eligible to become masters in a teaching corporation (university). Thus, the ceremony of "graduation" was also the students' "commencement" as certified teachers.

The liberal-arts curriculum of the university was normally a prerequisite to the professional courses. Its outlines had been developed in the monastic schools, which in turn had followed late Roman educational practices. The liberal-arts subjects were seven in number: grammar, rhetoric, and logic (the *trivium*); arithmetic, geometry, astronomy, and music (the *quadrivium*). Grammar, of course, meant Latin grammar. This was the language used by members of the clergy, lawyers, physicians, and scholars all through the Middle Ages. But the trivium went beyond the mechanics of language; it included the study of works of philosophy, literature, and history. The quadrivium was based on the reading of ancient texts and was almost entirely theoretical. Today we refer to the subjects of the trivium as humanistic studies and to the subjects of the quadrivium (excepting music) as mathematical studies.

The students in medieval universities did not enroll for course "credits" or "units." In order to earn a degree they did not have to complete a given number of courses with a prescribed "grade-point" average. Instead, degrees were granted on the basis of comprehensive oral examinations. After attending lectures and reading for several years in the subjects of the trivium, a student would ask to be examined by the members of the faculty. If he performed satisfactorily, he was granted the preliminary degree of bachelor of arts (B.A.). This degree was of no particular use in itself, except as a prerequisite for going on to the quadrivium. After several additional years of study, the student would present himself for examination once again. If he passed, he was awarded the degree of master of arts (M.A.), which certified that he was qualified to teach the liberal-arts curriculum.

The higher degrees were, similarly, *teaching* degrees. The Latin word *doctor* (teacher) was customarily used for the degrees in theology, law, and medicine. (The doctor of philosophy degree came later — philosophy meaning advanced study in the liberal-arts area.) Each of these degrees normally required four or more years of study beyond the master's. Again, however, the award was based not on the time spent in study or on the number of credits earned, but on the candidate's performance in a rigorous examination. The candidate usually presented a "thesis," or proposition, which he explained and defended orally before a faculty board.

Student life was quite different from what it is today. Since most females were thought to have no need for a formal education, the universities were for males only. There was no campus of the sort that Americans are accustomed to today. Professors lectured — at least at first — in their homes or in hired halls, and students lived independently, according to their means and tastes. This unregulated life sometimes led to ill health, "immoral" conduct, or both. As a corrective, private donors established residential "colleges" for scholars at many universities.

The first notable "college" was founded about 1250 by Louis IX's chaplain, Robert de Sorbon; he provided it with a dormitory, in which theology students at the University of Paris could live. Later, faculty members were assigned to the college, and lecture and library facilities were added. Thus the "Sorbonne" became a separate living-and-learning unit under the university's general control. (Today it is the instructional center for the faculties of literature, science, and theology.) This pattern was adopted for students in other curriculums at Paris, and it gradually spread to universities beyond France. It took firm root in England (at Oxford and Cambridge), where it has persisted until the present time. Elsewhere in Europe, universities are no longer organized into separate living-and-learning units.

During the Middle Ages students had few books and no laboratories. They inscribed their lecture notes on wax tablets and then transferred them to sheets of parchment. More stress was placed on memorizing and analyzing a small number of highly respected books than on extensive reading. Of special interest to scholars were some of the ancient classics that had reappeared in the West during the eleventh and twelfth centuries. Growing contact with Constantinople and the Muslim world prompted Latin translations, from Greek, Arabic, or Hebrew, of many of the works of Aristotle as well as books of Hellenistic science, mathematics, and medicine (pp. 185, 195). These were accompanied by original writings and commentaries by leading Muslim and Jewish scholars, who had formerly been unknown in western Europe.

Chief among the Muslim commentators on Aristotle was the twelfth-century philosopher Averroës (ibn-Rushd), a Spanish-born Arab. But many Christians were disturbed by his doctrine, drawn from Aristotle, that the universe had always existed and was therefore *not created*. He also denied the immortality of the human soul. More acceptable to Christians were the writings of Averroës' contemporary, the Jewish philosopher-physician, Maimonides (Moses ben Maimon). His *Guide for the Perplexed* addresses the "big" philosophical and religious questions that confront Jew and Christian alike: What is the purpose of God's universe? Will it last forever? How is God's will related to *natural* causes? Maimonides' answers to such questions consist of a closely reasoned mixture of Aristotle, the Old Testament, and traditional Jewish authorities (Sages).

Scholastic Philosophy

The stimulus from the East lifted the intellectual life of Europe beyond the level of earlier monastic and cathedral education. The creative response by scholars (schoolmen) gave rise to the major philosophical method of the Middle Ages, called *scholasticism*. The scholastics were primarily interested in religious matters. Thus, Anselm, a learned Italian monk and one of the first scholastic philosophers, put together arguments to prove *logically* the existence of God. In another treatise (about 1100) he explained why God had chosen to take on human form as Jesus. In defense of his studious efforts, Anselm asserted that *understanding* was a proper supplement to Christian *believing*.

In the twelfth century, the French scholar Abelard argued that the authorities of the Church should not be read without questioning, for they often contradicted one another (*Sic et Non*). He insisted, therefore, that all writings be subjected to the light of logic. "By doubting," he observed, "we come to examine, and by examining we reach the truth." Thus, Abelard had returned to the position of Socrates, who had sought knowledge through persistent questioning. Abelard sought to replace the general medieval habit of ready belief with an insistence on critical examination; no subject, henceforth, would be shielded from doubt and reason.

Though theological matters remained the focus of scholastic concern, medieval philosophers debated every subject under the sun — some grand and divine, some trivial and worldly. (Substantial attention was given to ethical questions associated with the rise of commerce and moneylending.) One of the most absorbing issues was that of "universals." Do "Man," "Horse," "Beauty," and "Justice" exist *independently* of particular things? Or are these terms merely convenient *symbols* for referring to various classes of objects and characteristics? The argument paralleled the ancient one between Plato and the Sophists. Plato believed that Ideas (Forms) had a perfect and independent existence, while the Sophists thought that only particular things existed. In the Middle Ages, those who held that "universals" were real were called "realists"; those who declared that they were just names (*nomina*) were called "nominalists."

The argument was (and is) important to one's philosophical outlook. The extreme realists attached little importance to individual things and sought through sheer logic or divine revelation to know the universals. The extreme nominalists, by contrast, saw *only* specific objects and refused to admit the existence of unifying relationships among particular things. The realists tended to ignore the observed world; the nominalists could scarcely make sense of it.

Most scholars took a middle position on this question. Among the moderates, Abelard expressed a view approximating that of most scientists today. It is called "conceptualism." Abelard held that only particular things have an existence in and of themselves. The universals, however, are more than mere names. They exist as *concepts in individual minds* — keys to an understanding of the interrelatedness of things. Thus, the concept "horse" exists in our minds and adds something to our understanding of all quadrupeds of a certain general description. Once we have identified such a creature, we can assign to it the specific features drawn from our concept. By means of many such concepts,

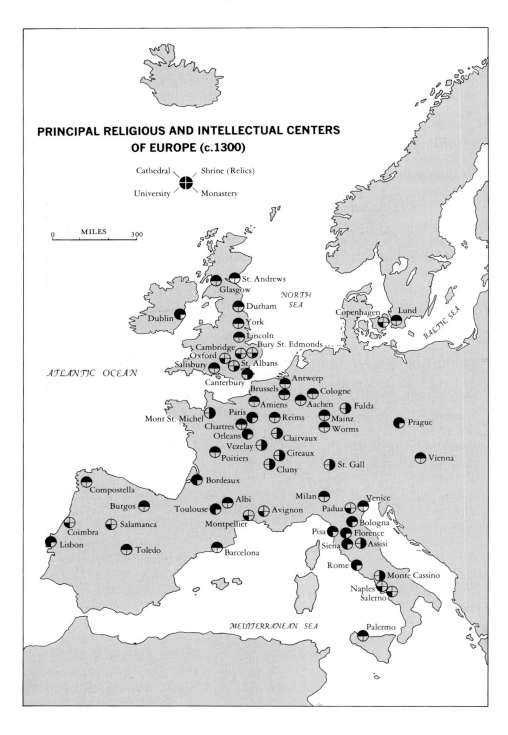

PRINCIPAL RELIGIOUS AND INTELLECTUAL CENTERS OF EUROPE (c.1300)

Cathedral ⎯⎯ Shrine (Relics)

University ⎯⎯ Monastery

MILES
0 ⎯⎯⎯⎯ 300

NORTH SEA

BALTIC SEA

ATLANTIC OCEAN

St. Andrews
Glasgow
Durham
Copenhagen   Lund
Dublin
York
Lincoln
Cambridge   Bury St. Edmonds
Oxford
Salisbury   St. Albans
Canterbury
Brussels   Antwerp
Amiens   Cologne
Mont St. Michel   Paris   Aachen   Fulda
Chartres   Reims   Mainz   Prague
Orleans   Worms
Vezelay   Clairvaux
Poitiers   Citeaux
Cluny   Vienna
St. Gall
Bordeaux
Compostella   Milan   Venice
Burgos   Albi   Padua
Toulouse   Avignon   Bologna
Coimbra   Salamanca   Montpellier   Pisa   Florence
Lisbon   Toledo   Siena   Assisi
Barcelona   Rome
Monte Cassino
Naples
Salerno
Palermo

MEDITERRANEAN SEA

inferred from individual observations, we can make the world (to a degree) comprehensible, manageable, and predictable.

Thomas Aquinas, the greatest of the scholastic philosophers, was a moderate realist. Born near Monte Cassino (Italy) of an aristocratic family, he joined the order of Dominican friars in 1244 (p. 237). A brilliant pupil, he studied at Cologne and Paris and spent his adult life teaching at Paris and Naples. He wrote an enormous number of scholarly works. Reflecting the medieval desire for unity, or oneness, Aquinas sought in these works to harmonize various approaches to truth and to bring all knowledge together. In his most comprehensive work, *Summa Theologiae* (*Theological Summary*), he clarified Church teachings about the nature of God and humanity. (In his view, theology embraced the full range of divine and worldly affairs.)

Following the lead of Anselm, Abelard, and other scholastics, Aquinas set a high value on human reason. By this time the full impact of Aristotle (pp. 72–73) and the new learning from the East had struck the schools and universities of Europe, and Christian teachings were being challenged by pagan, Jewish, and Muslim logicians — especially Averroës (p. 256). Instead of answering their arguments by denying the power of reason, Aquinas adopted Aristotelian logic and turned it to the defense of his faith. He sought to demonstrate that revealed truth (as in the Bible) is never in conflict with logic, *properly exercised*. Both faith and reason, he argued, were created by God, and it is illogical to hold that God could contradict himself.

Aquinas's methodology is most plainly set forth in the *Summa Theologiae*, in which he divided each major subject into a series of questions. For each, he explained the arguments *pro* and *contra*, in accordance with the usual scholastic method of presentation. The arguments are generally *deductive* in form and rely heavily on both pagan and Christian authorities. Thus, in an effort to support a particular point, Aquinas may join a generalization from Aristotle's *Politics* with Jesus' Golden Rule. He presented his own conclusion for each of the questions he posed — a conclusion that generally agreed with official teachings. (Six hundred years after Aquinas's death, he was declared by Pope Leo XIII to be the preferred philosopher of the Roman Catholic Church.)

The *Summa* is a masterful combination of quotations from Scripture, formal logic, and "common sense." It pays scant attention to *observation* and *induction* and none to *experimentation*. Aquinas saw truth as a closed system, complete and unchanging. Though his grand synthesis ("harmonization" of knowledge) does not meet modern scientific standards of proof, it stands as an impressive monument to the discipline and resourcefulness of the human mind.

By the end of the thirteenth century the intellectual life of the West had achieved a new vigor. The communities of university scholars had succeeded in their efforts to preserve and advance learning. Though lacking in originality, the scholastic philosophers had refined the methods of logical thought and had laboriously collected, compiled, and classified sources of information. Above all, they had established the essentials of scholarship: comprehensive research and precise expression.

Modern science owes much to these medieval seekers after truth. They built upon classical learning, reconciled it with Christian teachings, and absorbed new ideas from the Muslim world. Bernard of Chartres once compared himself and his fellow scholars with the philosophers and scientists of ancient times. "We are like a dwarf," he said, "standing on the shoulders of a giant." There is modesty in this statement, but also pride — pride in the fact that he and his colleagues could see a bit farther than their intellectual ancestors.

Medieval Science

The scholars of the Middle Ages cannot be called scientists in the modern sense. In the first place, they were not *specialists*; they regarded the *whole* of knowledge as their field of inquiry. Secondly, they did not observe what has come to be known as the "scientific method," which depends on the processes of observation, experimentation, and verification (pp. 415–16). Yet certain "scientific" knowledge passed on by the ancient Greeks and the Muslims attracted their attention; and a few medieval scholars, in the course of their studies, did contribute to that body of knowledge.

The German scholar, Albert the Great (a teacher of Thomas Aquinas), wrote on the broad range of philosophical and theological questions that challenged thirteenth-century thinkers. But he also found time to observe systematically many of the animal species of western Europe, including bees, spiders, hawks, beavers, whales, and eels. Albert rejected medieval accounts of mythical animals, like "griffins" and "harpies" — simply because he had never observed any.

Robert Grosseteste, an outstanding English scholar of the same period, wrote commentaries on the Bible, Aristotle, and a wide variety of philosophical topics. But he wrote, too, about the sun, weather, tides, colors, comets, and other objects in nature. Grosseteste was a pioneer teacher (and chancellor) at the new Oxford University, where he helped to establish the study of science and mathematics. A generation afterward, his pupil, Roger Bacon, continued to emphasize experimental methods. Bacon, who died in 1294, is remembered also for his predictions of such technological innovations as flying machines and powered ships. Other, lesser-known scholars of the Middle Ages made modest advances in optics, astronomy, and medicine.

LANGUAGE AND LITERATURE

The language common to western Europe during the Middle Ages was Latin. Passed down from pagan Rome, it had been carried beyond the old

Roman frontiers by the Church. Although it remained the formal language of education, law, medicine, and commerce, Latin began to disappear from spoken conversation. It was gradually supplanted by a variety of regional tongues (vernaculars), from which the modern languages would develop. By the thirteenth century the vernaculars had gained predominance in popular literature as well as in everyday speech.

Latin Writings

Medieval Latin did not hold to the classical standards of ancient Rome. The study of pagan authors was sometimes viewed with suspicion; some, such as Cicero and Vergil (pp. 113–114) continued to be widely read, because it was felt that in spite of being pagan, they had valuable moral lessons to impart. Christian writers who had lived at the time of the Roman Empire, such as Jerome and Augustine (pp. 162–64, 167–68), were deeply studied for the religious guidance they offered. But pagan or Christian, the ancient authors were not read for the sake of their language and style. As a result, the writing of classical Latin was neglected, and a modified Latin evolved that itself became the medium for notable literary achievements.

The finest creations in medieval Latin were the prayers and hymns of the Christian worship services. Some of these were incorporated into the Mass and are notable for their poetic beauty (*Stabat Mater* and *Dies Irae*). Latin was also used in new forms of religious drama: "Passion" plays (which grew out of the Easter ritual), dramatizations of the lives of the saints, and Christian "morality" plays. Classical dramas were not performed in the Middle Ages and did not begin to influence European literature until the fifteenth century. By then a secular (worldly) branch of dramatic literature had grown out of the religious performances and had detached itself from the Church.

Though Latin was the language of worship, it also was sometimes used to express dissent from Christian ideals. A substantial body of verse written by wandering scholars began to appear in the twelfth century, the best of which is known as Goliardic poetry, because it was dedicated to a mythical patron, St. Golias. Although few of the poets have been identified, it is clear that they were men of learning, schooled in Latin and familiar with the classics. One Goliard refers to his band as a "vagrant order" of runaway students and clerics. Their verses were mainly satirical, aimed at the clergy and the ascetic ideal. They were pagan in spirit, lauding the pleasures of drinking, eating, and lovemaking. One of the Goliardic poets, called "Archpoet," declared,

> My intention is to die
> In the tavern drinking;
> Wine must be at hand, for I
> Want it when I'm sinking.

Angels when they come shall cry,
At my frailties winking:
"Spare this drunkard, God, he's high,
Absolutely stinking!"*

Vernacular Writings

Goliardic verse could be understood only by the educated few who knew Latin, but the vernacular tongues were more suitable for the circulation of secular ideas. These tongues fell into two broad groups: the Romance (Romanic) and the Teutonic (Germanic). The boundary between the two was roughly the frontier of the ancient Roman Empire. In those areas that had long been occupied by Rome, spoken Latin served as the foundation of the vernacular tongues. It was modified only slightly as a result of the Germanic invasions, and it evolved, as living languages do, into local dialects. In areas north and east of the Roman imperial frontiers, the Teutonic-speaking peoples continued to use their age-old tongues. Western Europe to this day is divided into these linguistic groups: the national languages of Italy, Spain, Portugal, and France are derived from the Romanic; those of the Netherlands, Germany, and Scandinavia from the Germanic. Central and eastern Europe were occupied by the Slavs after the ancient Germanic tribes moved westward (p. 187). They, of course, speak their own *Slavic* languages, such as Russian, Ukrainian, Polish, Czech, and Bulgarian. All these languages, whether Romance, Teutonic, or Slavic, are descended from Indo-European dialects spoken by different groups of barbarian tribes in prehistoric times (pp. 47–48).

England, in the West, is a special case. It was less thoroughly Romanized than the other portions of the empire, and the Anglo-Saxon invaders were able to impose their Teutonic dialect upon the native Britons. The later Danish and Norman conquests (pp. 208, 211, 212) brought additional influences. By the middle of the fourteenth century Anglo-Saxon (Old English) had become modified into what we now term Middle English. Out of this evolved *modern* English, a mixture of Teutonic and Romance elements.

As early as the eleventh century the spoken vernaculars began to be set down in writing. These writings appealed chiefly to the nobility, and this "literature of chivalry" had a modifying influence, no doubt, on the values and behavior of those rough warriors. A leading work was the epic *Song of Roland* (*Chanson de Roland*), written by an unknown author in the dialect of northern France (around 1200). Though it grew out of traditional songs about the earlier hero-king Charlemagne and his courtly companions, this poem expresses the values of the medieval Christian knights.

Its chief hero is Count Roland, nephew of Charlemagne (p. 203). Roland personifies the warrior ideals of bravery, loyalty, and military prowess — and

*From George F. Whicher, *The Goliard Poets*. Copyright 1949 by George F. Whicher. Reprinted by permission of New Directions Publishing Corporation.

the Christian faith in God and salvation. The tradition of the Greek epic can be seen in this poem. It glorifies France and its heroes as Homer had glorified the champions of Hellas (p. 74). Roland is the counterpart of proud Achilles; the field of battle runs red with the blood of the courageous; and Roland's fellow vassals observe strictly the code of honor and revenge. Other national epics were written at about the same time in neighboring countries: the *Nibelungenlied* (*Song of the Nibelungs*) in Germany and the *Poema del Cid* (*Poem of the Cid*) in Spain.

But the troubadours (professional singers) of the Middle Ages did not confine themselves to epic tales. They also sang of "courtly" manners and *romantic love*. For the first time since the days of the pagan authors, a poetry of passion appeared in Europe. But it was, for the most part, passion on an "elevated" plane. The romantic knight placed his ideal woman on a pedestal and adored her from afar — with thoughts of physical fulfillment repressed or postponed. This "cult of love" also brought forth elaborate manuals of behavior for lovers. Courtly love, it should be noted, was a pastime for the nobility only; commoners were considered unsuited to the delicate art of romance. Even so, the code of conduct that held love as a noble ideal made a distinguishing mark upon the whole of Western culture.

Clearly, the hearty masculine culture of the early Middle Ages was giving way to a more tranquil, confident, and leisurely society. The noble's castle was becoming less of a barracks for fighting men and more of a theater for refined pleasures. Aristocratic ladies were accorded more and more attention and were able to exercise greater control over the men.

The feudal society of the later Middle Ages is splendidly portrayed in the so-called Arthurian romances, a cycle of prose stories composed in the twelfth and thirteenth centuries by French and Norman writers. One of the first and best of these was Chrétien de Troyes, who lived for a time at the court of the countess of Champagne, in eastern France, and who also enjoyed the patronage of the strong-willed Eleanor of Aquitaine. (Eleanor, who had been queen of France before becoming queen of England, regarded herself as the queen of courtly love and its laws of conduct.) Chrétien's most popular story, *Lancelot*, helped to shape the heroic mold of that mythical knight.

The central figure of the Arthurian romance is, of course, King Arthur, a Celtic chieftain of sixth-century Britain who fought against the Anglo-Saxon invaders (p. 181). But the legends of Arthur's Round Table are told in the manner of the late Middle Ages; they are tales of forbidden love, knightly combats, and colorful pageantry. Successive poets and musicians have turned again and again to Camelot, the legendary site of Arthur's court; Guinevere (Arthur's queen), Sir Lancelot, and Sir Galahad have become familiar characters in Western literature.

Toward the close of the Middle Ages the narratives of chivalric love became less fanciful and more realistic than the Arthurian tales. Most successful was the work of Christine de Pisan, the first woman to support herself entirely from her earnings as an author. Born in Italy, she spent most of her years at or near the French court in Paris. Her best-known story, *The Book of the Duke of True Lovers* (c. 1400), reads much like the earlier aristocratic romances. But it is based on actual events rather than legend, and its lovers act in response to common sense rather than to the dictates of passion and the cult of love.

These aristocratic tales were of little interest to the bourgeois. Finding little of their own lives in such stories, they turned to a different sort of secular literature. This, too, originated in France, and consisted of *fabliaux* (fables). Unlike the heroic and idyllic tales of chivalry, the fabliaux were about everyday life. Frank, sensual, and witty, they ridiculed both courtly and priestly life. One of the most popular fables was *Aucassin and Nicolette*, by an unknown author. Its hero, Aucassin, spurns knighthood in order to pursue his passion for a beautiful young Muslim captive. Indifferent to his soul's salvation, he subordinates everything to his desire for union with Nicolette. He even prefers hell to heaven, on the ground that the company there will be more attractive and entertaining.

The peasantry — the largest element of the population — could not read books of any sort. But they could listen to folk tales, legends, and ballads and could learn to recite them. A typical hero of folk literature was Robin Hood, a glorified English yeoman (freeman) who stole from the rich and gave to the poor. Robin's deeds corresponded to the commoners' desire for adventure, rebellion, and social justice.

Two works of the late Middle Ages rise above ordinary classification. One is *The Canterbury Tales* of Geoffrey Chaucer, written in the fourteenth century. This collection of stories is in the general spirit of the fabliaux but includes all classes of society and a wide range of topics. Born of a merchant family, Chaucer spent most of his life in the service of the English aristocracy. He read broadly and traveled extensively on the continent. His outlook was cosmopolitan and urbane, and he displayed a rare combination of scholarship, insight, and humor. In the *Tales*, a group of people exchange stories as they ride on pilgrimage to the holy shrine at Canterbury (p. 213). The stories, of "good morality and general pleasure," appealed to all literate persons in fourteenth-century England. In them, as in a mirror, they could see themselves and their society.

The other monumental work of the period is the *Divine Comedy* of Dante, which is regarded as the masterpiece of Italian literature. More profound than Chaucer's work, the *Comedy* is a grand synthesis of medieval theology, science, philosophy, and romance. Dante, a Florentine scholar and poet, was immersed in the political and intellectual currents of his time. His heroic poem is an *allegorical* tale describing the experiences of human souls after death. Escorted by the Roman poet Vergil (p. 114), Dante travels in his poem through the regions beyond the grave. He descends into the terrible Inferno (hell) and then moves on to Purgatory, where the souls of pardoned sinners are struggling ever upward. At last he is permitted to enter Paradise (heaven), where the blessed enjoy, in fitting ways, the gifts of God. For this final portion of the journey

Dante must leave the pagan Vergil behind. Now he is guided by the pure Beatrice, his ideal of Christian womanhood, who represents the blending of romantic and spiritual love that leads Dante at last to a climactic vision of God.

Dante called his work a comedy (*Commedia*) because he believed the story suggests a happy ending for all who choose to follow Christ. (Later admirers added the compliment "divine.") It is a moving and intensely personal story. At every turn of the narrative, Dante makes sharp comments on the characters of history and myth, who serve as dramatic symbols for his moralizing. Readers may agree or disagree with Dante's judgments, but they will long remember the vivid images created by his words.

WEST AND EAST: THE CRUSADES

The flowering of European literature and art reflected the mounting self-confidence of the West. Latin Christendom had come a long way from the troubled, precarious days of the ninth century, when western Europe had been a besieged fortress, struggling to hold out against determined invaders (pp. 207–9). As between the two variants of European civilization that had come into existence by the year 1000, that of the Latin West and the Byzantine East (pp. 188–89), the balance of power was swinging toward the West; and the West was even strong enough to take the offensive against the rival religion and civilization of Islam.

The Western Counteroffensive

To a large extent, this counteroffensive was the work of the feudal society that had grown up in the turmoil of the early Middle Ages. Kings and great lords were eager to enlarge their holdings and acquire land with which to reward their vassals. Among lesser warriors, there were crowds of younger sons and landless knights who dreamed of finding fiefs that would enable them to acquire the wealth and status of landowners. Thus there was a tendency among feudal warriors, once the pressure of outside attack slackened, to go immediately over to the offensive — not just to eliminate enemies but so as to conquer and colonize land. Any non-Christian nation, whether pagan or Islamic, was regarded as fair game for this purpose. That was why, during the tenth century, Norman warriors hastened to Sicily to reconquer it from the Saracens (and then went on to wrest southern Italy from Christian Byzantium, which was already coming to be considered an enemy of the Latin Church because of its persisting refusal to admit the supremacy of the pope — p. 155). For the same mixed reasons, great lords and knights from all over Europe participated in the gradual reconquest of Spain (p. 212).

But feudal warriors were not the only ones involved in the Western offensive. Conquest and colonization usually also opened the way for trade, and were therefore in the interests of the townspeople as well. Especially in the south, the pushing back of the frontiers of Islam cleared the western

Mediterranean for the rising commerce of Christian Europe. In the eleventh century, while feudal knights were fighting to reconquer Spain and Sicily, the islands of Sardinia and Corsica were seized from the Saracens by an Italian city-state, Pisa.

Besides feudal land hunger and commercial enterprise, the West was also possessed by religious faith. The power of religion in guiding the Western offensive is shown by the fact that religion was sometimes actually strong enough to rein the offensive in. Pagan tribes several times saved themselves from attack by timely conversion: this was one of the reasons why the Poles and Hungarians adopted Latin Christianity (pp. 212–13). On the other hand, religion also drove the warriors forward, particularly once the idea grew up in the eleventh century that to fight against pagans and Muslims — unlike other kinds of warfare, which the Church regarded as in principle sinful — was actually pleasing to God and conducive to eternal salvation. Once the popes took up this idea of Holy War, the stage was set for the most dynamic forces in western European civilization — the feudal warriors, the townspeople, and the Latin Church — to cooperate in a vast but ill-fated enterprise: the crusades.

Triumph and Tragedy in the Holy Land

Though crusades were fought against various non-Christian enemies in different regions of Europe, the most important of them were directed against the Muslims in the Holy Land — for the professed purpose of recapturing the birthplace of Christianity. These "great" crusades were, in fact, international mass movements that fired the imagination of all classes of society for two centuries (1095–1270). Though the crusades failed to achieve their declared aim, they provided a dramatic expression of the confidence and zeal of a reviving West.

It was the preaching of Pope Urban II that set Europe off on the "First Crusade." But the response to his call can be understood only in the light of longstanding tensions, which can be traced back as far as the fourth-century division of the Roman Empire (p. 135). Latin Christendom and Byzantium (pp. 185, 202), though linked by Christianity, had become increasingly hostile to each other. The rivalry between the Latin and Greek churches (p. 155) had grown in bitterness over the centuries. To the Westerners the Byzantines seemed decadent, pompous, and effeminate. They, in turn, looked upon the Westerners as rude and grasping barbarians. In the long centuries between the fall of Rome and the start of the crusades, relations between the West and Byzantium had gone from bad to worse.

The relations of the West with Islam (pp. 189–92) were less complicated. The Saracens were openly recognized as enemies, who had long fought the Christians in Spain and in the western Mediterranean. Though the Muslim religion was known to Westerners only in caricature, it was condemned by the Church as a devilish heresy. Western Church leaders remained continually

c. 750	c. 1050	c. 1300
Muslim Rule in Spain	Christian Reconquest of Spain	

fearful lest Islam resume its expansive sweep of earlier centuries. Nevertheless, until after 1000 there were few signs of general hostility on either side: the Christian faithful who remained in Muslim countries continued to enjoy freedom of worship, and pilgrims to the Holy Land were permitted to visit without interference. As more and more pilgrims visited the precious shrines, however, there was mounting resentment among Christians that these places should be held by "infidels" (betrayers of the True Faith).

The series of events that sparked the crusades had its beginning, actually, in central Asia. During the ninth century a militant nomadic people (pp. 45–47), the Turks, had entered Persia from the north. They were quickly converted to Islam and for more than a century held control over a portion of the Islamic empire. In the eleventh century the Turkish Seljuk dynasty conquered Baghdad, and won the title of "sultan" or ruler from its caliph (p. 191). Members of this warlike family pushed westward from Baghdad into Syria, Palestine, and Asia Minor. They established themselves as sultans of several small states in those areas and reversed the tolerant policies of their predecessors. Having crushed one Byzantine army in Asia Minor, the Turks then began to move toward the imperial capital itself. It was this emergency that caused the Eastern emperor, Alexius, to send an urgent appeal for help to the West. Thus was triggered the European movement known as the crusades.

Pope Urban II heard the plea of Alexius' ambassador early in 1095 and found the idea of sending a rescue force to the East well suited to his own far-reaching aims. Heir to the Cluniac reform movement and to the policies of Gregory VII (p. 238), Urban realized that a successful holy war against the Turks would do more than free Palestine and reopen the roads of pilgrimage. It would in all likelihood compel the Byzantine emperor, in repayment, to recognize the supremacy of the pope over the whole Christian Church. Moreover, the triumph would lift the prestige of the papacy to such a height that the Cluniac ideal of church supremacy over the state would surely be realized.

Later in the year 1095, Urban used the general Council of Clermont, in central France, as his forum for launching the First Crusade. His speech, a masterpiece of persuasion and emotion, appealed to both the highest and the lowest of human motives. As he addressed the assembled clergy, he was really speaking to all the classes and interests of Europe. He knew that some of the churchmen listening to him at Clermont had a deep dislike of violence. Yet his call for action was so effective that as he ended the oration his listeners shouted, "God wills it!" This became the battle cry of the crusaders.

In his speech, the pope kindled ugly prejudices and fanned them into a flame of hatred for the Turks. He reported, in horrific detail, atrocities that the "vile" and "accursed" race had allegedly committed against Christians. In the

name of Christ, Urban appealed to men of all ranks, rich and poor, to extermi-
nate the infidels. He reminded his listeners that such a response would be in
keeping with the grandest traditions of Western Christendom: Charlemagne,
for example, had proved his manhood and achieved glory by destroying paganism and extending the territory of the Church (p. 201). The same objectives
could be accomplished once more — and with a guarantee of safety for the soul
of each participant. The pope, citing his authority as vicar of Christ, declared
that all who died while journeying or fighting on this "holy pilgrimage" would
be automatically pardoned for all their sins.

Urban was aware, however, that it would take more than religious excitement to defeat the Turks. He aimed his call directly at the military class — the
knights and landholders. Quoting Scripture, Urban told them that they must
not hold back because of their concern for family or possessions: "Everyone
that has forsaken houses, or brothers, or sisters, or father, or mother, or wife, or
children, or lands for my name's sake shall receive a hundredfold and shall
inherit everlasting life." Then Urban observed that Europe was a narrow and
confined space — too small to support its growing population. For this reason,
he explained, you "murder and devour one another" in endless private warfare. Let your quarrels and hatreds cease, the pope concluded: "Enter upon the
road to the Holy Land; take it from the wicked race, and keep it for yourselves.
That land which, as the Scripture says, 'flows with milk and honey,' was given
by God into the possession of the children of Israel."

Thus presented, the crusade appealed to many Europeans' desire for
wealth, for Christian unity, for personal honor and sacrifice, for excitement
and adventure, and for spiritual salvation. The Italian merchants, though Urban had not been addressing them directly, saw a special advantage to themselves in the crusade. They would gain profit by providing ships and supplies.
And, if the crusaders succeeded, fabulous commercial opportunities would be
opened to them.

Of the successive expeditions to the East, by land and by sea, the First
Crusade was the only one to attain (temporarily) its professed goal. French
noblemen, responding to the call of Urban (who was himself a French aristocrat), made up the main body of crusaders. Godfrey, Duke of Lorraine, joined
by other dukes, counts, and barons, set out in 1096 with an army of some fifteen
thousand knights. They took the land route to Constantinople and then
crossed into Asia Minor to confront the Turks.

The crusaders suffered severe hardships, disease, and some defeats, but
they were at last victorious. Their leaders, having turned back the Turkish
threat to Constantinople, moved on to establish dukedoms in Asia Minor and
abandoned their original plan to march on to Jerusalem. The survivors of
lesser rank, however, insisted that the crusade be resumed. Responding at last
to their demands, Raymond, Count of Toulouse, advanced on Jerusalem and
took the city, after a six-week siege, in 1099.

The crusaders' entry into the Holy City was an orgy of looting and killing
of Muslims and Jews. One crusader reported in his journal,

The amount of blood that they shed on that day is incredible. . . . Some of our men (and this was more merciful) cut off the heads of their enemies; others shot them with arrows, so that they fell from the towers; others tortured them longer by casting them into the flames. Piles of heads, hands, and feet were to be seen in the streets of the city. . . . It was a just and splendid judgment of God that this place should be filled with the blood of unbelievers, since it had suffered so long from their blasphemies.

With the help of fleets from Venice, Genoa, and other Italian cities, the crusaders moved on to take the coastal towns of Palestine and Syria. (For this aid the Italians received, as they had hoped, rich privileges in the trade of the Orient.) The various conquered territories were then drawn together into a loose feudal state called the Latin Kingdom of Jerusalem. Baldwin of Flanders was chosen as its first king and accepted the usual homage and services of the landholding nobility. The feudal system of western Europe was thus transplanted to this Christian "beachhead" in the Middle East. But the kingdom proved short-lived. Half a century later, having rebuilt their forces, the Muslims launched a counteroffensive from surrounding territories. They won out, despite the arrival of Christian reinforcements from Europe. In 1187 Saladin, their resourceful leader, recaptured Jerusalem, and for all practical purposes the Latin Kingdom was dead.

There were countless other expeditions to the East, only some of which have been given a "number" by European historians. Even before the First Crusade was launched, a motley crowd of commoners had set out from southern Germany for Constantinople. Their enthusiasm, sparked by the pope's call to arms, was whipped to a fury by a maverick preacher known as Peter the Hermit. The Peasants' Crusade, as it came to be called, distinguished itself chiefly by the massacre of Jewish communities along the way. Lacking provisions of their own, these commoners lived off the country as they marched. When they at last reached Constantinople, the Byzantine emperor grew alarmed and hastily ferried them across the Bosporus waterway to Asia Minor. There the Turks made quick work of the misguided peasants.

The Second Crusade (1146) — called in response to Turkish success in recapturing part of the territory won in the First Crusade — was inspired by a reforming monk, Bernard of Clairvaux (p. 237). An extraordinarily persuasive man, he induced two monarchs and thousands of fighting men to "put on the Cross." The main force of this expedition was cut to pieces as it moved across Asia Minor. Bernard, convinced that his cause was just, concluded that the failure must have been due to the sinfulness of the crusaders.

Bernard's view was accepted by his more ardent followers. Some of them went still further: they reasoned that if purity of soul was a requirement for victory, young children would be the most favored of all crusaders. Somewhat later, in accordance with this notion, thousands of innocent German and French boys marched off on a Children's Crusade (1212). They never reached the Holy Land, however, for they fell victim to accident and disease or were captured by slave-dealers along the way.

Additional crusades of various sorts continued until the end of the Middle Ages. Though papal propaganda continued to stress the recovery of the holy places, the principal motive of the later expeditions was to guard against the rising power of the Turks. Actually, the crusades had increased the danger to Europe by undermining the Byzantine Empire. When Emperor Alexius called for aid in 1095, he had hoped that the Western knights would help his armies drive the Turks from Asia Minor and restore imperial control over that strategic area. But, as we have seen, the feudal lords had different intentions. The counts and dukes pursued their private ambitions and divided Asia Minor and Syria into principalities for themselves. These fell like houses of straw when the Turkish storm broke again in the twelfth century.

The cruelest blow to Byzantium occurred during the Fourth Crusade, which was turned against Constantinople itself. The crusade was organized by leading French barons and was to have gone by sea from Venice to Egypt. But the leaders, while on their way, plotted with the Venetians to switch the expedition from its original objective. They knew that Constantinople was a richer prize than all the Holy Land — and that it could be taken more easily.

The imperial capital was stormed in 1204 by the very men whose forefathers had promised its rescue a century before. Untold treasures of gold, silver, and holy relics were seized during the subsequent pillage and rape (see p. 483). Vandalism and fire consumed irreplaceable works of Greek art and literature. The city and the European portion of the empire were then divided among the chieftains of the crusade, and these remnants were brought together as the Latin Empire of Constantinople. The count of Flanders was proclaimed its first emperor, and a new patriarch (head) of the Greek Church was installed — one who was loyal to the *pope* in Rome. Venice secured special trading privileges, and the farmlands were parceled out in feudal fashion to the plundering knights. Thus, long-desired and ill-concealed goals were momentarily realized by the papacy, the Venetians, and the French aristocracy — all at the expense of Byzantium.

The Latin Empire of Constantinople was a freak of history, and its life was even briefer than that of the Kingdom of Jerusalem. What the Western forces really accomplished by this infamous crusade was a fatal weakening of Europe's key point of defense against the Turks. A Byzantine emperor carried on (in exile), clinging to a small piece of territory in Asia Minor; and in 1261 he managed to regain Constantinople and the area around it. But Byzantine power had been so shattered that it proved unable to check a later advance by the Turks (p. 284); and the rivalry between the Greek and Latin churches hardened into outright schism (p. 155).

The Anti-Jewish Crusade

The Christian expeditions against the East were accompanied by rising hostility toward the Jews in Europe. During the early Middle Ages, following a grudging decree of toleration by the Roman Emperor Theodosius I (p. 161), the Jews and their culture had survived. While remaining outside the Christian community, restricted by special laws and customs, they were spared the abuses and outrages that came later. The Jews remained small in numbers, constituting perhaps one or two percent of western Europe's population by the year 1000.

Medieval Jews were usually forbidden to hold land, serfs, or slaves and were, in fact, a class entirely separate from the Christian social order. Cut off from the land, they had sought to establish themselves in the towns. The professions, guilds, and most other occupations were closed to them, however, so they supported themselves in enterprises that were for the most part shunned by Christians. These occupations included metalworking, pottery-working, sewing, butchering, peddling, trading in precious jewels, and moneylending (p. 287).

The Jews congregated in their own quarters of medieval towns, partly to enhance their physical security and partly to maintain their distinctive pattern of life. There they were allowed a kind of autonomy by the governing officials, and the synagogue, with its rabbi (teacher), became a center of Jewish religion, law, and life. Despite the limitations on their freedom of action, some Jews rose to positions of power and distinction in commerce and royal administration. These individuals, however, could not match the achievements of the Spanish Jews, who enjoyed the generous tolerance of Muslim rulers (prior to the Christian reconquest of Spain). Notable Jewish scholars, poets, philosophers, and statesmen made, in Muslim Spain, a Golden Age of Jewish history. They contributed, at the same time, to the intellectual development of Christian Europe by helping to bring into Western circulation the wisdom of the ancient Greeks (p. 256).

The Christian attack on the Muslims in Spain (p. 265) and the expeditions to recapture the Holy Land brought a disastrous end to the relative security of Jews everywhere. The First Crusade, launched in 1096, set off a spasm of religious fanaticism and violence (p. 269). During the next two centuries, as prejudices against Jews were stirred up by Christian leaders, mob attacks on Jewish communities became commonplace.

Sporadic outbursts of anti-Semitic feeling had occurred in earlier times, but now the burnings and massacres became epidemic. In 1215 the Fourth Lateran Council of the Church encouraged public humiliation of the Jews by ordering that they must wear a yellow patch or cap for identification. In most countries of Europe, strict laws were enacted confining Jews to a marked-off zone (ghetto) in each town — usually the foulest and most congested part. Punishment and intimidation often took the form of seizing and burning copies of the Jewish Talmud (ancient rabbinical writings about their Scriptures), on the ground that the contents were offensive to Christ. At last, because they were thought to be an intolerable "contamination" to Christians, all Jews who refused conversion to Christianity were expelled from country after country:

England in 1290, parts of Germany in 1298, France in 1306, Spain in 1492. Compelled to leave their properties behind, thousands of Jews settled in eastern Europe and the Middle East (p. 282). Some found refuge in the kingdom of Naples, Poland, and lands under Turkish rule.

Some Christians were, of course, shocked by the violence and injustice directed against the Jews and gave them aid and protection when they could. But, from the twelfth century onward, the Jews could expect repeated humiliations and persecutions from the Christian societies in which they lived. This record is one of the longest and gloomiest chapters of Western history — a compound of Church teachings, popular ignorance, mob hysteria, and individual aggression.

THE MEDIEVAL SYNTHESIS

The crusades against the Muslims (and Jews) were a dramatic expression of the contradictions that characterized medieval civilization. The impulse that sent many of the knights to the Holy Land, at great personal sacrifice, was noble and genuine, but personal courage and high-mindedness were often overshadowed by baser motives. These contradictions marked European society as a whole. Though every civilization reveals some gap between ideals and reality, in the Middle Ages the gulf was extremely wide. The Christian goals of love and peace were generally professed, but the years were heavy with hatred and war. Humility and voluntary poverty were praised as holy virtues, but the most admired individuals were both proud and rich. The idea of a "Christian commonwealth" was preached, but the actuality was a narrow provincialism and constant struggle between church and state.

In other ways, too, the civilization of the Middle Ages was marked by contrasts and contradictions. Its intellectual leaders made a virtue of rigidity and conservatism, at least in theory and to a considerable extent in practice. For much of the period, most people of all classes (except the higher clergy) were marked by ignorance; literacy and education were not the common right of all, but a requirement only for certain vocations. And even the educated few believed in many crude superstitions. Their image of reality was blurred by ancient errors and an exaggerated belief in the *miraculous*; most minds were closed to systematic factual investigation. Though the medieval philosophers were thorough and well-disciplined, they held to a methodology and a concept of truth that did not meet the needs of the expanding Western world.

The society of the Middle Ages stressed the value of groups over individuals. Most people belonged to a village, a guild, a town, a fellowship, or a religious order. Their active Christian faith told them that their role in life, whether high or low, was determined by God, and all that was required of them was to live out their days according to Church-approved custom. It also gave them the consoling hope that the "life to come" would make up for the hardships of this world.

Yet the Middle Ages were also an era of remarkable creativity, when people improvised, improved, and innovated in every field. This was as true in farming, commerce, warfare, and technology as it was in law, education, and the arts. The spread of towns and universities is impressive evidence of resurgent human enterprise. The growth of agriculture and the development of new machinery and industrial methods are proof of economic expansion and technical inventiveness. The building of the Gothic cathedrals ranks among the greatest feats of engineering skill, artistic imagination, and spiritual striving of any civilization.

Many modern scholars regard these contrasts between ideal and reality, conservatism and innovation, rigidity and creativity not as contradictions, but as different aspects of an all-embracing harmony — the "medieval synthesis" as it is often called. Some have gone so far as to regard the medieval synthesis as the crowning achievement of Western civilization, for which the pagan civilizations of ancient times were a mere preparation, and from which the materialistic, secular civilization of the modern world represents a regrettable decline. Yet no amount of romanticizing can hide the other side of the medieval record — famine, filth, disease, violence, intolerance, and oppression. In these aspects, the Middle Ages were far from being a pinnacle of civilization.

It would also be a mistake, however, to regard evils of this kind as unique to the Middle Ages. Classical Greece, with its oracles to which humble citizens and proud city-states alike resorted in hopes of learning what the gods had in store for them (p. 65), had its own superstitions. In ancient Rome, with its citizens driven to ruin by the all-powerful tax-collectors, and its aristocrats who owned much of the population as slaves (pp. 101, 129–30, 135), oppression of the humble by the mighty was as ruthless as in the Middle Ages. And in the twentieth-century world, which boasts of abundance, peace, and progress amid bouts of famine, genocide, and social decay, the gap between ideals and realities looms just as large.

At the present day, no doubt, both the admirable and the evil sides of the Middle Ages seem more vivid to us than those of Greece, Rome, or other remote civilizations. But this is not because medieval civilization was exceptional, either in its achievements and strivings or in its follies and crimes. The reason is simply that we ourselves are nearer in time to the Middle Ages; for out of the changes that marked the end of the medieval period there evolved the Western civilization of the present day.

7-1 Hans Holbein the Younger. Detail from *The Ambassadors*, 1533. National Gallery, London.

PART THREE

THE COMING
OF MODERN TIMES

	POLITICAL, SOCIAL, AND ECONOMIC DEVELOPMENTS	RELIGION, SCIENCE, AND PHILOSOPHY	HISTORY AND LITERATURE	ART AND ARCHITECTURE
1300	Travels of Marco Polo			Florence Cathedral
				Giotto
	Black Death (bubonic plague) Hundred Years' War (1338–1453) Decline of feudal and manorial systems	"Babylonian Captivity" of papacy (1309–76) Renaissance humanism (1350–1600)	Petrarch Boccaccio	
	New weapons of war: longbow and crossbow			Renaissance style of architecture: Brunelleschi
		Great Schism (1379–1417) Wiclif		
1400	Domestic system of production (1400–1750)	Hus		Donatello Masaccio Van Eyck Ghiberti
	Age of despots in Italy: Cosimo de' Medici Francesco Sforza New-style armies: cannon and muskets		Valla Gutenberg	
	Fall of Constantinople to Ottoman Turks	Platonism (Florentine Academy) Ficino Pico Machiavelli		
	Expulsion of Muslims from Spain Jacob Fugger			Botticelli

	Politics & Events	Religion & Science	Literature	Art
1500	Overseas exploration: Columbus, da Gama, Magellan; Establishment of European colonial empires: Cortez, Pizarro; Rise of national monarchies: Henry VIII, Francis I	Luther (beginning of Protestant Reformation); Calvin; Pope Paul III (beginning of Catholic Reformation); Copernicus; Loyola and Society of Jesus; Council of Trent	Erasmus; Castiglione, More, Rabelais, Cellini	Leonardo; Michelangelo, Titian, Holbein, St. Peter's Basilica
	Charles V, Holy Roman Emperor; Philip II; Elizabeth I; Spanish Armada		Montaigne	Brueghel, Escorial Palace, Baroque style
1600	Religious Wars (Thirty Years' War in Germany)	Francis Bacon; Kepler, Galileo; Descartes	Cervantes, Shakespeare, Jonson	Globe Theater; Rubens; Rembrandt, Bernini
1650	Peace of Westphalia; Louis XIV			Taj Mahal; Versailles Palace

CHAPTER

7

The Transformation
and Expansion
of Europe

Unlike the Roman world, medieval civilization did not "fall." There were no waves of invading barbarians, no collapse of civic order and commerce. On the contrary, western Europe at the "close" of the Middle Ages displayed a remarkable vitality and an expansive spirit. It moved, without a noticeable break, into "modern" times. Thus, we cannot point to any historical event or series of events and say, "Here ended the Middle Ages." We might even say that our present civilization is an extension of medieval times, for the evolution of Western institutions has been continuous over the past thousand years, and the seeds of each new era have been nurtured in the old. Clearly, though, the *visible pattern* of Western life has changed profoundly. This transformation began already during the thirteenth century, and it accelerated during the fourteenth century, through a series of social calamities.

DISSOLUTION OF THE MEDIEVAL SYNTHESIS

The "modern world," as that term applies to the West, was several centuries in maturing. In some parts of Europe it arrived sooner than in others. But, for Western civilization as a whole, the medieval pattern had begun to *dissolve* by 1400, and by 1650 a new pattern had come into being.

The forces that dissolved the old synthesis and created the new were varied but related to one another. When a change began in one sphere of human affairs, it was reinforced by changes in others. The primary force appears to have been economic. In the thirteenth century, out of the bustling towns and cities and the increasingly populous and productive countryside that had developed since 1000, a truly commercial and capitalist economy was emerging. New social ranks appeared; serfdom grew obsolete in western Europe; and the entire class structure became more fluid. The bonds of caste and group were thereby loosened, and the freedom of the *individual* was enlarged. With economic and social change came political change. When stability and prosperity returned to Europe, monarchs found that they could exert a larger measure of direct authority over their kingdoms. Feudal states gradually gave way to centralized national states.

With the world changing in so many ways, ethical and philosophical views were bound to change, too. In the sharpened competition for wealth and power, the medieval ideals of asceticism, poverty, and humility were thrust aside by the "modern" aspirations for pleasure, money, and status. In formal thought, the scholastic approach to knowledge was challenged and discredited (pp. 256–60). (We will discuss the new view of human nature and its expressions in philosophy, art, and literature in Chapter 8.)

The breakup of the medieval pattern proceeded, during most of the transitional period, in a gradual, undramatic fashion. Many of the changes were hardly noticed when they took place, and few people could tell where they were leading. But one change was observed by all: the seamless garment of Western religious faith was torn by the Protestant movements of the sixteenth century. These movements set in fairly late in the course of the medieval dissolution, and they served to convince reflective men and women that a new age had indeed arrived. For, if the Catholic Church had been the core of western European life, its division confirmed the end of the traditional synthesis. We will consider forces underlying this religious upheaval in Chapter 9. In the present chapter we will examine the economic, social, geographic, and political factors that changed the face of Western civilization.

The Calamitous Fourteenth Century

Deep-running historical currents were already transforming European institutions by 1300, but the events of the years that followed speeded up the process. The fourteenth century was a time of turmoil and disaster, comparable to the late fifth century B.C. in Greece (pp. 87–88) and the turbulent third century A.D. in Italy (pp. 129–31). Social unrest, growing out of the deprivations and indignities that the common people had suffered for centuries, grew acute in western Europe after 1300. Revolts by peasants against their feudal masters had occurred at various times and places throughout the Middle Ages, but they had always been crushed by the feudal nobles. In the fourteenth century, however, social unrest threatened the very foundations of the political and economic order.

The trouble started with the weather. Early in the century Arctic cold and heavy rains swept across Europe, flooding farmlands and shortening the growing season. Hunger and starvation became widespread. (These natural disasters are a reminder that all societies live within a delicate ecological balance. A climatic shift of a few degrees can upset that balance, as it did in the fourteenth century.) The resulting famine had further effects: lower human resistance to disease, severe dislocations in agriculture and commerce, and fiercer competition among individuals, classes, and nations.

In 1320 a peasant uprising started in northern France. Its leaders expressed the grievances of the poor and a religious hope that the lowly would overthrow the highborn and establish a "Christian commonwealth" of equality for all. Farmers and poor people from the cities joined excited mobs as they made their way across the countryside. The rebels seized arms, attacked castles and monasteries, and destroyed tax records. As tales of atrocities circulated, the nobility and the clergy grew alarmed. Finally, after Pope John XXII had condemned the outlaws, mounted bands of knights took to the field and ruthlessly slaughtered the weary peasants. But the resentment and anger of the poor persisted.

Another uprising occurred about a generation later, in 1358. It was called the "Jacquerie," from Jacques, the popular catch-name for a peasant. Kindled in a village near Paris, the revolt spread like wildfire across the country. At its peak, perhaps one hundred thousand men, women, and children were on the rampage. Though better equipped and organized, the Jacquerie suffered the same fate as the earlier rebels. For two months both the peasants and the avenging nobles engaged in burnings, lootings, and killings.

France was not alone in her ordeal. During the century similar uprisings occurred all over Europe. In England the Peasants' Revolt of 1381 followed the pattern of the Jacquerie. Marked by murders and burnings, it was finally crushed by the ferocity and treachery of the nobles and the king.

Adding to these miseries were the drawn-out struggles between the English and French monarchs. (This prolonged conflict, which began in 1338, was later referred to as the Hundred Years' War.) Though combats were limited mainly to the noble class, they brought ruin to the farms and towns of France, the principal battlefield. The long-term political consequences of the Hundred Years' War will be discussed later in this chapter (pp. 309–14); the widespread physical damage was the immediate and most distressing result.

The cruelest blow of all to fourteenth-century Europeans was the bubonic plague, or Black Death, which struck in 1348. This infection, which is carried by black rats and their fleas, had already devastated much of Europe in the sixth century (p. 184). For several centuries thereafter, there were no massive outbreaks; but now the rats carried the plague to all parts of the continent and to the British Isles. Having had slight prior contact with the infection, people were highly susceptible, and their capacity for resistance had been weakened by widespread malnutrition. The first symptoms of the disease appear as ugly sores, or buboes, at the spot of the flea bite. Fever and chills follow, along with dark spots on the skin. (Since the dark spots usually precede death, the pestilence came to be known as the "Black Death.") After the primary form of the plague has become established in humans, it can be transmitted directly by breath to other humans. This second form, which invades the lungs, is even more lethal than the first and causes death within a few days.

The plague was at its height during its first two years and then continued to flare up from time to time. It killed perhaps a quarter of all the inhabitants of Europe during the fourteenth century (twenty-five million out of a population of one hundred million). In addition to its toll in death and suffering, the plague had drastic economic, social, and psychological effects. *Death* became a universal obsession. Many people interpreted the plague as a punishment from God that called for severe personal penitence; some thought the end of the world was at hand.

By the close of the century the effects of the plague had diminished, and life returned more or less to normal. But the medieval patterns of society had been severely strained by the plague and by the other catastrophes that had struck the people of Europe. The bonds holding people and institutions together were close to the breaking point: between serf and lord, journeyman and master, noble and king, lay person and priest, priest and pope. The bonds held, for yet awhile. But new forces, new ideas, and new relationships were on the rise; with the gradual recovery of European strength and confidence, the new ways would shortly overcome the old.

Eastern Europe in the Later Middle Ages

The crisis of the later Middle Ages affected eastern Europe even more severely than western Europe. Whereas the western countries mastered the crisis and rebuilt European civilization, those of the east never completely recovered. Instead, they took on the role in European civilization that they have retained down to the present day: that of "junior partner" to the western European countries, and the bulwark against threats to Europe from further east.

The differences between western and eastern Europe were partly religious and cultural, originating in the divergences between Roman and Byzantine civilization and the schism between the Latin and Greek churches (pp. 155, 183–89). The capture of Constantinople by Western crusaders in 1204 (p. 268) was far from spelling the end of Byzantine civilization. Though the restored Byzantine Empire from 1261 onward was small and feeble, its spiritual and cultural hold over the Orthodox peoples of eastern Europe was as strong as ever. (The Greek Church usually called itself "Orthodox," meaning "correct," just as the Latin Church called itself "Catholic," meaning "universal.") Most of the territories in southeastern Europe that Byzantium lost after 1204 came to be dominated by two rival successor states, Serbia and Bulgaria, which were both ethnically Slavic and Orthodox in religion. The rulers of these states, and even the Byzantine emperors, sometimes tried to strike bargains with the popes, submitting to papal religious authority in return for western military and political support. But these bargains never lasted; for as a result of the disaster of 1204, most of the Orthodox faithful now regarded the Catholic Church as an enemy and a traitor to Christianity. The rulers and people of Russia, the largest Orthodox country, were even more suspicious of Rome. Thus, the estrangement between the Catholic and the Orthodox churches hardened into bitter religious hostility.

The divergence between western and eastern Europe was also social, economic, and political. With the rise of a dynamic urban trading and industrial economy from 1000 on, western Europe forged ahead of the east. While the ruling families of western Europe came to accept the principle of primogeniture (p. 209) in the eleventh and twelfth centuries, those of eastern Europe continued to divide their dominions among numerous heirs until the end of the Middle Ages, thereby weakening their dynastic power. Europe came to be divided into a group of stronger and more highly developed western countries and a group of weaker and less highly developed eastern countries. The second group included not only the Orthodox countries but also Catholic Poland and Hungary, and the eastern territories of the Holy Roman Empire (p. 210). This division has persisted down to the present day.

In the Middle Ages, the western countries gained many advantages from the presence of a group of less advanced countries on their eastern borders. For western Europe, the east provided territories for colonization and emigration, and sources of foodstuffs and raw materials. In the twelfth and thirteenth centuries, crusaders from the Holy Roman Empire conquered many still-pagan tribes on the southern and eastern shores of the Baltic Sea (p. 214). Throughout these eastern borderlands of the Holy Roman Empire and on into Poland and Hungary, masses of German colonists moved in, clearing the land for agriculture and founding new towns and cities — a migration that nationalist-minded German historians centuries later christened the "Drive to the East." Along with the migration of Germans, there was also a mass movement of Jews, fleeing eastward from western European anti-Semitism (pp. 270–72).

In the newly colonized territories, and throughout much of the rest of northeastern Europe, farmers grew grain and flax, and lumberjacks logged timber, for export westward. The towns of eastern Europe functioned as trading outposts of the important German coastal cities that headed the dominant commercial organization of northern Europe, the Hanse (p. 285). Further south, the commerce of Hungary, Serbia, Bulgaria, the Byzantine Empire, and the Black Sea regions (p. 210) was controlled in the same way by the Italian city-states (pp. 303–7).

Sometimes, this western expansion into eastern Europe led to conflict. For more than two hundred years, the rulers of Poland vied for control of the Baltic coastlands with the Teutonic Knights, a group of crusading warriors that had led the German conquest of the pagan tribes of that region. The kings of Hungary likewise contested the hold of Venice on the eastern shores of the Adriatic Sea, Hungary's main outlet for seaborne commerce. In Bohemia, which was inhabited mainly by the Slavic Czechs, resentment at German immigration, along with religious disputes, led eventually to a bitter internal and international struggle, the Hussite Wars (pp. 356–57).

But these conflicts were exceptional. So long as the rulers of eastern Europe did not feel directly threatened with the loss of their local power and independence, they usually accepted western immigration and commercial domination. The kings of Bohemia, Poland, and Hungary welcomed and even invited Germans and Jews to settle in their countries, for the sake of the increased prosperity — and increased tax revenues — that the newcomers brought. Noble landowners were glad to supply foodstuffs and raw materials to the west; and with the kings weakened by the division of their territories and family disputes, it was often the nobles who wielded the greatest share of power. Their main concern was to ensure that they and not the peasants would pocket the profits to be made from trade with the west, and that (with far fewer peasants on the land following the Black Death), enough labor would be available to grow the profitable crops. For this reason, from the fifteenth century onward the nobles of eastern Europe began to reimpose the burdens of serfdom, which had earlier been loosened there as in the western countries (pp. 222–23, 288–89). As a result, from the eastern territories of the Holy Roman Empire through Poland, Hungary, and on into Russia, serfdom persisted down to the nineteenth century (pp. 404, 407, 493, 559).

In these ways, the government system and the social structure of the eastern countries began to diverge from those of western Europe. In the east, the ordinary person remained unfree, and the nobles retained a great deal of governing power in their own hands. Moreover, in eastern Europe social differences were also ethnic. In any particular region, the peasants belonged to one ethnic group, the townspeople to another (usually German or Jewish), and it was not unusual for the nobles and rulers to belong to yet a third ethnic group. In the Middle Ages, eastern Europe was on the whole more tolerant of religious and ethnic diversity than western Europe. But in modern times, under the impact of new religious, nationalist, and class ideologies — all of western European origin — eastern Europe would be torn by savage strife.

There was yet another important difference between eastern and western Europe: the eastern countries, unlike the western ones, were constantly exposed to Asiatic attack. Though the barbarian peoples of Europe itself had mostly entered the orbit of civilization by 1000, the nomadic peoples of Asia (pp. 45–47) remained a formidable threat. This threat reached its height in the thirteenth century when a nomadic people from the Far East, the Mongols under Genghis Khan, built an empire that stretched from Europe to China. Between 1237 and 1240, Genghis's grandson Batu devastated Hungary and Poland, and conquered Russia. The ancient capital city of Kiev and most of southern Russia came under the rule of the Tartars, a nomadic people allied with the Mongols, while the northern regions were ruled by native Russian vassals of the Tartars. Among these vassals, the most prominent were the rulers of the city and surrounding territory (principality) of Moscow. Over the generations, even while acknowledging Tartar overlordship, the rulers of this principality extended their power over most of northern Russia. In this way they formed the nucleus of the Russian state of modern times.

Meanwhile, southeastern Europe was the scene of renewed conquest by another Asiatic people, the Turks. Under the Seljuk dynasty in the eleventh and twelfth centuries, the Turks had already conquered most of Asia Minor (p. 267). In 1299 they came under the rule of a new dynasty, the Ottomans, who led them into Europe itself. Combining the warlike prowess of their nomadic ancestors with the patience and diplomatic skill of a civilized people, the Turks commenced a career of conquest on almost as grand a scale as the Mongols. In the fourteenth century, Serbia and Bulgaria fell victim to the Turks. There followed the final destruction of the thousand-year-old empire of Byzantium. In 1453, Constantinople was taken. The city founded by Rome's first Christian emperor became the capital of the Ottoman sultan, and Justinian's cathedral of St. Sophia was turned into a mosque (pp. 134, 185–86).

But this was far from being the climax of Turkish expansion. In the century after the fall of Constantinople, the Turks went on to conquer much of Hungary and the lands surrounding the Black Sea, as well as the Arab lands of the Middle East and North Africa. Most of the peoples conquered by the Turks retained their ethnic identity, and in the case of the peoples of southeastern Europe, their (mostly Orthodox) Christian religion as well. But they lived as subjects of an Islamic empire, and would remain so for hundreds of years until the decline of Turkish power in the eighteenth and nineteenth centuries (pp. 404–7, 488, 551, 555).

As for the western European countries, on the whole they left eastern Europe to its fate. The popes generally strove for friendship with the Mongols, in hopes of converting them to Latin Christianity and turning them against the Muslims. Such western help as came to eastern Europe against the Turks was mostly too little and too late. Up to the end of the Middle Ages, what prevented the invaders from advancing still further into Europe was above all the huge size of their empires: both the Mongols and the Turks found their territories difficult to control, and they had to fight wars on many other fronts besides Europe. Later, in the sixteenth century, powerful central and eastern European rulers emerged who mounted effective resistance to the Asiatic conquerors (pp. 316–17, 404–7). Thus, with little effort of their own, the western countries were insulated from attacks from the east as they pursued the innovations that would create modern Western civilization.

THE NEW ECONOMY

We have already pointed out that the rise of trade and towns was a crucial development of the eleventh and twelfth centuries (pp. 223–29). But from 1200 onward European commerce began to take on a new look. Medieval guilds and merchants had generally operated within limited areas and had been subject to local regulation (pp. 227–29). The system fostered the growth of trade and industry while Europe was still relatively backward, but by 1200 its very success was beginning to reveal its limitations. The masters of the workshops paid money wages and hoped to make a profit from their enterprises, but most prices were fixed, and the scale of business was small. As a result, the master's profit was seldom large, and whatever he made usually went to the upkeep of his shop and the care of his family. Though capital was used in trade and industry, very little capital *surplus* could be built up. The *entrepreneur* (organizer of a business) still thought primarily in terms of "production for use" in a limited market; he had not yet grasped the idea of the unlimited accumulation and expansion of capital. The *true capitalist* had not yet emerged.

The Birth of Modern Capitalism

Italian merchants had taken the lead in the revival of trade in the eleventh century (p. 225), and in the thirteenth they pioneered the development of capitalism. They dominated the profitable trade of the Mediterranean, and many of them made quick fortunes in their dealings. Finding that they could not spend all their profits immediately, they hit upon the idea of *reinvesting* the surplus.

This novel idea made it possible for the successful trader to launch new, more ambitious enterprises. Soon he was no longer traveling about as an ordinary merchant but was minding his account books at home as a "capitalist." He directed his energies to extracting profits from his varied enterprises and reinvesting them to gain *more* profits. Thus emerged the features that have characterized the "capitalist system" for the past five centuries: its boundless profit-seeking and its dynamic spirit.

For merchants to accumulate really substantial capital surpluses, they had to expand their trading activities constantly. What the Italians achieved as the middlemen between Europe and the Orient, the merchants of the port cities of Germany achieved in the Baltic Sea area. They found that by pooling their resources they could build fleets and win joint trading privileges abroad, and by the fourteenth century, the leading towns of northern Germany had formed an effective commercial league (the *Hanse*). The cities of the Hanse monopolized the foreign trade of northern Germany and set up outlets in the trading centers of Russia, Poland, Norway, England, and the Low Countries. From these far-flung outposts, rich profits flowed in to the capitalists of northern Germany (p. 282).

The merchants of the Low Countries prospered, too. The wharves of Antwerp and Bruges saw a steady stream of Italian ships carrying oriental spices and silks, and vessels from the Baltic loaded with furs, timber, and herring. The industries of England and the German Rhineland also sent their products into the Low Countries. By the fifteenth century a truly international commerce had developed — extensive enough to provide for the accumulation of profit surpluses and for the growth of a capitalist class.

Innovations in Business Organization

The new leaders of enterprise scrapped many of the traditional methods of doing business. In the eleventh and twelfth centuries, the masters of each guild, collectively, had served as its directing force; and within a framework of rules, individual masters had run their own shops. After 1200 several industries cast off the shackles of the guilds. Still, enterpreneurs found that they could seldom go it alone. Commerce was becoming more extensive and complex, requiring a pooling of capital and of managerial talent. Gradually the *partnership* came into favor as a unit of business organization. A special form of partnership, the family firm, was the most common. A group of relatives could best handle matters demanding secrecy and mutual trust and could assure the continuance of the enterprise.

The displacement of guild control is best illustrated by the woolens industry, in which the traditional association of master weavers, journeymen, and apprentices had disappeared in most areas by 1400. The industry was taken over by enterprising merchants, who bought the raw wool and put it out to semiskilled laborers for processing — first to spinners and then to weavers, dyers, and shearers in succession. The workers were paid by the piece or by measure, but ownership of the materials stayed with the merchants. They sold the finished cloth (or garments) in the international market at whatever price they could get.

The wool merchants thus reaped the profits of both industry and commerce. They paid the laborers at a low rate and permitted them no say in the conduct of the business. Moreover, the laborers were forbidden by law to organize or strike. This "putting-out" or "domestic" system was the principal mode of production in early modern Europe. It destroyed the close relationship between master and journeyman that had existed in the medieval guilds. It made profit the sole concern of the entrepreneur and diminished the worker's sense of creativity. The antagonisms that grew up between these entrepreneurs and the workers foreshadowed the fierce conflicts that were to mark the later industrial world.

The Rise of Banking and Bankers

As Europe moved from a largely self-sufficient economy to an economy geared to trade, the old techniques of exchange and finance proved inadequate. Relatively little money had circulated in the early Middle Ages; most exchange was by barter. From the thirteenth century onward the supply of coins grew steadily. However, the expansion of enterprise depended not so much on money itself as on new instruments of exchange and credit.

Perhaps the most important substitute for money payments was the *bill of exchange*, which was similar to a modern bank draft or check. A merchant with branch offices in various countries usually made a side business of selling drafts that were payable by his firm in some other city. A Venetian who bought linen from Antwerp, for example, would find it inconvenient to ship money to the Low Countries every time he placed an order. Instead, he could go to a Venetian firm that did business in Antwerp and purchase a draft payable by its office there. The seller of the linen in Antwerp was perfectly willing to accept this bill of exchange, for he knew he could collect on it in his own city. Rather than demand cash for it, however, he would probably endorse the bill and use it as a means of payment in a later business transaction.

The first bankers were successful merchants who had accumulated a profit surplus and who wished to reinvest it. They found that the business of moneylending, though risky, could bring high returns. Commencing in the thirteenth century, large-scale moneylending became normal. It had been practiced in earlier times, but on a smaller scale — partly because the economy was not so prosperous, and partly because the Church condemned all interest-taking as usury (lending at an *excessive* rate). In consequence lending at interest had been done chiefly by Jews, whose faith did not forbid it. This particular role of the Jews no doubt contributed to the periodic anti-Semitic outbursts in Europe (pp. 270–72).

With the expansion of commerce, however, many people came to realize that lending was a useful and acceptable activity. The traditional argument against interest payments was based on a revulsion against taking high rates from individuals "in distress." But loans to businessmen engaged in profitable enterprises, or to kings and popes, were obviously of a different sort. These loans could be *productive*, and they exposed the lender to risks that justified some reward. Many theologians agreed that this kind of lending was not sinful, and the popes themselves were among the biggest borrowers. Consequently, small-scale Jewish moneylending came to be overtaken by large-scale Christian banking.

Italian merchants first moved into the banking business during the thirteenth century. In the next century Florence became the leading center of international finance. The Bardi and Peruzzi families, for example, advanced huge loans to Edward III, king of England. Later, Edward refused to repay the loans and thereby forced those families into bankruptcy. But in the fifteenth century a new house of bankers, the Medici, emerged in Florence. This family restored the financial power of the city and came to dominate its political and cultural life.

Banking spread north from Italy to the rest of Europe. Jacques Coeur, a French merchant who had made a fortune in trading with the Orient, was appointed royal treasurer by Charles VII, king of France (1439). Taking advantage of his position at the court, Coeur acquired extensive holdings in mines, lands, and workshops and thus became one of Europe's most powerful international bankers. He used his enormous wealth for the benefit of his family and built a palace worthy of a king in his native town of Bourges.

The wealthiest and most famous banker of the period was Jacob Fugger of Augsburg. Southern Germany, in the fifteenth and sixteenth centuries, was sharing in the prosperity of growing commerce — and had the added resource of copper and silver mines. Some years earlier, capital had been put into the mining industry for the first time, permitting miners to dig more deeply and more efficiently with improved tools. The leading entrepreneurs of the industry soon took control of smelting and metalworking as well as mining, concentrating the direction of all operations in a few hands. The workers, who formerly had been independent producers, now became voiceless employees of the capitalists.

The Fugger family drew immense wealth from these and other enterprises and channeled their surplus into banking. Jacob pushed the family business beyond Germany by opening branch offices in the major commercial centers of Europe. He ventured into buying, selling, and speculating in all kinds of goods, and he provided financial services to merchants, high clergy, and rulers. One of his more spectacular operations was to lend half a million gold coins to Charles I, king of Spain. Charles wanted to "buy" the office of Holy Roman emperor through payments to the imperial Electors (pp. 316–17). A good capitalist, Jacob was also a good *philanthropist*. He and his brothers built, as evidence of their piety and generosity, an attractive group of dwellings for the "righteous" poor of Augsburg. It still stands, near the center of the city, as a memorial to the Fuggers' wealth and charity.

The Impact on Social Structure and Values

The forces released by the rise of capitalism disrupted European society and economic life by undermining the guilds and weakening the manorial system (pp. 218–23). The customs associated with manorialism had seemed almost unbreakable, even in the later Middle Ages; they survived long after the reasons for their existence had vanished. Even so, important features of manorialism were soon altered by the capitalistic economy.

The most far-reaching change, which affected all relationships between nobles and peasants, was the substitution of *money* for payments in goods or services. During the Middle Ages the lord of the manor had received, as rent, a share of the *crops* from his peasants' strips. In addition, the serfs had been required to cultivate the lord's "demesne," the land reserved exclusively for his benefit. This forced labor was not very efficient, however, and the lord himself usually cared little about better land management. Toward the close of the medieval period, the nobles often found it advantageous to rent out their demesnes to *free tenants*, who were now able to sell their produce at nearby markets and pay their rents in cash. The feudal landlords had also been entitled to extra labor in return for the serfs' use of their "common" fields and woodlands (p. 219). This service, too, was gradually converted into money payments. The serfs preferred this arrangement because it released them from extra work; the lords preferred it because they could usually find cheap day labor and still have cash left over from the serfs' payments.

The next step was the emancipation (freeing) of the serfs. Now that the nobles no longer depended on forced labor, they were willing to grant the serfs freedom. In most instances, the freedman remained on the land as a tenant and in exchange for his freedom paid his lord a lump sum or extra rent. But in so doing he normally lost his former hereditary right to stay on the land, which meant that he could be ousted when his lease expired.

By 1500 serfdom had disappeared from England and had become a rarity in western Europe. The medieval lord, with his rights to the produce and services of the peasantry, had become a capitalist landowner living off his *rents*. Though many of the great estates remained intact, the pattern of relationships had been changed. In short, the spirit of commercial enterprise had spread to the countryside. Merchants began to buy estates and play the role of landed aristocrats, while intermarriage between bourgeois and landed families further blurred the old distinctions. Serfs were becoming freemen, merchants were becoming landholders, and noblemen were becoming capitalists.

This social change, like other significant changes in history, brought loss as well as gain. The sense of personal security and community solidarity declined, but no longer was one class arbitrarily subjected to another. Equality of opportunity did not arise immediately, for the new circles of privilege were tightly drawn; but there was greater freedom of movement, both upward and downward.

Dislocations in society led to dislocations in ethics. Capitalism has been called the major heresy of the Middle Ages — by those who see it as opposed to some of the central teachings of Jesus. The merchants and bankers of the early modern period made profit their immediate and constant concern; they separated commercial dealings from Christian ethics. In their desire for gain they differed only in degree from the landlords and rulers of medieval times. The latter, however, could cover their activities under the cloak of feudal and royal rights and customs; the upstart bourgeois had no such camouflage at hand. Materialism came to be openly approved and systematized, leading to the overturn of traditional values. Pride, envy, and greed — branded by the Church as cardinal sins — were now regarded as the mainsprings of economic life. The religious ideals of meditation, prayer, and giving were overtaken by the goals of hard work, punctuality, and saving.

One might suppose that the Church would have mobilized its forces against this challenge to its ancient ideals. With its widespread organization and its control over public opinion, it could certainly have done so. But it no longer wanted to. Though it continued to profess its attachment to spiritual goals, the Church itself had in large measure succumbed to materialism. Nowhere was this more apparent than in the top ranks of the clergy. The popes, like almost everyone else in Europe, were dazzled by the new riches and became obsessed with wealth, elegance, and power.

The active carriers of the new morality were the bourgeois, or middle class. Some members of this class, like Jacques Coeur and Jacob Fugger, attained high levels of influence, equal to that of counts or princes. The position of the class as a whole, however, advanced much more slowly. The bourgeois enjoyed one long-run advantage in their competition for power with the landed nobility: they controlled the *movable* assets of the economy (commodities, ships, and money), and these assets were growing in value, while the nobility controlled the *fixed* assets (mainly land), and these assets were declining in value. Money, furthermore, was infinitely more flexible than land, and with it the middle class could buy the goods and services that secured influence.

Several centuries were to pass before the bourgeois attained social dominance. The nobility maneuvered to retain its inherited privileges, and the weight of tradition slowed the advance of the middle class. But from the sixteenth century onward the bourgeois ideals had a growing influence on society as a whole. Bourgeois "virtues" included, in addition to the habits of work and thrift, the qualities of reliability and inventiveness. These competed successfully against the "romantic" ideals of the nobility: physical prowess, courage, and chivalry. Middle-class ideas, dress, and manners, by the middle of the nineteenth century, would become the main standards of Western civilization.

THE NEW GEOGRAPHY

The impact of capitalism and materialism was magnified by expansion overseas. The voyages of Columbus, da Gama, and Magellan gave Western peoples a vision of ever-growing markets and fathomless riches. The expansion of Europe was more than just economic, however. It was a climax to the outward thrust of Western civilization that dated back to the tenth century (pp. 265–66).

Had the mariners of ancient Greece or of early medieval Europe crossed the Atlantic and "discovered" America, it is almost certain that nothing significant would have followed from that discovery. The reported finding by the Norwegian Leif Ericson (p. 208), around 1000, made only a slight impression on the West. The fact is that Europeans learned about the New World at the very moment when expansionist forces were rising. And, by an accident of history, the explorations took place at a time when the Europeans held decisive technological advantages over the peoples of the rest of the world. Nothing in the history of world relations has proved more fateful than this far-flung (and unequal) encounter between Europe and the other continents.

The Impulse to Overseas Expansion

Before 1500 few Europeans had given much thought to the regions beyond their shores. The crusades (pp. 265–70) had carried them to the Middle East and had excited their curiosity about the lands beyond. They knew the Black

Sea and, of course, the Mediterranean. But the areas to the west and southwest of Spain were great blanks on their maps — reaching, perhaps, to the edge of the earth.

Popular conceptions about the uncharted world were full of fanciful notions. Tales of sea monsters abounded, and sailors, fearful of the unknown, hugged the coasts in their tiny vessels. There was, however, a considerable body of reliable information about the world, and crude instruments of navigation were in use. One was the north-pointing magnetic compass, which helped the navigator set and hold the course of his ship. Another was the astrolabe, which indicated the altitude (angular degrees above the horizon) of the sun and stars; knowing this figure, the navigator could calculate the latitude of his position (degrees north or south of the equator).

Though geography was not taught in the schools or universities (none of the applied sciences were), cartography (mapmaking) and seamanship were well-developed arts. Most of this information had been handed down from ancient times. Greek observers had concluded that the earth was a sphere and had computed its circumference with extraordinary accuracy. Oddly, the Hellenistic scientist Ptolemy (A.D. 150) substantially reduced their estimate. His error was passed on to medieval geographers, with interesting consequences for later mariners. (Columbus, for example, accepted Ptolemy's figure.)

Marco Polo, a thirteenth-century merchant of Venice, contributed more than anyone else to Europe's awareness of exotic lands. Members of the Polo family, after establishing trading contacts with the Mongol empire in western Asia (p. 283), decided to journey to the far side of that empire. A long trek by caravan took them from the Black Sea to the Chinese city of Beijing, where Kublai Khan held court as emperor. The Polos were welcomed with courtesy, and Marco remained there for many years. When he returned to Italy he wrote of his travels and revealed to astonished Europeans the fabulous wealth of the Orient.

Through the Middle Eastern trade, the West had for several centuries tasted sweets, spices, and other luxuries from afar. Now the desire grew to acquire these goods directly, without paying a middleman's profit to Muslim merchants. The desire was especially strong in countries outside the Mediterranean area. The Italian cities, as sole carriers of the profitable spice trade to the West, were quite content with things as they were. But the merchants of Spain, Portugal, France, and England dreamed of bypassing *both* the Italians and the Muslims.

By the fifteenth century a race was under way to find sea routes between western Europe and the Far East. Europeans knew that no water passage existed between the Mediterranean and the Indian Ocean; hence, only two possibilities lay open. One was to try the way *south*, around Africa, then eastward to India. This was a relatively conservative plan, since ships could hold close to land during most of the voyage. The other was a much bolder, more theoretical plan: sailing due *west* across the open Atlantic. Though Africa and the Indian Ocean appeared on existing maps of the world, the Atlantic was uncharted. Geographers agreed that China must lie on the farther side, but none knew for sure what distances or barriers might have to be crossed before reaching it.

Both alternatives were costly and risky to test, and European merchants, though eager to find new routes, were reluctant to finance voyages of exploration. This could better be done, in any case, by governments, because to set up commercial routes and bases would require political and military power. The ambitious monarchs of Europe grasped the opportunity. They saw that by bringing wealth to their lands they could strengthen the economic base of their countries and their personal glory. In backing these ventures, the kings had the blessing and encouragement of the Church. For the clergy, responding to their Scriptural obligation to spread Christianity (pp. 147–48), were eager for new converts. Thus, three central motives combined to launch the brave sailors and their ships: the desire of the clergy to spread the gospel, the ambition of the monarchs for power and glory, and the hunger of the merchants for gold.

The Voyages of European Discovery: The New World

The little kingdom of Portugal took the lead in sponsoring exploration. It had only a short history of independence, having emerged when the Muslims were being expelled from the Iberian peninsula. Portugal had been a fief for a period, subject to the Christian rulers of Castile, but in the twelfth century its count proclaimed himself a king. The Portuguese monarchy, with its capital at Lisbon, reached the height of its power during the sixteenth century. With astounding will, enterprise, and ruthlessness, the Portuguese exploited vast territories and peoples overseas. Portugal became the early model of that form of cultural aggression known as Western imperialism.

The Portuguese favored the proposed route around Africa. In the course of developing it, their forces occupied the nearby Madeira Islands and the Azores, and opened trade for gold, ivory, and slaves along Africa's western coast (Guinea). At last, in 1498, Vasco da Gama rounded the Cape of Good Hope and sailed across the Indian Ocean to the west coast of India (p. 293), thereby linking Europe with the Orient. The Portuguese, having won that race, moved swiftly to secure their prize.

Prior to this achievement, a Genoese mariner named Christopher Columbus had sought support for a plan to sail *west* to China and Japan. The son of a weaver, he had turned to the sea and to dreams of fame and fortune. Finding his way to Lisbon, the center of activity in geography and navigation, Columbus went into the business of making maps and sea charts. On occasion he accompanied ship captains on voyages down the African coast. He also gained sufficient social status to marry a daughter of the governor of Madeira, thereby gaining access to the royal court of Portugal.

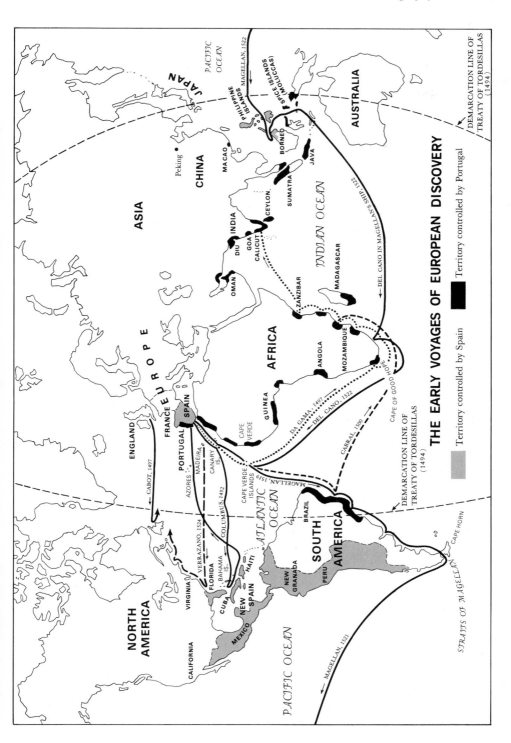

THE EARLY VOYAGES OF EUROPEAN DISCOVERY

■ Territory controlled by Portugal

▨ Territory controlled by Spain

When Columbus described his bold project to the king and asked for ships and provisions, the royal advisers pronounced his plans unsound. Columbus's scheme was based on the inaccurate calculations of Ptolemy and on an exaggerated notion of Asia's eastward projection; the king's advisers correctly reckoned that China was too distant to be reached by sailing westward across the Atlantic. Columbus believed China to be about three thousand nautical miles west of Lisbon, while his critics put the figure at about six thousand. The actual distance is more than twelve thousand miles.

Though disappointed, Columbus was not a man to give up. He turned next to the Spanish rulers, Ferdinand and Isabella, who were now driving the last of the Muslims from the Iberian peninsula (p. 265). His proposal was at first rejected by a commission of experts, for the same reason that had been advanced by the Portuguese. However, when the queen learned that Columbus was journeying north to offer his plan to the French king, she called him back. Attracted by his winning personality, Isabella decided to give him her personal support and agreed to an extravagant contract whereby Columbus was to become governor of all the lands he discovered and was to receive one-tenth of the wealth he extracted from them. Further, he was to be known as "Admiral of the Ocean Sea, Viceroy, and Governor."

Columbus personified the early modern spirit. A modest capitalist, he invested some of his own money in the venture. When his tiny vessels dipped below the horizon in 1492, they carried with them a high faith in the individual — and a passion for wealth, power, and glory. His courage brought him to the "discovery" of the New World, though he never understood the true nature of what he had found. By a bizarre coincidence, he sighted land (the Bahama Islands) at precisely the point where he expected to find the shores of Asia (p. 293). This convinced him that his geographical theories and calculations were correct and that he had reached his true destination. Yet if a continent unknown to him had not lain across his path the admiral would have returned to Spain empty-handed — or sailed on to his death.

Still seeking Japan or China, Columbus spent several months exploring the Caribbean, whose islands he mistook for the "Indies." He sighted and claimed Hispaniola (Haiti) as well as Juana (Cuba). On three subsequent voyages, he strengthened Spain's claim to the Western Hemisphere. He died in 1506 still believing he had opened a westerly route to Asia.

After 1500 most geographers were convinced that Columbus had not reached Asia but had stumbled across a land mass hitherto uncharted. They decided to name it for another explorer, one who first grasped the true nature of Columbus's discovery. Amerigo Vespucci was a Florentine adventurer and mapmaker who was once connected with the banking firm of the Medici (p. 287). Although knowledge of his activities is uncertain, he apparently took part in several Spanish and Portuguese voyages along the mainland coasts of the hemisphere, from Brazil to Florida. Vespucci wrote colorful letters about what he saw and coined the term "New World." Copies of his letters were widely circulated in Europe, and literate persons were soon discussing the "land of Amerigo" (America).

Conflicts quickly arose over the rival overseas claims of Spain and Portugal. To avoid trouble, the monarchs of the two countries agreed, in 1494, to draw a line between their spheres of interest. In the form of a circle of longitude, the Demarcation Line of the Treaty of Tordesillas passed through a point approximately fifteen hundred miles west of Cape Verde, the westernmost tip of Africa (p. 293). The Portuguese were to confine their claims to territories *east* of the line, while the Spaniards would limit themselves to areas *west* of the line. The Spaniards believed that this division would give them all the lands in the area of Columbus's discoveries; they had miscalculated the eastward extension of the southern continent. As it turned out, a large portion of it (Brazil) reached into the Portuguese zone. Lisbon thus gained, unexpectedly, a claim in the Western Hemisphere.

After Vasco Nuñez de Balboa sighted the Pacific Ocean, from the isthmus of Panama (1513), Europeans came to realize that beyond the New World lay another great stretch of water. The Spanish were disappointed that Columbus had failed to reach the Orient and still hoped that portions of it might fall within their treaty sphere. It was mainly with this in mind that Ferdinand Magellan set out in 1519 to find a *passage* to the Pacific through which he might sail on to Asia.

Magellan, a Portuguese in the service of Spain, guided his fleet of five ships down the coast of South America. After a false start up the broad Plata River, he continued his search until he entered the straits near the southern tip of the continent. He managed the hazardous passage into the Pacific and then sailed northwestward into the greatest of oceans. Following a frightful crossing of about one hundred days, during part of which his men lived on leather and rats, Magellan reached the island of Guam. With fresh provisions, he sailed on to the Philippine Islands, claiming them for Spain. There he was killed in a skirmish with the natives, but the expedition pushed on to the Spice Islands (the Moluccas), and the one remaining vessel, with a remnant of the original crew, finally returned to Spain by continuing westward around Africa (p. 293). Magellan's expedition thus revealed that there was a water passage *around* the New World and demonstrated that a westerly route could be followed from Europe to Asia. More significant, it demonstrated conclusively that the earth was round, it dramatized the vastness of the Pacific, and it gave a truer idea of the globe's size.

Though Spain and Portugal felt that the overseas world was to be shared by them alone, the northwestern countries of Europe did not intend to stand idly by. The English, the French, and the Dutch were also seeking routes for direct trade with the Orient. A Genoese mariner, whom the English called John Cabot, was sent out in 1497 to seek a "northwest passage" to the Indies.

Cabot touched the shores of the New World somewhere around Labrador and Newfoundland and thereby provided England with a claim to North America (p. 293).

Shortly afterward a Florentine, Giovanni da Verrazano, explored the North Atlantic coast for the king of France. Neither he nor anyone else ever discovered another water passage, but the search led to a close examination of the hemisphere's eastern shores from Labrador to the Straits of Magellan. It was only after hope of finding a shorter passage had been abandoned that the French and English took steps to settle the northern lands.

The Colonial Empires

The Portuguese had won the race to the Orient when Vasco da Gama brought his ship into the harbor of Calicut, India. They had seen their goal clearly, attained it, and exploited their victory to the full. What they wanted was a monopoly over the richest trade in the world, and this they held for more than a century.

When the Portuguese arrived in India, they found a heavily populated land with substantial resources. India's civilization dated back to 3000 B.C., when settled communities first appeared in the Indus River valley (pp. 15, 42). Indian culture was not firmly established, however, until after Indo-Europeans (Aryans) from the north had completed their conquest of the subcontinent about 1500 B.C. (p. 47). The civilization that evolved came to dominate not only India but all of southeast Asia. It was marked by profound religious and philosophical teachings, an imaginative and moralistic literature (Sanskrit), and a sensuous art and architecture.

Though most Indians held to a common faith (Hinduism) and lived under a common caste (class) system, they had enjoyed only brief periods of *political* unity — and that unity was usually imposed by foreign conquerors. The conquerors, after the tenth century A.D., consisted of successive armies of either Turks or Mongols, all converts to Islam (pp. 189–98). A Muslim sultan (ruler) at Delhi controlled most of India from about 1250 until 1398, when Delhi's power was smashed by yet another Mongol raider, Tamerlane (Timur).

At the moment of the Portuguese landing in 1498, India was divided into a number of separate kingdoms and was torn by hostility between Hindus and Muslims, friction among the various castes, and warfare among local warlords. Consequently, the inhabitants raised no effective resistance against the intruders. Moving in with superior ships and weapons, the Portuguese quickly established permanent trading settlements along the western (Malabar) coast.

The next strategic step for the Portuguese was to wipe out Arab shipping, which for centuries had carried luxury goods from the Indian ports to the Middle East. Having seized this trade from the Arabs, they extended their operations eastward to the Spice Islands and entered the ports of China and Japan. Here, too, they sought to monopolize commerce, reserving the transport of silks, lacquer, and spices to their own ships and restricting all sea trade in the area to ships licensed by the Portuguese crown.

The cost of maintaining naval vessels, bases, and men was high, but the crown and a few chosen companies reaped sensational profits — for a time. The Portuguese were too few in number to colonize the oriental lands, and their grip on key positions was insecure. When the Dutch and English cut into the spice trade during the seventeenth century, the golden empire began to crumble. Nevertheless, Portugal managed to cling to the remnants of its overseas possessions for nearly five centuries after da Gama's initial voyage.

The Spanish looked on enviously as the Portuguese piled success on success. The demarcation treaty of 1494 had tied their hands east of the dividing line, and Columbus's failure in the west had destroyed their dream of breaking through from that direction. True, Magellan had finally reached the Orient, but the miseries of his journey only proved that the route was impracticable. At first, the New World appeared to the Spaniards as a monstrous obstacle to their ambitions.

The Caribbean natives were peaceful enough, but they offered little of value to European traders. The only hope left to the Spanish adventurers was to fall upon some precious store of wealth — gold, silver, or gems. This they did in a manner and on a scale that surprised even those hardy soldiers of fortune. It was Hernando Cortez who first struck it rich. Attracted by rumors of wealth on the mainland, he organized and equipped a small expeditionary force in Cuba. He sailed off in 1519, without authorization from his superiors, and made for Mexico; there he had his soldiers proclaim him the legitimate ruler of the land, subject only to the king of Spain. Then he scuttled his ships, so that his men had no means of escape.

Cortez's conquest of the Aztec empire was both daring and cruel. The Aztecs, like the Mayas before them (and the Incas of Peru), were by no means primitive; their civilization boasted rich cities, splendid temples and palaces, and superb artistic creations. In the Caribbean islands the Spanish had looted and destroyed as they pleased, but in Mexico they faced an organized power, capable of resistance. The Aztecs suffered serious disadvantages, however. They had not invented the wheel, could not make iron utensils or weapons, and lacked horses and cattle. The government was oppressive and constantly threatened by tribal unrest. Finally, like the other natives of the Western Hemisphere, the Aztecs had not been exposed to the European diseases; they were therefore open to the deadly germs that the invaders brought with them.

Cortez played upon the natives' superstitious fears, drew up his cannon (recently developed in Europe), and set one tribe against another. In the face of constant personal danger, he succeeded in overthrowing the emperor, Montezuma. While the defenders were falling ill with smallpox, Cortez then destroyed the Aztec capital and laid out a new one on the old site, which later became Mexico City. Rich prizes were sent back to the Spanish court, and the king recognized Cortez as captain-general and governor of "New Spain."

Within a decade his lieutenants had taken over most of Central America, from the Rio Grande to Panama.

This caesar of the New World had many freebooting companions and rivals, though none surpassed him as a conquistador (conqueror). South of the Panamanian isthmus, the most notorious adventurer was Francisco Pizarro. Learning of gold and silver in the Inca territories, he organized an expedition with royal approval. The Inca empire, like that of the Aztecs, rested upon an advanced society; it stretched southward along the Andes Mountains from Ecuador through the modern states of Peru and Bolivia. Pizarro discovered, however, that the empire was torn by internal unrest and infected with small-pox — to which his own soldiers were resistant. Like Cortez, he made the most of the situation. Armed with superior weapons, Pizarro's men captured the ruler (Atahualpa) and held him for an extravagant ransom. After Pizarro had received tons of gold and silver, carried in from all parts of Peru, he had his prisoner baptized a Christian and then had him strangled. He next marched to the magnificent Inca capital of Cuzco, looted it, and took over the empire (1534).

The exploits of these European adventurers were to be repeated over and over again in the New World. Small bodies of armed and determined men were able to overturn impressive civilizations. They did so under exceedingly difficult conditions, operating far from home and with little knowledge of the strange lands, languages, and cultures. But they had decisive advantages on their side. While the native leaders and peoples were usually divided among themselves, the conquistadors were united by their purpose of plunder.

Their greed was accompanied by a driving sense of superiority and a fanatical conviction that Christianity was the one true faith and that they were responsible for spreading it. Priests came with the invaders; missionaries and bishops soon followed. The superior weapons of the Europeans provided them with the tools of victory, and through a combination of force, terror, treachery, and infectious disease they subdued the New World.

The court of Spain was delighted with the wealth taken from Mexico and Peru. The king received his royal share, and nobles close to the throne were granted vast estates in America. But soon it became evident that the quick-and-easy prizes of the New World had been consumed. The Spaniards came to realize that Columbus's discovery was an asset of unmeasured dimension, richer than all of Europe. But that wealth — which existed in the form of land and people — had to be cultivated in order to be harvested. By 1550 the monarchy had begun to lay the foundations of royal administration in the Americas. The era of conquest and plunder was over, and the long period of *construction* and *development* had begun. Thus, driven by the twin desires for material gain and Christianization, the Spanish set out to impose the institutions of Western culture on the New World. (Most legal experts and philosophers of the time *justified* these actions with arguments based on Christian teaching, "natural law," and ancient Roman law.)

After 1600 the Portuguese, too, turned their attention from commerce alone to the longer, harder task of developing the wealth of America. They established in Brazil a system of autocratic control similar to the Spanish. In both colonial empires the natives were forced into virtual serfdom, working huge estates (*encomiendas*) for the white landlords. Because the native Indians, generally, proved unable to endure certain types of labor, the Spanish and Portuguese brought large numbers of African slaves into the Western Hemisphere. These exploited blacks were procured by European merchant "slavers" from native African slave markets (p. 292). In the Caribbean, they quickly replaced the Indians, who succumbed to the maltreatment and diseases of the whites. Blacks and mulattoes today make up about one-sixth of the total population of Latin America, while whites constitute about one-quarter; most of the remainder are mestizos (mixed white and Indian). From early times, the Spanish and Portuguese permitted intermarriage between Europeans and Christianized nonwhites.

For much of the sixteenth century, the efforts of the English, French, and Dutch to explore, trade, and colonize overseas were overshadowed by the fabulous successes of Portugal and Spain. Yet these northwestern European countries were just as ambitious in this respect as the southwestern countries. France and England were powerful national monarchies whose rulers, nobles, and merchants were all eager for land and profits overseas. The Dutch, who rebelled against Spanish rule and formed their own independent republic (the Netherlands) in the second half of the sixteenth century (pp. 398–99), were now the most dynamic commercial nation of Europe. Three such competitors could not forever be kept on the sidelines.

As the sixteenth century drew to a close, the English, French, and Dutch redoubled their efforts to gain a share of world trade and world empire. They explored the coastlines of North America and northern Europe, vainly searching for northwest or northeast sailing passages — routes not dominated by Spain and Portugal, which could take them to the Indies. (Though such routes do exist, they are too icebound to have been used by sixteenth- and seventeenth-century ships.) More successfully, the northwestern countries began to *settle* in areas not yet occupied by Spain and Portugal, chiefly in North America. In addition, the new competitors began to encroach on the trade and territories held by the Spanish and Portuguese themselves. An era of "world wars" began, in which European armies and navies fought for control of distant overseas lands.

By the end of the seventeenth century, England, France, and the Netherlands had successfully stepped into the inheritance of Portugal and Spain. They now dominated the trade of the Far East, and most of Portugal's possessions there were now in the hands of the Dutch or English. The northwestern countries had driven the Spanish from much of the Caribbean, and Dutch ships carried much of the overseas trade of the Portuguese and Spanish empires in South and Central America. English, French, and Dutch colonies in North

America were thriving, with those of the English already harboring tens of thousands of settlers.

The northwestern countries struggled as fiercely with each other for trade and empire as they did with Spain and Portugal. During the eighteenth century, with the Dutch exhausted by wars within Europe, the overseas struggle narrowed to one between France and Britain (from 1708 on, Britain was the name for the union formed by England and Scotland — pp. 444–45). Every major eighteenth-century war, including those of the American and French revolutions (pp. 451–52, 460, 465–66), was part of a worldwide conflict between these two most powerful western European nations. By the end of the eighteenth century, in spite of the loss of its American colonies, Britain had come off best. It had won the position it was to keep down to the twentieth century, as the world's leading commercial and imperial nation.

Consequences for the Conquered

In the long run, the European discoveries and conquests were to have a profound impact throughout the world. As Europe became the heart of an expanding system that reached into all parts of the globe, changes occurring at the center of the system reverberated in far-off places. In the sixteenth century, however, the impact of the Europeans was felt mainly in the Western hemisphere. While commercial contact by the Europeans had comparatively little immediate effect on the civilizations of the *orient*, actions in the Americas were more devastating than any other invasions of recorded history. The killing, burning, looting, raping, and enslaving were not unusual. But there was, in addition, a rare psychological shock, arising in part from the clash of very different cultures.

The trauma was intensified by the suddenness and strangeness of the encounter. The dark-skinned Indians had no knowledge of the existence of the white men and no warning of their coming. When the conquerors stepped ashore from the great ocean — with their pale skin and unfamiliar dress — it was as if they had descended from another world. They rode animals never before seen, wore armor stouter than anything known to the natives, and spoke in the name of the "one true God," who was stronger than all the rest. The astonished Indians readily became believers when they observed that the white Christians stayed healthy while they themselves fell ill from smallpox.

In fact, the confrontation between the Europeans and the Indians was really a clash between the Old World and the New, in which the advantage was overwhelmingly on the side of the former. Europe was but *one* among many Old World civilizations, which over the centuries had influenced each other in many ways, and which had a longer and broader history than those of the New World. At the time of the European discovery of America, about forty-five hundred years had passed since the civilizations of Sumer and Egypt had first arisen, whereas it was only about twenty-five hundred years since the earliest civilizations had appeared in the Western hemisphere (p. 14). The European horses that amazed the Indians had first been domesticated in central Asia; the invaders' armor was made of iron, a metal first worked in the Middle East; and the gunpowder of their terrifying firearms had been invented in China. Thus, the Europeans had behind them the collective achievement of all the Old World civilizations. That was why their impact on the Aztec and Inca empires was so catastrophic, while in places such as India and China, it was at first hardly noticeable.

After the conquests were over, the routine of exploitation was less painful (except for the continuing outrage of the slave trade and the persisting toll of European diseases). The Spanish and Portuguese monarchies, in intimate partnership with the Church, endeavored to bring a new order of existence and Christian salvation to their subject millions. On the whole, considering the immense geographical distances involved, they succeeded remarkably well. The *Pax Hispanica* (Spanish Peace) covered an area far broader than the Roman Empire. And, while Rome imposed its civilization upon only a portion of its domain, Spain (and Portugal) determined to Christianize and Westernize the *whole* of the Americas.

The Spaniards, in a sense, carried the historic Roman mission to the New World in the sixteenth century. Heirs to Rome, they would build as well as or better than their forebears. During three centuries of rule they organized new cities and towns, churches and missions, plantations and industries. They constructed fine bridges, aqueducts, and highways. While destroying the native civilizations, the Spanish (and the Portuguese) brought to America, long before anyone else did, the Western legacy of art, literature, and learning. These contributions were enjoyed mainly by a privileged few — the European-born whites. For the colonial administrations differed from those of the Roman Empire in one vital respect: Rome permitted the native peoples to participate in the imperial prosperity (p. 111); Spain viewed them primarily as "wards" of the monarchy — to be Christianized and "civilized" — but to serve the interests of the crown and its supporters.

Consequences for Europe

What effects did the overseas expansion have on Europe itself? The most immediate *motive* for the explorations had been economic, and their first *effect* was economic: expansion nourished the roots of capitalism. As trade with the Orient and the Americas increased, profits accumulated; and the huge investments required for the long voyages and the colonial ventures brought handsome gains to bankers and capitalists. The flow of gold and silver from the New World stimulated general business activity. By 1600 the volume of money in existence in Europe had risen to nearly $1 billion (in today's terms). This more adequate supply of coins promoted trade and strengthened the incentive of all classes to produce for the market; and it also made for *price inflation*. This, in turn, gave an added push to business, for merchants and investors are eager to buy goods and properties when they see that prices are moving upward.

The overseas trade brought an abrupt shift in the geographical distribution of prosperity and power. Venice, Florence, Genoa, and the smaller Italian cities had long enjoyed a strategic position between the Middle East and northern Europe. Italy had sparked the revival of trade in the eleventh century and had helped the growth of early capitalism (p. 285). But after the Portuguese reached the sources of oriental commerce in the sixteenth century, the Mediterranean routes dwindled in importance; for the countries of western Europe facing upon the Atlantic now had the advantage of geographical position. Venice, the queen of the Adriatic, fell into decline.

As Britain, France, and Holland became the main trading gateways between Europe and the rest of the world, the center of prosperity and power shifted to northwestern Europe. Antwerp, Amsterdam, and London were to become, in turn, the leading financial centers of expanding world commerce. These cities had the first organized "money markets" in which large private and government loans were arranged. Exchange houses arose there for trade and speculation in commodities, currencies, bonds, and stocks. Stocks began to appear in the seventeenth century with the creation of "joint-stock companies," the forerunners of the modern corporation; these companies made it possible to raise large sums of capital for long-term investment. Though limited at first to commercial ventures, joint-stock companies were later formed in the mining and manufacturing industries.

The triumph of capitalism was assured by the acceleration of trade and production. The wealth of Europe mounted steadily, and the variety and quantity of goods increased with every day. Commodities and habits (like tobacco), formerly unknown in Europe, were introduced from both America and Asia. New foods added nourishment and novelty to European diets, notably potatoes, Indian corn, tomatoes, citrus fruits, chocolate, coffee, and peanuts. (Syphilis was also introduced from America — in exchange, perhaps, for the European gift of smallpox to the Indians.) Chinaware, oriental furnishings, and art objects began to appear in the homes of the privileged classes. The taste for luxuries had been whetted by medieval commerce, and the well-to-do could now indulge it to the full.

The fact is that after 1500 the world became a treasure house for the West. Europe, whose people made up a tiny fraction of humanity, was in a position to seize and exploit vast areas of the globe. In no other period of history has a major cultural group enjoyed so favorable a ratio between its population and its available resources. Although the Europeans were to squander this advantage on endless wars, it served to lift their standard of living and their sense of power.

This success in winning the riches of the world had a profound effect on the outlook and psychology of Western men and women. By confirming the usefulness of curiosity, daring, and ruthlessness, it raised the value they placed on these traits. The success also strengthened *materialism* by making more widespread the enjoyment of wealth and the chances of acquiring it. It broadened the intellectual horizons of Europeans to some degree, but contributed little to their respect for non-Western ideas and institutions. On the contrary, the startling victories of the Europeans fortified their optimism and strengthened their faith in their own *superiority*.

Most important of all, the overseas penetration triggered the expansion of capitalism into a *worldwide* system. For the first time in history, a civilization was to leap every barrier of race and geography and spread its influence around the globe. Some areas, of course, would be touched only superficially, but European values and ideas would become familiar almost everywhere. And within the emerging world of associated cultures the West would continue to serve as the chief carrier and transformer of ideas and institutions.

THE NEW POLITICS

Intimately bound up with economic evolution and expansion were new developments in the patterns of government. The feudal system, with its divisions into small, loosely related political units, gave way to larger units of *centralized* power. Had it not been for this trend, which was well under way in the fifteenth century, overseas exploration and settlement could not have been adequately supported. The successes of Spain and Portugal in the New World rested in part on their new political strength. As the monarchs of France and England consolidated internal authority, they, too, began to press their claims overseas. Political power thus promoted expansion, capitalism, and wealth; wealth, in turn, strengthened the hands of the rulers. The new politics and the new economy reinforced each other.

Absolutism in Practice: Italy

Italy did not become a unified national state until the nineteenth century, but it was in the Italian *city-states* that the practice and theory of strong government developed in the early modern period. The Italian city-states also pioneered in the practice of *diplomacy* and in the development of the law that would one day govern *international relations*. A tribute to the early ambassadors is the portrait by Hans Holbein the Younger (*Fig. 7-1*, p. 274).

One reason for the late unification of Italy was the long struggle that took place between the popes and the Holy Roman emperors. Each party wanted to win overlordship of the Italian peninsula and was willing to sacrifice the country and its people to gain that end. The state under the direct rule of the popes began with the Donation of Pepin (p. 200), which had granted the papacy a substantial portion of Italy. With Rome as its capital, the States of the Church cut across the peninsula, dividing it in two (p. 305). Lesser states were to rise and fall in Italy, and the Holy Roman emperors were often busy north of the Alps. But until near the close of the nineteenth century the pontiffs of the Roman Church proved to be constant foes of Italian *unity*.

Reinforcing the popes' opposition to unification were Italian "localism" and factionalism, forces deeply rooted in history. Like the ancient Greeks, the Italians identified strongly with the *city* of their region, rather than with any broader territorial unit. The city was near and familiar; it was worthy of reverence and sacrifice. Dante, for example, was more a Florentine than an Italian. As a result of this attitude, Italy had come out of the Middle Ages as a collection of rival city-states struggling among themselves for survival and mastery. By the middle of the fifteenth century the stronger ones had expanded their boundaries, absorbing weaker neighbors. A kind of "balance of power" developed among the five leading city-states: Milan, Florence, the States of the Church, Naples, and Venice.

During these turbulent years significant changes occurred in the internal politics of the Italian cities. By the end of the thirteenth century most of the cities had won self-rule from the feudal nobility and had emerged as *sovereign* (independent) republics. Their citizens, however, proved incapable of stable self-government. The usual source of trouble was the rivalry among factions: the bankers and capitalists, rising rapidly in wealth, tried to take political control from the more numerous small merchants, shopkeepers, and artisans. At the same time, wealthy families competed with one another for special advantage.

Out of the struggle, which was marked by corruption and violence, political "strong men" had emerged during the fourteenth century. Sometimes they were invited to assume power by one or another of the factions looking for an alternative to chaos; sometimes they invited themselves. In the main they supported, and were supported by, the bankers and capitalists. The rest of the citizens submitted (except for occasional plots and uprisings), for they, too, preferred stability to the disorders of freedom.

The new rulers, generally known as "despots," had been schooled in the arena of Italian politics. Men of few illusions, they trusted no one, yielded nothing, and resorted to any means to advance their interests. They put power first. In the past, weak governments had given rise to rebellion and disorder; the despots used an iron hand to restore peace and economic well-being and relied on hired soldiers to preserve their power. Since there was no citizen militia to speak of during this period, professional warriors decided the conflicts within and between cities.

The soldiers were organized in armed bands (mostly cavalry) led by enterprising captains (*condottieri*). The condottieri, in the spirit of the times, were a special sort of "merchant" — their merchandise was military service. With no sentimental attachments, they generally sold their services to the highest bidder.

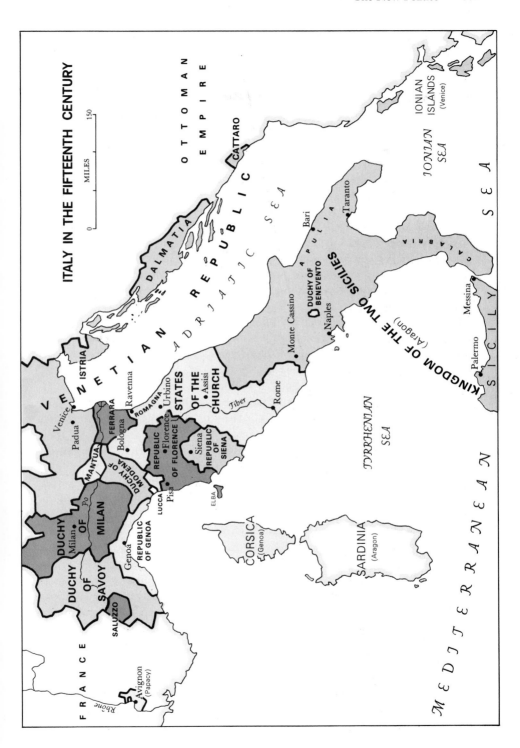

ITALY IN THE FIFTEENTH CENTURY

MILES

0   150

FRANCE

OTTOMAN EMPIRE

CATTARO

DALMATIA

ISTRIA

VENETIAN REPUBLIC

ADRIATIC SEA

IONIAN ISLANDS
(Venice)

IONIAN SEA

Venice

Padua

DUCHY OF SAVOY

SALUZZO

DUCHY OF MILAN

Milan

REPUBLIC OF GENOA

Genoa

Po

MANTUA

DUCHY OF MODENA

FERRARA

Bologna

ROMAGNA

Ravenna

Urbino

STATES OF THE CHURCH

Assisi

Tiber

Rome

Monte Cassino

LUCCA

Pisa

REPUBLIC OF FLORENCE

Florence

REPUBLIC OF SIENA

Siena

ELBA

CORSICA
(Genoa)

SARDINIA
(Aragon)

TYRRHENIAN SEA

DUCHY OF BENEVENTO

Naples

Bari

APULIA

Taranto

CALABRIA

KINGDOM OF THE TWO SICILIES
(Aragon)

Messina

Palermo

SICILY

IONIAN SEA

MEDITERRANEAN SEA

Rhône

Avignon
(Papacy)

(The bankers usually made the best offers.) On occasion they turned down all bids and seized power for themselves. These hardened and crafty adventurers, thirstier for money than for blood, remained an unpredictable force in the politics of Italy.

One of the most famous was Francesco Sforza, who made himself ruler of Milan in 1450. Assuming the title of "duke," which a preceding despot had purchased from the Holy Roman emperor, he governed from his moated *castello* (fortress-palace). Under the shrewd policies of Sforza and his heirs, Milan enjoyed a half-century of peace and prosperity. In the fashion of the times, the despot supported the arts and attracted scholars to his city.

The city of Florence, though it had experienced numerous upheavals and short-lived tyrannies, remained a republic. In 1434 authority settled in the hands of Cosimo de' Medici, heir to a wealthy banking family. He and his successors generally held no major political office, but through persuasion, manipulation, bribery, and force they controlled the machinery of government. The Medici advanced their own financial interests and the interests of their supporters and treated rival groups harshly. Despite their methods, they enjoyed the support of most citizens — for they put an end to a previous period of rioting and confusion in the city. The most illustrious member of the family, Lorenzo the Magnificent, was a man of extraordinary ability and artistic taste. Under his rule, in the latter part of the fifteenth century, Florence reached its peak as the cultural center of Italy.

The States of the Church belonged to the popes, but the pattern of despotism there was barely distinguishable from that in the rest of the country. The popes hired condottieri to reduce subject cities to obedience, engaged in wars and alliances, and used their office to further the wealth and rank of their families. The Borgia pope, Alexander VI, was notorious for his faithlessness and immoral behavior; Julius II had a fondness for waging war; and the Medici Leo X was noted as an elegant connoisseur of the arts. Such qualities were hardly those of Peter the fisherman, but they were typical of the despots of the new era.

South of Rome, the development of commerce had been interrupted by successive military conquests. The Byzantines and Muslims had invaded this area (including Sicily), and the Normans had established a feudal state there in the eleventh century. French and Spanish claimants had fought over the territory during the thirteenth and fourteenth centuries, and at last, in 1435, the larger portion of it (the kingdom of Naples) was taken by Alfonso of Aragon, who already held Sicily. His joint realm, called the Kingdom of the Two Sicilies, was equal in area to all the rest of Italy (p. 305). Though the south Italian countryside was agrarian and backward, under Alfonso's "benevolent" despotism cultural life flourished in the capital at Naples.

The only major city to escape the trend toward absolutism was Venice, whose government had been stable since the beginning of the fourteenth century. A small group of rich merchants managed to keep political control over the city and saw to it that the rest of the citizens were excluded from participation. The constitution of Venice, the envy of its less fortunate rivals, provided that the city be governed by councils and committees elected from and by the merchants. The "official" head of state was a *doge* (duke), who was chosen for life by the leading families. Though the doge was treated with respect, he had no independent authority.

The Theory of Absolutism: Machiavelli

Fifteenth-century Italy was throbbing with individualism — in commerce, in learning, in the arts. And yet in politics there was a pronounced tendency, as we have seen, to curb individual freedom. The citizens of the city-states were proud and competitive men who by no means relished submitting themselves to absolute authority. But their long experience with factional rivalries and political instability had been disheartening. And so one city after another had accepted the rule of a despot. This submission to political authority did not check individualism in other spheres, however; Italy's "age of despots" was also the age of its greatest artistic flowering.

In the judgment of many Italians, their whole nation would benefit from a unified, absolute government. Despotic rule had put down internal dissension in Milan and Florence, for example, but in relations between city and city anarchy still reigned. If a despot could bring all of Italy under his rule, these wasteful conflicts would cease. After 1500 the argument for unity grew stronger. The French and Spanish monarchs found that they could sweep into the Italian peninsula and easily subdue the divided cities, which were protected only by corrupt mercenaries. The invaders, with their loyal, well-equipped armies, kept Italy in turmoil for a century.

The most able spokesman for Italian unification and political absolutism was a Florentine, Niccolo Machiavelli, a one-time diplomat and a close observer of Italian affairs. He set down his basic views in a kind of manual, which he intended as a guide for the despot who would one day liberate Italy. *The Prince*, written in 1513, was dedicated to the Medici rulers of Florence.

Machiavelli's book marks a sharp turning in Western political thought. Medieval philosophers had seen government as one aspect of God's administration of human affairs: the Church and its officers direct Christians toward *spiritual* salvation, which is eternal; the state looks after their physical wellbeing, which is *temporal* (limited in time). Yet both branches of authority are subject to divine law.

Thomas Aquinas had discussed this matter in his *Summa Theologiae* (p. 259). He reasoned that temporal power is invested by God in the people as a whole, who delegate it to suitable persons. The state, then, whether monarchical, aristocratic, or democratic, is not a power in itself. It receives its authority from God (through the people), and it must exercise the power for *Christian* purposes and in a Christian manner. To be sure, medieval practices often seemed to contradict this doctrine, but these were explained away as the result of human frailty or error.

Machiavelli met the doctrine head on, rejected it, and stated the "modern" view of politics and the state. He felt no uneasiness in breaking away from traditional Christian teachings. He blamed the papacy for keeping Italy divided and felt that Christian teachings, in general, did not contribute to good citizenship. In his commentary on the ancient Roman Republic (*Discourses*), Machiavelli observed that the pagans had encouraged civic pride and service, whereas the early Christians had urged people to turn away from public affairs.

The state, he thought, does not rest on any *supernatural* authority. It provides its own justification, and it operates according to rules that have grown out of the "facts" of human nature. He thereby removed politics from Christian ideology and placed it on a purely secular (worldly) level. As noted earlier in this chapter, economic life had already become secularized, and literature, art, and science were soon to follow. This trend toward the *secularization* of life heralded the arrival of a new age.

Machiavelli's view of government won general acceptance in European thought and practice. Largely through his influence, the word "state" came into use to mean a sovereign political unit. And the evolution of European states from the sixteenth century onward moved in the direction outlined by Machiavelli. The state was to become the central force of modern times, a law unto itself, subjecting both institutions and individuals to its will.

Means, as well as ends, were a matter of concern to Machiavelli. As he saw it in *The Prince*, the central problem of politics is how to achieve and maintain a *strong* state. Much depends on the character of the citizens. He admired the Romans of the ancient republic and the self-governing Swiss of his own day, but he concluded that a republican form of government could prosper only where the citizens possessed genuine civic virtue. This he found lacking in sixteenth-century Italy. And, in giving advice to his ideal despot, he wrote in the context of his own time and place. His book was not a blueprint for utopia; it was a manual for present action.

His advice to rulers is geared, therefore, to a particular view of human nature. The Italians of his day were evidently people of exaggerated defects and exaggerated virtues. Machiavelli regarded them as corrupt beyond correction (except, possibly, by a strong prince). He wrote that they were, in general, "ungrateful and fickle, fakers, anxious to avoid danger, and greedy for gain; they offer you their blood, their goods, their life, and their children, when the necessity is remote; but when it approaches, they revolt."

With citizens of such character, how was a state to be founded and preserved? Machiavelli advised that a ruler first turn his attention to military strength. The prince, he believed, must devote himself to the training and discipline of his troops and must keep himself fit to lead them. He must practice maneuvers and study the decisive battles of the past; it was thus that Caesar had learned from Alexander. Machiavelli had only contempt for the condottieri and their hirelings, for they had proved ruinous to Italy and incapable of defending the country from invasion. He advised the prince to build an army of citizens drawn from a reserve of qualified men under a system of compulsory military training, for their interests would be bound up with his own. Machiavelli thus introduced to modern Europe the ideas of universal male conscription (draft) and the "nation in arms."

Military strength is not enough in itself, however. For the prince must be both "a lion and a fox." The lion, Machiavelli explained, cannot protect himself from traps, and the fox cannot defend himself from wolves. A ruler, in other words, must have *both* strength and cunning. Machiavelli noted that the most successful princes of his time were masters of deception. They made agreements to their advantage, only to break them when the advantage passed. He declared that the ruler should hold himself *above* normal rules of conduct, Christian or otherwise — that the only proper measure for judging the behavior of a prince is his *power*. Whatever strengthens the state is right, and whatever weakens it is wrong; for power is the end, and the *end* justifies the *means*.

Machiavelli cautioned the prince never to reveal his true motives and methods, for it is useful to appear to be what one is not. Though the prince must stand ready, when necessary, to act "against faith, against charity, against humanity, and against religion," he must always *seem* to possess those qualities. Machiavelli summarized his advice to the ruler as follows:

> Let a prince therefore aim at conquering and maintaining the state, and the means will always be judged honorable and praised by everyone. For the vulgar [common people] is always taken in by appearances and the result of the event; and the world consists only of the vulgar, and the few who are not vulgar are isolated when the many have a rallying point in the prince.

Building the National Monarchies: France and England

The rising monarchs of Spain, France, and England were cut to the Machiavellian pattern. Their efforts to build state power were aided, in each country, by growing national sentiment. In Spain, the spirit of patriotism had been ignited during the fierce struggle to expel the Muslims. When the kingdoms of Castile and Aragon, which had led the fight, were linked through marriage in 1469, the way was open for a unified Spain. Though the Portuguese remained independent, the other peoples of the peninsula welcomed this consolidation of territories once ruled by the Muslims. With popular backing, the young King Ferdinand broke the independence of the feudal lords, who had taken over most of the lands from the defeated enemy. He also reformed the Spanish Church, gaining the right to name its bishops. So vigorous were the centralizing efforts of Ferdinand (and his queen, Isabella) that the foundations of royal absolutism were completed by the close of his reign (1516).

In France, the nobles were more firmly rooted, and the challenge to the monarchy was therefore greater. France was also the richest and most populous kingdom of Europe, with some twelve million inhabitants. As France became increasingly unified, it would move irresistibly to the forefront of European power and culture. The most powerful stimulant to national feeling was the Hundred Years' War (1338–1453), an off-and-on struggle with the English that arose out of conflicting feudal claims. William of Normandy, after conquering England in 1066, had left his heirs properties in both France and England. Through marriage and inheritance, other provinces of France (Aquitaine and Gascony) were later acquired by the English crown. These provinces, however, were held as fiefs, subject nominally to the overlordship of the French monarchs. In the thirteenth century the Capetian king of France (p. 211), Philip Augustus, declared the fiefs forfeit and put most of them under his royal control. He was motivated in part by a desire to extend his own power and in part by a growing sense of national identity among the French. Medieval fiefs had generally been granted and held without reference to nationality, but Philip now resented English control over *French* soil.

In the fourteenth century the English rulers, stronger than they had been earlier, decided to recover the lost fiefs. Their king, Edward III, laid claim to the throne of France as well. (The succession was in doubt, and Edward was the grandson of an earlier French king.) And so the long campaigns began. By 1420 the English had triumphed, and most of France north of the Loire River (p. 315) was given to Henry V, now the English king. The French forces also agreed to accept Henry as heir to their throne.

This humiliation at the hands of foreigners brought forth a surprising reaction among the French people, who traditionally had been indifferent toward feudal struggles. After the throne fell vacant, they found an inspiring leader in a peasant girl called Joan of Arc, who in 1429 persuaded Charles, the disinherited son of the former French king, to march to Reims (the ancient crowning place of French monarchs). Claiming divine guidance, Joan herself took command of a small military force and vowed to drive the English from the soil of France. The young prince, responding to Joan's appeal, was crowned in Reims Cathedral as Charles VII and went on to lead his armies to final victory over the English. Joan did not live to see that day, however. Soon after Charles's coronation she fell into the hands of the English, who tried her as a witch and burned her at the stake. The martyred Joan has been revered for centuries as the glorious symbol of French patriotism.

The Hundred Years' War was frightfully destructive to France (p. 280) and interrupted the growth of royal authority. But when it was over the French monarchs were able to proceed more rapidly than before with the work of political centralization. The nobles, great and small, had been reduced in number and power, and a new spirit of national consciousness had spread through the land. The majority of the people, especially the bourgeois, now looked to the king for security and economic well-being. Charles VII and his son, Louis XI, completed the building of a strong national state.

In their struggle with the feudal nobility, the kings of France were able to take advantage of dramatic new developments in the techniques of waging war. During the Middle Ages mounted knights had been virtually invincible in battles against foot soldiers. As we have seen, the early Frankish kings had shared their lands and their power with the knightly class in their efforts to build up a strong *cavalry* force (p. 199). So long as the French monarchy depended on the services of these nobles, neither their independence nor their lands could be taken away from them. But during the fourteenth and fifteenth centuries new weapons came into use: first the longbow and the crossbow (which could penetrate the armor of mounted knights) and then gunpowder and cannon (which could penetrate their walled castles). As a result, the noble cavalrymen were reduced to *support* forces, and battles were now fought mainly by foot soldiers (musketeers), backed up by artillery. Once the feudal warriors had become less effective, Charles VII could build and maintain a standing army (mostly infantry) that was more than a match for his aristocratic opponents. He also placed his soldiers under strict *military discipline*, something that had been lacking in feudal fighting units. Charles's new army became a model for other European rulers.

To maintain a standing army required more revenue than the monarch had ever received through ordinary feudal dues, but Charles succeeded in raising this revenue. In preparing for his final thrust against the English, he summoned the Estates-General of France in 1439. This body, which represented the three estates, or classes, of France (p. 218), had the sole power to authorize new taxes. In a burst of patriotic fervor, the Estates-General approved Charles's national army and voted a permanent tax for its support. This tax was called the *taille* (cut); it was a kind of income tax levied on all persons in the country. With this substantial new revenue, supplemented by income from his own lands, Charles could now afford to act independently of the nobles. He acted by deception, threats of force, and marriage alliances to bring the great fiefs back into the royal domain (his personal holdings). He permitted the lesser nobles, if they were cooperative, to remain on their ancestral estates and to keep their inherited titles. But he eliminated feudal officeholders and replaced them with *royal* administrators recruited from the nobility.

Charles's son, Louis XI, pursued his father's methods and more than doubled the size of the royal domain. His final victory was to win back the duchy of Burgundy, which had long been independent even though it was legally subject to the French crown. Its last duke, Charles the Bold, had tried to expand his holdings into a major state between France and Germany. But his plans had miscarried; and when he died without a male heir, Louis took over the duchy (1477).

In their contest with the resisting nobles, the kings of France enjoyed the support of the middle class. The merchants and capitalists had much to gain from a secure national market, and they despised the pretensions and arrogance of the aristocracy. Wealthy individuals gave financial aid to the monarchs. (Jacques Coeur, it will be recalled, was treasurer for Charles VII and financed his later military campaigns — p. 287.) And the expanding towns became firm allies of the king.

The success of the monarchy in consolidating its power changed the role of the nobility. The nobles had no choice but to submit to these new conditions. By the end of the fifteenth century, most of them had adjusted and had begun to seek favored positions as military or civil officers of the king. The monarch, for his part, now had at his command the services of an *elite* class.

The Estates-General lingered on, meeting from time to time at the request of the crown. It might have developed into a constitutional body of importance, as did Parliament in England, but class and sectional rivalries, coupled with skillful manipulation by the monarchy, prevented this from happening. The Estates-General never became a serious challenge to royal authority, and it was to be swept into the dustbin of history in 1789 (pp. 456–57).

Nothing now checked the king's control over secular matters. But absolute power, to be absolute, must embrace ecclesiastical matters as well. While taming the nobility, Charles did not overlook the clergy. In some respects the spiritual lords were more powerful than the lay aristocracy. The archbishops, bishops, and abbots held vast properties in France and had a strong influence over the people. They generally supported the king in his efforts to centralize authority and end feudal warfare. They were jealous, however, of their own privileges, and they wavered in their loyalty between king and pope.

After the extreme ambitions of the papacy collapsed at the end of the thirteenth century (p. 242), the French clergy had tended to act independently of Rome. Although the French bishops and abbots had no thought of overturning traditional Church doctrines and institutions, they resented papal interference in local administrative affairs. The popes, however, continued to insist on the right to fill important ecclesiastical offices, a privilege that brought them handsome fees. They also siphoned off a substantial proportion of Church revenues to Rome.

As national feeling grew in the country, there was mounting sentiment for establishing a self-governing "Gallican" (French) Church. In 1438 the clergy, with Charles's approval, formally declared its *administrative* independence of the pope at the Council of Bourges. The decree limited papal interference and forbade payments and appeals of local decisions to Rome. This move gave clear control of the Gallican Church to the French bishops under royal protection. Louis XI revoked the decree, however, and his successor, Francis I, struck a bargain with the pope that extended the influence of the crown over the

Church. In a treaty with the pope (the Concordat of 1516), Francis secured the right to appoint French bishops and abbots. In return for this right, the papacy was granted the first year's income of Church officeholders in France. The pope thereby gained additional revenue and the alliance of a powerful monarch; the king, outflanking his own clergy, brought the Church within his grip.

The rise of absolute monarchies contributed to the general rise of secular forces in Europe. During the Middle Ages, when governments were weak and decentralized, the popes had sought supremacy over them. Having failed then, they had lost their chance forever. Rulers of the new states were growing in power and tried to remove every sort of external influence; they therefore became increasingly hostile to a *universal* Church, which could not be put under their control.

The despots were also good Machiavellians, however. They had themselves crowned with religious pomp and declared their zeal for a unified Christendom. But behind these ceremonial demonstrations they nourished their real interests and intentions. Thus, Francis, the "Most Christian King" of France, allied himself with the infidel Turks against Charles, "His Most Catholic Majesty of Spain." Henry VIII of England, whom popes had named "Most Christian King" and "Defender of the Faith," denounced the papacy in 1534 and proclaimed himself the supreme head of the Church of England (p. 371).

Before Henry became king, however, England had suffered through a long period of struggle for power. The Hundred Years' War had had an effect on England quite different from its effect on France. Though it had strengthened the national feeling of the English, it had weakened the position of the monarch. For one thing, it had permitted the nobles to build up large bands of armed men, who subsequently became their personal retainers. Moreover, in order to raise the substantial sums of money needed for the expeditions to France, the kings of England had been compelled to make concessions to Parliament.

The origins of Parliament go back to the thirteenth century, notably to the "Model Parliament" of 1295. In that year Edward I, seeking to enlarge the base of his support in the country, summoned representatives from the shires (counties) and boroughs (towns) to meet with his feudal council of barons. During the next century Edward's successors called Parliament frequently in their need for additional funds to carry on the war in France. Parliament evolved into two chambers: the House of Lords and the House of Commons. In the former sat the great barons and clerics of the country — lords who held fiefs and offices directly from the crown. In the latter sat representatives of the shires, and of certain towns. The Lords were the more important house for several centuries, but the Commons would ultimately have the upper hand in lawmaking.

The king had to turn to Parliament for approval of new revenues, and its members took advantage of that to gain privileges and redress of their grievances.

c. 900		1066	1154		1399	1461	1485
UNITED ANGLO-SAXON KINGDOM		NORMAN KINGS	HOUSE OF PLANTAGENET		HOUSE OF LANCASTER	HOUSE OF YORK	

HUNDRED YEARS' WAR (1338-1453)

It will be recalled that the Estates-General, a similar body in France, voted a royal income tax without demanding concessions from the monarch. Parliament did not agree so readily to the desires of the king and kept a firm hold on the purse strings.

Its control over lawmaking and general administration came only slowly, however. By 1399 Parliament had won the right to determine the line of succession to the throne. It chose the Lancaster house (family), and the monarchs of that line (who reigned from 1399 to 1461) worked closely with Parliament. At the close of the Hundred Years' War, however, England suffered a series of calamities. Confidence in the crown was shattered by the defeat in France, and the nobles proceeded to slaughter one another in a *civil* war led by the house of York against the house of Lancaster (Wars of the Roses). Henry Tudor, who would become Henry VII, was a relative of the Lancasters. When he at last emerged victorious from these wars in 1485, the strength of the nobles had been broken, and the nation was yearning for peace and unity.

Henry restored law and order and put an end to private warfare. Aware of the value of the bourgeois to the nation, he supported measures to protect home industries and commerce from foreign competition, and, by means of treaties, he extended markets abroad. As the influence of the old nobility declined, that of the middle class rose. And the English middle class, like the French, rallied to the service of the king as its position improved.

The sixteenth century, the century of Henry VIII and Elizabeth I, was an era of despotic power in England. Parliament, however, unlike the Estates-General, did not disappear. In fact, in the century to follow it would replace royal absolutism with *parliamentary* government.

The Eclipse of the Universal Empire: Germany

Strong central government did not come for centuries to other parts of Europe. Neither Germany nor Italy became a unified state until 1870. The reasons for this contrast with the rest of western Europe are many and complex, but the main one is the long conflict between the Holy Roman emperors and the popes during the Middle Ages. The emperors, distracted by their campaigns in Italy, failed to give sufficient attention to building a solid political foundation in Germany. Over and over again they gave up powers north of the Alps in order to win support for their expeditions to the south. As a result, the German princes became so entrenched and so independent that they could not later be reduced to obedience. Another reason was that the emperors did not identify strongly with any national group. Traditionally they were German,

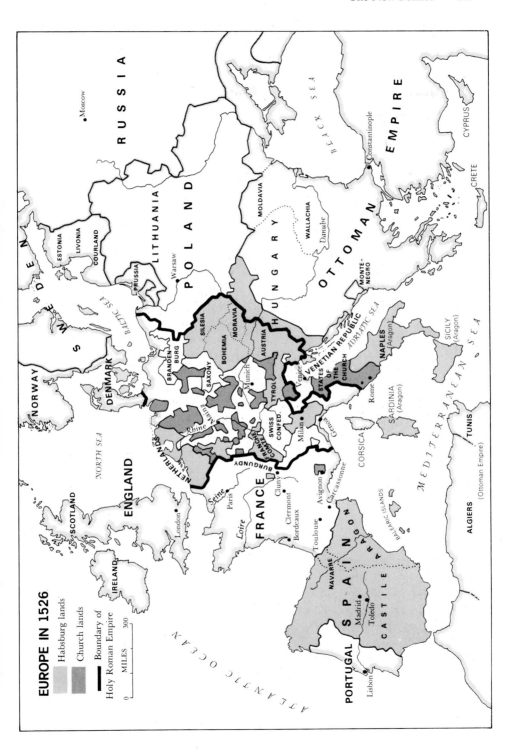

EUROPE IN 1526

Habsburg lands

Church lands

Boundary of
Holy Roman Empire

MILES 300

0   300

MOSCOW

RUSSIA

SWEDEN

NORWAY

DENMARK

ESTONIA

LIVONIA

COURLAND

PRUSSIA

LITHUANIA

POLAND

Warsaw

BALTIC SEA

BRANDEN-
BURG

SILESIA

MORAVIA

BOHEMIA

SAXONY

AUSTRIA

TYROL

HUNGARY

MOLDAVIA

WALLACHIA

Danube

BLACK SEA

Constantinople

OTTOMAN

EMPIRE

CYPRUS

CRETE

MONTE-
NEGRO

VENETIAN REPUBLIC

ADRIATIC SEA

Venice

STATES
OF
THE
CHURCH

Rome

NAPLES
(Aragon)

SICILY
(Aragon)

SARDINIA
(Aragon)

MEDITERRANEAN SEA

TUNIS

(Ottoman Empire)

ALGIERS

CORSICA

BALEARIC ISLANDS

Munich

Rhine

Mainz

SWISS
CONFED.

Milan

Genoa

FRANCHE-COMTÉ

BURGUNDY

NETHERLANDS

NORTH SEA

ENGLAND

London

SCOTLAND

IRELAND

Seine

Paris

Loire

FRANCE

Cluny

Clermont

Bordeaux

Toulouse

Avignon

Carcassonne

ATLANTIC OCEAN

SPAIN

NAVARRE

ARAGON

CASTILE

Madrid

Toledo

PORTUGAL

Lisbon

but the office was elective and legally open to any European candidate. Further, so long as the emperors made *universal* claims, they could not build a truly *national* state.

As a consequence, while Spain, France, and England were growing into strong centralized powers, Germany lingered on as a patchwork of hundreds of fiefs. It was a pleasant and prosperous country (except for the endless quarrels) but politically out-of-date. There were landed nobles with a bewildering array of ranks and titles, wealthy officials governing "free" cities under imperial charters, and powerful Church lords. The ranking princes of the empire had won the status of permanent "electors" as the result of an imperial decree of 1356 (known as the Golden Bull). Three of these electors were ecclesiastical: the archbishops of Cologne, Mainz, and Trier. Four were lay: the Count Palatine of the Rhine, the Duke of Saxony, the Margrave of Brandenburg, and the king of Bohemia. When an emperor died, these seven men met to choose his successor. This was often an occasion for lengthy bargaining — even bribing (p. 288); for the imperial office, though its power was declining, remained the political position of highest prestige in the West.

Dynastic (family) considerations, more than concern for national feeling, guided the politics of central Europe. The family that played the dynastic game most skillfully was the Habsburg, whose influence on the continent endured for centuries. Rudolf of Habsburg, a south German prince, had been elected Holy Roman emperor in 1273. The main reason for his being chosen was that he was a minor figure who could be counted on not to create trouble for the independent-minded barons and bishops. And, in fact, he took his imperial responsibilities lightly, choosing to concentrate on expanding his family holdings. In a struggle with a defiant vassal (Ottokar of Bohemia), Rudolf won the duchy of Austria and surrounding territories. He assigned these lands to his sons as imperial fiefs, and Austria thus became the base of the family properties.

The Habsburgs' mounting power worried the electors, who, when Rudolf died, chose an imperial successor from another, less affluent family. For nearly two centuries the Habsburgs were then passed over, but in 1438 another member of the family (Albert) was elected emperor. Thereafter, until the end of the Holy Roman Empire in 1806, the Habsburgs managed to keep the office in their possession, while extending their wealth and power by means of carefully arranged marriages.

The family holdings reached their greatest extent when they passed to the young man who was to become Emperor Charles V. His inheritance included the ancestral lands on the Danube River, Luxembourg, and the Netherlands, as well as Spain (with Hispanic America), Sardinia, Naples, and Sicily. When he secured the imperial title in 1519 (by buying the votes of the electors), he added to his family's domains the overlordship of Germany and northern Italy (p. 315). In 1526 the death (in battle against the Turks) of the king of Hungary and Bohemia, to whom Charles was related by marriage, brought him those two kingdoms as well. This was by far the greatest aggregation of territory, both in and outside Europe, that any European monarch had ever ruled.

But the aggregation proved exceedingly hard to control. Charles's empire was a hodgepodge of holdings, like those of the Middle Ages. The emperor encountered an endless series of political, military, and personal frustrations, and he at last retired to a monastery in 1556. Before abdicating, Charles divided the Habsburg properties into an eastern and a western portion. The western portion consisted of Spain, the family's other territories in western Europe and the Mediterranean, and the vast Spanish overseas empire. The eastern portion included Austria, Bohemia, Hungary, and the rule of the Holy Roman Empire.

Far from weakening the Habsburgs, the division of their territory into more manageable portions actually strengthened them. Working closely together, the Spanish and Austrian branches of the dynasty dominated Europe for a hundred years. The Europe of today still feels the effect of their power: it was they who sustained the Roman Catholic Church against the Protestant revolt, and who finally fought the Turks to a standstill (pp. 284, 399–400, 405). Yet in the long run, the far-flung Habsburg territories, assembled by conquest and marriage and united only by their ruling dynasty, were destined to crumble. The future lay with the rising national states and their despotic monarchs.

CHAPTER

8

The Renaissance: Upsurge of Humanism

The political and social changes that swept over Europe after the end of the Middle Ages were accompanied by fresh ideas about the nature of human beings and their place in the universe. To continue our examination of the changeover from medieval to modern times (1400–1650), we will now look at the mind and spirit of the West as expressed in the worldview, literature, and art of the era and then, in the next chapter, round out the picture by viewing the reformation of the Church.

THE RENAISSANCE VIEW OF HUMAN NATURE

So exciting were the fresh ideas about human affairs that some observers felt civilization itself was being "reborn." In fact, some historians later used the word "Renaissance" (rebirth) to describe the era as a whole. Modern scholars, however, tend to restrict the use of that term to the revival of interest in *classical* (ancient) literature, art, and values. Thus limited, the Renaissance was but one side of the transition to modern times; its core was an upsurge of *humanism*.

The Revival of Interest in the Classical World

Humanism can be most broadly defined as any view that puts the human person (*humanus*) at the center of things and stresses the individual's creative, reasoning, and aesthetic powers. Such a view is at least as old as the Greeks and Romans. Although the word "humanism" was not used in the classical age, Cicero (pp. 113–14) referred to *humanitas* as the quality of mind and spirit that distinguishes human beings from mere animals. That quality, he thought, is best nurtured and expressed through literature (including history, philosophy, and oratory). Renaissance scholars, following Cicero's lead, identified the study of classical literature (both Greek and Latin) with humanism, and they applied the term "humanist" exclusively to classical scholars.

Interest in the classics had not altogether disappeared during the Middle Ages. By the twelfth century many scholars had made themselves familiar with works of antiquity, and Dante and Chaucer drew heavily from the Latin poets. Before the fourteenth century, however, there had been little to equal the enthusiasm of Renaissance scholars for classical writings. It was in those works that they caught their "new" vision of humanity. Moved by this vision, they searched eagerly for ancient documents and developed a deep respect for the literary culture of antiquity. Their enthusiasm was not caused primarily by dramatic finds of "new" documents; it resulted, rather, from a quickening change in the European *state of mind*.

The medieval intellect, steeped in a God-centered, otherworldly view of the universe, had been largely closed to the naturalistic, pagan spirit. The schoolmen fingered classical manuscripts through thick gloves, so to speak; their religious training normally kept them from a truly sympathetic contact. But with the passing of the Middle Ages the ideals of asceticism and Christian poverty receded before advancing worldliness.

Caught up in this trend were many groups among the educated elite of Europe. In the developing towns, the bourgeois found medieval ideals increasingly unattractive, and were looking for standards closer to their hearts. Kings and nobles glimpsed through the classics the worldly elite of Greece and Rome, whose elegance, refinement, and heroic achievements they hoped to imitate. Even popes and bishops, coming as they mostly did from bourgeois and noble families, often dropped their suspicion of the pagan ancients and became patrons of humanist learning. Bourgeois, aristocrats, and high churchmen all hoped, by imitating the best in ancient thought and behavior, to re-create classical standards in their own times. They failed to bring back the past, or even to imitate it faithfully, but their efforts to do so helped shape modern values.

To most Renaissance thinkers the classical view of humanity was the proper view. They, like the ancients, saw human beings as active *egoists* whose interests were centered in the *here* and *now*. Though they seldom renounced religion, they regarded it as a formality or as an extension of *human* knowledge and power.

The good life, they thought, is the life that is pleasing to the senses, intellect, and aesthetic capacities. Human desires are generally good, though they need to be cultivated and kept in balance. The greatest wrong, to most Renaissance humanists, was *negation*, the absence or repression of spontaneous expression. Well-born and educated individuals, they believed, should be free and proud. They should strive for mastery of all the worthy arts, because their ultimate value as human beings would be measured not in humility, but in talent and accomplishments. Successful individuals, as the Italian humanists put it, possess the quality of *virtù* (strength, virtuosity). Their minds are so filled with thoughts of *this* world that they have little time (or desire) to think about the next.

The ideas of the humanists plainly ran counter to many Christian teachings. They seemed to reject the doctrine of Original Sin and *natural* human sinfulness. They suggested that individuals could perform mighty deeds without divine assistance. And yet (especially in northern Europe) a Christian humanism developed alongside this secular humanism. Some pious scholars shared the growing enthusiasm for the classics and ancient languages. They shared, too, the heightened appreciation of human capabilities, especially the powers of reason and creativity. But they insisted that all human powers were a gift of God — and that this life, though rewarding, fell short of the glory of heaven.

The New Scholarship: Petrarch, Boccaccio

It is no accident that the Renaissance arose in Italy (as did capitalism and absolutism). The force of social change were most advanced there; the development and spread of urban life, for example, had progressed further in Italy than they had in northern Europe. There was another reason, however, independent of those forces: the growing consciousness of *nationality*. While this consciousness did not produce a unified state in Italy (as it did in Spain and France), it caused Italians to embrace their past more warmly than ever before. As Italian humanists studied the Latin classics, they began to dream of restoring the grandeur of ancient Rome. Few Italians had forgotten those glories, for their land offered eloquent architectural reminders. The humanist "road back to Rome" was shortest in Italy, and it was traveled by *patriotic* pilgrims.

Francesco Petrarca (Petrarch), who is regarded as the founder of Renaissance humanism, was born in 1304 of an exiled Florentine family. Urged by his bougeois father to study law, he came upon the works of Cicero in the course of his reading. His admiration for Cicero's thought and style led to a passion for all the classics, and when his father died Petrarch gave up his study of law and turned to a life of scholarship.

It was Petrarch who first undertook the collection of ancient manuscripts. He persuaded others to join him in a search through monastic and cathedral libraries that took him all over Italy and into France and Germany as well. Among his finds were some lost orations and letters of his beloved Cicero. He employed copyists in his home and built up an admirable collection of pagan documents and books. His private library, the first of its kind, became a model for scholars and other intellectuals.

Petrarch's enthusiasm was contagious. Following his example, many of the well-to-do took up the search and began to build their own libraries. Wealthy patrons became interested and by the fifteenth century had founded such famous libraries as the Laurentian in Florence, St. Mark's in Venice, and the Vatican in Rome.

Petrarch set the style as a scholar as well as a collector. Though he led a busy life and spent much of his time in cities and at the courts of aristocrats, he expressed a love of solitude and the peace of nature. But this was a different solitude from that prescribed by the ascetic ideal; it was closer to the ancient Roman model. He spent his private hours not meditating and praying, but studying literature; for isolation without books, he declared, was "exile, prison, and torture." He alternated writing with reading, in the fashion of the modern scholar. What a glory it was, thought Petrarch, "to read what our forerunners have written and to write what later generations may wish to read. . . ."

He preferred to write in classical Latin, because he had only contempt for the vernacular tongues (p. 262) and the corrupted Latin of the Middle Ages. Many of his writings were in the form of epics, dialogues, and letters patterned after the style of Cicero and Vergil (pp. 113–14). He is hardly remembered for those efforts. More successful were his love poems (sonnets), which he wrote in Italian. He addressed most of them to Laura, a beautiful young married woman whom he loved and idealized (though she was unaware of his passion). A record of his most intimate thoughts upon seeing her and thinking of her, these sonnets to Laura became a model for many generations of romantic poets.

Petrarch lived only a generation after Dante, the supreme poet of the high Middle Ages (p. 264), but in these two figures we can see the shift from medieval to modern times. Though Dante knew the classics, he remained a medieval man. Petrarch knew them better, and, while continuing to profess the Christian faith, he warmly embraced pagan values. His irrepressible pursuit of fame led to his being crowned with the *laurel wreath* in 1341; he thus became the first *poet laureate* of modern times. Originally the laurel wreath had been placed upon victors in the ancient Greek "Pythian" games honoring the god Apollo; later, it was conferred upon outstanding public officials and artists. The Romans had adopted the custom, and it was revived late in the Middle Ages. Dante, significantly, refused the offer of a laurel crown, but Petrarch was pleased to strengthen his link with antiquity and to bask in the "immortal glory" of the prize. After the formal examination before King Robert of Naples, he was crowned in a classic ceremony in Rome.

One of Petrarch's followers, Giovanni Boccaccio, was among the first Westerners of modern times to study the Greek language. The son of a Florentine banker, Boccaccio grew bored with the humdrum of credits and debits and set out to learn Greek. Once he had done so, he instructed his tutor to translate Homer into Latin and thus helped to introduce his generation to their first reading of the *Illiad* and the *Odyssey* (p. 74). Like Petrarch, Boccaccio searched far and wide for ancient manuscripts. One of his prized discoveries was a work of the historian Tacitus, which he uncovered in the monastery library at Monte Cassino. When he first saw the neglected condition of the archives there, he broke into tears.

Though Boccaccio was nominally a Christian, his own writings are markedly pagan in spirit. *Fiammetta*, which is sometimes called the first psychological novel of the West, makes no reference to the world of Christian faith and morals. When the heroine is torn by the question of whether to give herself to her lover, she is answered not by the Virgin, but by Venus. The characters in *The Decameron*, Boccaccio's best-known work, are similarly un-Christian in outlook and behavior. The tales in this collection, which Boccaccio borrowed from various countries of Europe and the Middle East, feature sensual escapades, deceits, and clever revenges.

Now other Italian scholars began to study Greek; they were aided by refugee scholars from Constantinople, who had begun to flee the city before its fall to the Turks in 1453 (p. 284). These scholars offered Italians instruction in Greek, Hebrew, and Arabic. Moreover, they brought thousands of manuscripts from Byzantium for safekeeping in the libraries of Florence, Venice, and Rome. By 1500 nearly all the Greek authors had been recovered by the West and translated into Latin and Italian. This was an accomplishment of lasting importance. While medieval scholars had become familiar, through Arabic, with many of the writings of Aristotle and the Hellenistic scientists, they had no direct knowledge of Greek *literature*. It was the humanists who restored to our Western heritage the works of Homer, Herodotus, Thucydides, Aeschylus, Sophocles, Euripides, and Plato.

Humanistic Education and the "Gentleman"

This new body of knowledge challenged traditional patterns of education and thought. Along with new social forces and the rising secular spirit, it set off a revolution in European schooling. Medieval education had been almost exclusively by and for the clergy. Professional training in law and medicine had been introduced into Italian universities during the Middle Ages and had spread to the north. But, for medieval Europe as a whole, religion remained the focus of higher learning. The *trivium* and *quadrivium* centered on scriptural texts, the writings of the Church Fathers, and the logic of Aristotle (p. 255).

The Italian humanists made up the first substantial body of *secular* (nonreligious) scholars in Europe. Most of them were sons of the middle class or the nobility and had no connection with the clergy. Nor had they any use for the tiresome scholasticism that still dominated education (pp. 256–60); in fact, they regarded it as irrelevant to the new society. In Greek and Roman literature they saw the means of providing students with a truly *liberal* education.

It was fairly easy to eliminate scholasticism from the Italian universities, for it had never taken deep root there. The new learning was introduced in its place by humanist professors of rhetoric (speaking and writing), whose lectures drew enthusiastic students from all over Europe. The humanists were not welcomed at most northern universities, however. In the scholastic strongholds of Paris, Cologne, and Heidelberg, the faculties looked with disdain upon the unfamiliar Greek studies. Some Oxford masters condemned them as "dangerous and damnable." Not until the end of the sixteenth century did Greek and Latin literature — the "classics" — supersede philosophy as the foundation of liberal education in the north.

Humanism reached into elementary as well as higher education. The private schools that arose in the towns to serve the sons of the well-to-do were secular in tone and concentrated on Latin and Greek studies. But they aimed at more than the cultivation of the intellect. The schoolmasters saw the ancient leaders (like Pericles and Cicero) as models to inspire young men to lives of fruitful citizenship. The Greeks and Romans had lived in cities and had enjoyed a sophisticated social life; so it was their example, rather than that of the monks and saints, that seemed relevant to the new society. Literature and moral instruction were balanced by training in music and athletics. The Greek ideal of the well-rounded man, mentally and physically fit, was at the heart of humanistic education.

During the sixteenth century this pattern of education spread from Italy throughout western Europe. The private secular school largely replaced monastic and cathedral schools in the education of Europe's leaders. Like the classical model on which it was based and the privileged society it served, the private school was aristocratic in purpose and style. (Its most famous descendants are the "public" — actually, private — schools of England, notably Eton, Harrow, and Winchester.)

Although the curriculum of Greek and Latin studies often became rigid and sterile, it helped shape a new type of personality: the "gentleman." As an ideal, the gentleman now took the place of the medieval knight or the ascetic holy man. Whether of noble or bourgeois background, the ideal gentleman was a man of refinement and self-control. Just as chivalry had tamed the warriors of the Middle Ages (p. 263), humanistic education taught the new landowners and capitalists the ways of urbane living.

The true gentleman possessed a disciplined mind, graceful manners, and excellent taste. For those impatient to acquire such virtues, manuals of proper behavior began to appear; the most influential of them, *The Courtier*, was published in 1528 by an Italian nobleman, Baldassare Castiglione. As Machiavelli was advising rulers on the art of statecraft, Castiglione advised young aristocrats, both male and female, on education and manners. The gentleman (and the lady) would flourish as an admired type in the West for some four hundred years. In the twentieth century the gentleman seems to have disappeared as a model — replaced, perhaps, by the "expert" or the "organization man."

Philosophy: The Appeal of Platonism

Though the recovery of Greek learning revolutionized European education, its influence on philosophy was comparatively modest. Its main effect was to put Plato (pp. 70–72) in Aristotle's place as the foremost philosopher. Aristotle had ruled over the medieval universities because his methods of logic proved so useful to the scholastic thinkers (p. 259). His works were better known than Plato's, and his moderation appealed to men like Aquinas. But the humanists found his writings difficult and without literary appeal. As the complete dialogues of his teacher, Plato, became available during the fifteenth century, the humanists were struck by their charming style as well as their ideas. Here was philosophy that was at the same time literature, and literature that was philosophy. Plato became the new master.

Florence was the leading center for Platonic studies. Cosimo de' Medici, a scholarly ruler who was keenly interested in Plato, founded the Platonic Academy there about 1450. The Academy served as a center for the translation of Platonic writings and for discussions of Plato's philosophy. Just as thinkers of the Middle Ages had sought to reconcile Aristotle with Christian doctrines, so the Italian humanists tried to do the same for Plato.

The Academy was more of an intellectual club than a school. It consisted of only a few select scholars, subsidized by the Medici, and their circle of friends. Their talk and writings were of a rarefied sort that meant little to ordinary people. And yet the influence of the Academy was substantial — especially in art and literature. Almost every artist of the later Renaissance was influenced by Platonism, and some, like Botticelli and Michelangelo, became deeply absorbed in it. Through them the Platonic influence passed on to later generations — ultimately to such nineteenth-century writers as Wordsworth and Goethe (pp. 477–78, 479–80).

Marsilio Ficino was the shining light of the Academy. Chosen by Cosimo at an early age, he was carefully educated and then installed in a villa in the hills near Florence. From that time until his death, he devoted himself to translating Plato's writings and explaining his doctrines. He presided over polite seminars at the villa and corresponded with notables all over Europe, seeking to demonstrate that Platonic teachings were in agreement with Christianity. For those who could not accept religion on the basis of "revelation," he suggested that Plato could open another way.

Pico della Mirandola, a disciple of Ficino, went beyond his master and attempted a synthesis (bringing together) of *all* learning, Eastern and Western. This genius of the age knew Arabic and Hebrew, as well as Greek and Latin, and he studied Jewish, Babylonian, and Persian records. He refused to ignore any source of truth merely because it was not labeled Christian. He felt that by employing all the records and resources of scholarship he had achieved a comprehension of humanity and the universe beyond that of scholastic philosophy. Actually, Pico added little to the view of the world shared by others of his times. He did, however, emphasize human freedom and capacity for learning, and, by breaking through the bounds of medieval theology, he opened a door to the study of *comparative* religion and philosophy.

Like the other members of Cosimo's circle, Pico embraced the Platonic view of creation and existence, which held that by some accident of prehistory humans had become separated from their divine home of pure spirit. Though each soul (spirit) had fallen prisoner to matter (the body), it struggled for liberation and a return to God. This view corresponded to the Christian doctrine of the Fall and the human longing for salvation.

An interesting offshoot of this idea had a profound effect on the arts. The feeling for *natural beauty*, said the Platonists, came from the soul's remembrance of the *divine beauty* of heaven. Hence, aesthetic expression and enjoyment took on a religious connection. Finally, the Platonists linked the emotion of physical love to the higher urge that moves individuals toward their divine source (Platonic love). These teachings raised the arts, even when they dealt with secular subjects, to a higher level. According to the Florentine intellectuals, *art* stimulates appreciation of beauty, and *love* brings the individual closer to the ultimate goal of spiritual reunion with God.

The widespread acceptance of this idea helps to explain the Renaissance "cult of beauty" and the toleration by devout Christians of a frankly sensual art. It reinforced the naturalistic thrust of humanism and the rising secular taste of the times. Thus, by the fifteenth century most painters and sculptors had turned their backs on the "otherworldly" style of art and had plunged eagerly, sometimes ecstatically, into *realistic* representation.

The Critical Spirit and the Beginnings of Empiricism

Beyond its influence on aesthetics, the Platonic revival had only a limited effect on European philosophy. Of greater importance were the methods of scholarship that were introduced by the humanists, although the philosophical implications of those methods were not fully recognized at the time. Petrarch, Boccaccio, and the others who collected classical manuscripts sought to recreate, from the various documents, *correct* texts of the ancient authors. Their intention was simply to reassemble old learning, but their method led to a more *critical* attitude toward the written word and greater attention to *observed facts*. The downfall of scholasticism, with its system of knowledge based on authority and reason, encouraged scholars to find truth by *empirical* methods (observation and experiment).

The Roman humanist Lorenzo Valla was a pioneer of modern textual criticism. An expert on Latin style, he abhorred the carelessness of medieval writers and was bold enough to attack even the Latin of the Vulgate (the Bible as translated by Jerome — p. 156). He also challenged the popular belief that the Apostle's Creed, the traditional confession of Christian beliefs, had actually been composed by the apostles. His most shocking discovery, in 1440, was that the Donation of Constantine (pp. 200–201) was a forgery. This document, which served as a basis for papal claims to secular supremacy over the West, had stood unchallenged for centuries.

Using his new tools of scholarship, Valla demonstrated that the *language* of the Donation could not have been that of the fourth century but was more likely that of the eighth or ninth. Going beyond grammatical analysis, he also pointed out (as a careful scholar should) that the manuscript contained terms of a period later than the date when it was supposedly written. In the words of the Donation, the Emperor Constantine assigns vast powers to Pope Sylvester *before* leaving Rome to build a new capital at Byzantium. Yet he declares that the pope shall have supremacy over all patriarchs, including the one at "Constantinople." How could this be, asked Valla, when at that time Constantinople was not yet a city and there was no such patriarch? So conclusive was Valla's criticism that the Donation was recognized by all as a fraud.

It speaks for the spirit of the age that the popes made no move to punish Valla. On the contrary, they asked for the scholar's services. He was secretary to King Alfonso V of Naples when he published his exposé of the forgery. Afterward, Pope Nicholas V hired him away and brought him back to Rome to translate the ancient Greek historian, Thucydides (p. 79). Nicholas, a patron of humanism, also founded the Vatican (papal) Library as a depository for ancient manuscripts.

Valla was bold, critical, and independent, but, as a practicing humanist, he limited his attention to what could be learned from the literature of the past. The methods of Niccolo Machiavelli went further. He wanted to see what could be learned through direct observation of the world around him. As we noted in the preceding chapter (pp. 307–9), Machiavelli's work was a watershed in the history of political thought. We have seen how his view of the state contrasted with that of Thomas Aquinas, but even greater was the contrast in the *methodology* of the two scholars. Aquinas, the scholastic philosopher, had sought truth mainly by reasoning from authority (*deduction*). Machiavelli sought it mainly by generalizing from collected data (*induction*). He drew his facts from recorded history *and* personal experience. Though he lacked the system, precision, and control of modern social scientists, Machiavelli was clearly moving toward a new conception of knowledge and its verification.

He was not alone in this. Leonardo da Vinci, a fellow citizen of Florence, grew discontented with bookish learning and determined to see things for himself. Though Leonardo is best known for his great paintings (pp. 340–42), his love of art was matched by a desire to unlock the secrets of nature. In order to improve his skill in drawing human and animal bodies, he dissected cadavers and set down his on-the-spot sketches and comments in notebooks. He found dissection difficult and distasteful, but he insisted that observation was the only means to true knowledge. He also experimented with mechanics and drew up plans for ingenious practical inventions. A man of his times, Leonardo both typified Italian humanism and foreshadowed the age of empiricism.

Christian Humanism: Erasmus

So far we have spoken about humanism only in Italy, without tracing its spread beyond the Alps. During the fifteenth century a number of northern scholars journeyed to the Italian centers of learning and carried home with them the seeds of the new scholarship. But the soil of the northern countries produced a different variety of humanism — the pagan flavor, so strong in Italy, was missing.

When humanism came to the north, the intellectual leaders there were filled with Christian piety (deep reverence), and were eager to reform the Church. Dissatisfied with scholasticism, they seized on the rediscovered classics of antiquity. Unlike the scholars of Italy, however, they were not looking for models of sophisticated secular life. Rather, they sought guides to a purer religion and found in the ancient writings those ideals that would encourage *spiritual* reform.

Humanism as represented by Pico and his circle was an outlook based upon many faiths and systems. In the north, however, it emerged as a strictly Christian framework. The northern leaders believed that the example of disciplined and balanced living found in Cicero and the Stoics (pp. 116–18) could well be followed by Christians. Above all, they sought to use the new linguistic and textual skills developed by the Italian humanists as a means of establishing a "truer" Bible. They hoped with these tools to cut away the "false growths" of medieval religious practice and to restore thereby a "pure" Christianity.

There were many devout and vigorous humanists in the north, especially in Germany and England. But the greatest of them all was Desiderius Erasmus. Born in Rotterdam in 1466, he became a cosmopolitan scholar, at home in many lands. His learning and scholarship won him acclaim throughout Europe as the "prince of humanists."

Erasmus, an illegitimate child, had little knowledge of his family background. His father, of middle-class origin, was a priest at the time of Erasmus's birth. Little is known of his mother. Sent off to school as a boy, he lacked the comfortable bourgeois background characteristic of the Italian humanists. His school was supervised by an order of devout laymen, the Brethren of the Common Life. The Brethren, who were dedicated to a pious, mystical Christianity, taught that individual lives should be modeled on the example of Jesus. While subjecting themselves to rigid spiritual discipline, they emphasized the ideals of service and love. Erasmus was deeply touched by this early influence, and he adopted the "philosophy of Christ" as his lifetime ideal.

After Erasmus left school, he was persuaded to enter an Augustinian monastery, where he received little formal instruction but was free to read as he pleased in the classics, both Christian and pagan. At the age of thirty, looking to wider and deeper scholarship, he secured a release from his monastic vows. He went to the University of Paris, where he completed a course in theology. From then on he devoted his life to research and writing, visiting the major centers of learning. Though he was ordained a priest, Erasmus never served a parish. He lived, sometimes meagerly, on the support of patrons and on income from his books.

In the classics Erasmus found models of behavior that could well be followed by genuine Christians. Socrates, Plato, and Cicero were worthy, he thought, of a place among the saints. But he read the ancient writings as a firm believer, and he was persuaded that such studies should serve to strengthen faith, not undermine it. He mastered Greek, for example, not in order to find a truer Homer or Thucydides, but to discover a truer Christ.

Erasmus used his scholarly skills to prepare a more accurate version of the New Testament. Like Valla, he felt certain that the Vulgate Bible, respected though it was, contained errors. After collecting a number of the earliest available New Testament manuscripts in the original Greek, he produced a fresh Greek version based on a comparison of texts. He finished this work in 1516, along with his own Latin translation and commentary, hoping that these efforts would lead to a clearer understanding of the message of Christ — and to translations in the vernacular tongues. He was one of the first to believe that the Bible should be read by the *people* themselves.

Erasmus also prepared improved texts of the writings of the Greek and Latin Church Fathers as well as revised editions of pagan authors. He carried on an extensive correspondence with fellow scholars, and the influence of his ideas, expressed in clear, polished Latin, was extraordinary. He was feared by suspicious conservatives among the clergy but was welcomed everywhere by admiring humanists. Unlike many of them, however, Erasmus was not content to bask in the adulation of an elite; he wanted to make his thoughts available to all literate people.

He published a great many works, often satirical, through which he tried to call attention to the need for reform. He wished to cleanse the Church and society of selfishness, cruelty, hypocrisy, pride, and ignorance — and to replace them with tolerance, honesty, wisdom, service, and love. Repelled by violence and disorder, he hoped that appeals to *reason* would bring about peaceful change. But he sometimes questioned if reform could be achieved peacefully. His most widely read and most entertaining work, *The Praise of Folly*, is filled with doubts and double meanings. Paraded before the reader are the lovers of Folly, a character that personified for her creator the strongest forces in human nature.

Erasmus has Folly sing her own praises: "Without me the world cannot exist for a moment. For is not all that is done among mortals, full of folly; is it not performed by fools and for fools?" People find happiness in light-heartedness and light-headedness — in spontaneous, animal-like behavior. They delight in deceiving and in being deceived. Society rejects the person who pulls off the masks in the comedy of life; the "well-adjusted" person adapts to the game, mixes with others, and encourages their delusions.

At one point Folly observes that sober reason puts an unwelcome damper on natural impulses. The preacher's congregation yawns when he discusses a serious matter but perks up when he tells some silly anecdote. And human behavior is governed less by reason than by the emotions. According to Folly, anger holds the fortress of the breast, and lust rules "a broad empire lower down."

Erasmus spoke of the foolishness of war and war-makers and of the peculiar conceits of individuals and nations, but he reserved most of his barbs for the clergy. The Church, he thought, had grown unduly fond of Folly and had drifted far from the teachings of Christ. He criticized the hair-splitting theologians, the vain and ignorant monks, and the power-loving bishops and popes. He also ridiculed the excesses of the popular cult of the saints and their relics (pp. 234–35), and the purchase of indulgences (p. 239).

The Praise of Folly was written in 1509. Although Erasmus spoke with tongue in cheek, contemporary events tended to confirm what he said. The literate men and women who read his books were impressed and amused, but neither they nor the Church nor society at large was much changed by his sharp words. His criticism of clerics, it is true, helped to bring on the Reformation, but that religious revolt took a shape that he despised. What he hoped for was a *peaceful* reform of Christianity as a *whole*. He wanted a purified Church, not a divided one.

Erasmus was just as critical of the passions and violence aroused by Martin Luther as he was of the errors of the popes. This made him appear to be, in the eyes of Protestant reformers, a moral and physical coward who would not stand up for his convictions. Actually, Erasmus stood fast upon his own convictions — that Christian unity should be upheld, reason promoted, and rebellion shunned.

THE REVOLUTION IN ART

The spirit of humanism could not be confined to literature and philosophy, and as early as the fourteenth century it burst forth splendidly in the visual arts. It appeared first, as one might expect, in Italy — in Florence, the capital of humanism, which remained for some two hundred years the leading center of European art. Few places on earth, over a comparable period, can match that city's output of painting, sculpture, and architecture.

The Pioneer of Naturalism: Giotto

In point of time, Giotto di Bondone was a medieval man, living at the same time as Dante. But he was, in fact, a transitional figure who foreshadowed the modern spirit. In his own day (the early fourteenth century) Giotto was hailed by the citizens of Florence for having achieved a revolution in artistic technique.

In 1305 he was commissioned to paint, on the inside walls of the Arena Chapel in Padua, the New Testament story of Mary and Christ. This was an enormous task, calling for some thirty-five separate scenes. Giotto worked in a common technique known as fresco. Each morning a small area of the wall, covering the space the artist planned to finish that day, was plastered fresh (fresco). The paint, consisting of powdered pigment mixed with water, was applied to the wet plaster and became part of the wall surface when it dried. Because of its size and excellence, Giotto's work in the Arena Chapel was a milestone in European painting. Later artists would be commissioned to follow Giotto's grand example; their efforts reached a peak in Michelangelo's stupendous fresco on the ceiling of the Sistine Chapel (p. 342).

Giotto's paintings reveal the new techniques that were just beginning to emerge. He was not satisfied with the flat look of medieval altar panels and the painted figures of manuscripts. These served well enough to tell a story, and they were often superb in color and design. But Giotto wanted to re-create an actual scene, to give the viewer the feeling of being an eyewitness. In order to accomplish this, he sought to produce the illusion of "depth" (perspective) on a flat surface and to make the figures look solid and real. This he did by skillful use of light and shadow and by *foreshortening* the hands and feet. He also gave careful attention to the *composition* of each scene, arranging individual figures and groups as in a stage setting. Finally, he suggested the emotional state of his subjects through careful attention to facial expression and gesture (*Fig. 8-1*).

8-1 Giotto. *Lamentation.* Arena Chapel, Padua, Italy.

Later painters were to go beyond Giotto in the development of naturalism. But he was the pioneer and was recognized as such. His tomb, in the cathedral of Florence, bears this inscription: "Lo, I am he by whom dead painting was restored to life, to whose right hand all was possible, by whom art became one with nature. . . ." Giotto's influence touched every artist of the Renaissance and extended beyond mere technique. He established himself as a model to follow: the artist as hero, a famous individual. Medieval painters and sculptors had rarely put their names on their works, but Giotto, in the new spirit of the times, signed his paintings and amiably accepted popular acclaim. He demonstrated, further, the humanist ideal of the many-sided genius, the person of *virtù*. A man of many skills, he became the official architect of Florence and designed the graceful campanile (bell tower) of the cathedral. Rising some four hundred feet, it overlooks his beloved city and the valley of the Arno River (*Fig. 8-2*).

New Artistic Techniques: Brunelleschi, Van Eyck

Giotto left a technical challenge to his successors: How could painting be made *more* naturalistic? It was not until a century later that a significant advance in this direction was made. Again it was a Florentine, Filippo Brunelleschi, who pointed the way. A master of sculpture and architecture as well

8-2 Cathedral of Florence.

as painting, he designed a stunning Gothic dome to match Giotto's tower (*Fig. 8-2*). But he shared with his fellow humanists a distaste for medieval forms and set out, after a close study of Roman ruins, to create a *new* style. Adapting classical forms to the needs of his day, Brunelleschi set the tone of Renaissance architecture. His distinctive style marks many of the churches and palaces of Florence; proofs can be seen in his own work (*Fig. 8-3*) and in the work of architects influenced by him (*Fig. 8-4*).

8-3 Brunelleschi. Church of Santo Spirito, interior.

8-4 Michelozzo. Medici-Riccardi Palace.

Brunelleschi made a unique contribution to drawing and painting through his study of *perspective*. He was the first to lay down the mathematical rules governing the reduction in size of pictured objects, according to their placement toward the rear of a scene. The ancient Romans, and Giotto, had been skillful in suggesting depth and distance, but they did not have at their command precise mathematical laws. Brunelleschi formulated them by means of observation and measurement, the "new tools" of Renaissance learning.

One of the first painters to make use of the laws of perspective was Masaccio, some years younger than Brunelleschi. In 1427 he finished a fresco in the church of Santa Maria Novella (Florence). It was a startling innovation. The subject matter was common enough: the Holy Trinity, with the Virgin, St. John, and the donors of the painting (*Fig. 8-5*). What was striking about it was that it presented the illusion of a Roman tunnel vault reaching back through the church wall. The placement and handling of the figures increased the sense of depth. Perspective drawing is familiar to us today, but its unveiling in the fifteenth century provoked amazement. As viewers stood back from the wall, they must have gasped at what seemed to be a group of sculptured figures placed within a classical, three-dimensioned chapel.

8-5 Masaccio. *Trinity with the Virgin, St. John, and Donors.*
Soprintendenza alle Galerie, Florence.

In northern Europe, artists were taking a different approach to naturalism. Among the most influential was Jan Van Eyck, a painter of Flanders (in the Low Countries). The Flemish towns, it will be recalled, were thriving in the fifteenth century as centers of the expanding international trade (p. 285). Well-to-do patrons began to appear there, as in Italy, and Flemish art set the style for northern Europe during most of the Renaissance period.

Van Eyck, less radical than Masaccio, observed most of the traditions of late Gothic painting. But he carried to an unprecedented degree the recording of precise detail. He worked, for example, on the famed "Ghent Altarpiece" (completed in 1432). It contains twelve separate panels, with *The Adoration of the Mystic Lamb* the central subject. The painting was conventional in style, but Van Eyck was far more exact in his treatment than any previous painter had been.

Van Eyck's realism was distinct from that of the Italians. Giotto and Masaccio sought to give their figures roundness and solidity, set against a receding and darkened background, whereas Van Eyck treated objects in the background of his paintings with the same close attention that he gave to those in the foreground. His work has been described as both microscopic and telescopic. In the detail from one of his portraits, *Giovanni Arnolfini and His Bride* (*Fig. 8-6*), he seems to have counted every hair on the little dog, and he shows each one in a precise gradation of light and shadow.

In his efforts to achieve such effects, Van Eyck experimented with various paint materials. He was among the first to develop and use *oil* paints. Before this time, painters had mixed powdered pigments with water, or with a white-

8-6 Jan Van Eyck. Detail from *Giovanni Arnolfini and His Bride*. National Gallery, London.

of-egg liquid (called tempera). The latter gave fairly good results, but it dried out rather quickly. Van Eyck discovered that by mixing his pigments with linseed oil he could work more slowly and produce the special effects he desired. The quality and brilliance of his painting, as well as its accuracy, soon led most European artists to follow his lead.

The Liberation of Sculpture: Donatello

Sculpture, even more than painting, can be used for the faithful reproduction of nature. Sculptors have no need to create an illusion of depth, for they work in *three* dimensions. Yet medieval sculptors usually had to fit their figures into the narrow spaces assigned to them by architects and were therefore unable to realize the full potential of their art. Donatello, a contemporary of Masaccio and Brunelleschi, restored sculpture to an independent status and gave to his art the character of naturalism and humanism.

Donatello made a careful study of the remains of Roman sculpture. Discarding the copybook methods of medieval workmen, he also began to work (as the Romans and Greeks had done) from live models. One of his earliest statues, a marble *St. George* (1416), reveals the contrast between the new technique and that of the Middle Ages (*Fig. 8-7*). The young warrior, standing

8-7 Donatello. *St. George.* Marble statue from the Church of San Michele, Florence.

firmly by his shield, does not have the "otherworldly" gaze of most medieval figures; he looks straight ahead with an expression of readiness. This realistic appearance reflects Donatello's painstaking observation of the human body.

Donatello's fame spread swiftly from his native Florence. Just as Giotto had been called to Padua to paint the murals of the Arena Chapel, so Donatello was commissioned to work in one city after another. (The rival city-states of Italy competed with one another not only in arms and politics, but in art as well.) Near the close of his life, Donatello spent some ten years in Padua, which was then part of the Venetian Republic. There he produced a monumental equestrian statue in bronze (*Fig. 8-8*). The rider, "Gattamelata," is a Venetian general (condottiere) with the assured bearing of a caesar. One of the first equestrian statues to be made since ancient Roman times, it was modeled after a monument to the emperor Marcus Aurelius. That splendid work, the only one of its kind to survive from the ancient world, was discovered by humanists in the fifteenth century (*Fig. 3-6*, p. 128).

The *Gattamelata*, which still stands in the cathedral piazza (public square), was Donatello's largest free-standing statue. He created smaller carvings and *relief* sculptures as well. His most striking relief is *The Feast of Herod*, a bronze

8-8 Donatello. *Gattamelata*. Padua.

8-9 Donatello. *The Feast of Herod.* San Giovanni, Siena, Italy.

panel for the baptismal font (holy water basin) of Siena's cathedral (*Fig. 8-9*). In the Biblical scene shown, King Herod is being presented with the head of John the Baptist. Herod had ordered John's beheading reluctantly, at the urging of his stepdaughter, Salome. (She wanted John killed, because he had condemned the king's unlawful marriage to Salome's mother.) Now Herod and his guests, seated at the banquet table, recoil in horror. Though Donatello's panel measures only about two feet on each side, it is rich in dramatic detail. Having learned the trick of perspective from his friend Brunelleschi, he created a marvelous illusion of *depth*. One can look through the rounded arches to Herod's musicians and beyond, through other archways, into the far background.

Though less revolutionary, Lorenzo Ghiberti surpassed Donatello as a sculptor of reliefs. His fame rests on the gilded bronze doors of the cathedral baptistry at Florence, on which he labored for nearly thirty years. Michelangelo later called them fit to stand as the "Gates of Paradise," and so they have been known ever since. They are divided into ten large panels, each presenting a scene from the Old Testament. One of the panels, *The Meeting of Solomon and the Queen of Sheba* (*Fig. 8-10*), shows the artist's mastery of composition, perspective, and dramatic effect. The "Gates of Paradise" were hung in 1452, an event that may be regarded as the crossing point in Renaissance art between the period of revolution and the period of fulfillment.

Art Triumphs over Nature: Botticelli, Leonardo

The painters and sculptors of the late fifteenth and early sixteenth centuries were challenged by a task even greater than that of their predecessors. Masaccio, Van Eyck, and Donatello had shown the way to naturalistic representation — an impressive achievement, made possible by intensive study and technical innovation. But once naturalism had been established it revealed its own limitations. A "literal" presentation of subject matter did not necessarily result in harmonious composition. It did not always carry a message, mood, or emotion in the most effective way. Finally, if it was a perfect imitation of reality, it could not, as art, *transcend* (go beyond) nature.

Sandro Botticelli, a fifteenth-century Florentine, wanted to preserve the liveliness and realism typical of the work of the Renaissance pioneers, and yet he wanted to create an art that would be more appealing than nature itself. This meant "taking liberties" with the actual appearance of things, subordinating it to *form* and *color* — even injecting elements of *mystery*. One of his most successful efforts was *The Birth of Venus* (*Fig. 8-11*).

Botticelli was among the first painters to use figures from classical mythology in a major work. During the Middle Ages the Church, the chief patron

8-10 Ghiberti. *The Meeting of Solomon and the Queen of Sheba.* Baptistry, Florence.

8-11 Botticelli. *The Birth of Venus*. Uffizi Gallery, Florence.

of art, had forbidden the glorification of pagan traditions. The humanists admired antiquity, however, and during the Platonic revival in Florence (pp. 323–25) the Greek myths rivaled the Christian stories in popularity. In fact, Botticelli was commissioned by one of the Medici to paint *The Birth of Venus* for his private villa.

The work is full of color, movement, and grace. In the center, being wafted to shore on a seashell, stands the goddess of love. The picture is harmonious and unified, and it conveys the mystery of beauty that so fascinated the Florentine intellectuals. It will be recalled that they associated love of beauty with man's desire for reunion with the divine. Venus, symbolically, was the fountain of beauty and love. Though Botticelli used a flesh-and-blood model, his Venus appears detached, unearthly — an *idealized* beauty.

The cult of beauty encouraged patrons and artists alike to select pagan themes. Even when the myths were not completely understood, the humanists assumed that they contained hidden wisdom. Under this cloak of intellectual respectability, some artists went on to portray their subjects in a frankly sensual manner. The Venetian painter Titian is a notable example. His *Venus of Urbino* (*Fig. 8-12*), which he painted in 1538, concentrates the viewer's attention on a reclining, seductive nude. This is not the spiritlike Venus of Botticelli, but an enticing woman who seems aware of her naked loveliness and the eyes of the viewer. Titian's remarkable technique is revealed in his flesh tones and textures. His works were to serve as models for every painter of nudes who followed him.

8-12 Titian. *Venus of Urbino*. Uffizi Gallery, Florence.

The innovations in treatment and technique were, indeed, more significant than changes in subject matter. And the leading experimenter, in both art
and nature, was Leonardo da Vinci, who fulfilled the humanist ideal of the
"universal genius" (pp. 319–20). His *Notebooks* demonstrate the astonishing
breadth of his curiosity. He began his artistic training toward the end of the
fifteenth century as an apprentice in a Florentine workshop, where he learned,
under the guild system of supervision, the standard methods of observing and
sketching models and objects. He studied the optics of perspective, the mixing
of colors, and the techniques of metalwork. But when he left the shop of his
master, Leonardo had only started his education. For he was less interested in
the surface appearance of things than in what lay underneath, and so he undertook his ceaseless exploration of anatomy, physiology, and nature (p. 326).

He left many of his projects unfinished. We have only a few of his major
paintings, and some of these are in poor condition. In those we have, his genius
is clear. He resolved the difficulties of combining lifelike representation with
artistic form and an element of mystery. By comparison, the mirrorlike paintings of Van Eyck appear rigid and lacking in focus. In his use of light and
shadow, Leonardo found that shading lends grace and softness to facial features and reduces stiffness of line. By blurring his contours, especially at the
corners of the mouth and eyes, he left something to the imagination of the
viewer. Each time we look at his *Mona Lisa* (*Fig. 8-13*) her expression (and
thought) seems to change.

8-13 Leonardo da Vinci. *Mona Lisa.* Louvre, Paris.

Leonardo's most famous painting is *The Last Supper*, completed in 1497 (*Fig. 8-14*). This sacred subject had been treated countless times before. How could an artist do anything special or original with it? Most earlier paintings had shown Christ and his disciples quietly seated around the supper table in varying settings and kinds of dress. Leonardo introduced drama and excitement.

8-14 Leonardo da Vinci. *The Last Supper.* Convent of Santa Maria della Grazia, Milan.

He chose the precise moment after the Lord had said, "One of you will betray me" (Matt. 26:21). While Christ sits calm at the center of the picture, waves of disbelief, amazement, and distress sweep to the right and left of him. Only Judas, among the disciples, is motionless. And, even with the agitation and tension of the recorded instant, the painting forms a harmonious whole.

The Artistic Climax: Michelangelo

Though Leonardo was the most versatile of Renaissance figures (artist, musician, and scientist), he was overshadowed as an *artist* by Michelangelo Buonarroti. Leonardo observed and investigated nature as a whole; Michelangelo concentrated on anatomy, convinced that the inmost urges and sensitivities of human beings could best be expressed through the human figure.

Michelangelo preferred to represent the body in three dimensions of sculpture, but he was required to do numerous works as a painter. In 1508 he was called to Rome from his native Florence by the pompous and militant Pope Julius II. The pontiff, desiring a monumental tomb for himself, had turned to Michelangelo, the best sculptor of his day, to make it. Complications arose, however, and Julius asked Michelangelo to paint the ceiling of his private chapel instead. The chapel had been built by Pope Sixtus IV (hence, the name Sistine), and its walls had been painted by an earlier generation of masters (including Botticelli). The ceiling vault, however, remained blank.

Michelangelo, disappointed when his sculpturing commission was put off, accepted the new task with reluctance. But, having once decided to undertake it, he plunged into the work with his customary vigor. Some four years later the fresco was finished. It covers about ten thousand square feet and includes more than three hundred figures. In plan, execution, and magnitude no other painting in history (by a single individual) has surpassed it.

In the Sistine Chapel painting, as in all his creations, Michelangelo expressed his deep religious concern about humankind. Tormented by a sense of sin, his own and that of the human species, he suffered from a feeling of personal frustration, of unfulfilled ambitions. His conviction that individuals struggle helplessly against destiny led him to a tragic view of life. He felt that the human spirit, of divine origin, desires to return to God but is held fast by the flesh and by the sins of the flesh. In *The Last Judgment*, which he painted late in life on the end wall of the Sistine Chapel, he portrayed a severe and muscular Christ condemning crowds of sinners to the eternal fires of hell.

Michelangelo was clearly influenced by the Platonism of the Academy (p. 324). In an effort to reconcile his Christian convictions with the teachings of the Platonists, he merged the two in his pictorial layout for the chapel vault. The main feature, on the ceiling proper, is a series of nine panels showing the Hebrew-Christian stories of the Creation and the Flood. (The story from

Noah to Christ had already been painted on the lower walls.) Perhaps the most appealing of these panels is *The Creation of Adam* (*Fig. 8-15*). The Father, borne by the heavenly host, is about to bring the inert Adam to life by the touch of his finger. Evident here is Michelangelo's ability to suggest *latent* (reserved) power and to inject light and movement.

After finishing his backbreaking labor on the Sistine scaffolds, Michelangelo returned to his first love, sculpture. From solid blocks of marble, he began to carve several figures for the projected tomb of Julius II. The special quality of his sculpture can be understood in part by his attitude toward the stone: before taking up his chisel, he always visualized the human form within each block. He then proceeded, with furious energy, to "liberate" the form from the stone.

One of his finest works, carved some years earlier, expresses the spirit of athletic youth. His eighteen-foot-tall *David* (*Fig. 8-16*) was at first placed in the main piazza of Florence. A copy stands there today, but the original is housed in a Florentine museum. The *David* shows the influence of Greek sculpture on Michelangelo's work. Later creations, such as the figures for Julius's tomb, show the influence of Platonism. In one of these, known as *The Dying Slave*, Michelangelo shows a mature, powerful body falling into repose as death approaches, releasing the slave from life's futile struggle. Among Michelangelo's other sculptural works are a *Pietà* (the sorrowing Virgin mourning for the dead Christ) and a wrathful, monumental *Moses*.

Later in life, having won fame as a painter and a sculptor, Michelangelo turned his attention to architecture. Here, too, he was without peer. He continued the development of the Renaissance style that had been initiated by Brunelleschi. Much of his work was done in Rome, and the touch of his hand is revealed there in countless places: the Farnese Palace, the church of St. Mary of

8-15 Michelangelo. Detail from *The Creation of Adam*. Sistine Chapel, Vatican, Rome.

8-16 Michelangelo. *David*. Accademia, Florence.

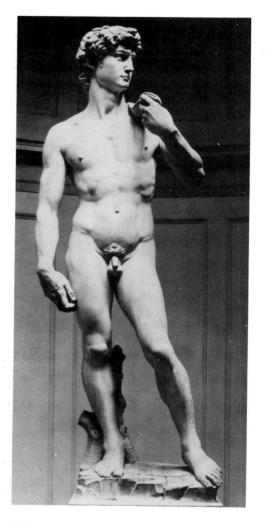

the Angels (which he converted from a great hall that had once been part of the Roman Baths of Diocletian), and the Campidoglio (a piazza atop Capitoline Hill, enclosed by civic buildings).

His last masterpiece was the dome of St. Peter's. The new St. Peter's (replacing the original church of the fourth century) was planned early in the sixteenth century by the tireless Julius II. He wished to erect, over the tomb of the first apostle, a structure that would surpass all others in Christendom. Several architects had a hand in the design, but in 1547 Michelangelo was put in charge. During the remaining years of his life he devoted most of his energies to planning the mighty basilica (church of special distinction).

The floor plan was for a colossal structure laid out in the form of a Greek (square) cross. A central dome was to be the crowning feature. Earlier schemes had called for a shallow dome modeled on that of the Pantheon (*Fig. 3-4*, p. 125), but Michelangelo wanted something greater for the "capitol" of Christendom. Inspired by Brunelleschi's dome in Florence (*Fig. 8-2*), he planned one even steeper and higher — one that would tower over every other building in the Eternal City.

Although he died before St. Peter's was completed, the dome was finished according to his designs. The square plan of the basilica, however, was altered into a Latin (oblong) cruciform plan (*Fig. 6-2*, p. 244), which meant that a long nave (central aisle) had to be constructed. As a result, the view of the dome from the front of the church is partially blocked. The view of St. Peter's from the *rear* (*Fig. 8-17*) shows the dome as it would have appeared from all sides had the original plan been carried out.

The magnificent dome, the largest in the world, has been copied by architects everywhere. Equal in diameter to that of the Pantheon, it rises *three hundred feet* higher. It stands as a splendid symbol of Christianity and a fitting monument to Michelangelo.

8-17 Michelangelo. St. Peter's, Vatican, Rome.

LITERATURE AND DRAMA

While the visual arts of the Renaissance reached their climax in Italy, striking accomplishments in literature were appearing beyond the Alps. The north could not match the best painting and sculpture of the south. It proved equal or superior, however, in the *written word*.

The Invention of Printing

The influence of scholars and writers everywhere was vastly extended by the invention of printing and the introduction of paper. During the Middle Ages literature had to be copied by hand on parchment (sheepskin). Books were therefore rare and expensive and could be afforded only by the wealthy. The art of making paper had originated in China before the birth of Christ. The Arabs, in the eighth century, had learned it from the Chinese and had carried it with them to their conquered lands. Cheaper than parchment, paper was coming into use in western Europe when Johann Gutenberg of Mainz began printing with movable metal type in 1447.

Printing by woodcut blocks had been known for centuries in both Asia and Europe. A whole page of text and illustrations could be carved out of a single block, and the block could then be inked to print on paper. But this process was slow and wasteful, since each block could be used for only a single purpose. Gutenberg's invention of individual letters cast in metal meant that the characters could be arranged and rearranged as many times as desired. By drastically reducing costs, the new method of printing brought a revolution in communication and education. By 1500, there were more than a thousand printers at work in Europe, and nearly ten million books had been printed.

The early printers desired to match the artistic standards of medieval scribes, and most of these "cradle books" (incunabula) were of excellent quality in type, paper, and binding. As the reading public grew, however, and as price competition became more pressing, the general quality of printing declined. Still, the influence of the printed word was infinitely greater than it had ever been before. The invention of movable type ultimately made possible free public libraries, mass education, and cheap newspapers and magazines. Its immediate effect was to accelerate the spread of humanism by making the classics more readily available.

The Libertarian Humorist: Rabelais

Printing also brought a wider readership to humanist authors. Erasmus probably had more contemporary readers than any previous writer. In France the most popular author was François Rabelais, an enthusiastic humanist with a talent for satire and parody. Though his books were condemned by religious and civil authorities (the issue of censorship arose soon after the invention of printing), they had a warm appeal to readers. Rabelais was (and still is) a most popular author.

Like Erasmus, who was born a generation earlier, Rabelais knew the Church and the universities from the inside. From a middle-class family, he had entered a Franciscan monastery in order to become a scholar. But he was a rebel from the beginning; his absorption in the classics disturbed his superiors and led to trouble. He switched from one religious order to another, for a time wore the garb of a priest, studied at various universities, and later took up law and medicine. His career, like his writing, followed no visible plan. With a vast appetite for life and learning, he was the personification of a vigorous and spontaneous humanism.

Though Rabelais loved the classics and knew them intimately (especially the Roman), his own temperament was by no means classical. It was the content, not the style, of the classics that appealed to him. He wrote in vernacular French, rather than classical Latin, and he detested all rules and regulations. One should follow, he insisted, one's own inclinations. Rabelais thus represented a humanism that did not copy classical models (or any other) but stood as a purely *individualistic* philosophy. Rejecting the doctrine of Original Sin (and most other doctrines), he stressed *natural goodness*; he held that most people, given freedom and proper education (in the classics), will live happy and productive lives.

This idea is central to Rabelais's great work, *Gargantua and Pantagruel*. The story, about two imaginary giant-kings, was published in several volumes over a period of years (beginning in 1538). Rabelais often used the giants, father and son, as spokesmen for his own views. He wrote the work primarily for amusement, because he believed that laughter (like thought) is a distinctively *human* function. However, in telling of the heroes' education and adventures, he voiced his opinions on the human traits and institutions of his time. In a tumble of words, learned and playful, he mingled serious ideas with earthy jokes and jibes.

Monasticism was a prime target for Rabelais, as it was for most humanists. Its stress on self-denial, repression, and regimentation was to him inhumane and hateful. He had Gargantua give funds to a "model" institution that *violates* monastic practices in every possible way. At this "abbey of Thélème," with its fine libraries and recreational facilities, elegantly dressed men and women are free to "do as they please." Monks, hypocrites, lawyers, and peddlers of gloom are barred from the abbey; only handsome, high-spirited people are admitted.

Rabelais disliked pretense and deception and praised the natural instincts and abilities of free persons. Rejecting the ascetic ideal, he expressed secular humanism in its most robust and optimistic form. In doing so, Rabelais also reflected the views of the ancient Greek *hedonist*, Aristippus (pp. 68–69) — and he anticipated the *modern* appetite for unlimited experience and pleasure (p. 634).

The Skeptical Essayist: Montaigne

Michel de Montaigne, born a generation after Rabelais, lived through the same troubled times of religious struggle between the Protestants and Catholics and shared Rabelais's keen interest in the classics. But some critical difference of personality turned him toward quite another kind of humanism. His temperament was nearer that of Erasmus (pp. 326–29). Both men remained loyal to the Roman Catholic Church and both were dedicated scholars, but Montaigne was more secular-minded and detached than Erasmus. He had no strong desire to reform society, and he was not concerned with what others thought of him. (His *own* opinion was all that mattered.) The son of a landowning family near Bordeaux, Montaigne received a superb education. His father held public office, traveled abroad, and believed in a humanistic upbringing for his children. When he died, Michel inherited the family estate and was able to retire at the age of thirty-eight to his library of a thousand books.

Privacy and leisure, which Montaigne treasured above all else, gave him an opportunity to read and think. He chose only those books that gave him pleasure — pleasure in the Epicurean sense (p. 116). These were the Latin authors (and some Greeks in translation), whom Montaigne considered superior in style and content to other writers. From his reading he developed a desire to live his personal life according to classical ways, and, like Petrarch, he began to record his own thoughts and observations.

Out of this activity came the first two volumes of *Essays* (1580). Unlike Rabelais's books, these were models of clear French prose. They were immediately popular, and Montaigne was encouraged to publish a third volume soon afterward. Altogether, he wrote more than a hundred essays on such topics as the emotions, superstition, customs, education, marriage, scholarship, and death. His usual manner was to begin with the opinions of traditional authorities on the topic, inserting quotations from their works, and then to explain his own views. Sometimes he would present opposing answers to a given question and then suggest a compromise solution — or, perhaps, no solution at all.

Montaigne's essays were a new form of literature, though they owed much to the example of Seneca, a Roman writer of the first century A.D. (p. 114). They were not systematic studies of the sort written by scholars but were simply *essais* (personal views). Montaigne did not attempt to change the minds of his readers, but wrote, in large measure, for his own satisfaction. And, because the essays were based on his own experiences and thoughts, they were also a form of *autobiography*. The notion that every person of worth should pass on some record of that person's life and ideas became widespread during the Renaissance. The boastful Florentine artist Benvenuto Cellini was among those who accepted this idea; he dictated his *Autobiography* in 1560. Gradually the *essay* and the *memoir* became standard literary forms, further expressions of the individualism and self-confidence of the age.

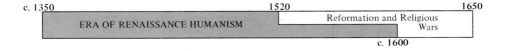

In one of Montaigne's most notable essays on the subject of knowledge and reason (Vol. II, Essay 12), he showed himself to be a philosophical *relativist* (p. 69). He spoke of the limits of reason in efforts to comprehend the universe: neither theology, classical wisdom, nor science can provide final answers to the "big questions"; all knowledge is subject to *uncertainty* and *doubt*. The human mind, observed Montaigne, is erratic; and the senses, which are unreliable, often control the mind. Beliefs, no matter how firmly held, cannot be regarded as constant; for they, too, have their seasons, their birth and death. He thus challenged the self-assurance of both Christians and earlier humanists.

Montaigne did not suggest that people should not use their minds. On the contrary, he thought that every individual capable of reason should seek answers satisfactory to that individual. The thinking person should never embrace the ready-made views of others, no matter how impressive their authority; they ought to consider various ideas and then make a choice. And if one feels unable to make a choice, one should remain in doubt. The uncertain character of knowledge ought to teach us, above all, that *dogmatism* (absolute self-assurance) is unjustified — and that persecuting people for differing beliefs is wrong.

Montaigne made his eloquent plea for tolerance in the midst of the frightful struggle among religious fanatics that raged through sixteenth-century France. He could see that war and homicide are often the outcomes of absolutistic thought and belief. Like Erasmus, Montaigne was a *political conservative* and opposed to violence; he felt that firm authority was indispensable to peace and order. Though he cherished independence of thought, he did not rebel against established institutions, hoping that those who held power would see the light, ultimately, of moderation and decency. In any event, he stuck to his personal philosophy — a blend of skepticism, Epicureanism, and Stoicism (pp. 115–18) — and remained aloof from other people. In the quiet and security of his library, Montaigne could meditate on one of his favorite sayings: "Rejoice in your present life; all else is beyond you."

Rabelais and Montaigne were among the few writers on the continent whose devotion to humanism was not disturbed by the religious upheavals that broke out around 1520. Another was Miguel de Cervantes, the greatest author of Spain. He began his masterpiece, *Don Quixote*, well past midlife (about 1600). It was a satire on the tales of chivalry (pp. 262–63) that were still being written (and read) in his native land. Cervantes's hero is a caricature of the romantic *knight*; he imagines windmills to be evil giants and vainly charges against them. While Don Quixote is a hopeless idealist, his squire, Sancho Panza, sees the world in simple, down-to-earth terms. (As the story unfolds, the dialogue between them produces a reversal of values in each.) Cervantes succeeded in ridiculing chivalric literature and revealed, through the Don's adventures, a panorama of the Spain of his day. On the philosophical level, the contrasting and shifting values of Panza and Quixote remind one of the *relativity* of truth that Montaigne had noted in his essays.

The Master Dramatist: Shakespeare

Humanism came late to England. It had hardly been established there by 1500, and it might even have vanished in the religious turmoil that erupted shortly thereafter. One of the casualties, indeed, was Sir Thomas More. A dedicated scholar and a friend of Erasmus, he wrote the visionary *Utopia*, in which he set down the humane features of a decent, planned society (pp. 514–16). But he later paid with his life for refusing to swear loyalty to the king as head of the Church of England (pp. 371–72). Humanism and the secular spirit proved hardy, however, and attained their full expression in literature around 1600. The leading genius of this expression was William Shakespeare.

Shakespeare was not a classical scholar. As his friend Ben Jonson said, he knew "small Latin and less Greek." But he was familiar (in the original or in translation) with many of the ancient authors. Moreover, he was filled with the *spirit* of humanism, which characterized the Elizabethan age (1550–1600). For England this was a period of rising national strength, bourgeois prosperity, and lusty living. Shakespeare's plays contain elements of the classical and the timeless, but they speak in the voice of the Renaissance.

The roots of Elizabethan drama go back to the Romans and the Greeks, for during the Middle Ages there had been only religious pageants and "Passion" and "morality" plays. But the classical revival of the fifteenth century stimulated the reenactment of Roman dramas at the courts of Italian rulers, and in time a new form of *secular* drama, based on the Roman model, came into being and spread across Europe.

Although the Italian playwrights followed the classical tradition of lengthy recitations, a chorus, and little action, the English introduced modifications to suit their national taste. They also began to build permanent theaters for dramatic performances; none had existed in medieval times. When Shakespeare arrived in London about 1590, both the new drama and the new way of designing theaters were approaching maturity.

The Globe Theater of his day is a good example of the Elizabethan playhouse. Octagonal in outward plan, it faced inward on a large courtyard (*Fig. 8-18*). The stage, or platform, was built on one side of the inner circle and projected some ten feet into the yard; ringing the yard were three tiers of balconies, or covered boxes. Those who could not afford boxes stood or sat in the yard itself.

The stage lacked the scenery and equipment available to our contemporary theaters. A curtained area in the rear could serve as a chamber or an inner

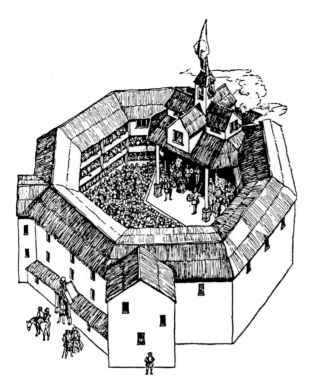

8-18 The Globe Theater.

room; when closed off, it became the backdrop for a setting on the main stage. The front of the platform often served as a street or passageway. Because there was no main curtain, the script had to provide action to clear the stage at the end of each scene.

A balcony directly above the stage could represent the window of a house, the deck of a ship, or the top of a castle wall, while trapdoors in the floor and roof of the stage enabled witches and spirits to ascend or descend. Lighting was no problem, since this was an open-air theater and performances were given in the afternoon. Though much of the setting was left to the viewer's imagination, the Elizabethan theater proved remarkably flexible and enabled the actors to establish close contact with their audience. As in classical drama, all the roles were played by men or boys. (The stage was not considered a fit place for females, and "respectable" women were seldom seen in the audience.)

The dramas themselves still bore the mark of the classical tradition. The length of the plays, their division into acts, and the types of characters and themes came from ancient comedy and tragedy. Greek plays were known in Elizabethan times only through their Roman versions, particularly those of Seneca (p. 114). Drawing from well-known Greek myths, Seneca had written gruesome dramas peopled by crudely drawn characters, ghosts, and phantoms, and dealing with themes of betrayal, revenge, and madness.

Renaissance drama differed from ancient drama in significant ways, however. It was not associated with religious festivals, as Greek drama had been (p. 76), and, though it often dealt with moral issues, its spirit was markedly secular. Supernatural touches were occasionally introduced (the audience expected them), but the plays were emphatically "of this world." Though Shakespeare himself was nominally a Christian, his dramas lack any doctrinaire Christian tone; in some of them there are even hints of religious doubts and fatalism.

The range of Shakespeare's themes and locales is greater than that of the classical dramatists. "All the world's a stage," declares one of his characters (Jaques, in *As You Like It*) — speaking to an audience that had daily reports of adventures in newly discovered lands. Many other features of his work reflect the values and concerns of humanism. The urge to *power* is the central theme in many of his plays, and the rising sense of *nationality*, or patriotism, fills his historical dramas. Shakespeare's deep interest in character and inner psychological conflict reflects the Renaissance concern with *individualism*. Many of his passages reflect, too, an emphasis on *materialism* and *sensuousness*. Finally, he demonstrates the same concern for *realism* that was displayed by the humanist painters and sculptors.

Hamlet, one of Shakespeare's greatest tragedies, illustrates his dramatic methods. The story comes out of a medieval Danish history book, though Shakespeare probably based his work on an English dramatic adaptation of the early sixteenth century. *Hamlet* is a tragedy of *revenge*, a type of drama popular at the time. Shakespeare gave it the elements of conflict, suspense, violence, and poetic imagery that his audience enjoyed. Since the audience consisted chiefly of well-read individuals, he was able to bring moral and philosophical ideas into the course of the dramatic action.

As a character, Hamlet typifies the ideal "gentleman" of the new Europe (pp. 322–23). He also embodies the conflict between meditation and action that fascinated the intellectuals of the age. Hamlet knows that it is his *duty* (by custom) to avenge his murdered father, but he insists on using the humanistic tool of *reason* to guide his actions. While he delays *acting*, a series of miserable deaths occurs. Shakespeare leaves it to his audience to decide whether reason should bow to custom, and whether humans are the masters of their destiny.

We know little about Shakespeare's life except that he prospered in London and retired to his native Stratford some years before his death (1616), but we do have the legacy of his works. No one has had a surer feeling for the sense and sound of the English language. In addition to his poetry, he left some forty plays, among them several masterpieces. These make superb literature as well as good theater; his collected writings have been referred to as the "English secular Bible." The Renaissance, which admired the individual genius, produced one in Shakespeare. Moreover, as Ben Jonson observed, he was "not of an age but for *all time*."

9

The Reformation: Division and Reform in the Church

As with all major cultural movements, it is difficult to say precisely when the Renaissance began or when it ended. The influence of the classics on art and literature, so marked in the Renaissance, has continued with diminishing force into the twentieth century. Humanism as a general point of view has persisted, too, but by 1600 it was no longer a leading influence in European cultural life. Other ideas (and systems) — capitalism, political absolutism, and national self-consciousness — continued to grow in strength. And added to these in the sixteenth century was the explosive force of religious revolt and reform. The resulting division of the Church completed the dissolution of medieval civilization.

The bitter religious struggles that broke out in 1520 did not end until about 1650. They so absorbed Europe's attention and energies that the years between came to be known as the era of religious reformation and religious wars. The Reformation was a complex affair. The primary impulses behind it were, of course, religious, but religious matters were closely bound up with political, social, and economic matters. And actually there were *two* concurrent reformations: the Protestant, which was carried out in defiance of papal authority, and the Roman Catholic, which had papal approval. The former led to many *separate* Christian churches, each with its own organization and doctrines; the latter led to correction of clerical "abuses," a redefinition of doctrines, and a freshening of Catholic spiritual life.

BACKGROUND OF THE REFORMATION

From the view of the established Catholic organization, the Protestant reformers were *heretics* who defied the pope. Differences on matters of doctrine had arisen early in the life of the Church, but for many centuries unity had been maintained in the West. (Differences between the Latin [Catholic] and the Greek [Orthodox] churches had arisen following the breakup of the Roman Empire; the final separation occurred following the capture of Constantinople by Catholic crusaders in 1204 — p. 155.) To preserve Western unity, the popes and bishops had exercised continuous watchfulness and strong discipline. During the Middle Ages thousands of heretics had been burned at the stake in the name of Christian purity and unity. How was it that the Protestant heretics survived where their predecessors had perished? One reason is that the late medieval Church had suffered a fateful decline.

Decay of the Church

During the thirteenth century the medieval Church had reached the height of its power. This was when the great cathedrals were built, when powerful reform orders were founded, and when scholastic philosophy achieved its greatest influence. Under Pope Innocent III the papal monarchy had dominated the rulers of Europe as well as the Church organization (p. 242). But the fourteenth and fifteenth centuries saw a steady fall in the condition of the Church, and by 1500 the organization had reached its low point.

The fortunes of the Church as a whole were closely tied to those of the papacy. Medieval popes like Gregory VII and Innocent III had done much to strengthen the Church structure. But the popes of later centuries had been less successful in their undertakings, and their failures affected the entire institution. Boniface VIII, for example, was defeated in his struggle with the French king Philip the Fair (p. 242). After Boniface's death (in 1303) Philip moved to avoid future trouble with Rome by forcing the election of a French bishop as the new pope. Thus, the papacy was drawn into French politics. The new relationship was demonstrated shortly thereafter when the pope (Clement V) transferred his court from Rome to Avignon.

Avignon was a papal holding on the lower Rhone River, just east of the border of the French kingdom. Clement went there voluntarily, chiefly because conditions in Rome were unsafe. But his move confirmed a widespread feeling that the papacy had become a *captive* of the French monarchy. Clement secured a French majority in the College of Cardinals (p. 238), and for some seventy years a succession of French popes reigned at Avignon.

Outside France, these popes were looked upon with suspicion and hostility. Because the pope holds office by virtue of his being the bishop of Rome, it seemed improper that he should reside anywhere but in the Eternal City. The English, who were then at war with the French, regarded the papacy at Avignon as the ally of their enemy. Actually, the popes acted quite independently during these years, but that did not prevent the Italian humanist Petrarch from labeling their stay at Avignon as the "Babylonian Captivity," a reference to the forced removal of ancient Jewish leaders to Babylonia (p. 41).

1303	1417	1520	1650
Avignon Papacy and Great Schism	Continued Spiritual Decline of Papacy	Reformation and Religious Wars	

1534

More serious embarrassments to the Church were yet to come. In 1377, Gregory XI decided to return the papal court to Rome; upon his death there, the Roman populace pressured the cardinals into choosing an Italian as pope. But the French cardinals then fled the city, pronounced the election invalid, and chose another pope. This one, with his supporting cardinals, moved to Avignon, while the Italian pope, with *his* cardinals, stayed in Rome. Each declared the other to be a *false* pope and excommunicated him and his followers.

The Great Schism (split), as this division was called, lasted some forty years (from 1378 to 1417). Europe now endured the spectacle of a Church divided into opposing camps, with *two* popes and *two* colleges of cardinals. Conscientious Christians were distressed, for they had no way of being certain who was pope and who was "antipope." Civil rulers supported whichever side seemed more useful politically. Thus, France and its allies recognized Avignon, while England and the German princes recognized Rome. The schism was at last settled by a general council of the Church (at Constance), which deposed both rival popes and elected a new one. But by this time the papacy had suffered serious damage. The foundation of papal power had previously been its immense *moral* authority. That position was now gravely weakened, opening the way to contempt and defiance.

The humiliation of the papacy contributed to the decline of the clergy as a whole — a decline that had begun after 1300. Worldliness and abuses had swept the Church once more, and the brave reform efforts of earlier centuries were forgotten (pp. 235–36). The monastic orders, traditionally the conscience of the clergy, fell into scandal, corrupted by comfortable living. Many of the seculars (priests and bishops) also slipped into self-indulgence, lust, and greed. While there doubtless remained thousands of honest, chaste, and pious clerics, the general situation was nevertheless distressing.

Vigorous reform of these abuses became urgent. But the popes of the fifteenth century, themselves deep in worldliness, were not interested in reform. The "princes" of the Church were more interested in politics, wealth, and art than in spiritual affairs. The Medici pope Leo X is reported to have said, after his election in 1513, "As God has seen fit to give us the papacy, let us enjoy it!"

The Awakening Reform Spirit: Wiclif, Hus

Many devout Christians realized that moral reform of the Church would have to start at the *top*, but they feared that the papacy lacked the will to reform. As a consequence, they began to turn *inward* in their devotions. In northern Europe, the fifteenth century saw a revival of *mysticism* (p. 237) and *pietism* (deep reverence). One response there was the founding of the Brethren of the Common Life (p. 327), whose members turned away from the formalism of established rituals. They joined together in semireligious communities stressing Christlike simplicity, purity of heart, and direct communion with God. Other Christians were moving, at the same time, toward a new idea of what the Church should be. Their model was "primitive" Christianity as practiced during the first century after Christ.

John Wiclif, a leading Oxford scholar and teacher, was among the first to question openly the need for a *priesthood*. His ideas, preached late in the fourteenth century, provided a foundation for later Protestant doctrines. After a lifetime of study, Wiclif concluded that the Church was suffering from more than just the misbehavior of some of its clergy. He challenged the established role and powers of the clergy itself — arguing that God and the Scriptures are the sole sources of spiritual authority.

Wiclif made an English translation of the Vulgate Bible (p. 156). In doing so, he sometimes chose English words that supported his own Scriptural interpretations, as opposed to those of the Church authorities. (Later translations of the Bible into the various languages of Europe would often, in a similar way, bear significantly on doctrinal disputes.)

More important, Wiclif urged laymen to read the Bible for themselves. Every individual, he said, can communicate directly with the Lord and can be saved without the aid of priests or saints. For challenging the accepted doctrines of authority and salvation, he was condemned and forced to retire from teaching. (Civil disturbances in England and the Great Schism in the Church saved him from more drastic punishment.) Wiclif was thus silenced, but his ideas were not.

Most of Wiclif's followers in England (who were known as Lollards) were executed as heretics. John Hus, the hero of Bohemia, met the same fate. Hus was a priest and a professor at Charles University in Prague (p. 380), in the kingdom of Bohemia. Already active in efforts to reform the clergy, he was inspired by the writings of Wiclif to launch stronger, more radical attacks. Hus had the support of most of his compatriots, partly because many of the clerics he criticized were Germans, whereas the majority of the population in Bohemia were Czechs (pp. 212–23, 282–83). (National feelings, here and elsewhere, showed themselves in the religious disputes.)

Bohemia was part of the Holy Roman Empire, and the Emperor Sigismund had grown disturbed by the mounting agitation among the Bohemians. When Hus was summoned by the Council of Constance in 1414 to stand trial on charges of heresy, the emperor promised him safe-conduct to and from the trial. After a long and cruel imprisonment in Constance, Hus was tried and found guilty. The emperor did not keep his promise of protection, and Hus, refusing to recant (withdraw) his beliefs, went to his death at the stake. The reaction in Bohemia was instantaneous. Anti-German and antipapal sentiments were inflamed, and a bloody uprising erupted in the country. This was but the beginning of a long series of political-religious wars in Europe.

During the fifteenth century, the criticisms by heretics like Wiclif and Hus were reinforced by the writings of the Christian humanists (pp. 326–29). Erasmus poured ridicule on the high clergy, monasticism, and popular devotional cults. But his intellectual approach did not stir the common people, and he never challenged the authority of the Church. For these reasons, and because of the humanistic leanings of the Renaissance popes, Erasmus escaped personal harm.

Nevertheless, there was a link between the Christian humanists and the rebels against authority. The leaders of the Protestant revolt found justification for their actions in Erasmus's call for a purer religion, one freed from ritualism and superstition. They were prepared, of course, to go much further than Erasmus: they would defy authority and split the Christian community if necessary in order to achieve their goals.

The Influence of Political and Social Forces

By 1500 ideas for religious reform were in broad circulation. All that was needed was the opportunity to start an effective *movement*. A century after Hus, the political, economic, and social conditions in Europe were shifting in such a way as to present that opportunity. The new situation would permit the rise of religious *founders* instead of religious martyrs.

National sentiment and political absolutism, whose growth was discussed in Chapter 7, were working against the principle and practice of the universal Church. As distinctively national cultures took shape, people grew increasingly conscious of belonging to a particular *nation* — a nation independent of all others. The citizens of the northern countries, especially, came to regard the popes as "foreigners" who had no proper business outside Italy.

This popular feeling supported the desire of kings and princes to gain control over the Church in their own territories and to build *state* churches. By 1520 the monarchs of Spain and France had virtually achieved this end by securing the right to appoint the bishops within their kingdoms. One reason for the failure of heresies in those two nations is simply that their kings had nothing to gain from religious changes. In Germany and England, however, where the kings and princes expected to enlarge their powers in the event of a religious break with Rome, heresies were to prove successful.

The higher social classes also began to sense that they might benefit from a break with Rome. In Germany the Church was immensely wealthy, holding from one-fifth to one-third of the total real estate. The landed aristocrats looked on those holdings with covetous eyes, and members of the middle class, though not particularly interested in acquiring land, disliked the fact that Church properties were exempt from taxes. Their own tax payments would be reduced, they reasoned, if Church holdings were shifted to private hands. And all classes of German society deplored the flow of Church revenues to Rome; the feeling that the "foreign" papacy was draining the homeland of wealth thus created another source of support for a religious revolt.

These economic, social, and political factors must be kept in mind if we are to understand the nature and success of the Protestant reform movements. The reformers, to be sure, did not act upon a *calculation* of these factors; they acted, rather, in response to their religious thoughts and feelings. But this had been true also of the less fortunate heretics who preceded them. The success of the Protestant leaders was due primarily to the new political and social forces. The time was ripe for religious revolt in northern Europe; the division of the Roman Church was at hand.

THE REVOLT OF LUTHER: "JUSTIFICATION BY FAITH"

The reformers did not intend, at the outset, to *divide* the Church or to start new churches. Each believed that he had the correct vision of the *one true* church, and he set out to convert (or force) all Christians to his point of view. (The Protestant leaders, to the disappointment of Erasmus, were to prove as intolerant as the papacy.) But, because no one of them managed to dominate the others, the end result was the division (and subdivision) of the Church.

The Provocation: The Sale of Indulgences

In 1517 Martin Luther struck a spark that set religious passions aflame. The event did not appear at the time to have far-reaching significance, but it started a chain reaction of dissent and rebellion. A Dominican friar (p. 237) named Tetzel, who was selling papal *indulgences* in Germany, had set up shop near the Saxon town of Wittenberg (p. 380). In Catholic teaching, indulgences may reduce or eliminate penalties due for sins, both on earth and in purgatory. (Purgatory, in Catholic doctrine, is a temporary state or condition, after death, for the cleansing of pardoned souls on their way to heaven.) Tetzel, however, made extravagant claims for indulgences, implying that they would *automatically* remove a sinner's *guilt* as well as the penalty.

Tetzel's claims were unacceptable to the local professor of theology, a priest named Martin Luther. In protest, he prepared a long list of criticisms of the sale of indulgences (the "Ninety-five Theses") and reportedly nailed it to the door of the Wittenberg Castle church. Luther charged that the money from Tetzel's sale of indulgences was going to Rome for the building of a new St. Peter's church (p. 345). (He resented having Germans pay for an undertaking that would be of no benefit to them.) He also challenged indulgences in general, implying that they were of doubtful value. His charges brought an immediate attack from the clergy, but they struck a sympathetic chord with the laity. Copies of the "Ninety-five Theses" were distributed throughout Germany; the revolt from Rome, aided by the new technique of printing, was under way.

The pope, Leo X (a Medici), directed that a reply be made to Luther's theses (arguments). In answering this reply, and in the series of exchanges that followed, Luther began to question the basic authority of the papacy and the whole Catholic system. When it became clear that his radical views could not be reconciled with the doctrines of the Church, Luther chose to stand by them, rather than recant. Unlike Erasmus and other humanists, he did not hesitate to defy authority in matters of personal belief. He would obey only his conscience. When he was warned that his unyielding position might lead to "division, war, and rebellion," Luther answered that *one cannot compromise on what one believes to be true.*

Luther's Spiritual Search: His Doctrine of Salvation

The force of Luther's personal conviction was due in part to his temperament. He relished a fight and was capable of quick, violent, and sustained anger. He was also a man of instinctive frankness and courage. But his beliefs were mainly the product of a long spiritual pilgrimage marked by doubt, agony, and, finally, conviction.

Luther was of peasant stock. His father, who had once been a miner, made wise investments and became a respected bourgeois. He wanted his son to study law in preparation for a career as a middle-class civil official. But Martin, who had attended a school run by the Brethren of the Common Life (p. 327), had fallen into deep spiritual fears in his early years. By the time he completed his liberal-arts course at the University of Erfurt (in Saxony), he had decided to abandon secular life and enter a monastery. His decision was sealed, he later explained, when he was caught in a violent thunderstorm and, terrified, interpreted the thunder as a call from God.

Luther took vows at an Augustinian monastery in Erfurt. Fearing that his soul was in danger of damnation, he hoped that an ascetic life would afford him a better chance of salvation. But he found no peace of mind either as a monk or as a priest. No matter how strictly he fasted, prayed, and punished himself, his sense of unworthiness persisted. The Church taught that "good works" helped to "justify" one's soul before God. But Luther continued to be oppressed by the fear of God and despaired of doing *enough* good works to gain his favor. While he was in this torment, he was sent by his superior to a new university in Wittenberg that had been founded by Frederick, the Elector (Duke) of Saxony. After receiving his doctor's degree there in 1512, he stayed on as professor of theology.

At Wittenberg Luther began to discover his path to spiritual peace. While preparing some lectures on the Bible, he was struck by certain passages that seemed to suggest an answer. In Paul's Epistle to the Romans, for example, Luther read, "The just shall live by faith" (1:17). After days and nights of pondering, he concluded that "by grace and sheer mercy God *justifies* [saves] us through *faith.*" The whole of the Scripture, he explained later, then took on new meaning for him. Whereas the "justice of God" had formerly filled him with hate, it now became "inexpressibly sweet in greater love. This passage of Paul became to me a gate to heaven. . . ."

Now Luther understood why his own self-punishment and works as a monk had gained him nothing. Man, by his nature, cannot please God without faith: but faith, a free gift of God's mercy, "justifies" a person and ensures salvation. We are saved not by works, concluded Luther, but by *faith alone*. Those of us who accept Christ as our Savior have the right to feel that true faith has been given us. From our love of God, we will freely perform good works — not because we *need* to, but because we *want* to.

These ideas afforded Luther immense personal relief, but when he began to apply them to the institution of the Church he grew troubled. If people received faith according to God's secret judgment, of what use was the ordained priesthood? If every Christian was, in effect, a priest, were not the claims of the clergy absurd and hateful? And what good were the special vows and way of life undertaken by monks and nuns? If *works* were no help to salvation, what was the benefit of sacraments, pilgrimages, and papal indulgences?

In 1517 Tetzel's selling of indulgences brought Luther face to face with what he regarded as a flagrant distortion of religious teachings. Up to this point he had shared his views only with his students; now he felt compelled to speak out. And so it was that he prepared, in traditional form for academic debates, his "Ninety-five Theses."

The Widening Split with Rome

As the dispute over indulgences dragged on, Luther busied himself with writing theological pamphlets in which he broadened his attack on the Church, especially the papacy. At the same time he appealed to the German nobles *(Address to the Christian Nobility of the German Nation)*, and to the laity in general, by speaking of the "priesthood" of *all* baptized Christians. Ordained priests and bishops, he argued, had no more *special* powers than other Christians; they were simply fulfilling the duties of their office (as princes fulfilled theirs). He also attacked monasticism and declared that priests should be permitted to marry.

In addition to challenging the doctrines of apostolic succession (p. 153) and "good works," Luther struck directly at the number and meaning of the holy sacraments (pp. 231–32). Of the seven traditional sacraments, he asserted that only *two* were called for by Scripture: baptism and the Eucharist. And, contrary to Catholic doctrine, he insisted that in the Eucharist there is no miraculous *change* of substance (*transubstantiation*) from bread and wine into the body and blood of Christ. Luther taught, instead, the "Real [Corporeal] Presence" of Christ *along with* the bread and wine; and the Presence, he insisted, is not brought into being by the priest, for God is *everywhere* present *always*.

Pope Leo, whose main interests appeared to be in art, hunting, and politics, was annoyed by the excitement Luther had stirred up in Germany. He referred scornfully to the dispute over indulgences as a "squabble among monks." But when he realized how serious the implications were he moved against Luther — cautiously. One reason for this caution was that Luther, as a professor at Wittenberg, enjoyed the protection of the Elector Frederick of Saxony; and the pope, for political reasons, was trying to stay on friendly terms with Frederick.

Ultimately, however, Leo had to act. In 1520 he ordered Luther excommunicated. Luther responded by burning the *bull* (the papal document of excommunication) before the city gates of Wittenberg, thus demonstrating his defiance of Rome. The clergy now called on the Holy Roman emperor, Charles V, to seize Luther (it was considered the duty of the civil ruler to punish confirmed heretics), but Luther had such strong support among all classes of the laity that the emperor hesitated. The Elector Frederick then insisted that Luther receive a hearing before the imperial Diet (assembly) of princes. At the Diet of Worms in 1521 Luther was afforded a last chance to recant his heresies. He refused, declaring eloquently that Scripture was the sole source of authority and that he must obey his conscience. The Diet then condemned Luther and issued a decree prohibiting *all* new religious doctrines within the Holy Roman Empire.

Luther had been guaranteed safe-conduct on his journey to Worms. After he left the assembly, however, the emperor ordered him put under the ban — which meant that he was branded an outlaw. Subjects of the empire were forbidden to shelter him, and, if seized, he could be killed. Frederick, however, had planned for Luther's safety in advance. His soldiers kidnapped Luther as he left Worms and took him secretly to Frederick's castle at Wartburg, where Luther remained for about a year working on a German translation of the Bible. His "people's" version of Scripture helped shape the modern German language as well as Protestant doctrines.

Building the Lutheran Church

When Luther thought it safe, he returned to Wittenberg to lay plans for a reformed church. He spent the rest of his life not as a rebel, but as an organizer and administrator. It was in this part of his career that he met some of his severest tests. Many of his followers had responded in extreme ways to his teachings of the "priesthood of all believers" and the sole authority of Scripture. Some developed disturbing notions about Christian practices and about the relation of religion to society. Numerous sects began to appear, not only in Germany but in Switzerland and Holland as well.

The principal group of extremists went under the general name of Anabaptists — a name derived from their views on baptism. They insisted that baptism was meaningful only after someone old enough to comprehend Christian doctrines had made a voluntary confession of faith. They therefore opposed infant baptism and held that grown-up Christians who had been baptized as infants must accept the rite *again* (*ana*baptism). The sects within the Anabaptist group varied considerably in their social ideas, which often proved troublesome to established laws and customs. Applying New Testament teachings *literally* to their own times, they refused military service and sought to establish a more equalitarian community. Some, including a group of Mennonites in Holland, resisted all forms of *modernization*; like the Amish (their descendants in America) they considered the acceptance of new fashions as a "compromise with the world." Still other sects advocated acts of violence against "ungodly" persons and against officials who declined to punish them.

Luther, who was extremely conservative in his views on the social order, was alarmed by such proposals. He believed in unquestioned obedience to the *state* and opposed any sort of rebellion against established *political* authorities. In 1524 Luther responded angrily to a peasant revolt that swept over Germany; the serfs were seeking relief from new burdens laid upon them by their feudal lords. (Germany had lagged behind France and England in abolishing serfdom — pp. 288–89.) He urged the aristocracy to put down the violent uprising without mercy, to slay the rebels as they would "mad dogs." He later admitted that it was he who commanded the slaughter of the peasants: "All their blood is on my head. But I throw the responsibility on our Lord God, who instructed me to give this order." (Luther also urged harsh measures against Jews, reinforcing the popular anti-Semitism of his times.)

He was equally severe with preachers who disagreed with his doctrines. He considered them "blasphemers" and believed that they, like persons guilty of rebellion against the state, should be executed. Though claiming for himself the freedom to interpret Scripture, he denied it to those whom he judged to be not properly "qualified." The Lutheran Church developed an orthodoxy of its own, resting on the "Augsburg Confession" of 1530. This document, largely the work of Luther's friend and disciple Philipp Melanchthon, was a moderate statement of Luther's doctrinal views, including those on justification (salvation), sacraments, and the relation of faith and works.

The Emperor Charles, though busy with war and politics outside Germany, still hoped to suppress the Lutheran Church by force. In 1529 Charles and the Catholic members of the imperial Diet reaffirmed the earlier Worms decree prohibiting all new religious doctrines in Germany. The Lutheran princes (of northern Germany) *protested* this action and thus acquired the name "Protestant." In time, this name came to be used for all the rebellious creeds.

Soon Germany was split into armed alliances; Catholic states lined up against Lutheran states. By the time the emperor could send his forces against the Lutheran princes, he found them too powerful to overcome. The result was a truce, known as the Religious Peace of Augsburg (1555), in which the members of the imperial Diet agreed to leave each prince free to choose either Catholicism or Lutheranism for his realm. (Other sects were still prohibited.) Under the Peace of Augsburg religious warfare among the German states was suspended for some sixty years.

The people living in the Lutheran states found no great difficulty in accepting the decisions of their respective princes. Though the peasants had been embittered by Luther's harsh attitude toward them, their bitterness softened with time. For their part, the princes, nobles, and bourgeois enthusiastically supported the reformed church. It appealed to German patriotism by rejecting the Roman papacy, and its support of the established order pleased all who held office or wealth. The laity as a whole tended to feel comfortable in Luther's church. According to his doctrine, all baptized Christians were on the same spiritual level as their ministers; the devout man of property could feel equal, before God, to the ascetic, propertyless cleric. Secular society and values had won the approval of the church.

The kings of Scandinavia recognized the advantages of a state church, and they, too, established the new faith as their official religion. In each Lutheran country the ruler appointed superintendents to oversee his religious establishment — thus subordinating church to state. The formerly Catholic religious buildings and grounds were assigned to the new churches, but the extensive landholdings of the bishops and abbots were seized by the crown.

In accordance with Luther's views, monastic orders were abolished in all these states, and ministers were permitted to marry. Luther himself married a former nun, who bore him six children. By his acts and teachings he raised the value placed on marriage and upheld the rights of wives to sexual satisfaction; he did not, however, urge any basic changes in the social role of women. The veneration of saints and relics (pp. 234–35) and all manner of formal "good works" were rejected. Luther did, however, retain the principle of church *authority* and many semblances of medieval religious practice. The worship service, in German, was not much different from the Catholic service. Unlike some other reformers, Luther also kept art and music in his church; he composed a notable book of hymns as well as several *catechisms* (handbooks for oral expression of church teachings).

CALVIN AND THE ELECT: "PREDESTINATION"

Luther was by no means the only religious rebel at work during the 1520s. And, though he tried to impose his doctrines on the others, he failed to do so outside northern Germany and Scandinavia. The logic of his own thought, in fact, worked against a unified reform movement. He had taught that each individual, guided by the Holy Spirit, must see the truth of Scripture according to his or her own conscience. While the papal theory of Petrine supremacy (pp. 154–55) had offered a logical basis for *one* interpretation of truth and for *one* church, Luther's view led naturally to *many* churches. Once papal authority had been overthrown, there was no logical limit to the number of creeds and denominations.

Of the countless separations that followed Luther's revolt, two require special attention because of their far-reaching historical impact. One of these is the Church of England, the most conservative of the major splits from Rome.

The other, initiated by John Calvin, departed most radically from the Catholic tradition — in doctrine, spirit, organization, and ritual.

Calvin: The International Reformer

Younger than Luther by some twenty-five years, Calvin was born and raised a Frenchman. Fear of persecution by the Catholic king forced him to flee to Switzerland, however, and he settled down in the city of Geneva in 1536. The city, which had just revolted from its feudal overlord (a bishop), was in the midst of political and religious turmoil. Within a short time Calvin and his version of reformed Christianity achieved dominance in the community. For some twenty years, until his death in 1564, he guided the church, the state, and the Academy (university) of Geneva.

Calvin's influence extended far beyond the boundaries of his city. He corresponded with rulers and theologians alike, and reformers from all over Europe came to Geneva to study his doctrines. When they returned to their homelands, they carried Calvinism with them. Calvinism thus became the leading Protestant force in France (the Huguenots), Holland (the Reformed Church), Scotland (Presbyterianism), and England (Puritanism).

Calvinism is important not only because of its international influence but because of its special appeal to the bourgeois. Born to a middle-class family, Calvin accepted business as a normal Christian vocation. He took for granted (as Luther and the Catholic theologians did not) the functions of capital, banking, and large-scale commerce. Though urging entrepreneurs to be honest and reasonable in their dealings, he did not question the correctness of their occupation. He was the first theologian to praise the capitalistic virtues: hard work, thrift, and the accumulation of money. He praised the creation of wealth through industry so long as that wealth was not used for self-indulgence. The businessman should be sober and disciplined, dedicated to the "service of the Lord."

It is not surprising that these ideas were warmly received in such commercial centers as Amsterdam, Antwerp, and London. (In Switzerland, the mountain regions remained Catholic, while the urban centers embraced Calvinism.) Calvin's faith suited the economic realities of the day and was attractive to the most progressive and venturesome class of Western society. Carried to New England in the seventeenth century, Calvinism (Puritanism) contributed significantly to the shaping of American life.

As a young man, John Calvin had prepared for the priesthood in Paris and then, at his father's urging, had turned to the study of law. His legal training sharpened his logic and strengthened his ability to express himself, but he found a career in law distasteful. He became active in humanistic scholarship (p. 326) and, after receiving his law degree, took up the study of Greek and Hebrew. His taste for the classics was reflected in a book he wrote about a work of the Stoic philosopher Seneca. A year later (in 1533) Calvin had a sudden conversion to the idea of religious reform. France, like the rest of Europe, was the scene of heated disputes about the Church; the writings of Erasmus and Luther had stirred the youthful Calvin. He remained a keen scholar all his life, but after his "conversion" Calvin the humanist gave way to Calvin the *reformer*.

He turned to a systematic explanation of his religious views and finished the first edition of the *Institutes of the Christian Religion* when he was only twenty-six years old (1536). He wrote the original in Latin but soon made a translation in French. This work was to stand as the principal statement of Protestant theology for some three hundred years and as such is comparable to the Catholic statement by Thomas Aquinas (*Summa Theologiae* — p. 259).

The Doctrine of God's Omnipotence

Calvin was very close to Luther in his basic theology. He saw the Bible as the sole source of authority and rejected a priesthood based on apostolic succession. He agreed that salvation was determined by God's grace (power) alone, unaffected by man's works. Like Luther, he scorned monasticism and such "Romish" practices as pilgrimages, indulgences, and the veneration of saints and relics (pp. 234–35).

The difference between the two men, and it was a real one, lay in what each chose to emphasize. Luther was obsessed with his soul's salvation, and it was this that led him to his doctrine. Calvin, on the other hand, was obsessed with a sense of God's *omnipotence* (unlimited power) and human *depravity* (wickedness). He argued that everyone must do what God wills not as a means to salvation, but *because God wills it*. Calvin's position may well have been a reaction to his contact with humanism, which *praises* human abilities. But he drew his vision of God's glory and perfection directly from the Old Testament, and no other theologian has followed through with such relentless logic the implications of that vision.

The best known and most controversial of Calvin's doctrines is that of "predestination" and "election." God, declared Calvin, foreknows and determines everything that happens in the universe — even those events ordinarily credited to *chance*. It follows that he certainly determines who shall be saved and who shall be forever lost. All individuals, because of Adam's sin and their own wickedness, would disobey God if left to their own puny powers. But God gives to those he "elects" the ability to persevere in his service. The rest, for his own reasons, he allows to fall. Calvin unflinchingly defined this doctrine in his *Institutes*:

> Predestination we call the eternal decree of God, by which he has determined in himself, what he would have become of every individual of mankind. For they are not all created with a similar destiny; but eternal life is foreordained for some, and eternal damnation for others. Every man, therefore, being created for one or the other of these ends, we say, he is predestinated either to life or to death.

In his discussion of predestination, Calvin warned that the subject is dangerous and delicate, since it touches on a guarded *secret* of the Almighty. To the charge that God could not be so unfair as to condemn most of humankind to damnation, Calvin answered that *no one* deserves salvation and that it is only through God's gracious mercy that *some* are saved. Further, it is wrong to question the plans and judgment of God. Man has only a worm's-eye view of Creation. Whatever God has willed is right, because he has willed it. Calvin admitted that the Lord's predestination was an "awesome decree," but he held that all must nevertheless accept it.

But many would not accept so harsh a doctrine. Luther accepted it, though he did not stress it in his teachings. Most Protestant groups, in time, would turn away from the doctrine for two reasons: it is very gloomy, and it denies free will. The Roman Catholics (including Erasmus) condemned Calvin's teachings, declaring that they reduce human beings to mere puppets. Catholics did not deny that God's grace is indispensable to salvation, but they believed that it is offered more generously than Calvin suggested. They also insisted that each individual can either cooperate (through good works) in achieving salvation or can *refuse* to cooperate. By refusing, a person chooses the path to hell, but this is the person's own doing. Calvin answered that the Catholic argument is an insult to God's majesty. It suggests that God's will is not all-powerful and that his grace, alone, is insufficient.

In reply to the charge that his doctrine would destroy all incentive for following a worthy Christian life and cause some people to throw themselves into reckless indulgence, he made this reply: nothing in the doctrine of predestination excuses any person from striving to obey God's commandments. On the contrary, argued Calvin, no one knows for certain who is of the "elect" and who is "reprobate" (condemned). All individuals, therefore, should act as if they enjoy God's favor. If they do enjoy that favor, they should want their lives to be shining examples to others; if they do not enjoy it, they should obey God anyway. It is surely the duty of those who feel moved by the Spirit to do God's will themselves and to see that others, whether or not they are to be saved, also honor God. The divine will can be clearly read in Scripture; all should shape their lives accordingly, regardless of the decree of predestination.

Calvinist Ethics: The Puritan Discipline

Calvin applied this line of reasoning with strict logic to the entire field of Christian morals. Though a person's behavior is not the means of his salvation, it must nonetheless be subjected to close scrutiny. *Puritanism* as a social discipline was thus born of Calvin, for he wanted the behavior of all Christians to be held under tight control. To Calvin, God is a righteous, demanding judge, under whose searching eye Christians should conduct themselves humbly and soberly.

Calvin gave a further justification of his ascetic doctrine. For the faithful to truly *glorify God*, they must first rid themselves of the "distractions" of the flesh. This belief followed that of Paul, Augustine, and the medieval ascetics; it was opposed to the humanism of Calvin's day. Yet his acquaintance with humanism gave him some appreciation of its values. He was even willing to tolerate a moderate enjoyment of the fruits of the earth, such as wine, since they are part of God's creation. But, because moderate indulgence often leads to excess, he urged *abstinence* as a practical policy.

Calvin criticized any form of decoration lest it lead to vanity and pride — and any form of cardplaying lest it lead to gambling. The theater, because of its historical associations with paganism, was closed down in Geneva; art was seen as a distraction from God's word. Drinking was condemned as a prelude to intoxication, and dancing was prohibited as a stimulant to desire. The clothing of women had to be plain and ample; he regarded the display of personal ornament or the exposure of flesh as a signal to sexual instincts. In living a "puritanical" life, concluded Calvin, one follows the teachings of the Lord, who "condemned all those pleasures which seduce the heart from chastity and purity."

To Calvin, a person's *conscience* is the prime defense against ungodly distractions and against sin itself. But conscience must ever be on guard. One should not yield to "natural" inclinations to sin; they are in all probability the temptings of Satan, and God wants us to overcome them. This compelling, inward sense of sin is difficult for most modern minds to comprehend. But in the sixteenth century the sense of sin and the fear of its consequences haunted God-fearing men and women. Luther himself confessed that he was harassed by the Devil and once threw his inkpot at him.

If the individual could not avoid wrongdoing, Calvin believed, it was up to other Christians to be their "brother's keeper." He used his pulpit to warn and frighten potential sinners. When his sermons failed, he resorted to force in prohibiting unseemly acts and words. The Consistory of Geneva was a special body of pastors and lay elders responsible for public morals and discipline. Alleged offenders were called before this court, which might reprimand the accused or impose bread-and-water sentences upon them. Common offenses were profanity, drunkenness, dozing in church, criticizing ministers, dancing, and other "immoral" acts.

More serious offenses were handled by the town council. One man, accused of placing an insulting placard on Calvin's pulpit, was tortured until he confessed; later, he was beheaded on a further charge of conspiring against Calvin. Accused heretics were also brought before the council. The most notorious trial was that of the Spaniard Michael Servetus, who challenged the Christian doctrine of the Trinity. Calvin, after warning Servetus to stay away, had him arrested when he visited Geneva. Calvin then charged him with heresy and supported his conviction and execution (1553). With firm logic, Calvin justified the destruction of "false prophets" by referring to the harsh thirteenth chapter of Deuteronomy:

God makes plain that the false prophet is to be stoned without mercy. We are to crush beneath our heel all affections of nature when his honor is involved. The father should not spare his child, nor the brother his brother, nor the husband his own wife, or the friend who is dearer to him than life.

Erasmus, now in his grave, was spared knowledge of Servetus' agony and Calvin's unyielding severity. The Protestant reformer had come full circle to the papal position of *intolerance* toward dissenting views. By excommunicating "wrongdoers" from his church, Calvin drove most of his critics from Geneva; refugees from Catholic persecution, meanwhile, kept slipping in from other lands. By the end of Calvin's rule (1564) the citizens of Geneva had thus been won over to support of his principles and policies.

Relations of Church and State

Though Calvin dominated both religion and government in Geneva, he held no public office. He opposed the union of spiritual and civil authority. But he desired legal separation as a means of safeguarding the independence of the church and of assuring its position *above* the state. In this he again followed papal policy, especially as conducted by Gregory VII (pp. 238–39): ministers of the Church must stand as *teachers* and *judges* of civil rulers. To Calvin, the purpose of government was to regulate society according to the will of God, and the *Church* was the appointed interpreter of God's will: "Great kings ought not to think it any dishonor to humble themselves before Christ, the King of Kings, nor ought they to be displeased at being judged by the church. . . . They ought even to wish not to be spared by the pastors, that they may be spared by the Lord."

Geneva was legally a republic whose principal governing organ was the town council. As we have seen, the council served to protect Calvin's church against critics, rebels, and heretics. And in the manner in which Pope Gregory had held the threat of excommunication (and disgrace) over kings and princes, so Calvin held it over the politicians of Geneva. His Consistory watched their public and private behavior for the slightest evidence of anything "improper."

For some twenty years Geneva served as a model of theocracy (church-controlled state). The organized church, Calvin asserted, is essential for the supervision of the state as well as for the salvation of souls. This view, too, paralleled the papal pronouncement that individual salvation is possible only within the Church. The idea of dependence on church membership may seem to contradict Calvin's doctrine of predestination and election. If God has already determined that a person is to be saved, why must that person remain in Calvin's church (or any other church)? This was a difficult question for both Luther and Calvin, because their very doctrines suggested that they themselves were not essential. Yet "inner voices" told them that this could not be. Calvin's explanation was simple: it is God's will that the elect be saved *through* the True Church. And through its inspired teaching and discipline the ways of Heaven might be reflected on earth.

Calvinist Ministry and Ritual

Calvin saw nothing inconsistent in holding to certain Roman Catholic principles. But he differed sharply from them with respect to the ministry and ritual of the Church. Calvin accepted, with Luther, the principle of the "priesthood of all believers"; his church gave to its ministers no special powers that set them apart from baptized laymen. Their authority came only from their assigned *office*, as did the authority of civil officials.

Calvin guarded against preaching by self-proclaimed ministers. A "legitimate ministry," he declared, is formed when suitable persons are appointed by the lay elders, subject to the approval of the congregation and the pastors of the community. In the administration of each church, the minister was assisted by elders elected by the congregation. Thus developed the *presbyterian* theory and practice of church government. (The word *presbyteros* is the Greek word for "elder.")

Today, at each level of the Calvinist church (local unit, district, and nation), control rests in the hands of ministers and elected elders. Thus, the ultimate power in Calvinist churches (and others that follow its model) is the highest "presbytery" of baptized believers. The ultimate power in the Roman Catholic Church, on the other hand, resides in one person — the pope.

Calvin insisted that Church ritual be based exclusively on Scripture. He found, with Luther, that only baptism and the Eucharist are clearly established there as sacraments. (But, unlike Luther, he held that the presence of Christ in the Eucharist is *spiritual* only.) Beyond the administration of these two rites, Calvin permitted little except the singing of psalms and the preaching of sermons. He regarded *images* of the saints as a distraction from the exclusive worship of the Almighty, and he therefore barred their use.

He believed that music, art, and ornamentation had no place in the Church; the awesome Catholic cathedrals, with their stained glass, gilt, and statuary, he branded as pagan temples. Jesus and Paul, according to Scripture, had conducted their ministries in simple fashion by preaching. And preaching was the core of the Calvinist service. There were no processions, genuflections (bending of the knee), embroidered garments, incense, or Latin chants. The minister wore simple black and spoke only in the ordinary language of his congregation (as Jesus had). The typical Calvinist service was once described by a critic as consisting of "four bare walls and a sermon."

HENRY VIII AND THE CHURCH OF ENGLAND

Calvinist austerity found little acceptance among Lutherans or among English reformers. While Protestant ideas from the continent influenced the doctrine of the Anglican Church (Church of England), organization and ritual remained close to the Catholic tradition. Thus, the Anglican Church came to represent a sort of compromise between extreme Protestantism and Roman

Catholicism. Radical reformers would criticize it as a muddled and illogical institution, subservient to the state; Roman Catholics would condemn it as divisive and heretical. The Anglicans, however, insisted that theirs was the True Church, that it was both Catholic *and* reformed. This is still the view of the worldwide Anglican churches, including the Protestant Episcopal Church of America.

Although John Wiclif had preached reform during the fourteenth century (p. 356), there was no English counterpart to Luther or Calvin in the sixteenth century. Religious reform in England, though supported by numerous critics of the Catholic Church, was carried through by its monarchs. From the time of Henry VIII, who initiated the reform, to the time of Elizabeth I, who completed it, changes were prompted primarily by the wishes of the crown. The reformed Church of England does not bear the mark of any one spiritual leader, though many devoted clergymen helped establish it.

The first Tudor monarch, Henry VII, had laid the foundations for royal absolutism and bourgeois prosperity (p. 314). His policies were vigorously pursued by his son and successor, the youthful Henry VIII. Henry proved to be a popular king, a robust Renaissance despot. He had had some training in theology, for, as a younger son in the royal family, he had been started by his father on a career in the Church. The plan was dropped on the death of his elder brother, Arthur, which left Henry heir to the throne. His interest in religious matters continued, however, and after his coronation he formally defended the Catholic view of the sacraments against Luther's public attack (1521). As a reward, Leo X gave Henry the title "Defender of the Faith."

Henry's Desire for Independence

Henry accepted Roman Catholic doctrine, but he soon came to resent Roman interference in the affairs of his kingdom. The rising tide of national feeling had already stripped the pope of much of his influence in European states. In Spain and France the monarchs controlled the Church within their borders, but in England the pope still confirmed the appointment of high-ranking clergy. Appeals from Church courts (in keeping with canon law) and a portion of Church revenues continued to go to Rome.

But it was a personal matter, related to the welfare of the state, that led Henry VIII to break with Rome. In order to preserve the alliance between the ruling families of England and Spain, he had married Catherine of Aragon, the widow of his elder brother. Because it was contrary to canon law to marry so close a relative, he had sought and received a papal dispensation (p. 239) permitting the union. In the course of their marriage, Catherine bore six children, but all except one were stillborn or died in infancy. The single survivor was a girl (Mary). The English had only recently emerged from a bloody civil war over the succession to the throne, and they feared that a female ruler might prove unable to maintain national strength and unity. When it appeared that

Catherine would have no more children, Henry and his advisers began to think about his taking a new wife.

Henry's sense of duty was accompanied by his fondness for Anne Boleyn, an attractive young lady-in-waiting to the queen. In 1527 he decided to marry her and directed his chancellor (chief minister) to have his marriage to Catherine *annulled*. The Church did not permit *divorce*; but if it found a marriage to be invalid, both partners were free to marry again. It was thought that Pope Clement VII, a Medici, would grant Henry's request, just as a previous pope had approved the original union. Because the marriage to Catherine had been contrary to canon law, it would have been easy enough for papal lawyers to find some *defect* in the earlier dispensation.

But the infatuated Henry was to be disappointed. The Habsburg emperor, Charles V, was Catherine's nephew. He informed the pope that there were no proper grounds for annulment and that such action would be cruel and insulting to his aunt and his family. Charles did not wish Henry to remarry, for Henry's daughter, Princess Mary (Charles's cousin), was heir to the English throne. If Henry had no son, Mary would ultimately become queen, bringing another state into the Habsburg circle of power.

Charles was busy at the time in a campaign to win control of Italy, and his army happened to be in Rome when Pope Clement received Henry's appeal. Charles added to the pressure on Clement by offering to restore the Medici family to power in Florence if the pope would refuse to grant the annulment. But Clement decided to do nothing, hoping that something would happen to spare him from making the choice. After nearly six years of waiting, Henry's patience ran out. He married Anne Boleyn in 1533, after his newly appointed archbishop, Thomas Cranmer, had declared his marriage to Catherine annulled. Clement promptly excommunicated the king and released Henry's subjects from their obligation of obedience to the crown.

Break with Rome: The Act of Supremacy

Infuriated by the pope's delaying tactics and by what he considered to be Clement's interference in state affairs, Henry determined to free himself of the pope once and for all. He was backed by both Parliament and the people, for the papacy had become exceedingly unpopular in England. Having first submitted the issue to the assembled English clergy, Henry had the Act of Supremacy passed by Parliament in 1534. This act declared that the king was the "only supreme head on earth" of the Church of England and approved his power to "repress, redress, and reform" all errors, heresies, and abuses in religion.

A series of supplementary acts made the break with Rome complete. Communication with the pope (who was now referred to as the "Bishop of Rome") was forbidden; payments to Rome were stopped; the crown was given sole right to appoint bishops and abbots; and any denial of the king's supremacy was labeled as treason. Sir Thomas More, a Christian humanist (p. 350) and former chancellor, refused to take the required oath of supremacy and was beheaded. Other men of strict principle followed More to the cutting block, and some minor rebellions had to be put down. But Henry imposed his will on the clergy, Parliament, and his subjects.

Henry's taking control over the Church of England did not mean that he wished to reform its *doctrine*. On the contrary, he disliked the Protestant tendencies in the country and had Parliament pass the notorious Six Articles, which defined heresy. Individuals who denied any of the "test" articles of faith could be executed. These articles included belief in transubstantiation, celibacy of the clergy, and the necessity of oral confession in the sacrament of penance (p. 231). Henry thus showed his determination both to rule the Church and to keep it "true." Those who challenged his authority were sent to the block as traitors; those who questioned Catholic doctrine were sent to the stake as heretics.

Henry's only important departure from Catholic tradition was his suppression of monasticism. The monks had acquired an unfavorable reputation, and as leaders of the pro-papal faction they had aroused Henry's anger. Further, the religious houses possessed great wealth and extensive lands, and Henry was hard pressed for money. His obedient Parliament voted to close the monasteries and to turn over their property to the crown. The income from a portion of this property was assigned to the support of older ("retired") monks, some of the property was taken for the king's own purposes, and the rest was distributed to his favorites and supporters.

Henry — a shrewd manipulator of people and institutions, a true Machiavellian prince (pp. 307–9) — was thus able to create new ranks of landed noblemen who now had a vested interest in his break with Rome. In those troubled times, moreover, many of the English (like many Italians) preferred despotic power to liberty and disorder. The success of Henry's undertakings, as well as his hearty manner, endeared him to most of his subjects despite his greed, cruelty, and marital misadventures.

Three years after marrying Anne, he accused her of adultery and treason, had her beheaded, and then went on to take, in succession, four more wives. Anne Boleyn had borne him a daughter (Elizabeth), and Jane Seymour gave him a son at last. But the boy proved frail. He came to the throne as Edward VI when only ten years old (1547), and his powers had to be exercised by a guardian *regent* (an appointed officer acting for the crown). He died before coming of age, and the crown passed, after all, to his elder sister Mary (the daughter of Catherine of Aragon).

The Struggle over Doctrine: Protestant Advance and Catholic Reaction

During the regency period of Edward, Protestant factions in England brought about significant changes in the Anglican Church. Cranmer, the Archbishop of Canterbury, had Lutheran leanings; after Henry's death, he

1485	1509	1547 1553 1558	1603
Henry VII (House of Tudor)	Henry VIII	Ed. VI	Mary	Elizabeth I

led the way to reform by persuading Parliament to repeal the Six Articles and to pass an Act of Uniformity (1549). This act required that all church services follow a uniform text, composed in English by Cranmer himself; this was then put into the *Book of Common Prayer*, which is still (as revised) the basis of Anglican ritual. All subjects of the kingdom were required by the act to attend services regularly; other forms of public worship were outlawed. Cranmer also issued a summary of doctrine, the Forty-two Articles, which was a moderate statement of Protestant doctrines.

When Mary succeeded Edward in 1553, the religious pendulum swung back. Mary, who had been raised a devout Catholic, was determined to restore the nation to allegiance to Rome. She replaced Protestant-minded bishops with Catholics and compelled the clergy to give up their wives. (Under Cranmer, priests had been allowed to marry, in keeping with the Lutheran practice.) Latin replaced English in the services of the Church. When Mary invited Cardinal Reginald Pole to England as papal ambassador, he ceremoniously pardoned her subjects from "heresy" and restored England to communion with Rome. Mary's most unpopular act was to wed her relative, Philip, heir to the Spanish throne and a bitter enemy of Protestantism.

In the face of Mary's ruthless policy against dissenters, most people adjusted their beliefs to avoid execution; but several hundred, including Cranmer, went to the stake for their convictions. The monarch thus earned the name (among Protestants) of "Bloody Mary." She was no more ruthless than her father, Henry, but she offended national feeling by subjecting the country once again to the pope and by marrying a despised foreigner. As Mary bore no child, her reign proved to be only a reactionary interlude whose net effect was to make Catholicism more unpopular than before.

The Elizabethan Compromise

Elizabeth, the daughter of Anne Boleyn, inherited the crown upon Mary's death in 1558. She had been raised a Protestant but, unlike her half-sister, was neither devout nor fanatical. During her early years she could observe for herself the frequent shifting of loyalties in religion and politics. As queen, she stood firmly for a Protestant church and independence from Rome. But her first concern was for the security of the crown and the unity of her subjects.

A true child of Henry, she managed Parliament and her ministers with shrewdness. She had Mary's Catholic legislation repealed and the Act of Supremacy reenacted (1559). But she avoided giving unnecessary offense to those of her subjects who were pro-Catholic. Her new laws established the "Elizabethan Compromise" (or Settlement), which remains to this day the foundation of the Anglican Church.

Parliament, with Elizabeth's approval, enacted a revised summary of official doctrine known as the Thirty-nine Articles. Similar to Cranmer's earlier statement, it was designed to satisfy all but extremists. The Thirty-nine Articles were Lutheran or Calvinist on certain matters, including the exclusive authority of Scripture, salvation by faith alone, the number of sacraments, and the freedom of the clergy to marry. But on many points the language was obscure, leaving a wide range of interpretation. There was also a firm insistence upon respecting the *traditions* of the Church, except those that were clearly "repugnant to the Word of God." Under the cover of tradition, pro-Catholics would continue to venerate the saints, go on pilgrimages, and engage in other "Romish" religious practices.

In internal organization the Anglican Church was very like the Roman Catholic. The monarch was its "Supreme Governor," but only in the sense that she was responsible, under God, for ruling all classes (religious and secular) in the country. This idea was similar to the priestly role of kings David and Solomon in the ancient Jewish state and to the position of Constantine, Theodosius, and Charlemagne in relation to their empires (p. 203).

The actual ministering of the Word and the sacraments was restricted to the ordained priesthood, in accordance with the doctrine of apostolic succession. The Anglican bishops traced their authority back to the twelve apostles, as did the Roman Catholic bishops (and those of the Orthodox Church). They rejected, however, the theory of *Petrine supremacy*, which was the cornerstone of papal claims to universal authority (pp. 154–55).

It is in the theory and role of bishops that Anglicanism differed most sharply from other Protestant denominations. This distinction is reflected in the designation "Episcopal Church" in America (*episcopus* is the Latin word for "bishop"). Most other Protestant groups developed a presbyterian form of church government, a form we encountered in our discussion of Calvinism (p. 369). The presbyterian form may be characterized as *representative*, the episcopal form as *aristocratic*. Roman Catholic government (to complete our comparison) is *monarchical*.

The Elizabethan Settlement brought stability because most of the English (who by this time were weary of religious quarreling) were prepared to conform. Only a handful of the clergy — who had called themselves Catholic under Mary — now refused to accept the new Act of Uniformity. Elizabeth, who cared little about the *private* views and doubts of her subjects, was content with outward obedience. She would not tolerate open dissent, but penalties were softened and offenders were few. Not until the seventeenth and eighteenth centuries would new religious stirrings disrupt the established Church in England. These would lead to further divisions of Christianity: Baptists, Quakers, Methodists, Unitarians, and others. But all that lay in the future. For the rest of the queen's long reign, her firm hand brought internal peace and prosperity.

The age of Elizabeth also brought England to the threshold of world power. Philip of Spain, who had become Philip II in 1556, sought the hand of

Elizabeth after the death of his wife, Mary. Elizabeth had held him off, so Philip finally decided to take her kingdom by force. (The pope excommunicated Elizabeth in 1570, declared her deposed, and thus opened the way to Philip's adventure.) In 1588 Philip sent a mighty fleet (the Spanish Armada) against England, expecting that once his soldiers had landed on the island, the thousands of unhappy Catholics in the country would rally to his banner. But the Armada was routed in the Channel by the English navy and was smashed by storms on its return home. With Spain, the leading power of the continent, thus humbled, the English became conscious of their strength on the seas. Elizabeth's reign marked a turning point in the nation's history. Thereafter, English sea power, commerce, and diplomacy were to exercise a mounting influence over European and world affairs.

THE ROMAN CATHOLIC RESPONSE: REFORM AND REAFFIRMATION

The Protestant movements — the revolt of some religious leaders and civil rulers against the Roman Catholic Church — grew out of a mixture of motives and were shaped by varying political and social conditions. But they all led to one result: the division of Western Christendom. Within half a century after Luther's challenge at Wittenberg, most of northern Europe had broken away from the papacy. Protestants dominated the cities of Switzerland; they formed a militant minority in France; and a few had even penetrated the Catholic strongholds of Spain and Italy.

Finally the Roman Catholic Church, after hesitation and uncertainty, moved to check the spreading revolt. Too late to reverse the major losses, these efforts did recover some ground and kept the remainder of Europe loyal to Rome. The response took two main courses: reform within the Catholic Church and *counter*measures against Protestanism.

Relation to Protestant Movements

Catholic reforms were inspired, in part, by the same ideas and ideals that had motivated Luther and the other religious rebels. As we have seen, the condition of the late medieval Church had caused widespread discontent and sharp criticism. The Christian humanist Erasmus was the most eloquent spokesman for reform without rebellion. Other sincere Catholics, both lay and clerical, worked for correction of abuses. A groundswell of reform, similar to that which had started the Cluniac movement in the tenth century (p. 236), now began to rise. There can be no doubt, however, that Catholic reform in the sixteenth century was also prompted by the Protestant actions. The papacy, whose leadership was essential to effective action, had long remained indifferent. But when Paul III became pope in 1534 he was forced to respond to the events in both Germany and England.

Though some aims were common to both the Catholic and the Protestant reform movements, there were important differences between them. Both conservatives and liberals among the Catholic leaders accepted the central doctrines, traditions, and organization of the Church. What the Catholic reformers desired was a purer Christian life within the established Church, in keeping with its historic tradition of *self*-reformation. The Protestant leaders, on the other hand, were not content with purification alone. As we have seen, they wanted a *reconstruction* of the Church, in accord with different theories of authority, priesthood, and salvation.

While the Protestant movements arose in the north, Catholic reform efforts were centered in Spain and Italy. The Spanish reformation had begun in the late fifteenth century, led by Cardinal Ximenes (Archbishop of Toledo), with the full support of the monarchy. The Spanish reform served as a model for Catholic action elsewhere in Europe. This was reform distinctly in the medieval tradition: it included a rigorous campaign to improve the morals and education of the clergy, military action against infidels (the Muslims — p. 266), and a strong effort to wipe out heresies.

In Italy, too, some churchmen had urged similar actions. But the Renaissance popes had dampened the hopes of reformers, and the princes of Italy were either indifferent or unwilling to make the necessary effort. As in the Middle Ages, however, new and reformed religious orders now arose to improve the quality of Christian life. One was the priestly order of Theatines, which was dedicated to education. Another was the order of Capuchins, a reformed branch of the Franciscan friars (p. 237). The Capuchins modeled themselves upon Francis of Assisi and carried his message of love, piety, and simplicity to the common people.

Loyola and the Society of Jesus

One man and one order above all others, however, were to play a decisive role in the Catholic reformation and in stemming the Protestant tide. Ignatius Loyola, a Spanish nobleman and soldier of the king, was the founder of this new order. At about the time Luther was standing before the Diet of Worms (1521), Loyola was seriously wounded in a battle. His leg was shattered by a cannonball, and he lay for months in painful convalescence, during which time he experienced a profound spiritual conversion.

Loyola was burdened, as Luther had been, by a sense of sin and unworthiness. After a lengthy period of confession, fasting, and nightly vigils (watches), visions of Christ and Mary appeared to him and relieved him of his fears. Now he resolved to give up all thought of resuming his former life and enlisted himself as a "soldier of the Lord." He turned the strong military and chivalric traditions of his country to a spiritual purpose, dedicating his services to the Virgin, as a knight to his lady. And he held also to the Spanish tradition of religious orthodoxy, finding satisfaction not in revolt but in absolute obedience to God and the pope.

Loyola realized that if he was to save souls from heresy or indifference he would need a thorough religious education. After preparing himself in Latin, he went on to the University of Paris, where he studied for some seven years, gathering about him a small band of devoted followers. Working at first as an informal association bound by common vows, they formed a regular religious order in 1540.

The order was named the Society of Jesus, and its members were commonly called Jesuits. Loyola was elected its general, or commander, for life, and he placed himself and his Society at the service of the pope. The general shaped the internal organization along strict military lines, with a "chain of command" reaching down to the ordinary Jesuit "soldier."

The Jesuits took the usual monastic vows of chastity, poverty, and obedience and required, in addition, absolute acceptance of orthodox doctrines and the authority of the pope. In his manual for members, Loyola laid out both "spiritual exercises" and rules of conduct. One of the rules stated, "To be right in all things we ought to adhere always to the principle that the white which I see I will believe to be black if the Church so rules. . . ."

The organization and discipline of the Society of Jesus were well suited to its broad purpose: "to employ itself entirely in the defense of the holy Catholic faith." The Jesuits sought to accomplish this goal chiefly through widespread education and preaching. They founded schools and colleges to inculcate young minds with the "true" doctrine, and they sent out missions to convert heathens and heretics. The Jesuits also tried (mainly through oral confessions) to keep wavering Catholics on the path to *correct* belief. And, by serving as confessors and advisers to civil rulers, they tried to guide states in policies favorable to the Church. Though the Jesuits were highly effective in their education and preaching, these political activities ultimately brought heavy criticism and attacks.

The Reforming Popes and the Council of Trent

When Loyola died in 1556, the Society had grown to nearly fifteen hundred members. All were carefully selected men, well trained and well disciplined, who could be counted on to support the pope without question. They proved especially effective in imposing papal control over the important Council of Trent in the mid-sixteenth century.

Paul III was the first of the reformation popes. Unlike his Medici predecessor, Clement VII, he was seriously committed to reform. A report by a committee of cardinals on abuses among the clergy he found so shocking that he decided to keep it secret. He did, however, launch an overhauling of papal administration, and he summoned a council to deal with reform and heresy.

Many Catholics, as well as Protestants, felt that a church council might help settle the deep troubles of Christendom. The conciliar (council) tradition was long established; the first general council, held at Nicaea in 325 (p. 159), had successfully faced a serious division over doctrine. The Council of Constance

(p. 355) had faced an equally trying problem in 1414 with respect to the Great Schism of the Church. Some believed that another meeting of all the high clergy might once again restore unity and purity to the Church.

Others, however, though they favored a reform of practices, feared that a council might be drawn into a compromise on *doctrine*. The pope was hesitant for an additional reason: past councils had tried to limit the papal monarchy and to establish the council itself as the supreme authority in the Church. Although Paul III at last summoned a council, he made sure that the papacy would control it.

The Council of Trent met, with interruptions, over a period of some twenty years (1545–63). The Jesuits at the council sought to keep a balance favorable to Roman policies; they were aided in this by the facts that papal ambassadors presided over the sessions and that Italian bishops outnumbered those of any other nationality. (The French clergy, who were committed to a "national" church, did not participate fully.) Because the Italians (and Spaniards) were loyal to Rome, they could be relied on to support the papacy.

By the time the council opened, the pope had decided on a definite course of action. Earlier, a few of his advisers had recommended that some effort be made to bring about reconciliation with the Protestants, but this had proved futile. The pope settled instead on a program of reform and reinvigoration, while refusing to compromise on doctrine. He was willing, apparently, to accept the Catholic setbacks for the time being and to concentrate on holding the line against further losses. This, he thought, could best be done by correcting abuses and by restating beliefs.

The Council of Trent sent its final decrees to the pope for approval, thereby reaffirming the supremacy of his authority. In general, the decrees gave the papacy what it wanted. They fell into two main parts: reform decrees and statements of doctrine. Bishops were ordered to regain strict discipline over their clergy in such matters as keeping vows, morals, behavior, and dress. (Special attention was given to the problem of restoring chastity and putting aside concubines.) And they were required to provide better education for the priesthood by establishing a seminary (theological school) in each diocese. Among the higher clergy, the practice of *simony* was forbidden. (This was the selling of Church "offices" [positions] that had regular incomes attached.) Also forbidden was the holding of more than one office at a time. Though the granting of papal indulgences was not altogether stopped, the *sale* of indulgences or of sacraments was outlawed. Had these reforms been launched fifty years earlier, they might have blunted the criticisms of Erasmus and other conscientious Christians. In any case, Trent was a turning point in Catholic history, and the clergy and laity both experienced a reawakening of piety and devotions.

Although the Protestant revolt no doubt stimulated the reform and revival of the Church, it also prompted a hardening of Catholic doctrine. The Council of Trent made no compromise with Luther or Calvin on theological issues; in responding to the Protestant challenge, it not only reaffirmed traditional doctrines but stated them more distinctly. The result was to make orthodoxy clearer and narrower and to leave Catholic theologians with less freedom of interpretation than they had had before Trent.

The special powers of the priesthood, the necessity of the Roman Church and the seven sacraments, the doctrine of transubstantiation (p. 360), the veneration of saints and relics, the belief in purgatory and indulgences (p. 358) — all were specifically confirmed by the council. At the same time, the council condemned the opposing Protestant doctrines. Headed by the papacy, the Church was now prepared to carry out the reform decrees of Trent and to restore "correct" doctrines throughout Christendom. Under the zealous popes of the second half of the sixteenth century, the Roman Church moved from stagnation and defensiveness to a bold offensive.

In addition to the Jesuits, two other agencies worked to crush heresy and to keep the faithful safe in "true" beliefs. The first was the Inquisition, of medieval origin (pp. 239–40), that was now revived in Spain, Italy, and the Low Countries. Directing its efforts against those accused of heretical ideas, its secret trials, torture, and burnings aimed at *conformity* through *terror*.

The censorship of books had been ordered by the Council of Trent as another means of checking "false" beliefs. The council authorized an Index (list) of prohibited books, including all those that attacked the Roman Church or contained ideas contrary to its doctrines; and it established a Congregation of the Index to publish the list and keep it current. Church members were forbidden to read any work named in the Index, which soon came to include much of the serious literature of Europe. Censorship, of course, had long been used by both Catholics and Protestants, but the new effort was more comprehensive and was executed with greater energy than ever before. Although the prohibited books continued to circulate even in Catholic countries, the Index no doubt contributed to a narrowing of the exchange of ideas. It remained in force until 1965, when it was dropped by order of the Second Vatican Council (pp. 632–33).

The vigorous response of the Roman Church to the Protestant challenge prevented further Catholic losses. Switches in religion among Europeans have been few since 1570, and the divisions of that time (map, p. 380) generally remain today.

Historical Significance of the Reformation

Viewed from the perspective of the twentieth century, the struggles of the Reformation period seem strange in some respects. In the first place, it appears odd that theological issues should have called forth so much attention, energy, and bloodshed at a time when religion generally was a declining force in European affairs. In the second place, while looking *backward* to primitive

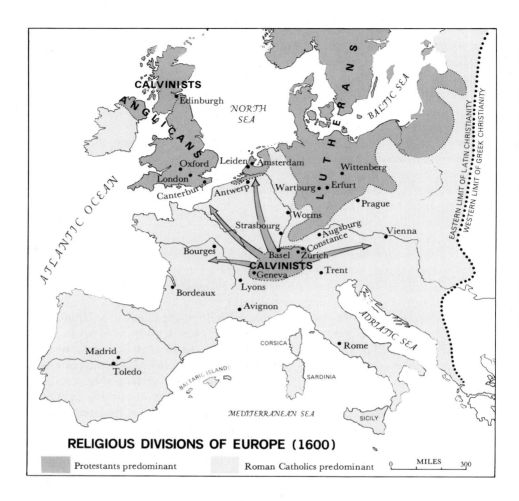

RELIGIOUS DIVISIONS OF EUROPE (1600)

Protestants predominant   Roman Catholics predominant

MILES
0   300

Christianity, the Protestant movements actually drew strength from *new* social developments and gave them strength in return. The growing sense of *nationality*, for example, helped Luther's cause in Germany and was, at the same time, stimulated by Luther's revolt. The turning away from Rome helped the power-seeking princes of northern Europe, while putting the church under state control (in Lutheranism and Anglicanism) was both a response and a stimulus to *secularism*. Also, Protestantism and *capitalism* tended to be mutually reinforcing. Calvin, for instance, though urging businessmen to behave ethically, gave his blessing to their occupations. And by praising hard work and thrift, he supported bourgeois morale and encouraged the accumulation of capital.

Perhaps the leading trend in Western culture from the close of the Middle Ages onward was toward *individualism*. It can be observed in the breaking down of the medieval social order, the growth of commercial enterprise, and in

overseas exploration (see Chapter 7). The trend continued in the Renaissance — in art, literature, and society. The Protestant movements, too, reflected
this tendency and gave it new force. Luther and Calvin stressed the right and
power of all believers to read the Bible for themselves and to communicate
directly with God. True, both soon came to the position of placing their authority over others. But the initial thrust of Protestantism — its spirit of rebel-
liousness and its appeal to individual conscience — could not be checked.

We see, then, that although Protestantism was in one sense reactionary
(backward looking), it was at the same time in harmony with the "progressive"
forces of its time. It may, indeed, be interpreted as an *adjustment* by the Christian religion to the forward movement of national consciousness, secularism,
capitalism, and individualism. But such an adjustment was by no means the
aim of the reformers; they saw their movement, rather, as an adjustment,
within Christianity, to strictly *religious* issues.

In any case, the Reformation radically altered the position of Christianity
in Western civilization. The Christian Church, after the sixteenth century,
could no longer speak with a single voice, and thoughtful individuals found it
hard to accept absolute truth and absolute authority when the claimants to that
truth and that authority contradicted and fought one another. This division
brought dismay to many and led some to atheism or skepticism (p. 422).

More than a century of wars over religion ended eventually in stalemate in
1650. The surviving religious denominations did not abandon their claims to
absolute truth, but most people in western Europe came to agree that "truth"
should no longer be imposed by force. And religious toleration, which thus
emerged as a byproduct of the Reformation, created a new intellectual climate
of open questioning and reasoning. The binding faith of medieval Christendom, with its intensity and its ecstasy, was gone forever. Religious doubt had
made its mark on modern Western culture.

ART DURING THE REFORMATION

For many Protestants, sacred paintings and sculpture were associated with
Rome, and the revolt against "popery" was often accompanied by attacks
(physical and verbal) on art images. Calvin, as we have seen, saw works of art as
a distraction from the word of God. He objected to any attempt to "paint or
carve" subjects that went beyond ordinary observation: "God's majesty, which
is too exalted for human sight, may not be corrupted by fantasies which have
no true agreement therewith."

The Protestant reformers (and some pious Catholics as well) were also
offended by the *sensuality* in some Renaissance art. The "cult of beauty"
(pp. 325, 339) had produced works that were shocking to puritanical viewers, and
a reaction now set in against the portrayal of nudity. Reforming popes of the
sixteenth century ordered artists to paint clothes on the figures in numerous
Renaissance masterpieces, and many of these works simply disappeared from
public view.

The Impact of Protestantism: Holbein, Brueghel

The Protestant artists of the sixteenth century faced two problems: they stood in the shadow of the Renaissance giants, and their main source of patronage had been cut off by the Reformation. In many areas, especially those under Calvinist influence, works of art were banned from the churches, and even for private homes paintings and decorations were frowned upon as frivolous. Erasmus, writing from the Netherlands in 1526, reported, "The arts here are freezing." For individual painters or sculptors, the chill was often fatal. They might lose income, acceptable subjects, and useful work — which could be a psychological as well as a financial blow. The sense of "alienation" (feeling "left out"), familiar to artists today, had its beginnings in the period of the Protestant Reformation.

The career of the German painter Hans Holbein is illustrative. Born in 1497, he mastered the techniques of his day and produced works that combined the best of the Italian and the northern styles. Most of his early paintings were designed for church altars, but with the coming of the Reformation Holbein had to turn to portrait painting. By good fortune and with the help of Erasmus (p. 327), he was able to move to England, where he secured commissions from the aristocracy; eventually, he became court painter to Henry VIII. He produced hundreds of lifelike portraits of the monarch, his family, and the royal courtiers (close officials of the king). Working with oils and in the realistic tradition established by Jan Van Eyck (pp. 334–35), Holbein usually showed his subjects in their customary setting and surrounded by the symbols and tools of their office or profession. A notable example is *The Ambassadors* (*Fig. 7-1*, p. 274).

Other Protestant painters explored the possibilities of landscapes and scenes of *ordinary* life ("genre" painting). The Flemish master of genre was Peter Brueghel; though he produced many splendid landscapes, he is best known for his pictures of common folk. Brueghel was himself a townsman, but he showed a keen understanding of plain, unsophisticated peasants. His interest in rustic subjects is evident in his paintings of peasants at work and at rest, and in his scenes of hunting, feasting, and playing.

Brueghel's *The Wedding Dance* (*Fig. 9-1*), painted in 1566, near the end of his life, is a striking example of *perspective* and *organization*. With its lively movement and rhythm, it suggests the healthy animal spirits of the dancers. Brueghel was one of the first artists to break with the aristocratic tradition of Renaissance painting to show us, bluntly and honestly, the ordinary men and women who made up the bulk of European society.

The Development of the Baroque: Rubens, Rembrandt

Although many Catholic painters were also skillful at treating secular subjects, they were encouraged to direct their talents to religious art. The Catholic Church, after the Council of Trent (pp. 377–79), was eager to check

9-1 Brueghel. *The Wedding Dance.* Detroit Institute of Arts.

the spread of Protestant ideas, and one way was to bring the teachings of the Church directly to the faithful. Art had provided religious instruction during the Middle Ages; it was now called upon to renew its role in defense of Catholic teachings.

The response was an outpouring of magnificent art ranging from the mystical to the sensual. Though the new artists built on Renaissance models, they threw off the restraints of classical rules. Their work came to be called *baroque* — meaning excessive or ornate. But the movement generated its own standards and must not be measured by classical norms. At its best, baroque has an impressive originality and impact.

The leader of baroque art is the Flemish painter Peter Paul Rubens. In 1600, as a young man of twenty-three, he journeyed to Italy, where he learned to create heroic, large-scale canvases. After returning to his native Antwerp, Rubens combined the traditional Flemish attention to detail with his newly learned Italian style. He worked chiefly for the court of the ruling Habsburgs, the Flemish aristocrats, and the Church. A man of enormous energy and versatility, he created fine portraits, altar paintings, and huge murals for palaces and religious houses. His subject matter ranged from romantic and mythological themes to the central mysteries of the Catholic faith.

Rubens was one of the few painters in history who were successful, prosperous, and generally respected in their own day. So great was the demand for his work that he set up a well-organized workshop in which he trained specialists to paint certain elements — heads, hands, animals, or backgrounds. He supervised the production of each work and finished the key features with his own hand. His paintings are notable for their organization, color, and texture.

He was blessed by good fortune and a happy disposition, and his paintings are charged with movement and vigor. His well-nourished nudes reflect the spirit with which he viewed the world. In his treatment of a traditional subject from Greek legend, *The Rape of the Daughters of Leucippus* (*Fig. 9-2*), he arranged powerful men, horses, and women into a tight group of solid figures. There is little "philosophical" intent in this kind of painting, but it combines exciting elements of form and action.

As Rubens was the artistic master of Catholic Flanders, Rembrandt van Rijn was the master of Protestant Holland. But a greater contrast in person-

9-2 Rubens. *The Rape of the Daughters of Leucippus.* Alte Pinakothek, Munich.

9-3 Rembrandt. *Portrait of the Artist.* Greater London
Council, The Iveigh Bequest, English Heritage, London.

alities can hardly be imagined. A generation younger than Rubens, Rembrandt
won substantial recognition early in his career. After his beautiful and well-to-
do wife died in 1642, however, his fortunes began to decline. He fell into debt,
his popularity vanished, and he turned more and more *inward* in his thoughts.

Yet it was in the dark days of tragedy and self-examination that Rembrandt did his most profound work. He painted no longer for rich patrons, but
for himself. Although he often painted religious subjects, all his works possess
a mysterious spiritual quality. Unlike Rubens, he usually took his subjects from
the middle or lower classes. He portrayed them with remarkable economy of
line and without affectation, shunning bright colors and extravagant movements and relying on contrasting lights and shadows. His colors appear dark
or drab to those who see his paintings for the first time; Rembrandt favored
browns, dark reds, and golds. For he did not wish the surface of his canvases to
blind the viewer to the "inner" person. When we look closely at a Rembrandt
portrait, we sense the essential *character* of the subject (*Fig. 9-3*).

Rembrandt spent most of his life in Amsterdam, but he put into his work
many of the qualities of Italian painting. These included careful organization

9-4 Rembrandt. *Supper at Emmaus*. Louvre, Paris.

and balance and, above all, *psychological interest* (as stressed by Leonardo — pp. 340–41). An illustration of Rembrandt's religious painting is the *Supper at Emmaus* (*Fig. 9-4*). A good Protestant, he was a devout reader of the Bible, and in this picture he dramatized a moment from the life of Christ as recounted in Luke (24:13–31). The Gospel states that on the day of the Resurrection Jesus appeared, unrecognized, along a road. There he joined two of his disciples, who invited him to eat with them at an inn. Rembrandt shows Jesus at the moment when he blessed and broke the bread and was revealed to his disciples as the risen Christ.

Baroque Sculpture and Architecture: Bernini

The main source of the baroque style was Rome, where the Catholic Reformation was centered. The climax of that style came during the seventeenth century in the work of the sculptor and architect Lorenzo Bernini (who died in 1680).

A leading characteristic of baroque artists was their effort to *fuse* architecture, sculpture, and painting into a single structure of grandeur and "truth." Bernini was trained as a sculptor, but he thought of himself as an artist who combined several talents. "I render marble as supple as wax," he declared, "and I have united in my works the resources of painting and sculpture." Bernini's most distinctive contribution was the revival of the Italian sculptural tradition, which had fallen into decline with the passing of Michelangelo (pp. 342–45). In the cold and hard medium of stone, Bernini succeeded in catching the fleeting instant, the throbbing passion, the rhythm of movement.

He learned much from the muscular, twisting figures of Michelangelo, but his work displayed even wider range and inventiveness. By means of extraordinary technical skill, he brought sculpture to new heights of drama and emotion. *The Ecstasy of Santa Theresa* (*Fig. 9-5*), which Bernini prepared for a chapel in a small Roman church, shows the mystical Spanish nun after her heart has been pierced by the arrow of divine love. As a smiling angel looks on, the face and body of the saint express indescribable rapture.

9-5 Bernini. *The Ecstasy of Santa Theresa*. Church of Santa Maria della Vittoria, Rome.

Bernini skillfully blended sculpture with architecture. Under Michelangelo's dome in the great basilica of St. Peter's he created an elaborate decoration for the apse (p. 244); and directly above the central altar (which rests over the tomb of Peter) he built a huge bronze canopy, or baldachin (*Fig. 9-6*). The scale and character of its swirling columns capture the spirit of Catholic baroque.

Some years later, Bernini fashioned a dramatic setting for the *exterior* of St. Peter's to match what he had done inside. He designed the vast oval piazza that stands before the largest church in Christendom. (More than a hundred thousand people crowd into this space on special days to await the blessing by

9-6 Bernini. Baldachin, St. Peter's, Vatican, Rome.

9-7 Bernini. Colonnade, St. Peter's.

the pope.) To enclose its two sides, Bernini constructed a huge, curving colonnade (*Fig. 9-7*), consisting of 284 Greek-style columns. They carry a roof more than sixty feet high, surmounted by seventy giant-sized statues. Visitors entering the piazza from its open end are embraced, symbolically, by the "arms" of the Church.

Baroque architecture (like baroque painting and sculpture) was an *adaptation* of Renaissance models. Such classical elements as columns, pediments, and arches were used freely, but without following strictly the ancient "rules" for their use. From the late sixteenth century to our own day, many of the public buildings of the West have been designed in this flexible style.

The Catholic monarchs of Europe were quick to adopt the style for their own purposes. Philip II of Spain, the most powerful ruler of his time (pp. 374–75), started in 1563 to build a new royal palace, choosing for its site the village of Escorial, in the mountainous country near Madrid. Philip's architects laid out a vast complex of buildings and courtyards, with an elegant church at the center. Beneath its main altar was placed a burial vault in which the Spanish kings and queens have since been entombed. The Escorial complex also included a monastery, a seminary, and a library. Its architectural style is generally restrained, but its plan is baroque.

A better-known monument to royal conceit is the Versailles palace, built a century later by Louis XIV. The French monarchy had by then replaced the Spanish as the leading royal house of Europe, and Louis wanted to erect a residence and a center of government and the arts that would surpass all existing palaces. Like the Escorial, Louis's residence was built in the countryside (about twenty miles southwest of Paris). It was a high point of the secular baroque style, combining architecture, landscaping, sculpture, painting, and the minor arts into a grand synthesis.

Built at staggering cost, Versailles matched Louis's love of display. The enclosed areas cover seventeen acres and housed some ten thousand people. The formal gardens, courts, parade grounds, and surrounding woods stretch over many square miles. The overall plan is a masterful realization of the baroque idea of "integrated" design. While the exterior of the Versailles palace is relatively modest, the interior is lavish in the extreme. One of the most dazzling chambers is the Hall of Mirrors (*Fig. 9-8*), a shimmering room designed to overawe visitors to the French court.

9-8 Hall of Mirrors, Versailles, France.

In many respects, Versailles proved to be highly "functional." Though wasteful of the nation's resources, it helped the king to centralize his authority within France, and it strengthened the role and image of France as cultural leader of the West. A milestone in politics as well as in civic planning and the arts, Versailles called forth a hundred imitations by the monarchs and princelings of Europe.

10-1 United Nations Educational, Scientific, and Cultural Organization Building, Paris. Built in 1958.

PART FOUR

THE MODERN WORLD

	POLITICAL, SOCIAL, AND ECONOMIC DEVELOPMENTS	RELIGION, SCIENCE, AND PHILOSOPHY	HISTORY AND LITERATURE	ART AND ARCHITECTURE
1600	Religious wars (Thirty Years' War in Germany) Grotius and emergence of inter-national law	Copernicus (died 1543) Francis Bacon Kepler, Galileo Descartes		Baroque style of architecture
	Peace of Westphalia			
1650	English Revolution Cromwell	Royal Society founded Hobbes Bossuet Locke		Versailles Palace
	Mercantilism Louis XIV Age of absolutism	Newton		Wren
1700	Rise of Prussia and Russia: Peter the Great Frederick the Great	The Enlightenment: Deism Rousseau	Age of classicism: Racine Pope	St. Paul's Cathedral Rococo style: Watteau Boucher Fragonard
				Reynolds

	Events		Literature	Arts
1750	Industrial Revolution and beginnings of factory system	Smith	Voltaire, Diderot	Classical revival style
	American Revolution	Kant	Jefferson	David
	U.S. Constitution			
	French Revolution	Condorcet, Burke		
1800	Napoleon I and empire of the French	Ricardo	Goethe	
	Conservative reaction	Hegel, Dalton, Schwann	Age of romanticism: Wordsworth, Scott, Byron, Shelley, Keats	Romanticism: Goya, Gothic revival style
	Congress of Vienna			
	Metternich System "Concert of Europe"	Utopian socialists: Saint-Simon, Fourier, Owen		Houses of Parliament
	Spread of political and economic liberalism	Comte	Balzac	Turner, Constable, Delacroix

	POLITICAL, SOCIAL, AND ECONOMIC DEVELOPMENTS	RELIGION, SCIENCE, AND PHILOSOPHY	HISTORY AND LITERATURE	ART AND ARCHITECTURE
1850	Growth of nationalism French Second Empire: Napoleon III German unification and empire: Bismarck Rise of corporate big business Rise of labor unions Urbanization of Western society Exploration of Africa The new imperialism Triple Alliance	Mazzini Marx, Engels, Bakunin Darwin Kierkegaard Mill Spencer Pasteur and germ theory of disease Leo XIII Nietzsche Freud Jung Einstein	Dickens von Ranke Ibsen Dostoevsky Tolstoy Shaw	Courbet Daumier Impressionism: Monet Cézanne Expressionism: van Gogh
1900	British Empire at full extent Russo-Japanese War Triple Entente First World War League of Nations Russian Revolution: communism, Lenin, and Stalin Rise of fascism and nazism: Mussolini, Hitler, Franco The Great Depression (1930–40) Roosevelt and New Deal Second World War and Holocaust Atomic bomb: "unlimited" warfare United Nations	Pavlov Rutherford, Bohr, Curie Barth Existentialism Tillich	Joyce Proust Eliot Orwell	Organic style: Wright International style: Gropius Mies van der Rohe Le Corbusier Kandinsky Picasso

Date	Politics and Society	Religion and Science	Literature	Art

1950	The Cold War (U.S. and U.S.S.R.)
	End of colonialism:
	  Gandhi, Kenyatta
	Mao Tse-tung (Mao Zedong)
	Indochina War (Vietnam):
	  Ho Chi Minh
	European Economic Community
	  (Common Market)
	End of "bi-polar" world
	National liberation movements:
	  Castro, Allende
	Israeli-Arab wars: Sadat, Begin
	Student movement and
	  youth culture
		Researchers
		
		John XXIII
		Second Vatican Council
		
		Paul VI
		New sexuality
		Revival of hedonism
		
		Man on moon: Armstrong
			Huxley
			
			Mailer
			
			Pasternak
			
			Solzhenitsyn
				Moore
				Calder
				Niemeyer
				Saarinen

1970	Emergence of "Third World"
	Struggle against racism:
	  King, Jackson
	Women's movement:
	  Beauvoir, Friedan
	World population and resources
	  crisis
	Resurgence of Japanese power
	
	U.S.–China renewal: Nixon
	East–West détente
	Conservative reaction
			Updike
			
			Heller	

1975	Iranian revolution: Khomeini International terrorism	John Paul II Islamic revival		
1980	Cold War renewal: nuclear arms race Thatcher, Reagan "revolutions"	Christian "fundamentalism"		
1985	Gorbachev revolution in eastern Europe	Space probes of solar system		
1990	End of Cold War; German reunification Persian Gulf War: Iraq vs. the U.N.			

CHAPTER

10

Science and
the New Cosmology

During the age of the baroque, beneath the flourish of grandiose art and architecture, new ways of thought were developing that were to have a profound effect on the position of all established authorities. Even more important, the new ideas were to revolutionize the accepted concept of the universe and the means of comprehending it.

NATIONAL AND INTERNATIONAL DEVELOPMENT

Before we turn to the seventeenth-century revolution in science and philosophy, we will summarize political developments in western Europe. By 1650 the shift from the political patterns of the Middle Ages had been largely completed. The principal new forms were *absolute monarchy* and the *nation-state*. And the monarchs of the seventeenth century, in addition to strengthening order within their own kingdoms, laid the foundations of modern *international relations*.

Foundations of the European State System: The Peace of Westphalia

A miniature model for the new European state system had appeared in Italy during the Renaissance, when city-states such as Florence, Milan, and Venice had worked out a system of relationships among themselves as sovereign powers. They established embassies and agreed on diplomatic rules for peace and war; they made alliances and sought to maintain a "balance of power" inside Italy (p. 304). The rising *national* states, beyond the Alps, drew on the Italian experience in shaping their own international relations.

The European state system grew out of a combination of forces, including dynastic ambition, national sentiment, and religious antagonism. In the Dutch

Spanish Rule of Dutch Provinces	DUTCH WARS OF INDEPENDENCE

revolt against Spain, for example, all three forces were present. Calvinism had won many converts in the Netherlands, which formed a rich part of the Habsburg domains; the Catholic rulers had responded in 1567 by imposing repressive measures in the Netherlands. In addition to admitting the Inquisition (p. 379) to the area, the Habsburgs had introduced harsh political and economic restrictions. The northern (Dutch) provinces reacted by declaring their independence in 1581; leading their struggle was William "the Silent," prince of the house of Orange. When Philip II of Spain (the Habsburg ruler) tried to bring the provinces back under his control he met with armed resistance. The defiant Dutch, with English help, fought the Habsburg forces on land and sea and at last forced them to withdraw. In 1648 the United Provinces of the Netherlands (Holland) was formally recognized as an independent state by the principal powers of Europe (p. 400).

Religion and politics were similarly mixed in France, where the Catholic monarchy viewed the Calvinist minority (known there as Huguenots) as disloyal to the crown. After the death in 1547 of Francis I, the country had a series of weak rulers, and an aristocratic reaction against the monarchy had set in. Many nobles, seeking to regain their independence from the crown, had associated themselves with the defiant Huguenots.

The resulting civil strife was mainly a contest between monarchists and the aristocratic faction in France; the religious convictions held by many on both sides tended to become submerged in the struggle. King Henry IV, seeking a truce in the political-religious warfare, secured civil rights and a limited religious tolerance for the Huguenots by his Edict of Nantes (1598). In the course of the seventeenth century, however, the royal government broke the military power of the aristocratic Huguenot faction, and Louis XIV canceled the edict in 1685.

In Germany, religion and politics combined to produce the most tragic consequences. As we have seen, the Lutheran military revolt had ended in 1555 with the Peace of Augsburg (p. 362), which left each German prince free to decide whether the religion of his subjects would be Lutheran or Catholic. This settlement had brought a kind of peace for sixty years, although divisive pressures mounted steadily. Guided by the Jesuits (pp. 376–77), the Catholic princes during these years stamped out the remnants of Protestant dissent in their territories. The zeal of the Lutheran princes, on the other hand, was weakened by bitter squabbles with Calvinist minorities. Sensing danger, some of the Protestant princes joined together in an armed league in 1608, an action promptly countered by the formation of a Catholic league.

As each camp eyed the other, watching for any move that might upset the religious and territorial balance, revolt exploded in Bohemia, which was part of the Holy Roman Empire. Most of the population of Bohemia were Czechs who were both anti-German and antipapal, and the trouble there had its roots in the Hussite rebellion of the fifteenth century (pp. 282–83, 356). During the sixteenth century the Protestants of Bohemia had enjoyed toleration under moderate Catholic rulers. But when Ferdinand of Styria, a Habsburg and a fanatical Catholic, was forced upon them as king, they feared that their religious and political rights were in jeopardy. Accordingly, in 1618 the Bohemian nobles announced their open defiance of Ferdinand and chose a Calvinist prince of the Rhineland to be their king. The Catholic league of princes moved swiftly to help Ferdinand crush the poorly organized rebellion, and Ferdinand's election as Holy Roman emperor in 1619 gave him added strength.

But as he proceeded to destroy Protestantism in Bohemia, other anti-Catholic and anti-Habsburg countries became alarmed. The king of Denmark decided to intervene in Germany in order to protect Lutheranism and to acquire territory for himself. He was promised help by the English and the Dutch, who for their own reasons, also wanted to check the advance of Habsburg (and Spanish) power. Later, Sweden and France joined the struggle against Emperor Ferdinand, chiefly for political reasons. During this Thirty Years' War (1618–48) Germany was turned into a ghastly battlefield, fought over by mercenary armies. As time passed, the aims of the warring powers grew ever more blurred.

The Peace of Westphalia, which concluded the war, is a landmark in European history. With the militancy of both Catholics and Protestants reduced by the long struggle, the so-called religious wars came to an end. In Germany the terms of the Peace of Augsburg were restored and extended to include Calvinism as well as Lutheranism and Catholicism. Each prince retained the right to prescribe one of these faiths for his subjects, but conditions throughout the country were so wretched that none of them used force to compel conformity. Thus, a kind of religious "coexistence" emerged from the exhausting struggle.

The end of the wars left Germany in a desperate condition. Having long suffered from political disunity, the country had then endured the ravages of warfare, plunder, famine, and pestilence (typhus). The population had been cut by a *third*, and the loss of property had been severe. At the Peace of Westphalia, the German princes won recognition as independent sovereigns, and the Holy Roman Empire was thus reduced to a shell. Switzerland and the Netherlands, which had once been subject to the Habsburgs, were also recognized as independent states. With the decline of Germany and of Habsburg power, the Bourbon dynasty (founded by Henry IV) took the lead in Europe, and a century of French dominance was at hand.

Thus, Westphalia marked a shift in the balance of dynastic power and the emergence of the modern European state system. Gone were the remains of imperial and papal claims to authority over the political life of Europe; gone was the medieval idea of a unified "Christian commonwealth." The settlement, whose principal provisions held until the Napoleonic Wars (1800), transformed

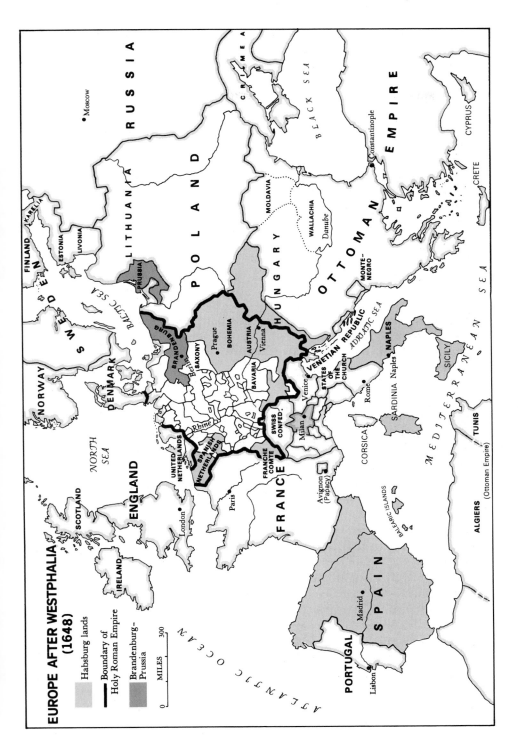

EUROPE AFTER WESTPHALIA (1648)

Habsburg lands

Boundary of Holy Roman Empire

Brandenburg-Prussia

MILES

0   300

the continent into an area of independent states (p. 401), with each free to wage war or make peace and generally to act in a sovereign manner. The earlier Italian practices of diplomacy, alliances, and balance of power were now followed throughout Europe.

The seventeenth century also saw the emergence of the idea and practice of international law, aimed at regulating relations among these independent states. Some rulers, of course, were more careful in following the law than were others, but the law at least provided *standards* that were widely respected. The classic statement of those standards is the *Law of War and Peace* (1625), written by the Dutch lawyer Hugo Grotius — partly in response to the atrocities committed during the Thirty Years' War. Though Grotius recognized war as a "legitimate" state of affairs, he distinguished between just and unjust conflicts and laid down some guidelines for "humane" methods of waging war. Grotius condemned such acts as poisoning wells, mutilating prisoners, and massacring hostages. Drawing on the ancient Roman principles of natural law (p. 119), he also spelled out the rights of neutral states and of *civilians* in war zones.

With later extensions and refinements, Grotius' statement remained the recognized authority on international law until the global upheavals of the twentieth century. The introduction of "total" war and weapons of mass killing have largely bypassed the "law of war and peace" and traditional notions of sovereignty and neutrality.

The Absolute Monarch: Louis XIV

By the end of the Thirty Years' War (1648), nation-states governed by powerful rulers had shown themselves to be stronger than city-states, princedoms, or loose collections of states. France, the wealthiest and most populous of the nation-states, had moved steadily toward political centralization during the fifteenth and sixteenth centuries (pp. 310–12). After a temporary setback following the death of Francis I, the trend toward absolute monarchy proceeded steadily during the seventeenth century. Cardinal Richelieu, the astute minister of Louis XIII, led the way in crushing provincial and aristocratic revolts and in fashioning effective instruments of royal power. His aim, he declared simply, was "to make the king supreme in France and France supreme in Europe." Richelieu died in 1642, but his work was completed during the reign of Louis XIV.

The idea of absolutism was not new, but in Louis it found its most spectacular fulfillment. Having come to the throne as a boy in 1643, he took personal charge of state affairs in 1661. Louis held firm control for half a century, laboring ceaselessly at perfecting his royal image and performing his royal tasks. His style of governing became the model for all Europe, as did the French army, language, manners, and culture.

1328   1589   1792

House of Valois	House of Bourbon

Louis XIV (1661-1715)

Louis ignored the traditional checks on royal power as he concentrated all authority in the *crown*, which became the symbol of national power. (He is credited with having declared, *"L'état, c'est moi,"* or, *"I* am the state.") Louis overawed the nobles (whose fathers had notions of regaining their independence) and used them as officers of his court. His minister of finance, Colbert, strengthened the tax system and promoted economic development. Internal trade was aided by improved roads and waterways; colonies and trading companies were founded overseas; and French industries were sheltered by protective tariffs and export subsidies.

The purpose of Colbert's program was to increase employment, profits, and state revenues — and to secure for France a "favorable balance of trade" with other countries. (This means *selling* goods abroad whose total value is more than that of goods *purchased* abroad; the balance due must then be paid for with gold or silver, which were thought to be especially useful by the monarchs of that day.) Regulation of business was not novel in Europe, for the towns and guilds had practiced it for centuries (pp. 228–29). But the chief economic controls now shifted to the *national* governments; this system came to be called "statism" or "mercantilism." It was well-established in seventeenth-century France and was also practiced, with similar measures, in Spain, Holland, and England.

Louis had a passion for territorial expansion and a love of war and glory. By siphoning off the nation's wealth and manpower into costly military adventures, he spoiled many of the accomplishments of his long reign. His driving desire was to gain and hold France's "natural" frontiers — the Rhine River, the Alps, and the Pyrenees — and he tried, beyond that, to bring Spain under French control. This bold challenge to the European balance of power gave rise to a Grand Alliance of the other leading states against France. Despite the brilliance of his generals and the sacrifices of his subjects, Louis failed to realize his grandiose ambitions. On his death in 1715, France lay exhausted, its military power spent.

Eastern Europe: Prussia, Austria, and Russia

From the sixteenth to the eighteenth centuries as in the Middle Ages, eastern Europe remained a distinctive region, though closely linked to the dominant western countries. During the Middle Ages, two powerful forces had tied eastern and western Europe together: immigration and trade (pp. 282–83). In the following period, the rulers of Hungary, Poland, and Russia continued to welcome German settlers, but by the eighteenth century, most western European emigrants preferred to seek land and religious freedom in North America. On the other hand, the trading links between the two halves of Europe grew stronger than ever. Barred by geography from ready access to worldwide trade and empire, the eastern countries looked to western Europe for overseas products; to pay for these, they sent grain, timber, and cattle westward in ever larger quantities. The rulers and nobles of the region, for whom these exports were their main source of income, redoubled their efforts to control and exploit the producers of these valuable resources: the peasants. By the beginning of the eighteenth century, *serfdom* in eastern Europe, far from dying out, had become more oppressive than it had ever been in the Middle Ages.

In eastern Europe as in the western countries, the leading rulers worked to build up absolute monarchies and struggled with each other for control of territory. Their task was complicated by the facts that the nobles were stronger and more independent-minded than those of western Europe, and that the mixture of religious and ethnic groups in the region made it hard to build truly national states (p. 283). Some rulers, unable to overcome these domestic problems, became vulnerable to external attack. From the late seventeenth century, the formidable Turkish empire went into decline and lost part of its European territory. Poland, a leading contender for power in eastern Europe until the eighteenth century, was actually swallowed up by its rivals (p. 407).

But the ruling dynasties of three other states, the Hohenzollerns of Brandenburg-Prussia, the Habsburgs of Austria, and the Romanovs of Russia, proved more successful. By the end of the eighteenth century they dominated eastern Europe; and they built up states that, at least in terms of military power, could stand comparison with the wealthy imperial countries of western Europe.

The Hohenzollern dynasty rose to power from comparatively small beginnings in the Middle Ages, as vassals of the Holy Roman emperors. The center of their properties was the north German princedom of Brandenburg, but the family also held the territory of Prussia, to the east, and claimed several smaller territories in western Germany. Through the Peace of Westphalia, Prince Frederick William gained additional lands and then spent the rest of his life tightening his control over the family's holdings. Following the example of Richelieu in France, he built up a centralized treasury and civil service and greatly strengthened his army. By 1688, when Frederick William died near his capital of Berlin, Brandenburg-Prussia had become the most efficient state in Germany. His successor joined the coalition against Louis XIV, and the Holy Roman emperor awarded him the title of "King in Prussia" (in addition to Prince of Brandenburg). The higher title soon displaced the lesser one, and the name, Prussia, soon was applied to the whole of the Hohenzollern lands.

During the eighteenth century the Hohenzollern rulers continued to increase their power — regulating economic activities, raising larger and better-equipped armies, and demanding *strict discipline* from their soldiers and subjects. Prussia's landed aristocrats accepted the monarch's authority in return for complete control over their serfs. They also supplied the king with a hereditary officer class. Since the army was essential to the survival of the Prussian state, it enjoyed high status and special privileges. It was at this time that the extreme militarism — "Prussianism" — emerged that was to mark modern Germany's destiny.

Frederick II (the Great), who was crowned king of Prussia in 1740, personified the new ideal of power. A product of the international anarchy and the political cynicism of his time, he became a master of the arts of war and diplomacy. With Machiavellian keenness, Frederick expanded his possessions to the east at the expense of the less efficient Habsburgs of Austria, and the dissolving state of Poland. He proved shrewder than Louis XIV, whom he first looked to as a model. In his palace at Potsdam (whose design had been inspired by Versailles), he could boast at the end of his reign that he had made Prussia a power of the first rank in Europe.

In Austria, the Habsburg rulers of the sixteenth and seventeenth centuries succeeded in maintaining control of their various possessions in spite of rebellions by Protestant nobles and peasants, and in gaining territory at the expense of the Turks (pp. 317, 356). However, their position was weakened by the declining power of the Spanish branch of their family (p. 317), which died out at the end of the seventeenth century. They also suffered from the increasing feebleness of the Holy Roman Empire, of which they were the nominal rulers. Increasingly, they were forced to depend on the resources of the other central and eastern European territories that they ruled; the government of these lands, however, was unwieldy and inefficient. In the eighteenth century, defeats at the hands of Frederick II of Prussia galvanized the Austrian Habsburgs into making administrative and social reforms. Empress Maria Theresa and her son Joseph II made considerable progress in centralizing control of their territories, improving the administrative and tax systems, and limiting noble exploitation of the serfs so that the latter would be able to pay higher taxes to the government. In this way, the Austrian rulers hoped to build up an army that would be a match for Prussia's. Though Habsburg Austria never achieved the degree of unity and discipline to be found in Prussia, it nevertheless counted as one of the leading European powers.

Perhaps the most spectacular change in eastern Europe was the rise of Russia. At the end of the Middle Ages, the principality of Moscow, from which modern Russia originated, had been a tributary state of the Asiatic Tartars (pp. 283–84). But the Muscovite princes were ambitious men, with a strong sense of mission. The Russians, like the other eastern Slav peoples, were Orthodox Christians with strong religious and cultural ties to Constantinople (pp. 155, 213). The Muscovite ruler Ivan the Great (who died in 1505) had married Sophia, the niece of the last Byzantine emperor. Since the Byzantine ruler had been regarded as the legitimate successor of the emperors of ancient Rome,

Ivan accordingly saw himself as heir to that empire. He assumed the title of "tsar" (caesar), and a Russian writer of the period referred to Moscow as the "third Rome." Thus, from early times Moscow was driven by a sense of imperial mission.

Over the generations, in spite of many setbacks, Ivan's successors were true to this mission. In the sixteenth century, they first threw off the overlordship of the Tartars, and then made the Tartars their subjects. Russian colonists penetrated ever farther east into the wilderness of Siberia, until by the beginning of the eighteenth century the tsar's dominions stretched all the way to the Pacific Ocean. At the time, this vast land empire was not nearly as profitable to its owners as the overseas empires of the western countries. All the same, it made Russia what it has remained ever since: a country that dwarfs (geographically) all the other countries of Europe, and whose sheer size has made it impossible to conquer.

From the accession of the Romanov dynasty in 1613, however, the efforts and ambitions of the tsars were mainly focused on Europe. They struggled with two principal competitors, Poland and Sweden, for control of the territories lying between the Black and Baltic seas. Though not always the aggressors in this struggle, the tsars were ultimately the victors. By the end of the seventeenth century, they had reached the coasts of the Black Sea, and were pressing forward to the Baltic. In the eighteenth century, Peter the Great, the most energetic and ruthless of the Romanov tsars, at last broke through.

Russia's rival in the Baltic area itself was Sweden. The Swedes for centuries had sought power beyond their home in Scandinavia: during the Viking era they pushed successfully into the east Slavic heartland (p. 208); later, having absorbed Finland, they fought for control of the Baltic shore across from Sweden. By the sixteenth century, under the Vasa dynasty, the Swedish monarchy had succeeded in making itself the dominant power of the Baltic region. But a grand alliance of eastern states, including Russia, at last put a hold on Swedish imperialism. After a lengthy war, in 1721, Peter took from Sweden the eastern Baltic provinces of Karelia, Estonia, and Livonia (p. 401). In this region, close to the border of Finland, he built a new capital, St. Petersburg (now called Leningrad). This "window on the West" was a symbol of his determination to make his empire into a well-organized state on the western European model.

When Peter died, a bitter struggle broke out between those Russians who supported a Western orientation and those who opposed it. Catherine II, who became tsarina in 1762, looked toward Europe. She had gained the throne after marrying a grandson of Peter; and though she was the daughter of a German nobleman, she devoted herself to the interests of her adopted country. Within the limits of her subjects' toleration, Catherine followed Peter's lead in encouraging Westernization. Forced to compromise with stiff-necked nobles, she never managed to secure the same degree of internal control that prevailed in

France and Prussia. (Her sprawling empire embraced many nationalities, and nine-tenths of its population were serfs.)

In external affairs, Catherine continued the Romanov policy of expanding their power further into Europe. In wars against the Turks, many of whose subjects shared the Orthodox Christianity and Slavic ethnic origins of the Russians (pp. 185–89, 281–82, 284), she extended her territories to the south. On Russia's western frontier, Catherine intervened in the neighboring country of Poland. Once one of the strongest powers in eastern Europe, Poland had gradually been reduced to anarchy and helplessness as a result of the overweening power and endless factional disputes of its nobles, whom the rulers could never bring under control. Between 1772 and 1792, Poland was "partitioned" (divided up) among its neighbors. Russia gained the largest share, and the rest was taken over by Prussia and Austria (partly so as to prevent Russia from advancing still further westward). By the end of the eighteenth century, Russia had become a major force in the power balances of Europe and the Middle East.

For all their successes, Prussia, Austria, and Russia remained in some ways weak and vulnerable. This was partly because the rulers of these eastern European states had built upon societies that were backward and poor compared with the western countries. In spite of the efforts they put into reorganizing their governments, increasing the yield of taxes, and recruiting and training soldiers, the eighteenth-century Hohenzollern, Habsburg, and Romanov rulers could not fight a war for any length of time without massive financial help from Britain or France. (Because these western countries were worldwide rivals — p. 300 — an eastern European ruler could generally get money from one of them, in return for using his or her armed forces against the other.) In spite of their autocratic government, the eastern rulers could not overcome the resistance of their nobles to abolishing serfdom. And this was a reform, as the wiser of these "enlightened despots" well understood, that offered the main hope of modernizing their economies and making their countries truly wealthy and powerful.

A further handicap, for the Habsburgs and Romanovs in particular, was linked to the fact that they had expanded into regions of eastern Europe that were ethnically very mixed. Once-powerful independent nations — Poles, Czechs, Hungarians, Ukrainians, and many others — were now under the rule of foreigners. Russia and Austria were not *national*, but *multinational* states, in which no single ethnic group formed the overwhelming majority.

In the seventeenth and eighteenth centuries, serfdom and the subjection of nations to foreign rulers were generally accepted as legitimate, but in time this would change. Already in the seventeenth century, changes in another area, that of religion, had brought widespread suffering to eastern Europe. The Protestant Reformation and the Roman Catholic countermeasures (Chapter 9) had disrupted the relative religious harmony of the region; tens of thousands had suffered exile or death as a result of systematic campaigns of expulsion and massacre directed by Catholics, Protestants, and Orthodox against each other — and by Catholics and Orthodox against Jews. In the serf societies and multinational states of nineteenth- and twentieth-century eastern Europe, social and national conflicts would arise that would dwarf these earlier religious struggles; instead of tens of thousands, millions of people would be expelled or killed.

Justifications for Absolutism: Bossuet and Hobbes

Absolutism was the predominant form of government in the seventeenth and eighteenth centuries. In those times it appeared superior to other forms for very practical reasons: despots were able to check civil strife within their realms, and in the struggles with competing rulers they could command the full resources of their states. Nevertheless, no form of government enjoys the unquestioned respect of every subject, and absolutism, by its very nature, aimed for total control. Consequently, the despots sought ideological *justification* for absolutism. They wanted to show why it was *right* for subjects to submit to them — no matter what their policies or demands.

The seventeenth-century monarchs might have turned to the absolutist theory of Machiavelli, who had viewed politics as a purely secular art and science (p. 308). This was, indeed, the thought and practice of the new monarchs, but they were themselves too Machiavellian to admit holding to his theory. (Machiavelli had advised rulers to cloak their purposes in piety and religion.) For personal and political reasons, the despots preferred a "higher" justification for their authority; they found it in the doctrine of *divine right*.

This was not, however, a return to medievalism. In the Middle Ages all authority was thought to be sent from heaven, but authority was believed to be *distributed* and *limited*. The theorists of the seventeenth century went further: they sought to reconcile *absolutist* concepts and practices with traditional Christian doctrine. James I of England, the Stuart king who succeeded Elizabeth I in 1603, did not hesitate to speak out for himself. "The state of monarchy," he lectured Parliament, "is the supremest thing on earth, for kings are not only God's lieutenants upon earth, but even by God himself are called gods." Parliament, however, was not to be won over; in fact, time was running out for English defenders of absolutism. (The English Revolution will be discussed in Chapter 11.)

It was in the France of Louis XIV, the "Grand Monarch," that divine right truly held sway. The theory was stated most precisely by a favored bishop of the court, Jacques Bossuet. In a booklet prepared about 1670 for the instruction of Louis's heir (*Politics Drawn from Holy Scripture*), Bossuet set down the royalist arguments. Referring to the Bible as the ultimate truth, he supported his points with appropriate quotations. Royal authority, he concluded, is sacred, fatherly, and absolute. The king's judgment is subject to *no* appeal on earth, and the king must be obeyed for reasons of religion and conscience. Whoever resists the king's command in reality *resists God*. For, declared Bossuet, "the royal throne is not the throne of a man, but the throne of God Himself."

The monarchs of France and other European states found these ideas appealing and, having heard them from childhood, probably believed them. They were less enthusiastic about the *secular* argument for absolutism developed by Thomas Hobbes. An English scholar and philosopher, Hobbes was a royalist who supported the Stuart kings. His writings (around 1650) did them little good; nevertheless, his analysis proved significant for later generations.

Hobbes broke completely with religious traditions and drew instead on the mathematical and scientific advances of his time. (These will be discussed in the next section of this chapter.) In a sense, Hobbes took up where Machiavelli had left off; accepting politics as a purely secular matter, he tried to make of it a deductive *science*. His philosophy rests on materialism and mechanism and reduces the human being to a mere physical machine, the product of complex motion and countermotion. From this it follows that the physiology and psychology of human beings are the true bases of political organization and consequently, the true bases of the state.

Hobbes held that every organism has an instinctive drive for self-preservation. Individuals cannot achieve this goal once and for all, but they can move constantly to enlarge their *means* of security. As Hobbes wrote in his classic study, *Leviathan*, "I put for a general inclination of all mankind, a perpetual and restless desire of power after power, that ceases only in death." In a "state of nature," with no governing (coercive) authority, the general human condition is a "war of every man against every man." To Hobbes such a life was "solitary, poor, nasty, brutish, and short." He did not look at history or primitive cultures to prove his generalizations; his method was logical rather than empirical, *deductive* rather than *inductive*. His dismal picture of the original (precivilized) condition of human beings arose from his assumptions regarding their physical makeup.

Fortunately, said Hobbes, humans have a power of *reason* that enables them to provide an alternative to the *anarchy of nature*. Because they are selfish egoists, unable to trust one another, they cannot create a cooperative society of equals. What they can do is agree to surrender their personal strength to a higher authority, which alone will have the power to curb individual aggression. Hobbes believed that human society, the state, and civilization itself arose from this imaginary "contract" of each individual with all others:

> I authorize and give up my right of governing myself, to this man, or to this assembly of men, on this condition, that you give up your right to him, and authorize all his actions in like manner. . . . This is the generation of that great Leviathan, or rather (to speak more reverently) of that Mortal God [king] to which we owe under the Immortal God, our peace and defense.

Once civil government is established in this manner, all subjects are bound by their contracts to *obey* it. They do so not for moral or religious reasons, but, again, because of the underlying motive of *self*-interest. *Law* is preferable to anarchy — because it better serves the *individual*. Hobbes supported absolute monarchy, or any other authority, on these grounds. But it is clear why his logic was not appreciated by the monarchists of his day. He demolished their claim to divine right and brushed aside all moral arguments, appeals to tradition, and personal sentiments. Though a royalist, Hobbes was, in fact, a most radical Englishman. While defending the *old* (monarchy), he turned people's minds to the *new* (in politics). His thought contains some errors and confusions, but it was a breakthrough in the study of human behavior. And it provided a justification for the modern *authoritarian* state.

THE SCIENTIFIC REVOLUTION OF THE SEVENTEENTH CENTURY

We will turn now to the intellectual changes that influenced Hobbes's ideas and that would have such a profound effect on Western life and thought. By comparison with these changes, the development of political institutions (which absorbed the attention of kings and ministers) was of passing importance. The scientific revolution of the seventeenth century produced a radically different *view of the universe* and a new *mode of thinking*.

The methodology of modern science seems natural enough to educated persons of the twentieth century. Because we are accustomed to it, we do not appreciate how *un*natural it is and how difficult it was to achieve. Yet our scientific method is unique in world history, a very special creation of the human mind. Science may be defined as a series of interconnected concepts and conceptual patterns related to "stubborn facts." It is a fruitful union of precise observation, mathematics, and general principles. Through science, we have penetrated the "mysteries" of nature and have learned to predict and manipulate it.

Our unaided "common sense" could never have produced science (any more than it could have produced theology or philosophy). In fact, one of the greatest barriers to scientific thinking was the tendency of human beings to accept as truth the judgments of their senses. The fantastic world that science reveals to us is often concealed under natural appearances. Through countless centuries, in every corner of the globe, people accepted the "obvious": that the earth, for example, stands still, while the sun and stars wheel past overhead. It was only through a rare combination of circumstances and high creative impulse that science was "invented." The methodology has not been perfected even yet, but it had its principal beginnings during the seventeenth century. The fertile minds of that time produced a stunning intellectual triumph and made the West the teacher of the world.

This achievement rested, of course, on a rich intellectual heritage, starting with the science of the Greeks, which had been recovered in the late Middle Ages. The medieval philosophers added refinement in *logic*; strengthened the idea of an *ordered* universe; and made modest contributions in some scientific fields (pp. 259–60). Then Renaissance men undertook geographical exploration and stressed the precise observation of nature. During the sixteenth and seventeenth centuries instruments for observation were invented or improved; and mathematics, that indispensable tool of the mind, was sharply advanced. Equally important, the founders of science displayed the ability *to see old things in new ways*. The result was the overthrow of a universe — that of Aristotle and Aquinas. As the new universe took form, the methods that produced it became a new way of thinking.

Discoveries of a New Cosmos: Copernicus, Kepler, Galileo

Aristotle's system must be looked at before the revolution of the seventeenth century can be understood. That system was far more in harmony with the world of *appearances* than was the system that would take its place. As adapted by Ptolemy, a second-century Greek astronomer (p. 118), Aristotle's scheme placed the solid, immovable earth at the *center* of things. Rotating about the earth, in perfect circular motion, were the luminous heavenly bodies, each embedded in a transparent sphere (globe). Closest to earth was the sphere that carried the moon; then, at successive intervals, were the spheres of Mercury, Venus, the sun, Mars, Jupiter, Saturn, and the fixed stars. Beyond the sphere of the fixed stars was the Primum Mobile (Prime Mover) — a sphere whose daily rotation from west to east drove all the other spheres in the opposite motion, from *east* to *west*. Beyond the Primum Mobile was the Empyrean (the highest heaven).

This ancient view was accepted into Christian thought and went unchallenged until the sixteenth century. It fitted everyone's ordinary observations, and by means of clever adjustments it could be made to correspond to observed data. Moreover, it suited people's awe of the heavens and their instinct for "rank" by placing the heavenly bodies in a "higher" zone, distinct from the earth. Scholars taught that imperfection and decay ruled over the human zone but that the revolving spheres were governed by a *superior set of laws*. This explained the apparent permanence of the heavenly bodies (in contrast to the temporary nature of things on earth) — and the regularity and harmony of their motions.

Now, Ptolemy was aware of a heliocentric (sun-centered) theory of the universe that had been taught by Aristarchus, an earlier Greek astronomer, in the third century B.C. According to his theory, the apparent motion of the heavenly bodies was due to the *earth's rotation* on its axis. But Ptolemy rejected this theory, as did other astronomers, because it did not fit his recorded observations so well as the geocentric (earth-centered) theory. Further, it was impossible to reconcile Aristarchus' notion of earthly rotation with existing beliefs about *motion*. Again, the authority of Aristotle was decisive. He had held that *earthly* objects remain in a *state of rest* unless they are moved by a *force* and that continued motion requires continued force. Because it was held that these rules did not apply in the heavenly zones, the rotation of the crystalline spheres presented no difficulty. But in the earthly zone, motion depended on force; and the astronomers could find no existing force strong enough to keep the earth's mass *turning*. Because of this, and because of the *appearance* that the earth stood still, the heliocentric theory had failed to convince the ancient thinkers.

Nevertheless, Nicolaus Copernicus revived it in the sixteenth century. A learned Polish cleric with a passionate interest in astronomy, Copernicus grew dissatisfied with the geometrical complexities and discrepancies of Ptolemy's system. He allowed himself to imagine various patterns and found that the *heliocentric* one offered the simplest geometrical explanation of observed movements. His major work, *Concerning the Revolutions of the Celestial Bodies*, was published in the year of his death (1543). Although other astronomers of the time shared his dissatisfaction with the Ptolemaic system, they did not accept the Copernican theory.

Copernicus's book was condemned by religious leaders, including Luther and Calvin, on the grounds that it contradicted Scripture and thus offended God. In one respect his theory was but a limited departure from the accepted view; it did not challenge the "motion mechanics" of Aristotle. Copernicus accepted the idea of the revolving spheres and only exchanged the positions of sun and earth. This alteration, however, upset the traditional view, for it shifted the earth into the *heavenly* zone of laws and forces — and that made his theory unacceptable.

A further objection was that Copernicus could furnish no observational proofs of his belief. If, as he thought, the earth revolved around the sun, then the position of the fixed stars should show a shift when sighted from opposite sides of the earth's orbit. As astronomers know now, they do shift; but the shift is so small (because of the enormous distances) that Copernicus could not detect it. Copernicus also faced a problem that had baffled the ancients: How could he account for a force sufficient to keep the earth in rotation? He offered an answer, but it was hardly persuasive. He argued that it was the "nature" of spheres to rotate and that the earth could not keep from doing so.

It was more than a century before the Copernican theory gained substantial acceptance. Religious criticisms were not the only obstacle; a great deal of observational work had to be done before its correctness could be properly checked. We should remember that Copernicus had no telescope to use in seeking proof for his theory; he worked from the ancient observational data handed down by Ptolemy. His mathematical mind constructed a neater system into which to fit the data, but he failed to reconcile his system with the prevailing physics of his day.

Though Copernicus did not overcome the limitations of traditional science, he inspired later generations to resume the search for a simpler and more satisfying truth. Toward the end of the sixteenth century a Danish astronomer, Tycho Brahe, made new and more comprehensive observations of the skies. These were assembled and analyzed by his co-worker, the brilliant German mathematician Johannes Kepler. As a test of the Copernican theory, Kepler tried to fit Brahe's data on the planets to *circular* courses (orbits) around the sun. When that effort yielded a negative result, he tried fitting the data to *elliptical* orbits. This gave him a positive result, and his finding came to be known as Kepler's First Law (1609).

Kepler next studied the data in order to find if there was *consistency* in *all* planetary motions. His resulting Second and Third Laws hold that every planet, though traveling its course at varying speeds, sweeps out equal areas of its "elliptical plane" in equal times, and that the *square* of the time a planet takes to complete its orbit is proportional to the *cube* of its mean distance from the sun. Kepler thus appears as the first man to work in the manner of modern scientists: he first formulated hypotheses and then tried to check the deduced consequences empirically (by observation). He also bridged the supposed gap between heavenly bodies and the earth by demonstrating the consistency of mathematical relationships *throughout* the solar system. Of still broader significance, he was the first to glimpse the universe as a vast, intricate machine subject to *exact and knowable* laws.

Though Kepler described the movements of the planets in precise mathematical terms, he was less successful in explaining what *made* them move. He assumed that some force might be holding the planets in orbit and moving them continuously along their courses. This force he concluded to be the *sun*. Basing his view largely on the experiments of William Gilbert, an English physicist, Kepler suggested that the planets were magnetic. The sun, he held, was a giant rotating magnet; as it turned it pulled the planets along in their orbits. Here Kepler was clearly reaching toward the modern concepts of *universal gravitation* and *inertia*. But it was left to the Italian genius Galileo Galilei to complete the overthrow of Aristotle, confirm the heliocentric theory, and bring the laws of motion to the point of a grand *synthesis*.

Galileo, a contemporary of Kepler, was less a mathematician and more an observer and experimenter. An astronomer as well as a physicist, he was the first, in 1609, to construct a *telescope* that could be used to examine the heavens. (The instrument had been invented a few years earlier by Dutch lensmakers.) Galileo's telescope was a lead tube about three feet long, with a two-inch glass. Crude and low-powered by modern standards, it nonetheless revealed a world previously unknown to earthlings.

To his excitement, Galileo saw that the planets were not mere points of light but bodies of dimension like the earth and the moon. Venus showed "phases" that corresponded to its position with respect to the sun and earth; this disproved the older notion that the planets were self-lighted, and gave further support for their heliocentric arrangement. By discovering the moons of Jupiter, Galileo provided support for the idea that there could be more than one center for heavenly orbits. And as he peered into the depths of space, looking past the fixed stars, he was overwhelmed by the incredible distances revealed by his telescope. Tens of thousands of stars, previously unseen, came into view, and he was convinced that uncounted millions lay beyond. The "familiar," closed universe of the Greek and Christian worlds vanished forever; earth and humans were now seen as wanderers through dark and boundless space.

The Catholic Church was quick to challenge Galileo's proofs and to condemn his conclusions. Because its authority and doctrines were linked to the Ptolemaic system, it regarded the new ideas as a menace to Christian truth and salvation. To the Church authorities (Catholic *and* Protestant) it mattered not that Copernicus, Kepler, and Galileo were deeply religious men, awed by God's wonders; their teachings contradicted both Scripture and sacred tradition.

Warned to give up his view that the "earth moves," Galileo had managed to keep his convictions private for some time. But he fell into trouble after publishing his *Dialogue on the Two Chief Systems*. In 1633 he was charged with heresy and brought before the Roman Inquisition; threatened with torture, he formally recanted. Through the *Dialogue*, however, his devastating attack on the conventional astronomy continued to spread. The book was placed on the Index (p. 379), along with the works of Copernicus and Kepler, where it remained until 1835. But the banning of a book could not alter the order of the heavens.

After his ordeal before the Inquisition, Galileo was allowed to work quietly in a villa near Florence. During these years he turned to a subject that in itself would not disturb the authorities — but that opened the way to the ultimate victory of the new view of the universe. The subject was *motion*. Though Aristotle's picture of the *heavens* was by now entirely discredited, his beliefs about motion were still accepted. It was clear that the overthrow of his universe must include the rejection of his "motion mechanics," but no one had yet shown how that was to be done.

Earlier in his life Galileo had experimented with *falling bodies*. He later built special structures in order to study the acceleration of polished balls rolling down frictionless wooden surfaces. These permitted him to make more precise measurements of time and distance than he could make when objects were dropped through the air. In 1638 he published the results of his experiments and set forth his general conclusions on the subject of mechanics. He rejected the traditional beliefs that objects are "normally" in a state of rest, that there are "natural" directions of motion for certain substances, and that heavy objects fall faster than light ones.

His observations convinced him that a body in motion (with friction disregarded) continues at a constant speed without any continuing force; a *change* in either velocity or direction *requires* a force. He also found that the distance covered by any falling body is proportional to the square of its time of descent. These conclusions, known today to most schoolchildren, were revolutionary in the seventeenth century. Galileo did not quite see that his "law of falling bodies" was the same law that kept the planets in their orbits. But he completed the overturn of Aristotle's universe and contributed the important new idea of *inertia* (the tendency of objects to remain in their *existing* state of either "rest" or "motion").

Makers of Scientific Method: Bacon, Descartes

Though the most striking accomplishments of the scientific revolution were in astronomy and mechanics, swift advances were taking place along the whole frontier of knowledge. One of the most significant was the development of science itself as a *methodology*. Here two men stand out: Francis Bacon and René Descartes.

Bacon, born in England in 1561, was a man of wide interests, a public official as well as a scholar. But his chief concern was the advancement of learning. He complained of the stagnation of knowledge, blaming the condition on undue reverence for the ancients — above all, as we have seen, on the authority of Aristotle. While Aristotle's ideas were being upset by Kepler and Galileo, Bacon struck at the *root* of his system–its *methodology* — thereby adding force to the intellectual revolution.

Bacon favored the practices of observation and experiment that had sprung up during the Renaissance (pp. 325–26). Experiments in themselves were not new, but he saw in them the foundation for a planned structure of useful knowledge. He criticized Aristotle's reliance on *deduction*, which he viewed as a mere manipulation of words. Bacon's proposed system called for *induction* — that is, repeated experiments that would lead to a *general* statement or conclusion. Following each induction, new observations and experiments would be undertaken that would permit further inductions to be made. In this fashion a *total system* of descriptive truth could be built up, he thought, in a relatively short time.

Bacon was mistaken in many of his own beliefs about nature, but he was confident that future experiments would correct his errors. He also urged scientists to *record* their experiments and to exchange data, in the interest of mutual assistance. Bacon's philosophy and practical suggestions stimulated the budding science of the seventeenth century. True, he subordinated the role of mathematics in scientific activities, but that fault was remedied by the Frenchman, René Descartes.

The advance of science requires, indeed, *two* modes of thought. One of these is induction, stressed by Bacon; the other is deduction, emphasized by Descartes. Descartes's classic *Discourse on Method* appeared in 1637; along with

Bacon's writings, which had been published somewhat earlier, this book gave new direction to both science and philosophy. Descartes and Bacon had at least one thing in common: they were dissatisfied with traditional learning and sought to construct a completely new methodology of knowledge.

Descartes was a brilliant mathematician, and his accomplishments in mathematics affected his approach to knowledge as a whole. A private scholar of independent means, he was disgusted by the absence of certainty and precision that he found in most areas of study. He therefore tried to apply to other subjects the methods of *geometry* and *arithmetic*, which start with "clear and simple" propositions of unquestioned truth. From these propositions, all consequences are *deduced*; plane geometry, for example, is built upon a single axiom (self-evident assumption): "A straight line is the shortest distance between two points."

In adopting the method of mathematics, therefore, one must commence by *doubting* all present ideas ("Cartesian doubt"); the slate must be wiped clean, so to speak. If an idea can be questioned for any reason at all, it must be discarded. Descartes did just that, reducing knowledge to a single idea that he could accept absolutely: "I *think*" — from which he deduced, "therefore, I *exist*." Upon this foundation he set out to construct, by a series of *logical* steps, a complete picture of the universe (including God).

In this ambitious effort, Descartes committed errors and fell short of success. But his rejection of existing knowledge, intellectual authority, and traditional ways of reasoning undermined those old ways of looking at the world. Especially challenging was his vision of a *mechanical* universe governed by *mathematical* rules, a vision that would profoundly influence philosophy and religion as well as science.

The Grand Synthesizer: Newton

The final statement of seventeenth-century science was left to Isaac Newton, who perfected and refined the new cosmic system first outlined by Kepler and Galileo. It was Newton, also, who established the rules of scientific method as a union of Baconian and Cartesian theory. Genius though he was, he could not have accomplished what he did without the knowledge and techniques developed by countless predecessors.

Newton was a simple country youth whose rare talents won him a place at Cambridge University. After earning his degree, he became deeply absorbed in mathematics and shortly developed the system of *calculus*, which is essential for the continuous measurement of complex variable quantities. While still in his twenties, he was appointed professor of mathematics at the university, where he continued his far-ranging research. Motivated by the pure love of knowing, he had little interest in publishing the results of his work. He soon turned his inquiring mind to the puzzles posed by the new astronomy.

Galileo had virtually established the principles of earthly motion but had failed to demonstrate how those principles applied to bodies beyond the earth. Why did the planets move in curved orbits rather than in straight lines? Galileo mistakenly answered that curved motion was as "natural" as straight-line motion and therefore had its own kind of *inertia*. The solution to the mystery, of course, lay in the pull of gravity. While Galileo recognized and gauged the earth's gravity in his observations of falling bodies, he had not made the stupendous leap to the concept of universal gravitation.

Ideas about the magnetic attraction of physical masses had begun to be formulated during the seventeenth century. Around 1600 William Gilbert had built a spherical magnet and had noted that its properties were similar to those of the earth. He reasoned that the heavenly bodies must also resemble the earth in this respect, each one exerting a pull toward its own center. The moon, he said, keeps the same face toward us because of its magnetic attraction to the earth. But the sun, the largest body in the solar system, is the *focus* of magnetic power. It will be recalled that Kepler also held this belief and said that the motion of the planets is due to the sun's rotation (p. 413).

Suspecting that the relation between inertia and gravitation was the key to understanding planetary motion, Newton studied the problem over a period of years. In order to prove his theories, he had to translate masses and motions into mathematical terms. He succeeded in calculating the masses of the sun, the planets, and their satellites. One of the first important consequences of these calculations was his discovery that each planet would travel according to Kepler's laws only if the gravitational pull upon it was inversely proportional to the square of its distance from the sun. He next applied this gravitational formula to the motion of the moon around the earth. Treating the moon as a body with inertial movement in space, he theorized that its curved orbit was due to a continuous "falling" toward the earth. And, after making due allowance for its distance from the earth, he concluded that the moon behaves in the same way as do falling bodies on earth. Newton thus linked Galileo to Kepler, eliminated the barrier between forces acting in space and those on earth, and established by *empirical and mathematical proof* the existence of *universal* laws.

Such was the message of Newton's *Principia (Mathematical Principles of Natural Philosophy)*, published in 1687. In this work he unraveled the mysteries of planetary motions and demonstrated the fact that human beings have the means to achieve far greater understanding. For he demonstrated that, on the basis of experiments conducted in a tiny corner of the universe, and aided by the lever of mathematics, he had discovered the nature of gravitation *everywhere*. Newton was able to express this discovery in the most precise terms: "Every particle of matter in the universe attracts every other particle with a force varying inversely as a square of the distance between them, and directly proportional to the product of their masses." Newton also set down *rules of scientific reasoning* to guide others in finding the fundamental principles embodied in nature, stating those principles mathematically, and in verifying them through observation and experiment.

Not surprisingly, Newton was hailed by his generation as a lawgiver, a scientific Moses. As Alexander Pope put it:

> Nature and nature's laws lay hid in night;
> God said, "Let Newton be," and all was light.

Although the *Principia* was not so widely read as Descartes's more literary *Discourse on Method*, it soon became the undisputed source and symbol of science — the new testament of a new faith. Some of Newton's ideas about matter and motion have been modified by twentieth-century physicists (p. 523), but his methodological principles remain a model.

The Organization of Science

The story of science since Newton has been one of continuous acceleration in the growth of knowledge. Even in Newton's time, discovery was proceeding in numerous fields, and findings in one subject suggested and aided investigations in others. Robert Boyle identified physical "elements" and thereby fathered chemistry. William Harvey explained the function of the heart and the circulation of the blood, thus beginning the science of physiology. The Greek physician Galen (p. 118), whose authority had ruled for centuries, fell from favor; medicine and pharmacy now achieved a scientific foundation.

Rapid strides were also made in optics, and the development of the microscope (as well as the telescope) opened promising new areas of exploration. The microscope paved the way for the sciences of botany and zoology and made it clear that human beings stand near a midpoint on the scale of *size* in the universe — halfway between the giant stars and the tiniest particles of matter. Along with optical devices, various types of instruments were invented for *measurement* — to give experimenters the *precision* they needed. And the idea of the *laboratory*, where experiments could be conducted under controlled conditions, took shape by the end of the seventeenth century.

These developments reflected the growing *interdependence* of scientific investigators and their equipment. The isolated, casual experimenter of the Renaissance (like Leonardo — p. 326), had given way to a new type. No matter how proud or self-centered scientists might become, they fully recognized that science was a *social* enterprise. No one individual or nation was alone responsible; the advance of science was an international achievement that depended on generally accepted procedures and continuous communication among investigators. Curiously, while religion and politics were breaking down into *national* and subnational units, science took the *opposite* direction.

The universities were painfully slow in promoting the new learning. Still in the grip of religious and humanist traditions, they were generally hostile or indifferent to science. In the education of young men, two centuries were to pass before the "classical" curriculum (pp. 322–23) would make room for scientific subjects, and new institutions had to be created for the support and coordination of experimental studies.

The earliest societies for the advancement of *research* were founded in Italy. Rome set up an academy in 1603, of which Galileo was a member; a half-century later the Medici established a scientific institution in Florence. More influential and longer lasting, however, was the Royal Society of London, which was chartered in 1662. It consisted of scientists and mathematicians as well as interested merchants, nobles, and clerics. In an effort to support Francis Bacon's idea for building up a total system of knowledge (p. 415), the society aided experiments, listened to learned discussions, corresponded with foreign societies, and published a scientific journal.

The society was interested in the *practical applications* of science as well as in "pure" research. Bacon himself had declared that the true goal of science was to give human beings greater *power* for human benefit. And Robert Boyle, an early member of the Royal Society, confessed that he did not desire merely to talk and write about nature; he wanted to learn to *master* it. Traditional philosophy, he pointed out, had been barren of practical advantage to humanity. Science, properly understood, would strengthen the useful arts and raise the people's standard of living.

This emphasis on practical applications attracted support from commerce, industry, and government, on the continent as well as in England. Louis XIV, at the suggestion of his finance minister, Colbert, endowed the Academy of Science in 1666, and similar institutions were founded in other European states. Thus, pure science (the search for truth) was wedded to technology (the creation of material goods and control over nature).

THE IMPACT OF SCIENCE ON PHILOSOPHY: THE ENLIGHTENMENT

The link between science and technology could soon be observed in the increased output of workshops and military arsenals. More subtle and complex was the influence of science on the general ideas, values, and attitudes of society. For science gave to educated Westerners a radically new view of their universe and the forces that move it. Most ordinary people, of course, continued to pass their days, as millions of people always have, in childlike innocence of the world of science.

Even illiterate people, however, could not wholly miss the consequences of the change. A new intellectual climate enveloped Europe in the eighteenth century and spread outward to the ends of the earth. The generators of the new

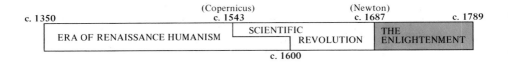

point of view were the educated classes of Europe, whose way of looking at life came from their underlying beliefs about the nature of the universe. While only a few intellectuals were trained scientists, most of them accepted (sooner or later) the scientific description of the natural order. And from this base they proceeded to construct a new philosophy and a new society.

A Revised Cosmology: The "World-Machine"

The scientists themselves had little to do *directly* with the philosophy that took shape during this era. Men like Kepler and Newton tended to be conservative in their religious and social views; Descartes, though a promoter of intellectual doubt, urged people to conform to traditional habits of life. Nor did professionally trained philosophers play a very significant role. The shift in thinking was mainly the work of gifted amateurs — "literary" persons. Most of them were French, and although they did not establish any formal system of philosophy, they came to be known in their country as the *philosophes* (philosophers).

The *philosophes* were so dazzled by Newton's brilliance that they considered themselves living in an unprecedented age of "light." It was this notion that gave rise to the term "Enlightenment" as a name for the period that reached from 1687, the date of Newton's *Principia*, to 1789, the start of the French Revolution. Those who glimpsed the new vision of the universe thought of themselves as the "enlightened" ones, and they were eager to spread the light to others.

The universe they held up to view contrasted sharply with the traditional Christian one. The most evident and disturbing differences were that the new universe was heliocentric and that it extended through boundless space. The devout Catholic mathematician Blaise Pascal had confessed, "I am terrified by the eternal silence of those infinite spaces." But the humanist as well as the Christian felt humbled: the human being was no longer the *center* of nature's plan. The architecture of Newton's universe made humans insignificant, both in time and in space. It was still possible to believe that a personal God existed, that he had a special plan for humanity, and that human life had supreme value. But such a faith was no longer supported by the evidence of astronomy. It seemed, rather, to be *contradicted* by the extravagant dimensions of the cosmos.

Other supports for traditional beliefs collapsed. With Aristotle's laws of motion overthrown, no role remained for a Prime Mover (p. 411), or for

Moving Spirits. The hand of God, which once kept the heavenly bodies in their orbits, had been replaced by universal gravitation. Miracles had no place in a system whose workings were automatic and unvarying. Governed by precise mathematical and mechanical laws, Newton's universe seemed capable of running itself forever.

People had long been familiar with such complex machines as watches and clocks. Was it not logical, after Newton, to believe that the universe itself was a grand machine? Not all its rules of operation had yet been discovered, but scientists knew enough to be able to sketch the nature of the whole. The French astronomer Pierre Laplace expressed the mechanistic idea of the eighteenth century when he said, "Give me the present location and motion of all bodies in the universe, and I will predict their location and motion through all eternity."

The View of God: Deism

If the "enlightened" concept of the universe had profound implications for the meaning of human freedom, responsibility, and ethics, it raised even more disturbing questions about religious convictions. What was to become of the belief in God? Some scientists hailed the marvels revealed by science as a confirmation of the wonders of the Almighty, while others chose to keep their scientific knowledge locked in a tight compartment in their minds, completely insulated from their religious beliefs. But it was extremely difficult to bring the two systems together, to fit Christian teachings and practices into the new cosmology. The "world-machine" had no *need* for supernatural guidance, prayer, priests, sacraments, or penance; these seemed superfluous, if not contradictory.

Churches and synagogues went on as before, with large bodies of followers. The certainty of individual belief may have weakened somewhat, though there was no external evidence of this. Religious leaders at first denounced the new scientific concepts as untrue and subversive; later, when the concepts could no longer be denied, they asserted that such ideas made no difference anyway. (Such responses suggest another sort of "law," which Newton had not set forth: the inertia of *belief systems*.)

Many scientists and intellectuals, however, persuaded that they could not logically reconcile Christianity with scientific truth, rejected the former. This does not mean that they necessarily gave up the idea of God. Newton had explained the *operation* of matter in motion, but he gave no hint of its *origin*. Because common sense still made it difficult for people to think of something as existing that had not been *made*, the question of creation remained unanswered. Here was a role for God that appeared reasonable to the *philosophes*. It also satisfied the urge to believe, which remained a part of their cultural inheritance.

Newton himself stated that the First Cause is not mechanical and suggested that God, "in the beginning," had formed matter in the particular way he desired. Thus, God was referred to in scientific circles as the Creator, the Maker, or the Author. It was equally logical to believe that he had established the governing rules of the universe as well as its substance; hence, he was given such alternative names as the Great Mathematician, the Great Engineer, and the Governor. Though scientists like Newton and Boyle suggested that the Divine Watchmaker might occasionally intervene to correct an irregularity in the operation of the world-machine, their belief was that God had long since removed himself from the affairs of the physical universe. Only *nature* remains, so it is nature that must be understood and respected.

This was a religion of sorts, but it was clearly not Christianity, Judaism, or any other revealed system of belief and worship. Vaguely labeled "Deism," this new religion had been started in the seventeenth century. An Englishman, Lord Herbert of Cherbury, tried to make of it a universal faith that would include and surmount all the others. He posed five basic truths as common to the foremost religions of the world — and not incompatible with science. These were: the existence of a Supreme Power, the necessity of worship, the requirement of good conduct, the benefit of repentance of vices, and the existence of rewards and punishments after death.

Lord Herbert's efforts failed to bring all believers together. He had dreamed of an end to sectarian strife and the beginnings of accord among all people of good will. Though Deism became popular with such eighteenth-century intellectuals as Voltaire, Franklin, and Jefferson, for most churchgoers it was an inadequate substitution for traditional religion. It lacked mystery, ritual, emotional appeal, and discipline. And it was offensive to the clergy of all denominations, for it challenged the authority of their sacred books, doctrines, and offices.

Deism gradually lost its appeal even to the converts of science. By the close of the eighteenth century many of them had decided that there really is no need even for a Creator. Newton had shown that motion is as natural as nonmotion. Is not matter, then, as natural as nonmatter? Was it not old-fashioned to think that things must be *created*? The universe and its motion had always been and always would be. This line of reasoning led some to deny God absolutely *(atheism)*; others said they could not or did not know whether God existed *(skepticism* or *agnosticism)*. Religious doubt was by no means new in Western civilization, but the scientific revolution gave it new vigor and appeal. Though the number of doubters remained small (and the number of *professed* doubters even smaller), they would continue to challenge traditional faiths.

The View of Human Society

If God played an inactive role (or none at all) in the view of the Enlightenment, the place and powers of *humans* were dramatically enlarged. The humanists (pp. 318–20), after recovering from the initial shock of Newton's astronomy, saw that humans became more important as God's role declined. Writers began to emphasize the grandeur of reason, which had enabled human beings to unveil the mysteries of the universe. Though humans could not control its movements, they had touched the cosmos with their minds. And they had, at the same time, vastly expanded their power over life on earth. Through science and technology, they could improve their well-being and press nature itself into their service.

Human beings might be viewed as not only stronger but *better*. The *philosophes* did not deny the existence of evil in human affairs, but they generally blamed it on bad *social institutions*. Nature, as revealed by Newton, is orderly and harmonious. Because of ignorance, however, humans had failed to follow nature's ways and had made customs, laws, sanctions, and beliefs that twisted and shackled the individual. Humans would regain their birthright and exhibit their true character when the chains of unreason were broken.

This growing optimism about human prospects had its roots in the Renaissance, but it was strengthened by the new science. The doctrine of Original Sin appeared out of place in the new cosmos, and the observed laws of motion showed no built-in movement in the direction of evil. Within the boundaries of human freedom, it seemed likely that individuals would choose good rather than bad — so long as they followed nature and reason. Some of the *philosophes* took an extreme position: as knowledge advanced, they held, individuals would become increasingly capable of good, and when at last they reached complete harmony with nature they would be judged perfect. Thus, they concluded, humans are not only good but *perfectible*.

No doctrine of the eighteenth century proved more controversial than this doctrine of human perfectibility. It runs counter to traditional Christian teaching and is hard to reconcile with much of history. The ablest thinkers among the *philosophes* did not accept such an extreme view, but they joined with others in working for social improvement. They became tireless *reformers*, aiming to remake social institutions according to the lights of reason. The "humanitarian" movement, as an organized force, was in large measure a product of eighteenth-century thought. Voltaire in France (pp. 429–30) and the Marquis de Beccaria in Italy, for example, worked for more effective ways of dealing with crime and punishment. The reformers focused attention, too, on helping the poor, the orphaned, the enslaved, and the sick; in these efforts they were often supported by traditional Christians acting in the spirit of holy charity. The *philosophes* worked, above all, for broad freedom of expression, tolerance, and a cosmopolitan outlook.

Faith in Nature and Reason

The humanitarian and ethical goals of the Enlightenment were similar to those of Christianity, and the "rational" criteria of goodness came, in fact, from the Judeo-Christian tradition. But the core of the new cosmology was alien to established religion. Whereas the latter evolved out of centuries of human experience, the philosophy of the Enlightenment sprang from the newly found method and vision of science. The essential differences may be summed up this way: Christianity rests its faith in the power of God as known through *revelation*; the Enlightenment puts its trust in nature as understood through *reason*. The supreme goal of one is *heaven* (spiritual bliss after death); the goal of the other is *progress* (physical happiness in life on earth).

To the ancient Greeks, as well as to the Christians, nature had been an uncertain force, more likely to be hostile than friendly. To the thinkers of the Enlightenment, nature had virtually replaced God and had been shown to be regular and knowable. They believed that the secrets of nature could be discovered and applied usefully to ordinary affairs — the farmer, for example, could make the soil more productive by observing and following physical laws. They believed, too, that legislators and judges could provide justice by applying moral and social "laws" to human relations. This confusion of *moral principles* with *physical laws* was to lead to bitter disappointments.

The eighteenth-century "cult of nature" was an outgrowth of excessive enthusiasm. Respect for the harmonious motions of the heavenly bodies led some philosophers to an unscientific, sentimental attitude toward *all* objects in nature. Alexander Pope (pp. 428–29) attributed to nature a grand intelligence and purpose:

> All Nature is but art, unknown to thee;
> All chance, direction which thou canst not see;
> All discord, harmony not understood;
> All partial evil, universal good.

Others turned to a romantic worship of *wildlife*. Jean-Jacques Rousseau (p. 459) inspired a "back to nature" movement that carried into the nineteenth and twentieth centuries. He helped popularize hiking and camping as ways of bringing one nearer to earth, rocks, and scenery unspoiled by human beings. The cult went so far as to glorify some of the least-civilized individuals and some of the lowliest occupations, on the ground that they were *closer to nature*. Even the French queen Marie Antoinette had a rustic village built for her near the lavish palace of Versailles. There, on sunny days, she and her ladies frolicked as milkmaids.

Most eighteenth-century intellectuals, however, kept their eye on the central idea: the extension of useful knowledge through the exercise of reason. Perhaps the most exciting discovery of the age was that nature behaves in a reasoned, even mathematical, manner; therefore its workings correspond to *human logic*. From this the *philosophes* concluded that reason is the key to nature's secrets and powers and is the proper means of judging and regulating human affairs.

An acceptable model for explaining the working of the mind was supplied by the Englishman John Locke (pp. 448–49). Though interested in science, Locke followed the guide of common sense rather than a strict methodology. He studied medicine, economics, political theory, and philosophy, and he associated with many of the leading political figures of his country. Perhaps because of his familiarity with practical affairs, his writings were readily received by the educated public, and several generations of hard-headed revolutionaries found reassuring arguments in his political writings. His ideas about the nature of human knowledge were especially persuasive, for he rested his case on the ordinary sense experience of his readers. Locke may not have been profound, and he was certainly not scientific. Nevertheless, his writings swept away many ancient beliefs and showed what the "new" reason could do when it was applied to questions about human beings and society.

In his *Essay Concerning Human Understanding* (1690), Locke stated that all knowledge comes from *experience*. This was in line with Bacon's empiricism (p. 415) and challenged long-established convictions that knowledge is *inborn* or *revealed*. Descartes, for instance, held that some ideas are implanted by God, while Socrates and Plato had taught that all knowledge is inborn. According to Christian doctrine, truth is revealed by God.

Locke's theory, however, rested on a very simple model of the mind, whose functioning depended on no concealed or supernatural elements. The mind at birth, said Locke, may be likened to "white paper, void of all characters, without any ideas." The ideas that come to be written on this paper come from but one source: *experience*. By this Locke meant not only immediate sense perceptions (sensation), but the operations of the mind in sorting and arranging those perceptions (reflection). Thus, the intelligent person uses the senses with care and systematically arranges and compares the impressions received through them. These processes are the substance of both reasoning and knowledge, and they enable individuals to understand and control the world about them.

Though Locke's notion of the "thinking machine" was naive (simple), it did call forth further study. Physiologists and psychologists have found that the mind is far more complex than Locke imagined. Still, the Lockean theory proved useful; it suited the eighteenth-century view that people are shaped by their *environment*. According to Locke, ideas are totally dependent on outside stimuli. Hence, if the correct environment is provided, the individual will receive only the "right" ideas. This suggests, in turn, that through the reform of institutions, especially education, rapid improvements can be made in human nature and society.

These beliefs help explain the devotion of eighteenth-century intellectuals to both science and education. To them, ignorance had replaced sin and the devil as the principal enemy. Sinners were to be redeemed not by the grace of God, but by human reason. Research had to be encouraged so that investigators could learn more; education had to be overhauled and extended so that the new knowledge could be carried everywhere. The *philosophes* threw themselves into these endeavors with the enthusiasm of missionaries. They felt that education should be for adults as well as for children. As propagandists of "truth," they took to writing pamphlets, books, and encyclopedias. (The most notable encyclopedist was the brilliant French editor and critic Denis Diderot.) The world would never be quite the same again; the belief in science and education became a feature of the modern world. In the United States, founded at the peak of the Enlightenment, that belief has remained an article of national faith (though it is being questioned today more than ever before).

The Vision of Progress

The extreme apostles of reason had no doubt that they were on the path to paradise on earth. No Christian heaven existed in their philosophy, but they found its counterpart in their vision of *progress* — a vision they expected to fulfill within a few generations.

Progress, as these *philosophes* understood the term, was a new idea in history. The ancients had been more "realistic" in this respect, for they believed that life on earth would always be hard and uncertain. If they wished to think of something better than their own lives, they had looked *backward* rather than forward — to an age of heroes or a Garden of Eden. Christianity had taught that sinful mortals must live in this world as "pilgrims" awaiting perfection in the *world to come*. Even the humanists of the Renaissance, though their estimate of human capacity was higher than that of the ancients, did not believe in the certainty of progress. Erasmus saw folly without end, and Montaigne sought the consolation of books (pp. 328, 348). Perhaps their attachment to the classics confirmed such scholars in their pessimism.

But seventeenth-century science at last broke the spell of antiquity. Scientists began to point out how much more they knew than the ancients. They felt moved to say what was plainly true: it was the Greeks and Romans who were "children" in time; and it was the most recent generations, those who had the advantage of accumulated experience, who were in fact the "ancients." Science thus dissolved the myth of classical superiority in knowledge and, with its new tools, pointed the way toward a grander future.

The Marquis de Condorcet made the most eloquent statement of this unbounded faith in progress. A well-educated nobleman trained in mathematics and science, Condorcet served as secretary of the French Academy of Science. He is especially remembered for his *Progress of the Human Mind*, written, ironically, during a chaotic year of the French Revolution (1794). Though an active reformer, Condorcet had broken with the more radical leaders of the revolution and was then in hiding as a fugitive. But he wrote that his sorrow over temporary injustices and barbarities was overbalanced by his vision of the *future*.

Condorcet's expectation of universal happiness on earth would prove mistaken, but his writing was nonetheless prophetic. He declared that nothing could stop the advance of knowledge and power "as long as the earth occupies its present place in the system of the universe, and as long as the general laws of this system produce neither a general cataclysm nor such changes as will deprive the human race of its present faculties and its present resources." He forecast that rapid technological advances would lead to a world in which "everyone will have less work to do, will produce more, and satisfy his wants more fully." He saw the eventual achievement of *equal rights for women*, the *abolition of poverty*, and the ordering of economic affairs so that *every individual*, guided by reason, could enjoy true independence.

Condorcet proposed a *social-security system* and suggested that population growth would ultimately have to be checked through *birth control*. He also predicted an *end to colonialism and warfare*, declaring that wars would "rank with assassinations as freakish atrocities, humiliating and vile in the eyes of nature." His vigorous optimism, characteristic of the eighteenth-century *philosophes*, marked the high point in the rise of secular values and human self-confidence that had begun in Europe after 1400 (pp. 318–20).

THE RATIONAL SPIRIT IN LITERATURE AND ART

The new ideas in science and philosophy had a marked effect on the literature of the seventeenth and eighteenth centuries. The leading cultural fashion was "classicism," which was an extension of Renaissance ideals — given fresh force by the new stress on logic and universal laws. Bernard Fontenelle, who preceded Condorcet as secretary of the Academy of Science, called attention to the significance of mathematical principles for literature:

> The geometrical spirit is not so tied to geometry that it cannot be detached from it and transported to other branches of knowledge. A work of morals or politics or criticism, perhaps even of eloquence, would be better (other things being equal) if it were done in the style of a geometer. The order, clarity, precision, and exactitude which have been apparent in good books for some time might well have their source in this geometric spirit.

Condorcet insisted that all expression must accept "the yoke of those universal rules of reason and nature which ought to be their guide." The endeavor of writers and artists to apply such rules led to the curbing of the extreme individuality that had developed during the late Renaissance and baroque periods (pp. 346–47, 386–91).

The leaders of classicism sought, through the use of reason, to construct a view of humanity that would be *universally* valid. They also sought to perfect exact *forms* of expression, based on ancient models, and to give to modern languages the precision and charm of classical tongues. Rejecting the force of current usage in determining what is "correct," they looked instead to recognized judges of style and taste. Nicolas Boileau (in France) and Alexander Pope (in England) were respected critics whose opinions were taken as literary *law*. Each wanted to be the Newton of his art.

The advocates of classical standards favored the founding of national academies to promote and enforce those standards. This idea appealed to the monarchs of the period — Louis XIII, for example, created the Académie Française in 1635. Because patronage flowed chiefly from the court and its dependent aristocracy, most writers now felt compelled to observe the official rules of style and taste. The Académie succeeded in imposing classical standards on French writers for more than a century.

Classicism: Racine, Pope

As we saw earlier in this chapter, France was the center of European power and culture during the seventeenth century (pp. 402–3). And in France classicism had its strongest roots, inspiring one of the richest periods in French literature. In addition to philosophical writers like Descartes and Pascal, there were outstanding individuals in every branch of letters. Chief among them was Jean Racine, France's greatest dramatic poet and a leading promoter of classicism.

Educated by a Catholic religious order, Racine received thorough training in Greek and Latin as well as in theology. His middle-class family wanted him to become a priest, but an urge to write poetry took him to Paris in 1663. When a poem written to Louis XIV brought him to the attention of the king, Racine's literary career was begun. He received a post at the court the following year and was elected to the Académie Française in 1673.

The plots of Racine's tragedies were drawn from classical themes and invariably centered on a single moral issue. Like other plays of the period, his were intellectual in nature, with long speeches and little action on stage. He relied on the spoken word to reveal character and passion under stress. The simplicity, precision, and dignity of his poetry brought Voltaire's comment: "Beautiful, sublime, wonderful."

Classicism was expressed in another literary form by Alexander Pope. In *An Essay on Criticism* (1711) he set down his guidelines for critics and, later, in his *An Essay on Man* he put forward in verse a *rationalistic* view of the universe. Pope, an English Catholic by birth, but strongly influenced by Deism (p. 422), tried to reconcile the discoveries of science with the idea of a benevolent God. He stressed the elements of order in nature, which had been confirmed by the mathematics of Newton. But, while admitting the power of reason, he urged his readers to restrain their curiosity and pride: God's works are ultimately beyond understanding; it is best to accept one's limited place in the scheme of things and to believe that "Whatever is, is Right."

Pope's *Essay on Man* is classical in form as well as substance. It consists of hundreds of rhyming couplets, many of which are cleverly turned and well-remembered:

> Know then thyself, presume not God to scan;
> The proper study of mankind is man.
>
> Hope springs eternal in the human breast;
> Man never is, but always to be blest.

The work as a whole illustrates the strengths and weaknesses of *didactic* verse (poetry with a "message") — and the classic *form*. Strict form has a power and beauty in itself; at the same time, it may limit the development of ideas and feelings.

Satire: Voltaire

Literature in the eighteenth century, responding to the Enlightenment, reached out to an ever-widening public. The classicists, like Pope and Racine, had written mainly for the royal court and a small group of educated readers. The *philosophes*, however, were less interested in the refinement of literature than in the circulation of new ideas. With literacy on the rise, they found that men and women of all classes, but especially the bourgeois, wanted to be informed. A group of writers appeared whose chief aim was to digest important ideas and put them in readable form for "the public." Along with encyclopedias, dictionaries, and surveys of knowledge, there was a rapid spread of newspapers and magazines.

The most successful and famous of the new writers was Voltaire; he was, in fact, one of the first individuals to make a fortune by his pen alone. The son of a Parisian lawyer, he was schooled by Jesuits, who evidently sharpened his talent for argumentation. Though he was formally trained in law in his homeland, his real education began in England. In trouble in France because he had insulted a nobleman, Voltaire accepted exile across the Channel in 1726. Through private study and conversation he quickly absorbed the ideas of English philosophy and politics.

When Voltaire returned to France, he began to write all sorts of works — plays, histories, poems, scientific surveys, and philosophical essays. The best known and most widely read of his more than a hundred books is the satirical novel *Candide* (1759), which reflects his reasoned outlook, his irony, and his strong convictions. The story is a swift-moving, rollicking caricature of an idea popularized by Pope — that "this is the best of all possible worlds." The "hero," Candide, is an innocent young man who has been brought up to believe that *everything is for the best*. In the course of incredible misadventures he learns differently. At the story's end, Candide and his companions are living on a small farm trying to shut out the stupidities and indecencies of the world. One of them concludes that the only way to do this is to "lose oneself" in some form of satisfying work. "It's the only way to make life endurable."

In the course of the novel, Voltaire struck out with rapier (and bludgeon) at many targets: the bigotry and hypocrisy of organized religion, the atrocities of war, the "inhumanity of man to man." He expressed contempt for arbitrary authority and disgust with ignorance and prejudice. Though a man of the Enlightenment, he criticized many of the new ideas as well: he ridiculed "pseudo" reason, which spins out unsupportable theories and seeks to find "cause" and "effect" in every event; scoffed at the nature cult; and turned the dream of "progress" into a nightmare.

Yet Voltaire had faith in the method of science and the power of reason. He stood courageously for freedom of expression; he admired simple honesty, moderation, humaneness, and tolerance. "Tolerance," he wrote in his *Philosophical Dictionary* (1764), "is the natural attribute of humanity. We are all formed of weakness and error; let us pardon reciprocally each other's folly. That is the first law of nature. It is clear that the individual who persecutes a man, his brother, because he is not of the same opinion, is a monster." If Voltaire sometimes grew bitter, it was because the world seemed so full of what he hated and so empty of what he loved. Like Erasmus, he was no revolutionist, but he and his fellow *philosophes* nevertheless helped prepare the ground for revolution.

The Architecture of Reason: Wren, Jefferson

The Enlightenment was only partly reflected in the visual arts. On the continent, the style of baroque architecture (pp. 386–91) carried over into the eighteenth century and was gradually modified into the lighter, more delicate style of "rococo" (shell-like). Both styles were elaborate and elegant, suited to the pomp of monarchs and aristocrats. By 1750, however, the *classical* spirit in the other arts led architects back to the simplicity of Roman and Greek models.

In England, the baroque had been more restrained, and the return to classicism came earlier there than on the continent. The most influential architect of the time was Christopher Wren. The Great Fire of London (1666) gave him a unique opportunity; as the king's principal architect, he was charged with replanning the city and rebuilding St. Paul's Cathedral. As might be expected, Wren had to accept many compromises, and his master plan for London was never realized. He did, however, succeed in having many of the city's churches constructed according to his designs.

Wren's triumph was St. Paul's *(Fig. 10-2)*, completed in 1710. The clergy had wanted a tall Gothic building (like Chartres Cathedral — p. 172), but he won approval for a plan that was essentially classical. Wren was influenced by Michelangelo's plan for St. Peter's and by later Italian architects, but he shunned the curving lines and extravagance of the baroque. He desired a simple though impressive structure crowned by a great dome. In order to satisfy

10-2 Wren. St. Paul's Cathedral, London.

the clergy, he placed tall bell towers above his classical façade and a tall "lantern" on top of the dome. The result was something of a hybrid, though Wren strove to preserve the basic harmony of the plan.

In his designs for parish churches Wren again came into conflict with his clients. The churchmen wanted tall Gothic spires, symbolic of Christian striving. Wren wanted simple, classical structures. The problem of combining the vertical thrust of the Gothic with the horizontal line of the classical was formidable, but somehow he managed to solve it. A well-preserved church of Wren's style and generation is James Gibb's St. Martin's-in-the-Fields *(Fig. 10-3)*. This church and others like it became models for churches in both England and America.

Subsequently, the trend was toward a strict classicism. The preferred manual of taste was now a book by the Renaissance architect Andrea Palladio, who had methodically measured ancient ruins. The "Palladian manner," with its Roman-style porches, rotundas (circular halls), and domes, became the standard for eighteenth-century England. Noblemen who built villas in this style believed that their homes were a reflection of an age of reason — the reason of

10-3 Gibbs. St. Martin's-in-the-Fields, London. Engraving drawn by Thomas Shepherd, engraved by H. W. Bond.

Newton and Pope. In the second half of the century, admiration for ancient architecture was further stimulated by the excavation of the Roman cities of Pompeii and Herculaneum (at the foot of Mount Vesuvius). The beauty and grace revealed in those ancient buildings had a powerful effect upon the houses, furnishings, and dress of the well-to-do.

Thomas Jefferson was one of the many intellectuals who became enamored of the classical style. On a visit to France in the 1780s he saw the ancient Roman temple, the "Maison Carrée" *(Fig. 10-4)*, in the provincial town of Nîmes. He reported that he gazed at it for hours at a time, "like a lover at his mistress." When Jefferson returned to America, he designed numerous public and private buildings, thus popularizing the classical style in America. His plan for the Virginia state capitol at Richmond *(Fig. 10-5)* was inspired by the Maison Carrée, and his designs for the Rotunda of the University of Virginia and his home at Monticello were patterned after the Roman Pantheon *(Fig. 3-4, p. 125)*. The public architecture of Washington, D.C., has borne the impress of Jefferson and the classical revival. Officials of the new nation were proud to demonstrate visually their enthusiasm for the Enlightenment and its ideals of reason and order.

The leaders of the French Revolution also favored Roman models. And the revolutionary heir, Napoleon (pp. 462–65), continued to support the style for personal reasons: he thought it fitting to his role as a "modern Caesar," and he wished to distinguish his own monuments from the baroque structures of

10-4 Maison Carrée, Nîmes, France.

10-5 State Capitol, Richmond, Virginia.

the French kings who had preceded him in power. Classicism thereby carried over to the nineteenth century. It was followed by a Gothic revival, which was an expression of the nineteenth-century *reaction* against the ideals of the Enlightenment.

Academy Painting: Portraits of Aristocratic Elegance

Painting, of all the arts, was least affected by the radical changes in science and philosophy. In the seventeenth century classical rules had continued to govern; during the eighteenth century the rules became less rigid. The painters of France, supported largely by royal and aristocratic patronage, were serving a doomed social order. But their works show no sign of an impending calamity and are marked by unique charm, repose, and grace.

The Belgian master Antoine Watteau was the finest representative of the eighteenth-century style known as *rococo*. He came to Paris in 1715 and went to work on various projects for the nobility. As a designer of interior decorations for courtly festivals and pageants, Watteau caught the spirit of refined ease and gallantry associated with the aristocratic ideal. He began to create oil paintings of picnics in the woods, music parties, and mythical scenes peopled by graceful ladies and gentlemen in lustrous silks and satins (*Fig. 10-6*). But these are not

10-6 Watteau. *Music Party*, ca. 1719. Wallace Collection, London.

lifelike portrayals. They arise out of a dream world, where ugliness is absent and beauty touches all.

Watteau worked, like his fellow artists in France, under the watcheful eye of the Academy of Painting. Yet his paintings have an unmistakable individuality — with an air of melancholy. Destined to die in his thirties of tuberculosis, Watteau seems to have sensed the fleeting character of life and beauty.

More sensual and lighthearted (but no more realistic) were the paintings of François Boucher and Jean Fragonard (*Fig. 10-7*). These artists painted mythical subjects and the frivolities of the nobility in a delicate and delightful manner. Their works, corresponding to the aims and taste of their patrons, had no important function other than playful entertainment.

Painting in England was more sober and solid. The leading figure there was Joshua Reynolds, who became the first president of the Royal Academy of

10-7 Fragonard. *The Meeting*, 1773. Frick Collection, New York.

Art (1768). Reynolds is best known for his portraits of the wealthy and for his support of traditional "laws" of painting. "I would chiefly recommend," he told the Academy, "that an implicit obedience to the Rules of Art, as established by the practice of the great Masters, should be exacted from the young students." He regarded the Italian Renaissance, rather than ancient Greece or Rome, as the "classic" source for the rules of painting. But he agreed with the classicists that there existed *universal* standards of taste and excellence.

The English upper classes were willing to pay a good price to have their portraits painted in the grand manner. Reynolds felt that historical or mythological subjects offered a greater challenge to his intellect, but he made his fortune by painting the rich. With high skill in texture and composition, he created hundreds of flattering portraits. His *Duchess of Hamilton* (*Fig. 10-8*) is typical of Reynolds's "classical" style.

10-8 Reynolds. *Duchess of Hamilton.* The Trustees of the Lady Lever Art Gallery, Port Sunlight, Cheshire, England.

THE CLASSICAL AGE OF MUSIC

The seventeenth and eighteenth centuries, taken together, constitute the classical age of European music; during that formative period most of our modern instruments and forms of composition were established. If, however, we use the term "classical" in a narrower sense — meaning the musical *style* corresponding to the style of classical literature and architecture — we find that it applies to the *eighteenth* century only. The music of that century, as we shall see, echoed the general accent on order, balance, and restraint. Seventeenth-century music, on the other hand, is usually called "baroque," because its variety and power corresponded to similar elements in baroque art and architecture (pp. 382–83, 386–91).

Music in Western Civilization

Music has always been a vital part of the life and expression of Western culture. If we have given it slight attention in our account of ancient and medieval civilizations, it is because we have so little information about the musical instruments and compositions of those times. Almost all the music and instruments we hear today go back no further than the Renaissance. Yet ancient and medieval peoples believed that music had important powers, and they used it for both sacred and secular purposes.

In prehistoric cultures music was regarded primarily as a vehicle of *magic*. Singing and playing on a variety of simple instruments were intended to win supernatural assistance for the individual or the tribe. Certain types of music were thought to lend strength in battle; others promoted fertility; still others preserved health or drove away sickness. With the rise of early civilizations, music began to be viewed also as a medium of pleasure and moral uplift. The further development of music as an art "for its own sake" ranks, in fact, as one of the prime achievements of the human spirit.

Though we possess only a few fragments of ancient Greek music, we know that music held a high place in the Greek scale of values. Belief in its power is symbolized by the ancient myth of Orpheus; his playing on the lyre (harp) tamed wild animals and even secured the rescue of his wife, Eurydice, from the underworld. Music was customarily used also to heal sick bodies and minds and was thought to influence the development of character and temperament. Thus, we find that the study of music was fundamental to Greek education. Aristotle stressed the psychological impact of various combinations of harmony and rhythm: some depressed the emotions, some inspired enthusiasm, while others produced a moderate mood.

Greek music, like that of the Orient, was primarily vocal, as might be expected of the Greeks, who were a highly verbal people. (Plato considered melody and rhythm useless, except as accompaniment for *words*.) Instrumental music was therefore neglected, and singing was confined to a simple tune (*mono*phony) with no harmonizing chords. The monophonic pattern is still characteristic of music outside Western civilization, but complex melodic forms (*poly*phony) began to appear in the West around A.D. 1000.

Most Greeks were amateur musicians, but there were professional singers and players as well. Wandering poets recited or sang their tales to the accompaniment of the lyre (pp. 73–75). The only other standard instrument was the pipes, which usually consisted of two slender tubes joined at the player's mouth. Its sound, scholars believe, was something like that of the modern oboe. Playing and singing were indispensable to Greek religious and civic processions, and they were vital parts of the drama, that high achievement of Hellenic art and intellect. The actors chanted their poetic lines, and the chorus sang and danced solemnly according to set steps and patterns (p. 76).

We know little about the music of ancient Italy, except that the Romans readily adopted Greek forms. We know, too, that they contributed a family of instruments, the military horns. Later, the Roman papacy was responsible for passing on a portion of the musical heritage of antiquity to western Europe. Pope Gregory the Great, the leading figure in shaping the medieval Church, collected and organized Christian sacred music in the sixth century.

This music had originated in a variety of oriental sources, chiefly Hebrew. Exclusively vocal, it was used only in liturgical services (the Mass) and canonical prayers (the Offices), and it was sung by the priest, the choir, or the congregation. It consisted of a monophonic chant, or plainsong. The music collected by Gregory or attributed to him is known as the Gregorian chant. For centuries it has been the principal sacred music of the Roman Catholic Church.

We have reason to believe that secular as well as religious music was popular during the sixth century, but most of it seems to have disappeared in the disorders of the early Middle Ages. There was a cultural recovery, however, from the tenth century onward. Poems and songs were presented by wandering scholars, who called themselves Goliards (p. 261). Still later came the troubadours, who composed and sang love songs and romances of chivalry (p. 263). They, too, used only the monophonic form with simple accompaniment.

Polyphony ("part" singing) had its beginnings in the tenth century. This more complex form demanded a superior means of *musical notation*, and during the twelfth and thirteenth centuries the basis was laid for the modern system, with its staff, time signature, and syllables. Meanwhile, new instruments were appearing. Most important were the clavichord and the harpsichord, the forerunners of the piano. The pipe organ, which was commonly used to accompany sacred music, underwent successive improvements.

During the Renaissance, polyphony reached its full development in both sacred and secular music. It was applied to scriptural texts, Masses, and to dramas of the Lord's Passion. The most popular songs were "madrigals," which consisted of secular poems put into "part" singing. Instrumental music (written mainly for dances) also gained favor. The recorder, a wooden relative of the flute, was introduced at this time, while the most common stringed instrument was the lute, similar to a mandolin. Most of the instruments of the period are no longer in general use, although we sometimes hear performances on re-created instruments of the period. More often we hear this music adapted to modern instruments.

Birth of the "Modern" Style: Monteverdi, Bach

The transformation of music to its "modern" form began rather late in the Renaissance and reached full force during the baroque era of the seventeenth century. So sweeping were their innovations that the baroque composers believed they were bringing about a musical revolution. In fact, they referred to the Renaissance manner as the "old style" (in Italian, *stile antico*) and to their own as the "modern style" (*stile moderno*).

In contrast to the even-tempered, complex themes of traditional polyphony, baroque compositions were marked by a heavier stress on a dominant melody. Elaborate harmonic chords and dramatic effects were also characteristic, and, in order to create a wider range of tonal effects, larger numbers and types of instruments were used: flutes, oboes, trumpets, and bassoons, as well as violas, violins, and the harpsichord. Composers now began to write instrumental music for *listening*, not just for dancing. Reflecting the growing social role of the bourgeois, concerts were held in public halls as well as in the private courts of royalty and nobility. This was a secular age, and secular music now became as important as sacred music.

Perhaps the most important cultural development of the time was the appearance of a new art form: the opera. This "music drama," consisting of expressive speech heightened by melody and rhythm, originated in Italy. Its chief creator was Claudio Monteverdi, who had spent the earlier years of his life writing madrigals and Masses but who in middle age turned enthusiastically to the modern style. The most appealing of his operas, *Orfeo (Orpheus)*, was first performed in 1607. Exhibiting most of the elements of modern opera, it contained the first operatic overture (musical introduction) and a number of instrumental passages to heighten dramatic action. Monteverdi, who was also a singer, viol player, and conductor, supported the operatic action with an effective combination of instruments. His ensemble (musical group) was close to that of the modern orchestra.

Opera, however, did not find a ready acceptance outside Italy. Nearly a century passed before the new art form spread north of the Alps, thanks partly to the work of George Frideric Handel (born 1685). Of German origin, Handel spent much of his youth in Italy before settling in England. Admired by the king and aristocracy who acted as his patrons — and beloved also by the growing English middle classes who attended his performances — Handel was enormously successful in his adopted country, and died a wealthy man.

Endlessly prolific and versatile, Handel could express in music almost any situation and emotion. These ranged from the sensual passion that marks many of his operas, through the magnificence of his works for royal occasions such as the *Water Music*, to the religious grandeur of his sacred music, notably the oratorio *Messiah*.

Meanwhile, another prolific German composer was writing in every form except opera. Johann Sebastian Bach (also born in 1685) is a giant of the baroque period and one of the great musicians of all time. A devout Lutheran, he composed profound and inspiring scores for religious texts (cantatas and oratorios), Masses, and Passions. Bach was equally talented in secular music, creating superb pieces (chamber music) for performance by small groups at aristocratic courts. He is notable for the power and grandeur of his expression and for his mastery of polyphonic themes.

The Classical Spirit: Mozart

The death of Bach in 1750 marked the end of the baroque and the beginning of yet another style of musical expression. As in the visual arts, a reaction had set in against the elaborateness and the complexity of seventeenth-century music. The Enlightenment valued rationality, clarity, and restraint; in France, the Academy of Music attempted to impose these qualities in a manner similar to that of the Academy of Painting. Melodies and rhythms were simplified, and form rather than content was stressed. Music, the classicists believed, should not be disturbing but should express balance and repose through perfect craftsmanship. The compositions of this era, which were mainly secular, were designed for enjoyable listening. They appealed as much to the intellect as to the heart.

Not surprisingly, instrumental music was more highly regarded than singing. The sections of the modern orchestra were well established during the eighteenth century, when the first important symphonies were written. Most popular, however, was music intended for *chamber* performances, normally given in small halls. The string quartet was the leading new musical form; the violin was the chief ensemble instrument, and the piano was the foremost keyboard instrument.

Among the most gifted of all the classical composers were Franz Joseph Haydn and Wolfgang Amadeus Mozart, both Austrians. Haydn, the light-hearted Viennese composer, brought the chamber and symphonic forms to a high point of perfection and in doing so created works of enduring appeal. Mozart, a child prodigy, was composing serious works before the age of five. Though he died in poverty in 1791, at the age of thirty-five, he created an astonishing number of magnificent compositions.

Mozart was himself a superb harpsichordist and pianist and wrote many pieces for keyboard instruments. He was a master of all types of composition, however, and displayed the clarity and grace of classicism at its best. But his ultimate triumph was in opera, where his understanding of human character combined with his gift for melody to produce immortal works. Among his most popular operas today are *Don Giovanni*, *The Marriage of Figaro*, and *The Magic Flute*. Though he was truly a man of the eighteenth century, trained in classicism, Mozart transcended both the style and the age.

CHAPTER
11

The Revolutions of
Liberalism and Nationalism

The eighteenth century — classical, rational, and aristocratic — marked the high point of a whole era of European history. Order, balance, and reason were the passwords of the day. Yet reason, joined with science, was undermining the foundations of the old ways. When the *philosophes* (p. 420) turned the light of reason on the culture and society of this age, they exposed its institutions to harsh criticism. The impact of the new science on religion has already been described (pp. 421–22); attacks upon royal absolutism were also being started. Clearly, an atmosphere leading toward political and social revolution had developed during the years of the Enlightenment.

Many people found the new atmosphere exciting. This was particularly true of the *bourgeois* — businessmen, property-owners, lawyers, civil officials — who were to play an important role in the revolutionary movements of the eighteenth and nineteenth centuries. In fact, this *middle class* embodied the forces that had been rising since the late Middle Ages — capitalism, materialism, secularism, and individualism (pp. 284–90). In the language of the eighteenth century, the bourgeois sought "liberty" and "equality." But these words had a very special meaning for them.

In economic terms, liberty meant the freedom of entrepreneurs from the restraints of *mercantilism*. In *political* terms as well, liberty had a narrowly restricted meaning. Voltaire saw it as a right of the educated classes: to speak freely, publish, hold property, and be protected by the law. None of these things, he thought, had much to do with the working classes, who were generally too "stupid and brutal" even to be aware of such matters. Most of the *philosophes* shared Voltaire's view, and not until a century afterward did the idea of liberty — full liberty for *all* people — begin to take hold.

Similarly, the idea of equality must be understood in its bourgeois sense. The middle class, bitterly resentful of the privileges of the aristocracy in law and property, sought to rise to equality of status with the landed nobility; and to this end it put forward, with passion, the doctrines of natural law and universal rights. With few exceptions, however, the bourgeois did not want the lower classes to rise to equality with themselves.

What came to be known as "liberalism" was a mixture of these and related ideas, centered upon individual liberty and equality (in the bourgeois sense) and faith in reason and progress. Liberalism was never a unified ideology; it had a wide range of interpreters. One area of agreement clearly emerged, however: liberalism was opposed to *hereditary privilege* and *political absolutism*.

Because those who hold power rarely surrender it voluntarily, a clash of forces became certain. The initial challenge to absolutism occurred during the seventeenth century in England, and the success of that challenge brought into being the first "liberal" state. About a century afterward, liberal forces erupted in North America and in France. These three revolutions inaugurated a new political order in Western civilization. Each had its own set of causes, and each followed its own course, but the end result of all three was to extend personal freedom and equality of rights to more and more people.

The clash between liberalism and absolutism, however, was not a clear-cut struggle between two uncompromising opponents. Though the liberal middle classes were united in opposition to hereditary privilege and political absolutism, they disliked revolutionary dictatorship and social anarchy just as much. For this reason, every revolution began with "moderates" in control, who tried to set limits to their own revolutions. In England, France, and other European countries that eventually underwent revolutions, these efforts were unsuccessful — in contrast to North America, which did indeed undergo a "limited" revolution. Many European middle-class revolutionaries, terrified by the forces they had unleashed, ended by cooperating with kings and nobles to bring about "restorations" — that is, more or less reformed versions of the social and political order they had originally hoped to abolish.

As for the kings and nobles, very few of them were idealistic enough to wish to surrender their privileges and power. Particularly after the French Revolution brought violent change to the mainland of Europe, their instinctive reaction was to meet liberalism with repression and force. But often, their instincts were overruled by considerations of realism and tactical prudence, which led them to accept or even sponsor liberal reforms. They did so in order to avoid revolutions that might overthrow them; or as the price for being restored to power once overthrown; or simply in order to make their countries more stable and efficient — and hence stronger — than those of rival rulers. Several of the greatest social and political changes of the eighteenth and nineteenth centuries, such as the abolition of serfdom in the countries of eastern Europe or the national unification of Germany, were brought about principally by monarchs who had come to believe that only by such measures could they hold on to power at home and strengthen themselves against foreign rivals.

With all these factors both pushing liberalism and nationalism forward and holding them back, it is not surprising that their spread was a lengthy yet inexorable process. In the short term, the English, French, and other European revolutions of the seventeenth to nineteenth centuries all fell more or less short of fulfilling the aims of their originators. But by the twentieth century, the social and political order that had developed fifteen hundred years earlier — out of the merging of Greek and Roman civilization and the warrior societies of barbarian Europe (Chapter 5) — was finally dead.

The liberal movements had a further result: they established the principle of *revolution* in the modern world. Civil struggles and seizures of power were of themselves nothing new, but the extent and success of the liberal struggles — and the influence of their defenders, from Locke to Robespierre — made revolution a *human right*. And time would show that the makers of these revolutions could no more restrict this right to themselves than they could restrict the rights of liberty and equality. The *collectivist* revolutions of the twentieth century (pp. 558–76) — shocking to many upholders of the *liberal* tradition — found their justification, in large part, in the precedent and justifications of the liberal revolutions.

THE ENGLISH REVOLUTION: PARLIAMENTARY SUPREMACY AND THE BILL OF RIGHTS

The English Revolution of the seventeenth century arose from a mixture of political, social, and religious tensions. In the wake of the Reformation (pp. 369–75), religious issues continued uppermost in many minds; and, as most of the king's opponents were of Puritan (Calvinist) leanings, the term "Puritan" was attached to the revolution. This revolution clearly was more than a struggle for liberalism, but it shared many of the aims of later liberal revolutions in America and France. Equally important, John Locke's *justification* of the English Revolution contributed to liberal ideology everywhere.

Challenge to the Divine Right of Kings: The Civil War and Cromwell

Why did absolutism fall into disfavor in England after having been strongly supported since the time of Henry VII (p. 314)? One reason seems to be that the middle class and other commoners had backed the monarch in his efforts to end the near anarchy of feudalism, but once order had been established they were eager to reduce his authority. Tudor despotism died with Elizabeth I in 1603. She was succeeded by her nearest relative, James I of the Stuart family, who was already king of Scotland. (England and Scotland remained separate kingdoms, though ruled by one and the same monarch, down to 1708, when they merged to form the "United Kingdom" of Britain.) James upheld the royal tradition of *divine right* (p. 408), but he was not an Elizabeth or a Henry: he failed to win the personal following they had enjoyed, and Parliament (p. 313) refused to agree to his demands. The House of Commons consisted of elected representatives of the gentry (small to medium rural land-holders) and of middle-class townsmen. Most of them were Puritan Dissenters, and they had no affection for the highly structured Church of England (p. 371). Moreover, they disapproved of James's foreign policies and his extrava-gance. When he asked them to approve new taxes to support his projects, they stubbornly refused. And so James governed without Parliament during most of his reign.

James's son, Charles I, fared worse. His insistence on his divine right to govern won little response from Parliament. Unable to make Parliament do his bidding on new taxes, he resorted to forced "loans" and to increases of estab-lished taxes. Resentment toward Charles was aggravated by what the House of Commons considered his violation of English constitutional traditions that went back to the Magna Carta of 1215. This "Great Charter," the first *written* statement of feudal liberties, had been signed by King John upon the demand of rebellious nobles. In it, he accepted strict limitations on royal authority and guaranteed the customary rights of all free subjects. When Charles summoned a Parliament in 1640, after a decade of ruling without one, the stage was set for an open clash between the king and his opponents.

The Long Parliament (as it was later called) proceeded to enact measures against the king's ministers and against the king's exercise of illegal power. When, in 1642, Charles tried to arrest the parliamentary leaders, the House of Commons answered by raising a citizens' army for its own protection. Charles, with a minority of the Commons and most of the House of Lords, then with-drew to Oxford; the rest of the Commons held London and prepared for war.

The loyalties of the English people during the struggle followed no fixed lines of social class or religious affiliation. In the main, however, Charles was supported by the great nobles, the high clergy of the Anglican Church, and the Roman Catholics. Parliament was backed by the bourgeois, by most of the gentry, and by Puritan Dissenters from the Anglican Church. In strictly politi-cal terms, the Civil War was a showdown between two rival power groups and two theories of government. The king and his hereditary lords were defending their privileges and the idea of absolute *monarchy*; Parliament, representing the smaller landholders and businessmen, was fighting for rule by a broadened *aristocracy*.

In the test of arms, the parliamentary forces kept control of the chief cities and seaports and enjoyed the support of the navy. On land, their campaigns were fought by a "new model" army, which had been organized by Oliver Cromwell—a landowner, a militant Puritan, and a member of Parliament.

1485		1603	1642	1660	1714
House of Tudor		House of Stuart	CIVIL WAR AND CROMWELL	House of Stuart Restored	

The first *citizen army* to be recruited in the era of revolutions, this force consisted chiefly of volunteer yeomen (independent farmers), who disliked royal absolutism and the established Church. Showing Puritanical zeal and discipline, Cromwell's army decisively defeated Charles's forces in 1646.

But the victorious coalition could not agree on what to do next. Cromwell and his army fell out with the majority of Parliament over questions of religion and the future of the king. Calvinism replaced Anglicanism as the state religion for a few years, but in 1649 a limited sort of *religious toleration* was adopted. Leadership of the revolution fell more and more upon Cromwell himself. At last he decided that Charles must be executed, on the grounds that he was untrustworthy and attracted "ungodly" persons to his cause. When Parliament balked, Cromwell drove out the members who opposed him. The surviving "Rump" Parliament of some sixty members put the king on trial and had him executed in 1649. It then declared the title and office of king abolished and proclaimed England a *republic* (the "Commonwealth").

The beheading of Charles was a psychological shock to most of the English, who still believed (with Shakespeare) that "divinity doth hedge a king." The execution was the work of a determined minority, and the majority of the nation's subjects recoiled from the deed. With the revolutionaries divided among themselves, Cromwell found that he could maintain orderly governmet only through strong personal rule backed by the army. He sought to institutionalize his control through several written constitutions, including one that called his government a "Protectorate." But, no matter what the name or outward form, Cromwell ruled in fact as a military despot.

The Restoration of the Monarchy and the Glorious Revolution

The Protector (Cromwell) conducted foreign affairs to the general satisfaction of his subjects, and he advanced the interests of the business class by encouraging trade and shipping. But this was not the kind of state that supporters of the Puritan Revolution had wanted. The English learned, as the people of other nations would learn again and again, that revolutions can take unexpected courses; that they can be bloody and chaotic — often forcing, at last, a choice by the people between *disorder* and *despotism*.

Sentiment in England swung steadily toward a restoration of the Stuart monarchy (and a "free" Parliament). Shortly after Cromwell's death in 1658, a new Parliament assembled — the first to have been freely elected in twenty years. One of its early acts was to invite the dead king's son, an exile in France, to return as Charles II. He was cheered on his arrival in 1660 by an emotional show of loyalty on the part of his subjects, and the nightmare of regicide (royal execution) and Puritanical tyranny faded into the English past. The Restoration, an era of relaxed tensions and enlarged individual freedom, had begun.

Parliament did not intend, of course, to restore divine right. It made clear to Charles that his was to be a *constitutional* government, based on the traditional rights of the crown, Parliament, and the people. Though the Anglican Church became once again the established church, it no longer upheld political absolutism. Bloody revolution and Cromwellism may have been viewed as mistakes, but few desired to turn back the clock to 1600.

Charles II accepted all this on the surface though he was suspected of having private reservations. Whatever his inner convictions, he could not forget the shadow of exile or the block; hence, he avoided extreme policies. The same cannot be said for his younger brother, who succeeded him as James II. A convert to Roman Catholicism, James raised the fear that "popery" might return to England. Moreover, he antagonized both the Anglican clergy and major factions of Parliament, justifying his unpopular acts by claiming the king was "above the law."

Though his critics were exasperated by James's behavior, they expected that matters would improve after his death. The "heir presumptive" (probable) was his Protestant daughter Mary, the wife of William III of Holland. But in 1688 a son was born to the middle-aged English king, who had him baptized a Catholic. Now faced with the prospect of continued political reaction and "Romanization," the leaders of the Parliament secretly invited William to land military forces in England. After William's landing, James found himself without support and quickly sailed for France. Parliament, alleging that James had "abdicated," then declared the throne vacant and offered it to William and Mary. Thus was the Glorious Revolution of 1688 carried out — glorious because it was decisive and bloodless.

Determined to keep the new rulers in check, Parliament in 1689 passed the Bill of Rights, which declared parliamentary supremacy over the crown and spelled out English civil liberties. This historic measure completed the revolution that had started in 1642. It stated that the king could suspend laws, raise armies, and levy taxes *only* with the consent of Parliament; it also provided for frequent meetings of the lawmakers and unlimited debate within their Houses. The Bill of Rights also guaranteed every citizen the right to petition the monarch, to keep arms, and to enjoy "due process of law" (trial by jury and freedom from arbitrary arrest and cruel or unusual punishment). This was a restatement of the guarantees in the Magna Carta (p. 445), but they were now expressed in more specific language.

The triumph of Parliament in 1689 was important for two main reasons. It put an end to absolutism and established a governing aristocracy (of property-owners); at the same time, it strengthened the exercise of individual freedoms for all. The wider enjoyment of civil rights led, eventually, to a demand for wider sharing of political power as well. Thus, the Glorious Revolution prepared the way for true *representative government* in England.

Locke's Justification of Revolution

A byproduct of the English upheaval was John Locke's political theory, which would have a profound influence on future revolutions. Locke, as we have seen (p. 425), was in touch with the scientific, philosophic, and political ideas of his day. He approved of Parliament's fight against absolutism and felt that both the Puritan Revolution and the Glorious Revolution were justifiable. In 1690, in order to satisfy his conscience and that of other English citizens — and in order to defend the parliamentary settlement — he published *Two Treatises on Government*. The first treatise (study) rejected the theory of divine right, while the second defended the right of rebellion. Though Locke's political ideas were not original, his second treatise became an ideological handbook for liberal revolutionists everywhere.

Locke believed that the English Civil War could be properly understood and judged only in the broadest context of human society and nature. Like his older contemporary, Thomas Hobbes (p. 400), Locke saw the state in a purely secular light and denied that it had been founded by God. Both insisted that the miserable condition of people in the "state of nature" had given rise to an agreement to establish civil government. Both also shared an *atomistic* view of society, regarding it as a collection of self-serving individuals. Starting from these common beliefs, Hobbes and Locke each attempted to set forth universal rules of political behavior and morals.

But there was an important difference between some of their assumptions. Hobbes reasoned that human aggressive tendencies had made life unbearable under "natural" conditions; hence, he argued, individuals must have turned over *all* their rights to the state as a means of securing order. This being so, people are bound to obey the absolute dictates of their ruler. Revolution, therefore, constitutes a breach of contract as well as a return to chaos.

Locke accepted the theory of "social contract," but he disagreed with Hobbes about its *terms*. He held that all people possess certain "natural rights," just as physical objects possess certain natural properties (mass, density, shape, and so forth). Individuals had *retained* most of their natural rights and powers and had agreed (in the contract) to transfer only *one* power to society: the power to preserve their life, liberty, and property. A society, said Locke, holds this power as long as the society lasts, but it delegates the use of this power to political agents. Should any agent (such as a king) push beyond set limits, the society is free, legally and morally, to *resist*. Who should decide whether a ruler's action is, in fact, a step *beyond* the set limits? *"The people shall judge,"* Locke replied, using as an analogy the relation of a private person to a trustee or deputy. And if, in face of this judgment, a ruler refuses to yield, the people have the ultimate right to resort to *force* — to "appeal to Heaven."

Thus, by building on the ancient Roman ideas of "natural rights" and "natural law" (p. 119), on the seventeenth-century style of reasoning, and appeals to common sense, Locke constructed a "universal" political theory.

Though it rested neither on scientific facts nor on actual historical events, it served as a "myth" (fiction) to justify the acts of the Parliamentary side in England's civil war. It justified not only acts of rebellion but even the execution of a king. And Locke's atomistic view of society suited the rising spirit of *individualism*. In the next two centuries of liberal revolution, it is clear how the Lockean "myth" proved useful in the large, historical sense. It was heartily embraced by Thomas Jefferson and other liberal leaders as a "self-evident," absolute truth.

THE AMERICAN REVOLUTION AND CONSTITUTION

Though he wrote the Declaration of Independence nearly a century after Locke's treatise appeared, Jefferson formed a direct intellectual link between the English and American revolutions. Jefferson expressed many of the liberal ideas of Locke and the Enlightenment and gave them wider circulation. Liberalism, however, was but one element of the American Revolution of 1776. That rebellion also brought about the first expulsion of a European colonial power, replaced monarchical government with a *republic*, and established the principle and practice of popular sovereignty (democracy). As a result of these achievements, the American Revolution served as a hope and model for later revolutions around the world.

The American Colonies and Their Aspirations

The overseas expansion of Europe had brought English settlers to the North American continent in the seventeenth century. Most of them, after driving back the native Americans and carving homesteads from the wilderness, inhabited the thirteen colonies of the seaboard between Nova Scotia and Florida. By 1750 the white population of these colonies (including settlers from the continent as well as Britain) amounted to about two million. Viewed from London, they made up but one part of a far-flung empire; some thirty chartered colonies and companies, in America and Asia, were then controlled by the king and Parliament. (The total number of Britain's subjects was approximately fifteen million at the time.)

The colonies were considered valuable chiefly for economic reasons — as a source of raw materials and as a market for exports. But the costs to the mother country for defense and administration probably equaled or exceeded the commercial returns. After 1750, therefore, Parliament tightened up the regulation of trade and the collection of taxes. Until this time the colonists had paid little more than the local taxes enacted by their colonial legislatures. They had achieved this "immunity" by means of wholesale smuggling and disregard of the British Navigation Acts. At the same time, they showed little desire to provide for their own military defense. The Americans thereby gained a reputation in England for lawlessness, and Parliament began to suspect that the Americans were unworthy of trust and incapable of self-government.

Not surprisingly, the colonists resented British efforts to collect existing taxes or to impose new ones. This was especially true after 1763, when the close of the Seven Years' War (known in the colonies as the French and Indian War) brought England victory over France. With French power on the North American continent broken, there was no longer a serious foreign threat to the thirteen colonies. Feeling more secure than before, the Americans grew even more defiant toward their absentee rulers.

Parliament cast about for some kind of tax that the colonists would pay, but the objections were so violent that most were repealed soon after their enactment. One exception was a tax on imports of *tea*; Parliament refused to repeal this one, mainly to emphasize its *right* to tax British subjects everywhere. But the Americans refused to admit that right. "No taxation without representation!" became the rallying cry of colonial protest.

English leaders argued in vain that the colonies enjoyed "virtual" representation, since members of Parliament, in theory, represented not individual electoral districts, but national and imperial interests as a whole. Thus, although many English towns, cities, and individuals had no elected representatives in Parliament, it was held that their interests were nonetheless represented there. The argument, though accepted in England at the time, did not impress the Americans. In their own colonial governments, legislators represented *particular* districts. This view of representation was firmly rooted in the American experience, and it now suited the economic interest of the colonists.

The squabble over taxation was only one evidence of the rising antagonism. Actions and counteractions led to a firming up of positions and a heightening of emotions. Though a minority remained loyal to the British flag and British law, most colonists were moving toward the point of no return. They saw themselves as heirs of the Glorious Revolution of 1688 and the British king and Parliament as *tyrants*, who went beyond their legal limits.

The Americans at first sought redress of their grievances, but gradually they began to think of seizing control of their own destiny. The urban middle class took the lead, and soon other groups began to sense that they, too, would be better off under self-rule. They realized that British *mercantilism* (p. 403) would check their own economic development and that, under colonialism, their general well-being would always be subordinated to imperial aims. Thomas Paine, a shrewd revolutionary propagandist, described the situation in a geographical perspective. Using the language of the Enlightenment, he declared that America's subjection to England was "contrary to reason." He went on:

> There is something absurd in supposing a continent to be perpetually governed by an island. In no instance has nature made the satellite larger than its primary planet; and as England and America, with respect to each other, reverse the common order of nature, it is evident that they belong to different systems. England to Europe; America to itself.

Paine did much to advance the cause of rebellion in America. Later he aided the radicals in France and England, thus becoming the first international revolutionist of modern times.

War and the Declaration of Independence

By 1774 the colonists had begun to commit acts of violence and sabotage (notably the Boston "Tea Party"), and the British responded with tough measures. Parliament passed what Americans called the Intolerable Acts, which closed the port of Boston and virtually canceled the charter of Massachusetts. The British may have thought that this hard-line policy would bring the colonists to their senses (or to their knees), but it had just the opposite effect. County assemblies were called together in Massachusetts to protest; one of them declared that no one should obey any part of the acts, which it described as "attempts of a wicked administration to enslave America." Shortly thereafter, representatives from all the colonies assembled at a Continental Congress in Philadelphia. There they drew up a statement of grievances and formed an association to cut off all trade with Britain. The conflict of words had given way to "direct action."

When the British governor of Massachusetts ordered its legislature dissolved, the legislators defiantly met again and proceeded to raise a defense force of "minutemen." This step was, of course, illegal; it brought into existence a condition of armed rebellion. Conciliatory measures were now proposed in Parliament, but it was too late. The first clash of arms occurred in April 1775, when British troops set out from Boston to destroy a reported supply of rebel weapons stored near Concord. They accomplished their mission but suffered heavy losses to sharpshooters on their return march. The war for independence was on.

The Continental Congress reassembled shortly after the skirmish in Massachusetts. The minutemen around Boston were enlisted as the core of a Continental Army, and George Washington was named as commander in chief. The war dragged on for six years. Britain, though a leading European power, was hampered by long lines of communication, uneven generalship, and troubles in other parts of its empire. The colonials suffered from the internal differences that normally divide revolutionists, and the Continental Congress was unable to provide enough troops, supplies, or money. Although the rebels fought bravely and endured severe hardships, they could hardly have won without the aid of foreign powers.

The French monarchy, eager to even the score with Britain after the humiliation of 1763 (p. 450), decided to aid the rebels. From the beginning, the French had sent officers and arms to the Americans, whose first significant victory, at Saratoga, was won chiefly with French weapons. Impressed by the American success in that battle, the French became formal allies and declared war on Britain. Spain and Holland followed, swinging the European balance in the Americans' favor. The surrender of the encircled troops of Lord

Cornwallis at Yorktown (Virginia) in 1781, which ended the British military effort, was forced by a French fleet controlling the waters off shore. Two years later, by the Treaty of Paris, the United States of America won recognition as a sovereign territory stretching from the Atlantic to the Mississippi River.

The independence of the new government, as well as its bid for allies, had been formally proclaimed in 1776. In fact, the most memorable achievement of the Continental Congress was its adoption of the Declaration of Independence. Drafted by Jefferson, it aimed to justify the resort to force against Britain and to win support *abroad* as well as at home. It is significant that the preamble gives this reason for publishing the document: "a decent respect to the opinions of mankind. . . ." In 1776 (as today) the influence of foreign opinion on the outcome of a struggle for independence could not be ignored.

The Declaration is a masterpiece of revolutionary literature fitted to the American cause. Jefferson omitted any mention of the colonists' reluctance to pay their share of defense costs, overlooked the long story of smuggling, civil disobedience, and provocative acts, and gave no hint at all of the deeper motives of the rebel leaders. He knew that Parliament had been supreme in England since 1689 (p. 447), yet he shrewdly focused his charges of wrongdoing upon the *king*. He did so because the king, in an era of absolute monarchs, could more readily be painted as a tyrant.

The ringing paragraph that links the American Revolution with "universal truths" is a paraphrase of Locke, but Jefferson's version is marked by greater simplicity, clarity, and power. Jefferson declares:

> We hold these truths to be self-evident: That all men are created equal; that they are endowed by their Creator with certain unalienable Rights; that among these are Life, Liberty, and the pursuit of Happiness. — That to secure these rights, Governments are instituted among Men, deriving their just powers from the consent of the governed, — That whenever any Form of Government becomes destructive of these ends, it is the Right of the People to alter or abolish it. . . .

In these few lines, Jefferson sets forth a view of humanity, government, and revolution that remains an inspiration to believers in human dignity, liberal principles, and progressive social change.

The Constitution of the United States

The Americans emerged from their war of independence with relatively few scars. Serious divisions had appeared within the colonies, but they were moderate compared with those of revolutions elsewhere. The fact that the enemy was an *absentee* ruler served as a unifying force among Americans of all classes. Even so, there was a minority of die-hard "loyalists" (loyal to Britain) who opposed the "patriots" (revolutionists). Subjected to confiscation of their property and rough treatment by the majority, some sixty thousand fled to Canada. Their departure eased the internal conflict in the colonies, and most of the émigrés (refugees) did not return to stir up trouble. (Canadian colonists remained loyal to Britain.)

After independence, the most pressing need of the former colonies was to agree on a plan for self-government. Each new state drew up a written constitution for itself, but there was disagreement over what form the *union* of the states should take. The "states' rights" feeling, arising from the experiences of the separate colonies, was very much alive. Many citizens preferred complete independence for their states but grudgingly accepted the idea of a loose union, as provided by the Articles of Confederation. When the Confederation proved unable to meet the common needs of commerce and defense, the states sent delegates to Philadelphia (1787) to revise the Articles. Instead, they drafted a new constitution aimed at forming a closer union.

The federal Constitution, approved after bitter debate in the thirteen states, was the earliest *written* constitution of a major country — and is the oldest still in use. The very act of Americans in framing their own basic law fired the imagination of European intellectuals. Here was Locke's "social contract" made real! Here also was a reasoned statement of the new doctrine of *popular sovereignty* (rule by the *people*). Starting with a clean political slate, the Americans rejected the notion of any privileged persons or bodies. The foreword identifies the sole source of civil authority in its opening words: "We, the people . . . do ordain and establish this Constitution for the United States of America."

The new document also launched a successful experiment in *federalism*, in which individuals hold citizenship both in their state and in the nation. The authors of the Constitution tried to strike a balance between powers delegated to the central government and those reserved to the states. With changing conditions, the balance has had to be readjusted through constitutional interpretation or amendment. Thus, a peculiar tension was built into American politics in 1787, with results not wholly satisfactory to anyone. Nevertheless, federalism stands as a noble endeavor to harmonize the requirements of centralized planning and power with the desire for local control.

The Constitution was, above all, a charter of eighteenth-century liberalism. It followed Jefferson's maxim, "That government is best which governs *least*." Fearing possible tyranny by one person or one body, the framers put their trust in a system of "checks and balances." The best protection against the human urge to power, they thought, is to establish *separate* political authorities and to leave them in jealous competition. Thus, the states were to keep a watchful eye on the *national* power; and within all government units a division of executive, legislative, and judicial powers was established.

Although the Constitution provides defenses against the invasion of individual rights, fears of an overly strong central government continued to be voiced. And so, at the insistence of many citizens, the Bill of Rights was added to the Constitution in 1791. Comprising the first ten amendments, it spells out and extends the historic rights of the English people (p. 447). Freedom of worship and freedom from an established church head the list. Every person is also guaranteed freedom of expression, petition, and assembly; the right to keep and bear arms; security of person and home; and due process of law.

By and large, the liberal principles embodied in the Constitution proved well suited to the self-reliant temper of the American people and to the conditions of life during the republic's first hundred years. With no strong enemies on their borders, and with vast resources to be exploited, Americans were free to exercise their inventiveness and talents. The federal power survived secession and civil war during the ordeal of the 1860s. But great forces were not needed for external defense, for eliminating counterrevolutionary elements, or for restraint of *private* powers. Not until the end of the nineteenth century — with the closing of the frontier, the swelling of population, and the rise of giant industry — did conditions develop that were less suitable to limited government.

The Growth of American Democracy

The desire of the "founding fathers" to maintain checks and balances was frustrated, from the beginning, by the growth of political parties. This development opened the door to "excessive" power by the people, something the founders had feared. They wished to avoid the tyranny of either one person or many. A majority party, however, by securing control of the various branches of government, could rise to a position of virtual dominance. An early example of the effect of parties was their undoing of the constitutional provision for electing the president. The Constitution calls for the indirect election of the chief executive through a college of electors, who are presumably independent. But *parties* almost at once began to nominate *lists* of electors to be chosen by the voters in each state, and the winning list was expected to vote as a unit for its party's candidate.

The opening up of the country and the exploitation of its resources brought a steady expansion of government activities in the United States. This trend stimulated parties and the spirit and practice of democracy. The relation between *liberalism* and *democracy* requires close examination. After the successful challenge to divine-right monarchy in the seventeenth century, the idea of liberalism had been joined to that of majority rule. Locke and Jefferson both believed that, *within the limits assigned to a liberal government*, the individual must submit to the *majority*. But there remained a persistent tension between liberal and democratic principles. What if the majority seeks to do something that the individual regards as a violation of "unalienable" *individual* rights? On this question, the strict liberal took the side of the individual, while the democrat supported the decision of the majority.

United States history shows, in fact, a progressive narrowing of individual rights and a corresponding growth in the power of the majority. Alexis de Tocqueville, a French observer of American institutions, identified this shift as early as the 1830s. In America, he reported, the *people* truly govern. Public opinion is king; its power applies not only to political decisions but to personal convictions and behavior. Tocqueville saw American democracy as the wave of the future and predicted (correctly) that it would soon extend to Europe and the rest of the world. Though impressed by the vigor and promise of America, he feared that the passion for equality and democracy would at last stifle individual liberty. His prophecy has not been altogether fulfilled, but the role of democratic government has grown enormously, and the Jeffersonian liberal state has long since passed from the scene.

THE FRENCH REVOLUTION: "LIBERTY, EQUALITY, AND FRATERNITY"

The American Revolution helped to spark the French Revolution of 1789, which proved to be the most violent and far-reaching of all the liberal upheavals. Not only did the French Revolution advance liberal ideals; it brought drastic changes in the legal, social, and economic order of France, the largest and most populous country in western Europe. The struggle was intensified by the passionate opposition of privileged groups at home and by the intervention of foreign powers. Even more than the English or American revolutions, it was a watershed in the flow of Western history. As Tocqueville later wrote, "The French Revolution had no territory of its own; indeed, its effect was to efface, in a way, all older frontiers. It brought men together, divided them, in spite of law, traditions, character, and language — turning enemies sometimes into compatriots and kinsmen into strangers. . . ." Not until the Russian Revolution of 1917 was an uprising to have such an impact on the Western world.

The Bourbon Monarchy and the Old Order

Living as we do in an age of revolutions, we have a special need to understand the nature of social revolts. Scholarly research on the French Revolution, which has been studied more intensively than any other, tells us a great deal about the "anatomy of revolution." What were the main causes, phases, and consequences of the movement that began in 1789?

First, let us survey the background of the rebellion. The splendor of the Bourbon monarchy had dimmed with the passing of Louis XIV, though his heirs upheld the grand style at Versailles (pp. 390–91). While preserving its claim to divine-right absolutism, the monarchy grew increasingly ineffective during the eighteenth century. Louis XV was a capable but pleasure-loving ruler, and his grandson, Louis XVI, was well-meaning but indecisive. Humiliating military defeats and the loss of the French overseas empire undermined royal prestige, while wars, extravagance, and insufficient revenues brought the monarchy to the edge of bankruptcy. Louis XVI tried to carry through reforms in taxation and administration, but he was frustrated by the privileged classes, who refused to accept their fair share of the tax burden. Though still capable of occasional action, the monarchy could not exert the absolute authority it claimed. Disclosure of its weakness led to mounting criticism of the government and encouraged the hopes of dissatisfied classes.

The landed aristocrats sought to regain historic rights that had been stripped away by the crown in preceding centuries. Their resurgent spirit expressed itself through the provincial *parlements* (judicial tribunals), which in 1763 vigorously protested attempts by the king to raise property assessments. The Parlement of Paris went further: it referred to the existence of the "fundamental laws" of France and declared that no decree of the monarch was valid until it had been approved by the Parlement. Thus, the Parlement virtually proclaimed itself the "supreme court" of France. The members of this haughty tribunal (and of the provincial *parlements*) were drawn from noble families and so reflected the desire of the aristocracy to modify royal absolutism in the direction of constitutional government (as in Britain). In short, the nobles hoped to regain some of the powers they had enjoyed in the Middle Ages (pp. 209, 214–15).

Other social classes sided with the aristocracy in its challenge to absolutism, feeling that some advantage would fall to them from a reduction in royal authority. The French bourgeois were especially eager to advance their social and political status. Growing in wealth and education, and sensitive to the winds of change, they longed for higher prestige and more active participation in the affairs of state. Through enlarged political influence, they also hoped to do away with the obstructions of mercantilism (p. 403) and reap the fruits of a freer economy.

The peasants, who made up by far the largest part of the population, were little concerned with prestige or politics. Their lot was a hard one, often marked by famine and disease. What they wanted was more land, freedom from ancient dues and services to the nobles, and relief from unfair tax collections. The years 1787 and 1788 were especially harsh for most peasants (and urban laborers). In their despair, they felt that *any* change in the existing order might result in some good. Ordinarily slow to act, they now showed themselves ready to play their part in bringing about change.

The Overthrow of the King and the Nobles

Though a "revolutionary situation" existed in France in the 1780s, it took a special chain of circumstances to set off the revolution. Having failed to get the revenues he wanted by means of existing laws, Louis XVI was compelled at last to seek additional taxing authority. According to tradition, such authority could be granted only by the Estates-General (p. 311). This body, representing the three major *estates* (classes) of France, had not met since 1614. The king's call for the election of delegates in 1788 created a stir of expectation, for if the monarch wanted new taxes he would have to offer something in return to the assembled delegates.

As planning for the meeting went ahead at the royal palace of Versailles, a split opened between the nobles and the bourgeois. The latter were legally commoners — members of the Third Estate. They resented this medieval classification, which lumped them with laborers and peasants; but, as leaders of the most numerous class, they sought greater power for themselves in the Estates-General. They demanded of the government that the Third Estate be allowed to send a larger number of delegates to Versailles than the two privileged estates (clergy and nobility) combined, and they insisted that votes be taken by count of individuals in the *total* body of delegates. They won the first demand, but the Parlement of Paris, to which the voting issue was referred, ruled in favor of the traditional method — *one* vote for each *estate*. It became apparent even before the Estates-General met in the summer of 1789 that rivalry and suspicion between the estates would complicate their dealings with the king.

After the session opened, matters soon came to a head. Unable to persuade the two higher estates to sit and vote with them as one body, the representatives of the Third Estate (most of whom were lawyers) decided to "walk out" of the Estates-General. Stating that they were the only true representatives of the people, they then declared themselves to be the "National Assembly" of France. This proclamation (June 17) was the first act of illegality, for it rested on no actual law. A crisis of decision was thereby thrust upon the king.

Louis, forced to choose sides between the nobility and the bourgeois, sided with the nobility. His initial response was to lock the meeting hall of the building where the Third Estate had been sitting. But the action failed; the Third Estate found another meeting place at an indoor tennis court nearby. There the members swore the "Tennis Court Oath," pledging not to return home until they had drafted a *new constitution* for France. Within a few days the National Assembly was joined by many priests from the First Estate and by some of the nobles. Having failed to persuade the rebels to back down, Louis next tried to intimidate them by a show of force. Toward the end of June, he called some twenty thousand soldiers to Versailles.

The National Assembly was rescued by the people of Paris. As order began to break down throughout the country, people everywhere began to arm themselves for defense against the king's forces. The excitement in Paris, fed by rumors of troop movements, rose higher and higher. Crowds began to roam the streets in search of weapons, and on July 14 they demanded arms from the Bastille. Though the old fortress was no longer of military importance, it was a hated symbol of despotism. When its commander refused to turn over arms, the mob attempted to push its way in. After an exchange of gunfire, in which about a hundred of the crowd were killed, the commander agreed to surrender. Then the mob rushed in, killed members of the small garrison (including its commander), cut off their heads, and carried them on spear points through the city streets.

Thoroughly alarmed, and doubting that his troops would fire on the people, Louis quickly sent his forces away from Versailles. He played for time by pretending to yield to the demands of the Paris mob and the Third Estate. The king recognized a self-appointed citizens' committee as the new city government of Paris and directed the representatives of the privileged estates to sit in the National Assembly. Thus, the revolutionary movement was saved for the time being and was strengthened by a new and powerful influence — the Parisian populace.

Violence broke out in the countryside as well. By late July it was rumored that the landlords were collecting hired ruffians to attack the peasants. While many of the nobles were away at the capital, the peasants seized the initiative. During the "Great Fear" of late summer they vandalized the manor houses of the nobles and destroyed the hated records of their required payments and services.

As the king had appeased the Paris populace, the National Assembly now tried to quiet the peasants. Many of the bourgeois, as well as the nobles, held landed estates. Frightened by the disorders in the country, they realized that they would have to take drastic action in order to save their families and properties. At a single night session (August 4), the Assembly removed all special privileges in landed property. Liberal noblemen led the way by surrendering their historic rights to peasant fees and labor, hunting on farmland, tax exemptions and advantages, and special courts of law for the nobility. A final decree, approved overwhelmingly, declared that "feudalism is abolished." Thus, a drastic overturn in property rights was the first major reform of the National Assembly. The chief losers were, of course, the nobles; the beneficiaries were the peasants, who now had a substantial interest in defending the revolution.

Now the Assembly could turn to its original task: the framing of a new constitution. Although this effort was to prove trying and divisive, there was wide agreement on the major liberal principles. Those principles were summarized in the most influential document of the liberal revolutions: the Declaration of the Rights of Man and the Citizen. Drafted as a preface to the constitution, it served as a guide to the new order.

The Declaration was the French counterpart of the English and American bills of rights. It went beyond them, however, in setting forth specific principles of government. After stating the "natural, inalienable, and sacred rights of man," it defined the *duties* of individuals in a society. "Every citizen summoned or seized according to law ought to obey instantly," but law must be an expression of the "general will." *All* citizens have the right to participate in the making of law, and its administration must be the same for all. (This statement, however, was not generally understood to include women — in spite of some feminist demands at the time.) "The source of sovereignty is essentially in the nation," the Declaration continues; "no body, no individual can exercise authority that does not proceed from it in plain terms."

This emphasis on the "general will" reflected in large measure the influence of the French-Swiss philosopher Jean-Jacques Rousseau. It is ironic that the Declaration, so clearly the product of Enlightenment *rationalism*, also bears the imprint of this *romanticist*. Rousseau had died in 1778, eleven years before the revolution. But his political ideas had stimulated the rebels of his own day and lived on in his writings. Rousseau's *The Social Contract* dealt with the same question of rights and authority that had been treated in differing ways, by Hobbes and Locke (pp. 409, 448). Though his explanations were often unclear, Rousseau claimed that the general will is the sovereign power in organized society.

Upon examination, the "will" of Rousseau turns out to be a vague, mystical notion, bound to "moral principles" and the "welfare of the whole society." The chief difficulty lies in discovering how, in practice, the general will is to be found. His interpreters have set forth three broad possibilities — each connected with a different form of government: the general will can be identified with the *decision of a majority* (democracy); it can be "revealed" by a charismatic *individual* (dictatorship); or it can be determined by a chosen *elite* (one-party rule). Thus, the National Assembly, Napoleon, and the modern authoritarian party could each speak in the name of the "general will" of the people.

Rousseau's ideas were raised against all political institutions that rested on a divine or historical right rather than on the general will. His arguments gave philosophical support to the French Revolution and served to justify the National Assembly's claim to sovereign authority. The planners of the new constitution accepted it as their duty to create a framework of government that would respond to and express the general will of France. But from the beginning there was sharp disagreement on how the framework should be built. Some wanted the new government modeled after that of England, with an upper and lower house and a king with executive and veto powers. Others, fearing that this arrangement would give undue power to the nobility, wanted a single legislative chamber and a figurehead king.

The rising distrust of Louis XVI shifted the balance toward the single-chamber (unicameral) plan. The leaders of the Assembly were properly suspicious of the monarch's loyalty to the revolution; his brother, the Count of Artois, had already fled the country, along with many noblemen. These émigrés proceeded to urge foreign powers to intervene in France, and Louis himself hesitated to accept either the Declaration of Rights or the Assembly's decrees abolishing feudalism. Demonstrating their doubts about Louis, crowds marched from Paris to the Versailles palace in October of 1789 and compelled him and his queen to move to the city (the palace of the Tuileries).

Moderates in the Assembly, sensing the coming violence, began to draw back from the revolution. This put increasing power in the hands of radical factions, of whom the most influential were members of the Jacobin Society. (The "Jacobin" name came from that of a former convent in Paris in which the society met.) Founded in 1789, this society soon had local chapters throughout France. By 1793 it had nearly half a million members and had become virtually a government within the revolutionary government. Serving as propagandists and administrators, the Jacobins were a prototype (model) for the revolutionary parties of the twentieth century.

The constitution completed in 1791 provided for a unicameral legislature and a suspensive veto for the king. (He could only *delay*, not prevent, legislation.) At the same time the well-to-do members of the Assembly managed to limit the right to vote. Moreover, candidates for the "electoral college," which was to name the legislators and administrative officials, had to be male citizens of substantial property. (Only fifty thousand men qualified as candidates in the first elections.) The reason given for these restrictive provisions was that the great majority of the people were uneducated; the *effect* was to hand control to the wealthy families of the country.

Louis XVI, who was named the titular ("official") head of the new government, had sealed his fate earlier in 1791 by attempting to escape from France. Captured near the northeast frontier and brought back to Paris in humiliation, he thus destroyed any serious hopes for a successful constitutional monarchy. Soon this government foundered, the king was deposed, and a new assembly was called (1792) to draft another constitution. (In the election of these delegates, *all* adult males were permitted to vote.) The new body, named the National Convention, met and proclaimed the (first) French Republic. The Convention governed France during troubled years of reform and war and completed its work in 1795 by approving a constitution for the Republic.

Foreign War and Internal Disorder

Reaction abroad deeply affected the course of the revolution. Whereas outside intervention had assured the success of the American Revolution (p. 151), it had destructive consequences for the French. It stimulated extremism and internal splits within the revolution, and it helped to bring about panic, dictatorship, and, ultimately, military defeat. The conflict between revolutionary France and the rest of Europe broke out in 1792. Some individuals outside France sympathized with the aims and deeds of the revolution, but the most influential groups — the royal and privileged ones — had become increasingly alarmed. Their feeling was strengthened by blood ties with the captive Bourbon king and by warnings from the émigrés. Over a hundred thousand aristocrats had left France, including more than half of the officers of the army; but they hoped to return one day to recover their lost positions and lands.

Foreign sentiment had led to a military threat in the Declaration of Pillnitz (August 1791). In this document, Leopold II of Austria, the Holy Roman emperor, stated that if the other European powers would join him he would use force to restore the Bourbon rulers to their full rights. Busy with matters in Austria, the emperor did not really wish to send troops to France, but his declaration encouraged the émigrés and alarmed the French leaders. It also helped the hand of those in France who wished to *internationalize* the revolution — who believed that the reforms could not be made secure in France unless they were also carried abroad.

The more aggressive revolutionists now pressed for an offensive against the reactionary powers of Europe. They pictured their armies carrying the banner of "liberation" into neighboring lands and uniting with native radicals to overthrow established governments. The desire for military action gained support also from those who believed that war would restore *unity* to France and from those who stood to lose should royalist armies invade the country. The government accordingly declared war on Austria in April 1792, thereby launching a period of continental revolution and war that lasted for twenty-three years.

At first the war went against the French, producing panic and disorder in Paris and the provinces. In the autumn a mob rushed the royal palace of the Tuileries and massacred the king's Swiss Guard. Later a band of enthusiastic army recruits invaded the Paris jails and seized a thousand or more prisoners who had been rounded up as suspected sympathizers with the aristocracy. After mock trials these unfortunates were put to death. The winds of violence, released by the revolution and whipped by nationalist hysteria, now swept across France. When the National Convention first met in September 1792, it faced the immediate problems of dealing with the king, restoring law and order, and conducting the war.

Louis's trial for treason opened a major split between the moderates and the radicals. The leaders of the Convention were all radical Jacobins (p. 460), but they were divided into factions reflecting a broad range of philosophy, interest, and temperament. Louis was voted guilty by unanimous decision, but the order of execution was passed by only a narrow margin. The majority of the Convention members thereby marked themselves as regicides (king-killers); the others were thereafter regarded as halfhearted, even *counter*revolutionary. The seeds of mutual distrust and hostility were thus sown within the revolution, and the rival leaders proceeded to devour one another. The guiding spirit of the Convention, the radical Maximilien Robespierre, ruled over the near anarchy of 1793 and 1794. (Violent uprisings, chiefly in the west and southeast, erupted out of opposition to the Convention's radical measures and the growing concentration of power in Paris.) Revolutionary trial courts were set up around the country to limit lynchings and to stifle local rebellions. At least fifteen thousand fell to the guillotines, usually on charges of treason (aiding the country's enemies) or sedition (rebellion against authority). Thousands more perished during the uprisings in the provinces.

As foreign peril declined, internal hysteria declined with it. The National Convention, having declared war on Britain, Holland, and Spain (as well as

Austria), approved the drafting of all able-bodied men. (This measure proved to be a fateful precedent for the mass armies of the future.) The French draftees, fired by revolutionary spirit, soon showed themselves more than a match for their enemies. By June 1794 they had turned the tide of battle and were overrunning the Low Countries. Within weeks the foes of Robespierre (both left and right) put an end to his political domination. He was *outlawed* by vote of the Convention and, with many of his associates, was executed.

The fall of Robespierre marked the end of the "Terror" and the return to power of the moderates. It was the moderates, chiefly representatives of the well-to-do, who secured the Convention's final approval of the republican constitution of 1795. The government so established (known as the *Directory*) restricted political participation to men of substantial wealth, even fewer in number than those who had held power under the constitution of 1791.

The triumphant bourgeois could well be satisfied with the trend of the revolution, despite its excessive violence and bloodshed. Their liberal principles and their leading political position were guaranteed by the new constitution. Feudal property rights, titles of nobility, and special privileges had been swept away; and the chaotic character of traditional administration had been replaced by self-governing cities and "departments" — units about the size of American counties. Freedom of enterprise had been advanced by the abolition of craft guilds and labor organizations and by the scrapping of the mercantilist regulations of the late monarchy.

The clergy, on the other hand, had seen its wealth and influence sharply reduced. In 1790 monastic orders had been suppressed, and the properties of the Church had been confiscated as a means of financing the revolution. In addition, the clergy had been placed under a Civil Constitution, with *elected* priests and bishops and with salaries paid by the state. These measures provoked not only the anger of most clerics but widespread popular opposition, particularly among women. The clergy, along with surviving members of the nobility, became a continuing source of *counterrevolutionary* activity.

Napoleon and the Revolutionary Empire

The bourgeois men of property failed, as they had in 1792, to meet the challenges of national political responsibility. The government of the Directory lacked effective leadership; many sincere reformers had either dropped out of public affairs or had been destroyed in the rivalry of factions. The politicians who remained were largely men of narrow vision and self-interest.

The popular spirit had shifted, too. High hopes had been turned into disappointment, animosity, and bloodshed. Economic conditions had worsened for the poor; families had been torn apart; and mothers, especially, bore a heavier burden of securing food and shelter for their children. Emotionally exhausted by five years of fevered excitement, many citizens fell into a mood of indifference or cynicism. Political officeholders not only failed to inspire but

showed themselves lazy, corrupt, and incapable of solving the nation's problems. Challenged from the right by reviving *royalist* sentiment and from the left by the still impoverished urban workers, the Directory clung to power only with the aid of the military.

A brilliant young general, Napoleon Bonaparte, was quick to grasp the facts of the political situation. He had first defended the government in 1795 against attacks by royalist mobs. (Afterward he boasted that he had dispersed them with a "whiff of grapeshot.") Two years later his troops were called on to enforce illegal measures that had been taken by the Directory, and in 1799 he plotted with some of its leaders to take over the state by a sudden seizure (*coup d'état*). The conspirators believed that only a strong government headed by a general could hold off royalism, establish internal order, and defeat France's foreign enemies. Napoleon proclaimed himself "First Consul," a title borrowed from the ancient Roman Republic (p. 96); later, after receiving a national vote of approval, he proclaimed himself *emperor* (1804). With warm public support, he ruled for fifteen years as a virtual dictator.

Napoleon had made his reputation as a general, but he was more than a soldier; he possessed a keen and wide-ranging intellect. Born on the Mediterranean island of Corsica in 1769, only a year after its annexation to France, he had become a fervent French nationalist. Though he distinguished himself as an officer of artillery, he would no doubt have remained in the junior grades had it not been for the revolution. But the flight of many aristocratic officers opened the grades above him, and the far-ranging wars of the republic offered him uncommon opportunities. (He once dreamed of conquering Egypt and India.) Owing his rapid advancement to the overthrow of the Bourbon monarchy, he heartily declared himself a "son of the revolution."

Napoleon was a master of politics and cunning, but there is no reason to doubt the sincerity of his professed devotion to revolutionary goals. He despised inherited and artificial privilege and was impatient with the inefficiency of the former government. He favored *equality of opportunity*, with careers (like his own) open to talent. Interpreting its meaning in his way, he readily embraced the revolutionary slogan of "Liberty, Equality, and Fraternity."

Napoleon was a child of the Enlightenment as well as of the revolution — a skeptic, a rationalist, and a believer in progress. There was a strain of mysticism in him, too, an ever-present faith in himself as a "man of destiny." Viewing himself as above ordinary people, he felt free from ordinary morality. He was the intellectual and moral heir of Caesar, Machiavelli, and Voltaire. With a firm sense of drama and history, he built an image of himself as the creator of a *new* Pax Romana — a *Pax Francica* (French Peace). This image, in turn, was to be transformed into a living myth.

The new master of France had no use for either the old aristocracy or the new democracy. Though his various constitutions gave voting rights to all adult males, the voters elected only lists of candidates, from which his government named the legislators and officials. Napoleon saw to it that only men loyal to him and to his purposes were appointed and advanced in office. The democratic "front" gave satisfaction to the populace and honor to his favorites, but Napoleon himself was the real power. Scornful of the democratic interpreters of Rousseau (p. 459), Napoleon presented *himself* as the spokesman of the general will of France.

It is inaccurate to conclude that Napoleon snuffed out democracy in France, for it had never existed there before. The great majority of the people — illiterate and uneducated — had enjoyed no political power under either the monarchy or the republic. Napoleon's overthrow of the Directory meant that a non-noble but propertied aristocracy had been displaced by an "enlightened despot" (p. 407). Declaring a general political amnesty, he invited back to France all the émigrés who were willing to work faithfully for their homeland. He called to his service men of widely varying backgrounds (from royalist to regicide) who would cooperate in consolidating the new order. By and large, every class gained from his statecraft, but his chief helpers and beneficiaries were the bourgeois.

His first task was to secure domestic peace and order. He arranged to have his opponents silenced by means of selective deportations, "exposure" of alleged plots, and the efficient work of his secret police. Catholic disaffection, springing from the earlier measures that had been taken against the Church, was dissolved by a dramatic concordat (agreement) with Pius VII in 1801. In this agreement, Napoleon formally accepted the fact that the Roman Catholic faith was the principal religion of the French, abandoning the attempt of the previous revolutionaries to replace traditional religion with a state-sponsored Deism (pp. 421–22) or "cult of reason." Church seminaries were reopened, and public religious processions were again permitted. Priests who had submitted to the revolutionary Civil Constitution were left to papal discipline, while those who had remained loyal to Rome were recognized as legitimate.

The pope, in return, accepted the new status of Catholicism in France. He dropped Rome's claims to confiscated church property and gave to the French government the right to nominate bishops. He tried, but failed, to eliminate the toleration of all faiths that had been secured by the revolutionary regimes. Although the settlement was criticized by some on both sides of the dispute, it established a peace between state and church in France that lasted for over a century.

Napoleon, privately a nonbeliever, recognized the importance of religion to the people and appreciated the advantage of having the Church on the side of the state. But he would not allow it to be the primary force in the shaping of citizens. The state, through its *own* schools, had to provide for the education and patriotic instruction of the young. He approved the earlier closing of Church schools by the National Convention and put into effect its comprehensive plans for a national educational system. By 1808 his subordinates had completed the structure of state-supported primary and secondary schools as well as public institutions of higher learning. The entire system, supervised from Paris, remains the basis of French education to this day.

Napoleon also carried through the plans of revolutionary leaders for reorganizing French law and administration. His appointed commissions cut through the centuries-old accumulation of rules and regulations and brought to completion the Napoleonic Code. This collection of laws and principles relating to persons and property was the product of a gigantic labor of sorting, eliminating, and condensing. The Code would become the new basis of law in major parts of Europe (and America) and is comparable to the ancient Roman codes that inspired it (p. 120). In later years Napoleon regarded the Code as his most durable accomplishment. While in exile he wrote, "My true glory is not in having won forty battles; Waterloo has effaced the memory of so many victories. What nothing can efface, what will live eternally, is my civil code."

Under Napoleon, the modern techniques of administering a centralized state took shape. The historic provinces of France, the local courts and offices, the administration of justice — all had been swept away by the revolution. Salaried officials ("prefects") responsible to the central government now presided over the cities and "departments" (p. 462). The reform of public administration extended to taxation, expenditure, and money and banking; the day of the *bureaucrat* was at hand and, with it, the equality of citizens before the law. All these changes, along with a grand design for public works, were in keeping with the rationalism (*logical* thinking) of the Enlightenment and with bourgeois ideas of efficiency.

But if Napoleon brought peace, order, and prosperity at home, he caused turmoil abroad. At the very outset of the revolution a sharp tension had developed between France and the rest of Europe. Any revolution, if it is a true revolution, creates such tension, for it is a threat to *established* social systems. The privileged classes of Europe, as we have seen, reacted in fear to the events of 1789; the French leaders, in turn, expected to be attacked. In the warfare that followed, the armies of the revolution extended the frontiers of France to the Rhine River and to central Italy, but the outcome of the struggle was still undecided when Bonaparte took over in 1799.

His first move in foreign affairs was to break the Second Coalition of powers (Britain, Russia, Austria, Portugal, and Naples), which had come together against France. By swift military moves and skillful diplomacy, he had achieved this goal by 1802. For the first time in a decade there was peace between France and its neighbors. But it proved to be only an uneasy truce.

Napoleon, in a position of strength, might have dug in on his advanced lines. The French state now held more territory than the Bourbon kings had dreamed of, and Napoleon pushed its control even farther by bringing Holland, Switzerland, and portions of Italy and Germany under his influence. He could have chosen a defensive military posture, against which his enemies might have struck in vain. But the momentum of the revolution, joined to his own driving ambition, worked against such a strategy. As the heir to what he believed to be *universal* ideals, Napoleon felt he had to *expand* the new order. His political and military moves led to another break with Britain, renewal of the war, and a Third Coalition against France.

Defense of the revolution merged, in Napoleon's mind, with personal and imperial glory, and he began to dream of dominating all of Europe. His genius and the confusion of his enemies brought him near to his goal. But the stubborn defiance of the British and their control of the seas, exhausting warfare against popular uprisings in Spain and Portugal, plus the vast manpower and distances of Russia, brought about his downfall.

A critical defeat for Napoleon was the bloody naval battle off Cape Trafalgar (1805), near the Atlantic entrance to the Mediterranean Sea. Ships of the British admiral, Lord Horatio Nelson, destroyed the French and allied fleets after Nelson himself was killed in battle. Compelled by this loss to abandon plans for invading Britain, Napoleon then tried to bring down the island nation through an economic *blockade* — ordering all ports on the continent closed against British exports. The British took countermeasures, however, and his "Continental System" proved a failure by 1810.

Napoleon's second failure was in Spain, which he invaded in 1807. His troops easily crushed the regular Spanish army, but the people of that country and neighboring Portugal continued to resist the French, using the methods of what they called the *guerrilla*, or "little war." Their tactics were those of ambush, surprise, and retreat before superior forces, and they were backed by the British with money, supplies, and an expeditionary force of regulars. As a result, the guerrillas held down tens of thousands of troops that Napoleon badly needed elsewhere.

Frustrated in the west, Napoleon turned eastward in a land attack on Russia in 1812. This proved to be his fatal blunder. His "Grand Army" of French and allied troops was annihilated (after initial victories) by the terrible winter, disease (typhus), and the stamina of the Russian guerrillas, using similar tactics to those of Spain and Portugal. Napoleon fought more battles after his disastrous retreat from Moscow, but his chance for final success was buried in the Russian snows.

After abdicating as emperor in 1814, Napoleon was banished to the Mediterranean island of Elba. Escaping a short while later, he raised a new army in a foolish gamble against the odds of power. On the battlefield of Waterloo (in modern Belgium) his last minutes as a maker of history ran out. But Napoleon had planted the seeds of a new order in Europe, and the continent would never again be the same.

THE CONSERVATIVE REACTION

While Napoleon was making his dash from Elba in the spring of 1815, the victorious powers were assembled at the glittering Congress of Vienna. Here the crowned heads of Europe and their chief ministers were trying to restore the continent to what it had been before the revolutionary disturbance. They were chilled by the news that the Corsican was once more at large. For the aristocrats of Europe viewed Napoleon not as a liberator, but as a vulgar upstart, a destroyer of the culture they were privileged to enjoy. A sigh of relief passed through Vienna when, after Waterloo, "that madman" was again shipped away — this time to the far-off isle of St. Helena, in the south Atlantic Ocean.

Metternich and the "Concert of Europe"

Though there were many signers of the settlement of 1815, the management of the treaty was in the hands of the four major powers that had brought about Napoleon's defeat: Britain, Russia, Prussia, and Austria. Prince Clemens von Metternich, the chief minister of Austria, was the leading spirit of the conference. An aristocrat of distinguished family, he had been a career diplomat in the service of the Habsburg dynasty (p. 405). He had demonstrated his shrewdness when Napoleon was at the height of power (1810) by arranging a marriage between the conqueror and Maria Louisa, daughter of the Austrian emperor. (At the same moment, though Austria was formally at peace, Metternich was working secretly for a new alliance against France.) Then, after Napoleon's disastrous defeat in Russia, Metternich threw Austria's weight against him. Though beaten many times by the French, Austria thus came out of the wars in a victor's role; and Metternich, to clinch the advantage, persuaded the allies to hold the peace congress in Vienna, the Austrian capital.

Metternich's cunning was matched by that of the clever Prince Talleyrand. Talleyrand was loyal only to himself and to France. He had served as a bishop under Louis XVI, as a statesman of the Revolution, and as Napoleon's foreign minister. When it appeared that the French emperor was overreaching himself, Talleyrand offered secret aid to Napoleon's enemies abroad, thereby preparing a place for himself in the postwar government. When the emperor fell, Talleyrand urged the victors to restore the Bourbon rulers in France; this, he explained, would follow the principle of "legitimacy" (legality). He hoped, by applying that principle, to hold for France the territories it had possessed before the Revolution.

The allies accepted the principles of *legitimacy* and *restoration*. The royal succession of France fell to the eldest surviving brother of the executed king, who assumed the title of Louis XVIII. (The late monarch's young son, who had died in 1795, was considered by the royalists as Louis XVII.) The restored monarch, having lived as an émigré in England, was brought back to Paris in

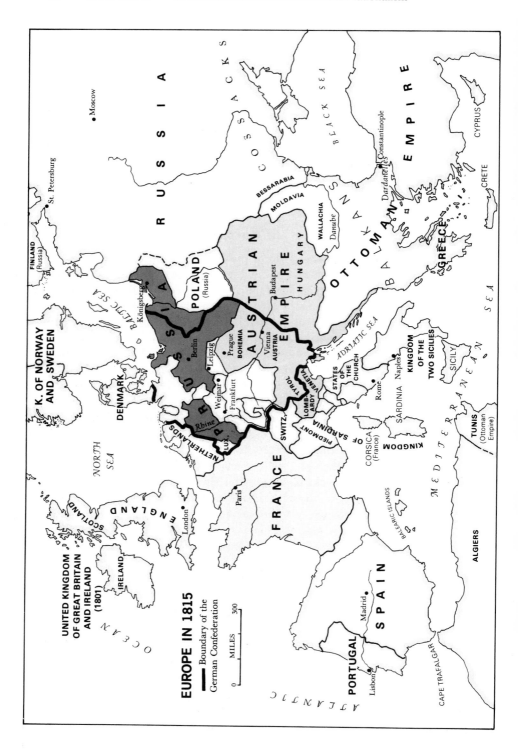

EUROPE IN 1815

Boundary of the
German Confederation

0   MILES   300

1814 by courtesy of the victors and at once rewarded Talleyrand by appointing him foreign minister.

At Vienna, Talleyrand played skillfully on the differences among the four principal victors, thus giving France, the defeated nation, a role in the settlement. The chief concerns of the conference were to restore, so far as practicable, the legitimate holdings of all titled rulers and the European balance of power. That balance, which had been established by the Peace of Westphalia (p. 401), had aimed to secure the independence of European states by preventing one or more of them from gaining too much power. In the course of the Vienna conference, for example, Talleyrand joined Metternich and Lord Castlereagh (of Britain) in a secret pledge to go to war should Prussia and Russia carry through their joint plans for expansion in central Europe. When word of the agreement leaked out, a compromise plan was proposed and accepted.

The Congress of Vienna by no means restored the borders of Europe exactly as they had been before 1789; it proved territorial *compensations* for those states that had contributed the most to toppling Napoleon. Russia, for example, was allowed to take Finland from Sweden, and Sweden was awarded Norway in exchange. (Norway regained its independence in 1905.) The redrawn map of Europe (p. 468) was to remain in effect, save for minor alterations, for half a century. The most unstable boundaries proved to be those in central Europe. There, Napoleon had given the final blow to the Holy Roman Empire in 1806 and had merged many of the smaller German states into a league of minor kingdoms (Confederation of the Rhine). The Congress kept this general arrangement, which was joined by Austria and Prussia and renamed the German Confederation. Subject mainly to Austrian control, this grouping forestalled for the moment Prussian desires for dominance in Germany.

Metternich was realistic enough to know that he could not completely undo the effects of the French Revolution. In France, the restored King Louis felt it necessary to grant a constitution that made the country a *limited* monarchy. The legal, administrative, clerical, and educational reforms of the revolution were retained. And beyond the borders of France the ideas of liberalism could not be altogether erased. Still less could Metternich prevent the rising sentiment of *nationalism*, which had been strengthened by the revolution's stress on "fraternity" and by Napoleon. The peoples of Germany and Italy, especially, were impressed by the power and accomplishments of the French nation-in-arms and by the psychological lift that accompanied national solidarity. Their hatred for the conquerors (which followed their initial admiration of the French as liberators) also stimulated their own sense of cultural identity. All across Europe, patriotic societies arose to champion the cause of national unity and independence.

But, for the time being, liberal and nationalistic movements were kept down. The privileged classes and the rulers of states with mixed nationalities saw them as threats to their interests. They agreed at Vienna to guard closely against them. Metternich arranged a "Concert of Europe" (in actuality, a Quadruple Alliance of Austria, Prussia, Russia, and Britain) that would use diplomacy and force against moves to change boundaries or social systems. Accordingly, several conferences ("congresses") of those states under Metternich's guidance, were called to meet threats to the established order. This "Metternich System" thus provided a type of collective security for the nations of Europe. It worked well for a while (until the middle of the nineteenth century), preserving order and forcing both liberal and national movements underground.

The Rejection of Revolution and Rationalism: Burke

Opposition to liberal ideas found wide support among ordinary people, as well as intellectuals. A longstanding division within Western culture had been deepened by the Enlightenment and widened by the Revolution. For generations afterward, those who stressed science and reason, equality and democracy, stood in opposition to those who stressed tradition and sentiment, aristocracy and authority. While some people straddled this broad division, most felt a sense of identification with one side or the other. Throughout the nineteenth century both sides appeared to make advances. The liberals succeeded in changing political, economic, and social institutions, and the conservatives made their influence felt in philosophy, the arts, and the general mood of Europe.

During the period immediately following 1815 the conservatives enjoyed a resurgence on all fronts. This was natural enough, for Napoleon, who personified the triumph of the revolution, had fallen. Victory had passed to the defenders of privilege and the old order, and the *ideals* of the Enlightenment had been dimmed by the *realities* of revolution, politics, and war. Many who had sympathized with the ideals now recoiled from the bloody cost of attempting to put them into practice.

One of the ablest spokesmen of the *conservative* point of view was the thinker and statesman Edmund Burke. As a British observer of French affairs, he had been one of the first to become alarmed by the events of the revolution. Opposing from the beginning the underlying principles of the revolution, he had feared that those ideas might win favor in his homeland. His *Reflections on the Revolution in France* appeared in 1790 and has remained to this day an important statement of conservative principles.

Burke's first point of attack was the doctrine of natural rights, which John Locke (pp. 448–49) and the revolutionary leaders had used to justify their actions. David Hume, a skeptical Scottish philosopher, had already demolished the proofs for natural law in his *A Treatise of Human Nature* (1740). Though Burke agreed that one might speak of natural rights in an *abstract* sense, he insisted that this had no bearing on the actual distribution of authority in a civil society. The liberties of the English people, wrote Burke, were those that had been slowly forged in the fire of history; he saw them as part of a specified "inheritance," handed down from generation to generation. And that inheritance was by no means equal for all. The king, the lords, and every other group within the English social body had the right to enjoy the particular privileges and liberties passed on to it from "a long line of ancestors." Burke thus expressed his belief in aristocracy and attacked efforts made in the name of equality to interfere with "legitimate" privilege.

Burke warned against undue reliance on human reason. He felt that each person's private stock of reason is pitifully small and therefore a poor guide to action. He much preferred the wisdom deposited in the "general bank and capital of nations and ages"—by which he meant *tradition*. It is arrogant for reform-minded thinkers, said Burke, to try to reconstruct institutions out of their own minds; such "progress" as might result from their efforts would prove a cruel disappointment. It is far better, he concluded, for people to follow the "prejudices" (established convictions) that bind them to tried and tested institutions.

Burke reserved his bitterest scorn for the Lockean-Jeffersonian belief in the right and benefit of revolution. Denouncing the social *atomism* of both Hobbes and Locke (p. 448), he thought of individuals as parts of a larger organism—*society*. He saw the state as a divine creation, binding past, present, and future generations. He referred to it as a *partnership* embracing all human purposes and not to be broken by individual human wills.

The state, being sacred, must be looked upon with awe and reverence. It should not be "hacked to pieces" by would-be innovators; such recklessness can lead only to anarchy. And, Burke felt, the absence of firm social control is "ten thousand times worse" than the blindest and most stubborn government. A devout Anglican, he held to the doctrine of Original Sin and rejected the Enlightenment faith in human goodness and progress. Only by strict social discipline, he believed, is the individual made decent and civilized. And once restraints are broken, people fall back to beastlike behavior. Thus, Burke argued, revolution leads to an intolerable chaos, which can be ended only by some form of despotism.

Burke did not think, however, that institutions should remain frozen. His view of society as an *organism* led him to think in biological terms. Thus, useless growths should be cut off and new shoots and branches allowed to develop. He was, therefore, a flexible conservative. He even stated that conditions in a given society might become such that a resort to revolution would be permissible. But it should never be a *calculated* action. Mystically (and dangerously) he declared that the justification for revolution must be "the first and supreme necessity only, a necessity that is not chosen, but chooses, a necessity paramount to deliberation, that admits no discussion, and demands no evidence. . . ." In other words, he placed his ultimate reliance on *intuition* (*inner* conviction), thus giving his approval to *irrational* social action.

Though Burke struck his critics as contradictory, hypocritical, and dangerous, he gave a classic expression of conservative thought, scoring hits on key points in liberal doctrine. Other writers soon joined in the assault. The English clergyman Thomas Malthus attacked the idea of human perfectibility, which had been put forward by some eighteenth-century writers (pp. 422–23). Noting the general misery of the poor, Malthus found the explanation in the pressure of population growth. Because of the sexual urge, said Malthus in *An Essay on the Principle of Population* (1798), people tend to increase faster than food supplies. Population growth is held down mainly by the "positive checks" of starvation, disease, and war. Seeing no way out of this condition (save the unlikely prospect of sexual restraint), Malthus predicted continued suffering for the human race. And without a favorable balance between food and people the material foundation for happiness (and perfectibility) is missing. Malthus thus called attention to one of the root problems facing the modern world.

A New Philosophical Synthesis: Kant and Hegel

The conservative reaction was also strong on the European continent, where the intellectuals of the Enlightenment were held responsible for the unhappy events of revolution and war. After 1815 liberal writers and critics were regarded with official hostility and general suspicion. The frequent persecution of authors and the suppression of their works were products of the haunting fear of new social upheavals. Defenders of the restored order concluded also that the weakening of religious faith had eased the way to social subversion. They therefore encouraged the revival of religious fervor that had arisen as a reaction to the secularism of the Enlightenment and the revolution. The Roman Catholic Church, traditionally conservative, played a leading role in this renewal of piety, morality, and respect for authority.

European philosophy was affected even more deeply than religion by the reaction against eighteenth-century thought. A German professor, Immanuel Kant, was a key figure in the shift from the outlook of the Enlightenment to that of the nineteenth century. Born in East Prussia, he spanned in his long lifetime (1724–1804) the confident period of science and rationalism as well as the aftermath of disenchantment. His keen, analytical mind, coupled with a profound moral and religious sense, gave his philosophy its special shape.

Deeply impressed by the achievements of Newtonian science (pp. 416–48), Kant retained much of the rationalist spirit and methodology. However, he set limits on its use and marked off areas of knowledge where religion and moral conviction applied. It was Hume's skepticism (p. 470) that first awakened Kant to the limitations of reason and observation as means of knowing. Hume had argued that science has no way of *proving* causal relationships; it can only note that a certain event is *preceded* by another. This relationship in time and space may be witnessed over and over again; yet the idea of *causation* remains a suggestion of the mind, not a proven fact.

Kant carried the point further, asserting that even "perceived objects" are in large measure a reflection of the mind. Locke had previously stated that knowledge comes chiefly from sensation—the result of external stimuli striking our sensory mechanism and registering upon our consciousness. But Kant was critical of this simple explanation. He insisted that our minds, *independent of experience*, establish certain internal structures, which impose their patterns on our perceptions. For example, we have the concept of "time" — which cannot be perceived and is therefore mental rather than experiential. Yet this concept, along with many others, controls and puts in order all our observations.

From this Kant concluded that scientific knowledge, though highly useful, is not knowledge of the "real" world but a creation of the human mind, drawn from bits of observation. While science thus provides a restricted means of knowing about material things, it cannot even ask the questions that go *beyond* material things. On such issues as the existence of God, immortality of the soul, and moral responsibility, science is mute. In these vital matters, Kant declared in his *Critique of Pure Reason* (1781), the individual must rely chiefly on *conscience* and *intuition*. Such teachings found ready response in Germany, where the Enlightenment (*Aufklärung*) had been comparatively weak. Cultural traditions there were more favorable to romantic hopes, mysticism, and faith.

Following Kant's lead, German philosophy in the nineteenth century reached its fullest development in the work of another professor — Georg Wilhelm Friedrich Hegel, an energetic and imaginative man who helped make the University of Berlin a center of philosophic activity. In response to the doubts and contradictions current among serious thinkers, he attempted nothing less than a complete reconstruction of formal thought. He sought a new methodological approach that would enable him to reconcile opposing philosophic tendencies and bring them into a unified system. He found that approach in the *historical method*.

Hegel steeped himself in the study of history, convinced that true understanding of any subject — whether politics, art, or religion — can be found only through examining its historical development. (This idea came to be known as "historicism.") He saw the general history of an age as more than a collection of events; politics, art, and religion are related parts of a cultural *whole* — guided by a unifying Reason, or Spirit (*Zeitgeist*). The scholar must employ his talent for synthesis as well as analysis in order to bring historical truth to light. This truth, claimed Hegel, is the fulfillment in time of a divine and logical *Idea*.

The Idea may be invisible to most individuals — before it takes shape as historical *happening*. Hegel illustrates this point by declaring: "Great revolutions which strike the eye at a glance [like the French Revolution] must have been preceded by a quiet and secret revolution in the *Spirit* of the age (*Zeitgeist*), a revolution not visible to every eye. . . . It is a lack of acquaintance with this spiritual revolution which makes the resulting changes astonishing."

Hegel's thought is related to Greek philosophical theories during the classical age (pp. 69–73). The Christian philosopher Augustine had also seen history as the unfolding of divine will (pp. 163–64). Hegel's special contribution was his development of the notion of *dialectic* in history. Like Augustine, he saw the continual struggle between opposing forces as the dynamic (power) behind events. But he defined those forces as opposing *ideas*, which become ever more inclusive at successive stages of the struggle. The dominant idea at any given stage he defined as the *thesis*, which (because it is imperfect and incomplete) calls forth a negative or opposing idea — its *antithesis*. In the conflict between the two, neither is entirely destroyed; the opposing elements are reconciled and absorbed into a higher idea, the *synthesis*. (This "Hegelian triad" was a *model* of the dialectical process — not always perfectly fulfilled in the flow of history.)

As an example of his theory, Hegel suggested that the idea of oriental *despotism* had been opposed by the Greco-Roman idea of limited freedom (*aristocracy*); both were being superseded by the German-Christian idea of *universal freedom* under monarchy. His concept of freedom was an *ordered* freedom governed by law. Hegel in this sense glorified the *state* and taught that it was approaching perfection in the Prussian monarchy of his day (pp. 404–5). Though discarding the eighteenth-century concept of progress and reform as naive, he regarded the dialectic of history as leading surely to a freer and happier condition for humanity. (This condition would not include equality for women, whom he regarded as, by nature, inferior to men.)

Since Hegel saw the development of *ideas* as the guiding force and the underlying reality of history, he is usually classified (like Plato) as a philosophical *idealist* — as distinguished from a *materialist*. "Whatever is rational is real, and whatever is real is rational." But he did not deny material existence; he merely subordinated it to the superior reality of ideas and logic. Human reason, in the eighteenth-century sense, he discounted, putting in its place the Reason of history. Hegel insisted that history provides its own solutions to problems that even the wisest of thinkers can understand only dimly.

The human individual, so precious to the *philosophes* (pp. 419, 426), was reduced by Hegel to a relatively minor role in history. Great leaders, he thought — in fact, all people — are instruments of the *dialectic*. Individuals, acting upon their own purposes and passions, can nevertheless accomplish notable deeds; political genius consists in identifying oneself with a *developing* idea. In this way he would explain the greatness of a Caesar, a Jefferson, or a Napoleon.

Though Hegel stressed the role of logic in historical development, he was at the same time both religious and mystical. He was not a practicing Christian, but he viewed religious doctrines and rituals as natural expressions of the total life of an age. (He saw *Christian* teachings as agreeing with his own philosophy.) Hegel's thought was indeed a blend of many elements that had previously been regarded as contradictory. It assigned value, on the one hand, to science, reason, and individual freedom — and, on the other hand, to faith, intuition, and authority. As might be expected, this comprehensive philosophy had a broad appeal: Hegel's books provided stimulus and support for a wide range of ideas. After his death (1831), his disciples branched off in many directions.

THE ROMANTIC SPIRIT IN LITERATURE, ART, AND MUSIC

The reaction against the Enlightenment showed itself in the arts as well as in philosophy. Here it was to take on the name of "romanticism" — a term that includes an extraordinary variety of creative expressions. Common to all of them was an emphasis on *emotion* and *imagination*, as opposed to "cold" calculation. Humanity and the world were to be viewed primarily through the heart, rather than the brain. The romantics were rebels not only against the eighteenth-century world view, but against everyday limitations on the individual. Thus, they fought the rules of bourgeois morality as well as the conformities imposed by industrialism (pp. 511–12). Most romantics desired, at the same time, a mystical identification with God, nature, race, or nation. They often turned to the past for inspiration — some to the classical age of Greece and some to Europe of the Middle Ages.

Nearly all romantic writers and artists had strong feelings about the political and social questions of their time, and many of them were active in politics as propagandists or leaders of movements. But they did not all fight on the same side. Some were conservatives, who blamed the thinkers of the Enlightenment for reducing human beings to mere thinking machines, disrupting the bonds of feeling that ought to link individuals and groups, and severing the mystical ties between man and God. Romantics of this kind usually supported the conservative reaction after 1815. Other romantics, on the other hand, saw absolutism, hereditary privilege, and traditional religion as the great enemies of human spontaneity and creativity. They looked to a future where liberty, equality, and national independence would give full freedom for individuals to develop and express themselves. Thus the influence of romantic ideals and yearnings was felt on both sides of the political struggle, lending additional intensity to the passion with which it was fought.

Appeal to the Heart: Rousseau

The many-sided nature of romanticism may be seen in the life and works of individual writers and artists. The pioneer was Jean-Jacques Rousseau, whose impact on the French Revolution we have already mentioned (p. 459). Though he lived during the Enlightenment, Rousseau's career was in part a revolt against the dominant thought of his age. His style and values became increasingly popular after his death, causing him to be known later as the "father of romanticism."

A man of little formal education or personal discipline, Rousseau had reacted spontaneously against the eighteenth-century emphasis on reason and science. Through a stormy career, which we know largely through his own *Confessions*, he found time to write hundreds of letters, as well as essays and books. His attacks on rationalism struck home not because he wrote from deep knowledge, but because of the power of his language and his appeal to *inner* experience. He wrote, he said, from the heart (and to the heart). Science, he declared, gives knowledge to people that they are better off without. The only knowledge worth having is knowledge of virtue (moral goodness) — and for this, science is not needed. The principles of virtue are "engraved on every heart."

The appeal of Rousseau was due chiefly to his intense sentimentalism. Readers who were unmoved by the theories of science and philosophy responded warmly to his emotional outpourings. In his novel *The New Héloïse* (1761), the hero is madly in love with one of his pupils, but she must marry another. The two frustrated souls experience many temptations and torments that end only after the death of the heroine. The theme of passion and suffering, of morbid self-examination, became a mark of romantic prose and poetry in the nineteenth century.

Another theme of *The New Héloïse* is Rousseau's criticism of sophisticated society and his glorification of nature. The hero of the novel seeks relief from his anguish by wandering through a wilderness. This provides the author with an opportunity to fashion eloquent word pictures of lakes, mountains, and flowers, which inspired such romantic nature poets as William Wordsworth.

Rousseau's individualism and his rejection of imposed patterns of behavior are best expressed in his famous *Émile* (1762). This is not really a story but an account of a proposed type of education for life. From infancy to manhood, the fictional Émile is cared for and taught in a manner contrary to the educational practices of the eighteenth century. Rather than forcing the boy into a succession of studies corresponding to the "knowledge" of the day, his teacher encourages Émile to *learn for himself*. When the need or desire strikes him, the youngster asks for instruction in reading and writing and in nature studies. Meanwhile, he lives a spare, simple, athletic life in the country. The teacher refrains from punishing his pupil for destructive acts, confident that such errors will be corrected through the boy's own experience of consequent loss. There are no naturally bad boys; real vices are learned from "civilized" elders.

Rousseau held that girls as well as boys deserved a sound education. But it must be suited to the female role in life, which he sharply distinguished from the male role. In Émile, he states that girls should be taught only what they will need as women, that is: "To please men, be useful to them, and make themselves loved and respected by them; to educate them when they are young, care for them when grown, counsel and console them, and make life agreeable and sweet to them. . . . The search for abstract and speculative truths, principles, and scientific laws is beyond the capacity of women; all their studies therefore ought to be of a practical sort."

There is much of Rabelais (pp. 346–47) in Rousseau's ideas about educational methods, but Rousseau wrote seriously rather than playfully. His *permissiveness* appealed to romantic individualists and impressed a number of educational reformers. Rousseau's religious sentiments, too, influenced succeeding generations. His was a romantic brand of Deism, rejecting theology and sacred books. As taught to Émile (at the appropriate time), this religion consisted of a simple faith in God and immortality. All that needs to be known about the deity and his commandments, wrote Rousseau, can be found in one's heart and in the study of *nature*.

Poets of Nature and Humanity: Wordsworth, Goethe

Rousseau's insistence on the divinity and beauty of nature was echoed by the lyric poets of the nineteenth century, especially in England. Lyric poetry, as a literary form, traces back to ancient Greece — to Solon and Sappho (p. 75). It was a perfect means of expression for the romantic writers, who desired to tell others of their innermost feelings and visions. William Wordsworth was one of the early romantics; his most moving verses deal with the excitement and meaning of wild nature. Schoolchildren of many generations have recited:

> I wandered lonely as a cloud
> That floats on high o'er vales and hills,
> When all at once I saw a crowd,
> A host, of golden daffodils.

But Wordsworth sensed something beyond the colors and movements of a landscape. His perceptions of nature opened the way to moral and spiritual insights. As he confessed in his "Lines Composed a Few Miles Above Tintern Abbey" (1798):

> . . . Therefore am I still
> A lover of the meadows and the woods,
> And mountains; and of all that we behold
> From this green earth; of all the mighty world
> Of eye, and ear, — both what they half create,
> And what perceive; well pleased to recognise
> In nature and the language of the sense,
> The anchor of my purest thoughts, the nurse,
> The guide, the guardian of my heart, and soul
> Of all my moral being.

Wordsworth shared Rousseau's contempt for formal learning as well as his passion for nature. In "The Tables Turned," Wordsworth wrote:

> Books! 'tis a dull and endless strife:
> Come, hear the woodland linnet,
> How sweet his music! on my life,
> There's more of wisdom in it.

• • • • •

> One impulse from a vernal wood
> May teach you more of man,
> Of moral evil and of good,
> Than all the sages can.

> Sweet is the lore which Nature brings;
> Our meddling intellect
> Misshapes the beauteous forms of things —
> We murder to dissect.

> Enough of Science and of Art;
> Close up those barren leaves;
> Come forth, and bring with you a heart
> That watches and receives.

Beauty, youth, and rebellion were common themes of three other poets — Keats, Byron, and Shelley — each of whom died young. John Keats saluted the ancient Greek ideal of beauty in a poem honoring a painted vase ("Ode on a Grecian Urn," 1820). Addressing this classical work of art, Keats concludes with these words:

> When old age shall this generation waste,
>   Thou shalt remain, in midst of other woe
> Than ours, a friend to man, to whom thou say'st,
>   "Beauty is truth, truth beauty," — that is all
>   Ye know on earth, and all ye need to know.

Lord Byron (George Noel Gordon) lived a turbulent life of passion and adventure, corresponding to the romantic quality of his writings. He died in 1824 at the age of thirty-six while taking part in the Greek war for independence from the Turks (p. 488). His famous poem, "Don Juan," includes a stanza (Canto IV:12) that explains Byron's admiration for youth and his contempt for life "after thirty":

> "Whom the gods love die young" was said of yore,
>   And many deaths do they escape by this:
> The death of friends, and that which slays even more —
>   The death of friendship, love, youth, all that is,
> Except mere breath; and since the silent shore
>   Awaits at last even those who longest miss
> The old archer's shafts, perhaps the early grave
> Which men weep over may be meant to save.

Byron's young friend, Percy Shelley, also lived an unconventional life — devoted to the cause of unrestricted personal freedom. Expelled from Oxford University because of his open profession of atheism (p. 422), Shelley continued to rebel against all forms of authority. He spent his last years in Italy, where he composed his most eloquent poems. In one of these ("Hellas," 1822), he ends by expressing anguish over the human sufferings of the past and hope that a better world may be dawning (signaled by the Greek war for independence):

> Oh, cease! must hate and death return?
> Cease! must men kill and die?
> Cease! drain not to its dregs the urn
> Of bitter prophecy.
> The world is weary of the past,
> Oh, might it die or rest at last!

Shortly after writing this poem, at age thirty, Shelley was drowned while sailing in the Mediterranean Sea.

Shelley's young wife, Mary Wollstonecraft Shelley, survived him. She, too, was a romantic writer, and an active feminist. (Her mother, Mary Wollstonecraft, had written *A Vindication of the Rights of Woman* in 1792 as an answer to the sexist views of Jean-Jacques Rousseau.) Mary Shelley's best-known book is *Frankenstein*, the story of a medical student who creates and brings to life a manlike monster. Her work cut a bold pattern, borrowed by countless authors afterward in the making of "horror" stories, plays, and films.

Though romantic writers sometimes focused on themes of horror, mystery, and death, they more often wrote about broader human experiences. One of the most popular prose writers in Britain was Sir Walter Scott, whose works made him a Scottish national hero. He created the *historical novel*, choosing the Middle Ages as the setting for most of his books. Novels such as *Waverley* (1814) and *Ivanhoe* (1820) show the drama, color, and imagination that marked his best romances.

In Germany the leading literary figure was Johann Wolfgang von Goethe. Born in the middle of the eighteenth century, he grew up during the Enlightenment and lived on into the age of romanticism. Goethe came from a well-to-do family of lawyers and administrators; his "conversion" to romanticism took place while he was studying law at Strasbourg. He later became a member of the court of Saxe-Weimar, a small German duchy. He remained for most of his life in Weimar, the capital of the duchy, where the duke's generosity allowed him freedom to study, travel, and write.

Goethe's interests embraced the whole range of the arts and sciences, in keeping with the Renaissance ideal of *virtù* (p. 319). A man of high intelligence and feeling, he wrote beyond the limitations of most romantic authors. But his personal life was notably romantic — a series of passionate love affairs, many of which he described in his writing. Goethe's lyric poetry reflects his fascination with love, nature, and death. In prose, the most striking expression of his youthful romanticism is *The Sorrows of Young Werther* (1774), which describes the extravagant sufferings of a forlorn hero tortured by frustrated passion.

Faust, a dramatic poem on which Goethe worked during most of his long life, parallels the conflicts and growth that took place in his personal development. Part One, published in 1808, retells the Renaissance legend of a learned professor, Doctor Faust, who bargained his soul to the devil in return for youth and power. (This portion was put to music by several romantic composers.) Part Two, which was not published until after the author's death in 1832, carries Faust on a kind of philosophical excursion in search of man's ultimate purpose and way to happiness. The soul of the hero, in Goethe's poem, is saved at last because he loves God and humanity and tries, in spite of errors, to serve both. Goethe's Faust is a literary model of "modern" man — the individual who seeks to understand and experience the lowest and the highest, and to harmonize sensual and spiritual urges.

The romantic spirit in literature brought forth an impressive response from Russian writers. As a result of Russia's turning toward the West (p. 406), eighteenth-century Russian literature had been largely imitative of the French. In the nineteenth century, however, it developed its own character. Alexander Pushkin (who died in 1837) was the first Russian writer to command serious attention in western Europe, with his romantic poems, plays, and short stories. In his homeland, he is still revered both as a writer of genius whose own short life was filled with romantic passion and adventure, and as the forefather of modern Russian literature in general. The grand tradition of the Russian novel was started by Nicolai Gogol. His *Taras Bulba* (1835) tells of adventures and conflicts among the high-spirited Cossacks, those warrior-horsemen who fought the Tartar enemies of Russia (p. 406). But the finest Russian novelists came later in the century — Feodor Dostoevsky and Leo Tolstoy. Both were concerned primarily with the inner life and struggles of the individual, while describing at the same time the color and detail of Russian life. The best known of their works are Tolstoy's epic historical novel, *War and Peace* (1868), and Dostoevsky's profound *The Brothers Karamazov* (1880).

Rebellion and Romance in Painting

The early-nineteenth-century reaction against rationalism in philosophy and literature was paralleled in the visual arts by a reaction against the classicism of the preceding century (pp. 432–35). In France, the main target of the aristic revolt was the classical style that had been established by Jacques-Louis David. David had turned away from the elegant, frivolous works admired by the aristocracy and had sought inspiration in ancient Roman and Greek sculptures. The classical revival in French painting may be said to have begun with the exhibition in 1785 of his heroic painting of Roman heroes in the *Oath of the Horatii* (*Fig. 11-1*); it became the official style of the French Revolution.

David, a middle-class man who sympathized with the radical political reforms of the period, was elected to the National Convention (p. 460) and helped abolish the royal Academy of Painting. The leaders of the revolution regarded art primarily as an instrument of *propaganda*; they destroyed the academy because it upheld aristocratic traditions. In its place they established the École des Beaux-Arts (School of Fine Arts), which adopted the classical style and sought to impose it on all French painters.

David reached the height of his influence later, under Napoleon. As "First Painter of the Empire," he made portraits of the new caesar, supervised the national galleries, arranged imperial ceremonies, and saw to the licensing of artists who wished to exhibit their works. After Napoleon's fall, David was ordered into exile, and the Academy of Painting was restored. But David's classicism remained the official style in France for a century afterward.

Romantic painters everywhere revolted against classicism, against official styles of any sort, and against academic rules of painting. One of the earliest rebels was Francisco Goya, a Spanish contemporary of David. Heir to the rich

11-1 David. *Oath of the Horatii.* Louvre, Paris.

legacy of Spanish painting of the baroque period (pp. 382–86), Goya preferred it to the restraints of classicism. However, he did not paint in the traditional aristocratic manner, which aimed to ornament or glorify. His portraits of Spanish royalty and nobility are proofs of his extraordinary honesty and powers of observation.

Goya's active social conscience also made him sensitive to the tyranny, civil strife, and poverty that he saw on every hand in his native land. (Hundreds of his etchings reveal the cruelty and desperation of the times.) In his painting *The Third of May, 1808* (Fig. 11-2), he presented an execution scene in the streets of Madrid; Napoleon's soldiers had been attacked by civilians the day before and are here making their reprisal. Goya chose to dramatize the horror of war and the human capacity for brutality — a side of war that David had preferred to ignore. Though he became more bitter as he grew older, he preserved his artistic independence to the end.

The romantic style achieved its fullest expression in France during the generation after Napoleon's downfall. Its most brilliant exponent was Eugène Delacroix. After a classical education, he decided to become a painter and began his training in Paris, which now eclipsed Rome as the art center of Europe. He became almost at once an enthusiastic convert to the new style. "If by Romanticism is meant the free expression of my personal feelings, my aloof-

11-2 Goya. *The Third of May, 1808.* Museo del Prado, Madrid.

ness from the standardized types of paintings prescribed by the Schools, and my dislike of academic formulas," he wrote later, "I must confess that not only am I a Romantic but that I already was one at the age of fifteen!"

Through the strength of his personality and talent Delacroix made the new style dominant in France, even though it was opposed by the academy critics. He was an excellent draftsman, but he disregarded formal rules of drawing and achieved his effects mainly through the use of color. He believed that imagination was more important to an artist than knowledge, and he sought above all to inject excitement and movement into his works. As did Goya, he often played down detail in the interest of sharp focus and strong impact.

Delacroix first gained public attention in 1822 through the showing of his *Dante and Vergil in Hell*. This scene, illustrating a passage from Dante (pp. 264–65), shows a group of tormented individuals writhing in the dark waters of the river Styx (in hell). Friendly critics saw in this work suggestions of the figures of Michelangelo and the colors of Rubens, the opposites of classical serenity. In his historical painting the *Entrance of the Crusaders into Constantinople* (*Fig. 11-3*), Delacroix raises the emotions of the viewer by contrasting the triumphant invaders with their crouching victims (see Fourth Crusade — p. 270). Responding

11-3 Delacroix. *Entrance of the Crusaders into Constantinople*. Louvre, Paris.

to the romantic taste for the exotic (foreign), Delacroix once traveled to Algiers, in Africa. Some of his most popular works, paintings of lion hunts and of the Muslim court and concubines, grew out of that experience.

The love of nature, which was a central feature of romanticism, was best expressed in painting by the English artists J. M. W. Turner and John Constable. Turner's paintings are visionary rather than realistic. A superb colorist, he gave his landscapes and seascapes a sense of grandeur and mystery. He often used a sentimental subject for his canvases, as in *The Fighting Téméraire* (*Fig. 11-4*), painted in 1839. English patriots were stirred by this picture of the ghostly *Téméraire*, a sailing ship of Lord Nelson's battle fleet (p. 466), being towed away for destruction. It is led to its inglorious fate by a squat black tug, symbol of the triumph of steam over sail, iron over timber, efficiency over beauty. Turner showed the ship against a sweep of sky and sea. The time, symbolically, is sunset and a reddish light is cast on the water. Turner's imaginative treatment of nature proved extremely popular; he sold hundreds of paintings and etchings and built up a fortune during his lifetime.

Constable, Turner's contemporary, approached nature in a different manner. His love of the English countryside was akin to that of his good friend the poet Wordsworth; but he studied nature with the eye of a scientist, and, though he finished his canvases indoors, he worked from oil sketches prepared in the

11-4 Turner. *The Fighting Téméraire.* National Gallery, London.

open. His paintings were so strikingly different from the commonplace studio landscapes of the period that they created a sensation when first shown. When *The Hay Wain* (*Fig. 11-5*) was exhibited in Paris in 1821, French painters were astonished by its truth to nature, and many set out to imitate Constable's technique.

Constable referred to Turner's works as "airy visions, painted with tinted steam," while he based his own painting on "observable facts." He wanted nature to speak for itself, without artificial effects. Limiting his subject matter almost entirely to rural scenes, he painted rich canvases — with people and animals (as in *The Hay Wain*) fitting into a scheme clearly designed for human satisfaction. The atmosphere of Constable's paintings is often set by his treatment of the sky, which he believed was "the key note, the standard scale, and the chief organ of sentiment."

The Gothic Revival in Architecture

In the nineteenth century, architectural style became more and more a matter of *individual* taste or fancy. This was a time of vast activity in construction, especially in the industrial cities; most of the older buildings still standing in Europe today were erected during the nineteenth century. They represent a confusing variety of styles springing from several architectural *revivals*. The architect sometimes aimed at a "pure" style, sometimes at a mixed one, and

11-5 Constable. *The Hay Wain*. National Gallery, London.

sometimes at an original design. But by mid-century certain "connections" had developed: banks and government buildings, for instance, were usually built in the Greek or Roman manner; churches and colleges, in the Gothic. There were, of course, notable exceptions to the rule, and all buildings, regardless of their design, suffered a general decline in workmanship.

Of the various styles, the Gothic is most often associated with romanticism. The Gothic *revival* first appeared in England before the French Revolution, as a reaction to the classical Palladian style (pp. 431–32). Horace Walpole, a writer and the son of a noted statesman, wanted to make his country house distinctive from other aristocratic houses. Feeling a romantic attachment to the medieval past, he decided to remodel the house in the manner of a Gothic castle. The result was anything but "pure" Gothic, despite the addition of spires and towers. As with many such attempts, Walpole's creation turned out to be a curious mixture.

The romantic movement, after the turn of the century, gave new force to the Gothic revival. The outstanding example of this period is the Houses of Parliament (*Fig. 11-6*). When the old building burned down in 1834, the lawmakers, remembering that English liberties and Parliament itself traced back to the thirteenth century, decided to rebuild it in the medieval style. At about the same time, across the North Sea in Germany, numerous "medieval" castles began to appear. All over Europe and America the Gothic revival proved popular.

Romanticism in Music: Beethoven, Wagner

The eighteenth-century classical style in music, as we have seen (pp. 440–41), stressed order, grace, and clarity; the nineteenth century cast off restraint and released the emotional power of music. The classical style did not disappear altogether, but it was submerged in the tide of romanticism. Ludwig van Beethoven, born in Bonn, Germany, in 1770, bridged both styles. His early works are similar to those of Haydn and Mozart, and he followed established compositional forms throughout most of his life. But he responded to the romantic spirit, and his later works are marked by heightened drama, suspense, and brilliant climaxes. Unlike some romantic composers, Beethoven never lost control of his musical themes; his works throb with energy but are contained within an orderly pattern. For this reason, he is sometimes called a "classical romantic."

Compositions in the romantic style were usually written for the concert hall, rather than for the small chamber or drawing room. They called for more volume and range of sound; Beethoven's orchestra was nearly twice the size of Haydn's. Although few new instruments were introduced, the number of strings, winds, and percussion instruments was enlarged. The symphony became the most popular form, but pieces for solo performance also found favor.

11-6 Barry and Pugin. Houses of Parliament, London.

Melodies were highly expressive and original; harmonies were rich and often dissonant; and rhythms were subject to sudden or subtle changes.

Leading composers in the romantic style were an Austrian, Franz Schubert; a Pole, Frederic Chopin; a Frenchman, Hector Berlioz; and a Russian, Peter Ilich Tchaikovsky. Much of the serious music performed today — in the concert hall, on the air, and on records and tapes — is by romantic composers. The high point of romanticism appeared not in the symphony hall but in the opera house. Richard Wagner, born in Leipzig in 1813, created a new concept of opera — or music-drama, as he preferred to call it. Wagner personified the deepest yearnings of the romantic spirit. Above all, he stressed the idea of the *unity* of thought and feeling and believed that this unity should be reflected in all art forms. He had contempt for art as mere entertainment or spectacle — "effects without cause." His new kind of opera, which was modeled on the performances of Greek tragedy (p. 76) joined poetry, music, scenery, and action into one unified whole.

Wagner's "Ring cycle," a sequence of operas drawn from Germanic legend, best illustrates his idea of form. Here the drama — which is concerned with the curse of gold and the lust for power — is central. Voices and orchestra combine to carry forward the powerful themes; instead of writing separate speeches, arias, choruses, and accompaniments, Wagner created an "endless melody" out of all the musical elements. His music is rich and complex, full of passion and suspense, wholly romantic.

Italian opera, it should be added, remained close to the tradition established by Monteverdi (p. 439). But it, too, reflected the new stress on emotion and the enlarged capabilities of the orchestra. Giuseppe Verdi, Wagner's artistic rival, is probably the most successful of operatic composers; his spectacular *Aïda* has been performed more often than any other opera. Verdi chose plots that focused upon the most elemental human feelings and set them to thrilling vocal music. A political activist, he also used stories in his operas that inspired the rising desire for liberty and nationhood in Italy (pp. 495–96).

THE SPREAD OF LIBERAL DEMOCRACY AND NATIONALISM

The defeat of revolutionary France, and the conservative reaction that followed, slowed the momentum of liberal and national revolution; but in the long run they could not reverse it. The forces making for change were too strong to contain. These included the resentment of the middle classes against absolutism and privilege, continued deprivation among the urban poor, the growing discontent of eastern European serfs, and the appeal of liberal romantic ideas to educated young people of all classes. On the other side, the conservative rulers and nobles, divided by traditional power rivalries and inclined to waver between repression and reform as the best way of preventing renewed violent revolution, were not so united and determined as they seemed. Down to 1871, the nineteenth century saw the gradual crumbling of conservative resistance and the emergence of a new Europe, dominated by the hopes and ideals — and the ambitions and rivalries — of liberalism and nationalism.

The Revolutions of 1830 and 1848

The struggles for liberal democracy and national unity and independence followed a general pattern in Europe during the nineteenth century. In the first decade after the Congress of Vienna, most of the uprisings were quickly suppressed (as in Naples, Spain, and Russia). Revolutionary successes were achieved only in Greece (against the Ottoman Turks — p. 284) and overseas, where the Spanish and Portuguese colonies in Latin America gained their independence by 1825. Waves of revolution continued to break across Europe, however — notably in 1830 and 1848. The most significant victory for the liberal forces came in France in 1830.

Even with the restoration of the Bourbon king, Louis XVIII, in 1814, France had preserved the principal reforms introduced by the Revolution and Napoleon. Louis reigned as a constitutional monarch, with a legislature that

1804	1814	1830	1848	· 1852	1870
FIRST EMPIRE (Napoleon I)	Bourbon Restoration	JULY MONARCHY (Louis-Philippe)	SECOND REPUBLIC	SECOND EMPIRE (Napoleon III)	

represented the restored nobility and well-to-do members of the business class. Though the limited voting rights displeased the majority of citizens, the arrangement was close to what the moderate bourgeois had sought in 1789. It was threatened in 1824, however, when Louis was succeeded by his brother (the Count of Artois) — Charles X.

Charles had been an enemy of the revolution, a leader of the émigrés who had urged other European nobles and princes to attack revolutionary France (p. 459). After becoming king, he and his reactionary friends moved to turn back the clock. They sought to require the government to make annual payments to former nobles whose lands had been confiscated during the revolution. They also wanted to bring back the old feudal law of *primogeniture* (exclusive inheritance of an estate by the firstborn son), and they favored a return of clerical influence in education and politics. Charles himself, proud and stubborn, was contemptuous of the popular criticism his measures caused. When the elective Chamber of Deputies refused, in 1830, to bend to his will, he violated the constitution that had been issued by Louis XVIII. By decree, Charles dissolved the Chamber, censored the press, and changed voting rights to strengthen the power of the former nobles.

Paris responded to this revival of absolutism by throwing up barricades in the streets. The "July Revolution" lasted only a few days, for the troops and police refused to fire on the populace. Charles, who had no desire to share the fate of Louis XVI, promptly abdicated and left for England. The rebels now found themselves divided on what to do next. The workmen, students, and intellectuals who had hoisted the revolutionary *tricolor* (flag) at the city hall, in place of the Bourbon *fleur-de-lis*, demanded that the monarchy give way to a republic. The bourgeois politicians, however, opposed such a change, feeling that their interests would be safer under a constitutional monarchy. All they wanted was a different kind of king, one who would serve their purposes. The politicians found such a man in Prince Louis-Philippe, who, though a member of the Bourbon family, had fought on the side of the revolution in 1789. They persuaded the aged and respected national hero, the Marquis de Lafayette, to support Louis-Philippe. This helped to make the "left-wing" Bourbon prince acceptable to those who wanted a republic.

The reign of Louis-Philippe brought a modest extension of liberal and democratic practices. Though the number of voters was still only a small fraction of the total citizenry, it was double what it had been before. The chief significance of the July Revolution was that it decisively ended the threat of counterrevolution in France and shattered the principle of legitimacy, hallowed at Vienna in 1815 — Louis-Philippe became king upon the *invitation* of an elected Chamber of Deputies. The French thus struck a blow against the "Metternich System" (p. 470), and their success encouraged liberals and patriots elsewhere.

The first uprising outside France occurred in the Belgian Netherlands. This territory, for centuries under either Austrian or Spanish control, had been joined to the independent Dutch Netherlands by decision of the Congress of Vienna. Metternich and his colleagues had hoped that a united Netherlands would serve as a barrier to the French, whose rulers had frequently sent armies northward toward the Rhine River. But there were deep-seated problems in the cultural relations between Dutch and Belgians. The Dutch were mainly Protestant, while the Belgians were mainly Catholic; and the French-speaking population of southern Belgium (Walloons) resented the required use of the Dutch language in most areas. Discontent with the Dutch king, William I, led to street riots in Brussels shortly after the July uprising in France. At first the Belgian leaders demanded only local self-rule. But when William took up arms against them they declared for complete independence.

Metternich and his allies in central Europe would have moved against this eruption of nationalism in the Low Countries had they not been occupied with threats nearer home. With French and British backing, the Belgians managed to hold off the Dutch king. Finally, in 1831, an international conference in London provided for an independent Belgium, with a German prince (Leopold of Saxe-Coburg) as constitutional monarch. In 1839, King William also recognized the new state, and its independence and neutrality were guaranteed by the major European powers.

Polish patriots, meanwhile, had tried and failed to establish the independence of their homeland (p. 407). After long diplomatic "trading" among the powers at the Congress of Vienna (pp. 417–68), Poland had been given over to Russian control as a separate kingdom — under the personal rule of Tsar Alexander I. Early in 1831 the Polish Diet (assembly) of nobles rejected Alexander's successor Nicholas I as their king; Nicholas sent a large army and crushed the brave but divided Polish forces. Revolutionary stirrings also arose in 1830 in various parts of Germany, Italy, Spain, and Portugal. In almost every case, they were put down by force, as they had been in Poland. But the widespread agitations demonstrated that liberal nationalist forces were rising throughout Europe, kept in check only by political repression and military measures.

In Britain, where substantial change could be brought about through legislation, liberal ideas and practices made a striking advance. Even during the 1820s, Parliament moved away from a mercantilist economy toward free international trade. It also gave to Catholics and dissenting Protestants political rights equal to those of Anglicans. But the most significant single act was the Reform Bill of 1832, which altered the voting franchise and the system of representation in the House of Commons. In response to shifts in the English population, this bill assigned seats to the growing urban centers of the North and the Midlands at the expense of districts in the South.

The individual right to vote remained tied to property ownership, but more lenient requirements almost doubled the number of eligible voters (men only) — to nearly one million. The new voters were chiefly of the middle class; the Reform Bill raised its share of power in Commons to roughly that of the landed gentry (p. 445). It also opened the door to further liberal and democratic reforms during the ensuing decades, including extension of the vote to women. ("Cabinet" government, responsible to the Parliamentary majority, had been established a century earlier by Robert Walpole, Britain's first "prime minister.") Although the British achieved this transformation without revolution or civil war, at critical moments the use (and threat) of violence was no doubt decisive. In 1832, for example, the Reform Bill was driven through Parliament under the pressure of street demonstrations and signs of possible insurrection.

Some of these pressures came from the English "Radicals" of the time, who wanted to go far beyond the liberals in overhauling British society and politics. The Radicals — chiefly from the working class, with some of the new industrialists like Robert Owen (p. 515) — were both philosophical and action-minded. Inspired by such older writers as the American Tom Paine (p. 450) and their own countryman Jeremy Bentham (p. 494), they demanded radical changes in voting laws, Parliament, courts, prisons, the Anglican Church, and the privileges of the lords. Many of these changes were brought about later in England. But for the time being, in 1832, the controlling powers in Parliament showed enough skill to permit *mild* reforms rather than face the risk of rebellion.

On the continent the strongholds of privilege proved more unbending. Rather than submit to change or attempt to guide its course, the conservatives generally sought to *repress* it. Liberal and nationalist discontent continued to build up, however, and another series of explosions came in 1848. In France, Louis-Philippe, the "citizen-king," had become exceedingly unpopular. Voting rights remained limited to a small fraction of citizens, and many of the bourgeois, as well as working people, became increasingly discontented. The critics of the government fell into two groups: the radicals, who wanted to discard the monarchy and establish a republic with *universal* voting rights, and the liberals, who wanted only a limited extension of voting rights. Had Louis Philippe yielded to the liberals, he could have gained broader support and kept his crown. But he stubbornly rejected *any* constitutional change, and in February 1848 the streets of Paris bristled once again with barricades.

In a virtual repetition of the events of 1830, the royal troops refused to march against the people, and the king sensibly sailed for England. The victors were again split between monarchists and republicans, but this time the disagreement developed into deeper civil conflict. The republican leaders of Paris were concerned about *social* as well as political reforms. They spoke for the growing number of workers, many of them unemployed, who had been drawn into the industrial centers. The victims of low income, insecurity, and poor working conditions, these "proletarians" were generally anticapitalist and antibourgeois.

In 1848 the republicans overcame monarchist opposition and forced the proclamation of a *republic*. They then arranged for the election, by a universal male vote, of a Constituent Assembly to frame a new basic law for France. The Assembly, which met in May, no doubt represented the sentiment of the nation as a whole (outside Paris). It favored democratic political changes but no substantial social or economic reforms. This view was assailed by the aroused workers of the city, most of whom wanted the government to establish industrial workshops as a means of providing employment.

Fearing that the majority of the Assembly would reject their demands, groups of workers attacked it and yet again the barricades went up. This time, however, the result was very different. An ugly class war started in Paris, and some ten thousand were killed or wounded in several days of bloody street-fighting. The regular army, called upon to defend the Assembly, crushed the revolt and thereby raised the bitterness of most of the urban workers. They concluded that the army had been used to defend the "exploitation" of laborers by the capitalist class. The bourgeois, for their part, were shaken by the threat of social revolution.

After those bloody "June Days," the Assembly drafted a new constitution that provided for a legislature and a president with strong powers. It decided to call for the president's election at once, even though the final work on the constitution had not been completed. Of the four well-known candidates who entered the contest, the victory went to the one who promised the most to both sides in the civil struggle. Prince Louis Napoleon Bonaparte, a nephew of the famous Corsican, represented himself as standing for both social *order* and social *change*. Playing upon his family name, he swamped his rivals and became president of the Second Republic in December 1848. Three years later, he brought about the dissolution of the legislature and had himself elected for a new term of ten years. In 1852 this shrewd politician proclaimed the Second Empire, taking the title of Napoleon III. (His cousin, the son and direct heir of Napoleon I, had died in 1832.)

The cycle of revolution and counterrevolution also took place beyond the borders of France. In central Europe liberal demands were mixed with nationalist hopes. Revolutionists rushed into the streets in a dozen capitals, proclaiming political rights and calling for the unity and independence of their own national groups. Monarchs and ruling classes were at first frightened by these demonstrations and generally responded by offering concessions or new constitutions. But the protesting movements lacked the internal cohesion and the organized force needed to hold their gains. When it became clear that they could be stopped by military action, the authorities recovered their poise, withdrew their concessions, and put down the rebels with troops and police. In the course of these uprisings, peasants who were still *serfs* won their freedom, but liberal reforms and progress toward national self-determination were checked.

Nevertheless, the movements of 1848 had significant consequences. The Austrian Empire felt the greatest shock, a warning of things to come. Until 1848 Prince Metternich (p. 467) had remained the outstanding leader of "legitimacy" and conservatism. Yet a liberal uprising in Vienna so unnerved him that he hurriedly resigned as imperial chancellor and departed for London. The flight of Metternich brought joy and hope to the advocates of change everywhere. These feelings were premature, however, for within two years imperial troops had suppressed the disturbances in the Habsburg domains, and Metternich could return to his beloved Vienna to write his memoirs. But he was no longer in power, and the Metternich System was broken.

Nationalist aspirations, though frustrated, were intensified throughout central Europe. Hungarians, Czechs, Italians, Serbs, Croats, and Rumanians became more dissatisfied within the Austrian Empire. Many Germans, meanwhile, were looking toward the creation of a large Pan-German state. The various German territories (including Austria proper) sent delegates to Frankfurt in 1848, with the aim of setting up a German federal union. This Frankfurt Assembly could not reach agreement, however, on the type of constitution for such a union. Upset by the political reaction that had set in by 1849, this assembly produced no solid results. Nationalist sentiment had nonetheless been stirred, and within a generation a united Germany would be created by the more "realistic" methods of diplomacy and war (pp. 496–99).

The Liberal Ideal: Mill

The immediate aims and actions of the liberal and nationalist movements were in keeping with their maturing ideologies. The liberal demands were for extension of voting rights, free expression, guarantees of legal protections, and constitutional checks on government power; the nationalist demands were for the political union and independence of distinct cultural groups. Neither set of aims can be fully understood without a knowledge of its underlying system of thought.

Nineteenth-century liberal thought was the outcome of a trend that had started in the Renaissance, or even as far back as the late Middle Ages. It was represented in succeeding stages by men like Rabelais, Erasmus, Locke, and Jefferson (pp. 328, 347, 448, 452). Central to the thinking of these men was their stress on human personality and its free development. This idea could be realized, they believed, only through each individual's exercise of personal *freedom*. The nature of freedom and the proper conditions for its use had been outlined before the French Revolution; after Napoleon, those views had to be modified considerably.

Nineteenth-century liberals were bitterly aware that something had gone wrong with the revolution — "Liberty, Equality, and Fraternity" had led to bloodshed and dictatorship — but they clung to the same basic beliefs, while studying the mistakes that had been made. They became more respectful of *history* than earlier liberals had been, observing that human rationality is not sufficient to overcome, in a short time, the lasting power of old institutions and habits of thought. They were also more wary of *popular* tyranny, concluding that the will of the majority can be as wrong and oppressive as that of a despot. Many liberals emphasized, finally, that freedom must be guided by morality if it is not to go astray. Thus, the nineteenth-century liberals held that a *tempered* doctrine of liberty is the best means to individual happiness and the fulfillment of human potential.

On the continent, liberal voices were generally overpowered by those of the conservatives and romantics. In England, however, they remained vigorous, and liberal speeches and writings accompanied the advance of political reforms. John Stuart Mill was the foremost spokesman of nineteenth-century liberalism. His conceptions of personal freedom, precisely and eloquently expressed, have had a persistent appeal to those everywhere who admire the ideal of liberty.

Mill was a follower of Jeremy Bentham, the founder of a philosophy called "utilitarianism." According to Bentham, who took an *atomistic* view of human society (p. 448), the most acceptable way of evaluating social institutions is to measure their total *utility* (usefulness) to all the affected individuals — looking to "the greatest good of the greatest number." Mill defended this view, explaining that the measurement of the "greatest good" must take into account *qualitative* differences in human satisfactions. He believed that the highest satisfactions can be reached only under conditions of personal freedom, and he set out to specify those conditions and work for their achievement. Mill's carefully reasoned *On Liberty* (1859) remains the classic statement of the historic liberal view of individual rights in relation to society.

The book accepts Aristotle's conviction that the purpose of human life is the harmonious development of one's abilities (p. 72). This purpose, declared Mill, requires two conditions: "freedom, and a variety of situations." He would give to each individual, therefore, the utmost freedom in relation to society and the state. (Like John Locke, he distinguished between freedom and *license*, for the latter means interference with someone else's freedom.) Each person's freedom he regarded as *sacred* — "the only purpose for which power can be rightfully exercised over any member of a civilized community, against his will, is to prevent harm to others." Mill justified this position not by resorting to the outmoded doctrine of "natural rights" or the "social contract" (p. 448), but on the *utilitarian* ground that freedom is essential to the greater happiness of the individual and the species.

He included females as well as males in his philosophical judgments. His partner in writing *On Liberty* and other major works was a woman, Harriet Taylor. A close intellectual associate for many years, she at last became his wife. Mill, unlike other writers of the nineteenth century, viewed women as equal to men in intelligence. He helped found the first woman's suffrage society in

England in 1867 and published, soon after, *The Subjection of Women*, a persuasive statement of the case for female political rights.

Mill abhorred the drift toward large bureaucracies and cultural conformity. The state itself, he insisted, is worth no more than the individuals who make it up: "a State which dwarfs its men, in order that they may be more docile instruments in its hands even for beneficial purposes, will find that with small men no great thing can really be accomplished. . . ." It is by cultivating individual *differences*, concluded Mill, that human beings become noble and enrich social life. As people become more valuable to themselves, they are capable of being more valuable to others. Each person thus "strengthens the tie which binds every individual to the race, by making the race infinitely better to belong to."

He opposed increases in public services by government, even when done for the benefit of individuals. He preferred that citizens and groups act on their own initiative to forestall the "deadening hand" of centralized power and uniformity. But his first concern was the preservation, at any cost, of liberty of *thought* and *discussion*. This, he thought, is crucial to the health of the individual and society. He denied the right of any government, popular or despotic, to interfere with free expression: "If all mankind minus one were of one opinion, and only one person were of the contrary opinion, mankind would be no more justified in silencing that one person, than he, if he had the power, would be justified in silencing mankind." The evil of forbidding the expression of an opinion is more than the injury to an individual, Mill asserted: it hurts the human race, and it hurts those who dissent from the opinion more than those who hold it. "If the opinion is right, they are deprived of the opportunity of exchanging error for truth; if wrong, they lose, what is almost as great a benefit, the clearer and livelier impression of truth, produced by its collision with error."

The Nationalist Ideal: Mazzini

While many people, especially in England and France, applauded Mill's sentiments, others subordinated individual freedom to nationalism. In Italy and Germany, still "geographical expressions" rather than national states, the desire for national unity and prestige overshadowed all other aims. Freedom, like every good thing, was seen to be rooted in the *nation*. Unlike Mill, who took Britain's power for granted, the nationalists on the continent did not glorify the individual, "free" of interference by the state; they regarded the building of a powerful state as the necessary means to full nationhood and individual realization. Hence, in Germany and Italy the moving ideology was national liberalism (or liberal nationalism). Its special form and tone, in the first half of the century, were expressed by the Italian patriot Giuseppe Mazzini. Though inspired by the humanitarian and egalitarian ideals of the Enlightenment, Mazzini was caught up in the romantic and nationalist passion of his own generation. In him, the "religion of liberty" became the "religion of the fatherland."

The nationalist ideal, as described by Mazzini, was linked to a sentimental concern for all humanity. Mazzini described his feeling in a series of essays, *The Duties of Man*, written at midcentury and directed to the Italian working class. "You are men," Mazzini told his readers, "before you are citizens or fathers." The "law of life" requires that individuals embrace the whole human family in their love, confessing their faith in the unity and brotherhood of all peoples. But the lone individual, declared Mazzini, is powerless to work for the benefit of all: "The individual is too weak, and Humanity too vast." Effective action requires fraternal cooperation among individuals who can work together — those of a common language and culture — in other words, a nation. Starting with this line of reasoning, Mazzini went on to glorify the nation as divinely created for serving *humanity*. But many of his readers, then and later, became so attentive to the glory of the nation that they forgot his teaching of a prior duty to humanity.

Mazzini saw the independent nation as a promoter of individual liberty and equality: "A Country is a fellowship of free and equal men. . . . The law must express the general aspiration, promote the good of all, respond to a beat of the nation's heart." But, in fact, the push for national strength through unity often reduced freedom, especially when freedom involved dissent from national objectives. Nationalism could readily become statism, as it did north of the Alps. The historian Heinrich von Treitschke, writing later in the century, declared that the individual's *first* duty is *obedience to the state*. This influential professor at the University of Berlin gave academic and philosophical respectability to the German drive for discipline, unification, and dominance.

The Achievement of National Unification: Bismarck

The unsuccessful liberal-nationalist uprisings of 1830 and 1848 had failed because of inadequate organization and power. It is significant that the eloquent Mazzini, who labored tirelessly to rid Italy of foreign occupation, spent most of his years as a revolutionary exile. But his patriotic propaganda paved the way for the diplomatic and military successes of others, notably Count Camillo di Cavour and Giuseppe Garibaldi. Though his liberal ideals were far from realized, Mazzini lived to see the achievement of a united Italy in 1870.

But in Germany the practical means to national unification were most forcefully demonstrated, and the consequences for Europe and the world were most profound. After the disappointment of 1848, German nationalists looked for more effective means of bringing their dreams to fulfillment. One of them, Count Otto von Bismarck, was sure he knew the way. Born into an aristocratic landowning family, he rose to power as a high official of the Prussian kingdom. In the tradition of Frederick the Great (p. 405), Bismarck admired autocracy and militarism. He had despised the liberal leaders of 1848 and had urged the

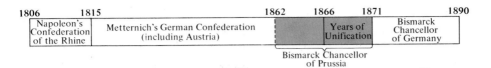

1806	1815		1862	1866	1871	1890
Napoleon's Confederation of the Rhine	Metternich's German Confederation (including Austria)			Years of Unification		Bismarck Chancellor of Germany

Bismarck Chancellor of Prussia

Prussian king to use the army to restore order and civil obedience. (Many German liberals later supported Bismarck, however, because his methods proved effective in building national power.)

He set out, after 1848, to make Prussia the dominant German power. His desire was both to glorify Prussia and to unify Germany. He was convinced that the German princelings would never join together through their own efforts, and he had only contempt for what the "people" might accomplish. The important decisions and acts had to be taken, he thought, by the ruler and ministers of the leading German state, Prussia. "Not by speeches and majority votes," declared Bismarck, "are the great questions of the day decided — that was the mistake of 1848 and 1849 — but by blood and iron." Acting upon this conviction, he proved to be Europe's master of the art of "power politics."

Appointed chief minister to the Prussian king in 1862, Bismarck determined to remove, by diplomacy and war, whatever stood in the way of German unification. Austria was clearly the chief obstacle, for Metternich had managed to establish and maintain Austrian dominance in central Europe, and he and his successors looked with distaste and fear upon the ambitions of Prussia. Prussia cooperated with Austria in a military campaign to take the duchies of Schleswig and Holstein from Danish control, but the two powers quarreled over the division of their conquests. In 1866 the argument turned into armed conflict, and Prussian troops invaded Austria and its allied German states. European diplomats were impressed by the efficiency of the Prussian military machine, which Bismarck had created at heavy expense. After the conclusion of the Seven Weeks' War, defeated Austria gave up all influence over northern Germany to Prussia. Metternich's German Confederation (p. 469) was abolished, and Bismarck raised in its place the North German Confederation, under the presidency of the king of Prussia. This new political grouping had a firm economic foundation, for Prussia had previously led the way in establishing a customs union (*Zollverein*) that equalized tariffs among the states that joined it. The union included most of the German states outside Austria.

It was now France's turn to be uneasy, for the French, like the Austrians, had traditionally opposed a strong and united Germany. Aggressive factions in both Prussia and France viewed a military showdown as inevitable; diplomatic maneuvering and reciprocal insults led, in 1870, to a declaration of war by France. The whirlwind Franco-Prussian War was another brilliant success for the Prussian armies, resulting in the death of one empire and the birth of another. Napoleon III, humiliated by defeat and capture, lost his throne, and in 1871 William I of Prussia was proclaimed the emperor (*Kaiser*) of a united

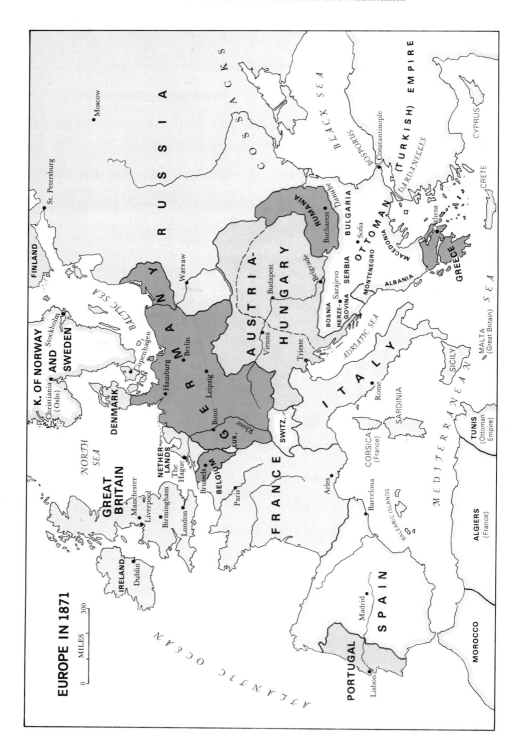

Germany. (William was a descendant of the Hohenzollern dynasty, which had come to rule Prussia by the eighteenth century — p. 404.) Four south German states, which had remained aloof from the North German Confederation, took their places in the proud new empire (p. 498). Bismarck, now the *imperial* chancellor, had achieved the central ambitions of his career: Prussia was supreme in Germany, and Germany was supreme in Europe.

During the Franco-Prussian War, Napoleon III (p. 492) recalled his troops from Rome, where they had been protecting the territory and political independence of the pope. (Rome was all that was left of the States of the Church — pp. 303–4.) The French withdrawal permitted the newly created kingdom of Italy to send in forces and annex Rome, thereby completing national unification in 1870. Italy and Germany, both of which had been divided for centuries, now became independent members of the European state system. This would be the central fact of international relations during the years to follow. The greater power, Germany, which had achieved unity and strength by the methods of authority, discipline, and militarism, was determined to win its "place in the sun" after its late arrival as a state. The successful revolutions of national unification were thus a prelude to European and global struggle, climaxed by the First and Second World Wars.

CHAPTER

12

The Impact
of the Machine

All through the nineteenth century, revolutions aimed at political and social reform attracted the attention of Europe. These were movements that rose and fell at various times and places. But there was also another force behind the nineteenth-century changes that operated unceasingly, and indeed accelerated throughout the century: the *technological* revolution and the accompanying development of *machines*. The political and social movements had many parallels in the past. But the acceleration of technology was without precedent; it set Europe on a new and irreversible course. The Industrial Revolution would prove comparable, in its impact on human culture, to the Agricultural Revolution of the New Stone Age (pp. 10–15).

Neither the machine nor technology was new to Western civilization. Just as modern science has roots in ancient and medieval thought (p. 260), so mechanization grew out of the practical devices of earlier centuries. The important craft of metallurgy traces back to the Bronze Age, which began in Europe around 3000 B.C. (p. 8). It made possible the manufacture of metal implements, weapons, armor, and objects of art. Mechanical devices, too, were invented and used during ancient, medieval, and early modern times. These included water wheels, pumps, catapults, windmills, compasses, telescopes, clocks, printing presses, spinning wheels, and cannon.

It was not technology, but rather the *rate* and *scope* of its development that proved revolutionary in the nineteenth century. Before 1800, in spite of the existence of simple machines, most of the world's food and other commodities had been produced by hand tools with the aid of human and animal power. After 1800, these necessities were produced increasingly by powered machinery — and the technological drive has grown ever stronger. Today the use of machines has passed beyond the abundant creation of material goods; machines are extending and replacing human functions of every sort. Technology and the scientific knowledge that undergirds it have given to modern societies a power for good and evil that is unique in human history.

One of the early consequences of the machine was the sweeping change in the conditions that had given rise to historic liberalism. As we saw in the preceding chapter, liberal ideas and institutions made striking progress during the nineteenth century, despite the countercurrents of conservatism and romanticism. "Free enterprise" and the encouragement of individual initiative spurred the invention and development of machines. Yet those very machines, by altering the structure of production and the organization of society, were to make obsolete the doctrine of unlimited economic freedom. That doctrine had been nurtured mainly in the eighteenth century, in a society that was rural (hence self-sufficient) and in which the units of production were small. The principle of *laissez-faire* (let alone) could not effectively meet the problems that would arise from mass production, class conflict, urbanization, and the concentration of private economic power. The twentieth century, which earlier liberals had predicted would be a century of widening decision-making by individuals, would in fact be a time of expanding control by huge corporations and governments.

THE INDUSTRIAL REVOLUTION

The Industrial Revolution was unplanned. Perhaps the most remarkable thing about it is that it ever happened. True, many of the developments that had transformed Europe since the end of the Middle Ages had also prepared the way for the Industrial Revolution. The growth of colonial empires had brought much of the world's trade to the countries of western Europe, giving them the wealth to invest in new technology and worldwide markets for their resulting products (pp. 301–3). The rise of capitalism had created a class of merchants and manufacturers who were willing to take risks, as well as new forms of business organization that were adaptable to the needs of large industrial enterprises (pp. 286–88). The Scientific Revolution had greatly increased the fund of scientific knowledge on which early machine technology rested (p. 419), and Europe possessed the raw material necessary for industrialization.

But the turning of an agrarian society into an industrial one is not something that comes about easily or "naturally." It is, in fact, an extraordinary development, and there is reason to believe that industrialization came when and where it did only because of an unusual set of circumstances. Those circumstances included a social system and entrepreneurial skills that could convert the *potential* of technology into the *actuality* of large-scale production.

The Agrarian Transformation

It was in England that the Industrial Revolution began; from there the pattern of change spread to the European continent and to the Americas.

Preceding and accompanying the Industrial Revolution were significant changes in agriculture. In the course of the eighteenth century, English landlords had substantially increased their holdings and revenues by speeding up the practice of *land enclosure*, which had been going on since the end of the Middle Ages. Under the old manorial regime the lord's tenants had enjoyed access to the common lands of pasture, meadow, and wood lot (pp. 219–20). By successive parliamentary acts of enclosure, these lands were gradually removed from common use and were *rented* to individuals to farm. Over the same period the "open fields" of cultivated strips were also switched into single plots and fenced in for individual use. In this process of redistribution, the landlords usually gained additional land, while tenants often found that they could no longer make a living.

Although the redistribution brought hardship to thousands of farm families, it put large tracts of land under more efficient management. Whereas the typical small farmer clung to old-fashioned ways, the more ambitious landlords were willing to experiment with improved methods. They tried new farming tools and fertilizers, planted soil-renewing crops, and developed scientific breeding of livestock. The result was a substantial rise in output. This revolution in agriculture also created a pool of displaced farmworkers, both men and women, who desperately sought employment. Some hired themselves out to successful farm operators; others turned to spinning or weaving. They were ready to go wherever they could earn better wages.

At about the same time British traders were discovering profitable new markets. By 1750 Britain had built up a globe-circling empire supported by a large navy and merchant fleet (pp. 299–300). Rich profits awaited those who could increase their exports. Woolens merchants, whose business was well established, were in a favored position to do so; all they needed was a larger production of woolen cloth. There was a brisk demand for cotton goods, too. If English cottons could be made competitive in price with goods produced in the Orient, quick fortunes could be made in the cotton-textile trade.

The Mechanization of Industry and Transportation

A series of inventions gave the textile merchants what they were looking for and led to the general mechanization of industry in England. The first breakthrough, about 1760, was a hand-powered, multispindled spinning wheel (jenny). Soon afterward came Richard Arkwright's water-powered spinning "frame," which spun stronger threads than the jenny. Advances in spinning were soon matched by the development of powered weaving looms. At first designed for use in the cotton industry, these inventions were eventually (from the 1830s onward) adapted to woolen production as well.

The logic of events led next to the building of factories. Spinning and weaving under the domestic system (p. 286) were to persist for many years, but the new machines were not well suited to household use. They were a substantial capital investment; therefore, they had to be operated around the clock. Moreover, they required a source of *power*, which at first was available only near swift-running streams. For these reasons, and for reasons of maintenance and supervision, power machines were set up in special establishments. Arkwright launched the first spinning mill in the 1770s, and within a few years he was employing hundreds of workers, who attended thousands of spindles. Other entrepreneurs soon followed his example.

The greatest boost to the building of factories was the development of an efficient steam engine, which furnished a mobile source of power. The story of the steam engine is one of continuous interplay between science and technology. The chief advances appear to have been made by practical inventors, but they could not have succeeded without the aid, direct or indirect, of accumulated scientific knowledge.

The steam engine initially was a response to a problem in coal mining. For deep shafts to be operated efficiently, there had to be some way to pump out the water that drained into them. Thomas Newcomen invented the first working machine for this purpose about 1700. Later in the century James Watt and others made important improvements on Newcomen's invention. The steam engine eventually became the chief source of power in the factories and was adapted to both water and land transportation. The "age of railways" opened in 1830, when George Stephenson's famed locomotive, the *Rocket*, made its first run on the Liverpool and Manchester line. Within twenty years, steam trains were running between all the principal cities of Britain. With its cities linked by steam transportation, with its mechanized cotton industry, and its coal mines deep beneath the earth, Britain now provided the pattern for future industrialization around the world.

Development of a "Permanent" Industrial Revolution

At the middle of the nineteenth century, Britain's industrial productivity and technical progress were unique. But it did not keep this position for long. In the second half of the nineteenth century, with astonishing speed, the Industrial Revolution spread to other countries of western Europe, North America, and the Far East.

In these regions, there were many countries possessing more or less the same features that had enabled Britain to pioneer the Industrial Revolution. They, too, had resources of coal and iron ore. They, too, had middle-class businessmen who were eager to build factories, and landless country-dwellers who were eager to earn wages in them. Even landowning nobles wanted to farm their land more efficiently and profit from the coal and iron ore that might lie beneath it. National monarchs, for their part, struggling to keep what they could of their political power, were well aware that industrial wealth and advanced weapons could only make them stronger. In addition, the progress of science, on which continued technical advancement came to depend (pp. 522–25), was international. In the second half of the nineteenth century, other countries besides Britain joined in the push for technical invention.

By the end of the nineteenth century, Britain was one among a global spread of industrial countries, and not even the most advanced or productive. In Europe, that position had been taken by Germany, while other countries such as France, Belgium, Italy, and Austria-Hungary were also important industrial producers. In the Far East, the ancient empire of Japan, responding to the threat of U.S. and European imperialistic control, was well on the way to becoming a modern industrial country (p. 544). But the most advanced and productive of all the industrial countries, thanks to its vast natural resources, its hardworking population (swelled by immigration), its scientific progress, and its technical know-how, was the United States.

Industrialization not only *spread* from country to country, it also *progressed*. That is, more and more traditional products came to be manufactured by the new methods, and more and more new products and manufacturing processes were invented. The main reason for this was that the machine itself, and the science and technology from which it sprang, were progressing at an accelerated rate. With the rapid increase in scientific knowledge in the nineteenth century (pp. 522–25), more and more industrial firms recognized the connection between "pure" and "applied" science, and sought to exploit it. Practical engineers and backyard tinkerers could still make significant breakthroughs, but more and more inventors were professionally qualified scientists. Indeed, invention itself became an organized activity, as industrial companies (and governments) began to invest large sums in *research and development*. Purposefully conducted and linked to the seemingly limitless progress of pure science, the surge of technological progress continued beyond the nineteenth century, down to the present day. The Industrial Revolution that began in eighteenth-century Britain has continued without interruption ever since.

The new age of "permanent" Industrial Revolution linked to science began shortly after the middle of the nineteenth century. It was inaugurated by the development of new processes in the iron industry — mostly arising from better understanding of the chemistry of metallic ores — that enabled iron to be rapidly and cheaply transformed into a stronger form of the metal, *steel*. By the end of the century, steel had largely replaced iron for rails, bridges, shipbuilding, and other types of construction where superior strength is required. Meanwhile, advances in the physics of heat, gas, electricity, and magnetism led to revolutionary inventions in the field of power production and distribution. A new and far more powerful form of steam engine, the turbine, was coupled with generators that turned steam power into electrical energy, so as to make electric light and power.

At the end of the nineteenth century, steam and electrical power were joined by the internal combustion (gasoline or diesel) engine. Fueled by previously untapped petroleum resources — which could be located thanks to the rapidly developing science of geology (p. 526) — the new type of engine brought about yet more revolutions in transportation. Small, light, and yet powerful, it made possible the twentieth-century development of both automobiles and aircraft. With petroleum available in vast amounts to supply the needs of motorists and pilots, chemists also found ways to produce from it an endless variety of textiles and plastics. Other twentieth-century scientists, building on basic discoveries in physics from the late nineteenth century onward, created a whole range of electronic devices that have transformed the transmission and processing of information: radio, television, recording devices, and computers.

Each of these and many other inventions of the last hundred and fifty years has amounted to a revolution in itself. Whole industries — such as steel, oil, plastics, electronics, automobiles, or aircraft — have sprung from nothing to produce and sell these inventions. Usually in not more than twenty or thirty years after the initial invention, each new industry has developed its giant corporations, its massive production plants, and its labor force of hundreds of thousands. As for the *consumers* of these new inventions — the motorists and television viewers, the owners of washing machines and refrigerators, and the users of countless more trivial devices — their way of life has been utterly transformed. Taken together, the new inventions have profoundly altered traditional views of the world, attitudes toward work and leisure, and personal and social habits.

This "permanent" worldwide industrial revolution has been far from painless. It has led to massive changes, usually accompanied by conflict and hardship, in the way businesses are organized and run, and in the patterns of work and life of ordinary people. It has given rise to radical ideologies that have promised relief from the evils of capitalism and industrialization, but in practice have often brought their own forms of mass suffering. It has altered the balance of power in the world, giving dominance to the advanced and productive nations, subjecting nonindustrial ones to imperialistic control, and providing the weapons to fight wars more terrible than any in history. Much of this and the following chapters is concerned with exploring these aspects of the impact of the machine.

THE BUSINESS CORPORATION AND CAPITALIST EXPANSION

As industrial operations grew in number and size, entrepreneurs had to raise capital from sources other than their own profits. Up to midcentury the single proprietorship and the partnership were the principal forms of business organization, but after that time those forms proved less and less able to raise the amounts of risk capital needed. Large undertakings, calling for heavy initial investment in buildings and equipment, required the pooling of money from hundreds of thousands of individuals. The apparatus that business leaders developed for raising and controlling such funds was called the *limited company* in England, the *corporation* in the United States. Its forerunner, the joint-stock company, had first appeared in the seventeenth century as a means of financing commercial and mining ventures.

The Structure and Control of the Corporation

The distinctive feature of the corporation (or limited company) is the financial protection it gives its stockholders. The earlier joint-stock company had sold transferable shares and had served as a means of risk-sharing, but the stockowners collectively had been liable for the debts of the enterprise. The corporation, on the other hand, is a clever *legal invention*, a fictitious "person" created by law. It is authorized to hold property, borrow money, and sue and be sued — without direct involvement of the stockholders. Should the assets of the corporate "person" be lost, the stockholders would lose only the value of their shares of stocks.

"Limited liability" is of crucial importance, since it permits individuals far removed from the control of a business to invest money in its stock without the risk of losing *other* property that they hold. They delegate direction of the firm's operations to a small body, the board of directors, who are elected (usually routinely) by an annual vote of the stockholders. The board, in turn, chooses the executive officers of the firm. So long as the managerial group — the directors and the executives — produces profits for the stockholders, it normally remains in control.

As corporations grew in size (especially after 1900), and as stockholders became increasingly numerous, more and more power went to the managers. The historic link between property *ownership* and property *control* was radically altered by the giant corporations of the twentieth century — a process that has been aptly called the "managerial revolution."

The modern large corporation, whose development was a direct response to the massive use of machines, has become the main functioning unit of Western capitalism. Because these enterprises affect the lives of people everywhere, it is worth examining how they function. The typical large corporation is *multinational*, conducting operations around the globe. It is owned by thousands of stockholders, whose primary concern is to receive regular dividends or an increase in the value of their stock. It employs thousands or hundreds of thousands of people, provides commodities for millions, and pays taxes to national, state, and local governments. The corporation's assets may run into billions of dollars; its gross income may exceed the revenue of many states and nations. Yet this vast economic empire is *controlled* by a small group of corporate managers and professional experts. Their decisions, made within the limits of law, finance, and consumer acceptance, determine the flow of investment, research, and development — and thereby influence the tastes and habits of the public.

The Global Reach of Capitalism

The large corporations, from the very beginning, usually had important *foreign* interests. They sometimes sought to eliminate competition in world markets through private agreements (cartels), and, by extending their investments abroad, they controlled the rate of economic growth in many lands. Industrial capitalism thus became a global force, with money and business seeking the best rates of return, and with an international elite of owners, managers, bankers, and promoters. The push of industrialization was a major factor, along with liberalism and nationalism, in shaping Europe and the world in the nineteenth century.

Risk capital was especially drawn to "backward" countries by the promise of extraordinary profits. Labor was cheap there, the demand for capital was high, and in some cases rich resources were awaiting exploitation. Overseas investments also aided the creation of an *interdependent* global economy — geared to the interests of the industrial ("advanced") countries. Thus, European capital built railways in Africa that brought out raw materials to be manufactured in Europe and sold in markets around the world.

The industrialists of Great Britain had the jump on those of other nations. By 1914 British private investments overseas amounted to more than $18 billion. French capitalists were next, with some $7 billion. These figures are a fair index of the two nations' comparative penetration and influence in the "backward" continents. (United States capitalists had only $3 billion in foreign investments by 1914; by 1970 the figure was close to $150 billion.)

As early as 1900, some thoughtful observers began to ask whether the concentration and expansion of economic power could go on without seriously disturbing political relations within and among nations. The corporate leaders knew well enough that their wealth was guiding politics both at home and abroad. They saw nothing wrong in this; in fact, they felt their political influence was essential to the full development of the world's resources. Encouraged by the doctrines of economic liberalism, they believed they could serve humanity best by the unrestricted pursuit of profit.

Economic Liberalism: Theory and Practice

Such political and economic views were quite different from the doctrine of mercantilism, which was widely accepted up to end of the eighteenth century. Mercantilism held that economic activities should be used to strengthen the state and that the state, in turn, should guide industry and commerce (p. 403). The Scotsman Adam Smith had been the most effective critic of mercantilism during the eighteenth century. His classic *The Wealth of Nations* (1776) attacked the system and called for a new order of "liberal" economics. Basing his ideas on Hobbes's atomistic view of society (p. 409) and the widely held idea of natural law, he argued that there exists a "natural" economy geared to *human selfishness*. People, if left free to follow their own nature and interests (laissez-faire), will be led by an "invisible hand" to promote the economic welfare of *all*.

Smith's writing had reflected the general optimism of the Enlightenment, but later theorists — the developers of "classical" economics — presented a darker outlook so far as the working class was concerned. One such theorist was David Ricardo, a financier who had made his fortune in England during the Napoleonic Wars. In his *Principles of Political Economy and Taxation* (1817), he set forth the main "laws" governing economic affairs, such as the "law of supply and demand." He is best remembered, perhaps, for his "Iron Law of Wages." Ricardo declared that in a *free-market economy* with a plentiful supply of labor, wages must remain close to the level needed for *bare subsistence* of the workers. More than that would allow more of the workers' children to survive; this would increase the supply, which in turn would *lower* the "natural" price (wages). On the other hand, should wages fall so low that some workers died off, the supply of labor would then decrease, which would *raise* wages back to the subsistence level.

One can see why the teachings of "free-market" economists gave a feeling of hopelessness to wage earners. But the "dismal science" (economics) did not dishearten the captains of trade and industry. On the contrary, it furnished them with respectable and compelling "reasons" for keeping wages down, for seeking profit when and where they could, and for working toward the elimination of unwanted government "interference." They proved generally successful in striking down controls that were not to their liking and in promoting government action that *favored* their interests. Toward the end of the nineteenth century and on into the twentieth, the latter practice became increasingly common, as economic and political realities moved further away from the models of Adam Smith. His doctrines nonetheless persisted — as a kind of mythology — to be called up or ignored, according to the interests of particular industries.

THE REACTION OF LABOR AND GOVERNMENT

"To every force, there is an equal and opposing force." Those familiar with this Third Law of Motion (of Isaac Newton) should have expected that bigness in business would call into being an opposing force (or forces). And, indeed, by the turn of the century Big Business was being confronted by Big Labor and Big Government. The "autonomous" (self-directed) individual found independent actions ever more limited by huge "autonomous" *organizations*.

The Appearance of Trade Unions

There is no doubt that in the long run industrialization raised standards of living and lightened the burden of manual labor. But the transfer of production to factories from family farms and workshops weakened the traditional *family* unit, for it took away one of its foremost functions. Work henceforth became associated, rather, with *class*. Further, working conditions in the early factories were dangerous and oppressive, hours were long, and wages were low. The factory-owners beat down the workers' protests and plowed profits back into more efficient machines. The capital accumulation and investment of the nineteenth century were thus drawn from the unhappy laborers, whose only choice was to work or starve.

The conditions typical of the early factories gave rise to bitter discontent. In some respects conditions were little worse than those under the "domestic system" of production (p. 286). But the factory system, by bringing large numbers of workers together, made workers more aware of their common plight and gave them a sense of what their *united* power might be. Alone, the laborer was at the mercy of a large-scale employer. With a surplus of hungry workers seeking jobs, an employer could run a factory without the help of any single wage-hand. Wage-hands, however, often had no place to turn should they lose their jobs. In the early part of the nineteenth century, therefore, there was no bargaining over wages and hours; they were set by the employer, and the worker could either take them or leave them.

Collective action for the purpose of bargaining with employers or influencing legislation offered some promise of relief to the laborers. They discovered, however, that whenever they tried to organize, the odds were against them. Local "trade clubs" had existed in England before the Industrial Revolution, but only in a few skills (printing, tailoring, weaving) and only in certain communities. When artisans tried to organize on a wider basis, their combinations were broken up by the joint action of employers and the government. Generally viewed by the courts as "conspiracies," trade unions had been prohibited in both France and England by 1800. Governments feared that they might lead to riots or uprisings; employers feared that they might lead to higher costs. Later legislation in England (1825) allowed unions to exist but closely limited their activities.

Workers themselves were far from unanimous in their support of unions, partly because of the harsh punishments given by employers to those suspected of belonging to such organizations. The charges of conspiracy were no doubt another discouraging factor. Nevertheless, by the middle of the nineteenth century steps had been taken in England to organize some skilled workers on a nationwide basis. The cotton spinners, for example, began to gain recognition for their associations and to develop modern collective-bargaining procedures (supported by the power of strikes). Many legal battles still had to be fought and won by British labor unions, but by 1900 two million workers (skilled and unskilled) had been organized into effective bargaining associations. A similar pattern of struggle — legal, economic, and political — followed in the United States and in other industrial countries.

The Trend Toward State Intervention

Many workers looked to *legislation* as a means of remedying certain evils of industrialism. Some believed that legislation was a helpful addition to direct economic action by unions; others thought legislation, eventually, might make direct action unnecessary. In England, the laboring classes themselves had virtually no political power until after midcentury; even before that, however, other social groups succeeded in bringing about some needed reforms through legislation. Most disinterested observers had come to agree that protective measures by the state (contrary to the doctrines of economic liberalism) were essential to the health and safety of the nation.

Reform legislation was initiated by the Tory party, which represented primarily the interests of the landed aristocracy. Since the landowners did not usually have large investments in industry, they could best afford to promote humane treatment of factory workers. Numerous intellectuals and humanitarians, without respect to party, also supported the Tory proposals. And it is only fair to add that some of the industrialists themselves, after accumulating their fortunes, supported reforms. Factory-owners as a group, however, bitterly fought all proposed limitations on their freedom to conduct their enterprises as they saw fit.

A series of parliamentary acts, beginning in 1833, removed the worst conditions in British industry. Employers were forbidden to hire children under nine years of age, and the labor of those under eighteen was restricted to nine hours a day. Women and children were excluded from mine labor, and better hours and safety devices were required in the mines. Government inspectors were hired to ensure that the regulations were observed. After wage-earners themselves gained the right to vote (in 1867), additional measures were enacted for their protection and welfare.

On the continent of Europe, France and Belgium began to catch up to the English in industrial growth. Napoleon III established the Second Empire in 1852 with the active support of the French bourgeois (p. 492). He took effective measures to promote agriculture, manufacturing, and commerce. The popular emperor also showed sympathy toward the industrial working class, legalizing labor unions in 1864 and providing many social welfare institutions. Workers benefited further from his grand public works projects, among them the rebuilding of Paris into a splendid city of broad boulevards and impressive public squares.

Germany was several decades behind England in industrial growth; but in the latter part of the century it took the lead in social legislation. Conditions in mines and factories were similar to those in England and France, and laws regulating job safety, age of employment, and hours of labor were passed in due course. Labor unions, intellectuals, and religious groups helped bring about these reforms. After Bismarck became imperial German chancellor in

1871 (p. 499), he used social legislation as a means of improving the nation's health, ensuring his own popularity, and increasing the loyalty of citizens to the new German Empire. The crowning regulatory measure was the Industrial Code of 1891, which guaranteed uniform protection to workers (with respect to hours and conditions) throughout the nation. Equally significant were later laws providing for sickness and accident insurance and old-age pensions for workers. The Social-insurance Code of 1911 became a model for other industrialized countries.

In adopting measures of this nature, the United States was at least a generation behind western Europe — though in another field of government intervention America was ahead. Giant industries developed rapidly after the Civil War; by 1890 mergers, trusts, and other forms of business combination were eliminating competitors and making huge profits. Many liberals, labor leaders, populists, and small entrepreneurs became alarmed by the growing concentration of economic power. They demanded legislation to check the expansion of monopolies and to keep enterprise "competitive and free."

Thus, in the name of liberalism, the power of the American government was called up as a *counterforce* to Big Business. The Sherman Antitrust Act of 1890 declared illegal "every contract, combination, or conspiracy in restraint of interstate commerce." The passage of this law was only the starting point of a long and tough contest in which government has sought to protect the public against the excesses of private economic powers; it was looked upon, however, by those powers as an encroachment upon *their* freedom. A further interference with wealth concentration was the enactment by the federal government of a *graduated income tax* in 1913.

URBANIZATION AND STANDARDIZATION OF SOCIETY

Personal freedom for millions of people was reduced by their crowding into large cities. This had been foreseen by the classic liberal Thomas Jefferson, who had written in 1800, "I view great cities as pestilential to the morals, the health, and the liberties of man." Population congestion calls forth regulation as a means of organizing essential services and protecting citizens from the trespasses of their neighbors. Although the move from farm to town had begun in the high Middle Ages as a response to the revival of commerce (p. 223), for centuries the flow was insignificant. It was the Industrial Revolution, along with a sudden rise in population — and in eastern Europe the belated end of serfdom, giving the peasants freedom to move and change their occupation (pp. 492, 559) — that brought about the rapid expansion of European cities.

Population figures before 1800 are only estimates, but it is evident that the number of people in Europe had risen very slowly until that time. The nineteenth century saw a startling increase, however. From 1800 to 1914 the population of western Europe grew from about 150 million to nearly 450 million — an increase greater than that of the preceding *ten* centuries (p. 222). (The total figure would have been still higher except for *mass emigration* — the largest movement of people in history. The big wave began to roll after 1870. From that year until 1914, over twenty-six million Europeans left their homes for the New World, more than half of them for the United States.) The extraordinary increase in population cannot be explained by a change in birth rates, for these remained fairly stable. The lowering of the *death* rate was the decisive factor, and this resulted from numerous causes. Chief among them were increased food production (aided by agricultural improvements), planting of more nutritious crops (the potato and Indian corn), decline of infanticide, advances in sanitation, and control of epidemics. In addition, the Industrial Revolution provided more purchasing power in the manufacturing countries, and that power was used to import more food from overseas.

By 1910 Germany, with fifty-eight million, had the largest population of any western European nation. Britain was next, with forty-two million; then France, with forty-one million, and Italy, with thirty-six million. The most striking growth, everywhere, was taking place in the cities. At the start of the Industrial Revolution there were only four English cities of over fifty thousand inhabitants. By 1850 there were thirty-one, and half the population of Britain was living in cities — a proportion unprecedented in European history. Manchester, in the cotton-manufacturing region, was the largest and best known of the new industrial communities. Formerly a market town of twenty-five thousand, it had grown to half a million by 1850. Its civic officials, like those of other urban centers, lacked the authority and organization they needed to meet the city's needs.

The nineteenth-century growth of cities led to a momentous change in the way of life of the Western peoples. For thousands of years since the Agricultural Revolution (pp. 10–15), the average man or woman had lived on the land, either as a smallholding peasant or as an agricultural laborer. As late as the year 1800, in most European countries eighty to ninety percent of the population was occupied in agriculture, with only ten to twenty percent gaining a living from industry or commerce. By the late twentieth century, the proportion was exactly reversed. In western Europe and the United States, less than ten percent of the population worked in agriculture, and much of the rest of the world was moving in the same direction.

The "backwash" from industrialization and the swift overflow of people from towns and farms overturned deep-set patterns of family and community life that traced back to the Middle Ages and even earlier. The end result in the countryside, as one observer concluded, was "the death of tradition itself."

As it brought an end to the traditional way of life, the factory carried the Western peoples from a world in which they were surrounded and dominated by nature to one more of their own making. And the new environment was ugly. The cities lacked sewers and paving. Housing for workers was cramped, rickety, and drab. Into the crowded, soot-blackened tenements poured the refugees from rural poverty — strangers in their own land. The chronic urban maladies of alienation, disease, and crime have persisted into the twentieth century.

Cities, in time, also brought much that was positive: better education, medical care, theaters, libraries, and merchandise from all over the earth. Even these advantages, however, were shared unequally, and poor people felt even more deprived in the presence of commodities they could not afford. Moreover, they seldom found the satisfaction in their daily labor that had brought meaning to the life of the craftsman in earlier times. The factory system reduced workers to the attending of machines and subjected them to its rigid discipline. Narrowing specialization of tasks chained them to deadening, repetitive motions. Workers, like the machine and all its parts, became standardized, replaceable cogs in a production line that turned out standardized, replaceable things.

Alongside the factory, there grew up another institution that shaped the lives of millions of people from the late nineteenth century onward: the office. Big business and big government needed office workers and other "white-collar" employees even more than they needed factory workers. In pay and standards of living, white-collar employees (including increasing numbers of women) did not differ much from ordinary "blue-collar" workers, but since they did not do heavy or dirty manual labor, they considered themselves more respectable. Together with self-employed small business owners and storekeepers, they formed the "lower middle class" as opposed to the "working class."

Mass production and maximum profits required not only *standardized commodities* but *mass demand*. In order to keep capital and plant capacity working up to their full potential, advertising was developed to force-feed natural desires. Organized "buy" appeals supported and expanded the media of mass communication — overcoming local resistance and tending to make the demand for goods uniform and universal. As the twentieth century proceeded, the individual came to be viewed increasingly as a *consumer* of goods, a permanent target of the commercial persuaders. Daily choices (whether conscious or not) would be governed to a mounting degree by enticing propaganda.

When technology was applied to the art of salesmanship as well as to production, it weakened many time-honored habits and customs. Mass culture thus came into being, essentially as we know it today — plastic, commercialized, and conformist. Though it included numerous and varied subcultures, it held to one constant value: concern for *material* things. The materialism and secularism of the West, on the rise since the Renaissance (pp. 318–19), had reached new heights by the beginning of the twentieth century. The Westerners' acquisitive character had always opened them to the lure of worldly goods. The machine now enabled them to produce wealth beyond their dreams, and the new salesmanship ensured that those dreams would never cease.

THE DEVELOPMENT OF SOCIALIST THOUGHT AND ACTION

The impact of the machine provoked a wide range of intellectual responses. Ever since the Industrial Revolution, people have been struggling with the vast problems and the vast promise of technology. In alternating moods of gloom, bewilderment, and hope, they have sought to understand where the machine is leading them and how to adapt it to human ends. Since the machine was identified in the nineteenth century with the system of industrial capitalism, that system became the focus of analysis and criticism.

The first reactions were to the factories themselves. Beyond the low wages, the oppressive working conditions, and the wretched housing was the misery caused by *unemployment*. Operating, in the main, according to "natural economic laws," nineteenth-century capitalism was a dynamic, unstable mechanism. Good times (booms) alternated with bad times (depressions), and the economic crises appeared to grow worse and worse. Wage earners, whose daily bread depended on their pay envelopes, were hardest hit when the factories laid off workers. Under the doctrines of economic liberalism, they were bound to suffer for as long as the system endured.

We saw earlier in the chapter that many workers turned to unions and social legislation to protect themselves and their families. But some workers and intellectuals became convinced that reform within the system was insufficient. Reacting to the social reality of *nineteenth-century capitalism*, they believed that the only hope for a better economic life and a just society lay in a radical change of the *system itself*. Most of these critics, though their ideas ranged across a broad spectrum, may be classified generally as *socialists*.

Utopian Socialism

Among the socialist thinkers of the nineteenth century the major division was between "utopians" and Marxists. The former belonged to a tradition reaching back as far as Plato (pp. 71–72). Their general approach was to turn from the evils apparent in the existing order and to seek in their imagination something closer to their ideal of life and society. Some of these thinkers were influenced by the *Utopia* of Sir Thomas More, written in the sixteenth century (p. 350). Sir Thomas despised the grasping landlords and entrepreneurs of his day; for his imaginary island of Utopia (literally, "no place") he envisioned a *planned* society of common ownership, tolerance, and equality.

In France, the utopians pursued two distinct lines of thought. Count Henri de Saint-Simon proposed a reorganization of society from the top, with state ownership of the means of production, and control by a national board of scientists, engineers, and industrialists (technocrats). The purpose of industry would be *production* rather than *profit*, and workers and managers would be rewarded according to individual merit. In his chief work, *The New Chris-*

tianity (1825), Saint-Simon stressed philanthropic motives: "The whole of society ought to strive toward the amelioration of the moral and physical existence of the poorest class; society ought to organize itself in the way best adapted for attaining this end." Saint-Simon's writings drew the sympathic attention of numerous European intellectuals. His disciples in France, some of whom became leaders in politics, were among the first modern advocates of a nationally planned society.

Charles Fourier, a younger contemporary of Saint-Simon, took a different approach. Resisting the idea of centralized economic control, he favored the creation of thousands of small production units, which he called "phalanxes." Limited in size to four hundred families, each phalanx would contain a residential hotel, school, market, health service, and other public facilities — in addition to its own farms and manufacturing plants. All these were to be *community* property, and the rule governing labor and distribution would be: "*From* each according to his *ability*; *to* each according to his *needs*." (The Marxists were later to adopt this slogan.) Surplus production would be exchanged for other goods by barter among the phalanxes; within each plant, workers would change jobs often, in order to reduce the monotony of performing repetitive tasks.

Fourier anticipated many of the problems of industrialism and believed that the free association of cooperative producers was the soundest way of meeting them. His ideas attracted numerous followers, and a few isolated phalanxes were actually established in America — notably Brook Farm, near Boston. Each phalanx had its own internal problems, and each was doomed to failure. Success for Fourier's plan would have required the development of an *extensive system* of phalanxes, and there was scarcely a chance that this could have come into being.

The efforts of Robert Owen, an industrialist and utopian planner, failed for the same basic reason. A successful cotton-mill owner in New Lanark, Scotland, Owen was distressed by the poverty, ignorance, and immorality of his employees. He determined to change matters and succeeded in setting up a model factory and community in New Lanark. He was not satisfied, however, with his own *local* reforms and sought to reform the whole industrial order.

Owen observed that the factory system had not freed workers — it had enslaved them. Under laissez-faire, their condition remained at a miserable level. Morals had fallen along with material standards of living, and the traditional ties of compassion between master and servant were missing in the new industrial order. Owen had fair success in promoting remedial factory legislation, but this served only to check the worst abuses. After failing to persuade factory-owners to follow his example at New Lanark, he proposed that the poor be organized into cooperative, self-sufficient villages.

Owen's plan won commendation in the British press and in Parliament, but nothing more. Abandoning his appeals to the leaders of government and industry, he next turned to the working people themselves. Out of his efforts grew several producers' cooperatives, including one overseas — at New Harmony, Indiana. Founded in 1824, this venture (like the others) lasted only a few years. Owen nonetheless left his mark on public thought and on the struggle to lighten the harshness of industrialism. But it took another, more rigorous thinker to produce a tougher brand of socialism that would meet the capitalist system head on.

Scientific Socialism: The Synthesis of Marx

Karl Marx brushed aside "utopian" ideas as sentimental and unrealistic; in this he shared the opinion of most of the capitalists of his time. Marx's study of history told him that events are shaped by underlying *economic* developments, rather than by idealistic reformers, and he believed that these developments were leading toward the collapse of capitalism. Therefore, he insisted, the proper task of workers and intellectuals is to *understand* the trend of history and to *participate* in its forward movement. While accepting some of the observations and principles of Owen and Fourier, he felt that their appeals distracted people from the "correct" course of thought and action.

It was in this sense that Marx and his followers regarded his own doctrine as "scientific." Marx set forth certain theories and sought to prove them by the evidence of history. He was not primarily an inventor of ideas; his achievement was a grand *synthesis*. Materialist, rationalist, libertarian, and revolutionist, Marx was an heir of the Enlightenment — who drew upon the leading scientific, economic, and philosophic ideas of the nineteenth century. But, reflecting also the romantic spirit of his age, Marx's teachings contain strong elements of faith and feeling as well as of reason and science.

Born in the Rhineland (Germany), of a middle-class Jewish family, the youthful Karl attended the universities of Bonn and Berlin. His father (a Lutheran convert) was a lawyer, and the son began to prepare for the same profession. Soon, however, Karl became attracted to the study of history and philosophy and would have liked to qualify himself for a professorship. But he feared that his Jewish identity and his liberal political views would block his chances of winning a university appointment, for this was the period of the conservative reaction in Germany. Caught up by the revolutionary stirrings of the 1840s, he turned instead to journalism and pamphleteering.

With his lifelong friend and partner, Friedrich Engels, Marx organized revolutionary groups and wrote *The Communist Manifesto* of 1848. After participating in the insurrections of that year in the Rhineland, he escaped to London, where he remained for the rest of his life. He was one of the first critics to stress the *international* character of working-class movements — thus placing himself in opposition to the mounting spirit of nationalism in Europe (pp. 495–96). From London, Marx continued his association with revolutionary movements in various countries, helping to found the First (socialist) International in 1864. And he spent long hours in the British Museum studying history and economics.

The most famous product of his labors, *Das Kapital* (*Capital*), appeared in part before his death and was completed by Engels. It consisted chiefly of theory and analysis and is closely related to the writings of the "classical" liberal economists (pp. 507–8). While Marx scorned their ignorance of history, he respected their understanding of the dynamics of nineteenth-century capitalism. Working largely from their stated "laws" and principles, he concluded that all economic *value* is produced by *human labor* and that the capitalist unjustly takes over a portion of this value. The system, he claimed, promises nothing but misery to the laborers and contains *contradictions* that ensure its own destruction. But Marx's economic conclusions were perhaps the least original, least proven, and least important of his ideas. His enormous influence would come from the fact that he was able to join his criticism of capitalism with a revolutionary program based on a *unified view* of history, politics, and morals.

The philosopher Hegel gave Marx the key to his general view. History is an unceasing process, said Hegel, governed at any moment by the struggle between a dominant idea and its opposing idea (pp. 473–74). This was a relatively simple explanation that made order and purpose out of the bewildering tangle of events. Marx was excited by Hegel's *dialectic* principle, but he had no use for the notion that *ideas* are the prime forces in history. After much study and reflection, he concluded that the "mode of production" (economic structure) is the main determining force in a given society; its *opposing* force arises from technological changes that are no longer suitable to the established economic structure. In Marx's own words:

> In the social production which men carry on they enter into indefinite relations that are indispensable and independent of their will; these relations of production correspond to a definite stage of development of the material powers of production. The sum total of these relations of production constitutes the economic structure of society — the real foundation, on which rise legal and political superstructures and to which correspond definite forms of social consciousness. The mode of production in material life determines the general character of the social, political, and spiritual processes of life. It is not the consciousness of men that determines their existence, but, on the contrary, their social existence determines their consciousness.

Thus did Marx "turn Hegel upside down." The flow of history and the growth of ideas and institutions, Marx thought, are all shaped by changes in the mode of production. And this evolution had passed through four principal stages: "the Asiatic, the ancient, the feudal, and the modern bourgeois methods of production."

Engels later sought to modify the rigidity of Marx's economic determinism (sometimes called "historical materialism"). What he meant, explained Engels, was that the economic factor is "the strongest, most elemental, and most decisive." But to admit the influence of *various* factors is to weaken the claim of *economic* determinism. Even non-Marxist historians agree that the system of production is *one* important factor among the "determinants" of a given culture.

Marx saw the "class struggle" as part of historical materialism — a view that had special significance because it related to the actual struggles of working people in the nineteenth century. Each mode of production, he said, serves a particular "ruling" class, which takes advantage of its opposing "exploited" class. The ancient world had its masters and slaves; the feudal age, its nobles and serfs; the capitalist age, its bourgeois and *proletarians*. (This last word, derived from the Latin name for *propertyless* citizens of ancient Rome, was applied by Marx to the swelling number of industrial wage-hands.) Marx believed that the ruling class of each age provides laws and institutions to guarantee its continued exploitation of the opposing class. The state itself thus becomes a mechanism of *suppression*. The executive of the nineteenth-century capitalist state, he declared, was "a committee for managing the common affairs of the whole bourgeoisie" (the bourgeois *class*).

Social revolutions occur, according to Marx, when a new mode of production — taking shape within the framework of the old — bursts the bonds of established laws and relationships. The agents of the revolution are the "new" class, which, in time, becomes the ruling class. Thus, he argued, the bourgeoisie had promoted the *liberal* revolutions, thereby paving the way for a new economic order — and for a new ruling class (itself). But the hour had struck for the bourgeoisie, as it had earlier for the European nobility. The potential of expanding technology could not be realized within the structure of private capitalism; and the capitalist system of production, hit by increasing severe depressions, was stumbling toward its end. In accordance with the dialectic principle, the old system had already brought into existence the class that would overthrow it and build a new order upon the ruins. This class, the proletariat, was being drawn into the industrial centers in ever larger numbers. All it needed in order to help history along was Marxist instruction and organization.

Though Marx had bitter feelings toward the bourgeoisie and regarded its exploitation of the proletariat as the most brutal in history, he felt that it had played, in preceding centuries, a constructive and progressive role. This was in keeping with his (and Hegel's) view of history as moving irresistibly toward higher and higher goals of human fulfillment. Marx also approved the liberal revolutions, whose results were chiefly *political*. The freedoms gained were of primary benefit to the entrepreneurial class, but they also increased the opportunities of the lower class to work for *social* revolution. Political freedom was meaningless to the hungry and the homeless, thought Marx, but it was a step toward achieving a new order of production that could provide a decent living for all — and liberate the worker from humiliation and servitude. Only after those changes had been brought about could individuals realize their full potential, the goal Marx desired for *everyone*.

Marx predicted that the mounting clashes between the proletariat and the bourgeoisie would lead to the triumph of the working class. This victory would bring an end to the historic class struggle, for all individuals would then be included in *one* body of workers. Dismantling the old social order and taking over the means of production would be carried out under a temporary "dictatorship of the proletariat." This would be followed, in turn, by an intermediate period of democratic "socialism," during which individuals would "work according to their ability and receive according to their output." Socialism would lead eventually to pure "communism."

Once *communism* had been reached, the state would "wither away," Marx believed, because without a class struggle there would be no reason for the existence of a state. Thus would come into being, for the first time in civilized history, "true" liberty for all. In the vaguely outlined communist society, voluntary associations would plan and carry out production; individuals would work according to their *abilities* and receive according to their *needs*; private persuasion and restraint would replace police, prisons, and war.

Close observers of human nature, from Aristotle and Augustine through Montaigne, Hobbes, and Voltaire, would no doubt have felt that this sketch of an earthly paradise is highly unrealistic. Even if we grant a measure of scientific truth to Marx's analysis of the past, his vision of the *future* was a romantic one — as demonstrated by failures of Marxist societies in the last decade of the twentieth century. If accepted at all, it had to be accepted on *faith*. Indeed, the followers of Marx found in his doctrines a kind of religion; they called it the *religion of man*.

Their "god," the prime mover, was "historical materialism," and Marx its prophet. There were Marxist apostles and saints — as well as despised heretics. The sacred books were his writings, defended by "dialectical" theologians. The Church was the Party, and true believers had to have unquestioning faith in its gospel and its works. The Marxist heaven was their idealized society to come.

This analogy with traditional Christianity, or Islam, each with its absolutistic doctrines (pp. 156–57), is to suggest the emotional quality of Marxism — and to stress the fact that it presented a *total* view of humanity and the universe. This is a crucial point to grasp if we are to understand the attraction of Marxism over the past century-and-a-half. At a time when the foundations of "old-fashioned" religion and liberalism were being challenged, Marx created a new worldview of the facts, theories, and hopes of the *industrial age*. Its promise appealed to the working poor, but it appealed also to many intellectuals who felt alienated from industrialism and were looking for some kind of total reorientation. Partial critiques and actions based on a mix of traditional values (as in utopianism) left such people unsatisfied. Marxism offered a unified view and psychological equivalent to traditional religion. If we use the term "myth" to mean a large complex of ideas that people *believe to be true*, and by which they try to understand and act, the Marxist myth served, in the West, as a modern competitor of the Christian and Lockean myths (p. 449).

The Interpreters of Marx: Revolutionary and Evolutionary

As with all such myths and doctrines, Marxist "truth" has been open to differing interpretations. The early Christians discovered that disagreement over doctrine was one of their most serious problems (pp. 156–57), and that problem has continued to the present day. The followers of Marx, similarly, have been divided by heresy (and schism — p. 155). Had capitalism faltered and collapsed during the nineteenth century, as Marx himself expected, the split among his followers might have been less profound. But the established order proved much tougher, much more adaptable, than he had expected. Reform laws and unions strengthened capitalism (as did Marxist criticism), improved the distribution of purchasing power, and bettered the conditions of the workers. The rich were getting richer, as Marx predicted, but the poor (at least in the West) were *not* getting poorer. And in the United States, the young giant of capitalism, no strong revolutionary feeling or class-consciousness appeared among the wage-earners.

How did the Marxists deal with this indefinite postponement of the day of revolution? Again, one is reminded of the parallel with the Christians of the second century, who had to face the fact that the Second Coming was evidently not going to happen right away (p. 151). Some decided to "overthrow" the world by withdrawing from it, but most decided to make their peace with the world — to remain "in" it, if not "of" it. Marx had considered two possible paths to the overthrow of capitalism: one by legal means, the other by force. He did not exclude either, and he recognized the power that an extension of voting rights might hold out to the working class. But he leaned toward the view that the ruling class was unlikely to surrender its property under democratic processes and that a resort to violence must ultimately be expected.

After Marx's death (in 1883), the capitalist states showed no signs of tottering, and most socialist workers tended to make their peace with the existing system. True, a small group of Marxists stuck by the "hard" line, scorning "legalism" and "gradualism." But the larger group recognized that such a stand would not appeal to the bulk of workers. They stated frankly that Marxist doctrine would have to be *revised* if it was to continue as a major force.

The "revisionists" mapped a much longer (and different) road to the ideal society. They stressed democracy, parliamentary methods, and class cooperation as means of achieving further reforms. Eduard Bernstein, a German socialist, was the leading advocate for this view. (The "Fabian" socialists of England, though non-Marxist, held a similar position.) The broad term "social democratic" can be applied to most of the labor parties in European politics after 1890; they represented the "evolutionary" wing among the heirs of Marx. The "revolutionary" wing remained significant only in eastern Europe, where

c. 1800	1848	1889 1914
Utopian Socialism	Development and Spread of Orthodox Marxism	Revisionist Marxism Dominant

Second —International—

First International (1864-72)

the absence of effective representative government prevented change by peaceful, legal methods. It was there, in a relatively backward country, Russia, that the revolutionary Marxists would achieve the first great victory of socialism (pp. 560–63).

A different sort of attack upon the established order of the nineteenth century took the form of *anarchism*. This view holds that any use of *authority* — economic, religious, or political — is an unjustified interference with the individual. Believing that human beings are basically *good*, the anarchists claim that voluntary, harmonious relationships could be achieved among individuals if the power of the state were removed. Some, like the Russian writer Leo Tolstoy (p. 480) and the American essayist, Henry David Thoreau, were anarchists only in a philosophical sense; they firmly opposed the use of violence as a means of realizing their ideas. But others pursued what they considered to be the direct and necessary route to the abolition of government: assassination of government officials, terrorism, and insurrection. Though these anarchist ideas were first expressed in western Europe, it was Mikhail Bakunin, a Russian nobleman, who exerted the largest influence. Bakunin died in 1876; his followers succeeded in killing (among others) Tsar Alexander II of Russia, President Sadi Carnot of France, King Humbert I of Italy, and President William McKinley of the United States. Such acts of *terror* horrified the powerful everywhere, but failed to produce an effective movement for social change or for the abolition of state power. (Nevertheless, these acts were forerunners of terrorist killings in the twentieth century — pp. 640–41.)

The Roman Catholic Response: Pope Leo XIII

It was unthinkable that the established churches of the West could ignore the impact of industrial capitalism *or* the Marxist (and anarchist) attack upon it. While the one appeared destructive of certain Christian values and virtues, the other appealed openly to class-hatred and violence. Both unrestricted (laissez-faire) capitalism and Marxist materialism were roundly condemned, at last, by the most powerful spokesman of Western Christendom, the pope. In 1891, Leo XIII addressed his bishops through a formal letter (encyclical) entitled *Rerum Novarum* (*Of New Things*). In this carefully drawn, comprehensive statement, he set forth the position of his Church on the relations between capital and labor.

The pope's immediate concern, as expressed in his letter, was for the "misery and wretchedness which press so heavily at this moment on the large majority of the very poor." The workers, he went on, "have been given over, isolated and defenseless, to the callousness of employers and the greed of unrestrained competition." Going still further, he declared that "a small number of very rich men have been able to lay upon the masses of the poor a yoke little better than slavery itself."

But the socialist remedy, the pontiff declared, called for the destruction of private property. Such action would be unjust to the present lawful owners of property and would deprive workers of the main object of their labors. He also rejected the socialist idea of equalizing wealth — as being "against nature." The overriding mistake of the Marxists, however, was their feeling that social classes must be mutually hostile, "that rich and poor are intended by nature to live at war with one another." On the contrary, stated Pope Leo, "it is ordained by nature that these two classes should exist in harmony . . . capital cannot do without labor, nor labor without capital."

Quoting freely from his favorite philosopher, Thomas Aquinas (p. 259), who was known for his efforts to harmonize conflicting positions, the pope urged a Christian "middle course." Moderation and cooperation should guide the common affairs of employers and employees. Working people must give honest work and never injure the owners or their property; the owners must never make excessive demands on their employees' labor or pay them less than the needs of their families require. For the purpose of mutual help and wage-bargaining, workers should be allowed to form unions; and if workers find themselves too weak to defend their rightful interests, the government must intervene with *protective legislation*. At the same time, however, the government must preserve absolutely the *sanctity of private property*.

The *Rerum Novarum* was significant not so much for its originality as for its authority. Approved by succeeding popes, including John Paul II (p. 633), it served as a rallying point for individuals (Catholic and non-Catholic) who were perplexed or frightened by the social crisis. The message gave little comfort to aggressive entrepreneurs on the political right, or to angry critics of capitalism on the left. But it offered a guide for moderates who wished to see the rewards of labor improved while avoiding industrial violence. It also prompted the founding of new Catholic trade unions and Catholic political parties in most of the countries of Europe. These organizations have exercised notable influence, continuing to the present day. Finally, *Rerum Novarum* pointed the way, morally and philosophically, to the democratic "welfare states" of the twentieth century (pp. 576–79).

THE ACCELERATING PROGRESS OF SCIENCE

Accompanying the technological progress, social changes, and class conflicts of the nineteenth century were great leaps in pure science. The scientific revolution of the seventeenth century had lost none of its force: the organization of science became even wider and better supported. As more and more trained minds were focused on the riddles of nature, their combined efforts and findings rose at a rapid rate.

Physical scientists continued to build on the foundations of Galileo, Newton, and Boyle (pp. 416–18). One of the most important subjects of their investigations was energy. Experimenters proved the equivalence of heat and energy and formulated two basic laws of thermodynamics. The First Law states that the total energy (or heat) in the universe remains constant, though it is continually changing its form. The Second Law states that energy systems tend toward degradation (heat, for example, flows from a hotter body to a colder one); hence, the amount of *useful* energy is diminishing in the universe. These generalizations, supplementing the Newtonian laws of motion (p. 417), gave fresh understanding to physicists, chemists, astronomers — even philosophers.

The first correction or modification of Newton's laws was made by the German mathematician Albert Einstein, who first stated his Special Relativity Theory in 1905 and later extended it into a General Theory. Though he recognized that Newtonian physics "worked" well enough for ordinary purposes, Einstein believed that it did not truly describe the universe of nature and that it could lead to hopeless error in *cosmic* calculations. Newton and his followers had conceived of space and motion as *absolute*. They assumed the existence of an "ether," a kind of immovable substance that fills the universal void (empty space). All changes in positions of objects, they thought, could be measured absolutely by reference to this ether. But experiments in the late nineteenth century proved that no such substance exists, thus destroying any fixed basis for reference.

Einstein met this puzzlement with a radically different approach. Matter and motion are not absolutes, he declared, but are *relative*. They can be measured only from a given point or system in time and space. (What is the velocity of a fly buzzing about inside a speeding aircraft?) Einstein believed, further, that objects have a *space-time* dimension that affects their length, breadth, and thickness. Bodies moving toward or away from a given point have shifting proportions of length and mass with respect to that point. The alterations are not noticeable in ordinary motions, but they become significant as bodies approach the speed of light. The speed of light is the one *constant* he found in the universe; it remains the same for *all* physical systems. Though Einstein's theory, expressed in mathematical equations, was incomprehensible to the average person, it exploded many of the fundamental assumptions of scientists. It reminded them (and others) that the scientific myth, too, while highly practical in its application, is by no means absolute or immune to change. One especially important practical application grew out of another Einstein equation ($E = mc^2$) — explaining the relation between *energy* and *matter*: E (Energy, in metric units called ergs) equals m (mass in grams) times c^2 (the speed of light squared, in centimeters per second). This now-famous equation led to the development of the atomic bomb during the Second World War (p. 585).

In Einstein's lifetime, the theory of matter was moving toward its current formulation. Until a century ago it had been believed that matter was solid, although the ancient Greek Democritus (p. 67) had theorized that matter was reducible to invisible, indivisible particles. John Dalton, a British schoolteacher, had accepted this general notion but found, early in the nineteenth century, that each chemical element was composed of atoms of different weights. Scientists later assumed the existence of *molecules*, which contained the atoms. All material substances, they concluded, are made up of molecules.

As molecular studies advanced, physicists further theorized that the molecules are *separated* from one another and are in constant motion. Increases in heat cause the molecules to vibrate more rapidly; increases in pressure slow them down. The discovery of X-rays by W. K. Roentgen in 1895 was followed by the discovery of radioactivity in certain molecules (like those of radium and uranium). This led, in turn, to the conclusion of Marie and Pierre Curie that the *cause* of radioactivity (particle emissions) is the slow breaking down of "unstable" substances. (Roentgen's discovery of X-rays also proved immensely valuable to medicine and technology.)

The "solidity" of objects dissolved still further when Ernest Rutherford and Niels Bohr introduced their *model* of the atom (about 1910), which they saw as a miniature solar system containing a nucleus of one or more *protons* with encircling *electrons*. These tiniest particles were explained as units of electrical energy. Later research would show the atom to be even more complex than Rutherford or Bohr had at first believed, but their concept was the starting point for modern atomic physics.

More immediately practical uses flowed from discoveries about the nature of *light* and *electromagnetic waves*. Newton had observed that when sunlight passes through a prism it spreads into a band of colors — red at one end and indigo (dark blue) at the other. Scientists of the nineteenth century discovered that each chemical substance, in the gaseous state, yields a spectrum distinct from every other. Spectrum analysis was developed as a tool for chemists — and for astronomers in studying the sources of light in space. The production, reception, and explanation of electromagnetic waves by Heinrich Hertz (about 1887) pointed the way to Guglielmo Marconi's wireless and all that followed in the field of radio communications.

Notwithstanding the advances in physical science, the nineteenth century was still more the century of biological and medical progress. Drawing upon seventeenth-century descriptions of cellular structure in plants, Theodor Schwann developed the cell theory to explain *organic* (*living*) matter. It was realized by about 1835 that all living things consist of tiny cells, whose health and growth determine the physical fate of the total organism, and a special branch of biology (cytology) was established for the study of *cells*. Embryology and bacteriology also became specialized fields of inquiry.

Bacteriology, an outgrowth of the germ theory of disease, opened for examination the world of microorganisms. These tiny forms of life had been seen through the primitive microscopes of the seventeenth century, but little attention was given to them until after 1850. It was a French chemist, Louis Pasteur, who first theorized that bacteria (germs) were the cause of many deadly illnesses. Physicians knew of the existence of bacteria but thought them the result, rather than the cause, of disease. After years of ridicule, Pasteur at last had the opportunity to demonstrate the correctness of his theory and the practice of preventive inoculation (vaccination). His first successful test was against an epidemic of anthrax disease in sheep.

Once the germ theory was accepted, it led quickly to the identification, treatment, and prevention of countless bacteriological and viral diseases, as well as to antiseptic procedures in surgery and improvements in public hygiene and sanitation. No other development in science can match the importance of the germ theory in its effect on the world's *death* rate — and the consequent upward curve of human population. The mass killers — bubonic plague, typhus, smallpox, and cholera — were at last subject to human control. (In the twentieth century an ancient crippler of children, poliomyelitis, would also be conquered, and improved vaccines and antibodies would aid the general fight against all germ-caused illnesses.)

Medicine was not the only area where the growth of scientific knowledge had an impact beyond the lecture-halls and laboratories. It was chiefly the progress of pure science that drove forward the Industrial Revolution after the middle of the nineteenth century (pp. 504–5). Science, further, provided a model for other branches of thought and investigation, or at least was called upon to make their views and theories more believable. Marxists, for example, and social thinkers of other persuasions, claimed that their methods and results were "scientific"; so, also, did some psychologists dealing with human feelings and behavior (pp. 516, 529–31). Moreover, due especially to the work of Charles Darwin, science once again called into question traditional ideas on the place of humanity in the universe and its relationship to God.

THE CHALLENGE OF DARWIN'S THEORY OF EVOLUTION

The discoveries about *bacteria* raised no serious controversy after Pasteur's classic proofs. But the emerging theory about the *origin of human beings* caused bitter disputes that continue more than a century afterward.

New Perspectives in Human Biology

The work of Charles Darwin may be compared with that of Isaac Newton, who lived two centuries earlier. As Newton completed the overturn of ancient ideas about the physical universe and its governing principles, so Darwin completed a revolution of thought with respect to the earth's *creatures* — the human species, in particular. Scientific opinion, until about 1850, had supported the idea of the *fixed nature* of each species, within a "Great Chain of Being." A Swedish botanist, Carolus Linnaeus, was in part responsible for the persistence of this idea. His work as a classifier (in the 1730s) helped to develop the notion that all creatures had been placed in a neat and permanent overall scheme. Linnaeus assumed, and most of his readers believed, that all members of a particular species could be traced back, without change, to an original pair formed at the time of Creation (the "creationist" theory).

Before the nineteenth century there had been insufficient evidence either to prove or to disprove this theory. But by 1850 discoveries in comparative anatomy, embryology, and geology were pointing toward one inescapable conclusion. Even before Darwin published his *On the Origin of Species by Means of Natural Selection* in 1859, the theory of *change* in species had been accepted by a number of naturalists and philosophers. Darwin focused his life's work on that theory and established it securely on the basis of his observations, collected data, and reasoned explanations.

Though the evolutionary theory raised many thorny problems, it won acceptance because it better suited known facts than did the competing "creationist" theory. According to Darwin, all forms of life are descended from a few original creatures. Each individual (and the species of which it is a part) has come into existence as the result of an unbroken competitive struggle. Continuing slight variations in physical qualities give an advantage to some creatures over others; the losers in the struggle die out, while the winners pass on, through heredity, their distinctive qualities ("survival of the fittest").

Without the concept of "geologic" time, Darwin could not have convinced even himself, for the process of "natural selection" required a sweep of centuries beyond human imagination—to produce, in tiny steps, the kind of changes that carried upward from plankton to mammals. But Charles Lyell, an English geologist, had opened the door to Darwin's theory. Prior to the appearance of Lyell's *Principles of Geology* in 1830, most educated individuals believed that the earth's history had been relatively short and that the earth's surface had undergone sudden and drastic changes ("catastrophism"). Lyell helped to reverse this view, holding that geologic change had been slow and gradual and that the earth's age ran into hundreds of *millions* of years.

Second only to Lyell in direct influence on Darwin was Thomas Malthus, whose *An Essay on the Principle of Population* (pp. 471–72) offered a key to the process of natural selection. Malthus pointed out that reproduction in animals advances at a rate that outstrips the supply of food. Hence, the fate of all nature's creatures is one of struggle for survival. This point was crucial to Darwin's doctrine, for without the elimination of some individuals and the *survival* of others, there would be no *selection* among the variant creatures.

The least satisfactory portion of Darwin's theory concerns the mechanism by which "survival" characteristics are transmitted to succeeding generations. He believed this to be essentially a matter of passing along to offspring the *physical characteristics* of superior *individuals*. He understood only dimly the mechanism of heredity and the fact that the species' supply of *genes* (units of heredity) is independent of the physical characteristics of individuals. Only *widespread* mutations (changes) in *gene supply* can make a change in the species. This fact was established by the experiments of the Austrian botanist Gregor Mendel (about 1870) and by later researchers in the new science of genetics.

Darwinism in Philosophy and Social Thought

Whatever may have been Darwin's limitations and his debts to other scientists, he fully deserves the acclaim that has been his. He combined a stirring new vision of living creatures with the courage to publish and defend his ideas. What others had hinted at or backed away from, Darwin at last expressed openly and honestly. Although his theory brought criticisms from all sections of the community, by the close of the century it had become generally accepted among educated people.

At first the more severe attacks came from religious thinkers and devout Christians. Though Darwin argued that the divine hand can (and does) work its will through evolution, his critics preferred to think that humans had been fashioned *directly* in God's image. The Copernican theory had dwarfed the importance of the earth in the heavens (p. 410); the Darwinian theory now reduced the importance of human beings by associating them with animal evolution. Moreover, it contradicted the literal reading of the Book of Genesis. It is small wonder that many Christians were shaken by what appeared to be another blow to their faith and pride.

On the other hand, there were philosophers, statesmen, industrialists, and theologians who welcomed the doctrine and sought to extend it beyond the biological field. Herbert Spencer, a brilliant and self-educated advocate of evolution, was one of those most excited by Darwin's writings. It was he who stressed Darwin's phrase "survival of the fittest" to describe the governing principle in nature, and, more significantly, Spencer asserted that the principle applies not only to physical creatures and galaxies but to human institutions, customs, and ideas as well. All of these, he reasoned, have their cycle of origin, growth, competition, decay, and extinction. Thus, there can be no "absolutes" of religious or moral truth; there is only the *passing* truth of those ideas that have evolved, and that have (so far) *survived*.

These convictions, however, did not drive Spencer to mechanism or atheism (p. 422). As did some church leaders of his day, he adapted his faith in God to the new facts of science. Behind these facts, he believed, there must exist a *supernatural* power — one that humans cannot fully know. He believed, however, that moral standards can be established on the basis of what we *do* know. Spencer put forward a "science" of ethics based on the principles of natural evolution: moral acts are those that contribute to human adaptation and progress. Moral perfection will be reached, he concluded, by "the completely adapted man in the completely evolved society."

Spencer's philosophy of morals did not pass unchallenged in the nineteenth century. If morality is geared to the evolutionary processes of nature, what becomes of one's own moral responsibility and freedom? What has science to do with ethics? Even if Darwinism explained the development of the moral sense, it could not lay down a particular code of behavior. A further objection was that nature itself had been shown by Darwin to be ruthlessly *amoral* (lacking in moral concern). How, then, could nature serve as a foundation for morals?

The "tooth-and-claw" nature of organic evidence does indeed present nature in a mixed light. Some saw magnificence in it; Darwin himself found it thrilling:

> Thus, from the war of nature, from famine and death, the most exalted object which we are capable of conceiving, namely the production of the higher animals, directly follows. There is grandeur in this view of life . . . from so simple a beginning endless forms most beautiful and wonderful have been, and are being evolved.

But this creation so admired by Darwin had been achieved through monstrous waste and universal conflict. The sweet Mother Nature of the romantic poets (pp. 477–78) had revealed another and terrible face.

It soon became clear that Darwinism could be interpreted and applied in conflicting ways. All could agree on one central point: the idea of a static world, of fixed relations and values, had been overthrown and replaced by the idea of continuous change and struggle. But how people should think and act in relation to the struggle, especially human struggle, was a question that drew profoundly different answers.

Philosophers of Hegel's school viewed Darwin's theory as a confirmation of the dialectical idea in history (pp. 473–74). Among theologians, Calvinists most often found support for their teachings in Darwinism, for their doctrine of human salvation by *election* is paralleled, in nature, by the survival of the few and the destruction of the many (pp. 365–66). As one Calvinist teacher put it, Darwinism is to science what Calvinism is to theology: it serves as a foe of sentimentalism and optimism and as a check on the reign of law and trust in reason.

The implications of Darwinism for social action had far-reaching consequences. After reading *On the Origin of Species*, Karl Marx declared that it furnished a "basis in natural science for the class struggle in history." He hoped that it would bring support to his revolutionary appeals. Marx gave Darwin a copy of *Das Kapital*, but it is doubtful whether the scientist read it. While Darwin sought to avoid controversy outside his own field of biological study, he rejected the notion that his theory was connected with socialism. He was, rather, inclined to agree with the classical economists of his time, who saw the social struggle as a "natural" expression of human competition. Like them, he opposed interference with the system of laissez-faire, no matter what the motives might be. As his friend Herbert Spencer explained, "The poverty of the incapable, the distresses that come upon the imprudent, the starvation of the idle, and those shoulderings aside of the weak by the strong, which leave so many 'in shallows and miseries,' are the decree of a large far-seeing benevolence."

The American billionaire, John D. Rockefeller, once used an attractive metaphor to explain how natural selection worked to the advantage of all. The man who had built Standard Oil into a giant monopoly by beating out his competitors compared his work with the breeding of a lovely flower. The American Beauty rose, with its splendor and fragrance, could not have been produced, Rockefeller told a Sunday-school audience, except by sacrificing the buds that grew up around it. In the same way, the development of a large business is "merely survival of the fittest . . . merely the working-out of a law of nature and a law of God."

Rockefeller and other titans of industry were unashamed promoters of what was later called *social* Darwinism. Essentially, it approved a no-holds-barred struggle of "all against all," in the manner of the jungle. And the idea readily passed from one of battle among individuals to one of battle among races and nations. Darwin's theory strengthened the convictions of slave-owners, racists, militarists, and extreme nationalists. Many individuals, including some respected philosophers, glorified *war* as a "pruning" hook for improving the health of humanity. "Making war is not only a biological law," declared a famous general, "but a moral obligation, and, as such, an indispensable factor in civilization."

Development of the Social Sciences

The nineteenth century saw the prestige of science rising to its apex. Generals, industrialists, statesmen, theologians, and philosophers sought to ally themselves with scientific doctrines. And social researchers of various sorts tried to model their methods of inquiry upon those of mathematics, physics, or biology — and, in the process, to establish new branches of "social knowledge" that might draw the kind of respect paid to natural science.

One of these individuals, the Frenchman Auguste Comte, was the first to use the term "sociology" as a term for the "science of society." A disciple of Saint-Simon (pp. 514–15), Comte was a lifelong reformer. He shared with Saint-Simon the view that society is best managed by "experts," but he believed that the experts needed a more reliable body of knowledge about people and their social relations than was at hand. Scorning "knowledge for its own sake" and narrow academic specialization, Comte believed that learning should serve *human needs*, and he felt that all studies should be directed to that purpose.

He believed that the most useful knowledge is the sort that rests upon empirical evidence (pp. 325–36) — "positive" knowledge, he called it — which was to be found in his day only in the natural sciences. But empirical methods can and must, he insisted, be extended to "social" science; human conduct is neither random nor altogether unpredictable, and it can be "quantified," analyzed, and classified. From the resulting social "laws," the proposed managers of society would be able to draw guidance for social regulation and planning.

Comte died in 1857, before he could complete his ambitious studies directed toward reconstructing knowledge *and* society. (Before breathing his last, he is said to have sighed, "What an irreparable loss!") But the foundations of sociology had been laid, and they were extended by the energetic Herbert Spencer (p. 527). At about the same time a companion discipline, anthropology, came into being. This word means, literally, the "study of man," but the study has focused on physical evolution, prehistoric cultures, and *comparative* social institutions.

While anthropology analyzed and classified the broad patterns of social conduct, observed over time and geographical space, a new discipline, psychology, concentrated on individual human actions. In 1872 Wilhelm Wundt established the first laboratory (in Leipzig, Germany) for the observation and testing of human and animal subjects. A Russian, Ivan Pavlov, soon afterward gained worldwide notice by his remarkable experiments with dogs. He discovered the "conditioned reflex," a principle that could (and would) be extended to humans.

By 1900 psychology was moving in several directions. Followers of Pavlov's experiments developed a view called "behaviorism." Believing that human thoughts and actions can be understood on a purely *physiological* basis, they dismissed as meaningless such concepts as "mind" and "soul." They studied the various systems of the body — nervous, glandular, muscular — and the mechanisms of "stimulus" and "response," and *measured* them. From the accumulation of such data the behaviorists hoped to develop "positive" knowledge of human nature. (Within a century of Pavlov's experiments, the American psychologist B. F. Skinner concluded that the time had arrived to construct a workable "technology of behavior." His *Beyond Freedom and Dignity*, published in 1971, proposed systematic management of human actions within the framework of a *planned society*.) Most theologians, philosophers, and humanists found such ideas distasteful. They argued that a person's true being is spiritual rather than physical — or, if only physical, that it is far more complex than the behaviorists imagined.

Other investigators, meanwhile, were trying to penetrate the dark *interior* of the individual by means of psychoanalysis. The Austrian physician Sigmund Freud was a bold leader in this effort to investigate the subconscious and unconscious depths underlying thought and action. His methods were neither quantitative nor statistical but rather, clinical. Each human subject was examined, by means of free discussion and dream recollection, for clues to the inner self. (The broader philosophical and social significance of Freud's thought will be developed in Chapter 15 — pp. 627–29).

Freud's one-time associate, the Swiss psychologist Carl G. Jung, also stressed the importance of the unconscious as a major part of "psychic wholeness." Jung believed that each individual, as a result of biological evolution, possesses a "collective" unconscious in *addition* to a "personal" unconscious. The "collective" contains those emotion-filled instincts and images connected with long-past experiences of the *species*. Jung called such images "archetypes" — such as the "Great-Mother" figure, the Hero, the Sage, the Betrayer, the Savior-God, and other types that appear widely in popular myths and religions. In keeping with this view, he held that "great" works of art and literature are seen as great because they portray such figures — projected from the collective unconscious of their creators.

We have reviewed the emergence of new branches of "social" knowledge in the nineteenth century, along with the startling advances in the natural sciences. The older branches of learning dealing with human relations were also influenced by the trends of the times. Political economy, which traced back at least to Adam Smith and the eighteenth century, reached its "classical" development in the nineteenth century in the formulation of economic "laws" (pp. 507–8). Later in that century, economists established a "scientific" vocabulary, statistical techniques, and instruments of *prediction*.

History, one of the most ancient studies concerned with human affairs, also flourished in the nineteenth century. Much of the writing, though marked by careful research and literary merit, was essentially romantic and nationalistic. The effort to apply *scientific methodology* centered in Germany, where Leopold von Ranke started the "objective" school of historical writing. He announced that he and his students would describe the past as it "actually happened." Sentiment and national bias were to be set aside, and historical documents were to be collected and interpreted in a rigorously critical fashion. Near the end of the century the "scientific" approach was carried by historians from German to American universities.

Ranke wrote some excellent histories, and his insistence on correct method was wholesome. He did not convince all historians, however, that it is possible to reconstruct a *single* true picture of what "actually happened." Serious philosophical and practical objections have been raised against his assumptions, and most twentieth-century historians have concluded that the account of individuals and societies can never be told with anything like the precision of natural science. There are indeed "lessons" of history, but they are interpreted in different ways by different writers and cultures. The Muse of history, Clio (p. 73), has never felt altogether at ease among the social sciences. She is more at home with the *humanistic* disciplines, especially philosophy, literature, and the arts.

LITERATURE AND ART IN THE MACHINE AGE

Writers and painters responded sharply to the changes in civilization triggered by science and the machine. They developed, by the middle of the nineteenth century, new goals and forms that would eclipse romanticism in European literature and art (pp. 475–85).

Expressions of Social Change: Dickens, Ibsen, Shaw

The new trend in literature was known as "realism." It started in France with Honoré de Balzac, who began writing successful novels in the 1830s. (His collected works were later published as *The Human Comedy*.) Balzac placed under close examination men and women of all stations in society. A keen observer, he set the style of insightful reporting of human strengths and weaknesses that marked French literature for the rest of the century.

In England, realism spotlighted the social effects of the Industrial Revolution. Charles Dickens, one of the most popular authors of the era, called the attention of his readers to the cruelties and hardships of the urban working class. In *Pickwick Papers* (1836) he exposed the grim debtors' prisons; in *Oliver*

c. 1800	c. 1830	c. 1860	c. 1890	c. 1905
ROMANTICISM	REALISM	IMPRESSIONISM	POST-IMPRESSIONISM	

Twist he revealed the horror of the English workhouses (places of forced labor for the poor). Though his many novels range widely over human themes and problems, they have a strong note of *social protest*; the world of Dickens's characters is not far from Karl Marx's view of a warped capitalist society. Dickens's books contributed, no doubt, to the reform legislation of the nineteenth century (p. 510).

The continental writer who addressed himself most directly to the problems of his day was a Norwegian, Henrik Ibsen. Though he is today recognized as one of the prime molders of modern dramatic form and technique, his reputation at first rested on the social content of his dramas. The son of a once-prosperous businessman, Ibsen grew up with contempt toward his own society, especially the new bourgeoisie. In *Pillars of Society* (1877) he revealed the corruption and hypocrisy he had observed among "established" Norwegian families. His next plays dealt with such issues as female emancipation (*A Doll's House*) and the conflict between commercial interests and personal honesty (*An Enemy of the People*). Not surprisingly, these works brought hostile reactions from the middle-class audiences. In his later plays, Ibsen gave up his challenges to the social system and created memorable portraits of *individuals* (*Hedda Gabler*).

George Bernard Shaw, a brilliant Irish author, was among Ibsen's admirers. He appreciated the intelligence and purpose that Ibsen had brought to the nineteenth-century theater, and he turned his own pen to the cause of social criticism. To Shaw, nothing was sacred; he even faulted Shakespeare for lacking a social message for his own time. One of the most prolific of writers, Shaw composed nearly fifty plays during the course of his long life. Virtually every one of them contains both satire and "message"; his characters, accordingly, tend to be two-dimensional, serving mainly as bearers of intellectual argument.

The relation of literature to social questions during the latter part of the nineteenth century is underlined by the fact that Shaw was a self-taught economist and one of the founders of English socialism. "In all my plays," he once said, "my economic studies have played as important a part as a knowledge of anatomy does in the works of Michelangelo." The drama that first attracted public attention was his *Widowers' Houses* (1892), a condemnation of slum landlordism. This was followed by *Mrs. Warren's Profession*, showing the economic roots of modern prostitution, and *Arms and the Man*, satirizing the military profession. Later dramas dealt with such matters as poverty, war, religious faith, and eugenics (human genetic improvement). By 1915 Shaw's fame was known around the globe, and in 1925 he was awarded the prestigious Nobel Prize in literature.

The Response of the Artist: Monet, Cézanne, Van Gogh

In the arts, social protest was expressed in the works of only a few individuals. Most prominent among them were two French artists of the realist school: Gustave Courbet and Honoré Daumier. Both rebelled against the romantic tradition, sympathized with the poor, and felt that art should correspond to social facts. While Courbet stressed the simple and truthful representation of nature, Daumier pictured the poverty and despair of the working class. He is best known, perhaps, for his thousands of lithographs (prints) caricaturing all levels of French society; they complement the *word* pictures of his contemporary, Balzac, in revealing the "human comedy." One of Daumier's masterpieces in oil, *The Third Class Carriage*, reveals his ability to paint, with sincerity and compassion, the ordinary people of his time (*Fig. 12-1*). He experienced in his own life the miseries recorded in his art — he died a pauper in 1879.

Daumier's artistic techniques, particularly the "unfinished" effect of his canvases, continued beyond his death. They influenced the style of "impressionism," the most important development in nineteenth-century painting. The impressionists, however, had nothing to do (as artists) with social satire or protest. They tended to be strictly *formal*, wishing to record images with optical accuracy and without concern for any kind of message.

The whole trend of painting after 1870 was toward "art for art's sake." This indicated, perhaps, an even deeper sense of alienation than that which

12-1 Daumier. *The Third Class Carriage.* Metropolitan Museum of Art, New York.

inspired the social realism of Daumier. Rather than trying to speak for the downtrodden or to change society, most artists now turned their backs on society, seeking escape into a *separate* world of art, where painters could impose whatever rules they desired upon elements of their own creation.

Claude Monet represented most fully the aims and achievements of impressionism. He desired to record physical appearances immediately as he saw them. In order to do this faithfully, he disciplined himself to suppress his prior *knowledge* of the shape and detail of things — a break with traditional painting. Fascinated by the change in appearances resulting from alterations in light, Monet insisted on working in the *open air*, putting his visual impressions to canvas in rapid strokes, almost as though he were making a sketch. As the eye, in glancing, sees only a few objects clearly, he deliberately left major areas of his pictures blurred or "unfinished."

This absence of clear detail in Monet's work at first called forth the scorn of critics. In 1874, in an exhibit with other painters of the new style, he showed a picture of a harbor seen through morning mists. He called it *Impression: Sunrise (Fig. 12-2)*. From this title, an unfriendly observer coined the term "impressionists" as a label for these artists. In time, critics and public alike grew to appreciate the special aims of this kind of painting. Some of the impressionists associated their techniques with the methods of scientific observa-

12-2 Monet. *Impression: Sunrise.* Musée Marmottan, Paris.

tion. Most, however, simply yielded to the delight of producing their riches of color and tone.

The ultimate success and popularity of the impressionists gave all artists a fresh sense of freedom and power. Any chosen combination of forms and colors might now be considered a legitimate work of art. Gone were the rules that had required "dignified" or "worthy" subjects, "correct drawing," "rules of perspective," and "balanced composition."

Impressionism itself, however, was a beginning, not an end. Toward the close of the nineteenth century there came new stirrings in art — largely reactions to impressionism. Paul Cézanne, who came to Paris in 1861, had adopted many of the techniques of the new style. He objected, however, to what he regarded as the airy, temporary quality of impressionist paintings; he longed to combine the brilliance of their coloring with more *substantial* forms.

As may be seen in his *Still Life* (*Fig. 12-3*), one of hundreds of such studies that Cézanne painted, he tried to develop *solidity* in his works. As a means of furthering this aim, he slightly shifted eye levels in looking at the various objects in the painting, thus creating several angles of view on a single canvas. He also *distorted* the natural shapes of objects and avoided symmetrical lines. These techniques make his paintings a source of continuing interest and pleasure.

12-3 Cézanne. *Still Life*. National Gallery of Art, Washington, D.C.

12-4 Van Gogh. *Cornfield with Crows*. National Museum Vincent van Gogh, Amsterdam.

While Cézanne sought to rearrange nature into what he considered a more satisfying balance of light and form, a younger artist, Vincent van Gogh, had different objectives. Like Cézanne, van Gogh learned the special brush techniques of the impressionists. But he was not really interested in the outward appearances of things; he wanted to express his own *deep feelings* about nature and life. Van Gogh was thus the pioneer of the modern school of "expressionist" painters.

Extraordinary spiritual and mental stress marked van Gogh's brief life. The son of a Protestant minister, he had experienced in his youth an urgent though unfulfilled missionary impulse. In later years he sensed a divine creative force within nature and all forms of life; he sought to show this force in his paintings. His works were the products of an emotional frenzy that passed into periods of mental illness. Finally, when he found himself no longer able to paint, he took his own life (1890).

But in the years before his death, especially during a final stay at Arles, he produced a series of remarkable canvases. Stimulated by the sun-drenched countryside of southern France, he painted it with fevered excitement, applying color with greater vigor and freedom than had any painter before. He did not try to imitate the hues of nature; the colors represented his feelings. Yellow, his favorite color, was his means of expressing the ever-present love of God. Blue, pale violet, and green expressed rest or sleep.

A striking example of van Gogh's last works is *Cornfield with Crows* (*Fig. 12-4*), finished just before his death. It presents "vast stretches of corn under troubled skies," expressing, as he wrote, "sadness and the extreme of loneliness." Such was the final response of a great and sensitive talent in the closing years of the nineteenth century.

CHAPTER
13

Imperialism, World War, and the Rise of Collectivism

As the twentiety century opened, scientific technology and industrial production gathered momentum. At the same time, powerful economic, political, and military developments were heading toward a decisive crisis, the crisis of the First World War (1914–18). That ruinous struggle marked the beginning of a profound change in Western civilization. Change in history is continuous, but most scholars agree that a radical shift took place in the West during the half-century following the First World War. As a result, the basic conditions and prospects of life today are far different from what they were before 1914.

In this chapter we will see how imperialism and world war came about and how far-reaching were the consequences. Chief among these was the breakdown of the liberal order in Europe and the rise of collectivist social systems. In the next chapter we will see how the *Second* World War accelerated the changes in Western civilization and furthered the transformation of the entire globe.

IMPERIALISM AND EUROPE'S WORLD DOMINION

The expansion of Western society, which made lasting marks on a large portion of the earth, began at the close of the Middle Ages (pp. 290–303). Overseas exploration and colonization proceeded steadily from the sixteenth century into the eighteenth and then, about 1750, slowed down for a time. For more than a century thereafter, Europeans were busy at home with their liberal-nationalist revolutions and the Industrial Revolution. But after 1870 new colonial ventures were undertaken in Asia and Africa. Because these differed in important ways from earlier colonial efforts, they are usually called the "new" imperialism.

Imperialism itself is as old as history. Broadly defined, it means *control* by one group of people over other groups beyond its borders. It takes a wide range of forms, from outright occupation and enslavement to the exercise of hidden and subtle influence. Imperialistic adventures fill the accounts of our most ancient writers—Homer, Herodotus, and Thucydides (pp. 74, 78–79). The most successful imperialists of ancient times were the Romans; the Pax Romana, though based on conquest, brought order and prosperity to the Mediterranean world for several centuries (pp. 107–11).

Imperialism, no matter what its form, may be divided into two main types. Roman imperialism was, on balance, *beneficent*: it provided for a sharing by the conquered in the advantages of empire and movement toward equal political rights. A second type is clearly *exploitative*: as with Cortez in Mexico (pp. 297–98), it aims primarily at using the resources and peoples of other lands for the gain of the conquerors.

Motives for Nineteenth-Century Expansionism

The imperialism of the late nineteenth century was *exploitative*; its impact (intended and unintended) was shattering. What was it that moved Europeans to strike out across the seas and force themselves and their technology upon the peoples of Asia and Africa? The economic motive, arising from the growth of industrial capitalism, was certainly powerful. We saw in the preceding chapter how surplus profits found their way to "backward" countries (p. 507). The urge to secure raw materials, markets, and investments gave a mighty push to overseas penetration.

J. A. Hobson, an English socialist, wrote an influential analysis of the economic causes of expansionism. His book *Imperialism* (1902) attacked the system of overseas exploitation as "a depraved choice of national life, imposed by self-seeking interests." Hobson suggested that the system had grown out of the maldistribution of profits from industry. Since wage-earners lacked the purchasing power to buy all they produced, manufacturers had to go abroad to sell part of their output and invest their profits. He claimed that colonial administration and defense were costly and dangerous, and that economic problems could be better solved by providing higher wages and better social services at home. By these means the home market would be expanded, and capitalists would have better opportunities to invest their funds there. In effect, Hobson was urging a change in policy that would bring British capitalism closer to humanistic aims.

Vladimir Lenin took a different tack. As a Marxist (pp. 516–18), he did not think it possible for "reformers" like Hobson to alter the preordained course of capitalism. He accepted Hobson's analysis of imperialism, but he viewed imperialism as the inevitable last state of capitalism. In *Imperialism, the Highest Stage of Capitalism* (1916), Lenin declared that profits flowed overseas because they produced a higher rate of return there. And only in a colony, under formal political control, did investments yield their maximum return.

Colonies had extended the life of capitalism by bringing into existence *new proletariats*. But now that the globe had been parceled out, the capitalist states were being driven by their economic systems to wage wars against one another. These, he predicted, would be followed by proletarian revolutions, the establishment of socialist states, and the death of imperialism. Though Lenin's argument is inadequate, its partial confirmation by events and its acceptance by communist leaders throughout the world made it enormously influential.

The economic motive, no matter how interpreted, was only one of the forces behind imperialism. Probably more important was the drive for national power and prestige. European nationalism had come of age by 1870, as we saw in Chapter 11 (pp. 495–99). Germany, proud and militant, now set out to find its "place in the sun." It is no accident that the renewed scramble for colonies began at about the time that Germany and Italy became unified nations. The pride and effort that go into achieving self-determination for a nation (nationalism) can lead easily to the desire to control other nations and peoples (imperialism).

The balance of power in Europe itself seems to have stabilized after 1870, and the field of conflict shifted overseas. The armed forces of the rival nations sought strategic fueling stations, military bases, and sources of raw materials. They also looked to colonies for new reservoirs of combat troops. But, above all, many Europeans came to regard overseas possessions as the measure and substance of national power and glory.

Now intellectuals began to speak and write of their nation's "civilizing mission." Many members of the upper and middle classes sought careers in the overseas services, where they could feel superior to the natives. Ordinary citizens, as well, thrilled to phrases like "advance of the flag," the "white man's burden," and "manifest destiny." Men, women, and children of all classes studied the new global maps showing their nation's overseas possessions in distinctive colors. The vocal minorities that protested against imperialism on practical or moral grounds were swept aside as "small-minded" or *unpatriotic*.

Methods of Penetration and Exploitation

Imperialism did not always mean colonies; control could be informal as well as formal. In fact, many economic and political experts preferred informal control, because it was cheaper and enabled a nation to avoid many risks and responsibilities. Prior to 1870 the British, with their shipping and financial responsibilities, had proved especially skillful in securing economic privileges abroad. But informal and formal relations were woven together into a single fabric of empire: trade with informal control if practicable, trade with *rule* when necessary. The United States pursued a similar strategy in the Western Hemisphere, where it was the dominant power. Though it annexed Puerto Rico and secured special constitutional privileges in Cuba (1898), the United States controlled the rest of the Caribbean republics through economic influence ("dollar diplomacy"), aided when necessary by the Marines.

c. 1860	1871		1914 1918
Unification of Italy and of Germany		ERA OF THE NEW IMPERIALISM	FIRST WORLD WAR

When rival states began to challenge British economic privileges in particular areas, Britain responded by seeking exclusive arrangements. Thus, after 1870 its Foreign Office sought treaty rights, "spheres of interest," and colonies. Germany and Italy, as well as the older European nation-states, joined in the sweepstakes. All employed various methods for gaining a foothold or an advantage and backed up their efforts by the threat or use of military force. The "underdeveloped" or declining countries of Asia and Africa found themselves helpless before this combined onslaught. As in the case of earlier confrontations between Europe and the non-Western world (pp. 297–98), the Europeans held the advantages of aggressive purpose, superior organization, and advanced technology.

The assault on Africa began in earnest after 1870. The "Dark Continent" (meaning Black Africa, south of the Sahara desert) had remained virtually unknown to the Western world until that time. As a matter of fact, most Africans themselves knew little about *other* Africans; they were separated by natural barriers and suffered from malnutrition and disease. The continent, second largest on earth, has a wide variety of climate and geography: deserts, prairies, farmlands, jungles, mountains, lakes, and mighty rivers. Its inhabitants were of many ethnic stocks, speaking hundreds of languages and dialects, and worshiping countless gods and spirits. Some were farmers, some were herdsmen or hunters, and some lived mainly by trade (gold, ivory, slaves).

As a consequence of persisting differences and obstacles, the Africans had never achieved a *unified* culture or political organization — though impressive cities and regional empires had arisen, with splendid arts and crafts, poetry, music, and ritual dances. Probably the chief hindrance to the development of sub-Saharan cultures was their isolation from the rest of the world (except for limited contact with Muslim and Christian raiders, traders, and missionaries). With only elementary technology, no written languages of their own, and no science, the various tribes and kingdoms had remained within the limits of their traditional cultures.

The conditions of Africa and the slight knowledge of it by outsiders restricted the avenues for penetration and conquest. Nineteenth-century ventures, nevertheless, showed the Western capacity for investigation, missionary activity, and greed for wealth. David Livingstone was the first white person to explore substantial areas of the interior. (Earlier expeditions had been turned back by tropical diseases, to which whites had proved susceptible.) Livingstone, a Scottish physician and missionary, survived some thirty years among the Africans doing medical and religious work; during that time he had traveled the upper courses of the great rivers. When he was reported in Europe and America as being "lost" in the jungles, a New York newspaper sent a reporter to find him — as a journalistic stunt. Henry Stanley "found" the good doctor in 1871, decided to conduct further travels of his own, and later publicized his adventures in a book called *Through the Dark Continent*. More important, Stanley saw the possibilities of extracting wealth from central Africa. He succeeded at last in interesting King Leopold II of Belgium in his promotional plans.

Belgium, a small country that had gained independence only a generation before (p. 490), had no overseas possessions. Leopold's venture was entirely *private* — in keeping with the individualistic, buccaneering spirit of the times. He formed a company, with himself as president, and sent Stanley and other agents into the Congo region. Taking the view that the African interior was open for sale to the white race, Leopold acquired "possession" of an enormous area by making "treaties" with hundreds of tribal chieftains. (The treaties were usually "signed" after the Belgians handed over trifling gifts to the native leaders.) He thus created a "Congo Free State" under his personal rule — recognized as legal by the major powers in 1885. The Congo boundaries enclosed an area equal to that of the United States east of the Mississippi River.

Though Leopold claimed scientific and humanitarian purposes for his venture, his prime purpose was personal gain. His eye was fixed on the booming industrial demand for rubber: the Congo had rubber trees and a large supply of native laborers. But the natives were infected by tropical diseases and proved unresponsive to European work incentives; they could be forced to work only by the harshest methods.

Leopold's agents used up the trees and natives of the Congo without restraint. But, though the annual value of its rubber exports reached $10 million by 1908, Leopold did not make operations there self-sustaining. He used much of the income for personal extravagance and borrowed huge sums from the Belgian government. In return, he mortgaged the Free State to the government, which took it over at his death. As the *Belgian* Congo, the region received somewhat better treatment, but it remained a shocking example of human and material exploitation.

Leopold's taking of the Congo attracted the attention of other European states to the prizes of Africa. A conference was called in 1885 to give some order to the carving up of the remainder of the continent. Certain ground rules were agreed on: a nation with possessions on the coast had prior right to the related hinterlands; but, in order for a claim to any territory to be recognized, it must be supported by the presence of administrators and soldiers. The conference agreement was thus a signal to all competitors to move in with civilian and military forces. Within twenty-five years Africa had been completely staked out by the Europeans (p. 542).

The methods employed were similar to those used by Leopold's agents. White men trekked into the interior in search of tribal chiefs who would sign treaties. The chiefs seldom understood what the treaties meant or had the authority to transfer property rights, but the whites acted as if they did. These "rights" were then transferred to some European government, and a colony

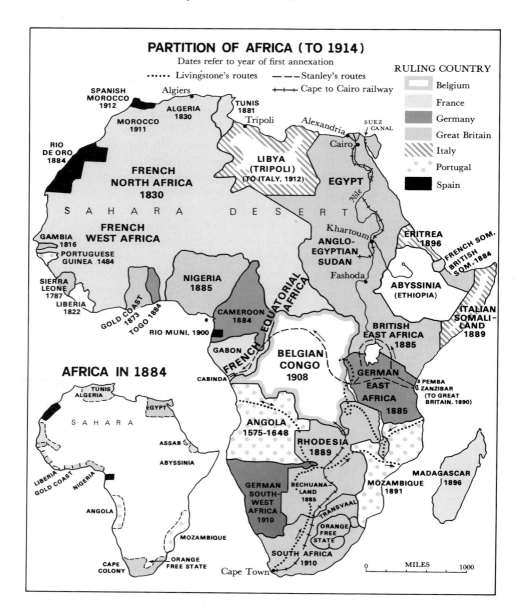

PARTITION OF AFRICA (TO 1914)

Dates refer to year of first annexation

•••••• Livingstone's routes   — — — Stanley's routes   +—+—+ Cape to Cairo railway

RULING COUNTRY

Belgium
France
Germany
Great Britain
Italy
Portugal
Spain

SPANISH MOROCCO 1912
Algiers
TUNIS 1881
Tripoli
Alexandria
SUEZ CANAL
ALGERIA 1830
MOROCCO 1911
RIO DE ORO 1884
Cairo
LIBYA (TRIPOLI) (TO ITALY, 1912)
EGYPT
FRENCH NORTH AFRICA 1830
S A H A R A   D E S E R T
Nile
Khartoum
GAMBIA 1816
FRENCH WEST AFRICA
ANGLO-EGYPTIAN SUDAN
ERITREA 1896
FRENCH SOM.
BRITISH SOM. 1884
PORTUGUESE GUINEA 1484
SIERRA LEONE 1787
LIBERIA 1822
NIGERIA 1885
Fashoda
ABYSSINIA (ETHIOPIA)
ITALIAN SOMALI-LAND 1889
GOLD COAST 1873
TOGO 1884
CAMEROON 1884
FRENCH EQUATORIAL AFRICA
RIO MUNI, 1900
GABON
BELGIAN CONGO 1908
BRITISH EAST AFRICA 1885

AFRICA IN 1884

CABINDA
GERMAN EAST AFRICA 1885
PEMBA ZANZIBAR (TO GREAT BRITAIN, 1890)

TUNIS
ALGERIA
EGYPT
SAHARA
ASSAB
ABYSSINIA
ANGOLA 1575-1648
RHODESIA 1889
MADAGASCAR 1896
LIBERIA
GOLD COAST
NIGERIA
GERMAN SOUTH-WEST AFRICA 1910
BECHUANA-LAND 1885
MOZAMBIQUE 1891
ANGOLA
TRANSVAAL
MOZAMBIQUE
ORANGE FREE STATE
SOUTH AFRICA 1910
CAPE COLONY
ORANGE FREE STATE
Cape Town

MILES
0   1000

was thereby established. The only serious difficulties arose when rival nations secured overlapping grants in the same region. Such problems were usually referred to the European capitals for settlement.

In Asia the situation was different. There were no "dark" or "unoccupied" zones. China, for example, was a historic empire, well mapped and administered. Chinese civilization, like that of India, traced back to 3000 B.C. A developed culture, including a written language, an agrarian economy, feudal political relationships, and splendid arts and crafts had become established by 1000 B.C. For many centuries the Chinese lacked a strong central government. This was achieved at last in the third century B.C. and led to a lengthy period of rule by the Han dynasty — 200 B.C. to A.D. 200 — about the same period as Roman rule in the West (pp. 98–111). The country afterward fell under continued pressure from Mongol nomads dwelling north of China's Great Wall. These barbarians repeatedly attacked (and sometimes ruled) China — as they attacked the Middle East, India, and Europe (pp. 46–47, 198, 283–84, 296). But China absorbed the invaders and pressed steadily forward with its brilliant and unbroken civilization. The excellence of Chinese practical and fine arts, scholarship, philosophy, and literature made a lasting impression on all of east Asia (including Japan).

China, however, did not match the scientific and technological advances of the West after 1500. Thus, when the Europeans eventually decided to penetrate the Chinese "wall" of isolation from foreigners, they possessed superior military equipment and made effective use of it. What the Europeans wanted initially were trading privileges. They coveted the luxury goods of China (silks, precious stones, porcelain), and they wanted to secure them in exchange for their factory-made products. Unfortunately, the Chinese did not want such articles. The one item they would buy in substantial quantities was the narcotic drug, opium, grown in India and sold by British merchants. When the Chinese government tried to check its importation, Britain started hostilities. (This was the so-called Opium War.)

The treaty forced upon China at the end of the Opium War (1842) was the first of countless impositions on that country. According to the treaty's terms, the opium trade was to be resumed without further interference. In addition, Britain demanded and won possession of the strategic Chinese city of Hong Kong. Within the next few decades other countries made their own demands. Under the "treaty system" a dozen Chinese port cities were opened to European traders (p. 546), and in each port city the leading European powers were allowed to establish their own settlements, free from Chinese authority. European nationals, under further agreements, were allowed to travel inside China, subject only to the laws of their *own* homelands. The Chinese government was deprived of control over its external commerce; the European powers required that no tariff of more than five percent be placed on imports and that the tariffs be collected by Europeans. A good portion of this revenue was then siphoned off as "war indemnities" to the invaders. Small wonder that the Chinese felt growing resentment toward the "foreign devils"!

No matter what technique the Europeans used to impose their control, the results were disastrous to native institutions and morale. Although most Westerners are seldom aware of the effect of their technology when it is brought into traditional cultures, historians generally agree that modern industrial civilization has been one of the most disturbing cultural forces ever known. It breaks down and transforms premachine social organization, habits of life, and ways of thought. In this sense, the damage brought by imperialism resulted as much from "culture shock" as from the economic exploitation of "backward" peoples.

China suffered the full consequences of economic and social dislocation. Before the British broke in, there had existed a kind of balance between farming and handicrafts. A merchant class had prospered in the cities, and there were some large-scale workshops. China had a lively export trade in silks and porcelains, and its superb craftsmen had been kept busy. But the entry of low-priced manufactured goods in the nineteenth century upset the entire structure. And, by building factories in the free ports and using the cheapest labor, the Europeans further undermined Chinese handicrafts and demoralized the regular work force. Quick fortunes were made from these enterprises by foreign traders and manufacturers, but the cost to the Chinese people was beyond measure.

The Japanese were more fortunate. Though they had long admired and accepted Chinese ways, their conservative leaders feared the influence of Western ideas on their tightly organized, traditional society. After unhappy experiences with Portuguese and Dutch traders, the Japanese had closed their ports to foreign vessels in the seventeenth century. They did not reopen them until 1854. It was then that the American Commodore Matthew Perry, by threatening naval bombardment, persuaded the ruling power to negotiate a commercial treaty. The Japanese soon yielded to the idea that they must accept industrialization if they were to survive in the modern world. But they were determined to develop it *themselves*, without disruptive interference by foreigners. They jealously guarded control over their finances and tariffs, and in an extraordinary national effort they modernized their economy and armed forces. By 1890, they were thus able to meet the Westerners on even terms. (Asians, generally, learned a lesson from the Japanese example. Today most Asian leaders prefer to build their own national economies, in accordance with the character and needs of their societies.)

The Partitions of Asia and Africa

The concessions of trade and treaty ports by China failed to satisfy imperialist appetites, and the major powers continued to jockey for advantage. The Russians began, about 1850, to develop their long-neglected Siberian possessions (p. 406), founding the city of Vladivostok (Ruler of the East) on the Pacific Ocean. Then they turned their attention to Manchuria and Korea, both of which had close historical ties to China. The Japanese, also infected by expansionism, shortly revealed that they had plans of their own in this area. They drew China into war over clashing rights in Korea in 1894, and their Western-style army won easily. China was compelled to cede to Japan the large island of Formosa (Taiwan), as well as its claims to Korea (p. 546).

The Europeans were astonished by this demonstration of Japanese will and strength. Now that it appeared that China might be falling prey to greedy neighbors, they decided to protect their interests by seizing control of whatever territories they could. The Germans, French, Russians, and British pressured the Chinese government to give them vital coastal zones, in addition to their settlements in the "treaty ports." Only suspicions and disputes among the great powers saved the rest of China from complete partitioning at this time.

The intervention of the United States, which had become a Pacific power in 1898 when it took the Philippine Islands from Spain, had only a minor effect on the situation. The Americans feared that their commerce with China would be cut off if the foreign interests already there succeeded in spreading their territorial holdings. The secretary of state, John Hay, therefore pushed vigorously (1899) for the acceptance of an "Open Door" policy in China, which would guarantee the "territorial integrity" of the country against further losses and extend to *all nations equally* the commercial privileges that had been won from the Chinese government.

Britain supported the Open Door policy, for it promised to block the threat of more annexations by China's neighbors. The other powers viewed it coolly, however, for they hoped to pounce upon portions of the faltering empire. Ignoring the Open Door principle, Japan determined to tighten and extend its grasp. In both Korea and Manchuria, Japan faced the Russian imperialists. After failing to negotiate an agreement for two separate "spheres of influence," and fearing further Russian advances, the Japanese decided to settle the issue by force.

Japan opened hostilities in 1904 with a surprise naval attack on the Russian fleet and base at Port Arthur, in China, declaring war a few days *afterward*. This strike was a glaring violation of international law (repeated by the Japanese some forty years later in their sneak attack on American forces at Pearl Harbor — p. 584). The tsarist government never recovered from this opening blow and was roundly beaten on sea and land (in Manchuria) during the Russo-Japanese War. As a result, Russian expansion in this area was checked, and Japan strengthened its special rights in Korea and Manchuria, as well as in Port Arthur. Japan also gained enormous international prestige for having humbled the (supposedly) mighty Russian Empire.

Meanwhile, the rest of Asia had been gobbled up. The French, over the years, had taken control of large areas of southeast Asia; they combined them in 1887 to form French Indochina (p. 546). The British had begun to plant settlements in India back in the seventeenth century; in the nineteenth century the crown assumed direct control of the Indian government and extended its grip to Burma and Malaya. The Dutch widened their earlier holdings in the East Indies (p. 299), while Persia and Afghanistan were split into British and Russian spheres of influence (1907). Russia also established a "protectorate" over Mongolia in 1913.

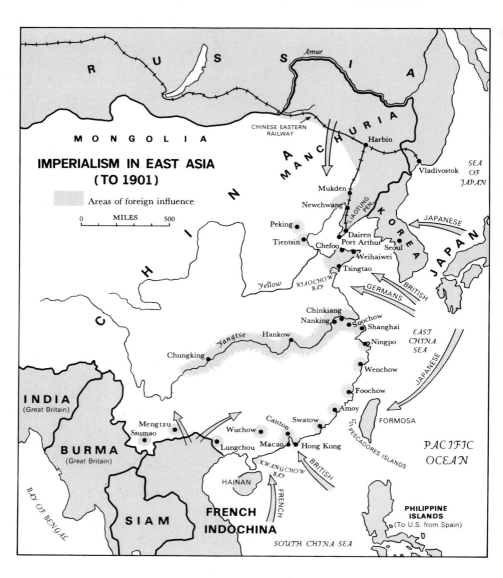

IMPERIALISM IN EAST ASIA
(TO 1901)

Areas of foreign influence

0   MILES   500

As for Africa, the entire continent had been partitioned by 1914. France held most of the bulge of west Africa, which was largely desert; the British held the richest lands, running from South Africa in the south to Egypt in the north. The main possessions on the southern and eastern coasts, and in the central region, were those of Portugal, Germany, Italy, and Belgium (p. 542).

At last this era of fabulous conquest came to an end. The "new" imperialism had added five million square miles to the British empire. (In 1900 Queen Victoria ruled nearly four hundred million subjects, with overseas territory *forty times* larger than the home island.) French possessions had expanded by almost as much; substantial though lesser areas had been acquired by Germany, Russia, Belgium, Portugal, and Italy. And Japan and the United States had joined the list of imperial powers.

The moral issue aside, imperialism brought some advantages to colonial peoples. It pushed them abruptly into the mainstream of world development. Roads, railways, sanitation, hospitals, and schools were introduced, while tribal wars and gross practices, where they existed, were stopped. Most significant, "modernization" was brought to the colonial territories — though it could have come in a less coercive fashion. But all these benefits must be measured against the physical and psychic blows inflicted by imperialism upon the subject peoples. It left them with a lasting sense of confusion, defeat, and degradation.

In 1914 Europe stood at its peak of power and arrogance. But its outward thrust had intensified the forces that were pushing the Western nations toward war among themselves. Europeans claimed to look after the problem of "backward" peoples, but they proved unable to solve their own. Europe was about to explode in a frightful conflagration, leading to the collapse, soon after, of their colonial empires.

THE FIRST WORLD WAR AND THE DECLINE OF EUROPE

The two "world wars," one starting in 1914 and the other in 1939, are closely linked. Both were products of the international political system created and legitimized by the European powers. The First War ended not with a stable peace, but with a truce; the Second War was its nightmarish sequel. It was 1914, rather than 1939, that was the major turning point of modern history.

Yet on the eve of 1914 there were few who could see what the future held. The trend of surface events had indeed been deceptive. Europe had been spared a *general* war for one hundred years — since the downfall of Napoleon (p. 466). The advance of science, liberal institutions, and material well-being was indisputable. The years before 1914 were a time of expansiveness and optimism, with the promise of the Enlightenment (p. 426) apparently nearing fulfillment. Given another half-century of peace, Europe might have made the *liberal order* secure.

As we look back, however, it seems evident that such an outcome was unlikely. The existing peace was shaky; and, even without war, it seems doubtful that the liberal order could have endured. For there was another, gloomier side of the European picture. Technology had created forces that were dissolving the foundations of liberalism, and imperialism had opened wounds, both in Europe and overseas, that continued to fester. There was, too, a rising romantic mood, irrational and illiberal, associated with mystical ideas of racial purity and national "soul." But Europe's fatal flaw was excessive *nationalism* — especially when it became connected with militarism and military alliances among the great powers.

Nationalism, Militarism, and the Alliance System

By the close of the nineteenth century the nationalist ideal of Mazzini (p. 495) had hardened into a self-centered and self-destroying passion. Its characteristics were the same in every Western land: the people of each nation believed in their own superiority, sovereignty, and special mission in the world. They saw the advancement of national power and glory as the supreme aim of all of its citizens.

Nationalism, the "religion of the fatherland," was, in fact, the true faith of most Europeans at the turn of the century. Each nation viewed itself as the chosen instrument of God; its founders and heroes were the apostles and martyrs; its political charters were revered as holy texts. The flag was the sacred symbol of each nation, and pledging allegiance to the flag — and visiting historic shrines — were honored rituals.

This patriotic enthusiasm fell hard on certain ethnic minorities within states — groups suspected of having less than *total* loyalty to the larger community. Most Jews, for instance, were seldom accepted as "full" citizens of the states where they resided. Reacting to this feeling, some Jews began to think of securing a national state of their own; this fitted in with an age-old yearning following the Jewish "Diaspora" of ancient times (p. 161). A "World Zionist Organization" was founded in 1897 by an Austrian journalist, Theodor Herzl. It sought to create a Jewish *nation* in Palestine; "Zion" is the name of the hill that had once been the site of King Solomon's temple and palace (p. 142). Herzl and his successors appealed to world leaders to support their cause — leading, in time (1948), to the creation of the state of Israel (p. 597).

The armed forces of each European nation became the principal embodiment of its sovereign spirit and honor. They served, at the same time, as the ultimate means of pursuing national aims; both pride and interest, therefore, moved public officials and citizens to respect and strengthen the army and navy. Bismarck, building on the military tradition of Frederick the Great (p. 405), had pursued this policy in Prussia. His forces had impressed the rest of Europe as they paved the way to the creation of the German Empire in 1871 (p. 497). The other powers had worked to catch up militarily as rapidly as possible; all except Britain adopted universal male conscription and military training. Competition in weaponry accompanied the rise of huge standing armies; by the end of the century Europe had become a bristling camp. Nationalism and militarism were thus fatefully joined.

Stated simply, militarism is the belief that preparation for war provides sound moral training and the best safeguard of peace and the national interest. Militarists scorn diplomacy except when it is used as an expression of force. They aim, therefore, to build ever stronger military power — greater, if possible, than that of any likely combination of enemies. "Peace through strength" is their slogan. But strength is *relative*, and each of the major nations wants to be the strongest. When the European peoples embraced militarism in the nineteenth century, they took off on an unrestricted *arms race*. All were caught up in it; for though a nation might never hope to win such a race, it dared not fall behind.

Unwilling or unable to agree upon principles for peaceful coexistence, the European powers were left to the deadly consequences of their own nationalisms. For in relations *between* states there was no enforceable law comparable to that which existed *within* states. Because each sovereign power recognized no authority superior to itself, the ultimate resort was to go to war. The situation then, as now, has been correctly called *international anarchy*. There is only one fundamental difference today: the weapons of war have become infinitely more destructive.

Metternich's "Concert of Europe" (p. 470) had been an attempt to deal with the problem of international anarchy by harmonizing the interests of the great powers. But this idea, basically at odds with nationalism, was doomed from the start. During the course of the nineteenth century, a few farseeing individuals tried earnestly to modify the sovereignty principle, strengthen international law, and establish international courts of justice. Peace conferences were called, notably those at The Hague (in the Netherlands) in 1899 and 1907. Representatives of twenty-six nations, assembled at The Hague, tried and failed to agree on a proposal for *arms control*, but they did conclude several treaties on the "law of war" and the "rules of warfare." They pledged not to use poison gas or other weapons that were considered especially inhumane or indiscriminate. They also created an international court of *arbitration*, to which countries might submit their disputes. Moreover, numerous "peace societies" were formed in various parts of Europe and America during the prewar period.

These efforts were forerunners of more substantial moves toward replacing anarchy with international order. But the responsible leaders of that era did not take them seriously. Those leaders believed that the only path to security, beyond keeping their own nation strong, was to enter into *alliances* with "friendly" powers. Thus, nationalism and militarism led to the alliance system of the late nineteenth century. Like the arms race, the alliances were competitive, and they added strength only in *relative* terms. The European states did not find safety from war in either arms or alliances. The pursuit of both served only to make the war fires hotter and more widespread when they flared up.

The Road to War

Though most of Europe's leaders, even as late as 1914, declared that war was *unthinkable*, we can see now that war was built into the existing international system. The pronouncements of the statesmen of that time are strong evidence of the human tendency to indulge in wishful thinking — to cling to comforting *myths* rather than face disturbing *realities*. Some said war would not happen because it was "too expensive," or "too frightful," or "too irrational." But we know now that those characteristics of war do not prevent it.

The research of countless scholars on the origins of the First World War shows how international anarchy leads, in fact, to international war.

Until 1914, there had been grounds for optimism about keeping the peace in the fact that a number of international crises had been settled without resort to arms. But the pressures for war were cumulative, and the right type of crisis at the right time was virtually certain to strike the igniting spark. Many countries were working at cross-purposes internationally; Germany, however, held the chief initiative. Its triumphal unification in 1871 made it the dominant power on the continent. The eyes of European diplomats were fixed on the Germans, watching what they would do and how far they would go. The acts of other powers were closely related to German actions.

It was Bismarck (p. 497) who started peacetime alliances, as a means of maintaining Germany's new dominance in Europe. His motives were no doubt defensive; he feared that the French, stung by their defeat in the Franco-Prussian War (1870), would seek revenge. And so he arranged an alliance with another vanquished rival, Austria-Hungary, in 1879. Italy joined this pact a few years afterward, making it the Triple Alliance.

The isolation of France, shrewdly arranged by Bismarck, was broken soon after he fell from office in 1890. His fall was due in part to the ambitions of the new German emperor, William II, who replaced Bismarck's cautious, *continental* policy with a policy that would propel Germany into its "rightful" place as a *world* power. The emperor's policy was an open challenge to Britain, whom Bismarck had sought to keep neutral in European affairs. Britain responded by developing closer relations with France.

Britain's island security and world position had depended for over a century on its superiority on the seas. But the new German kaiser (emperor), convinced of the importance of sea power to overseas commerce, colonies, and national prestige, was determined to have a great navy as well as the world's finest army. Beginning in 1898, Germany began to lay out huge expenditures for a fleet of warships. Britain, alarmed, reacted with still larger sums, insisting on the principle that its navy remain the equal of any other *two*. And, though traditionally committed to "splendid isolation" from European "entanglements," the British now began to consider European alliances to counter the rising power of Germany and the Triple Alliance. (Britain had already signed an alliance with Japan in 1902.)

The French, meanwhile, had not forgotten 1870, and they, too, were seeking military partners. They looked first to the power on Germany's eastern border. Russia — autocratic and conservative — was ideologically and socially in sharpest contrast to liberal and progressive France. But internal differences between states do not necessarily stand in the way of common goals in foreign policy. Already linked to each other by substantial French loans to the extravagant tsarist regime, the two countries entered into a Dual Alliance in 1894. This action confronted Germany with the threat that Bismarck had most feared—the possibility of a two-front war. From that time until 1914, the governments of Europe studied the military, diplomatic, and economic moves of the various powers with a view toward measuring their effects on the two opposing alliances. Any development that might decisively shift the balance of power between them could set off immediate and general war.

Britian found itself swinging ever closer to France and Russia. The French *revanchists* (revenge-seekers) accepted British advances in Africa and persuaded Russian diplomats to settle longstanding disputes with the British in the Middle East. For their part, the British were growing more worried with each "tough" move by the kaiser. They made no formal military commitments, but after 1907 there existed a "close understanding" (*entente*) between Britain, France, and Russia. British and French military officers began to carry on joint staff conversations. The Dual Alliance was thus extended into a Triple Entente. That "understanding" was to grow firmer as trouble erupted in the Balkan peninsula (southeastern Europe).

The "Balkans" and the narrow waterways (straits) of the Dardanelles and Bosporus had long been objects of great-power interest. The Ottoman Turks, in spite of losses of territory from the seventeenth century onward, continued to hold much of southeastern Europe, as well as the Middle East, until after 1815 (pp. 284, 405, 407, 415). Their subject nationalities, mostly Slavic, differed in language, religion, and general culture from their Muslim rulers, and they began to respond to the spirit of nationalism that was spreading through all of Europe. The Greeks, for example, had won their independence in 1829 (p. 488), and the Rumanians, Bulgars, and others were waiting for a chance to throw off the Turkish yoke. Slavic efforts to gain independence were supported by Russia, Austria-Hungary, Britain, and France—all of whom hoped to snatch for themselves some property from the declining Turkey, the "sick man of Europe." Intervention by these countries complicated Balkan affairs by fueling a dreary sequence of wars, treaties, conferences, and more wars. It was the grasping of the great powers, combined with the nationalist excitement in southeastern Europe, that furnished the tinder for the First World War.

The Russians had three objectives in the area: to liberate their fellow Slavs, to win control of the Black Sea coasts, and to secure a warm-water outlet for themselves at the straits. The tsar nearly achieved these objectives in 1878, when he invaded the Turkish Empire and crushed its forces. But Austria and Britain demanded, upon threat of war, that the Russians reduce their peace demands. At the ensuing Berlin Conference, presided over by Bismarck acting as an "honest broker," Russia gained only a few harbors and border territories. But Rumania, Serbia, and Montenegro were recognized as independent states, and Bulgaria secured self-rule under the Turkish sultan (ruler). Russia thus emerged as the protector of the Balkan peoples, having freed them from the hated rule of a crumbling empire.

The alarmed sultan now tried to check the decay of Turkish strength by inviting German experts to reform his army and finances. He tried, at the same time, to play off the great powers against one another. But he had to pay a price: in return for their continuing diplomatic aid against Russia, he permitted the British to occupy Cyprus and the Austrians to administer the provinces of Bosnia and Herzegovina (p. 498). Egypt, nominally part of the sultan's empire, was occupied by the British in 1882 as part of their colonial schemes in Africa. The island of Crete broke free from Turkey in 1896. Only a remnant remained of the dying empire, and that would be lost in the treaty ending the First World War (p. 555).

The conflicts of the Balkans reflected the deadly clash of opposing national aims. Russia, as we have seen, wanted to make the Black Sea a Slavic lake by controlling its outlet (the straits) at Constantinople. But Britain considered Russia's southward push a threat to its own "line of empire," which ran through the Mediterranean to India, and therefore sought to keep Russia bottled up in the Black Sea. Austria-Hungary, and Germany, too, had aims in the Balkans. Austria, which wanted to expand trade and influence in the region, resented growing Russian prestige there. And the Germans were building a Berlin-to-Baghdad railway, to open up the Middle East and India to German economic and political penetration. This ambitious project required understandings with the Balkan states through which the railway passed, as well as the Turkish sultan. Britain, Russia, and France regarded the German enterprise as a source of unwelcome aid to the Turkish Empire and an invasion into their own spheres of interest.

The most serious and irrepressible conflict, however, was between the Slavic nationalists and the empire of Austria-Hungary. The Habsburg rulers realized that their empire, consisting of a dozen different nationalities, would fall apart if they failed to contain the nationalistic forces within it. The little state of Serbia posed the most immediate threat. The Serbs, a Slavic people who had secured their independence in 1878, had an ambitious sense of national mission and wanted to unite all the "South Slavs" into a single political unit. Some of these South Slavs lived in the provinces of Bosnia and Herzegovina, which Austria annexed in 1908. The leaders of the "Greater Serbia" movement began agitation and subversion there in an effort to win over the allegiance of their fellow Slavs and bring about their liberation from Austria.

The statesmen in Vienna were understandably worried. A Serbian success would pull important territories away from the Austrian Empire. Still more dangerous was the force that such a success would set in motion. The Magyars (Hungarians) had already gained self-rule within the empire (in 1867), but the Czechs, Poles, Rumanians, and other minorities were still treated as subordinate peoples. They, too, were aroused by nationalist feelings and were eager to split the Habsburg domain into independent national states. The explosive situation also affected the alliance system, on which the general peace of Europe seemed to hang. If Austria-Hungary were to break apart, the Triple Alliance would be decisively weakened. Germany, the senior partner of the alliance, therefore kept in anxious touch with Vienna. On the opposing side, the Russians did all they could to *encourage* the Serbs to seek independence.

The Serbian nationalists, knowing that their country was militarily weaker than the Austrian Empire, resorted to *terror* to further their "holy" cause. Their efforts reached a climax in the streets of Sarajevo, Bosnia, in June 1914. A young terrorist assassinated the Archduke Francis Ferdinand (heir to the Austrian throne) and his wife. World leaders were shocked by the murders, and the Austrian government decided to use the occasion for a showdown with Serbia. Believing that the Serbian government was involved in the assassination plot, the Austrians sent a harsh *ultimatum* (a demand, backed by threat of action if not agreed to). The Serbs accepted in substance all but one of the requirements. But the Austrians rejected their response as unsatisfactory, broke off diplomatic relations, mobilized their army, and declared war on Serbia. The small Slavic nation, having received reassurances from Russia, also mobilized.

The responsibilities of the great powers in the face of this grave threat to European peace are difficult to assess. Germany, for reasons already suggested, had advised Austria to move ahead. Russia, having made a commitment to the Serbs, felt it could not back down. France, determined to preserve its alliance with Russia, urged its partner to be firm and to avoid any compromise that might cause a "loss of prestige" for the Triple Entente.

The decisive step in widening the war was the tsar's order to mobilize the Russian army. A week or more was needed before an army could be made ready for battle, and German leaders decided that they could not stand by while Russian mobilization went ahead. They sent a telegram demanding that the Russians halt their call-up within twelve hours. Failing to receive a positive reply, the Germans declared war on Russia on August 1, 1914. As Paris ordered mobilization, Berlin declared war on France as well. The catastrophe that "nobody wanted" had at last come about.

Though Britain had made no public pledge to aid France, its ministers had privately promised to help if the French were attacked by Germany. Parliament put aside any reluctance it might have had to make good this promise when the Germans, according to their war plan, invaded Belgium. Britain, as one of the guarantors of Belgian neutrality and security (p. 490), now had a legal basis for action. Parliament declared war on Germany on August 4. Japan, Britain's treaty partner in the Pacific, soon entered on the side of the "Allies," while the Turks, renewing their struggle with Russia, joined the "Central Powers" (Austria and Germany). Italy, a member of the Triple Alliance, did not enter the war at once, taking the position that its military obligation to its partners (Germany and Austria) was binding only if they were *attacked*. Italy remained neutral until 1915, when secret promises of extensive territorial rewards won it over to the Allied side. Many smaller nations were gradually drawn into the war (at least formally), but they did not influence its outcome.

The Course and Consequences of the War

The strategy of the First World War was basically simple. The Allies, with control of the seas, were sure of winning a *long* war of attrition. The Central Powers aimed for a quick, decisive victory based on superior military technique and forces already in place. They also enjoyed the advantage of interior lines of communication, which meant that they could concentrate their troops swiftly on chosen fronts. The Germans, wishing to avoid dividing their army between west and east, had planned to strike an overwhelming first blow against France and then turn against the Russian forces, which would be slower in mobilizing. In executing their plan, the German generals did not hesitate to sweep through tiny Belgium, violating the treaty guaranteeing Belgium's neutrality. The treaty, explained the Germans, was but a "scrap of paper"; the invasion was a matter of "military necessity."

The German attack, which aimed to roll up the French army in a grand wheeling movement, stalled at the Marne River, near Paris. After the first few weeks, the battle on the western front changed from one of movement to one of *fixed positions*. Now the advantage shifted to those who were on the defensive. Trench warfare, with its barbed wire, machine guns, artillery barrages, and bayonet charges, became a routine of slaughter for the next four years. Some new types of weapons were tried, aimed at breaking the military stalemate there: tanks by Britain, poison gas by Germany, and aircraft by both sides. These weapons failed to change the course of the conflict, but two of them — tanks and aircraft — would develop into decisive forces during the *Second World War* (pp. 583–84).

On the eastern front the Germans quickly gained the upper hand. The soldiers of the tsar, brave but poorly supplied, suffered disastrous losses and were practically out of the war by 1917. This military loss to the Allies was more than balanced, however, by the entrance of the United States on their side in 1917. Americans had been generally sympathic with the British and French from the start of the war, though there was a pro-German ethnic minority in the country. There was also a stubborn antiwar movement in the country that demanded that the United States remain *neutral*. But, in the end, opposition to joining the conflict was overcome by a combination of forces: the American government, fearing the strategic consequences of a German victory, pushed for intervention on the side of the Allies; and the public, alarmed by reports of German atrocities and the sinking by German submarines of commercial vessels, rallied to support the government. By bringing in fresh troops and equipment, and by pledging the resources of their continent, the Americans ensured ultimate victory for the Allies. Bowing to the inevitable, the Germans at last responded favorably to President Woodrow Wilson's offer of a moderate settlement, on Allied terms — a "peace without victory" (p. 580). In November 1918 they agreed to lay down their arms.

At the peace conference, which met at Versailles and other suburbs of Paris, separate treaties were arranged with each of the Central Powers. None of the defeated nations was given any effective voice in the settlements; it turned out to be a victor's peace after all. France, Britain, and the United States laid down the conditions, which were severe. (Had the Central Powers won, the conditions would probably have been even more severe — against the Allies. Evidence for this lies in the drastic terms imposed by Germany in its separate peace with Russia a year earlier — p. 562.) Delegates from the Central Powers protested bitterly but they were compelled to accept under threat that the war would be renewed. In a vengeful stroke, the French required the Germans to sign their treaty in the Hall of Mirrors at Versailles (*Fig. 9-8*, p. 390), where in 1871 Bismarck had proclaimed the German Empire.

The most objectionable part of the Versailles Treaty, from the German point of view, was the "war guilt" clause — which stated that Germany and its partners accepted responsibility for *all* loss and damage caused by the war. The Germans did not feel that they alone were to blame, and the historical facts indicate that other powers shared the responsibility. The guilt clause no doubt reflected popular sentiment in the Allied countries, which had been fed strong propaganda by their wartime governments. It was put into the treaty to justify huge damage claims by the victors. Only small amounts of these claims were ever collected, but the "war guilt" clause aroused among Germans a violent and lasting hatred of the treaty (p. 573).

Under the terrritorial provisions, Germany lost the provinces of Alsace and Lorraine (which had been taken from France in 1871), its overseas colonies, and valuable lands on its eastern frontiers. Germany also had to surrender most of its merchant shipping and to dismantle its armed forces. The treaties with the other defeated powers (1919–20) provided for the remaking of the map of central and eastern Europe, for now three empires (the Russian, Austrian, and Turkish) were in partial or total dissolution (p. 556). The guiding principle in drawing the new frontiers was Woodrow Wilson's principle of "self-determination" for nationalities. Seven new states came into being: Finland, Estonia, Latvia, Lithuania, Poland, Czechoslovakia, and Yugoslavia. (The last named fulfilled the dream of the Serbian patriots, who had started it all at Sarajevo.) Austria and Hungary were separated and reduced to small, landlocked states. All that remained of the Turkish (Ottoman) Empire was the "Republic of Turkey," limited to Asia Minor and a small area in Europe that included Constantinople (renamed Istanbul in 1930).

Despite the general application of national self-determination, the problem of nationalities continued to plague Europe. The diverse ethnic groups had become so intermixed that every fixing and refixing of state boundaries left some ethnic minorities under the political control of some other ethnic group.

PEACE SETTLEMENTS
IN EUROPE, 1919

TERRITORY LOST BY:

Germany

Bulgaria

Austria-Hungary

Russia

The deeper consequences of the war went far beyond the treaties and the breaking and making of states. The war had brought a catastrophic loss of lives and treasure from which Europe never fully recovered. Of the more than sixty million men mobilized, some nine million were killed. Total civilian deaths, direct and indirect, amounted to more than thirty million; economic costs ran into *trillions* of dollars.

France was the hardest hit. During the first year of war, French soldiers defended their homeland with a reckless courage due as much to the foolhardy tactics of the generals as to the bravery of the men. French military theorists before 1914 were committed to the doctrine of the offensive: "Attack" — always and everywhere. With disastrous results for the French, this doctrine was put to test at a time when offensive techniques were decisively inferior to defensive techniques. In the first sixteen months of fighting, France lost three-quarters of a million men — half its total losses in the war. Such casualties were unprecedented. During the first traumatic year nearly one family out of two received the dreaded message announcing the death of a loved one in action. As the struggle wore on, a sense of doom and despair spread across embattled France.

After 1916, a year in which the British suffered the highest losses in any single offensive (at the river Somme), all the combatants realized that such wholesale squandering of lives was futile. Yet the daily slaughter went on to the end, resulting in the destruction of half of a generation of young men. The spirit of Europe, especially of its surviving aristocracy, was broken. The youth who lived through the war, and wondered why, regarded themselves as the "lost" generation. The old beliefs and slogans had for them become mockeries; traditional morals, manners, and standards seemed, at best, irrelevant.

Men and morals were not the only casualties of the war. The *liberal order*, which in 1914 had appeared firm, was badly damaged. France and England, the leading liberal states, were crippled. In addition to their irreplaceable losses in manpower, their world positions had been shaken. In prosecuting the war, both nations had found it necessary to sell off a large portion of their overseas investments. Moreover, the spectacle of Europe at war with itself stripped away the awe with which colonial peoples had viewed their conquerors. The Western powers had given them reason to hope that they might one day send the imperialists packing.

The loss of physical and psychological power by the liberal states was equaled by the injury to their professed ideas and institutions. Liberalism was rooted in the Enlightenment, with its optimistic faith in humanity, reason, nature, and progress. But this faith had been crushed in the agony and futility of the war. Could liberalism survive after its supporting faith had collapsed? Disenchanted Europeans were unsure. Some drifted into skepticism (doubting all), cynicism (scorning all), or nihilism (rejecting all). Other Europeans were drawn toward socialism or toward a new and more violent strain of nationalism.

The war had undermined specific liberal institutions as well. This was most evident in the economic sphere, where "free enterprise" had been jealously guarded during the nineteenth century. Every nation at war was forced to clamp controls on business; just as the draft on manpower was compulsory, so was the call on economic resources. Raw materials, exports and imports, banking, wages, prices — all had been regulated in the pursuit of victory. Laissez-faire principles (p. 508) had been ignored "for the duration," and this experience of government planning and direction continued into the future. The war had also disrupted the intricate mechanism of international trade, and a chain of financial dislocations after 1918 marked the end of historic laissez-faire. It would be demonstrated time and again that private enterprise, both domestic and international, was not always "self-regulating" in the public interest. To maintain employment and save business from mass failures, Western governments would be called upon to take action.

The World War was fought, declared President Wilson, to make the world "safe for democracy." As he looked at Europe from Versailles in 1919, he might well have thought that the goal was now within reach. Prussian militarism had been defeated, long-standing empires had been reduced to ruins, and proud monarchies had been toppled. Democracy (as well as nationalism) appeared triumphant. Yet Wilson and others of liberal-democratic convictions were to suffer bitter disappointment. For most of the new democracies were only superficially democratic, and the older democracies were soon to lose their once liberal character. Moreover, the shock and aftershock of the war were to open the doors of revolution in several countries. From the underground of the nineteenth century sprang the promoters of new social orders — people who were radically opposed, in theory as well as in practice, to both liberalism and bourgeois democracy.

COMMUNIST COLLECTIVISM: THE RUSSIAN REVOLUTION

The most comprehensive term applicable to the entire range of antiliberal ideologies and systems is "collectivism." Collectivism opposes historic liberalism (individualism) most directly on the issue of the amount of personal freedom in society. The liberal idea favors *maximum freedom for each individual* from any kind of restraint. Each person is to be "let alone" — to do whatever pleases that person (without injuring the freedom and rights of others). The collectivist idea, on the other hand, favors active *social planning and direction* — to promote the "general welfare" of all members of the society. In pursuit of this idea, collectivist systems restrict some freedoms of individuals and leave many areas of decision-making to large organizations — above all, to *government*. (In their extreme form, collectivist systems are properly called *totalitarian*.) Collectivist organizations and governments may be controlled in various ways — from autocratic to democratic — but, no matter what the form of control may be, the individual is bound by decisions of others in many spheres of life. We should distinguish the collectivist state from the political absolutisms of the past, in which both the intentions of the rulers and their means of control were relatively limited. In fact, we can fully comprehend modern collectivism only in the context of the scientific, technological, and social conditions of the *twentieth* century.

Collectivist systems have shown a wide variety, arising from their differing values, ideologies, principles of action, and historical settings. They have come into being through one or the other of two modes of development: *revolution* or *evolution*. The former mode has appeared in countries where peaceful change had been blocked and where experience in liberal democracy had been slight, while the latter mode grew directly out of liberal democracy and with little or no violence. Most collectivist developments had this much in common: they were active responses to the failures of historic liberalism and to the deep troubles of modern industrial society.

Russia before the Revolution

Strangely, the first collectivist state was established in a country where modern forces had scarcely started to develop. Autocratic Russia was a century or more behind the changes that had swept over western Europe. In 1917, the position of the Romanov dynasty was not far different from what it had been more than two centuries earlier under Catherine the Great (p. 406). It resembled, in its pretensions and ignorance, the Bourbon monarchy of France in 1789 (pp. 455–56).

Russia had created a vast empire of many distinct nationalities, stretching eastward from central Europe to the Pacific Ocean (pp. 405–6, 544, 566). East of the Ural Mountains, the sparse population consisted of various Asiatic peoples, some of whom were seminomads. In European Russia (which then included Poland and the Baltic lands), the population was settled and dense; in 1900 it totaled about one hundred million. More than eighty percent of these people were peasants, and most of them had only recently been freed from serfdom (1861). They held more than half the arable land of the country, either as individual owners or through their village organization (*mir*), and they had gained limited political rights. Nevertheless, they remained largely illiterate and were regarded by the landed aristocracy (less than ten percent of the population) as an inferior caste. Over all was the heavy hand of the Russian Orthodox Church, which resisted Western ideas and supported the tsar's "divine" rule of Holy Russia and its empire.

Western influences had nevertheless reached into Russia. The late nineteenth century saw the rise of a new social element, the *intelligentsia*, made up of educated members of the aristocracy and the small urban middle class. Though the intelligentsia usually identified themselves with Slavic traditions, they were familiar with Western books and ideas. Writers like Tolstoy and

Dostoevsky were members of this group (p. 480). Their popularity in the West reflected a growing common ground of culture. Russia also produced musical composers, philosophers, and poets, as well as some outstanding mathematicians and scientists.

The Industrial Revolution served as the chief spearhead of Westernization. After 1880, with the help of outside funds, the capitalist pattern of economic growth began to take shape in Russia. Substantial investments went into factories, mines, and railroads, and Russia became active in the world trading system. Capitalist development, however, was still limited in comparison with that of England or Germany. Industrial wage-earners made up only a small fraction of the total labor force in 1914, and their working conditions resembled those in England fifty years earlier. The capitalist class was very small and had to share the economic field with numerous state-owned enterprises.

Though in theory an absolute monarch, Nicholas II was troubled by a wide range of domestic criticism and opposition. Around 1900 the rising business and professional class, in combination with liberal landowners, had formed a political party known as the Constitutional Democrats. Eager to follow the example of western Europe, they wanted to convert Russia's autocracy into a liberal, constitutional government. At about the same time two radical parties were founded — the Social Revolutionaries and the Social Democrats. The former, drawn mainly from the intelligentsia, was an agrarian party; its goals were to give more land to the peasants and to strengthen the functions of the *mir*. The Social Democrats were a Marxist group, also chiefly intellectuals. They viewed the peasants as hopelessly backward and believed that social change would have to follow Marxist theory — that is, the continuing growth of capitalism followed by the rise (and triumph) of an urban proletariat.

In 1905 a large body of protesting workers had gathered in front of the tsar's Winter Palace in St. Petersburg and had been fired on by troops. This "Bloody Sunday" set off insurrections across the country that were supported and used in various ways by the opposition parties. As a means of restoring order, the tsar promised a constitution and civil liberties and agreed, further, to the creation of an elected legislative body (Duma). Thus, by 1914 some concessions had been made to demands for political and economic reforms, but discontent still rumbled among most classes of the population. Only by means of a hated secret police was the tsar able to keep down the opposition. Even so, some revolutionaries resorted to *terrorism*, and no public official was safe from assassination. The grandfather of Tsar Nicholas (Alexander II) had been killed by a bomb, and Nicholas's prime minister was shot dead in 1911.

The Collapse of the Tsarist Regime and the Triumph of Lenin

Russia's military disasters in the First World War, following defeat in the Russo-Japanese War (p. 545), opened the way to revolution: they laid bare the inadequacy of the tsarist administration and heaped disgrace upon it. Soldiers and sailors, poorly supplied and hungry, at last refused to continue the hopeless fight against the Germans. In March 1917 food riots and strikes in Petrograd (formerly St. Petersburg) led to mutinies among the garrisons of the capital. The tsar, then at the front, abdicated upon the advice of his generals; thus the Romanov dynasty ended, and Russia became a *republic*. A provisional government, composed chiefly of the reformist leaders in the Duma, now assumed power. This government was challenged, however, by the Petrograd Soviet of Workers' and Soldiers' Deputies, a body representing the radical parties. The country's future now hinged upon the struggle for power between the provisional government and the Soviet.

In April, Vladimir Lenin arrived in Petrograd. The son of a middle-class civil official, Lenin had enjoyed a comfortable childhood. But at the age of sixteen, after the execution of his elder brother for alleged participation in a terrorist plot, he had thrown himself into opposition to the tsarist regime (1886). Depending on his friends for support, he made revolution his life career. Lenin spent most of his years in exile — first in Siberia and later in western Europe.

An early convert to Marxism, Lenin worked to make the Russian Social Democratic party a disciplined revolutionary organization. The "revisionist" wing of the party (p. 520) appeared to outnumber Lenin's faction, but at a meeting in 1903 he temporarily secured majority backing for the radical position. His followers thenceforth called themselves Bolsheviks, from the Russian word meaning "majority"; their reformist rivals came to be known as Mensheviks (minority). In 1912 the Bolsheviks broke away completely from the Social Democratic ranks and formed an independent revolutionary party. They changed their name to "Communist" in 1918.

During most of the war Lenin promoted international Marxist activities from Switzerland. His return to Petrograd in 1917 was aided by the Germans, who hoped that his activities there would help to overthrow the new government and take Russia out of the war — which is what Lenin succeeded in doing. First, however, he had to take power from the provisional government, which was making an earnest effort to restore internal order and uphold Russia's obligation to its allies to continue fighting the Germans. But conditions grew steadily more desperate in the country. Though Russia's economy had not developed to the point at which a proletarian revolution in the Marxist pattern could be expected, Lenin became convinced that the war had opened a *shortcut* to socialism. He saw that the bulk of the Russian people wanted three things above all: *peace*, *land*, and *food*. The provisional government, headed after July by Alexander Kerensky, a Social Revolutionary, had failed to satisfy these longings.

Lenin's road to power was through the Petrograd Soviet. Local soviets (councils) had first appeared during the insurrection of 1905; these "spontaneous" bodies had supposedly spoken for the peasants, city workers, and soldiers. Similar councils were formed in the crisis of 1917, and the Petrograd Soviet began to act as a "shadow" government. Though the Bolsheviks were a minority within the Soviet when Lenin arrived, he saw that the Soviet could be a key agency for seizing control of the state. He cleverly outmaneuvered his opponents (the Mensheviks and the Social Revolutionaries), and his repeated promises of peace and land won growing popular support for the Bolsheviks. In October 1917 Lenin's faction won the upper hand in the Soviet and elected Lenin's close ally, Leon Trotsky, chairman. As Kerensky's power slipped and as soldiers once more began to desert their units, Lenin decided to move against the provisional government.

The seizure of power (on November 7) was carefully planned and swiftly executed. With the support of the Petrograd military garrison, a revolutionary force occupied the telephone exchanges, power plants, and railway stations of the capital. The cruiser *Aurora*, stationed on the Neva River (fronting the Winter Palace) trained its guns on the building and fired the signal for the main attack. Kerensky found no troops to defend his government; he escaped, and the rest of his ministers fled or were captured.

On the afternoon of the coup, according to plan, Lenin arranged a meeting in Petrograd of delegates from soviets in other parts of the country. This "all-Russian" congress, controlled by the Bolsheviks, declared the provisional government at an end and claimed full authority. It approved decrees for an immediate peace with Germany and for the distribution of land to the peasants. (Under the terms of the subsequent peace treaty (1918) the Soviets agreed to surrender control of Finland, the Ukraine, much of Poland, and the Baltic territories of Lithuania, Latvia, and Estonia — all historically parts of the former Russian Empire.) The congress also elected a Council of People's Commissars (Deputies) to conduct the government, with Lenin at its head. These formalities could not conceal the fact that a small group, shrewdly and boldly led, had moved into the confused situation and had taken command. Thus was established the world's first communist state under the first "dictatorship of the proletariat." Could such a government, facing enormous internal and external problems, keep itself in power? Its only organs of administration were the Communist party, the soviets, and the Council of Commissars. The commissars established a secret police and authorized the recruiting of a Red Army. The war commissar, Trotsky, was to be its builder and leader.

One of the early tests of the new government came with the arrival in Petrograd (January 1918) of delegates to a national Constituent Assembly. This body had been authorized months before by the provisional (reformist) government and was to write a liberal constitution for the country. The delegates had been chosen in a general election in which thirty-six million citizens voted, and a majority of them belonged to Kerensky's Social Revolutionary party. But Lenin refused to surrender power to the "malignant bourgeoisie" and sent a company of Soviet sailors to stop the meetings of the Assembly.

A more severe challenge soon followed. Former tsarist generals organized and led counterrevolutionary forces ("Whites") in several regions of the country. They were joined by property-owners, reactionaries, liberals, and anti-

Bolshevik revolutionaries. In addition, the western Allies sent military units to aid the Whites against the Reds; the Allies were trying to keep Russia in the war and wanted to help destroy communism. But after two years of frightful civil war, marked by the use of *terror* on both sides, the hardened Communists emerged victorious. (Their ruthlessness, developed during this early period of their struggle for survival, established a pattern of behavior that led, ultimately, to the massive atrocities of Stalin.)

The Red triumph owed much to the extraordinary will of Lenin and to the military and organizing genius of Trotsky. And it owed something to the confusion and splits among the counterrevolutionary groups and their association with *foreign* powers. But, in the last analysis, it owed most to the attitude of the common people. Many of the commoners, to be sure, opposed the new regime. But the majority feared that a White victory would probably lead to the withdrawal of land from the peasants and to a restoration of the old order of autocracy, caste, and privilege. Though they also feared the Communists, they preferred them to the reactionaries. And popular support, in the fluid, guerrilla-type struggle, proved decisive. After 1920, with the bloody ordeal over, Lenin and his party sought to bring order out of chaos.

Building a Socialist Society

The task of pulling together a battle-torn country (formerly the multinational empire of the tsars), and at the same time overhauling its social structure, was staggering. The violence of civil strife had brought more distress than had the war against the Central Powers. During the fight with the counterrevolutionaries the government had resorted to temporary measures — later called "war communism." These included the drafting of workers into labor teams and forced deliveries of food from the peasants, in order to relieve hunger in the cities. Lenin was eager to start building socialism, but economic conditions were still so bad in 1921 that his plans had to be postponed.

Food was the primary problem; drought had made matters worse, and famine now stalked large areas of the country. Something had to be done quickly to spur the efforts of farmers and to encourage them to market their produce. The New Economic Policy (NEP) aimed at doing just that. Launched in 1921, it removed restrictions on the ways in which land could be held and operated. (The peasants now possessed *all* the farmland; in accord with the Soviet land-distribution decree of 1917, the peasants of each community had divided the properties of the landed aristocracy among themselves.) Now they were permitted to hire laborers and to sell or lease land as they saw fit. Forced food deliveries were stopped, and the growers could market as they wished. The NEP was also extended to industry and commerce. While the state kept its grip on public utilities and other large industries (which had been nationalized in 1918), it encouraged private entrepreneurs to undertake new business ventures.

1917	1924	1928		1953
Lenin	Trotsky versus Stalin		Stalin	

This temporary return to capitalistic methods brought about substantial recovery of production. But it fell short of the hopes and promises of the Communists. By 1928 output was at about the same level as it had been in 1913, and the momentum of the New Economic Policy seemed to slacken. Meanwhile, in 1924, the revered Lenin had died, and his former colleagues were maneuvering to take his place. Trotsky was the best known and probably the most talented. He, better than anyone else, expressed the impatience of the party with respect to economic development. In 1926 he openly criticized the NEP, complaining in particular about the new bourgeoisie and the richer landowners (kulaks). He called for the *collectivization* (government takeover) of agriculture, vigorous expansion of heavy industry, and a master plan for balanced and rapid economic growth.

Trotsky, who also urged the promotion of Marxist revolution in countries beyond Russia, could not gain the support of the majority of the party. Joseph Stalin, who held the post of party secretary, had quietly and skillfully built a following for himself as Lenin's heir. He appealed to those who wanted to concentrate on the revolution inside Russia, to those who looked inward rather than to the world. The party congress expelled Trotsky in 1927; he was first sent to Siberia and then deported. During his years of exile he attacked the Stalinist leadership as a perversion of Marxist ideals and tried to develop the "true" international revolutionary movement. Branded a communist heretic ("deviationist"), Trotsky was assassinated in Mexico in 1940 — probably by agents of Stalin.

With Trotsky and other rivals out of the way, Stalin in 1928 commenced the building of "socialism in one country." He announced the party's first Five-Year Plan, which concentrated on the collectivization of farming and the accelerated development of industry. State-controlled planning proved to be the most significant communist contribution to modern economics (though it came to be widely discredited in the late 1980s and 1990s). It was the fulfillment of an idea that had been worked out by Marx's partner, Friedrich Engels (p. 516), many decades before. Engels had noted that planning was indispensable to the efficient operation of individual factories and industries. The logical and ultimate goal, he thought, was the creation of a unified and complete *national* plan, embracing all parts of the economy. Since planning from above necessarily limits individual freedom of decision and action, it is clearly a *collectivist* idea.

Stalin's first plan ran into near-ruinous resistance. His officials scoured the countryside, joining private farms into large collectives of one thousand or more acres each. Strictly speaking, the farmers of each collective, as a "cooperative" unit, retained possession of the land, but individual farmers no longer controlled any portion of land as their *own*. The poorer peasants usually submitted to these forced measures, but the richer farmers, the kulaks, who possessed many acres, animals, and capital improvements, fought collectivization bitterly.

The government at last decided to coerce the resisting landowners and brutally removed, as a class, some two million kulaks and their families. Most were shipped off to labor camps in Siberia; others were forced into obedience; and many were killed. Some of them, in a final act of defiance and sabotage, destroyed their animals and implements before yielding. The heavy losses, and government manipulation of the surviving supplies, brought renewed famines in the early 1930s. Nevertheless, the collective-farm program was driven through; Stalin pursued it as a means of effecting complete state control over the rural population and of increasing agricultural efficiency and output. He believed that the collectives could make better use of machinery and scientific methods than could the single-owner farm. However, there was a loss of *personal incentive* in this system. (In the late 1980s, the government recognized this and began to permit limited production for market by individual farmers.)

Stalin's farm policy aroused sharp protests within the ruling bodies of the Communist party. His most notable critic was Nikolai Bukharin, a veteran activist and theoretician, who was a long-time associate of both Lenin and Stalin. Bukharin condemned the use of force against the peasants; he supported a flexible economic policy — based on persuasion, compromise, and *gradual* development.

But Stalin outmaneuvered his opponents. In 1930 Bukharin was shunted out of party influence and, later, was denounced as an "enemy of the revolution." Following a rigged "show" trial, he was sentenced to be shot in 1938. Had Bukharin and his allies succeeded in stopping Stalin, the course of Soviet history might have been quite different. (Bukharin's political reputation was gradually "rehabilitated" by Communist leaders over the years following Stalin's death in 1953. One of these leaders was the reformer, Mikhail Gorbachev, whose own pragmatic views were close to Bukharin's.)

While the painful and destructive events were taking place in the countryside, positive advances were being made in industry. The *rate of growth* in the decade of the 1930s surpassed that of any Western nation during that ten-year period. Much of the new development was located east of the Urals, in central Asia, where it altered the life and culture of a vast region. It was the combination of socialist planning and state exploitation of labor that made rapid modernization possible — and without the aid of foreign capital; this example captured the attention of other underdeveloped countries around the world. The industrial successes, of course, were trumpeted to Russian workers and peasants, who developed a fierce pride in Soviet material accomplishments. They found deep satisfaction in the feeling that "backward Russia" was at last catching up, scientifically and industrially, with the West. Access to education and the arts was also extended, and most Soviet children enjoyed greater opportunities than their parents had.

The price of all this, in addition to the early years of bloodshed, losses of property, and severe hardships, was the domination of life by the Communist party and government (*totalitarianism*). The Orthodox Church was stripped of its former influence, and other traditional faiths were barely tolerated. (Marxism became, in effect, the state religion.) There was no free press, free speech, free unions, or freedom of assembly. Political power remained a monopoly of the party, which was supported by the feared secret police. Dissenters, under Stalin, were put down or destroyed by systematic terror: "show" trials, purges, labor camps, and mass executions. In these respects, the political atmosphere resembled that under the tsars. But the new government was more efficient, used modern tools of control, and succeeded in deadening virtually every nerve of resistance. (Years after Stalin's passing in 1953, the full scope and nature of this repression were illuminated by Aleksandr Solzhenitsyn, a gifted Russian writer. His massive *Gulag Archipelago* (1974) reveals not only the island-like chain of inhuman labor camps and prisons but the entire apparatus for suppressing internal dissent.)

The major political institutions of the new state had been formed before Lenin's death. According to the constitution of 1923, the Union of Soviet Socialist Republics (U.S.S.R.) was a federal, democratic state. The former Russian Empire had embraced some fifty nationalities, and the Communists debated the question of how to deal with them. They wanted to preserve native languages and customs while guarding against *separatist* tendencies. Lenin decided on the *federal* principle (borrowed from the United States) as the most suitable answer. Each major nationality became a Republic (or a self-governing Region within a republic). By 1940 there were sixteen republics; by far the largest was the Russian, which contained over half the U.S.S.R.'s total population of two hundred million. The Ukrainian Republic (retaken by the Reds during the Civil War) had about half as many inhabitants as the Russian Republic and the White Russian (Byelorussian) about one-tenth. Most of the other republics were relatively small, with from one to six million inhabitants each.

Each republic had its own administration for its internal affairs. The highest body in the federal structure was the Supreme Soviet, which was composed of two chambers: a Council of Nationalities, having equal numbers of deputies from each republic, and a Council of Union, having numbers proportionate to the population of each republic. The Supreme Soviet enacted national legislation. However, this body met for only a short time each year, when it elected a Presidium of some thirty members, to which its functions were delegated. The Supreme Soviet also chose the Council of People's Commissars, whose members served as the executive heads of the federal government.

The controlling power of the U.S.S.R. lay in the Communist party rather than in the agencies of the state. It was not a party in the liberal-democratic sense, but a disciplined organization whose self-appointed mission was to run the country. Accordingly, the constitution of 1923 authorized it to carry out this special role. Thus, while one did not have to be a party member to vote or run for office in the Soviet Union, party representatives determined whose names would be placed on the election ballot. Within the party itself, organization and authority followed the principle of "democratic centralism": officers and delegates to higher bodies were elected at several levels — from the level of the smallest party "cell," to intermediate bodies, to the All-Union Party Congress, which normally met every other year. Though the congress was recognized as the highest party authority, actual control resided in its Central Committee, to which the congress delegated its power. After the time of Lenin, power tended to go more and more to the top. And, once policy was decided upon there, it was the duty of every Communist to work for its fulfillment. Without the party organization and its carefully selected and trained membership, the Soviet state could not have transformed, as it did, a country that covers one-sixth of the land surface of the earth. On the other hand, this monopoly of power by a single party — with its stultifying bureaucracy and lack of accountability — would prove incapable, in the long run, of satisfying the desires of the subject peoples.

International Communism

Although the Bolsheviks succeeded in "building socialism in one country," they were less successful in spreading socialism abroad. As Marxists, they believed in and worked for *world* revolution (as Trotsky had urged), but they made little headway in that direction. Marx himself had given to socialism its international character, regarding national states as narrow creations of the bourgeoisie. In 1864 he had organized the First (socialist) International. During the rest of the nineteenth century, however, the international socialist movement proved weak. It was troubled by internal differences — ideological and personal — and, ultimately, by rival patriotisms. A Second International foundered in 1914. An association of the socialist parties of many nations, it fell to pieces with the start of the First World War. A minority stuck to their convictions and refused to support their war governments, but most "reformist" socialists supported the "patriotic fronts" of their homelands.

Lenin, who had predicted the war as a natural outcome of capitalist imperialism, scorned the reformist parties as bourgeois. In 1919 he invited left-wing socialists throughout Europe to join the Soviet Communist party in forming a *Third* International. This, Lenin declared, would be a "pure" successor to Marx's original organization. Free of the reformist socialists, it pledged itself to worldwide revolution and the dictatorship of the proletariat.

Left-wing socialists of other countries, impressed by Lenin's stand and by the Russian Revolution itself, readily accepted Moscow's leadership. During the 1920s the methods of the Soviet party were adopted by the new association. Tight organization, centralized control, and the name "Communist" were imposed on the international body and on each of its national parties. As a result, sharp hostility arose between rival groups of Marxists outside the Soviet

Union. The reformist socialists viewed with horror the violence used by the Communists, especially under Stalin, and despised the intolerance of party leaders toward members with different views.

Having alienated the large majority of Marxists outside the Soviet Union, the Third International (known as the Comintern) had little chance of success. It was the reformist (democratic) socialists, strengthened by their break with revolutionary Marxism, who made impressive gains in the Western nations. After the failure of several communist-led uprisings immediately following the War, the reformists helped advance collectivism by legal and democratic means in France, Germany, Scandinavia, and Britain. Despite the predictions of Marx and Lenin, proletarian revolution was clearly not coming soon in the industrial countries of the West.

Meanwhile, communist parties, with Moscow's support and direction, were at work, usually underground, in fifty or more countries. (In most of the European democracies there were large and legal Communist parties, but they were generally excluded from governing power.) Though all of these failed during the 1920s and 1930s to bring about successful revolutions, they served as arms of propaganda and espionage for the U.S.S.R. The principal international influence of communism came not through the activities of the Comintern, but through the fact that the Soviet Union *existed* as a world power. Collectivists of all shades could point to it as a concrete alternative to liberalism and capitalism. Though they objected to many characteristics of the Soviet Union, they could use it as a working example of state planning and cooperative social principles.

FASCIST COLLECTIVISM: THE REVOLUTIONS IN ITALY AND GERMANY

The fear of communism helped push several European nations into revolutionary collectivism of another sort. In Italy and Germany, the fascist revolutions sprang from two conditions: a social crisis that arose in the wake of the First World War and the inadequacy of liberal-democratic government. (Wherever governments effectively met their problems, they were able to resist subversion.) Moreover, the revolutions in Italy and Germany were propelled by violent nationalisms growing out of the frustrations of the war. Whereas the communists focused on *class* and interclass struggle, the fascists stressed the *nation* and international struggle.

There is another significant difference between the two kinds of collectivist revolution. The communist uprisings in Europe had been anticipated in the decades of Marxist organization, propaganda, and threats of action. (Bolshevism was unwelcome but not unexpected.) Fascism, on the other hand, came as a surprise. As a doctrine, it had no ideological founders, no authoritative books, and no forces in evidence before 1918.

Its explosive appearance can now be understood as a breaking out of strong ideas and passions, some open to view and some hidden, that were opposed to liberalism, democracy, and rationalism. Though revolutionary, fascism had a broad appeal to privileged groups as well as to ordinary people. Its militant nationalism aroused all patriots, and its support of class interests (including those of the military) satisfied individuals of property and power. This appeal of fascism to national spirit and class power makes it a persisting (though veiled) threat to capitalist democracies everywhere. Fascism, we should remember, was destroyed in its major strongholds only by *external military force* (in the Second World War); should severe internal crises strike again in the industrialized countries, existing governments will no doubt find fascism a greater danger than communism. The relative ease with which fascists can take over a nation was *demonstrated* in the historical example of Italy.

Fascism in Italy: Mussolini

Italy after 1918 provided a favorable setting for the rise of fascism. Its parliamentary institutions, less than fifty years old, had never won much loyalty or enthusiasm from the people. Even before the war Italians often complained of graft and inefficiency in government, and the Italian legislature seemed incapable of dealing with the acute economic challenges of the 1920s. The majority of citizens, suffering from postwar inflation and unemployment, were disillusioned with the nineteenth-century ideas of liberty, reason, and progress. Moveover, they were bitterly disappointed over Italy's role in the war. Though they finished on the side of the victors, their armies had experienced hardships, losses, and humiliating defeats. And at war's end the Allies gave Italy only a portion of what they had promised as a reward for Italy's entering the conflict on the Allied side (pp. 553–54).

Many voters turned to the socialists in the hope that they would do something about the worsening economic situation. The elections of 1919 gave the Socialist party one-third of the seats in the national Chamber of Deputies; with the Catholic Popular party, the Socialists might have developed a constructive program for the country. Mutual distrust between Catholics and Marxists made such cooperation impossible, however, and the socialist trade unions began to take direct action. In 1920 unionists occupied a number of factories and tried unsuccessfully to operate them. The workers soon withdrew, but their action had given the propertied classes a fright. In the following year the Socialist party split over the question of whether or not to join the Communist Third International (the Comintern — pp. 567–68), thus losing what chance it might have had of becoming a dominant political force. It was on this scene of confusion, discontent, and fear of communism that Benito Mussolini presented himself as the national savior.

A shrewd propagandist and politician, Mussolini might be regarded as the Lenin of the Italian revolution. But, unlike the Russian hero, he did not find it necessary (as we shall see) to seize power by military force. Born into a socialist family, the son of a blacksmith, Mussolini was a man of the laboring class. He went to school to become a teacher but turned to journalism and radical agitation. In 1912 he secured the position of editor of the Socialist party newspaper

1860	1870	(March on Rome) 1922	1943
Period of Unification	Constitutional Monarchy	Mussolini (Fascism)	

in Milan, and he gained a reputation as a dynamic radical leader. As a Marxist, he had initially opposed war and had escaped military conscription by going to Switzerland; but in October 1914 he reversed himself by urging Italian entrance into the war against Germany. For this he was expelled from the party and from his newspaper. Thereupon he founded a journal of his own, which he used to publicize his new convictions and to advance his political career.

Mussolini served in the war as a corporal until he was injured in an accident in 1917. Resuming the editorship of his paper, he tried to stir popular support for the flagging war effort. He turned wholly against socialism after the Russian Revolution, growing more and more militant and nationalistic. He opposed the floundering parliamentary government of his own country; the legislature, he declared, was a collection of special interests and selfish individuals who lacked the desire and the ability to serve the national interest. Mussolini, like many other veterans of the war, became attracted to violence as a way of life and as a means of securing change. He started organizing his followers into paramilitary black-shirted units (*fasci di combattimento* — hence the name *fascist*). These units took it upon themselves to take part in street fighting with socialists and others they disliked, to smash opposing party and newspaper offices, and to assassinate some of the opposing leaders. The Blackshirts thus came to be regarded as the fighting arm of the new social movement.

Mussolini next organized his forces into a fascist political party, even though he had only contempt for the parliamentary party system. In the national election of 1921 he and his followers won thirty-five seats in the Chamber of Deputies. As their leader, Mussolini made fiery nationalist appeals and attacks on socialism. He began to gain widespread support, especially from the shopkeepers and white-collar class, but from the rich as well. Young people were strongly attracted by the uniforms, parades, mass rallies, and calls for *action*. During 1922 his Blackshirts drove the legally elected socialist governments from control of Italy's northern industrial cities, and later that year a huge Fascist assembly in Naples called for a march on Rome.

The constitutional king of Italy, Victor Emmanuel III, was now faced with the prospect of black-shirted bullies converging upon his capital. His prime minister, unable to secure an effective legislative majority, urged him to declare martial law. But the king decided to do otherwise; he invited Mussolini to come from Milan and form a new ministry. The Fascists, camped near Rome, marched on the city while Mussolini arrived by railway car to take over the government.

The new leader, who preferred his party title of *Duce* (leader), was not long in consolidating his position. The Chamber of Deputies, which had surrendered to the Blackshirt threat without a fight, quickly voted Mussolini dictatorial power for one year. During that time he altered the election law to allow the party that received the most votes (even though less than a majority) to take *two-thirds* of the seats in the chamber. A Fascist victory was thus assured (again, by "legal" means), and in the election of 1924 the party won about seventy percent of the total national vote. Despite its unclear aims and its fondness for violence, the party received the support of many moderates who hoped that they could exercise a restraining influence on the Duce. Within a few years he had eliminated almost all opposition and had established a fascist state.

The collapse of Italian democracy was clearly due to its own failures, but Mussolini's triumph resulted from a variety of factors. Critical among them was the backing of the army and the great industrialists of the country. Mussolini did not have to create a new army (as did Lenin), though his Blackshirts became a permanent military body. The regular army came readily to his side. Many of its high officers had had fascist sympathies from the beginning, and the Duce's glorification of militarism and his extravagant support of the army gained their active loyalty.

The industrial leaders, for their part, had been uncertain about Mussolini at first. They approved his smashing of the Socialist party and the unions, but they were worried about his intentions toward business. In 1925 the associated industrialists signed an agreement with the Duce. In return for their support of the Fascists, the industrialists were given a recognized position in the government, with the authority to regulate the nation's industrial affairs. The major employers in agriculture and commerce were later given similar authority. Together with hand-picked labor and professional bodies, these regulatory groups made up what Mussolini called the "corporate" state. In theory this state represented a harmonizing of all the economic and social interests in the country. In fact the corporate state was an instrument of the dictator, through which he permitted the leading capitalists to administer the nation's economic affairs.

Mussolini completed his structure of power by negotiating an alliance with the pope. Ever since the move for national unification had begun, in the middle of the nineteenth century, state and church in Italy had been in opposition (pp. 304, 499). After lengthy and difficult discussions, Mussolini and Pius XI signed the Lateran Treaty and Concordat of 1929. By their terms, the pope gained sovereignty over the area of Vatican City, which includes St. Peter's Basilica and its immediate environs. The Church also secured state financial aid and a special position in the educational system. In return, Pius gave his weighty support, and that of the Italian clergy and laity, to the Fascist state. Mussolini was himself an atheist, but, like Napoleon before him (pp. 464–65), he sealed his position as dictator by a bargain with the Church. Afterwards, not surprisingly, he violated the terms of the Concordat as he saw fit.

Though Fascism stressed action and was anti-intellectual in tone and character, it nevertheless developed a distinctive ideology. In the beginning, as

Mussolini himself admitted, it was largely a negative movement: *against* liberalism, democracy, rationalism, socialism, and pacifism. This negative feeling flowed from Mussolini's personal experience and that of countless other Europeans during and after the war. They had been cast adrift, let down by failed hopes of progress and happiness. Faceless in a mass society, they also felt *alienated* from *themselves*. The Fascists found an answer to this emptiness by arousing extreme nationalism. One could get an emotional lift by forgetting one's problems as a person and by giving oneself to something larger and grander — the nation. Mussolini and his associates developed this idea into the myth of the "organic state."

The Fascists asserted that the state is a *living entity*, above the individuals who compose it. Yet, though personal liberty in Italy was under the control of state authority, they held that the individual's power was enlarged through association with the body of citizens. This view contrasted sharply with liberal and Marxist ideas about the individual and the state (pp. 493, 519). "The state," declared Mussolini, "is a spiritual and moral fact in itself. . . ." It encompasses every sphere of life (totalitarianism); the state alone can "provide a solution to the dramatic contradictions of capitalism." And, as a living organism, the state must *expand* in order to express its vitality. This meant a continuous and disciplined *will to power*, which required unity within the nation, militarism, imperialism, and war.

The fascist myth rejected the liberal reliance on reason and replaced it with a mystical faith. Stridently anti-intellectual, it held that the "new order" would spring from the conviction of the "heart." Fascists therefore looked upon intellectuals in general as outmoded and suspicious characters, unduly concerned with their private mental fancies. Yet most Italian intellectuals willingly cooperated with the Fascists, thus confirming Mussolini's view that they were lacking in honesty and courage. The few who opposed the government were either silenced or forced into exile — the Fascist secret police struck down any active opposition.

Most ordinary Italians accepted Fascism with enthusiasm. The individual, who formerly felt alone and unneeded, enjoyed a new sense of "belonging"; this feeling of personal identification and participation was deepened by the paternalistic measures of the government and by various other means. Many types of workers wore distinctive uniforms, and mass rituals were staged in the great public squares of Rome and other cities. By 1930 Fascism appeared to have gained the firm support of most of the Italian people, as well as the admiration of many conservatives abroad.

The political institutions of Italy underwent a steady evolution under Mussolini. The corporate associations, which guided economic affairs, gradually became the basis for political representation in the national legislative body. But the true power in all fields was the Fascist party, headed by the Duce. The party resembled, in many ways, the Communist party of the Soviet Union (pp. 566–67). It was the only legal party; it consisted of only a fraction of the total citizenry; and its members were carefully drawn from the ranks of select youth organizations. Corresponding to the Communist Central Committee was the Grand Council of Fascism. Its members generally held high offices in the government in addition to their party positions; this connection, too, paralleled the interlocking of party and state officials that existed in the Soviet system.

Fascist ideology frankly supported rule by an elite (the "chosen" best). While Marxists taught that the state and its officeholders would gradually disappear after the abolition of capitalism (p. 519), the Fascists believed in *permanent* rule by their "natural" leaders. These would be individuals of rare intuitive power, capable of rising above self-interest and of sensing the character and desires of the nation. Their superiority, the Fascists declared, came chiefly from *action* rather than thought: it was basic that the leaders would have fought for the fatherland, taken part in the Fascist revolution, and helped to build the "new order."

The Nazi Compound of Fascism and Racism: Hitler

Just as the ideas of communism could not be confined to the U.S.S.R., so the fascist philosophy spread quickly across Europe — and the world. It won a substantial following in Austria, Portugal, Spain, and Argentina; but its world-shaking triumph was in Germany. Here fascism as a doctrine fused with deeper and older forces in the German tradition; here the fierce words of elitism and imperialism turned into deeds of conquest and genocide (race-murder).

Germany's humiliation at Versailles (p. 555), coupled with severe economic problems after the war, prepared the ground for Adolf Hitler and his National Socialists (Nazis). The Germans adopted a democratic constitution in 1919, but its success was unlikely from the start. The new government was inexperienced, it suffered from the usual stresses and divisions within liberal states, and it was associated with the crushing military defeat. (In the closing days of the war, the German generals had shrewdly withdrawn and left the country's surrender to a liberal civilian government hastily appointed by the kaiser.) Unlike the parliamentary regime in Italy, the German Republic did not collapse in the years immediately after the war. But it failed to win the full allegiance of the people, and in little more than a decade it fell under the weight of its unsolved problems.

One of its problems was Adolf Hitler, who had been born of middle-class parents in a small Austrian town. Early in life he had become an ardent German nationalist, and, though he spent some of his formative years in Vienna, he found its cosmopolitan atmosphere especially distasteful. A moody drifter, he did not find a place for himself until the outbreak of the First World War. When he enlisted in the German army, Hitler experienced the comradeship and discipline of military life and exulted in his service to his adopted fatherland.

In 1919, embittered by the war's outcome, he went to Munich, capital of the south German state of Bavaria. Large numbers of unemployed veterans and political dissidents had congregated there. Hitler joined a budding group that called itself the National Socialist German Workers' party and shortly became its leader (*Fuehrer*). This new role provided an outlet for Hitler's deep-seated animosities and ambitions. He attracted to the National Socialist banner others who shared his intense nationalistic feeling and hatred for Jews. Among his supporters were Hermann Goering, a swaggering pilot-hero; Dr. Josef Goebbels, a university-trained journalist; and General Erich Ludendorff, an arch-conservative and one of Germany's chief military commanders during the First World War.

Hitler threw himself fully into the life of politics and national "regeneration." Though he had but limited formal education, he had an intuitive grasp of the concerns that were disturbing his fellow Germans, especially the middle class. (Among their concerns were deep anxieties about the decline of "culture," the threat of social revolution, and the mixing of the races.) And, like Mussolini, he had a gift for rousing speech-making. The early 1920s were a time of restlessness and disorder in Germany; street clashes and rioting were commonplace. In 1923 Hitler led an attempted coup (*Putsch*) against the Bavarian state government. It was stopped in the streets of Munich by police fire, and the Nazi party seemed to have been crushed by the government reprisals. Hitler was imprisoned for nearly a year, during which time he wrote *Mein Kampf* (*My Struggle*), the statement of his life and beliefs. Upon his release from prison, he refounded the party. For a while it made little headway, but financial contributions, mainly from the middle class, enabled Hitler to purchase newspapers and periodicals through which he could spread Nazi propaganda.

The international economic crisis of 1930, a product of the dislocations stemming from the World War, gave the German revolutionary parties their great opportunity. Rising numbers of unemployed men were looking desperately for work. Many of them found "jobs" as brown-shirted Nazi storm troopers, similar to Mussolini's Blackshirts (pp. 570–71). The party gained electoral strength steadily during the years of economic hardship. And when at one point it ran out of funds, some powerful industrialists came to the rescue. In January 1933 Hitler received from them a promise to pay the wages of his storm troopers and the party's debts. German business leaders, generally, preferred the familiar conservative politicians to Hitler. But in this time of crisis, they turned to the Nazis as a "bulwark against communism" — and to insure themselves against the possibility of a Nazi victory in the elections.

A few weeks later, backed by conservative politicians and generals, Hitler succeeded in pressuring the aged president of the Republic, Paul von Hindenburg, to appoint him head of the national government (chancellor). The Nazis had the largest number of elected delegates in the legislature (Reichstag), but they still did not have a *majority*. However, after the Reichstag building was mysteriously burned, Hitler declared a suspension of constitutional guarantees. He banned the Communist party and had its leaders imprisoned; the Social Democrats were the only opposition party left. The Nazis, with the support of other conservative parties, then passed the Enabling Act of March

1871		1918	1933	1945
HOHENZOLLERN EMPIRE (REICH)		DEMOCRATIC REPUBLIC	HITLER THIRD REICH	

1933 — giving the government power to rule by decree for a four-year period. Hitler next replaced the flag of the Republic with the Nazi *swastika* (the "crooked cross") and declared the beginning of the "Third" Reich (Empire) — successor to the medieval and Hohenzollern German empires (pp. 498–99).

Soon afterward Hitler outlawed all parties save his own, duplicating the Fascist example; by mid-1933 his political opponents were either in jail or in exile. A year later, after Hindenburg's death, he assumed the office of president in addition to that of chancellor. This act was ratified in a vote of overwhelming approval by the German electorate. Thus, the mad Austrian became the sole ruler of one of the most educated and civilized nations of the world. He proceeded, with the cooperation of the army and leading industrialists, to marshal the country's manpower and resources. Hitler's aim was to make Germany the most powerful nation in Europe and, ultimately, the world.

Nazism had much in common with Italian fascism. Both rested on the myth of the "organic state," the importance of struggle and will, the glorification of militarism, an insistence on authority and discipline, rule by an elite, and a mystic faith in the leader. But in Germany there were added elements of violent racism, neoromanticism, and nihilism. The first two were largely out of the nineteenth century; the last were mainly an outgrowth of the war and took the form, essentially, of a mindless lust for power.

For the Jews of Europe the Nazi racial theories led toward genocide. During the Middle Ages the Jews had suffered from the religious prejudices of Christians (pp. 270–72), and persecutions and segregation had persisted up to the time of the French Revolution. In the course of the nineteenth century the liberal philosophy of equal civil rights for all had liberated Jews from the ghetto in some parts of Europe. However, the decline of discrimination on *religious* grounds was counterbalanced by the rise of new theories of *racial* differences. Some writers in France, England, and Germany began to assert the supremacy of Nordic "races" over others — especially over the Semitic and Negroid.

Hitler and his associates, resentful of resurgent Jewish social and cultural influence in postwar Germany, embraced these racial ideas and made them a central part of their program. They became vicious anti-Semites, portraying the Jew as a seducing, bloodsucking fiend who longed to pollute Nordic "purity." The Nazis, in the name of racial "science," thus revived the dark and primitive Jew-hatred of the Middle Ages. Building on that passion, they enacted discriminatory legislation, outlawed marriage and sexual relations between Jews and citizens of "German blood," forced Jews to wear a humiliating badge, burned their synagogues, and laid plans for the systematic annihilation of the Jewish people (Hitler's "final solution" — the death camps of the "Holocaust.")

Like the Fascists, the Nazis had contempt for reason and intellectuals. Hitler saluted the "simple and honest" values of the German peasantry and declared that those values were the foundation of Nazi goals. Yet under Hitler the country became increasingly industrialized and urbanized. Cleverly, the Nazis covered up the disturbing reality of technological change by encouraging popular belief in the myths of rustic purity and racial superiority. Millions became converts to the Nazi faith during the 1930s. It suited the traditional romantic yearnings of most Germans, offered a total view of life in place of fragmentation and alienation, and appealed strongly to national and racial pride. Finally, it released the urge to violence. Nazism led, by successive steps, not only to the murder of Jews and political opponents, but to the wider catastrophes of the Second World War.

DEMOCRATIC COLLECTIVISM: EVOLUTION OF THE WELFARE STATES

While collectivist societies built on totalitarian lines were taking shape in Germany, Italy, and the U.S.S.R., the shift from liberalism went forward in a different manner in the still-democratic countries of the West. In the Scandinavian lands, France, Great Britain, and the United States, the major prewar social institutions appeared to hold firm. But none was secure from the disturbances that followed the war or from the ceaseless march of science and technology.

In response to these forces, democratic governments intervened more and more in matters formerly considered to be "private." And as their functions expanded, governments left behind some of the principles and practices of historic liberalism. They created, without full-scale planning, forms of *democratic collectivism*. Some observers called this "social democracy" or "creeping socialism"; but a more fitting term is the capitalist "welfare state."

A European Example: Britain

Events in Britain after the war illustrate the evolution of a welfare state. This country had been identified, more than any other, with the historic liberal spirit and principles. John Locke and J. S. Mill were among many English men and women who had developed and promoted liberal ideas both at home and abroad (pp. 493–95). Britain in the nineteenth century had stood as the chief stronghold of capitalism and free trade; furthermore, its people enjoyed an extraordinary tradition of stability. Prior to 1914 one would hardly have expected this nation to move toward any form of collectivism.

Yet, as we have seen, even before the war the British had traveled a substantial distance away from liberalism (p. 510). Trade unions had become a force between individual workers and their employers; Parliament had passed numerous laws regulating industrial conditions. By 1914 the foundations had also been laid for compulsory national insurance, which protected workers against the costs of accident, sickness, unemployment, and old age. The revenues to support such programs were to be drawn in large measure from progressive income taxes.

The First World War brought new problems that demanded further action by the government. During the war itself, additional regulations were viewed as a matter of necessity; that experience made it easier for the British to accept growing state intervention in the postwar period. England had suffered severe losses of manpower and wealth during the struggle against Germany, and its most pressing problem at war's end was to recover its financial and trading position in the world. British investments overseas had been largely sold off, and many British markets had been taken over by American and Japanese firms.

It is a fact that Britain must "export or die," and both public officials and industrialists tried to improve the nation's competitive position. One obstacle to the effort was Britain's aging industrial plants. Another was organized labor: the unions, accustomed to high wages during the war, would not agree to lower wages afterward. For these principal reasons Britain failed to regain the lost markets, and after 1921 the country fell into a chronic depression that lasted until the Second World War. Unemployment and poverty became a way of life for several million Britishers.

Organized labor grew into a powerful force in British *politics* during the 1920s. The unions, in combination with moderate socialists, had formed the Labour party in 1892. By 1924 it had the largest number of seats in Parliament and stood as a challenge to the dominant Conservative party. Labor discovered, however, that its exercise of political power did not guarantee a better living for workers or a solution to the country's economic problems. The domestic policies of Labour governments did not, in fact, depart sharply from those of Conservative governments. Both parties agreed that they could not rely on "automatic" economic forces to produce business recovery. The protection and advancement of the public well-being required continuing and widening intervention by the state.

As the British depression grew deeper during the early 1930s, laws were passed that ended the traditional policy of free trade. Tariffs were enacted to guard the home market against imports, especially from the United States. (This action was explained as a countermeasure against high tariffs in America.) The government also went off the "gold standard" (1931) and devalued its money (the pound) in terms of other currencies. The latter step was taken as a means of aiding British exports, but its effect was shortly undone by corresponding devaluations of other currencies in capitals around the world. When key industries, like coal, proved unable to compete, they were voted subsidies by Parliament. Extensive plans were also laid by the government for the general development of British industry and agriculture.

Democratic governments on the continent were forced to adopt measures similar to those in Britain. Sweden was the most successful example (aided by having remained neutral in the two world wars). Its dominant Socialist party blended private capitalism with economic planning and social legislation — a "Middle Way" between laissez-faire capitalism and socialism. Sweden imposes steep income and inheritance taxes on its citizens. But its strong economy and "cradle-to-grave" security programs sustain a *general standard of living* that is perhaps the highest in the world.

The American Experience: Roosevelt

The United States, as a consequence of the First World War, became the strongest capitalist country. During the 1920s the nation pulled away from its military adventure overseas and from the domestic controls imposed during the mobilization for war. It was the decade of "normalcy," a word coined by the amiable and easygoing President Warren Harding. Though laissez-faire was more myth than reality, the power of big business and finance was seldom checked by the governing Republican party.

Normalcy, however, soon proved anything but normal, and the government of the United States, during the 1930s, was pushed into the kind of intervention that had become common in other Western democracies. The economic boom of the postwar years had brought temporary prosperity to the nation, but the boom was driven by artificial and unstable forces. In the spectacular stock-market Crash of 1929, many of the inflated values were wiped out within a few hours. More serious, the Crash signaled the coming of the Great Depression — a long and bitter experience for millions of Americans. During that time they discovered the underlying shortcomings of the "free-market" economy.

President Herbert Hoover, the Republican leader, was in office when the Crash came. A competent administrator and a well-meaning humanitarian, Hoover never understood that a system and an era had ended. Although he approved limited government measures to assist certain financial institutions and railroads, he held stubbornly to the view that business in general would recover by itself. (The restrictive fiscal and monetary policies of his administration actually dampened the prospects of business.) While Hoover was telling a worried public, repeatedly, that recovery was "around the corner," production and employment skidded downward. They struck bottom during the winter of 1932–33. By then, physical production had fallen nearly 40 percent from the 1929 level; wages were down by the same proportion; farm income was reduced to half. Construction had nearly ceased, and about fifteen million people were out of work.

Depressions were by no means a new experience in capitalist countries (p. 514). The ups and downs of the "business cycle" had been carefully studied, if little understood. This depression, however, was the worst in history, and there was reason to believe that "normal" recovery forces were unlikely to prove effective. This was due to several factors: the rigid price and wage structures, rapid technological advances in industry (which displaced workers), and the near-hopeless situation of farmers, who were producing for a depressed and uncontrollable world market. Given enough time some kind of balance in the economy would no doubt have come about through "natural" forces. But the economy had grown so complex and interdependent that these forces would have been too slow. So many individuals and families would have been crushed in the process that the strain on the social system could have proved intolerable.

In the presidential election of 1932 the American people turned to Franklin D. Roosevelt, who promised that he would *act* in this crisis — that he would lead the federal government in an attack on the depression as if it were an attack on a physical enemy. The temper of the country was such that, had he not promised to act, more radical leaders might well have gained a mass following. After an overwhelming electoral victory for the Democrats, Roosevelt began the first Hundred Days of his "New Deal" program. This program marked a shift from the traditional policy of limited government interference to one of acceptance by the government of responsibility for the "general welfare."

The New Deal was new only to a degree, since it built on the ideas and policies of earlier American "progressives" as well as the wartime experience of industrial mobilization (p. 558). But Roosevelt realized that the challenges were now far greater and that they demanded a new boldness. He proposed remedies in a frankly experimental fashion, with no developed ideology. The New Deal was not anticapitalist; on the contrary, it aimed at *preserving* and *strengthening* the capitalist system. Recognizing the *interdependence* of social and economic forces, the New Dealers turned their attention to all aspects of national life: finance, agriculture, industry, labor, foreign trade, natural resources, public works, education, and personal security.

Roosevelt classified his measures under the headings of relief, recovery, and reform. Those measures were too numerous and extensive to describe here, and they fell short of solving the fundamental problems of the economy. The significant thing is that most of the programs *worked*, at least to a degree, and they placed the government in a new and generally accepted role in the social and economic life of the country. (They also initiated a pattern of increased federal *spending* and *borrowing* as a means of stimulating business and relieving the distress of the poor.) Though FDR was attacked by some of his opponents as a devil and a "traitor to his class," it is more accurate to describe him as an *elected agent* of far-reaching adaptive social change.

The democratic welfare state, in America as in Europe, did not lose sight of the individual person. In a technological, mass society, it aimed to do what was needed for the protection and well-being of the majority of individuals. In many respects, Western men and women have had less economic freedom in the twentieth century than they had in the nineteenth. On the other hand, the greater wealth and economic security resulting from advances in technology and social organization have offered them expanded areas of freedom in their *personal* lives. These areas include education, leisure and travel, the arts, books and magazines, entertainment, and material consumption.

CHAPTER

14

Global Transformation: Dawn of a New Age

Human hopes for a better life through technology were threatened by the construction of ever more deadly *weapons*. After the First World War some observers thought that its terrible costs would lead to a scrapping of the "war system" as a means of settling international differences. Instead, the struggle unleashed more violent feelings of nationalism and hatred that led to another and more frightful *Second* World War.

THE SECOND WORLD WAR AND ITS CONSEQUENCES

When President Woodrow Wilson led the United States into the First World War in 1917, he had declared that it was a "war to end war." When that conflict ended, Wilson began a determined effort to make his promise come true. He urged the Allies to put into effect the peace proposals that had persuaded the Germans to quit the war (p. 555) — the widely publicized "Fourteen Points." These included the goals of "open" diplomacy (no more *secret* treaties), freedom of the seas, arms reductions, removal of trade barriers, and political "self-determination" (independence) for peoples everywhere.

The Fourteenth and crowning Point was Wilson's proposal for a "general association of nations," to guarantee their independence and boundaries. And with a view to ensure that this association be established, Wilson traveled to Paris after the war and took part personally in the peace conferences. At his insistence the plan for a League of Nations was written into the Treaty of Versailles in 1919 (p. 555).

The Failure of the League of Nations

Most of the European diplomats at Paris, still *nationalists* to the core, had little enthusiasm for the League. They approved it largely to please Wilson, who, in return, made concessions to them on the other provisions of the treaty. To Wilson, the League was the saving feature of a treaty that in many respects seemed harsh and unjust to the defeated peoples. He believed that the League, once established, could correct such injustices and lay the foundation for a *warless world* — an emerging idea, which now had substantial popular support. Ironically, the Treaty of Versailles, including the League plan, was later ratified by all the Allied governments *except* the United States. Its defeat in the Senate was due to a combination of factors: persisting nationalism, disillusionment with the late "crusade" in Europe, Wilson's refusal to accept amendments to the treaty, and the constitutional requirement of a *two-thirds* affirmative vote for ratification. (A simple *majority* did vote for the treaty.)

Whatever chance the League may have had to fulfill its high purpose was crippled by America's failure to join it. Both Germany and the Soviet Union were excluded from membership for a number of years, so the organization was far from being universal. Nevertheless, it had some strong supporters, and it carried on in the hope that the United States would one day become a member. During the economic boom of the 1920s, however, most Americans became absorbed in making money and showed a lessening interest in the problems of the world. The later miseries of the Great Depression turned them even more inward. By 1933 the United States was clearly committed to an *independent* course in foreign affairs.

The League performed many useful international functions, including the conduct of plebiscites (popular votes) in disputed territories, returning prisoners of war to their homelands, and providing aid to refugees. Through its commissions, it also arranged for the exchange of scientific and cultural information and the collection of social and economic statistics. Its sponsorship of disarmament conferences proved completely fruitless, for the participating nations viewed proposals for arms reduction as another arena for the continuing *power struggle*.

The primary purpose of the League, as planned by Wilson, was to *prevent war*. The treaty required that member states submit their disputes to arbitration (decision by an impartial umpire) and, if that failed, to the Council of the League. The Council, which consisted of representatives of the principal countries, could, by unanimous vote only, call for economic or military actions ("sanctions") by member states against any aggressor state. The principle underlying this provision was that of "collective security." This was a simple idea, one that Wilson fervently believed in. It held that if *all* "peace-loving" countries acted together (collectively) against *any* violator of the peace, the violator would be overwhelmingly defeated. Potential aggressors, once convinced that collective action against them was a certainty, would not start acts of conquest.

Collective security might have worked if the leading powers (including the United States) had put an overriding priority on stopping aggressors. Unfortunately, the idea was never taken seriously in the major capitals. In and out of the League, each nation continued to pursue its own particular aims and refused to act except when its own immediate interest seemed to be threatened.

Furthermore, a number of powers (notably Japan, Italy, and Germany) were conspiring to support one another's seizure of territory. The balance between countries wishing to preserve territorial boundaries and those prepared to use force to break them proved to be too nearly equal for the collective-security idea to succeed.

Japan was the first country to test the will of the League's members. In 1931 Japanese soldiers occupied Manchuria, driving out the legal Chinese authorities. Responding to China's appeal, the League sent an investigating commission to Manchuria; in 1932 the commission concluded that Japan was guilty of aggression and recommended appropriate action. But the Council of the League could not agree on sanctions. Britain, with extensive interests in the Far East, was reluctant to offend the Japanese, who had a powerful Pacific fleet. Unable to secure a guarantee of assistance from the United States should sanctions lead to war with Japan, the British decided that *nothing* should be done. And Britain was the most influential member of the League and its Council.

The exultant militarists in Tokyo, having successfully defied the League, strengthened their grip on Japanese politics and prepared for more ambitious conquests in China, and beyond. Had the League and the United States joined in placing sanctions on Japan, that island nation would have been compelled to back down. Instead, the League's failure encouraged aggressors in both Asia and Europe. Little more than a decade after the First World War, the Wilsonian hope for collective security lay shattered. The great powers were already on the road to the Second World War.

Fascist Conquests and Defeat

Benito Mussolini viewed the League's failure with special satisfaction. In keeping with the fascist ideology of militarism and imperialism, he was seeking to expand Italian control in Africa (p. 542). During the 1920s he had attempted by negotiation to gain a foothold in the ancient empire of Ethiopia. But the Ethiopian emperor, Haile Selassie, had stubbornly refused. Mussolini, after observing the impotence of the League, decided to move by force of arms.

Selassie's tribesmen, armed with primitive weapons, could not hold out against the artillery and aerial bombardment of the Italians. Within a year Ethiopia was beaten and annexed to Italy (1936). In this affair Britain had been more deeply aroused than in the case of Manchuria; it had persuaded the Council of the League to call for economic sanctions against Italy, the declared aggressor. The measure was only partially effective, however, and Mussolini continued to receive needed supplies from Germany. Italy resigned from the League; Japan and Germany had already pulled out.

By now it was becoming clear that these three nations were linked in a plan for wide-ranging conquest. The "Rome-Berlin Axis," joining the two fascist states of Europe, was formalized in 1936. In the following year the militaristic and profascist government of Japan joined Germany and Italy in signing an Anti-Comintern (Anti-Communist) Pact. The pact was intended, supposedly, to check the spread of communism; actually, it was a general defensive-offensive military alliance. And the strongest member of the alliance, Germany, was preparing to strike. In 1935 Adolf Hitler had announced his decision, in defiance of the Treaty of Versailles, to rearm Germany. His army and air force were growing steadily in strength. Though he moved cautiously at first, Hitler continued to violate the 1919 peace settlement. His troops crossed into Austria in 1938, and the Fuehrer announced the absorption of that state into the new German Empire (the Third Reich — p. 575).

A year earlier, Hitler had extended his influence southward by intervening in the Spanish Civil War. He supported an army rebellion, led by General Francisco Franco, against the newly established Republic of Spain. The government, which had been elected by a "Popular Front" of democratic, socialist, and communist parties, appealed to the Soviet Union for help against the rebels, and the war soon became a bloody theater for the ideological struggle between Left and Right in Europe. It also proved to be a testing ground for new weapons and tactics of war. Hitler and Mussolini sent equipment, troops, and pilots in decisive numbers to Franco (now called *Caudillo*, leader). The war ended in 1939 with total victory for the fascists. With the support of the Spanish Church, Franco established a tough, repressive government that was to endure until his death in 1975. He added Spain to the armed camp of Germany and Italy.

Britain and France by now were thoroughly alarmed, but popular antiwar sentiment and political incompetence kept them from responding effectively to the fascist threat. The Soviet Union seemed to be the only power that could check Hitler. France had concluded a defensive alliance with the Soviets in 1935, but the agreement proved short-lived.

One reason for the collapse of the Franco-Soviet alliance was the failure of France and Britain to honor their treaty obligations to defend Czechoslovakia. (The Soviets also had an agreement to aid the Czechs — but only if the French acted with them.) At Munich, in September 1938, the two Western powers, ignoring Soviet concerns, agreed to Hitler's demand for a portion of Czech territory. (Six months later the Nazis took over the rest of Czechoslovakia.) Joseph Stalin's suspicions of the Western powers were strengthened by their act of "appeasement." The Soviet dictator feared (rightly) that some British diplomats were secretly hoping that Hitler would smash eastward into the Soviet Ukraine, thus locking in mortal combat the two great land powers of Europe. Such a struggle could serve the British interest by reducing or eliminating one or both of the Nazi and Soviet threats. Stalin now chose to remove the threat of an invasion of his country by working out a deal with Hitler: the Nazi-Soviet Nonaggression Pact of 1939 came as a shock to British and French diplomats. It provided, in return for mutual pledges of nonaggression (and territorial promises to the Soviet Union), that Stalin would not interfere with Hitler's next territorial grab in Europe.

The ink was hardly dry on the pact when the Nazis, without warning, pounced on Poland on September 1, 1939. In a desperate effort to deter or contain Hitler, the British and French had given "last-minute" pledges of assistance to the Poles. This time they stood by their word and declared war on Germany. The Second World War was under way. Poland was crushed militarily within a month as the Germans displayed new tactics of mobile warfare. Swift tank formations, supported by aircraft and paratroops, paralyzed and surrounded the Polish troops. So successful were these tactics that the Germans appeared to be invincible. (Soviet troops, meanwhile, by prior agreement with the Nazis, moved into the eastern portion of Poland. To create a further "defensive buffer," on the Baltic Sea, the U.S.S.R. also occupied and annexed the newly independent states of Estonia, Latvia, and Lithuania — pp. 555, 556).

In 1940 Holland, Belgium, and France fell before the German blitzkrieg (lightning war), and Italy formally joined the conflict. Hitler, ignoring his nonaggression pact with Stalin, savagely attacked the Soviet Union in June 1941. In Russia and elsewhere in eastern Europe the Germans not only sought swift military victories; they launched a ruthless program of exterminating all Jews and a portion of the Slavic peoples, whom they regarded as racially inferior (*Untermenschen*). Six months after the German attack on Russia, the Japanese, pursuing their own conquests in Asia, struck the United States Pacific fleet at Pearl Harbor, Hawaii. (This daring and devastating assault by carrier-based bombers came without warning — while Japanese diplomats were "negotiating" in Washington.) By 1942 all the major powers were involved in the war by land, sea, and air.

The fascist forces, having seized the initiative, scored astonishing gains in the early period of fighting. They secured control of most of continental Europe and much of North Africa, while Britain held out defiantly against Nazi bombers and threats of invasion. In Asia, Japanese forces had occupied large areas of China before 1941. They now launched spectacular moves — winning mastery of the western Pacific Ocean and its islands, and conquering the British colonies of Burma and Malaya, French Indochina, the Dutch East Indies, and the American-controlled Philippine Islands (pp. 544–47).

The population and resources of all Allies were vastly superior, however, and in the end they achieved unconditional victory. By mid-1943, the Allies were counterattacking; thereafter, the Axis powers were generally on the defensive, both in Europe and the Pacific. Soviet ground forces and American air power were among the decisive factors in the outcome of the war. At Stalingrad (now Volgograd) the Russians completed the destruction of twenty-two German army divisions — numbering some three hundred thousand soldiers — in the largest single battle of history. In the air war, the Americans at first pursued a new military plan called "strategic" bombing; it aimed to destroy key transport and production facilities whose elimination would cripple the enemy's war machine. This type of bombing, which depended upon pinpoint accuracy and which spared the civilian population, was only partially successful, however. In the last year of the war (1944–45), the Americans switched to the British method of bombing: massed attacks upon enemy cities — contrary to traditional "rules of warfare" (pp. 402, 549). (The

1914 1918		1939 1945	
FIRST WORLD WAR	LEAGUE OF NATIONS	SECOND WORLD WAR	UNITED NATIONS

Allies were not the first to bomb cities, but they did so now on an unprecedented scale.) Fire raids on Hamburg and Dresden were among the deepest horrors of the war, and virtually every Japanese city was reduced to ashes by giant bombers.

This new kind of "unlimited" warfare was most dramatically demonstrated by the dropping of the world's first *atomic* bombs on Hiroshima and Nagasaki — cities that the Americans had spared from earlier bombings so that they could better measure the destructive power of the new weapons. The public justification for using atomic bombs against these defenseless cities was that this "shock" action was necessary to bring a quick end to the war — and thereby save millions of lives that would otherwise be lost in a military invasion of Japan.

Recent historical evidence throws serious doubt upon that public explanation. Japan, in fact, was ready to surrender *before* the bombs were dropped and *without* an invasion. Peace could indeed have come even sooner than it did if the Americans had not held back from negotiations while awaiting completion of their secret atomic tests. Emperor Hirohito, with his nation near collapse from prolonged air bombardment and naval blockade, had been seeking desperately for a dignified way out of the war. Washington knew this, for it had broken the Japanese communication codes. But President Harry Truman (in office only a few months) had become convinced that dropping the atomic bombs would strengthen the *strategic position* of the United States *after* the war. Upon learning that the tests were successful (in late July 1945), and after consulting with his military and civilian advisers, Truman ordered the Air Force to hit the preselected target cities as soon as the new bombs could be delivered.

Each of the two weapons (small in power by present-day standards) incinerated tens of thousands of men, women, and children. These superscientific devices for mass killing assured the quick and "total" victory of the Allies. (Germany had already surrendered.) More significantly, they also confirmed a radical shift in the nature of all-out warfare: from attacking opposing *armed forces* to destroying *whole populations*.

The Emergence of New Power Balances and the Cold War

The human toll in the Second World War exceeded that of any previous conflict. Of the more than one hundred million persons mobilized for military service, some seventeen million were killed. Civilian deaths, direct and indirect, amounted to more than forty million; among these were six million Jews, victims of the Nazi Holocaust (p. 576). The political consequences of the war were decisive: Japan was stripped of imperial sovereignty and placed under American military occupation, Italy lost its possessions in Africa, Germany was divided, and fascism was destroyed in all the defeated countries. The states of western Europe, which a generation before had dominated global affairs, had now fallen to the rank of secondary powers. The Soviet Union, though it had suffered enormous losses and damage from the Nazi invasion, extended its control in both Asia and Europe (p. 588). The United States, untouched at home by the ravages of battle, emerged as the dominant military and economic power of the globe. This "post–World War II Era" would last for about forty years — until the late 1980s.

President Franklin Roosevelt, who had been the principal leader of the victorious alliance until his death in April 1945, anticipated the new distribution of power. During the war he had joined in top-level ("summit") conferences with the British prime minister Winston Churchill and with the Russian leader, Joseph Stalin (pp. 564–65). The "Big Three," by working together despite grave differences, succeeded in defeating their common enemies. Roosevelt hoped that when the war was over the major powers could continue to cooperate for peace as they had for victory. The key to this accomplishment, he thought, was American-Soviet understanding.

It was in part to develop such understanding and cooperation that Roosevelt proposed a new international organization, the United Nations. Its general outlines were approved by the Big Three at the Yalta Conference (1945), and the organization came into being some months later, after Roosevelt's death in 1945. In planning it, Roosevelt had sought to avoid what he regarded as the visionary and rigid aims of his predecessor, Woodrow Wilson.

Though the United Nations was similar in structure to the disbanded League of Nations, it was not based on the failed principle of collective security (pp. 580–82). Nor was it viewed as a world government or anything approaching it. The organization, thought Roosevelt, might be a *step* in that direction, but its immediate function was to serve as an instrument that would enable the two "superpowers" (the U.S. and the U.S.S.R.) to maintain world order. This was a practical, short-range objective that might have been achieved had Roosevelt lived a while longer.

Within a few months of the president's death, a chill descended on East-West relations; as this chill deepened into the "Cold War," hopes for cooperation evaporated. The reasons for the deterioration in relations have been sharply debated by diplomats and scholars. On the Soviet side there was fear and suspicion of the Western powers, tracing back to their intervention in Russia after the Bolshevik (Communist) Revolution (p. 563). During the struggle against Hitler the Soviet leaders had developed a cautious trust in Roosevelt, but they had little faith in the word or intentions of Churchill. Shortly after Roosevelt died, Churchill had proposed to the new American president, Harry Truman, that prior agreements about Allied military occupation zones in Germany be ignored by the Western powers. Truman turned down that proposal but later (1949) joined with the British in merging the Western occupation zones into an *independent German state* (the Federal Republic).

As it became clear that the United States had decided to restore and rearm western Germany, contrary to the wartime understandings, Stalin showed more determination than ever to keep under communist control the countries that his troops had "liberated." The Soviet zone in eastern Germany became the German Democratic Republic, one of eight "satellite" states erected in eastern Europe (p. 588). Soon afterwards, Churchilll declared that Stalin had lowered an "Iron Curtain" between East and West. (What became the most infamous portion of this barrier was the "Berlin Wall," built in 1961 by the GDR to stem the outflow of its citizens to the more prosperous Federal Republic. Its physical destruction in 1989 would signal the end of the Iron Curtain and the Cold War.)

On the Western side there persisted a deep-seated fear of communist expansion. This fear also traced back to 1917, but now it was heightened by the presence of Soviet military power in central and eastern Europe. Churchill and Truman protested vainly against Stalin's failure to provide free elections (as he had promised) in Poland, Rumania, Bulgaria, and Hungary. Their concern rose when communist-led guerrilla fighters threatened the Western-supported government of Greece in 1947. President Truman responded vigorously by sending military and economic aid to Athens. More important, he declared a general American policy of communist "containment," which pledged military assistance to *any* regime threatened by "armed minorities or by outside pressure." In support of this policy, he undertook a multibillion-dollar program of aid for economic recovery and integration in western Europe (the "Marshall Plan," named for his secretary of state). In 1949 Truman concluded a twelve-nation military alliance (the North Atlantic Treaty Organization — NATO) for unified defense against the presumed Soviet threat. This treaty was later supplemented, for defense of areas outside Europe, with alliances in the Middle East (the Central Treaty Organization — CENTO) and in southeast Asia (SEATO). Huge arms expenditures by the United States, corresponding to these expanding overseas commitments, would lead to creation of the most powerful military strike forces ever assembled. The Soviets responded predictably with a military buildup of their own and formation of a military alliance to counter NATO. Consisting of the communist states of eastern Europe (except Yugoslavia), it came to be known as the "Warsaw Pact" (1955).

The American nuclear monopoly was the most decisive single fact in world politics immediately after the war. It caused deep worries in Moscow, where leaders feared that some American generals might gain backing for a "preventive" war against the U.S.S.R. (Such a proposal was, in fact, vigorously advanced before the National Security Council, the president's top military advisory body after 1947.) Soviet scientists worked feverishly to build a bomb of their own as a counter to the American weapon. This they succeeded in doing in 1949, much to the surprise of scientists and military leaders in the United States.

It soon became evident that the Russians, aided by secret information supplied by their agents in the West, were a match for the Americans in advanced technical undertakings. When the United States exploded its first hydrogen

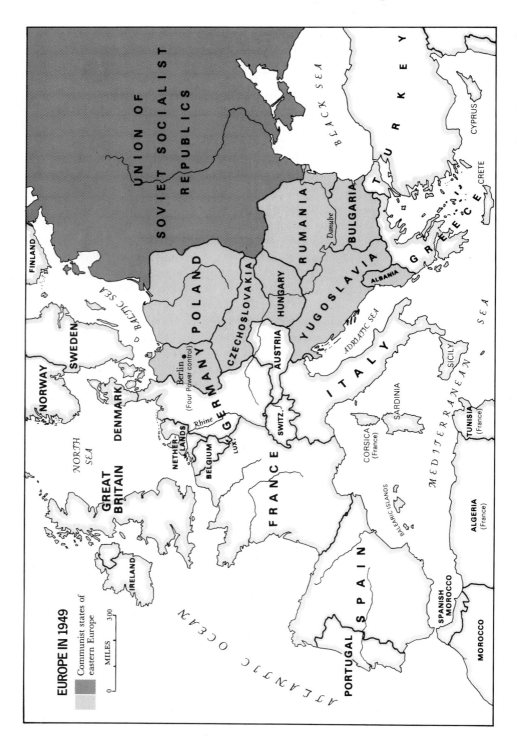

EUROPE IN 1949

Communist states of
eastern Europe

MILES
0   300

(fusion) device in 1952, the government revealed that the energy released was hundreds of times greater than that of the Hiroshima (fission) bomb. Within a year the Soviets announced the explosion of their own hydrogen bomb, and in 1957 they became first in space by rocketing *Sputnik* (a small satellite) into orbit around the earth. In a real sense, these Soviet demonstrations lent a degree of stability to the international situation. With each side in the Cold War capable of destroying the other (with aircraft or intercontinental missiles), a new kind of balance was struck — a "balance of terror."

Return to International Anarchy

No balance, however, could last for long, because the power alignments and the nature of power itself were continually changing. The *bipolar* world of American and Soviet power began to dissolve soon after it appeared. Stalin died in 1953, and his place was taken by Nikita Khrushchev. The new leader uncovered the massive crimes committed by Stalin, and initiated a policy of internal relaxation and "peaceful coexistence" among nations. Marshal Tito of Yugoslavia, though a communist, took actions that were increasingly independent of Moscow. After an anti-Soviet uprising in Hungary in 1956, all the satellite states displayed somewhat greater freedom of action.

The limits of such freedom, however, were driven home to the Czechs in 1968 by a Soviet-led military suppression of "too much" liberalization in that unhappy land. Leonid Brezhnev, who had succeeded Khrushchev, later declared that his country had the right to intervene in any country of eastern Europe where "socialism" was threatened. This declaration was labeled in the West as the "Brezhnev Doctrine," and it revealed the primary fear of Soviet military strategists. They were convinced that the defection of the satellite states, most of which were historically anti-Russian, would deprive the Soviet Union of its "defensive buffer" against the West, and swing the world balance of power against it. Awareness of these Soviet views caused Western leaders to worry when Polish labor unions (the "Solidarity" movement, led by Lech Walesa) challenged communist authorities in the 1980s. They feared that, as a final resort, the Soviets would use troops to hold Poland rather than risk the ultimate danger of a strengthened Europe, backed by American nuclear weapons, facing directly upon the borders of the Soviet Union. (As it turned out, the Polish government was able to repress Solidarity, temporarily, by placing the country under martial law. But the unions eventually brought down the communist government; and Walesa, in 1990, would become the first democratically elected president of the new Poland.)

Most weighty of the changes within other communist lands was the growing power of China (which faces the southern and eastern borders of the Soviet Union). In 1949 Mao Tse-tung (Mao Zedong) had led his revolutionary forces to victory over Chiang Kai-shek's Nationalists, bringing the most populous country on earth under the Red banner. After a period of dependency on

Soviet aid, the Chinese began to regard Mao as the principal ideologist of Marxism and Beijing as the true capital of proletarian revolution. By 1962 a bitter split had opened between the two communist giants. Mao accused the Soviets of ideological "revisionism" (backsliding toward capitalism) and collaboration with the United States; Brezhnev replied with charges of Chinese defection from the "socialist camp." The harsh verbal exchanges during the 1960s were accompanied by military clashes along their common frontiers in central Asia.

Soviet concern over the growing power of China grew stronger during the 1970s when the United States reversed its policy toward the People's Republic. John Foster Dulles, the American secretary of state under President Dwight D. Eisenhower, had previously sought to *contain* the communist regime through diplomatic and economic strangulation. But, as other nations recognized and opened commerce with China, it became apparent that the Dulles policy had failed. President Richard M. Nixon, a longtime opponent of communism, made the practical decision to abandon the American policy and come to terms with the People's Republic. Guided by his national security adviser (later secretary of state), Henry A. Kissinger, Nixon made a dramatic visit to Beijing in 1972. Diplomatic missions were soon afterward established in the two capitals, and "friendship" replaced hostility.

The Chinese aim was clear: to neutralize the American threat as a means of improving their position with respect to the Soviets. By pursuing at the same time a policy of relaxation toward the Soviets, Nixon and Kissinger thus initiated a *triangular* power relationship among the three rival nations. President Jimmy Carter strengthened the China ties by extending formal recognition in 1979. By then the dominant leader in the People's Republic was Deng Xiaoping, who rose to power after Mao's death in 1976. Deng actively sought American help for his country's technological advancement, and China became more outward-looking than before. He also moved to "liberalize" China's economy by decentralizing government controls and offering limited profit incentives to individual producers. (In the political field, however, Deng in 1989 forcibly repressed a swelling "democracy" movement centered in the universities and major cities.)

The new relationships with China disturbed diplomatic links around the globe. It became clearer than ever that earlier assumptions and alignments of the Cold War were being substantially modified. Communism, once seen by the West as a "monolithic" (single) force, had become a loose alliance of states that gave priority to their *national* identities and interests. As nationalism proved stronger than liberalism in the nineteenth century (p. 548), so it countered communism in the twentieth.

The Atlantic alliance (NATO) was similarly transformed, due in large measure to the swift recovery of western Europe. The recovery, made possible by large American loans, was linked to the creation in 1957 of the European

1921	1928		1945	1949		1976
China United by Nationalists	Nationalists Nominally in Control		Civil War	China under Communism and Mao Zedong		Deng Xiaoping

Japanese Incursions (1931-45)

Economic Community (EEC) — the "Common Market." It consisted initially of six countries: France, West Germany, Belgium, the Netherlands, Luxembourg, and Italy. In 1973 Britain, Ireland, and Denmark joined the EEC, which sought to draw the separate European economies into a single trading area. (Greece was added in 1981; Spain and Portugal in 1986.) Tariffs and trade restrictions were steadily reduced within the Community, and a common set of tariffs was adopted for imports from outside the Market. Free movement of capital and labor across Community frontiers was assured, and commissions were appointed to coordinate national plans for investment and development.

The consequences were dramatic: during the 1960s and 1970s Europe experienced the most rapid economic advance in its history, and the rising standards of living were shared in some degree by all classes of the population. Food and housing were better than before the war; travel became more widespread; and class lines were blurred by increasing social mobility. This prosperity also had its effects on internal politics and ideology: the radical, "proletarian" parties of western Europe turned away from the Soviet political model and worked out their own platforms of "democratic" Marxism (Eurocommunism).

While the western European nations now accepted lesser roles in global affairs, they felt a mounting urge to reassert their traditional character and independence. France in particular, under the guidance of President Charles de Gaulle, enjoyed a cultural as well as an economic resurgence. French leaders desired to reduce or eliminate the strong influence that American politicians, generals, and business representatives had exerted in Europe after the Second World War, and de Gaulle acted openly against the dominant role of the United States in NATO. By 1963 he had established, independently, a French nuclear strike force, and in 1966 he ordered United States military forces and bases out of France. Though somewhat softened, de Gaulle's policies were carried on by his political successors in Paris, including the socialist, François Mitterand.

A contributing factor in Europe's mounting spirit of independence was a lessening of the earlier fear of the Soviet Union. The American-Soviet "balance of terror" cast a protective cloak over Europe, and Kremlin policy after Stalin's death gave no indication of a desire for military adventure on the Continent. Britain, whose scientists shared atomic secrets with the United States during the Second World War, developed its own nuclear force in the late 1950s. The later spread of atomic weapons to France and to China (1965) further contributed to the equalizing of military strength and the consequent diminution of single-power influence. Responding to this new situation, the chancellor of the German Federal Republic, Willy Brandt, sought to turn off the Cold War on the Continent. In 1970 he undertook successful talks in Moscow, accepting for his prospering country the postwar political boundaries of central and eastern Europe. Brandt's initiative marked a dramatic step toward an easing of tensions ("détente") between once-hostile groups of states. It was capped in 1975 by a "summit" meeting at Helsinki, Finland, where heads of thirty-five countries (including the United States) signed a pact for European "security and cooperation."

The Helsinki agreement, pledging the signatories to assure "human rights" for their own citizens, gave formal support to East-West détente. European political leaders, like Helmut Schmidt of West Germany and Valéry Giscard d'Estaing of France, saw no alternative to détente in their dealings with the Soviet Union. But the continuation of eased relations proved shaky at best. This was due in part to alleged violations of human rights and to military moves by Russia outside Europe, notably in Afghanistan (p. 608), and in part to revival of the Cold War spirit in America. While Leonid Brezhnev alarmed the West in the 1970s by a rapid build-up to achieve nuclear "parity" with the United States, President Ronald Reagan alarmed the Russians in the 1980s with evident determination to regain American nuclear "superiority" (p. 620).

With or without the Cold War, existing treaty organizations and alliances (like NATO and the Warsaw Pact) grew less solid than in the earlier postwar period. The United Nations remained a forum of political discussion and debate, but it appeared unable to *act* as a "collective" power. The international scene during the 1980s was marked by growing national independence, a wide variety of sociopolitical systems, and numerous insecure governments. There was no evidence of a trend toward a *unitary* world or even a world "police force." Each nation desired to go its own way, without interference in its internal affairs by any outside power. This development, hopeful in one way, appeared nevertheless to be a return to the kind of international anarchy that prevailed before the First World War (p. 549).

THE SWEEP OF NATIONALISM AND MODERNIZATION

The trend toward collectivism, through either revolution or evolution (pp. 558–59), was accelerated during and after the Second World War. Total war, as waged by the main combatants, called for the total organization of the human and nonhuman resources of each country. When the fighting stopped, some of these controls were relaxed in the democratic welfare states. But collectivist patterns persisted elsewhere. The most dramatic expansion of collectivism, revolutionary style, occurred in Asia, when communism, after long and devastating wars, triumphed on the mainland of China (1949).

The Resurgence of Japanese Power

Korea, adjacent to China and formerly a Japanese possession (p. 544), was given divided "independence" by the victors of the Second World War. The northern half was turned into a communist state under Soviet guidance; the southern half, under American guidance, was organized as a "democratic-capitalist" state. Each area was ruled by a dictatorial strong man dependent on one of the superpowers.

In 1950, North Korean troops, with Soviet arms, crossed the dividing thirty-eighth parallel (of latitude), thus starting a bitter civil war. The government in the South was saved only by swift United States military intervention, directed by General Douglas MacArthur, hero of the late war in the Pacific and Supreme Commander for the occupation of Japan. (MacArthur acted, legally, as head of a United Nations "police force," authorized by the Security Council upon motion by the United States. In fact this "police action" was mainly an American operation.) After hard fighting, a cease-fire was arranged in 1951, but two more years of drawn-out negotiations passed before a final truce was signed. Korea, bloodied and devastated, remained divided at the thirty-eighth parallel. Each half, with substantial foreign assistance, quickly achieved reconstruction, however. Though still under authoritarian rule, South Korea became a model of Westernization and economic prosperity in the 1970s and 1980s.

Like much of the rest of Asia and Africa, Korea was caught up in the worldwide confrontation between opposing social systems and power balances. Japan, defeated in the Second World War, proved more fortunate than its former victims in that war. Under the umbrella of American arms, a newly democratized Japan made astonishing technological and economic advances. By 1970 this disciplined, creative nation (of one hundred million people) had surpassed its huge neighbor, China (eight hundred million), in gross national product (GNP) and ranked *third* in the *world*.

Japan was bound by its peace treaty and new constitution to a nonmilitary foreign policy. However, its strong *economy* made Japan the leading power of east Asia and the western Pacific. In the 1980s most experts agreed that this area had the brightest economic prospects of any part of the world. Borrowing Japan's industrial and commercial methods, numerous neighboring countries joined the Pacific boom: South Korea, Taiwan (Formosa), Hong Kong, Singapore, and Thailand all achieved high rates of economic growth in the 1980s.

The reasons for the success of these countries seem clear: their business leaders worked closely with each other and their governments; they vigorously promoted new factories and advanced technology; they pursued intensive market research and efficient management — and enjoyed the competitive advantage of low labor costs and low taxes. As a result, aggressive Asian entrepreneurs, led by Japan, attracted foreign capital and undersold most other manufacturers around the world.

The consequences for the older industrialized countries have been dramatic since 1980. Millions of jobs have been taken away, and the United States has run up huge trading debts to other nations, especially Japan. They, in turn, have used their trade surpluses to purchase billions of dollars' worth of American stocks and bonds, real estate, banks, and other businesses. The nations of the West have yet to find an effective response to this "Pacific challenge" to their standards of living and financial independence.

In most countries outside of the Pacific area, traditional institutions changed more slowly. In Africa and Asia, colonialism was repudiated wherever it existed and was replaced, usually, by some type of independent collectivist regime. This shift was closely tied to the rising spirit of nationalism there and the spreading passion for modernization.

The Liquidation of Colonialism

Even before the end of the Second World War, nationalist leaders in the various colonies were planning for independence. As we saw in Chapter 13, the impact of European intruders on native cultures had been shattering (pp. 543–44). Within a few decades after 1870, millions of people and millions of square miles had fallen under Western control. The conquered peoples had reacted in awe, confusion, and hatred, but they were pretty well convinced that the whites could not be driven out.

The Second World War, even more than the First, changed their feelings of apathy and despair. Though the British and French made free use of colonial troops and resources during the war, native leaders were mightily impressed by the defeats that the Western powers suffered. Between 1945 and 1960 most of the peoples of Asia and Africa gained their independence. The swiftness of European colonial takeovers was more than matched by the swiftness of colonial undoing.

The spurt to independence outran the hopes of native leaders and the fears of the colonial powers. Men like Mahatma Gandhi (India), Achmed Sukarno (Indonesia), and Kwame Nkrumah (Ghana) found that the force of nationalism in their countries, once unleashed, was irresistible. It was not surprising that the new spirit of pride was sometimes carried to excess. Though newly independent peoples had forgotten and forgiven much of the colonial past, they retained a residue of bitterness toward their former masters that could readily be stirred up.

For their part, Western political leaders sought to salvage what they could from the colonial wreckage. The British took the most realistic and enlightened view. For many decades the various portions of the British Empire had been evolving into a "British Commonwealth of Nations." Self-governing countries, like Canada and Australia, were sovereign states, but linked in friendship and cooperation with Britain. Recognizing that they could no longer play the role of masters, Britain's leaders sought to change once-subject peoples into friendly allies. They hoped thereby to keep a measure of political influence around the globe and to benefit from established ties of commerce and culture. In keeping with such aims, the British offered leadership training to a selected few in the colonies. These individuals, usually educated in Britain, aided in the transition of their homelands to independence and Commonwealth association.

The freeing of India from British rule was the largest single step in the ending of colonialism. The subcontinent, with its (then) four hundred million people, had been granted limited self-rule before the Second World War. This had not satisfied Indian nationalists, however, and at the war's end they insisted on full independence. The chief obstacle arose from the demand by Muslim leaders in India for a state separate from the Hindu majority. At last, in the hope of avoiding widespread violence, the last British viceroy, Lord Louis Mountbatten, agreed (1947) to partition the colony into two independent states. The larger, mainly Hindu portion of the subcontinent took the name of India; the smaller, mainly Muslim portion was called Pakistan. Both, by their own action, became members of the British Commonwealth.

The state of Pakistan originally consisted of two territories, east and west, separated by nearly a thousand miles. In 1971 the eastern territory rebelled against the central government, which was located in the west. After months of fighting, the rebels established an independent state, Bangladesh. This poor, war-torn land thereafter depended on aid from India and other outside powers. The remaining state of Pakistan encountered stubborn difficulties in achieving stability. After some ten years of military rule, a civilian government headed by a woman — Benazir Bhutto, was voted into power. But in 1990, under allegations of incompetence and corruption, her party suffered defeat at the polls — and a return to political influence by the military.

India, for its part, faced mounting economic and political problems. In 1975 the Indian prime minister, Indira Gandhi, suspended constitutional guarantees and tightened her personal control over the country. Shortly afterward, the voters reacted by defeating the prime minister and her Congress party in parliamentary elections. But the opposition groups soon fell apart, and in 1980 Gandhi and her party were swept back into power.

A few years later, the country suffered a severe shock — as a result of fighting between government forces and Sikh separatists in Punjab state (northern India). Sikh terrorists from Indira's bodyguard shot her dead in an act of revenge. Her son, Rajiv Gandhi, was elected to take her place as prime minister in 1984. He raised fresh hopes for national reconciliation. But tension and violence persisted, and Rajiv was voted out of power five years later by a coalition of opposition parties.

Though India has become a regional economic and military power, comparable in strength to China, its internal stability has steadily worsened. In addition to the troubles in the Punjab, the country has recently been torn by clashes between traditional Hindu castes, and between Muslim and Hindu

1763	1857	1947
India Controlled by British East India Company	Direct Rule by British Government	Independent India and Pakistan

religious zealots. The near-chaos in political life was driven home in May, 1991: Rajiv Gandhi, while campaigning to regain office and restore social order, was killed by a terrorist bomb.

Britain's postcolonial policy toward the Indian subcontinent was applied also to Ceylon (now Sri Lanka), Burma, and Malaya. In Africa, too, the British took steps to prepare their colonies for independence. Acting swiftly, they ended their previous treaty rights in Egypt in 1954 and granted freedom to the Gold Coast (Ghana) in 1957, and to Nigeria in 1960. Within a brief span most of Britain's other African territories became independent members of the Commonwealth (p. 601).

An exception was Kenya, in east Africa, where the white minority resisted black participation in the government. After a rebellion by blacks, involving "Mau Mau" terrorists, Britain in 1963 granted independence to Kenya under the leadership of Jomo Kenyatta. A true national hero, Kenyatta launched the first African experiment in multiracial government. In southern Africa, a longer and still more bitter racial fight took place. An all-white government, headed by Ian Smith, proclaimed Rhodesia independent in 1965. Britain reacted with economic sanctions against Rhodesia, and some blacks formed bands of armed resistance. It was not until 1980 that the British succeeded in bringing all parties to agree on a new constitution and free elections. The black majority chose a former guerrilla chief, Robert Mugabe, as the new leader, and changed the name of the country to Zimbabwe (an ancient capital of the region). Only one of Britain's former colonies remained under white rule: the Republic of South Africa (p. 609).

In Palestine, the British had taken political control from the dissolving Turkish Empire at the close of the First World War (p. 555). After the Second World War, however, Britain was prepared to give up authority there. One reason was the growing friction between the long-established Arab residents (Palestinians) and the recently arrived Jews, who sought to establish in Palestine a "national home" for their people. "Zionism" as an organized movement had appeared in Europe at the turn of the century (p. 548). It was seen by many Jews as the only permanent solution to their age-old problem of repeated persecution and discrimination in Christian states. During the First World War, the British cabinet had responded to Zionist appeals by promising support for a national home in Palestine (the Balfour Declaration of 1917). Following the Nazi extermination of an estimated six million Jews a generation later, the need for a place of refuge seemed even more desperate; thousands of Jews (chiefly from central and eastern Europe) made their twentieth-century exodus to the "Promised land." There they were joined by large numbers of Sephardic Jews, who had settled years before in Arab countries, and who came now as refugees.

The Arabs of Palestine (and elsewhere) saw this migration as a new form of Western imperialism. They believed the Jews, with their (mostly) European ways, to be an expansionist colony on the Arab shore. Violence broke out between Jewish and Arab armed factions in 1946; there were also *terrorist* acts, by both sides, against the British. Two years later Britain withdrew, and the United Nations voted for an independent Palestine, divided into two separate states. The Arabs, refusing to accept this division, tried unsuccessfully to overthrow the new state of Israel. Israel gained recognition from most non-Arab nations, however, and quickly established itself as an economic and military power in the Middle East.

In the years immediately after independence, Israel defended its existence against continuing Arab pressures and threats. Its most impressive demonstration of strength was in the "Six-Day War" of June 1967. In a lightning attack, Israel smashed a larger surrounding force of Arabs (mainly Egyptians) and occupied several Arab territories (p. 598). But the Arabs continued to refuse to recognize Israel and its occupation of their territories. They acquired new arms from the Soviet Union, which desired to expand its own influence in the Middle East. In the United Nations, the Arab states won passage of Security Council resolutions calling for Israeli withdrawal from the conquered lands in exchange for a settled peace. The Israelis, however, held on to the occupied territories; and the Egyptians and Syrians, after six years of waiting, opened a surprise attack in October 1973. Israeli forces, hastily reinforced by weapons from the United States, recovered from heavy initial losses and turned to the offensive. With the United States and Russia poised to enter the war, each to protect its client states, the United Nations stepped in and secured acceptance of a cease-fire.

The Middle East War of 1973 thus ended in a draw, but it appeared that Israel could not continue indefinitely to withstand Arab pressure to give up the conquered lands — including a place for the resettlement of Palestinian refugees from Israel. (Israel's population was less than one-thirtieth the population of the opposing Arab countries.) Pressure against the Jewish state mounted when the Arab oil-exporting states imposed, as a war measure, an embargo on shipments to all nations supporting the cause of Israel. Since the industrialized countries were critically dependent on oil, they pressed Israel to come to an agreement with the Arabs. Egypt, meanwhile, shifted from its reliance on the Soviet Union to a close relationship with the United States. It now realized that only the United States (by withholding its massive aid to Israel) was in a position to influence the Israeli course of action. Henry Kissinger, the American secretary of state, became an intermediary among the contesting parties in 1974, but his "step-by-step" diplomacy did not bring a peaceful settlement to the Middle East.

Anwar Sadat, the Egyptian president, next attracted world attention in 1977 by a surprise flight from Cairo to Jerusalem. With his nation desperate for peace, he proposed a permanent settlement to Menachem Begin, the Israeli prime minister. Begin responded favorably, and in 1978 the terms were painstakingly

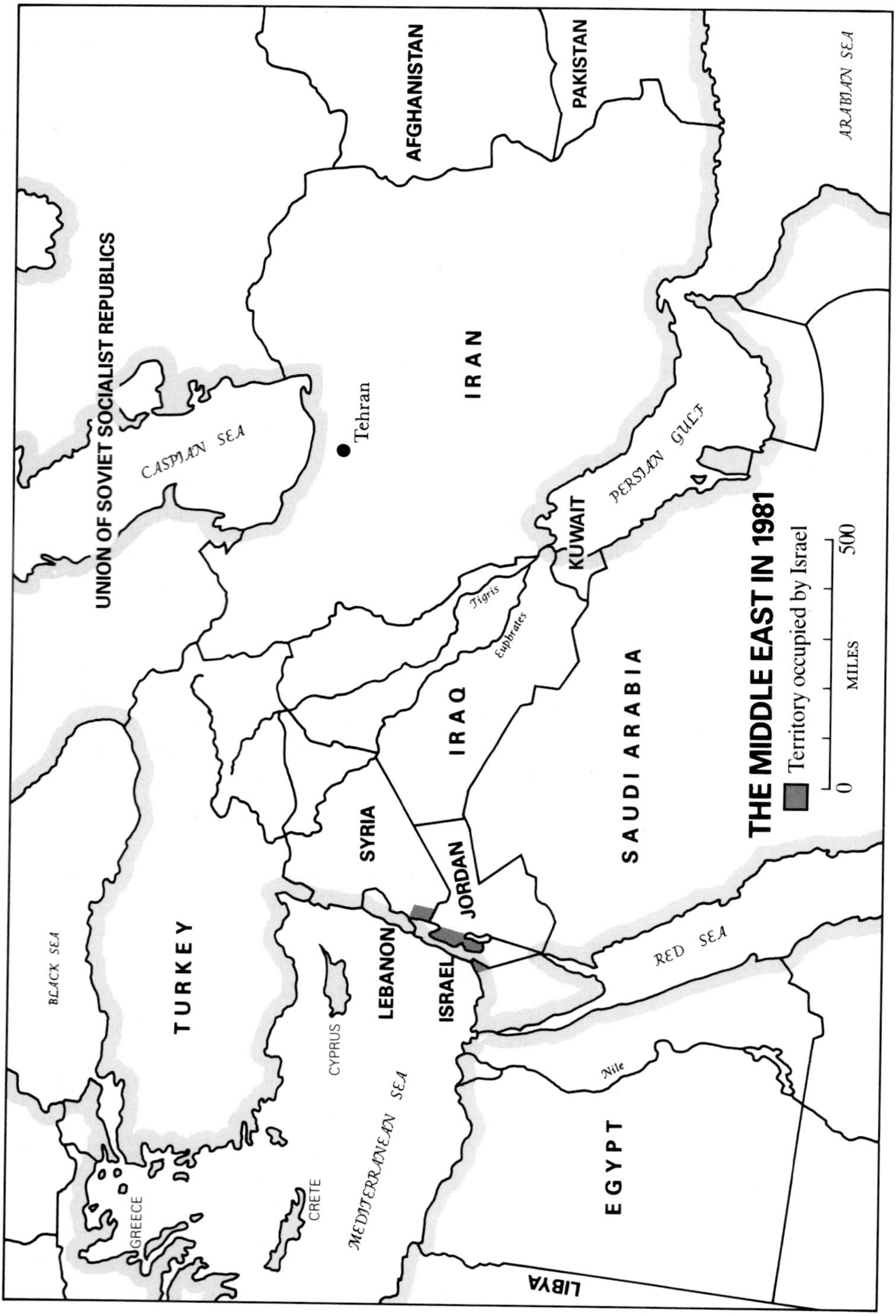

THE MIDDLE EAST IN 1981

UNION OF SOVIET SOCIALIST REPUBLICS

AFGHANISTAN

PAKISTAN

ARABIAN SEA

IRAN

CASPIAN SEA

Tehran

PERSIAN GULF

KUWAIT

Tigris

Euphrates

IRAQ

SAUDI ARABIA

SYRIA

JORDAN

TURKEY

BLACK SEA

CYPRUS

LEBANON

ISRAEL

RED SEA

CRETE

MEDITERRANEAN SEA

GREECE

Nile

EGYPT

LIBYA

■ Territory occupied by Israel

0 — MILES — 500

worked out at a series of "summit meetings" in Washington (Camp David), chaired by President Jimmy Carter. The Arab states (Libya, Syria, Jordan, Iraq, and Saudi Arabia) viewed Sadat's negotiations as a "separate peace" with a common enemy, and they furiously denounced the Camp David agreements. Nevertheless, the understandings between Israel and Egypt were largely fulfilled. The most controversial issue — a homeland for the Palestinians — remained to be settled. Sadat himself was killed by Muslim fanatics in 1981; Hosni Mubarak succeeded him as president.

As we have seen, the general policy of the British after the Second World War was to grant political independence to their colonial territories. In contrast, the French attempted to bring their colonies into *closer* political association. They offered them membership in a "French Union," which integrated overseas territories with continental France. This approach proved a failure; it appealed only to a limited number of colonial subjects who had been educated in French schools and who had come to respect and admire French culture. Moreover, Charles de Gaulle, who led the "Free French" movement during the Second World War, had promised the colonies that assisted him a free choice of status after peace was won. They chose independence, though most of them joined the French Community, a short-lived association that resembled the British Commonwealth. Regardless of their political choice, the former French territories in Africa have continued to rely heavily upon French military aid, investment, and trade.

In two areas — Algeria and Indochina — the French resorted to war in a vain attempt to hold political power. After brutal fighting and heavy losses, they were at last compelled to withdraw from both. Algeria became independent in 1962. Portions of Indochina — Laos and Cambodia — secured their independence from France in 1954, but the remainder — Vietnam — was temporarily divided by an international conference and soon fell into a prolonged and bloody civil struggle. Its agonies were worsened when the United States intervened to forestall an expected communist victory in the southern half of the country (pp. 603–5). The northern half, with its capital at Hanoi, was already under communist control.

The smaller colonial nations — the Netherlands, Belgium, and Portugal — tried to regain or hold on to their colonies after the Second World War. The Dutch, who had lost their rich holdings in the East Indies to Japanese forces in 1942, sought to reestablish their control. But they were compelled in 1949 to recognize the newly formed state of Indonesia, with a population of nearly a hundred million. Belgium made little preparation for the transition of its African Congo to independence, but in 1960 the rising tide of nationalism forced the Belgians to agree to freedom — without adequate preparation. The result was temporary chaos, followed by the formation of an independent state of Zaire under military rule (p. 601).

The Portuguese were determined to keep their grip on the vast African territories of Angola and Mozambique, which they continued to view as part of Portugal. The native resistance forces, however, through guerrilla tactics, at last broke the will of the colonial masters. Portuguese commanders in the field, observing the futility of their own military efforts, brought about a change in the imperial and dictatorial home government in Lisbon. The new Portuguese government, veering toward the political Left, granted independence to both these territories in 1975.

In Mozambique, where the resistance movement remained unified, the turn to independence went ahead on schedule. But in Angola the Portuguese withdrawal was followed by a civil war among three competing parties; this struggle was complicated by intervention from outside powers (South Africa, Zaire, the United States, the Soviet Union, and Cuba). By the spring of 1976 the "Popular Movement" party, backed by the Soviet Union and Cuba, gained control in most of Angola. South Africa, however, did not accept the new government and supported "UNITA" guerrillas in Angola. Thus, the civil war dragged on; an "official" peace was at last negotiated in 1991. In neighboring Namibia, formerly a German colony, South Africa continued an illegal occupation until 1990. An international agreement in that year provided for independence and free elections in Namibia.

All the new nations faced severe problems, for political independence did not automatically bring them prosperity and happiness. It became the responsibility of their new leaders to deal with the grave challenges of hunger, disease, ignorance, and *tribal* conflicts. They found, too, that they were seldom free of external influences. They were still bound to the economic structures developed earlier by the colonial powers; to a large extent their countries continued to serve the purpose of foreign capital ("neocolonialism").

Rising Material Expectations and the "Liberation" Movements

It was under these difficulties that the new leaders sought to satisfy their peoples' "revolution of rising expectations." Even as their own pride had been stirred earlier by the pride of their conquerors, the former colonials were now dazzled by Western affluence and technological mastery. Though glad to see the foreigners depart, they were impatient to learn their ways and enjoy their material advantages.

What, specifically, did the new nations desire? Their goals often seemed contradictory, for they desired to keep their cultural identity while adapting Western ideas and techniques to their own patterns of life. They did not often succeed; in the encounter between the old and the new, the old was usually destroyed. The ancient social structures of Asia and Africa proved no more capable than those of Europe of withstanding the impact of technology.

The emerging countries wished first of all to gain *economic* independence, for political sovereignty was hollow so long as foreigners ran the economy. In most instances there was only one practicable means of transferring control:

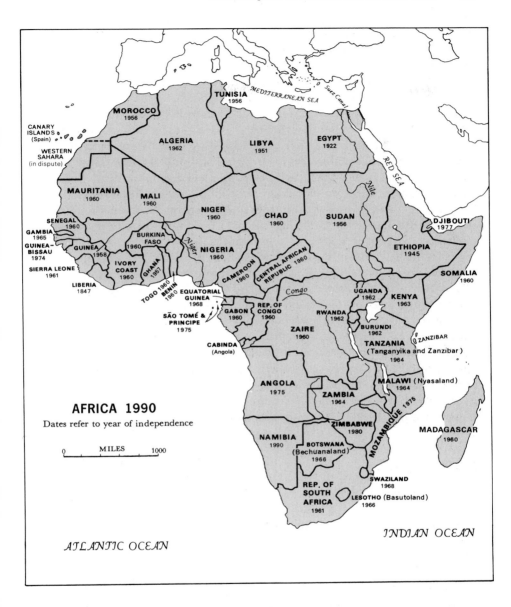

AFRICA 1990

Dates refer to year of independence

MILES
0 _____ 1000

CANARY ISLANDS (Spain)

WESTERN SAHARA (in dispute)

MOROCCO 1956
ALGERIA 1962
TUNISIA 1956
LIBYA 1951
EGYPT 1922
MEDITERRANEAN SEA
Suez Canal
RED SEA
Nile

MAURITANIA 1960
MALI 1960
NIGER 1960
CHAD 1960
SUDAN 1956
DJIBOUTI 1977
ETHIOPIA 1945
SOMALIA 1960

SENEGAL 1960
GAMBIA 1965
GUINEA-BISSAU 1974
GUINEA 1958
SIERRA LEONE 1961
LIBERIA 1847
IVORY COAST 1960
BURKINA FASO 1960
GHANA 1957
TOGO 1960
BENIN 1960
NIGERIA 1960
CAMEROON 1960
CENTRAL AFRICAN REPUBLIC 1960
Niger
Congo

EQUATORIAL GUINEA 1968
SÃO TOMÉ & PRINCIPE 1975
GABON 1960
REP. OF CONGO 1960
ZAIRE 1960
CABINDA (Angola)
UGANDA 1962
KENYA 1963
RWANDA 1962
BURUNDI 1962
TANZANIA (Tanganyika and Zanzibar) 1964
ZANZIBAR

ANGOLA 1975
ZAMBIA 1964
MALAWI (Nyasaland) 1964
MOZAMBIQUE 1975
MADAGASCAR 1960

NAMIBIA 1990
ZIMBABWE 1980
BOTSWANA (Bechuanaland) 1966
REP. OF SOUTH AFRICA 1961
SWAZILAND 1968
LESOTHO (Basutoland) 1966

ATLANTIC OCEAN
INDIAN OCEAN

nationalization. Foreign owners, supported by their home governments, naturally resisted such measures.

Nationalization went forward at a different pace in each developing country. In China, the communist revolution quickly took over all major sectors of the economy. Elsewhere, most of the new governments practiced some degree of socialism, though a number continued to protect established business interests, both foreign and domestic.

An example of the problems and achievements of nationalization was Cuba, where political independence from Spain (achieved in 1898) did not lead to economic independence either before or after the Second World War. The United States, which had driven the Spaniards from the island, had kept a heavy hand in Cuban affairs. From 1933 through 1959 it exerted its influence chiefly through one man, a former army sergeant — Fulgencio Batista. With or without elections, he remained the real force in most of the Cuban governments of that period. Batista was a friend and client of Washington and had kept Cuba open to American capital investment. But in 1959 Dr. Fidel Castro led a revolutionary movement that ousted the hated dictator. One of Castro's first acts in power was to *nationalize* the country's agriculture and industry, both of which had been owned in substantial part by Americans. Cuba thus became an authoritarian model of "national liberation" from a foreign-controlled political and economic establishment.

The underlying aim of Castro's movement, as of similar efforts to uproot the remains of colonialism, was to put the resources of the country at the disposal of its own people. But Castro and the other leaders were well aware that continued independence and the effective use of resources depended on health care and improved education; universal literacy was essential if their purposes were to be understood and their programs successfully carried out. They stressed technical education in particular, so that the young men and women of each new nation could operate the complicated machines that promised a better future. Ignorance was associated with the miseries and humiliations of the colonial era; "backwardness" had to be overcome at all costs. But the new leaders discovered that the cost of education was high indeed and that resources were usually unequal to requirements. The result, often, was popular disappointment and frustration. In Cuba, for example, many thousands fled their homeland to seek a freer and more comfortable life in the United States (usually in south Florida — only ninety miles distant).

In carrying his program forward, Castro faced not only grave internal handicaps but an external enemy as well: the United States. Despite public professions of the right of all peoples to *self*-determination, the American government (both Democratic and Republican) took a hostile attitude toward social revolutions — on the ground that they violated "human rights" and that they were or might become "communist." In keeping with this policy the United States has maintained a *trade embargo* against Cuba, and President John F. Kennedy in 1961 approved the "Bay of Pigs" invasion, guided unsuccessfully by the Central Intelligence Agency. (The CIA subsequently plotted for the assassination of Castro.)

Kennedy's successor, the Democrat Lyndon B. Johnson, sent troops into the Dominican Republic in 1965 for similar reasons; he further announced the "Johnson Doctrine" — that the United States would feel free to intervene in *any* country of the Western hemisphere that appeared threatened by communism. President Richard M. Nixon, a Republican, pursued the same general policy after his election in 1968; but his "Nixon Doctrine" proposed a shift in *means* for areas *outside* the hemisphere. Native troops (with American arms) would be expected to do their own ground fighting against rebel "communist" forces there. If United States combat assistance was needed, it normally would be limited to air and sea units. President Gerald Ford, Nixon's appointed successor, confirmed this strategy in 1975. The next president, Jimmy Carter, followed a more restrained policy of intervention; but Ronald Reagan, who became chief executive in 1981, ordered stronger action and a buildup of American military forces overseas (pp. 621–22).

Vietnam

Vietnam proved to be the key testing ground for American opposition to national-liberation movements. This was especially the case because in Vietnam the United States met a firm determination on the part of the Soviet Union and China to *support* the movement led by their ally, the nationalist (and communist) Ho Chi Minh. (The communist powers generally aided revolutionary movements everywhere — for their own ideological and political purposes.) What had begun in 1946 as a Vietnamese revolt against French colonial rule turned into a desperate civil war between North and South (p. 599). As part of his global anticommunist policy, John Foster Dulles, President Eisenhower's secretary of state, had provided substantial economic and military assistance to the French. After the French pulled out in 1954, Dulles persuaded Eisenhower to send military "advisers" to help the American-sponsored regime in Saigon, the chief city of the southern portion of Vietnam. Eisenhower's successor, President Kennedy, went further: he authorized United States special forces ("Green Berets") to conduct *sabotage* operations against communist-held northern Vietnam, whose capital was Hanoi. But it was the next president, Lyndon Johnson, who decided on a major escalation of American combat forces in 1965.

Johnson sent hundreds of thousands of troops to South Vietnam to aid the Saigon army; they were supported by hundreds of warships and thousands of aircraft, which also ranged northward to pour bombs on "enemy" installations. By the end of the war the total tonnage dropped by the United States in Indochina amounted to more than *three times* the tonnage dropped by the United States in all areas during the Second World War. It became clear by 1968, however, that the communist forces, supplied by the Soviet Union and China, would not give up — and that the American voters were becoming increasingly opposed to the continuing slaughter. American war deaths already exceeded forty thousand; Vietnamese deaths were estimated at more than a million; dollar costs had risen to hundreds of billions. (It was these huge expenditures and borrowings that opened the door to runaway price inflation and federal debt in the 1970s.) President Johnson at last stopped the military escalation and announced that he would not run for reelection.

Although Johnson did not run in 1968, his party's candidate (Hubert Humphrey) was defeated at the polls; the victor, Richard Nixon, was elected on a platform that included a "secret plan" for peace in Vietnam. The plan, as revealed during the Nixon years, called for the "Vietnamization" of the struggle and the gradual withdrawal of American combat forces. The plan also called for carrying the war into neighboring Cambodia and Laos as a means of "facilitating" United States withdrawal from Vietnam.

By 1971 it became apparent that what the Nixon administration desired was a "Korean-type" solution (p. 593) — by which limited United States units would remain in the South indefinitely as guarantors against a takeover by the Vietnamese National Liberation Front. (The Front consisted of guerrillas in the South, opposed to the Saigon government and closely linked to the northern communist forces.) But Nixon's critics in Congress called for *total* withdrawal of American forces from Vietnam and the rest of Indochina. The war had become a central issue of domestic politics in the United States. By the summer of 1971 the "antiwar" movement had displayed growing strength — in persistent acts of protest and mass marches on Washington and other cities.

Nixon, mindful of the approaching presidential election of 1972, sent his security adviser, Henry Kissinger, to conduct peace talks with the North Vietnamese. Kissinger found that there were irreconcilable differences in political objectives between the North and the South. Just before the election, he nonetheless claimed that he had negotiated "peace" in Vietnam and the withdrawal of all American troops "with honor." Most voters chose to believe that Nixon-Kissinger "magic" had ended the fighting for good and cast their ballots heavily for the president.

The following year, 1973, brought a time of reckoning and revelation for Nixon and the American people. The communist forces of Vietnam, convinced that South Vietnam would never permit the political compromises suggested in the Kissinger agreement, resumed hostilities. With most American forces now withdrawn, the Saigon armies began to give ground. The climax of the war came suddenly in 1975, when all of South Vietnam was swiftly taken over by "liberation" troops. Since then, the leaders from the North have been trying, painfully, to consolidate the two sections of the country, repair the damages of the war, and lay the basis for a workable national economy. (Their first symbolic act was to *rename* Saigon, the former southern capital, calling it "Ho Chi Minh City.")

A disastrous sequel to the Vietnam War unfolded in Cambodia (since renamed Kampuchea). Caught in the drawn-out Indochina battle, Cambodia fell to the Khmer Rouge, an extreme Marxist group that had fought for years as guerrillas against various governments in Phnom Penh (the capital). Its leader, Pol Pot, sealed off the country in 1976 (save for contacts with China) and proceeded to transform the nation by force into a collectivized agrarian society. People were uprooted from the cities and compelled to clear new lands or work on irrigation projects and farms. As a result of these shocking dislocations and accompanying repression, malnutrition, and disease, several million Kampucheans perished.

In 1978 this near-genocidal government was overturned by Cambodian rebels and Vietnamese troops, though the Khmer Rouge (and other groups) fought on as guerrillas. Pol Pot had been aided from the outset by China; in 1985 the United States and some of its Asian allies also began to send supplies to the guerrillas. The ultimate outcome of this conflict remains highly uncertain. Meanwhile, thousands of refugees have fled Kampuchea, as well as other parts of Indochina, by both land and sea (the desperate "boat people").

While Nixon's Vietnam operation was falling into ruin, his position at home was also collapsing. Starting in 1973, a Senate committee of inquiry, the "Watergate Committee," looked into charges of White House involvement in a political burglary at the Watergate apartment complex in Washington. It also investigated illegal financial contributions, misuse of government agencies, campaign "dirty tricks," and obstruction of justice. The charges were proved true, with decisive information coming from secret White House audio tapes the president had ordered made of conversations in his office. Facing impeachment by an aroused Congress, Nixon abruptly resigned from his high position — the first such action by an American president. Shortly before that historic happening, his vice-president, Spiro Agnew, had resigned to avoid prosecution for bribery and tax charges. Thus, the "law and order" administration, overwhelmingly reelected in 1972, fell in disgrace in 1974. Gerald Ford, previously appointed by Nixon to replace Agnew as vice-president, then moved up to the presidency. One of his first public acts was to proclaim a complete pardon of Nixon for any and all crimes that he might have committed in office. (Nixon's subordinates in the Watergate affair, however, were brought to trial and most were convicted.)

The disaster in Vietnam and the shocking disclosures in Washington drew American and world attention away from efforts by some "developing" nations to achieve modernization. A hopeful start in that direction had been made in a small country of Latin America — Chile. One of the few truly democratic states in the Western hemisphere, Chile was a test case for seeing if radical social change could be brought about through peaceful, democratic methods. Salvador Allende, an avowed Marxist, was elected president in 1970 by regular constitutional procedures. He had the direct support, however, of only a *plurality* of the voters, not a *majority*. While in office, Allende sought authority for sweeping landholding reforms and for state ownership of banks and basic industries; with equal vigor, he defended democratic methods, legality, and civil liberties. The president's conservative opponents made full use of the press, their control of the Chilean Congress, and their economic power to block Allende's legislative program and his efforts to increase national production. Faced with staggering inflation, internal unrest, and secret intervention by the American CIA, Allende had reached an impasse by 1973. Then, as some observers had predicted, his generals and admirals struck against his democratic government in a bloody military coup. Allende, holding to his principles to the end, stayed at his desk in the presidential palace; there he was gunned down by the rebel soldiers.

The new military government, headed by General Agusto Pinochet, proceeded to destroy its opponents by relentless harassment, torture, and executions. It was promptly recognized by the United States government, which later admitted having spent millions of dollars to "destabilize" (make unworkable) the Allende democracy. With the aid of American loans and financial advisers, Pinochet set out to establish a laissez-faire economy within the bounds of his anticommunist dictatorship. The Chilean economy was thus stabilized, though it later stagnated. After repeated popular protests against the military dictatorship, a citizens' *referendum* at last restored the substance of Chilean democracy in 1989.

Elsewhere in Latin America, most countries remained under the control of the wealthy, the Church, and the military — even when democratic *forms* of government were adopted. Though liberalism had been the declared ideal of the first independent states of Latin America (p. 488), the twentieth century brought chiefly dictatorships and repression. *Modernization* was the principal goal of the Latin nations after the First World War, and with it came the impact of foreign capital. American business was the major outside influence, buttressed in recent years by the CIA.

In the 1970s there was a determined effort to break away from "Yankee imperialism." Mexico, for example, attempted with some success to conduct a foreign policy free of American influence. In Brazil tough military rulers, while making use of foreign investment, pursued a generally independent course of "directed" economic growth. (This program ultimately failed and led to unmanageable inflation and foreign debt.) In the Caribbean area, tiny Panama in 1978 regained control of its Canal Zone, which had been occupied by United States forces in 1903. The treaty of transfer, submitted to the Senate by President Jimmy Carter, was ratified over furious objections by some Senators. And in 1990, United States power was once again asserted in Panama when a later president, George Bush, sent an invasion force to topple its dictatorial "strongman," Manuel Noriega.

In nearby Nicaragua, in 1979, the "Sandinista National Liberation Front" brought down the regime of the corrupt Somoza family, longtime American clients. The Sandinistas, headed by Daniel Ortega, quickly installed a socialist government, and this time, in spite of ideological reservations, President Carter responded with cautious friendship and assistance. However, his successor, Ronald Reagan, reversed this position in 1981 (p. 621).

Iran

Of all the "liberation" movements of recent years, the one that most disturbed the great powers broke out in the troubled Middle East — in oil-rich

Iran (p. 598). Called Persia until its change of name in 1935, this strategically located country has long been fought over by imperial states, especially Russia and Britain. After the Second World War, Iran turned to America as a counterweight against Soviet pressure from the north; in 1947 the United States sent military and economic advisers to Iran as part of a joint plan for the country's development. Its ruler, Reza Shah Pahlavi, was strongly supported by the Americans, whose primary interest was in the Iranian oil fields.

All went smoothly for the American (and British) oil companies until 1951, when the Iranian Parliament, headed by Premier Muhammad Mossadeq, nationalized the petroleum industry. Within two years the American president, Dwight Eisenhower, decided that Mossadeq must be turned out. Shah Pahlavi accordingly dismissed Mossadeq, but the populace rioted and forced the shah to flee the country. Then the American CIA, giving out large sums of money and military supplies, engineered a counteraction that drove Mossadeq from office and brought back the shah. Pahlavi's new premier at once negotiated a petroleum agreement favorable to the American oil companies.

Shah Pahlavi made full use of American aid and his government's oil revenues. He lavished funds on his armed forces and started a program of rapid modernization and industrialization. The oil prosperity was shared by many members of the Iranian middle class, but most of the benefits were channeled to a privileged few. The poor remained poor, their plight worsened by high inflation resulting from the swift influx of oil money. Public resentment rose in the 1970s against the shah's personal extravagance, foreign (especially American) influence, and the corrosive impact of Western secular ways on traditional Muslim culture. Numerous groups and parties became involved; but religious leaders (the *mullahs* and *ayatollahs*) were the principal promoters of the swelling protest. These leaders called for a fairer economic order as well as a return to religious fundamentalism. The protest continued to grow, in spite of harsh measures by the shah's security forces, which had been trained in part by American police experts.

In 1979 the pent-up pressures exploded against the shah. Riots and street demonstrations mounted in anger and violence. Thousands were imprisoned, tortured, or killed by the military during this period, but at last the shah's soldiers refused to shoot at their rebelling fellow Iranians. Though his American support continued, the monarch was compelled to flee for his life; and the Ayatollah Khomeini, who had been guiding the revolt from his exile near Paris, returned in triumph to the capital (Tehran).

Once the revolutionaries were in power, they moved to establish a theocratic (church-controlled) "Islamic Republic of Iran." The new Revolutionary Council tracked down hundreds of the shah's military and civilian officials, put them on trial, and executed them. At the same time it enforced strict Muslim rules and punishments respecting dress and behavior, especially for women. In November 1979, when the hated shah was received in New York City (for medical treatment), Iranian militants protested by seizing the American embassy in Tehran and taking the staff hostage. In return for their release, the militants demanded return of the shah (for trial), recovery of the enormous wealth he had transferred abroad, and an end to American interference in Iran's affairs.

The public reaction in the United States was one of surprise and anger. (President Carter had been previously warned of the possible seizure of the embassy and staff.) Some people called for a military response, but the president's concern for the lives of the hostages overruled the desire to resort to force. Carter did react with tough economic steps: he froze Iranian assets in the United States (worth many billions) and cut off all trade with Iran, including imports of oil. He also appealed to the United Nations and his European allies to take diplomatic and economic actions against these flagrant violators of international law. (Embassies have always been considered part of a nation's territory abroad.) But the Iranians did not yield. They remained in the grip of nationalistic excitement, hatred for the American government, and religious fanaticism. It was not until 1981, after a failed rescue mission by the Americans, that they finally released the hostages. They did so in exchange for the unfreezing of Iranian assets and a pledge of noninterference in Iranian affairs.

The "loss" of Iran was a heavy blow to American prestige and interests. The shah had been regarded as America's "policeman" in the Middle East, providing security for investments there as well as military bases for "monitoring" the U.S.S.R. (Iran's northern border runs parallel to the Soviet border — p. 598.) After the shah's overthrow, the Carter administration feared that the oil fields of the entire Middle East, needed by the American economy, were endangered. Carter saw the possibility of Iranian-style revolutions spreading to nearby oil states, and the possibility of a Soviet march southward into a weakened Iran. He responded by increasing the number of American warships in the Persian Gulf and by starting up a "Rapid Deployment Force" for use in the Middle East.

The Soviets, for their part, feared that the revolutionary Islamic tide might flow from Iran to a neighboring Muslim country, Afghanistan — or even to the millions of Muslims who live in the southern republics of the U.S.S.R. It was this concern, in part, that moved the Soviets to send troops into Afghanistan late in 1979 to install a pro-Soviet regime. This move, in turn, caused a negative reaction in the United States and Europe, jeopardizing the frail détente with Russia (p. 592). Thus, the liberation movement in Iran brought not only upheavals within that country but had serious effects beyond its borders. It also brought war to Iran from neighboring Iraq in 1980. This conflict further split the Islamic world and continued to run its bloody course until peace between these two countries was concluded in 1990.

The Struggle against Racism

Western colonialism had been laced with racist feeling; the fight against colonialism — and the liberation movement — were marked by *rejection* of racism. (There were, of course, some outbursts of "reverse" racism.) The memory of exploitation of dark-skinned peoples by whites did not vanish with the departure of the colonial masters. In the new black-controlled states of Africa, whites seldom displayed the racial arrogance of earlier times, but some still held feelings of superiority and contempt toward black citizens.

In the one remaining white-controlled state of sub-Saharan Africa (the Republic of South Africa), racism has continued to flourish. Attitudes are changing even there, but the system of *apartheid* (enforced racial separation) remains generally in effect. In the 1980s, however, pressure mounted against it. The chief white political leader, P. W. Botha, tried to reduce this pressure by offering limited reforms within the system; but he stuck to his pledge to keep black communities *separate* from whites and to keep *white control* over national policies. Botha's successor as prime minister, Frederik de Klerk, moved further in 1990 and 1991 — bringing about *repeal* of the laws that established apartheid. He also extended recognition to the African National Congress, the principal black organization seeking equality, and released from prison Nelson Mandela, its charismatic leader.

World opinion supported the blacks, who make up about seventy percent of the population. They were still denied basic civil rights and decent pay for their work. In fact, the South African labor system, for blacks, is thought to be worse than "old-fashioned" *slavery* (abolished in most parts of the world more than a century earlier). Growing unrest in the black communities has led to countless protest marches, clashes with police, and hundreds of deaths and imprisonments.

In addition to Mandela, another outstanding black leader is the eloquent (Anglican) archbishop of Capetown, Desmond Tutu. His world stature, as winner of the Nobel Peace prize in 1984, served to attract wide attention to the blacks' demands. Nation after nation has been persuaded to enact trade and financial penalties against South Africa. But with mounting white resistance, and some angry splits inside the black community, the final result of the struggle is not yet in sight.

The fight against racism has not been limited to South Africa or to former colonies. The most notable effort in the postwar period took place in the United States — where some black leaders declared that the black community (some twenty-five million people) remained, in effect, a colony within the larger nation. Their ancestors, indeed, had been brought to America from the slave markets of Africa, and their history, for some three hundred years, had been one of exploitation and unequal treatment. The end of legal slavery in 1865 left African Americans still in a very inferior condition. It was not until after the middle of the *twentieth* century that they began to approach equality with whites in civil, political, social, and economic affairs.

In spite of their subjection and disadvantages, blacks in America contributed creatively to the sciences, literature, art, and music of the nation and the world. Their aspirations were lifted in 1954 by a landmark decision of the Supreme Court of the United States. This decision put an end to the earlier principle of "separate but equal" education for black children and called for progressive *integration* of the races in public-supported schools and colleges. The decision was bitterly resisted by whites in many communities, but by 1970 the new *principle* appeared to have been widely accepted. (Actually, the tradition of the "neighborhood school" and resistance to "busing for racial balance" kept schools substantially segregated in spite of the ruling.) Black leaders also worked harder than ever to end "Jim Crowism" (separate seating in transportation and public-service facilities) and to place more blacks on voter-registration rolls. These efforts, backed by sit-ins, boycotts, mass demonstrations, and civil disobedience, proved largely successful during the 1960s. In the forefront of the drive were aggressive legal actions guided by the National Association for the Advancement of Colored People (NAACP) and the leadership of Martin Luther King, Jr. (He has since been honored by an act of Congress designating his birthday as a national holiday each year.)

Dr. King stood squarely for full integration of the races, equal opportunity, and nonviolence (pp. 640–41). In the late 1960s, however, some of the younger members of the black community began to fall away from his leadership. Blacks still endured poor food and housing, especially in the urban ghettos, and unequal opportunity for jobs, health care, and schooling. Some concluded that more forceful methods were needed to persuade the white power structure that more must be done for blacks. Cries arose for "black power," militancy, and violence. The police became a particular target of hatred; in the eyes of most blacks, they patrolled black neighborhoods like soldiers of an occupying army. Clashes with the police sometimes erupted into ugly riots, burnings and lootings — such as those in Watts, California (1965), and in Detroit and Washington (1967).

The assassination of Martin Luther King, Jr., in 1968 was a shocking and demoralizing blow to the black movement. It had the effect of pushing the movement temporarily toward militancy — toward more radical leaders. The "white blacklash," meanwhile, heightened racist feelings and sharpened the "law and order" issue in the country. Police forces were enlarged and more heavily armed; they sought out militants (like the Black Panthers), kept them under surveillance, raided their headquarters, and often brought court charges against their leaders.

In the 1970s and 1980s, violence and threats of violence diminished, but racial tension remained high. Within the African-American community itself, division grew between those who favored continued efforts toward integration and a small minority who favored racial *separation* as a goal. In any event, blacks who were "successful" displayed a stronger spirit of pride, independence, and energy than ever before. This spirit showed itself in virtually all the arts and professions — most visibly, perhaps, in the advance of black athletes in competitive sports.

The business recession of 1981–83 bore most heavily on nonwhites, especially the young. In spite of "affirmative action" programs designed to employ more minorities in industry and public service, the unemployment rate for

African Americans rose substantially. Cutbacks in government spending, which began at all levels in 1981, reduced the number of public jobs and decreased financial aid for the poor.

As a matter of fact, economic "entrapment" has brought more frustration to poor blacks than what remains of racial discrimination. African Americans still make up a disproportionate number of the nation's "underclass." Living mainly in the ghettos, these individuals suffer from severe handicaps — financial, social, educational, and psychological. Thus, while watching their traditional menial and unskilled jobs become fewer, they usually find the "better," middle-class jobs beyond their reach. The Reverend Jesse Jackson has become the most outspoken leader, nationally, in calling attention to this frustration. At the local level, African Americans have gained some help through the election of mayors of their race in the large cities — notably, Detroit, Chicago, Los Angeles, Philadelphia, Atlanta, and New York.

ECONOMIC REASSESSMENT AND THE "THREE WORLDS"

American public attention to world affairs during the 1970s and 1980s was largely absorbed by the troubles in Vietnam and the Middle East. For at least a generation, however, some experts had been warning of broader and deeper dangers: world population was rising to unsupportable levels and the limited resources of the planet were running short. In the late 1940s one expert, the Swedish-American food scientist Georg Borgstrom, had undertaken a broad examination of the world's life-support systems and their interrelationships. He reported his findings in a trilogy of books, commencing in 1965 with *The Hungry Planet*. Borgstrom was joined by growing numbers of scientists and other experts who were now looking with alarm at the prospects of humanity. The "ghost of Malthus" (p. 472), once forgotten, had reappeared.

The Interlocking Crises of Population, Resources, and Pollution

Advances in science and technology, as we have seen (p. 500), were primarily responsible for sweeping changes in social conditions. After 1800, the decrease in death rates, flowing chiefly from improvements in food production and medical practices, led to a sharp rise in the number of people in the world (p. 512). The rate of increase grew even steeper in the twentieth century; the numbers being added to the world's population each year were greater than ever before. In the decade of the 1980s, the cumulative *increase* amounted to more than one *billion* people — bringing the *total* to more than five billion in 1990. Experts now forecast a figure close to *seven* billion by the year 2000.

The fact is that the food supply is not keeping up with population growth. The poor two-thirds of the globe (Asia, Latin America, Africa), where numbers are rising the fastest, *already* suffer from malnutrition and periodic famines. The "Green Revolution," which introduced better grain seeds during the

1970s, lifted yields somewhat, but the increases were limited by inadequate supplies of water and fertilizer. Overconsumption in the rich one-third of the globe has intensified the feeding problem. The average American or European, for instance, consumes many times more calories and proteins than the average Asian or African. A primary explanation of these dietary differences lies in the fact that the Europeans, with their historic command of the oceans and their conquests in the New World, secured control centuries ago of immense resources outside their own countries (pp. 301–3). After 1850 some seventy million Europeans emigrated to the New World; they and their descendants thus relieved the pressure on Europe's food supply by putting to use the vast, fertile lands of North and South America and Australia.

Other resources have also come up short. In spite of the efforts of scientists and technologists, the earth's supply of water, minerals, and fossil fuels remains *finite*. Residents of the industrialized countries were shocked into an awareness of this reality by the unexpected Arab oil embargo of 1973 (p. 597). Suddenly the wheels of factories and automobiles slowed. For the first time in their lives, many consumers in the West became aware of the extended and intricate resource network on which their life-style rested.

Even after the embargo was lifted, the fourfold increase in oil prices indicated the true value of a substance that previously had been bought cheaply and squandered recklessly. The dramatic price hikes by the Organization of Petroleum Exporting Countries (OPEC) upset the importing nations, the flow of international monetary payments, and the world balance of economic power. Experts could see that all production based on the use of energy would cost more in the years ahead. Though temporary gluts in oil production would bring prices down at times, the long-run prospect for prices of *all* nonrenewable resources is *upward*.

Atomic energy, produced by nuclear reactors, has been urged as a replacement for fossil fuels (oil and coal). Here is another illustration of the predicament of modern technologists: while the reactors help fill energy needs, they create *new* problems such as operational safety, radioactive wastes, and the possible misuse by terrorists of the plutonium produced (p. 616). The world was sharply alerted to such dangers by the reactor disaster at Chernobyl, U.S.S.R., in 1986. And dozens of other nuclear plants around the globe could be similar disasters "waiting to happen."

Beyond these special problems is the general threat of environmental pollution caused by rising energy consumption, industrial wastes, and the use of chemicals. (These dangers were highlighted in 1985 by the accidental release of a deadly gas from an American plant in Bhopal, India. Thousands of people were killed by this gas in a matter of hours or days.) Degradation of the earth's air and water, as well as overheating of the earth's atmosphere, seems inevitable if the upward trend in energy use continues. The exploration of the world's seabeds and the exploitation of outer space might provide solutions to some of these problems in the long run, but neither activity promises much aid for earthlings in the foreseeable future. Many scientists believe, therefore, that the survival of the species demands a leveling off in total population and a *reduction* in energy and resource consumption. Some public recognition of these facts took place in the 1970s and 1980s, but more *action* is needed in the 1990s.

Economic and Political Divisions

With the world seen as a finite, interdependent whole, many traditional ideas and hopes have been challenged. Narrow nationalism, in particular, became outmoded. The nation-state could no longer assure either security or sustenance to its citizens. Accordingly, men and women in many countries found themselves more and more alienated from their "central" government, which they saw as too big and remote to command their allegiance, but not big enough to guarantee their safety. Hence, there was talk of "devolution" in Britain (the proposed transfer of certain powers from London to the Scots and the Welsh); "states rights" in the United States; and "separatism" (ethnic autonomy) in Canada, Spain, India, and other countries. These moves toward greater local control had a sentimental and practical appeal, but moves in the opposite direction — toward units of organization *larger* than the nation-state — were driven by economic and security requirements.

Nations have begun to group themselves into common-purpose blocs: the Organization of Petroleum Exporting Countries (OPEC), the European Economic Community (EEC), and the Organization of African Unity (OAU). And the tendency was toward still larger groupings. In the 1980s virtually all of the approximately one hundred fifty nation-states belonged to one of "Three Worlds." As seen by observers in the West (and in the Soviet Union), the *First* World consisted of the industrialized, noncommunist states, led by the United States; the *Second* World consisted of the communist states, headed by the Soviet Union; the *Third* World included the rest — the developing states — located mainly in Asia, Africa, and Latin America, whose peoples were, for the most part, nonwhite and poor. (Though the idea of the *Second* World appears to have dissolved with the breakup of the communist bloc, the distinction between First and Third Worlds remains valid.)

Within the Third World there is a further division based on unequal resources. A minority of the Third World countries, which possess rich oil reserves, enjoy large revenues and the potential for rapid development; but the majority, which have few natural resources, are very poor and have little expectation of development. These countries, since 1980, have become burdened with huge foreign debts (to the "developed" world); and in Africa, millions of people have suffered hunger and starvation, due mainly to droughts, lack of money for importing food, and (often) internal military conflicts.

The central issue in relationships between the poor of the Third World and their economic betters has to do with food and other necessities for existence. In order to reach at least survivable standards of living, the poor ("have-not") countries are asking for creation of a "new international economic order" based on fairness and sharing rather than on power and inequality. They want control, for their own benefit, of whatever resources and natural advantages they may possess. And they demand changes in the "terms of trade": the relation between prices received for their exports and prices paid for their imports.

For their part, the satisfied ("have") countries now accept the fact of global interdependence, but they insist on being the ones to decide what "adjustments" are to be made. The "North-South dialogue" of the 1970s and 1980s (between the rich and the poor nations) has produced little help for development of the Third World. The poor countries, partly because of their own mistakes in economic planning and execution, are *worse off* today than they were in the 1970s. And the present global economic situation gives little prospect of improvement.

The Nuclear Arms Race and Terrorism

The Three Worlds of the 1980s were frequently at odds with one another. And the relative distribution of strength, both military and economic, was what usually determined the outcome of disputes. Arab oil (more than Arab votes in the United Nations) brought to the Third World whatever influence it has gained in global affairs. Recognition of the importance of *power* speeded the race for weaponry, both nuclear and "conventional." The superpowers, notwithstanding their existing "overkill" capabilities and their lip service to "arms control," spent hundreds of *billions* of dollars annually in a technological struggle for "superiority." This contest struck many observers as futile and wasteful, for military power is only *relative*; as each side matched the escalation of the other, neither gained in security or influence.

The most dangerous and costly contest was in *nuclear* arms. The race had started in 1945 with the dropping of the first atomic bomb on Japan (p. 585). This action by the Americans let the world know of their *ability* and *will* to use these "ultimate" weapons when they saw fit. The Soviets responded by building nuclear bombs of their own (p. 587); during the 1950s the race went onward for more efficient warheads (explosive charges) — and for faster and more accurate means of delivery. In this race the Americans have generally been ahead, both in technological advances and in numbers of deliverable warheads.

Though many types of weapons were designed — for such purposes as short-range ("tactical") use against armies and for use at sea against submarines — the most critical area of competition was in long-range ("strategic") weapons that could reach the *homeland* of the other superpower. The Soviets put most warheads of this type into land-based missiles, placed in underground "silos." The United States put most of theirs in nuclear-powered submarines, as well as in land-based missiles and bombers.

No matter what the differences in numbers and locations, it was clear by 1970 that each side had more than enough warheads to wipe out the population of the other side. So why did both sides continue to spend billions for *still more?* The answer is that each side sought a "breakthrough," by technological advance or sheer numbers, that would give it "superiority" over the other side. Essentially, this means gaining a "first-strike" capacity: that is, the ability to destroy enough of the opponent's nuclear weapons (in a surprise attack) so that the opponent's retaliatory ("second") strike would cause only limited losses to the attacker. The nation that gained first-strike capacity would thus have "superiority" — and with it, supposedly, the final "say" in disputes with the other superpower. That is why each side *wanted* the advantage — and, even more important, why it could not permit the *other* side to gain it.

As it became obvious that neither side would be permitted to win superiority by adding *more* offensive weapons (because the other side would add more also), nuclear war planners turned to *defensive* weapons as a way to gain the advantage. If one side had a "near-perfect" defense against enemy warheads, while the other did not, the first side would then have gained the desired "first-strike" capacity. So, a race began about 1970 to build "antiballistic missile" defenses (ABM).

It was shortly realized, however, that this simply added *another* threatening and expensive side to the arms race — one that, again, neither side could win, nor yet afford to lose. In 1972 President Richard Nixon and the Soviet leader, Leonid Brezhnev (p. 589), signed a treaty limiting the building of ABM systems. This agreement was followed by further efforts to achieve "arms control" (limitations or reductions) of *offensive* weapons. A promising advance was achieved in 1979 when a Strategic Arms Limitation Treaty (SALT) was signed by Brezhnev and a new president, Jimmy Carter (p. 590). However, the Senate of the United States failed to ratify the treaty, and the race in offensive weapons remained open.

Britain, France, and China were also producing nuclear arms (p. 591). They did so chiefly for national prestige; a nation, to be considered a *first-class* power, now had to belong to the "nuclear club." But none of these nations was in the same "league" as the superpowers. Their relatively small supply could hardly give them a first-strike capacity, and they viewed their weapons only as a "last resort" — to be held as a "deterrent" threat against any nation that might plan to attack them. Some other countries possessed, or were trying to acquire, nuclear weapons; these included India, Pakistan, Israel, Iraq, and South Africa; a dozen more countries could be nuclear-capable by the year 2000. This "proliferation" (spread) raised the risk of a "small" nuclear catastrophe somewhere, which might also ignite a *total* catastrophe should the major nuclear powers become involved.

Most other countries, however, did not desire, nor could they afford to "go nuclear." They contented themselves with a buildup of other types of arms, whose power and accuracy were also growing remarkably. The poor countries found that they could not compete very well even on that level; this explains in large part the attraction of *terrorism* as a type of armed force. (Terrorism means the use of violence to achieve the aims of states or groups within states. These aims cover a broad range, including certain national goals, social revolution, expulsion of foreign influences, or revenge for injuries to ethnic pride and interests. By waging "mini-war" and thereby creating an atmosphere of *fear*, the terrorists hope to compel targeted governments or other groups to give in to their demands.) "Senseless" violence, such as bombing, sabotage, and hijacking, is cruel and indiscriminate (as are most other forms of warfare) — and usually ineffective. But in a world ruled by *force*, terror is often viewed as the only weapon left to those who lack "regular" military forces. (Further discussion of the use of violence appears on p. 640.)

The widespread use of terror by armed gangs — of both the Left and the Right — became an extremely nagging worry of government leaders from the 1970s up until the present. In addition to using standard police methods for countering violence, some officials were developing highly sophisticated devices for dealing with kidnapers, hijackers, and assassins. But the threats have persisted. The most frightening terrorist danger lies in the transfer of nuclear technology, equipment, and fuels to desperate Third World countries. Plutonium, diverted from power reactors into nuclear explosive devices, could become a nightmarish means of international blackmail.

END OF THE POSTWAR (COLD WAR) ERA

In the late 1980s an unexpected *change* began in the internal and external relations of many countries of the world — especially those in the European communist bloc. This change had *roots* in the past, not clearly perceived by outside observers, but which rose suddenly to the surface as the last decade of the twentieth century opened (1990). A new order was clearly in the making — affecting millions of individuals in both East and West. Its most important feature, no doubt, was the abrupt turn away from the "Cold War" toward a new era of *cooperation* among the leading world powers. In order to understand the nature and prospects of this new era, we must review the chief developments of the decade preceding this "historical surprise."

Political and Economic Changes in the West: Thatcher and Reagan

In western Europe, the 1980s saw continuing movement away from old-fashioned nationalism (pp. 580–81) to the idea of a "common European homeland." Progress in this direction took place mainly in the economic field; it had started as far back as 1957 with the creation of the European Economic Community (pp. 590–91). The purpose was to create a prosperous "free trade" zone, comparable in market size to the United States. More recently, the EEC established an Exchange Rate Mechanism (ERM), a system for stabilizing the currency exchange rates among the various Community members. And for the future, the EEC leaders are planning for a *common* monetary unit and for a *political union* of member states to complement their economic union. Thus, the world could soon see a "United States of Europe" — with no internal tariff walls or border controls. This concept was strengthened in 1990 by the upgrading of periodic meetings following the Helsinki "summit" (p. 592) into an active and continuing "Conference on Security and Cooperation in Europe" (C.S.C.E.). Including *all* the European nations, plus the United States and Canada, it has developed cooperative measures to assure their *military* security.

The unifying trends in western Europe during the 1980s were accompanied, within most of these countries, by a swing to conservative economic and political policies. (One notable exception was France, where the socialist François Mitterand held the presidency for the entire period.) The *conservative movement* was primarily a reaction against the *liberal* policies that had generally prevailed in the West from 1933 until about 1980. The terms "liberal" and "liberalism," of course, no longer meant what they had meant in the eighteenth and nineteenth centuries. In that earlier time liberalism had been equated with *individualism* and with the revolt against hereditary privilege and absolute monarchy (pp. 442–44). In the twentieth century liberalism still stood for individual rights (civil liberties) and openness to social reform, but came to be most strongly identified with "social democracy" and the "welfare state" (pp. 577–79). The social and moral changes that accompanied the welfare state also came to be linked with liberalism.

Although the conservative reaction to these changes proceeded unevenly in most countries of the West, it took decisive form in Britain and the United States. Margaret Thatcher was chosen as leader by Britain's Conservative party in 1979, and she led her party to victory in Parliament during the ensuing decade. With large majorities in the elected House of Commons, she was able to enact sweeping reforms: many government-owned enterprises were sold off to private corporations; the educational system was overhauled at all levels — and with reduced expenditure; the power of trade unions was curbed; and taxation policies shifted ever more to favor the rich. While these changes were not altogether pleasing to many British voters, Thatcher gained and held power largely because of splits within the opposition Labor party. By 1990 her public support had fallen sharply; she was replaced as party leader by John Major, a member of her cabinet. The Conservatives continued to hold their majority in the House of Commons, and new general elections would not be required until 1992.

In the United States the conservatives did not achieve a full grip on the federal government. This was due to the Constitutional provision for "checks and balances"—which *distributes* authority among the legislative, executive, and judicial branches. However, with Ronald Reagan as their leader and president, the conservatives made a deep impress upon public thinking and acting in the 1980s. Their ascendancy in national politics had been demonstrated even before that time—by the election and reelection of Richard Nixon to the presidency (1968, 1972). But his second term was undermined by the ugly "Watergate" affair (p. 605), and it took several years thereafter for the conservatives to regroup and rally around their emerging chief spokesman, Ronald Reagan.

By 1980, conservative opinion-makers were also setting the national mood. Writers and television commentators like William Buckley and George Will were displacing, in the public view, well-known liberals like Arthur Schlesinger and John Kenneth Galbraith. The conservatives, like the liberals, had a considerable range of interpreters. But the central thrust of the movement was becoming quite clear. Their common wish was to *conserve*—actually, to *restore* and keep American institutions and life-styles as they were thought to have been around 1930 (or even earlier). They therefore objected to many of the features of the welfare state (introduced in 1933 by Franklin Roosevelt's "New Deal"—p. 579) and to some of the social and ethical changes that had come about during the period of liberal control (pp. 633–41). *Opposition* was thus a principal part of the conservative program—opposition to the expanding functions of government (business regulation, "welfare" services, deficit spending, high taxes), and opposition to social "permissiveness," feminism, abortion, pornography, and busing to improve racial balance in the public schools.

The *affirmative* aims of American conservatives included a more nationalistic foreign policy, military "superiority" over the Soviet Union, restoring laissez-faire economic policies, strengthening "law and order," rejuvenating the traditional family and morals, and returning to religious "fundamentals." This latter concern reflected a widespread demand for prayers in public schools, massive responses to television preachers, and the "Jesus movement" among many young people. (The religious revival is not unique to this country or to Christianity; it parallels developments in Hindu India and the Islamic nations, notably in the Middle East—pp. 607–8.) American conservatives, generally, expressed less concern over global matters, such as the nuclear arms race, environmental pollution, excessive population growth, poverty, and resource shortages.

The issues between conservatives and liberals found clear focus in the elections of both 1980 and 1984. The Republican party, which had stood in opposition to most of the reforms of the New Deal, remained the political stronghold of conservatism. The Democratic party, beginning with the New Deal, had become identified with liberalism. The Republicans won the presidency for Ronald Reagan in 1980, as well as control over the United States Senate. At the same time, five leading liberal Senators were defeated, including George McGovern, the Democratic presidential candidate of 1972. The election results signaled that conservatives had gained the balance of power in the nation — politically, psychologically, and philosophically.

When Ronald Reagan took office in 1981, he was determined to lead a "second American revolution." He put himself at the head of the powerful forces that already supported conservative ideas, and he appealed to large numbers of voters, in both parties, who were antitax, anti-union, anticommunist, and antigovernment. President Franklin Roosevelt, the "father" of America's welfare state (pp. 579–80), had viewed government as a *positive* agency for solving the nation's problems and aiding its citizens. President Reagan, rejecting that view, declared that "government is not the solution; it is the problem."

The main direction of Reagan's first term was in keeping with that declaration. He sought to cut back on federal services and regulations — and in so doing, reduce taxes. The primary accomplishment of his first year in office was to carry through Congress a sharp reduction in tax rates on personal incomes. While the reduction was "across the board" — twenty-five percent — the largest *amounts* of money were saved by the wealthiest individuals.

The chief result of the Reagan tax cut — for the country — was that federal tax *revenues* fell far below what the government was spending. This put heavy pressure on Congress to make up for the loss in income by reducing spending. In response, Congress did make cuts in social programs, including those for the "truly" needy; but Reagan insisted, at the same time, on large *increases* in military spending. As a result, the federal budget could not be balanced, and the huge annual deficits (money shortages) had to be made up through extravagant government *borrowing*, much of it from foreign investors.

When Reagan came to power in 1981, the *accumulated federal debt* stood at about $1 trillion — after some *fifty* years of moderate increase. In the *eight* years of the Reagan administration, the debt tripled to nearly *$3* trillion. The substantial economic growth of those years was due chiefly to the stimulus of this borrowed money. But it left the country with a mountain of government debt (in addition to an unprecedented level of private debts). Payments of *interest alone* on the federal debt were estimated at $250 billion for the fiscal year 1991 — a sum equal to the appropriation that year for the entire Department of Defense.

Reagan and his advisers downplayed the deficit problem; he promised that his "low tax" policy would eventually correct it. But his Republican successor, elected in 1988, fell heir to the *reality* — as the debt soared ever higher. President George Bush, yielding at last to the views of financial experts around the world, decided (in 1990) to face up to making substantial cuts in the annual deficit. But success in accomplishing this proved to be minimal; the American people, accustomed to living beyond their incomes, were prepared to punish any politicians who voted for higher taxes. Thus, the burden of debt upon the economy — and essential public services — remains a continuing legacy of the Reagan years.

In addition to reducing tax rates, Reagan pushed for *deregulation* of the economy. This was favored by the business community, but contributed to some serious negative results. Lax supervision of the savings and loan industry, for example, was a factor in permitting gross mismanagement and fraud there. And since the Congress had guaranteed depositors' savings accounts, the *losses* to *taxpayers* would run into hundreds of billions of dollars. Reagan sought also to eliminate numerous federal agencies that had been established to safeguard the public (like the Environmental Protection Agency). In most cases he was unable to gain Congressional approval for abolishing them, but he often succeeded in cutting their funds — and in choosing agency heads who would limit their effectiveness. But his most lasting impact was upon the *courts* of the land. During his eight years in office, Reagan was able to name hundreds of federal judges, most of whom shared his conservative political and social views — and whose lifetime tenure on the bench will run many years beyond the time of their appointment.

Aside from domestic affairs, Reagan sought a "revolution" in the nation's military and foreign policies. He wanted, first of all, to "rearm" America — with more and better weapons, both "conventional" and nuclear. By 1980 the nuclear arms race with the Soviet Union had come to a standoff (p. 615). The superpowers had reached rough equality ("parity") in offensive power. But Reagan and his conservative advisers were not satisfied with "parity."

When he became president, he began steps to regain nuclear "superiority" — which the United States had enjoyed right after the Second World War (pp. 587–89). He believed this could be done through a massive buildup of arms: annual military spending *doubled* from $150 billion for the year 1981 to about $300 billion in 1985 — and continued to increase thereafter. The Soviets, though sorely pressed financially, matched the buildup; and the strategic standoff persisted.

With the effort to gain superiority through *offensive* weapons at a dead end, Reagan next proposed (1983) to build a *defensive* system against intercontinental nuclear missiles. This was a return to an earlier idea in the arms race, which had been rejected by both sides in 1972 (the ABM treaty, p. 615). But advances in technology — lasers, computers, space mirrors — had led some weapon scientists to advise the president that another try should be made.

In response, Reagan agreed to give up the "stability" of the existing nuclear balance and seek to construct a space-based system — one that could give the United States a "first-strike" capacity (p. 615). Reagan called his plan (estimated to cost hundreds of billions) the "Strategic Defense Initiative," but it was quickly tagged "Star Wars" by the news media. The Soviets, predictably, protested this new turn in the arms race and tried to raise world opinion against it. They saw it as "destabilizing" and declared that they could not reduce their offensive arsenal if "Star Wars" went ahead. Hence, the hopes of many observers for some *reduction* in nuclear weapons appeared to be dashed by Reagan's "Defense Initiative."

The Star Wars issue was one of the main subjects discussed at the Geneva "summit" meeting (November 1985) between Reagan and a new Soviet leader, Mikhail Gorbachev. This was Reagan's first meeting with a top official of the U.S.S.R., and its purpose was to reduce tension between the two superpowers. During his early years in office, Reagan had turned the previous relation of "détente" (p. 592) into one of hostility. His words and actions had been partly a response to Soviet moves around the world (in Ethiopia, Poland, and Afghanistan); but they reflected, chiefly, his intense anticommunism — going back to his earliest years in politics. As president he aimed, through a military buildup, to deal with the Soviets from a "position of strength" — which meant *superior* strength. He believed that this policy would stop communist "expansionism" — and, by overstraining the Soviet economy, would lead to the undermining of the "evil empire."

However, at the 1985 summit, responding to concessions and fresh initiatives from Gorbachev, Reagan displayed a definite shift in his tone and words to the Soviets. This shift was welcomed by America's European allies and by people everywhere who feared war between the superpowers. It proved to be a critical turning point, built upon later by both leaders, toward slowing down the arms race and ending the Cold War.

On other international fronts, Reagan improved relations with China, the NATO alliance, and anticommunist governments everywhere (including Japan, South Africa, and Chile). In Latin America, he held to a hard line against communists. When the Caribbean island of Grenada fell into a political crisis under its Marxist leaders (1982), he sent United States military forces to occupy the island and install a prodemocratic government there. Though contrary to international law and the United Nations charter, these actions were welcomed by most Grenadans — and cheered by a majority in the United States.

Reagan also defied international law in moves against the Central American republic of Nicaragua.* Though at first denying it, he later admitted that his goal was to help overthrow the established Marxist government there. Reagan steadily raised pressure on Nicaragua (p. 606) with hints of an American invasion and with direct aid to rebel guerrillas (the "Contras"). The president justified these actions by charging that the Cubans and Soviets were building bases in Nicaragua that threatened the United States. Eventually, the suffering Nicaraguan people voted for peace — by defeating the Sandinista party (p. 606) in a free election. A democratic coalition, headed by Violeta Chamorro, came to power in 1990.

In another part of the world, the Philippine Islands, Reagan continued American support for the dictatorial rule of President Ferdinand Marcos. (Reagan's main concern there was to keep United States lease-rights to important military bases in the Philippines.) However, there was a growing Filipino

---

*The International Court of Justice so ruled (by 12–3 vote) in June 1986.

opposition to the corrupt Marcos government — an opposition led, finally, by the courageous Corazon Aquino, widow of an assassinated popular leader. Following a national election in February 1986, the "people's movement," joined by some high military officers, brought about Marcos's removal from office. American forces rescued the tyrant from his capital, Manila, and flew him to the United States. At the same time, the newly elected President Aquino, having agreed to respect the existing military leases, gained official recognition from Washington.

Reagan's deepest frustrations were in the troubled Middle East (pp. 596–99). In 1982 America's ally, Israel, invaded the neighboring country of Lebanon. Its forces cleared out anti-Israeli guerrilla units of the "Palestine Liberation Organization" (PLO) that were based there. But in doing so, they killed thousands of Lebanese civilians and caused heavy damage to towns and cities by bombings. During the Israeli occupation, Reagan ordered American marines to the capital, Beirut, and sent a fleet of warships to remain offshore in the Mediterranean Sea.

These American ("peacekeeping") forces were seen by most Lebanese and other Arabs as military support for the Israeli effort to set up a client (dependent) government in Lebanon. During the battles around Beirut (between pro- and anti-Israeli militias), the marine barracks were a target of snipers; and one night (in 1983) a "terrorist" drove a truck full of explosives into the main barracks building. More than 240 marines died in their beds in one of the worst disasters in Marine Corps history.

The president accepted responsibility for the losses and declared that such terrorist acts would not force the United States to run out on its "commitments." Within a few months, however, American ground and naval forces were pulled out of Lebanon. (The neighboring Arab state of Syria then became the dominant influence there — p. 598.) Israeli troops withdrew gradually; after 1985 they occupied only a small "security" strip north of Israel's border. In 1989 they faced a new and persisting uprising (the "intifada") by Palestinians of the occupied territories (p. 597). In spite of violent episodes and killings, the demands of the Palestinians for a "homeland" continue to be resisted by the Israeli government.

The military, foreign, and domestic actions of the Reagan administration thus proved to be a mix of failures and successes. Nevertheless, widespread support for his conservative policies was demonstrated by his decisive reelection in 1984. His victory, however, was achieved in large part by his exceptional *personal* appeal — his charm, self-confidence, good looks, and speaking ability. The conservative forces, generally, did not fare so well at the polls. In subsequent Congressional elections, they lost their control of the Senate to the Democrats. With Democrats controlling *both* houses of Congress (after 1986), a virtual deadlock developed in the confrontation between conservatives and liberals. George Bush sustained the conservative position by keeping the presidency in Republican hands in the election of 1988, but he has proved unsuccessful in trying to bring about a majority for his party in either the Senate or House of Representatives. The conservative tide thus appears to have run its course in the United States — but the Reagan mark, for good or ill, remains imprinted upon the nation.

The Revolutions in Eastern Europe: Gorbachev

While conservative reforms were gradually taking shape in western Europe and America during the 1980s, the eastern (communist) bloc showed little change on its *surface* — until the end of the decade. Then that region commenced to *explode* in radical changes — political, social, economic, and cultural.

For some seventy years (since the Russian Revolution of 1917) the Communist party grip on the Soviet Union had appeared to be unbreakable. So, too, appeared its forty-year grip on the "satellite" countries of East Germany, Poland, Czechoslovakia, Rumania, Hungary, and Bulgaria. There had been some outspoken dissidents, like Aleksandr Solzhenitsyn (pp. 566, 643), but it seemed that the instruments of control and repression were so systematic and powerful that no *major* change could erupt from below. Yet the "historical surprise" of the century suddenly dawned upon those lands.

Although largely unknown to foreign observers, serious doubts about the viability of the communist system had begun to grow among some of the higher officials of the Soviet party even before 1980. As far back as the 1930s, Nikolai Bukharin had criticized the Stalinist regime and had called for greater flexibility in the economy (p. 565). And after Stalin's death (1953), Nikita Khruschev, as party chief, introduced some measures of relaxation (p. 589). Such views and actions, however, were not sustained by the party as a whole.

It was not until a generation after Khruschev that disenchantment with the system became a rising force. More and more party members (as well as ordinary citizens) were concluding that the long-time promises of communism — and centralized economic control — were not being fulfilled. They viewed with envy the rising prosperity of the capitalist West; they became convinced that *changes had to be made* to rescue their faltering economy. In 1985 the central committee of the party chose Mikhail Gorbachev as their agent of change. He moved quickly in two directions: what he called *glasnost* — the "opening up" (democratization) of Soviet society, and *perestroika* — the "restructuring" of the economy.

With respect to foreign affairs, Gorbachev urged "new thinking" — for his own and other countries. (He supported his words with action by pulling Soviet troops out of Afghanistan in 1988 — p. 608.) The Cold War and its confrontational policies had proved enormously wasteful "dead ends." A new era of *cooperation* in addressing the *real problems* of the planet was called for. These goals, articulated and vigorously pursued by Gorbachev, were the main factors that precipitated the revolutions of eastern Europe — still in progress.

Worldwide recognition of his historic role was symbolized by the awarding to Gorbachev of the Nobel Peace Prize in 1990.

The progress of change within the Soviet Union itself was uneven. Gorbachev had powerful domestic critics on both "left" and "right" (those who wanted to move *faster* and those who tried to *hold back* reforms). Nevertheless, swift action was taken to implement glasnost. Thousands of political prisoners were released and free expression and free assembly were permitted. Perhaps the most significant constitutional reform was the abolition of the Communist party's monopoly on political power (p. 567). New elections took place throughout the U.S.S.R., with rival nonparty groups vying for office.

Gorbachev's principal frustrations lay in the area of perestroika — the restructuring of the economy. Some individuals wanted to move as quickly as possible from the existing system of centralized control to a full-fledged "market economy." Others believed such a rapid move would be too disruptive and painful to workers and consumers; they favored a "go-slow" approach. Gorbachev, walking the tightrope, proposed a plan combining features from both sides. In October 1990 his compromise was approved by the newly elected Soviet Parliament — and he was authorized, as president, to set it in motion by executive decree. Up until that time, the public was becoming increasingly discontented as supplies in the shops continued to dwindle.

The prospects for success of the economic reforms were further shadowed by the unraveling of the ties that held the Soviet Union together. Gorbachev's general policy of repudiating the use of *military force* to keep the country together opened the door to long pent-up desires for independence from the multinational state. The Baltic republics (p. 584) were the first to declare their own individual *sovereignty*. The Russian Republic, the largest by far (p. 566), quickly followed, along with the Ukraine, Georgia, Azerbaijan, and most of the other republics. How could a countrywide economic plan work if the now "sovereign" states of the Soviet Union each took off upon its *own* plan? This dilemma was highlighted in the case of the Russian Republic. Boris Yeltsin, a former Communist turned radical reformer, was elected president of that republic in 1991. He declared, with the support of the republic's parliament, that Russia would press toward a market economy by a much faster route.

The momentous happenings of August 1991 gave added force to Yeltsin's plan. The political "right," backed by the secret police (KGB), ranking army officers, and Communist party conservatives, launched a coup against Gorbachev and the reformers in the Russian Republic. But the coup lasted only seventy-two hours as thousands of Muscovites filled the streets to defend their parliament — and the deployed army units were pulled back. Opinion elsewhere in the country, and in the world, strongly condemned the effort to overthrow the legal order. The failed coup thus damaged the reactionaries — and gave decisive impetus to the supporters of democracy, market economy, and independence for the constituent republics. Within days, the reformers initiated far-reaching measures: to deprive the Communist party of any effective role in government; alter drastically the functions of the secret police;

loosen controls over the media; and ensure that the armed forces were kept under the command of loyal officers. The way was also cleared for achievement of complete independence by the individual republics — whose elected leaders would now be free to negotiate their relations with one another and with foreign countries.

The unraveling of the Soviet Union was paralleled by the breaking away of the "satellite" countries of eastern Europe. They had been held as "allies" of the U.S.S.R. by *force* since the end of the Second World War (1945). At that time, the Soviet leaders had viewed them as a needed "buffer" — to help protect their war-ravaged homeland from any future attack by a resurgent Germany and the West. The economies of these states were suffering from the same growing paralysis that the Soviets were enduring. Once Gorbachev signaled that force would no longer be used to hold them in tow, popular movements exploded against their communist regimes (all the more despised because they were *imposed* by a *foreign power*). Thus, democratic revolutions (mostly nonviolent) followed in 1989 and 1990 in Poland, East Germany, Czechoslovakia, Hungary, Rumania, and Bulgaria. Though Yugoslavia had not been under the control of the Warsaw Pact, that country took a similar course of democratization — and *separation* into its component republics.

New Dangers and New Opportunities of the 1990s

These dramatic events were important and challenging to the citizens of those individual countries. They raised challenges as well in the broader arena of European and world affairs. The wholesale overthrow of a major, once-dynamic ideology (Marxism) had repercussions far beyond eastern Europe. The virtual coming apart of one of the two superpowers also had an unsettling impact upon international diplomacy and the global balance of power. And a special effect followed from the reunification of Germany, which occurred in October 1990. This was a direct result of the anticommunist revolutions and was adroitly managed by Helmut Kohl, chancellor of the Federal Republic (West Germany). Though apparently inevitable, the merger raised old fears — memories of what a united Germany did to Europe in two world wars of the twentieth century. Leaders in Europe and the United States hoped to keep that nation in bounds, through placing it in a cooperating role within some sort of federated Europe (pp. 616–17). But there was no assurance of such an outcome — or of the ultimate shape of the other postrevolutionary regimes.

Thus it can be seen that the post-Cold War era provides many uncertainties. The former "balance of terror" between the superpowers was fearsome, but at least it was well understood and relatively stable. With the erosion of a powerful controlling power within the Soviet Union and across eastern Europe, there looms the possibility of regional and local forces pulling apart the fabric of civilized order. Rising ethnic and national feelings, repressed for several generations, may burst into uncontrollable and destructive conflicts.

Warning examples have already occurred in the U.S.S.R.: in 1988 an enclave of Armenians, within the republic of Azerbaijan, saw violent clashes between the ethnic minority and the majority — with successive rounds of reprisals and counterreprisals. The newly declared "sovereign" republics now feel free to fight over boundary lines, minority rights, economic resources, and religious differences — while seeking to create their own *armed forces* to support their claims and counterclaims. And beyond the U.S.S.R., the "satellite" states have a long history of lethal disputes among themselves; some may now be moved to redress old injuries and "injustices" by the way of war.

On the other hand, as opposed to these prospects of spreading anarchy in international relations, there is an alternative prospect of better international *cooperation*. The unifying moves in western Europe, economic and political, have already been indicated in this chapter (pp. 616–17). And with the Cold War properly buried, the United States and a restructured "successor state" to the Soviet Union *could* combine their strengths and work together toward solving many of the critical problems facing this planet.

One of those problems is *war* itself. In September 1990, with an unprecedented show of unity and determination, the Americans led a coalition of powers within the United Nations (including the U.S.S.R.) to declare and enforce a total *trade embargo* against an aggressor state (Iraq). When, after five months of trial, this measure appeared insufficient to compel Saddam Hussein, the Iraqi leader, to withdraw his army from neighboring Kuwait, the U.N. Security Council authorized the coalition powers to resort to military action (January 1991). These forces, headed by the United States, quickly and decisively routed the Iraqis (Operation "Desert Storm").

This successful demonstration of *collective action* in turning back aggression raised hopes for developing effective means for providing global security. President Bush hailed the new level of international cooperation as the beginning of a "New World Order" (NWO). Converting this promise into reality will prove to be a formidable task; one has only to recall the fate of similar aspirations of two earlier presidents in this century: Woodrow Wilson (pp. 580–82) and Franklin Roosevelt (p. 586).

In a related area, the United States and the U.S.S.R. have made a start in agreeing to reduce their nuclear arsenals — with a view to turning away from their huge expenditures on weapons and working, instead, to meet the needs of civilian society. Other fields remain to be addressed: ecological concerns, overpopulation, widespread poverty, limited natural resources, and urgent health matters. But the end of the Cold War has brought at least the *hope* that new opportunities will overpower the new dangers of the 1990s — and beyond.

15

The Revolution
in Western Culture

The global transformation that came in the wake of two world wars was not limited to military, economic, and political matters. It brought changes in philosophy and religion, social roles and relationships, and the creative arts. These changes appeared first in Western culture and soon spread throughout the world.

RECONSTRUCTION IN WESTERN PHILOSOPHY AND RELIGION

The scientific findings of the early twentieth century affected nonscientists as well as scientists. It altered their worldview and their confidence in established knowledge. The common thread in the new scientific ideas is that the universe is not as knowable or as orderly as had been previously thought. Educated persons were coming to realize that Isaac Newton's "world-machine" (pp. 420–21) was as much a creation of the human mind as the God-centered universe of Dante (pp. 264–65).

Einsteinian theories had already contradicted the older concept of "absolute" physical laws (p. 523). And in 1927 the German physicist Werner Heisenberg announced the "principle of indeterminacy," which came from his findings that the motion of subatomic particles could not be predicted with certainty and that the very act of observing them affected their motion. It was not just a matter of the complexity of things or the limitations of their instruments; the new physics pointed to a radical disconnection between the way things *are* and our ability to *know* them. How could we imagine space that is at once finite and unbounded? Or light that is at once particle and wave? Researchers, of course, continued to produce huge amounts of data that could be put to practical use. But spiraling knowledge carried humankind ever further from a "true" grasp of the universe as a whole.

Philosophers, reflecting the new skepticism of the scientists, virtually abandoned efforts to explain objective "reality." They generally agreed that no such explanation was possible. The two most influential schools of philosophy in the twentieth century were those of the "linguistic analysts" and the "existentialists." The former held that nothing significant could be said about "being in general"; they focused attention, therefore, on limited intellectual problems, especially the applications of symbolic logic. The existentialists (p. 630) insisted that our very humanity prevents us from seeing things *in themselves.*

As in all times of change, inherited myths and ways died hard. The *idea of progress*, born of the Enlightenment, still persisted — especially in the United States. As we saw in Chapter 13, "old-fashioned" *liberalism* in Europe had become discredited by 1919 (p. 557); and the void was filled, in part, by Marxism, fascism, or extreme nationalism.

Some Westerners, in disillusionment, returned to traditional religion. The crimes and horrors of world wars and revolutions heightened their awareness of "evil" and man's "sinful nature." Hence, certain religious leaders rekindled Augustinian teachings (pp. 162–64) and called for a resurgence of orthodoxy and ritualism. But neither this effort, nor "consensus" Christianity, nor "born-again" fundamentalism wholly satisfied the intellectual challenge of the times.

The Implications of Depth Psychology: Freud

The source of the twentieth-century challenge lay as much in the new psychology as in the new physics: John Locke's simplistic view of the mind (p. 425) was as completely superseded as Newton's mechanics. The major figure of modern psychology was Sigmund Freud, whom we referred to in Chapter 12 as a pioneer in the discipline (p. 530). Freud was a practicing physician whose initial interest was in curing the mental ailments of his patients. In the course of his clinical work, however, he discovered aspects of the human mind and personality that had long lain hidden. Freud published his significant *The Interpretation of Dreams* in 1900, but his broader impact on thought was not felt until after the First World War.

Though Freudian psychology has been disputed and amended (especially his views on female sexuality), much of its substance gained acceptance. Freud held that human beings are not rational machines, consciously directing their appetites and will. On the contrary, reason plays a relatively minor and subordinate role in most people, for the conscious life and its expression are but a covering of the "real" person. Beneath the surface are unconscious and subconscious drives, which are the chief engines of motivation; these include the desire for sexual gratification, love, power, and death. In addition, behavior is influenced by physiological responses and acquired attitudes.

Society, Freud wrote in *Civilization and Its Discontents* (1930), compels individuals to *repress* many of their "natural" desires. In a highly organized civilization, these repressions take a heavy toll from the individual; yet without some repression civilization would be impossible. The "normal" person accepts the traumatic damage without breaking down, but the neurotic (or psychotic) person cannot do so. The Freudian view of the individual in relationship to society posed a sharp challenge to traditional morals, religion, and politics. All those had rested on a base of supposed rationality and conscious control. According to the new view, those traditions were not geared to psychological reality and might therefore be dangerously false. Freud believed that human personality would suffer even under "enlightened" codes of behavior, because there exists an inescapable conflict between personal drives and the social order. Hence, "perfectionist" social dreams can never be fulfilled, and the goal of complete individual happiness is a tormenting mirage.

Rejection of Traditional Systems and Values: Nietzsche, Kierkegaard, Sartre

Friedrich Nietzsche, a German philosopher who died in 1900, lived in Freud's time and shared many of his views on human nature. And the impact of both men was most strongly felt in the *twentieth* century. Nietzsche's influence was perhaps wider than Freud's, for he challenged not only the traditional view of human nature but the entire institutional and ideological heritage of the West. When he said, "God is dead," he meant not only the God of the Judeo-Christian faith but the whole range of philosophic *absolutes*, from Plato down to his own day. Because all Western values had been linked to those ultimate "eternal" values, they crashed to earth with "God's death." Facing the void alone, thought Nietzsche, people value but one goal: *power*. Thus would he explain the ceaseless drive for power by individuals and nations.

Nietzsche's most revealing work is his most poetic, *Thus Spake Zarathustra* (1884). In it he allowed his unconscious self to speak freely, without regard to logical organization. The book is a flowing stream of images, symbols, and visions, some of which have not yet been fully understood. In *Zarathustra* and other works, notably *Beyond Good and Evil*, Nietzsche considered the various conditions of human beings and their relation to the universe. He was one of the first thinkers to stress the *absurdity* of human existence: the inability of our reason to comprehend our surroundings — though we are born to try.

All existing systems, whether based on reason or revelation, appeared false to Nietzsche. He focused his attack on the bourgeois civilization of the late nineteenth century: on science, industrialism, democracy, and Christianity. As an untamed *individualist*, he rejected theism (belief in God as Creator and Ruler), mechanism, and any other idea that would deny human freedom. What he hated most was the reduction of people to narrowly specialized creatures and their subjection to a Christian ("slave") morality. Nietzsche presented these particular ideas most fully in *The Genealogy of Morals*, published in 1887. He longed for a return to the heroic Greek idea of the "whole man"; this goal could be achieved only by the overthrow of current values and the permitting of determined individuals ("supermen") to recover their wholeness through disciplined struggle and sacrifice. Nietzsche left unanswered many questions as to how these aims could be accomplished. His importance lay primarily in his bold challenge to "sacred" beliefs and in his shrill protest against the smothering of the individual by the "herd."

A thinker of different temperament was Søren Kierkegaard, a Danish theologian-philosopher. Though he was born a generation earlier than Nietzsche, the influence of both was felt at about the same time. Writing from widely separated points of view, they were the forerunners of twentieth-century "existentialism." It was, in fact, Kierkegaard who gave special meaning to the word "existence" (though his works were scarcely read until after the First World War). He defined "existence" as a unique attribute of human beings. They alone exist "outside" nature, possessing the power to *think* about the universe and to *choose* what they will believe and how they will act. This very freedom, thought Kierkegaard, gives individuals both responsibility and anxiety (*Angst*). They must suffer anxiety, for they can never be certain about the consequences of their own free choice.

Kierkegaard, like Nietzsche, attacked the rationalism and determinism of Hegel's philosophy (pp. 473–74). He branded as ridiculous the generalization that the world is rational and that it represents the unfolding of a divine plan. How can any person, a particular part of an uncompleted scheme, know what the completed form will be? If the world *is* a system, only God can know it! It follows, therefore, that people cannot presume that they occupy a specific place in a known scheme of things. Everyone must act, rather, from day to day, as best one can, always *unsure* of the consequences.

Kierkegaard had a profound influence on Christian theologians, but his writings appealed also to individuals of agnostic or atheistic leanings — especially, modern "existentialists." These people were impressed by Kierkegaard's assertion of the individual's nakedness and loneliness in the universe — "condemned to be free." They saw the individual increasingly depersonalized and alienated by the forces of modern society: huge economic organizations, mechanization, bureaucratization, and the high level of abstraction encountered in most phases of living. Following this observation, the existentialists sought to awaken in each person a sense of individuality and the possibility of an "authentic" life.

Jean-Paul Sartre, more than any other writer, brought the existentialist view to the educated public (through *Nausea*, *No Exit*, and other works). Sartre, partly through his own experience in the French Resistance against the Nazis, came to believe that personal commitment and action are essential to genuine living. He felt this especially during the war, in his daily decision-making and risk-taking. He proved to himself that, even in extreme situations, the individual possesses the *irreducible liberty* of saying "no" to overpowering force. Such a force, Sartre inferred, might be an occupying army — or it might be the conformist cultures in which most of us live (p. 513). The freedom to say "no," even to "disaffiliate" oneself from the system, is the individual's ultimate defense against being swallowed up as a *person*.

Sartre himself in later years severely modified his wartime view of the *degree* of individual freedom. He conceded (as a Marxist) the powerful grip of social conditioning—yet insisted that each individual nevertheless has the ability (and the *responsibility*) to "make something out of what is made of him." Sartre's idea of limited freedom contrasted with the optimistic, rational liberalism of the Enlightenment (pp. 422–23). It was closer to the "tragic view" of the ancient Greek poets and dramatists, who likewise saw pain and absurdity in the human condition, yet held that one remains *responsible* for what one is and does within an established order (pp. 77–78).

Revision in Christian Theology: Barth, Tillich

The blow to "systems" and "absolutes" in philosophy was paralleled by a rethinking of Christian doctrines. We have seen that Kierkegaard opened the way to philosophic existentialism; he was the pioneer also of profound *theological* changes. A deeply committed Christian, Kierkegaard insisted that rational proofs for the existence of God were irrelevant. The logic of Aristotle, Aquinas, or Descartes (p. 416) left him unconvinced. In order to become a Christian, asserted Kierkegaard, one must make an inward choice: *a leap into faith*. All other human choices, he insisted, are secondary to that *one*. And that choice must be made without knowledge of whether it will lead to salvation or damnation. Thus, a *true* Christian lives in a kind of despair. (Kierkegaard attacked most modern churches for enjoying and preaching a "comfortable," but counterfeit Christianity—"the *opposite* of what is in the New Testament.")

The leading theologians of the twentieth century advanced, in their own ways, this fundamental view of Kierkegaard's. While respecting the value of reason in connection with scientific and practical affairs, they insisted that it cannot answer the questions of "ultimate concern." Karl Barth, an influential Swiss Protestant theologian, stressed human dependence on God, but concluded that there is no *straight line* from the mind of man to God: "What we say breaks apart constantly . . . producing paradoxes which are held together in seeming unity only by agile and arduous running to and fro on our part." Rather than preaching that there are compelling reaons for believing in God, religious thinkers like Barth would say: "This community of faith invites you to share in its venture of trust and commitment."

In addition to seeing religious faith as a matter of trust instead of something "objectively" proved, many theologians of the twentieth century sought to reconstruct the ancient symbols and myths. They believed that the traditional Christian image of God and the universe had crumbled under the bombardment of scientific findings and historical scholarship. The "vision of reality" expressed in the Bible no longer served as a believable frame of reference for many educated people. They were convinced that if Christianity was to endure as a meaningful teaching, it would have to create images that fitted with scientific knowledge.

To some religious thinkers, this was another way of saying "God is dead." For the German-American theologian Paul Tillich, the phrase meant simply that the ancient image of God had passed into history. This did not mean that Christianity was obsolete, but that it had to find, as it had found in the past, new forms to carry its message to the living. The idea of a Supreme Being — "out there," or "up there" — is not an essential part of Christian truth. Tillich dissented from Barth's view that God lives *outside* humankind; he insisted that God is not a special *part* of creation, but, rather, Ultimate Reality itself. Modern men and women, Tillich suggested in his *Shaking of the Foundations* (1948), must look for God as the *ground of all being*, as the *depth* and *center* of their culture and their lives.

The Movement Toward Unity: Pope John XXIII

Though the Protestant churches were more absorbed than the Roman Catholic Church in theological reappraisal, all the major branches of Christianity gave serious attention to closer relations with one another. The period following the Second World War, especially, was marked by a lessening of interfaith hostility and a growing sense of Christian *oneness*. This was due in part to the consciousness that all churches were being challenged, as never before, by secularism in general and Marxism in particular. Religious leaders could see that many people were turning toward agnosticism (no belief) and that a more united front would strengthen the appeal and power of Christianity.

On the Protestant side an important step was taken in 1948 when the World Council of Churches was formally established at Geneva, Switzerland. One of its primary purposes was to bring some two hundred separate denominations into closer association. It included in its supporting membership most Protestant churches, Anglicans, and Eastern Orthodox groups. The Roman Catholic Church held aloof at first but later opened formal relations between the Vatican and Geneva.

The election of Pope John XXIII in 1958 gave a decisive boost to the movement toward unity. As leader of the largest organized body of Christians, John was in a position to aid greatly, and he did so with the full force of his warm personality. Though he did not abandon the papal claim to being the "one shepherd" of the Christian flock, John broke down centuries-old barriers to communication with Protestants. At the same time he started a sweeping program for *aggiornamento* (bringing the Roman Church up to date). This included a fresh attitude of humility and affection toward the "separated brethren" (no longer "heretics") — and toward "men of good will" beyond the fold (no longer "atheists"). John opened windows and let fresh air into the Vatican, while introducing a new era of hopeful dialogue between the Roman Church and all other Christian groups.

The most complete expression of Pope John's thought and feeling was his encyclical *Pacem in Terris*, issued in 1963. This document, an extraordinary appeal to reason and humane sentiments, called for the harmonious *coexistence* of all faiths and social systems. John's work for peace, both religious and secular, was carried on after his death by Pope Paul VI and the reforming Second Vatican Council (1963–65). Paul dramatized the new responsiveness of the papacy by breaking its historic confinement to Rome and making visits to such places as the Holy Land, India, Latin America, and the United Nations headquarters in New York. Paul secured friendlier relations with the Eastern Orthodox churches and renounced the traditional Christian hostility toward Jews. On issues of Catholic faith and morals he remained a conservative.

Equally conservative was his successor in 1978, John Paul II. Formerly the *primate* (chief Catholic official) of Poland, he was the first non-Italian to be elected pope in over four hundred years. A learned and appealing figure, John Paul declared that he would build upon the work of his two predecessors, John XXIII and Paul VI. He called on the clergy to support traditional rules and roles, but he disappointed millions of liberal Catholics eager for some hint of change on such pressing issues as clerical celibacy, women in the priesthood, and the use of contraceptives.

Though insisting that the Catholic clergy must not hold any *political office*, John Paul traveled widely around the world and freely expressed political views. He consistently urged national leaders to avoid war, and he approved an important "pastoral letter" of the Catholic bishops of the United States condemning nuclear weapons. Their letter, *The Challenge of Peace*, was sent out in 1983 as a "teaching" of the Church. It opposes *any* "first use" of nuclear arms (p. 615) and appeals for immediate international agreements to end their testing and production.

THE SHIFTING WAYS OF SOCIETY

Religious and philosophical teachings, no matter what their character, did not check the continuing social revolution in the West. *Technology* was the chief engine of this revolution, but psychologists, educators, and advertisers accelerated the rate of change.

The New Sexuality

The most visible, and perhaps the most profound of these changes were new sexual attitudes and practices (the "sexual revolution"). Sex has been a demanding concern in all societies: how to value sex, and how to deny, repress, or channel it. Sex can be regarded as any or all of the following: an instinctive impulse, a source of pleasure, the means of creating children, an expression of physical love, the bond of faithfulness in marriage, a sign of gender, and a personal property. Social and moral codes of behavior aim to contain and balance the multiple functions of both male and female sexuality.

During the nineteenth century, while scientific and technological innovations were altering the economy and society in the West (pp. 500–513), religious and civic leaders made a determined effort to prevent changes in traditional sexual mores. Thus, during the "Victorian Age" (1840–1900), a cloak of puritan morality obscured the realities of sexual behavior. It was Sigmund Freud who, by reporting his clinical observations, showed that *sexual repression* could cause psychic illness (p. 628). Freud, by bringing sexuality into the open, revealed it as a normal and powerful force in human behavior.

As the twentieth century progressed, other physicians, psychologists, and educators began to reexamine the human organism and its needs. They challenged all types of authoritarian controls over individuals — not only in sexual matters but in personal behavior as a whole. Traditional taboos began to fall, especially after the two world wars; the age of "permissiveness" and "self-fulfillment" was at hand. With moral, social, and legal restraints loosened, men and women gave freer rein to their instincts for self-gratification. In 1960 scientific medicine gave a liberating boost to worry-free sex: the "pill" made sex easy and "safe." (In the 1980s, however, the appearance of the "AIDS" disease [pp. 639–40] brought fresh worries to the sexual scene.)

The sexual revolution was quickly exploited by profit-seeking publishers, theatrical producers, broadcasters, and filmmakers. Sex manuals flourished; no one any longer had to be ignorant. Magazines and books catered to the newly released desire for titillation, and the walls of literary censorship were leveled in nearly every Western nation (p. 644). Pornography, hard and soft, became readily available — in both verbal and pictorial forms. The "ultimate" in pictorial porno seems to have been reached in X-rated video tapes — designed for home use.

Among magazines, the most respectable and successful in the United States is *Playboy*, first issued in 1953. Its self-made publisher, Hugh Hefner, also built a thriving entertainment business around his magazine — geared to the theme of guilt-free sensual enjoyment. His Playboy "philosophy" is a modern form of historic hedonism (pp. 68–69).

The new hedonism reaches, of course, beyond the frontiers of sexuality. Huge industries have been built around the popular hunger for every sort of pleasure. Given good health and sufficient income, people in the West today enjoy limitless opportunities for personal gratification. There is, unfortunately, another and dark side of the pleasures of freedom. This is best exemplified by the widespread consumption of illegal drugs throughout the "free world." The drug problem is now recognized as a serious threat to the health of millions of individuals — and to the functioning of every technological society. It also feeds a related problem: *organized crime*. Though enormous human and financial resources have been marshaled to fight against both drugs and crime, the battle seems far from won. A leading cause of this failure is the stress placed on *personal freedom* within most democratic countries. Though unlawful acts are supposed to be beyond its permitted "limits," the *dynamic* of freedom tends to counter the efforts of law *enforcement*. Thus, many activities ("evils") that "good citizens" deplore — such as drugs, crime, pornography — are closely linked to freedom itself.

The Youth Culture

The changing ways of Western society have had their main effect on men and women born after the Second World War. Their fathers and mothers were as a rule too rooted in older ways to alter their own views or behavior. But the immediate postwar generation, in most Western countries, grew up within a radically different culture. Especially for the middle classes, the postwar period was a time of widespread affluence and leisure. The dominant materialistic morality placed high value on competitiveness, achievement, and "success." As pointed out by the "existentialists" (p. 630), it was an era of bureaucracy, depersonalization, manipulation, and social "adjustment." All this, moreover, was seen and heard each day in the "instant" world of radio, television, films, records, and tapes.

While parents expected their children to accept these cultural gifts with appreciation — and many of them did — a substantial minority experienced a disturbing sense of *alienation*. Not having to struggle for a livelihood, as most of their Depression-reared fathers and mothers had done, they found more time to reflect on the surrounding culture and their relation to it. These young people found much to object to. Taking for granted the ability of the "system" to satisfy their basic physical needs and pleasures, they saw in its workings a lessening of their personal identity and a great deal of hypocrisy, violence, and injustice.

These perceptions arose at a time when the philosophical and psychological barriers to doubt and idol-breaking had largely dissolved, under the influence of thinkers like Freud, Sartre, and Tillich. By the 1960s many among the postwar generation felt free to move in their own way — toward creating a "counterculture." While uncertain and groping, they appeared to share some central goals: humaneness in personal relations, self-discovery and independence, sexual freedom and equality, simple enjoyments, love of nature, and peace. As a badge of these beliefs, the young revolted against adult styles of dress and began to develop styles of their own. The long hair, beards, fatigue jackets, and jeans — so repugnant to older believers in clean-shaven, starch-shirted efficiency and conformity — were symbolic challenges to the established order of values.

By the 1970s a new life-style was taking shape among many young people across the Western world. It allowed for a wide range of individual differences, but it displayed certain characteristics: an underlying "philosophy," flexibility and informality in family relations, an esoteric ("in") vocabulary, and its own brands of pop music (p. 656). The young tended to be suspicious of governments, corporations, and military organizations. And they often scorned intellectualism in favor of "spontaneous experience."

The freshness of their approach and their willingness to try something new offered promise of creative ideas and remedies where old methods had failed. The parents of this youth, having recovered from their initial shock and disapproval, seemed increasingly to recognize some promise in their children.

In the United States, for example, a constitutional amendment was passed in 1971 lowering the voting age from twenty-one to eighteen years.

The youth activity found its focus in colleges and universities; from there it spread, in considerable measure, to the rest of society. Students thus formed a leading part of the larger youth culture, but much of their concern naturally was with the campus environment. Universities had mushroomed after the Second World War. They had become, especially in the United States, vast aggregations of researchers, teachers, and students. They represented hundreds of millions of dollars in capital investment and served as the principal workshops for the production and spread of specialized knowledge. Many students saw their university as an example of corporate bureaucracy — a huge machine that reduced the individual to a *number*. They also saw it as a service center ("multiversity") for the larger society — preparing technicians for business and industry, conducting research for the military establishment, and turning young people into pliable servants of the state. Individual courses and curricular requirements often appeared to them as arbitrary and sterile — lacking in "relevance."

In the 1960s student discontent was translated into protest — then rebellion — at many educational centers around the world. In the United States, most adults first learned of the crisis through news reports from one of the most distinguished public institutions of learning, the University of California at Berkeley. The "Free Speech Movement" of 1964 sought a larger exercise of student political rights on campus; it also demanded (among other things) that the highly regarded and highly paid professors spend more of their time *teaching students*. Demonstrations, sit-ins, and classroom "strikes" followed in support of these demands.

The protests spread from Berkeley to Columbia, Harvard, MIT, and hundreds of other campuses. "Local" demands often were combined with demands on the nation as a whole: end the war in Vietnam (pp. 603–4), check the power of the "military-industrial complex," stop discrimination against blacks and other minorities. The student actions were generally led by small numbers of committed radicals, who hoped to bring on a general dislocation and change of the social order. Their immediate demands, however, often had sufficient merit and attractiveness to win the support of "moderate" students as well. When college administrations overreacted, still larger numbers of students joined the action.

Protest fever ran high in 1969 and reached a climax in May 1970, immediately following the United States invasion of Cambodia. In response to student violence at Kent State University (Ohio), National Guardsmen were called in to restore order. During a "clearing maneuver," they shot and killed four students; a few days later, state patrolmen killed two black youths in a confrontation at Jackson State College (Mississippi). A severe reaction against the student movement promptly set in. Many Americans were shocked by the killings; others blamed the students for damaging property and thus bringing on the ugly consequences.

After Kent State "the movement" lost much of its force. Most students recoiled from the violent turn it had taken; others became convinced it had reached a dead end; still others thought the "system" had been opened up a bit. Actually, the American student protests of the 1960s seldom achieved great immediate successes. In many instances, however, they gave added force to university self-reform that expanded student rights and benefits.

In Europe, Japan, and Latin America, during these same years, students protested against grossly inadequate facilities and outmoded curriculums. They also sought wider power over national affairs. A student revolt at Paris in 1968 very nearly toppled the government of President de Gaulle; strikes and demonstrations had to be forcibly put down in Mexico City and Tokyo. Discontent and protest are by no means novel among university students. But seldom before had protest been linked so closely to the profound alienation of youth from the established culture and order.

In the 1970s college campuses, particularly in the United States, grew peaceful once again. Some observers saw in this a return to the comparative apathy and conformism of the 1950s, but the reality was more complex. Students generally were reacting to the abnormal level of social concern that had marked the preceding decade. They withdrew to more personal concerns: to careers, greater "inner awareness," or even to self-centered ways that have been called "narcissistic" (the "me" generation). Students were sobered, too, by the fewer job opportunities in the late 1970s, and in the 1980s preparing for a "good" *job* became the first concern of a majority of students. But another important reason for their changed attitude and conduct was that most of them now *possessed* the freedoms of life-style that previous students had worked for in the sixties.

The Women's Movement

The youth culture, in its core values, was linked to the long tradition of *humanism* in the West (pp. 318–20). And that tradition, in its current expression, supports equality for both young and old — and for both *women* and *men*. It is a cruel yet undeniable historic fact that women have suffered severe deprivation in most civilizations; education and political rights have been withheld from them, and the professions (except the "oldest" one) have been generally closed to them. In the United States, after the close of the Civil War (1865), some energetic feminists undertook a long and painful campaign to win equality of opportunity with men. Women gradually moved into jobs in industry, commerce, and education and began to insist on broader legal and political rights.

Their demand for the right to vote (suffrage) met with strong resistance — from some females as well as males. Opponents charged that the feminine intellect was unable to deal with problems of government and that political equality with men would diminish feminine charm and loosen family ties. But aggressive leaders like Susan B. Anthony and her marching "suffragettes" pushed on toward their goal. Finally, the politicians responded. Impressed by the contributions of women to the American effort in the First World War, Congress at war's end proposed the Nineteenth Amendment to the Constitution. Eliminating all restrictions on voting based on *sex*, the Amendment was ratified by the states in 1920. Since then most other Western nations (and Japan) have extended the suffrage to women, but the female vote, by itself, appeared to make little immediate difference in the course of politics and legislation.

Interest in women's rights in America was subdued for some forty years after approval of the Nineteenth Amendment. But in the 1960s efforts started up again, and by the early 1970s a women's "liberation movement" was in full swing. Social conditions had altered a great deal since 1920: more women were working outside the home, and improved contraceptive devices (as well as easier abortions) were making it practicable for women to control their traditional role of childbearing.

At first the expanding ideas and goals of feminism were limited to a small number of "emancipated" women; but books, magazines, and the mass media shortly aroused the enthusiasm of hundreds of thousands. A key work, *The Second Sex*, by the French author Simone de Beauvoir, called worldwide attention to numerous false assumptions about women. But it was chiefly *The Feminine Mystique*, published in 1963 by an American, Betty Friedan, that sparked the popular response. She pointed to the social and psychological pressures that kept women "in the home," the false notions about female sexuality, and the persisting stereotypes of female intellect and behavior.

The women's movement — in part organized, in part unorganized — employed both propaganda and political action. Its leaders demanded an end to discrimination in legal rights, education, jobs, and politics. Feminists in the United States achieved a political success in bringing about the passage in Congress of a proposed "Equal Rights" amendment to the Constitution (ERA); it was submitted to the fifty states for ratification in 1972. Opposition to ERA came from men and women with traditional views, plus some women who feared it might take away from them such existing advantages as exemption from military conscription, protective laws for women in hazardous occupations, and other established legal benefits. The proposed amendment failed (narrowly) to win approval by at least thirty-eight states, as required by the Constitution for adoption. President Ronald Reagan and the Republican party have opposed ERA; but the Democratic leaders have supported it, and they reintroduced the amendment in Congress in 1985 and in subsequent years. The ultimate fate of the proposal remains in question.

Feminism embraces a wide spectrum of beliefs about social institutions (like marriage and the family), sexual relations, and life-styles. But contrary to what is alleged by some critics of the movement, very few feminists desire to *exchange* roles with men. Most of them desire, rather, to open all social roles to *both* sexes. An increasing number of men, for their part, express agreement with this goal and view its achievement as an enrichment of life for themselves as well as for women. In keeping with this growing feeling for sharing, family relations and responsibilities have become more flexible than in earlier times. In fact, the traditional family unit itself is being challenged by variant forms: the one-person household, the childless household, and the single-parent household are rising in numbers.

Probably the most controversial issue affecting American women during the 1980s and early 1990s was *abortion*. In most parts of the world abortion is and has been permitted, but in the United States it had been illegal up until 1973 — though it was in fact widely practiced. In that year, however, the anti-abortion laws of two states, Texas and Georgia, were under challenge in the federal courts — on the grounds that they violated the Constitutional protection of a woman's rights. The key decision of the Supreme Court, by a 7–2 vote, concluded that no state could prevent a woman from having an abortion during the first six months of her pregnancy. The Texas and Georgia laws were therefore declared invalid, and this principle obviously extended to similar laws in other states as well.

The landmark case (Roe *v.* Wade) was hailed by feminists and others as a triumph for a woman's "right to control her own body." But a fierce opposition to the ruling also erupted — from many church groups and individuals who asserted that a fetus is a *person* and therefore abortion is *murder*. They protested actively (under the banner of "pro-life") and were encouraged during the Reagan years to expect changes in the judicial makeup of the Supreme Court. Reagan's conservative appointments to the high bench (p. 620) did bring about a decided shift in its outlook on abortion and other civil rights matters. In a series of cases in 1989 and 1990 the Court reopened the issues raised earlier by Roe *v.* Wade and indicated that some state laws relating to abortions could be ruled Constitutional. It was even hoped by the antiabortionists that Roe *v.* Wade might be overturned in its entirety. The issue, still unsettled in 1991, continued to stir bitter debate throughout the nation and became a critical factor in electoral politics. Groups active for the cause of "planetary survival" generally support the "pro-*choice*" position, because they view legal abortion as one of the necessary means for checking the world's population explosion (pp. 611–13).

The women's movement, along with growing sexual permissiveness in the West, encouraged the rise of still another social movement — "gay" liberation. Homosexuals, historically subject to contempt and abuse, called for the right to live freely according to their own sexual natures. In the 1970s, "gays" (male) and "lesbians" (female) sought changes in laws and institutional practices that would prohibit acts of discrimination against them. Because their aims ran counter to traditional Judeo-Christian moral teachings and ingrained social attitudes, the movement to win public acceptance for sexual diversity encountered severe hostility. This feeling was intensified in the 1980s by the sudden appearance of a mysterious viral disease that seemed to affect, mainly, homosexual men. Called "AIDS" (Acquired Immune Deficiency Syndrome), this disease is transmitted through bodily fluids and is almost always fatal. Thus, health fears have been added to traditional prejudices toward gays, dimming prospects for further advances against discrimination.

Beliefs in Violence and Nonviolence

The frustrations of youth, women, and other "out-groups" gave rise in the 1960s and 1970s to a widespread rejection not only of some institutions but of the accepted ways of *altering* institutions. The liberal-democratic tradition had generally given citizens a healthy respect for "law and order." The principles of "majority rule," "proper channels," and "legitimate authority" had been emphasized by politicians, parents, teachers, and preachers. But in the years of the Vietnam and Middle East wars, some nonconformists began to raise provocative questions: Is it consistent to assert that individual or group acts of violence are "senseless" while governments spend billions on armaments for their own doubtful uses? Are laws necessarily *right* — or are they simply the products of *might*?

The answers to such questions are not self-evident. Some individuals argued that it is the *aim*, rather than the *means*, that is most important in social actions. The use of violence toward a good end, then, would be permissible; its use to defend a bad institution would be condemned. This line of reasoning led to a belief in "acceptable" violence, supported by arguments drawn from the writings of Luther, Jefferson, Marx, Bakunin, and Nietzsche. The belief appealed most directly to the frustrated and despairing person, the adventurous, and the instinctive rebel; its connection with *terrorism* (p. 616) is apparent.

"Idealistic" violence generated its opposite: idealistic *nonviolence*. Nonviolence, whether religious or philosophical, has been for centuries a *way of life* for some men and women (in both the West and East). In the twentieth century this historic practice was modified to serve as the basis for a new method of *social change*. Its advocates were convinced that the use of violence brings on counterviolence, and that even when violence achieves an immediate goal it creates new tensions and problems that perpetuate the chain of inhumane actions and counteractions. The leader of the Indian national independence movement, Mahatma Gandhi, saw this truth most clearly and turned to *satyagraha* (militant nonviolence) in order to free his people from British imperialism (p. 594).

Gandhi's ideas impressed Martin Luther King, Jr. (p. 610). Both Gandhi and King saw nonviolence as the preferred method for all social change. Their idea was by no means one of cowardly "passivity." They urged their followers to strive for social goals through courageous (but nonviolent) action; this often involved acts of *civil disobedience*, which might bring down violence on the "offender." They taught that one must never respond with *hate*; one must try, through feelings of *love*, to win opponents over to a just point of view. Their conviction rests on certain key assumptions: that everyone has an inner decency that can be appealed to and that people possess the capacity to live together nonviolently.

The principle of nonviolence, though it lost some support among blacks in the early 1970s, appeared to gather strength within the youth culture of the time. When, during the Nixon administration, the cycle of force-counterforce-repression appeared to have stalled the protest movement on college campuses (p. 637), some students began to feel that nonviolent methods were the *only* effective way of resisting "the system." These methods included refusal to register for or serve in the armed forces. Between such commitments to nonviolent action, on one side, and resorts to violence, on the other, stood the large majority of youth — and most older citizens as well.

FRESH DIRECTIONS IN LITERATURE AND THE ARTS

Literature and art were parts of the twentieth-century transformation of Western society, thought, faith, and action. We saw in Chapter 12 how writers and artists reacted to the impact of machine civilization during the nineteenth century (pp. 531–36). Some mirrored society; some wanted reform; still others turned inward upon themselves. In every age the arts are intimately involved in the life of the times, and as they respond to events they in turn influence events.

The Search for a New Language of Expression: Joyce, Eliot

"Contemporary" literature may be thought of, roughly, as that written since the First World War. (We noted at the beginning of Chapter 13 that the year 1914 marked a crucial divide in the course of Western civilization — p. 537.) The decades that followed brought radical innovations in the *forms* of writing; the *content* brought daring new insights into the human condition.

The key element in this literature was its emphasis on *subjectivity*. As in modern psychology, philosophy, and religion, the tendency was away from seeing the individual as an object geared to an orderly and purposeful environment. The new view held that everyone is unique and can be comprehended only through one's *internal* experiences. Authors felt, therefore, that they must assume a position quite different from the traditional one.

Before the First World War, most writers controlled their stories from the *outside*, furnishing dialogue and action for their characters. This technique seldom stressed the subjective life. New-style authors desired to penetrate more deeply the *minds* of their characters, to enter into the characters' private thoughts. The reader, then, also became intimate with their internal experiences. The effect was sometimes accomplished by the "stream-of-consciousness" technique, in which the author puts down words in the way in which ideas appear to the mind; the result is a running jumble of sense and nonsense, a mixture of past, present, and future.

Numerous literary experiments were tried in the endeavor to communicate "inner truth." In many of these, set plots and well-developed characters are missing. The traditional models of dramatic structure are abandoned as artificial. The moment-by-moment, *existential* reality is all. As one modern critic has commented:

> Recent novelists tend to explore rather than arrange or synthesize their materials; often their arrangement is random rather than sequential. In the older tradition, a novel was a formal structure composed of actions and reactions which were finished by the end of the story, which did have an end. The modern novel often has no such finality.

James Joyce was a pioneer of the new literature. Born in Dublin, Ireland, he abandoned his homeland and his Catholic faith to live on the European continent. He made *himself* the subject of his work, and by examining his own experience he sought to understand the general human problems of his times. In *A Portrait of the Artist as a Young Man* (1916), he drew on the first twenty years of his life.

The hero of Joyce's novel, Stephen Dedalus, struggles with major crises during his youth. In early years he is indoctrinated with religion, and a love affair at sixteen brings on a period of tormented guilt feelings. During his years in college, Stephen at last abandons religion, turns his back on conventional society, and takes up the artistic life. His departure from Ireland is also a symbolic rejection of his cultural heritage and a seeking for goals and forms of his *own* making. The escape does not bring him contentment; it is only the beginning of a lonely and bitter search. In his story Joyce deals hardly at all with action but presents an association of words that flow through consciousness.

In his later works, notably *Ulysses*, Joyce continued to draw from his personal experience. In doing so, he developed further his unusual use of language. In its complexity and obscurity his writing reflects the loneliness and alienation felt by many artists (and others) of the time. He was an inspiration to authors of his own and later generations. Many of them, using a variety of styles, have explored his method of "interior monologue." One of the most successful was the Frenchman, Marcel Proust, famous for his *Remembrance of Things Past* (1913–27). This seven-volume novel draws upon Proust's detailed recollections of figures in fashionable society that he had known in Paris around the turn of the century.

Some leading authors followed traditional methods of writing. The brilliant Englishman, Aldous Huxley, was one of these. He turned his talent to numerous topics; one was the "future" society. In his novel, *Brave New World* (1932), Huxley reveals a "probable" world to come, based on the rapid strides in the physical and social sciences. He sees a *world* state — achieved, at last, as the only means of avoiding suicidal nationalistic warfare. And to eliminate conflicts *within* the society, he sees the planned use of genetic engineering, social conditioning, easy sex, and safe drugs. Efficiency and "happiness" are the goals of this future society — at the cost of losing individuality, dissent, and struggle. Another "anti-utopia" of the period is a gloomier novel by another Englishman, George Orwell's *1984*. Published in 1949, it is the prophecy of a future society built on *totalitarian* lines, one even more repressive than *Brave New World*. It uses psychological terror, rather than pleasure, as the primary means of social control.

In the Soviet Union, where totalitarianism was a fact, not a prophecy, some great literature appeared in the tradition of Dostoevsky and Tolstoy (p. 480). Notable is Boris Pasternak's *Dr. Zhivago* (1958), an epic historical novel about Russia before, during, and after the Communist revolution. (It was also made into a memorable film.) Another giant is Aleksandr Solzhenitsyn, a voice of furious dissent against totalitarianism (p. 566). He first became known for his gripping novel, *One Day in the Life of Ivan Denisovich* (1963). It draws upon the author's experience as a prisoner in a labor camp, and highlights the struggle of one individual to uphold his personal spirit against determined efforts to crush it.

In the United States, some of the finest prose writing of the recent period is that of John Updike. Much of it is highly personal and subjective. His *Couples* (1968) reflects the intimate lives of well-to-do suburbanites, with heavy attention to sex; his four-volume series, starting with *Rabbit, Run* (1960), reflects the private lives of middle-class Americans caught up in the "success" ethic. More radical in his reactions to contemporary culture is Joseph Heller. His *Catch 22* (1955) is a hilarious story about combat airmen in the Second World War. *Something Happened* (1966) treats peacetime frustrations in personal affairs and in working for a large business corporation with insight and humor.

The major *poet* of the recent period was the American-born T. S. Eliot, who, like Joyce, became an expatriate. Eliot found his spiritual home in England, and he found deep meaning in the Christian religion. The writings of Eliot, like those of Joyce, are self-searching and rich in symbols and imagery.

Eliot moved to London in 1914 and soon began to write poems and literary criticism. His early works reflect a profound disenchantment with modern civilization, a sense of its emptiness and sterility. "The Love Song of J. Alfred Prufrock" (1917) was followed by other poems in the same mood, notably "Gerontion," "The Waste Land," and "The Hollow Men." These are scholarly works, full of echoes from the literary past. With subtlety and sensitivity, Eliot stripped bare the corruption within Western culture. These "confessional" poems blame the breakdown on the loss of religious spirit; after Eliot's confirmation in the Anglican faith, he began to write more hopefully about the human condition. If the waters of God's grace have dried up within us, he said, we must discover how to make them flow again. In a bid to reach a wider public, he turned to the theater; his most successful dramatic work, a modern "morality" play, is *Murder in the Cathedral* (1935).

Drama, like prose and poetry, came under subjectivist and experimentalist influences. Such notable playwrights as Eugene O'Neill, Tennessee Williams, and Arthur Miller dealt with ancient themes in new ways; they did not hesitate to alter methods of staging, as well as plot, form, and dialogue. The "theater of the absurd" reflected meaninglessness and the failure of human communication. The Irishman Samuel Beckett was perhaps the best known of the "absurdists." In *Waiting for Godot* (1948), his characters find themselves trapped in a nonsense world of neither "logic" nor "decency." Writers of dramas and musicals in the late 1960s pressed experimentation still further, including the novelty of having nude characters on stage (notably, *Oh, Calcutta!* and *Hair*).

A trend common to all forms of literature in the last decades was the steady sloughing off of *restraint*. Legal censorship of books and plays diminished in most Western countries, while reader resistance was shattered by rising shocks to traditional sensibilities. Each adult was thought to be the sole and proper judge of what he or she would see or hear. Thus the once-suppressed writings of authors who dealt frankly with sexual themes, like D. H. Lawrence and Henry Miller, became readily available — as did later works of sex and violence like those of Norman Mailer, Philip Roth, and Jerzy Kosinski. The Scandinavian countries generally took the lead in relaxing censorship. The Danish parliament, in an unprecedented act of 1969, authorized the printing of *any* sort of literature intended for adults.

The twentieth century brought three entirely *new* means of expression to world culture: the motion picture, radio, and television. Producers of motion pictures drew on most of the established arts, including writing, drama, and photography; but what they created was a *unique* art form. As a product of technology, this form seemed perfectly suited to the new era. It was associated with rapid movement and possessed virtually limitless capabilities (not always utilized). From experimental beginnings prior to the First World War, films grew into an immensely popular medium of entertainment. They are truly *international* in character, with writers, directors, and actors coming from many cultures. But the largest single source of filmmaking is in the United States (chiefly, Hollywood). Motion pictures have been generally subject to censorship, but by the 1980s restrictions in most Western countries had become minimal.

Radio broadcasting was developed during the 1920s, offering a flexible and powerful new dimension in the field of communications. It has flourished worldwide, featuring information programs and music of all types. However, radio has been overshadowed since about 1940 by still another new medium: television. In some respects, TV is a *projection* of motion pictures, but it has special capabilities that give it enormous influence on its own. Millions of viewers in Western nations are locked in on the daily "soaps," and most persons now rely mainly upon television for "news" and for watching sports events.

This medium has also become a prime carrier for commercial advertising — and has revolutionized the conduct of political campaigns in democratic countries.

The Private World of Painters and Sculptors: Picasso, Moore

Artists in the purely *visual* arts, like painting and sculpture, expressed many of the same feelings and ideas that moved the serious novelists and poets of recent times. The artistic protests of the late nineteenth century (pp. 533–36) became a storm of rebellion as the twentieth century proceeded.

Pablo Picasso, a Spaniard who made his home in France, is the giant of modern art. His productive life spanned the major developments in art since Cézanne and Vincent van Gogh (p. 535). A gifted draftsman, trained at the Barcelona Academy of Fine Arts, Picasso began painting in a fairly conventional manner. *The Old Guitarist*, produced in 1903, illustrates his early interest in portraying the poor, the outcast, and the alienated (*Fig. 15-1*). Through his distortion of bodily contours and his careful attention to composition, Picasso quickly achieved mastery of the "expressionist style" (p. 536). But he moved

15-1 Picasso. *The Old Guitarist.*
The Art Institute of Chicago.

restlessly on through successive experiments (he called them *discoveries*). From Cézanne he took the idea of building *solidity* into his works, of reducing natural subjects to their basic "cubes, cones, and cylinders." Picasso thus became a leading exponent of "cubism," perhaps the most fruitful movement in painting during the first half of the twentieth century.

Though it appeared in numerous varieties, cubist art involved essentially a *breaking down* and *reordering* of nature. For example, in Picasso's treatment of a violin (*Un violon, Fig. 15-2*), he not only has taken the instrument apart; he shows the parts at whatever angle and in whatever degree of distortion he desires. More correctly, he projects onto the canvas his own thoughts and feelings about a violin, about handling and looking at it. At the same time, he arranges the pictorial elements in an aesthetically pleasing composition. The finished work, then, is Picasso's private, disciplined response to the *idea* of a violin. Like Joyce's literature, Picasso's painting is *radically subjective*, personal, unique: it is not a copy or an imitation of something, but a *special creation* of the artist.

Such inward creations have not been easily understood by the general public. If alienation influenced artists to paint private and secret visions, such paintings only lengthened the distance between them and the public. But in-

15-2 Picasso. *Un violon accroché au mur*, 1913. Museum of Fine Arts, Berne, Switzerland.

formed and sensitive viewers were able to grasp Picasso's intent. They understood, too, that his technique could be more than a visual reduction of objects to geometrical forms; it might also reflect the breaking down of traditional culture and values. The latter possibility is starkly displayed in Picasso's *Guernica* (*Fig. 15-3*), a commemoration of the bombing of a small town during the Spanish Civil War (1937). The fascist general Francisco Franco (p. 538) had used German bombers in a terror raid against the civilian population. (The attack was a prelude to the mass killings of the Second World War.) Picasso, who was both antifascist and antimilitarist, responded by painting this large canvas (twelve by twenty-six feet) in black, white, and gray. It is a masterful protest — using techniques of cubism and expressionism — against the indiscriminate and hideous character of modern war.

Social protest, however, has seldom been the motive of contemporary painters. They were generally absorbed in problems of their craft, especially the problem of form. Since the Second World War the principal trend has been "abstractionism" — work completely divorced from any objective model. A Russian, Vassily Kandinsky, had begun to paint such works as early as 1911. His researches into the psychological properties of color, line, and shape led him to conclude that a "pure" art, not connected with representation, could be developed. This would be *visual* art on its own terms, corresponding to the purely *auditory* art of music.

Though the new idea took various forms, perhaps the most exciting was abstract expressionism. This combined spontaneity with nonobjectivity and was most forcefully advanced by an American, Jackson Pollock. Pollock used unorthodox techniques in order to express most fully his vigorous feeling for lines, shapes, and colors. He preferred to begin painting with no pattern in mind, allowing one stroke to lead to another and responding almost

15-3 Picasso. *Guernica*. Museo del Prado, Madrid.

subconsciously to his strong inner feelings. He spoke of his designs as *creating themselves*; he did not know what the final appearance would be while he was "still in the painting." In order to achieve desired effects, Pollock sometimes worked from a scaffold — pouring, spraying, and dripping his paints on a large canvas below. His techniques were regarded as extreme by some of his fellow artists; others moved beyond him in even freer uses of pigment and plastic materials. These far-out efforts, some sincere and some for sensationalism, created an "art of the absurd."

Similar trends could be observed in sculpture, where traditional representation was also abandoned. Considered the greatest modern sculptor, the Englishman Henry Moore is comparatively conservative in this respect. Many of his figures, though distorted, do suggest a *subject*. His primary interest, however, lies in the *materials* and *forms*. One of Moore's best-known works is his *Recumbent Figure*, done in 1938 (*Fig. 15-4*). The figure suggests the idea of woman, or femaleness; but it is at the same time a remarkably fashioned *stone* creation. The sculptor, by freeing himself from the requirement to reproduce naturalistic details, can concentrate on curves, texture, and the balance of masses.

In 1967 Moore produced a most unusual work, in cast bronze. His *Nuclear Energy* monument (*Fig. 15-5*) was created to mark the twenty-fifth anniversary of the world's first nuclear (atomic) "chain reaction" — a scientific feat that

15-4 Moore. *Recumbent Figure*, 1938. Tate Gallery, London.

15-5 Moore. *Nuclear Energy*, Chicago.

led to the making of the atomic bomb (pp. 523, 585). The sculpture, ten feet tall, is located near the site of the event, on the campus of the University of Chicago. Moore's design cleverly *combines* the shape of an exploding atomic cloud with a human skull.

The American sculptor Alexander Calder also took a novel approach to three-dimensional abstract form. He was the first sculptor to design works that moved; he called them *mobiles*. Typically, Calder linked together components of wire and flat pieces of carved metal and suspended them (usually from a ceiling) in a carefully balanced assembly. He preferred "natural" movement to mechanical means; his mobiles are usually activated by air currents or a slight touch. Thus, space and motion, rather than mass, dominate in his sculptures — transmitting a *kinetic* (moving) sensation to viewers as they watch the ever-changing assembly.

Calder, schooled in mechanical engineering, also found that he could construct *static* forms that transmit a feeling of motion. His *stabiles*, sometimes designed as large outdoor sculptures, project a sense of movement — and

15-6 Calder. *La Grande Vitesse*, Grand Rapids, Michigan.

change continually in appearance as the viewer walks around them. A splendid example is the Calder centerpiece for the civic plaza of Grand Rapids, Michigan: *La Grande Vitesse* (*Fig. 15-6*). Completed in 1969, it consists of giant, curved steel plates linked together in dynamic (energetic) unity of form.

Technology in Architecture: Wright, Gropius

Architecture was affected far less than painting and sculpture by the philosophical and psychological currents of recent decades. This was due, no doubt, to the generally *utilitarian* (service) character of architecture. Yet there have been striking innovations, spurred by the availability of new materials of construction. The twentieth century is one of the great ages of architecture.

Contemporary building is notable not only for its unprecedented quantity but for its distinctive *style* as well. Architecture in the nineteenth century had been a mixture of "revival" styles, none of which came from the spirit or technology of the times (pp. 485–86). During the 1890s a number of designers in Europe and America began to express dissatisfaction with the state of architecture. They pointed to the contradiction in putting up a structure by modern engineering methods and then covering it with a façade (facing) of "historical" ornamentation. They also complained about the mediocre workmanship of the façades, for *craftsmanship* in building declined sharply during the Industrial Revolution.

Frank Lloyd Wright, an American, was the pioneer of a new architecture. He concluded that the machine was here to stay and that the crafts could not be rescued. One should break entirely, he declared, with the forms and decorations of the past. One should try to utilize whatever kind of beauty the machine is capable of producing and allow *"form to follow function."* An authentic (true) style is one that provides the kind of space suited to a particular kind of human activity (work, rest, or play); its beauty will lie in the character of the building materials themselves. Because his structures were designed around the needs and desires of the individuals who occupied them, and because they preserved the natural appearance of the materials, Wright called his style "organic."

Wright began building residences at the turn of the century. In order to achieve the freest flow of space inside and to join that space with its natural surroundings, he made effective use of the "cantilever" method of construction. The cantilever, an outgrowth of the post-and-lintel method of the ancient Greeks (p. 80), provides for an *unsupported extension* of the horizontal members. Traditional construction materials, like stone, wood, or cememt, can be used only in a limited way as cantilevers. But steel or ferroconcrete (concrete reinforced by steel rods or mesh) can be boldly employed in this method of building.

Wright's "Falling Water" (1936) is a spectacular example of organic architecture using cantilevered elements (*Fig. 15-7*). This home, built over a rustic waterfall, appears to grow out of its surroundings. Inside the house, free space and a sense of contact with nature are maintained. While Wright is especially respected for his designs of private dwellings, he also created impressive structures for public and industrial uses.

Outside the United States, leading architects were deeply impressed by Wright's "functional" ideas. Perhaps the most influential among them was a German, Walter Gropius. He designed his school of art and architecture (the Bauhaus, at Dessau) according to the new principles (*Fig. 15-8*). Though it appears commonplace today, it caused spirited controversy when it was built in 1926. Gropius, like Wright, emphasized that attention to function is the first principle of architecture; a good *design* in an object (no matter what it is) ensures its *beauty*. His Bauhaus became a model of what today is called the "international" style. Especially as applied to large buildings — factories and offices — this style aptly expresses the precision and efficiency of the machine

15-7 Wright. "Falling Water," Bear Run, Pennsylvania.

15-8 Gropius. Bauhaus, Dessau, Germany.

age. A later example (1958) is the headquarters building of the United Nations Educational, Scientific, and Cultural Organization (UNESCO), located in Paris (*Fig. 10-1*, p. 392).

The most brilliant architect in the international style was Ludwig Mies van der Rohe, who held that function alone is not enough to assure beauty. His stunning skyscrapers please the eye because of their balanced proportions, richness of materials, and painstaking details. His shimmering glass walls hang upon frames of cantilevered steel. Mies's masterpiece, the Seagram Building in New York (*Fig. 15-9*), has been appropriately described as "dignified,

15-9 Mies van der Rohe. Seagram Building, New York. Ezra Stoller © ESTO.

sumptuous, severe, sophisticated, cool, consummately elegant architecture for the twentieth century and for the ages."

In lesser hands the "glass box" of the international style was often undistinguished and monotonous. In recent years this decline led to a turning away from that mode and a searching for more imaginative, if less efficient, designs. The French-Swiss architect Le Corbusier produced some striking examples of an architecture that appears to *reject* the machine. His mountain chapel near Ronchamps, France, completed in 1955, is startling and mysterious in its sculptured masses (*Fig. 15-10*). Lacking in symmetry or evident plan, its interior suggests a primitive sacred cave.

Numerous other architects subordinated function to interesting forms; one of them is the Brazilian Oscar Niemeyer, whose glass-crowned cathedral (1961) is among the number of marvelous structures he designed for his country's new capital of Brasilia (*Fig. 15-11*). Still others applied the freer design principles to utilitarian buildings. Outstanding was the Finnish-American Eero Saarinen. He is best known for his design of *airports*. An airport combines enormously complex movements of people, ground transport, and aircraft. Most world travelers are familiar with Saarinen's TWA Building (1961) at Kennedy International, near New York, and his Dulles International, near Washington, D.C. Architects like Niemeyer, Le Corbusier, and Saarinen had one thing in common with Wright and the internationalists: they all aban-

15-10 Le Corbusier. Notre Dame du Haut, Ronchamps, France.

15-11 Niemeyer. Cathedral of Brasilia.

doned the backward-looking imitativeness of the nineteenth century and committed themselves to an architecture that is modern in both spirit and
materials.

Novel Patterns of Tonality and Rhythm: Schoenberg, Stravinsky

The changes that swept through the visual arts around the turn of the
century affected music as well. Though romanticism continued to dominate
concert and operatic performances (p. 487), composers began to embrace new
aims and methods. Some turned to impressionism, which was inspired in part
by the movement in painting (p. 533). Musical impressionism, as developed by
the Frenchman Claude Debussy, was anticlassical as well as antiromantic. It
sought to record the composer's fleeting responses to nature (clouds, sea, moon-
light). Departing from traditional patterns of melody, tone scales, and rhythms,
Debussy's music has a dreamy, shimmering quality.

As in painting, impressionism in music was followed by expressionism.
Expressionist composers were not interested in responding to their environment; they sought, rather, to record musically their inmost, even subconscious
feelings. (This motive corresponded to the literary subjectivism of Joyce — p.
642.) Viennese composer Arnold Schoenberg was one of the earliest expres-
sionists. Just before the First World War he turned from the large orchestral

productions of the nineteenth century and began writing string quartets and other forms of chamber music (p. 440). Abandoning tonality, Schoenberg stressed melodic distortion and the chance coincidence of notes — often producing a harsh dissonance. Later in life he adopted a unique tone scale of his own invention. Musically, Schoenberg was not unlike van Gogh or Picasso (pp. 645–47) in seeking vigorous and disturbing means of expression.

Contemporary composers, like painters or sculptors, freed themselves from the traditions of their craft and chose whatever musical elements they wished. The result was an unbounded diversity of individual styles. One of the best known and most successful of the moderns was Russian-born Igor Stravinsky. Younger than Schoenberg, he, too, worked with established forms before discarding them. He also decided to ignore public tastes (as the painters had done) and to write "abstract" music to suit his own ideas. The chief characteristics of his mature works are stress on polyphony, free use of dissonance, and quickly changing rhythms.

In popular music, American jazz won growing numbers of enthusiasts throughout the Western world. Europeans, who had been creators and exporters of classical compositions for centuries, became eager *importers* of jazz. African rhythms are the foundation of this new musical form, which flowered chiefly among the talented writers and musicians of black America. But the principal feature was its unending novelty and the improvisations of its interpreters; among the greatest of these were the prolific composer-conductor, "Duke" Ellington, and the trumpet-playing "Ambassador of Jazz," Louis Armstrong. More than any other type of artistic expression, jazz seems to incorporate the spirit of rebellion against traditional forms and restraints. It is plainly an antidote for high tension, repression, and frustration. Jacques Ellul, a French sociologist and philosopher, believes that jazz appeals today because it offers an *illusion* of individual freedom in a culture that has stifled much of the *substance* of freedom.

Rock music, which became popular in the 1960s, has a similar appeal. It grew out of black "rhythm and blues" and white "country" music, but it is a unique form. Rock is directed mainly at adolescents; its sensual beat, electronic amplification, and frank lyrics excite youthful audiences around the world. By means of the mass media, it quickly created idols (and legends) like Elvis Presley, John Lennon, and Michael Jackson. The power of rock was further extended in the 1980s through another new art form: music video.

THE END OF THE BEGINNING: A NEW AGE OF HUMANITY

Music and the arts furnish strong proofs that Western civilization has entered a new age. Some writers use the word "postmodern" to describe it. But that term does not suggest the magnitude of change that has occurred since 1914 in the West (and elsewhere). *The new age marks a break with the past as decisive as that between precivilized and civilized times.* The lessons of the past, though still valuable as guides for the present and future, must be *adapted* to radically altered realities. Humans now stand on the threshold of a different world — one largely of their own making and subject, in substantial measure, to their own control.

The Radical Mutation in Human Culture

Today, literature, arts, philosophy, and religion show a disconnection from the past in both form and content. Also, varying types of "mixed" economies have largely displaced both laissez-faire capitalism and centrally planned systems. In international relations, the growing self-awareness of non-Western peoples is challenging the domination of the West.

But the distinctiveness of today's civilization arises from more than shifts in patterns and relationships. Totally *new* elements have emerged in human culture. One is *acceleration* itself: changes on every side are moving ahead, it appears, by *geometric* progression. Before a given problem can be identified and addressed, the problem is altered or obscured by new problems. People of no previous era have faced the prospect of living in a cultural *centrifuge*.

The machine, originally a simple tool, is in large part responsible for this bewildering rate of change. It has produced "automation," a system of integrated machines and robots that eliminates human labor. Human thought is at the same time being extended (and replaced) by informational systems (electronic computers, or "thinking machines," and microcomputers). The ultimate impact of these and other technological developments can hardly be imagined. Science has unlocked cosmic powers for the use (and abuse) of human society. The widening fields of genetic engineering, organ transplants, weather management, synthetic chemistry, lasers, and controlled nuclear energy illustrate the expanding ability to manipulate human beings and their environment.

Jet aircraft and rockets have annihilated distances on earth and have projected humans into space. Both the Soviets and the Americans have undertaken costly programs of exploration of the solar system; hundreds of millions of people around the world shared that televised instant in 1969 when an *earth*ling first set foot on the *moon.* "That's one small step for a man," declared the astronaut Neil Armstrong, "one giant leap for mankind." No one can predict how far space searches will go or what they may discover; science fiction is fast becoming reality. Meanwhile, a Damoclean sword hangs by a hair over life itself. Nuclear, radiological, chemical, and bacteriological weapons have passed the level of *overkill* — and their use could cripple or destroy the human species.

The Challenge of Survival and Mastery: A Summary

The new age thus confronts *Homo sapiens* with a profound challenge: Can humans preserve themselves from *self*-destruction? Can they use their new powers to create a more satisfying life for themselves? Having overcome nature, humans must now overcome many of their *own* values and institutions. History has been marked by endless competition and warfare, but it now appears that humans must learn to *cooperate* in order to *survive*.

Nuclear war is the most immediate but not the sole threat to existence. Exploding population, if unchecked, may shortly outrun the supply of food and other life-supporting elements. The air, water, earth, and sea are falling to levels of sterility and pollution that may prove fatal to human and other forms of life. "Spaceship earth" is flashing red warning signals.

In this perspective, current differences over ideologies and "national interests" must be subordinated to higher considerations. Disagreements and conflicts will doubtless persist, but the overriding priorities are survival and peace. These require, in turn, that concern for the *world* community supersede traditional concerns about national sovereignty. *Trans*national authorities to govern population levels, resource development, health services, arms expenditures, education, and research seem indispensable if the poor — and the rich — of the world are to survive in peace.

Such controls would impose restrictions on the freedoms and privileges of some individuals and some nations. Westerners, who have used much of the world for their own purposes, may find the prospect uninviting. But they cannot ignore the facts or the challenge. Perhaps they can find a fresh source of satisfaction in the *adventure* of the new age they have created. They cannot, in any event, turn back; Western men and women now share with all peoples the burden of godlike knowledge — and a *common fate*.

Recommended Further Reading

History embraces everything that human beings have said or thought or done — so there is no substitute for the widest possible reading. The most rewarding reading, no doubt, is in the original ("primary") writings of the past. Many such writings are cited in this book and can be read as individual works. (Most are available in paperback.) For practical reasons, however, a careful selection of portions of original works may better fit the needs and desires of the majority of students. Several suitable anthologies (collections) are available; especially recommended is the paperbound set prepared to accompany this book: *Classics of Western Thought* (Harcourt Brace Jovanovich, 4 vols.).

In addition to original source materials, many "secondary" works are of great value and interest. The authors of such works attempt to sort out and interpret human experience in the light of later events and differing points of view.

The books recommended in the list that follows are "secondary" works, chiefly by modern authors; titles followed by the date of publication (in parentheses) are in *hard covers* only. Fortunately, a great many books of high quality and appeal are available in *paperback*, and most of the titles recommended here may be found in paperback editions. They have been chosen for both their authority and their readability. Titles are arranged to correspond to the *chapter* and *section headings* of this book.

1 The Birth of Civilization in the Middle East

THE PREHISTORIC ERA

Sound and readable accounts of early humans may be found in R. J. Braidwood, *Prehistoric Men* (1957); J. G. D. Clark, *World Prehistory in New Perspective*; and K. P. Oakley, *Man the Toolmaker*. C. G. Starr, *Early Man*, is a brief, well-illustrated presentation of the first civilizations as well as prehistory. For the effects of disease on human cultures from earliest times to the present, see W. H. McNeil, *Plagues and Peoples*.

THE EARLIEST CITIES: MESOPOTAMIA

For the ancient civilizations of the Middle East, see C. G. Starr, *Early Man*. J. Finegan, *Light from the Ancient Past*, explains the archeological background. For Mesopotamia alone, S. N. Kramer, *The Sumerians: Their History and Character*, is the most comprehensive; H. J. Nissen, *The Early History of the Ancient Near East, 9000–2000 B.C.* (1988), is a recent brief account of the rise of civilization by a leading archeologist; and a cultural analysis is given by A. Leo Oppenheim, *Ancient Mesopotamia: Portrait of a Dead Civilization*. For focus on religion, see T. Jacobsen, *The Treasures of Darkness: A History of Mesopotamian Religion*; for social conditions, G. Contenau, *Everyday Life in Babylon and Assyria* (1954).

LAND OF THE PHARAOHS: EGYPT

Of the many histories of ancient Egypt, two detailed ones are recommended: A. H. Gardiner, *Egypt of the Pharaohs*, and J. A. Wilson, *The Culture of Ancient Egypt*. Authoritative specialized studies are H. Frankfort, *Ancient Egyptian Religion* and *Art and Architecture of the Ancient Orient*. See also I. E. S. Edwards, *The Pyramids of Egypt*.

THE FIRST UNIVERSAL EMPIRES: ASSYRIA AND PERSIA

The Assyrian empire is treated in C. G. Starr, *Early Man*, and in A. T. Olmstead, *History of Assyria* (1923). The standard account of the Persians is A. T. Olmstead, *History of the Persian Empire*.

THE EUROPEAN BARBARIANS

A readable survey by a leading archeologist, stressing the high level of organization and skills of barbarian peoples, is C. Renfrew, *Before Civilization: The Radiocarbon Revolution and Prehistoric Europe*. E. Phillips, *The Royal Hordes* (1966) is a succinct account of the Eurasian nomads of ancient times. For the origins and spread of the Indo-Europeans, and their influence on the language and way of life of the peoples of Europe and Asia, see J. P. Mallory, *In Search of the Indo-Europeans* (1989).

2 The Greek Beginnings of Western Civilization

THE AEGEAN BACKGROUND

J. W. Alsop, *From the Silent Earth* (1964), is a colorful account of Bronze Age Greece by an enthusiastic amateur archeologist. C. W. Ceram, *Gods, Graves, and Scholars*, provides a lively account of modern excavations in the Aegean area. M. Smith, *The Ancient Greeks* (1960), is a short, well-written introduction to the eleventh through the third centuries B.C. The *Oxford History of the Classical World: Greece and the Hellenistic World* is an authoritative and readable guide to the same period.

THE CITY-STATE

V. Ehrenburg, *The Greek State* (1960), is a classic analysis. Sir A. Zimmern, *The Greek Commonwealth* (1947), is an interesting account of fifth-century Athens; A. H. M. Jones, *Athenian Democracy*, is an excellent brief analysis; W. G. Forrest, *History of Sparta*, is reliable. K. Freeman, *The Greek City-States* (1950), focuses on cities other than Athens and Sparta. For everyday life, see T. B. L. Webster, *Life in Classical Greece* (1969), and F. J. Frost, *Greek Society*; for a lively study of women, see S. B. Pomeroy, *Goddesses, Whores, Wives, and Slaves: Women in Classical Antiquity*. Economic conditions are described in A. French, *The Growth of the Athenian Economy* (1976).

GREEK RELIGION

For an admirable summary of the Greek cultural achievement, see C. M. Bowra, *The Greek Experience*. This account may be balanced by E. R. Dodds, *The Greeks and the Irrational*, or by M. I. Finley, *The Ancient Greeks* (1963). H. D. F. Kitto, *The Greeks*, is a readable short account. Specifically on religion, H. J. Rose, *Religion in Greece and Rome* (1959), is brief but lucid on the civic cults; A. Festugiere, *Personal Religion Among the Greeks* (1960), deals with less formal aspects of worship. Detailed accounts may be found in R. Graves, *The Greek Myths*.

THE FOUNDERS OF WESTERN PHILOSOPHY

Of the many treatments available, B. Russell, *A History of Western Philosophy*, may be recommended for its lively style; W. K. Guthrie, *The Greek Philosophers: From Thales to Aristotle*, provides more detail. A. E. Taylor, *Socrates: The Man and His Thought* (1951), is an excellent brief introduction; also valuable are W. K. Guthrie, *Socrates*, and *The Sophists*.

GREEK LITERATURE

A. Lesky, *A History of Greek Literature*, and K. Dover, *Ancient Greek Literature*, are standard surveys. An attractive introduction to the drama is H. D. F. Kitto, *Greek Tragedy*.

ARCHITECTURE AND SCULPTURE

Of the many available accounts, J. Boardman, *Greek Art*; G. M. A. Richter, *The Sculpture and Sculptors of the Greeks* (2nd ed., 1950); A. W. Lawrence, *Greek Architecture* (2nd ed., 1962); and F. Chamonix, *The Civilisation of Greece* (1965), are authoritative treatments with excellent illustrations. Briefer are M. Robertson, *A Shorter History of Greek Art*, and J. J. Pollitt, *Art and Experience in Classical Greece*. For a general history of Western art, including Greece, a sound work is H. de la Croix and R. G. Tansey, *Gardner's Art through the Ages* (9th ed., 1991); a compact introduction and manual of art history is D. G. Cleaver, *Art: An Introduction*.

THE DECLINE OF THE GREEK CITY-STATES

Greek imperialism is thoroughly treated in R. Meiggs, *The Athenian Empire*. F. W. Walbank, *The Hellenistic World*, is excellent for the later period of Greek influence.

ALEXANDER THE GREAT AND THE WIDER SPREAD OF GREEK CULTURE

W. W. Tarn, *Alexander the Great*, is a scholarly and imaginative biography of the conqueror. F. W. Walbank, *The Hellenistic World*, is a useful survey.

3   The Roman Triumph and Fall

THE RISE OF ROME

R. H. Barrow, *The Romans*; C. G. Starr, Jr., *The Emergence of Rome as Ruler of the Western World*; M. Grant, *History of Rome*; and the *Oxford History of the Classical World: The Roman World*, are good scholarly surveys. Social conditions during the entire Roman era are clearly described in H. C. Boren, *Roman Society*.

THE OVERTHROW OF THE REPUBLIC

Starr, above, and E. Badian, *Roman Imperialism in the Late Republic*, are valuable brief accounts; R. Syme, *The Roman Revolution*, and P. A. Brunt, *Social Conflicts in the Roman Republic*, give more attention to the social aspects of the struggle.

THE IMPERIAL FOUNDATIONS

C. G. Starr, Jr., *Civilization and the Caesars* (1954), and H. Mattingly, *Roman Imperial Civilization* (1957), are readable books by outstanding scholars. The founding emperor is the focus in A. H. M. Jones, *Augustus*.

THE APPROACH TO ONE WORLD: PAX ROMANA

C. Bailey, ed., *The Legacy of Rome* (1923), which contains essays by several experts, is still valuable. J. Carcopino, *Daily Life in Ancient Rome*, is a spirited account by a French scholar.

ROMAN CHARACTER AND THOUGHT

H. Mattingly, *The Man in the Roman Street*, describes the empire as it appeared to the ordinary person; H. C. Boren, *Roman Society*, illuminates social and economic conditions at each stage of Roman development; J. P. V. D. Balsdon, *Roman Women* (1975), gives special attention to the female gender. H. J. Rose, *Religion in Greece and Rome* (1959), and E. Brehier, *History of Philosophy: The Hellenistic and Roman Age*, are standard accounts of their subjects. M. Grant, *Roman Literature* (1954), and R. M. Ogilvie, *Roman Literature and Society*, are valuable.

ROMAN LAW

P. Grimal, *The Civilization of Rome* (1963), and A. H. M. Jones, *The Later Roman Empire, 284–602*, have chapters on the law.

ARCHITECTURE AND ENGINEERING

Sir M. Wheeler, *Roman Art and Architecture*; F. E. Brown, *Roman Architecture*; and G. Daniel, *The Art of the Romans* (1965), are excellent. L. Sprague de Camp, *The Ancient Engineers*, chaps. 6–7, is a nontechnical account.

THE END OF ROME AND THE BEGINNING OF EUROPE

E. Gibbon, *The Decline and Fall of the Roman Empire*, is a monumental classic of historical literature (available in paperback in a one-volume abridgement, ed., D. A. Saunders). A. H. M. Jones, *The Decline of the Ancient World*, is a work of the highest authority; P. Brown, *The World of Late Antiquity* (1971), is the most recent account. On the Germanic invaders, see M. Todd, *The Northern Barbarians*; J. B. Bury, *The Invasion of Europe by the Barbarians*; and J. M. Wallace-Hadrill, *The Barbarian West, A.D. 400–1000*.

4   A Conquering New Faith: Christianity

SOURCES OF CHRISTIANITY

I. Epstein, *Judaism*, is an historical presentation by a rabbinic scholar; H. M. Orlinsky, *Ancient Israel*, is readable and comprehensive. For the immediate setting of Jesus' ministry, see E. Schürer, *History of the Jewish People in the Time of Jesus*.

THE LIFE AND TEACHINGS OF JESUS

A. Schweitzer, *The Quest of the Historical Jesus* (1968), is a classic work by a great humanitarian; H. C. Kee, *Jesus in History*, is a concise recent study.

THE EARLY CHURCH AND ITS EXPANSION

H. Chadwick, *The Early Church*; R. H. Bainton, *Early Christianity*; and E. J. Goodspeed, *Paul* (1947), are all works of deservedly high reputation. For the persecutions of the Christians, see W. H. C. Frend, *Martyrdom and Persecution in the Early Church* (1965).

THE GROWTH OF CHRISTIAN ORGANIZATION AND DOCTRINE

R. H. Bainton, *Early Christianity*, is again useful; J. Danielou, *The Development of Christian Doctrine* (1977), is a solid presentation of difficult materials.

THE WORLDLY VICTORY OF THE CHURCH

H. Mattingly, *Christianity in the Roman Empire*; A. H. M. Jones, *Constantine and the Conversion of Europe* (1948); and C. N. Cochrane, *Christianity and Classical Culture*, deal with various aspects of the rival traditions. An excellent biography is P. Brown, *Augustine of Hippo*.

EARLY CHRISTIAN MONASTICISM

D. Knowles, *Christian Monasticism* (1969), traces the idea and the movement from the beginning to the twentieth century. The principles of regulated religious communities are set forth in *The Rule of St. Benedict*, tr. by A. C. Meisel and M. L. Del Mastro.

5   The Creation of Europe: Political and Social Foundations

EUROPE IN THE EARLY MIDDLE AGES

C. Dawson, *The Making of Europe* (1953); H. Trevor-Roper, *The Rise of Christian Europe* (1965); and H. St. L. B. Moss, *The Birth of the Middle Ages, 395–814* (1964), are stimulating studies of both East and West and their respective cultures; J. M. Wallace-Hadrill, *The Barbarian West*, is brief and readable.

THE RIVAL CULTURE OF BYZANTIUM

Besides Dawson and Moss, just cited, there is the comprehensive account by A. Grabar, *Byzantium from the Death of Theodosius to the Rise of Islam* (1966). C. Diehl, *Byzantium: Greatness and Decline*, is an insightful French interpretation. D. Obolensky, *The Byzantine Commonwealth: Eastern Europe 500–1453* authoritatively analyzes the Byzantine influence on the Slavs and other eastern European peoples.

THE BOOK AND SWORD OF ISLAM

In addition to Dawson and Moss, H. A. R. Gibb, *Mohammedanism*; P. K. Hitti, *The Arabs*; and B. Lewis, *The Arabs in History*, are excellent introductions. A. J. Arberry, *The Koran Interpreted*, and D. Talbot-Rice, *Islamic Art*, are useful; and T. Andrae, *Mohammed: The Man and His Faith* (1970), is brief and balanced. A worthy survey of the Islamic legacy is G. E. von Grunebaum, ed., *Medieval Islam* (2d ed., 1966).

THE EMERGENCE OF MEDIEVAL CIVILIZATION

C. Dawson, *The Making of Europe*, continues to be valuable; S. Painter, *The Rise of the Feudal Monarchies*, is also a standard work. H. Fichtenau, *The Carolingian Empire*, and J. Boussard, *The Civilization of Charlemagne* (1968), are excellent studies of the emperor and his times; Einhard, *Life of Charlemagne*, is by a leading member of his court. J. Brondsted, *The Vikings*, is a good introduction to the Norse invasions; the Norman impact on England is well told in D. C. Douglas, *William the Conqueror*.

FEUDALISM

M. Bloch, *Feudal Society*, and F. L. Ganshof, *Feudalism*, are works of high scholarship; S. Painter, *French Chivalry*, is in a lighter vein.

MANORIALISM

H. S. Bennett, *Life on the English Manor*; M. E. Reeves, *The Medieval Village*; and E. Power, *Medieval People*, deal primarily with English conditions; G. Duby, *Rural Economy and Country Life in the Medieval West* (1960), provides broader geographical coverage. For perceptive essays on the life of women, see S. M. Stuard, ed., *Women in Medieval Society*. L. White, *Medieval Technology and Social Change*, relates innovations that changed history.

THE RISE OF TRADE AND TOWNS

H. Pirenne, *Medieval Cities*, is brief and readable; a more recent account, with source references, is J. H. Mundy and P. Riesenberg, *The Medieval Town*. S. L. Thrupp, *The Merchant Class of Medieval London*, is an interesting account of commercial activities. A comprehensive survey is R. H. Bautier, *Economic Development of Medieval Europe* (1971).

6   The Flowering of Medieval Culture

THE MEDIEVAL CHURCH

F. Heer, *The Medieval World*, is a first-rate account of the period 1100–1300, with chapters on such topics as urban, intellectual, and courtly life, Jews, and women, as well as on the Church. M. W. Baldwin, *The Medieval Church*, is by a Catholic writer; R. H. Bainton, *The Medieval Church*, is by a Protestant. G. Barraclough, *The Medieval Papacy*, is a penetrating study by an outstanding authority. R. W. Southern, *Western Society and the Church*, shows the relations between religion and the social order.

CHRISTIAN ART

C. R. Morey, *Medieval Art* (1942), is the best comprehensive treatment; J. Beckwith, *Early Medieval Art*, includes the Romanesque style; and E. Mâle, *The Gothic Image: Religious Art in France of the Thirteenth Century*, is authoritative and detailed. H. Adams, *Mont-Saint-Michel and Chartres* (1905), is a classic synthesis of medieval culture as a whole; another notable work of interrelation is E. Panofsky, *Gothic Architecture and Scholasticism*.

THOUGHT AND EDUCATION

D. Knowles, *Evolution of Medieval Thought*, by a distinguished Catholic scholar, is a most readable introduction; F. C. Copleston, *The History of Medieval Philosophy* (1972), and *Aquinas*, are valuable works by a learned Jesuit. A more secular assessment of the intellectual complexity and creativity of the period is G. Leff, *Medieval Thought* (1958). C. H. Haskins, *The Rise of Universities*, is a general survey; more specific is G. Leff, *Paris and Oxford Universities in the 13th and 14th Centuries* (1968).

LANGUAGE AND LITERATURE

For a general history of the new vernacular literatures, see W. H. Jackson, *The Literature of the Middle Ages*. G. G. Coulton, *Chaucer and His England* (1963), and T. G. Bergin, *Dante* (1965), are excellent biographies.

WEST AND EAST: THE CRUSADES
S. Runciman, *History of the Crusades* (1967), and H. E. Mayer, *The Crusades*, are complete accounts.

THE MEDIEVAL SYNTHESIS
H. O. Taylor, *The Medieval Mind* (2 vols., 4th ed., 1949), is an admirable general survey. C. G. Crump and E. F. Jacobs, eds., *The Legacy of the Middle Ages* (1926), is a collection of essays on diverse topics.

7   The Transformation and Expansion of Europe

DISSOLUTION OF THE MEDIEVAL SYNTHESIS
J. Huizinga, *The Waning of the Middle Ages*, is a work of subtle insight, dealing mostly with the Low Countries and France. A fine introduction to the coming of modern times is E. P. Cheyney, *The Dawn of a New Era* (1936). B. W. Tuchman, *A Distant Mirror*, tells the horrors of the fourteenth century.

THE NEW ECONOMY
H. Pirenne, *The Economic and Social History of Medieval Europe*, is a good introduction; R. de Roover, *The Rise and Decline of the Medici Bank* (1963), provides greater detail. A. von Martin, *The Sociology of the Renaissance* (1944), deals with the new society in Italy.

THE NEW GEOGRAPHY
J. H. Parry, *The Establishment of European Hegemony*, is an excellent survey; more detailed is J. H. Parry, *The Age of Reconnaisance*. B. Penrose, *Travel and Discovery in the Renaissance, 1420–1620*, deals with the opening up of Asia, Africa, and America; D. P. Mannix, *Black Cargoes* (1962), is a highly readable account of the brutal Atlantic slave trade. For African history, see R. W. July, *A History of the African People*. G. Pendle, *A History of Latin America*, is a brief popular account from the beginnings to modern times. An authoritative brief biography of the great discoverer is S. E. Morison, *Christopher Columbus, Mariner*.

THE NEW POLITICS
D. Hay, *The Italian Renaissance in Its Historical Background*, and G. Mattingly, *Renaissance Diplomacy*, are good introductions; J. R. Hale, *Renaissance Europe: The Individual and Society*, and H. Butterfield, *The Statecraft of Machiavelli* (1960), give additional detail. For individual city-states, see G. A. Brucker, *Renaissance Florence*, and D. S. Chambers, *The Imperial Age of Venice* (1970).

8   The Renaissance: Upsurge of Humanism

THE RENAISSANCE VIEW OF HUMAN NATURE
M. P. Gilmore, *The World of Humanism, 1453–1517* (1952), is a comprehensive study of the age; D. Herlihy, *The Family in Renaissance Italy*, makes interesting social history. P. O. Kristeller, *Renaissance Thought*, vol. I, is a summary of the classical, scholastic, and humanist strains. B. Cellini, *Autobiography*, is a unique record by a contemporary artist; J. Huizinga, *Erasmus and the Age of Reformation*, is a superior study of the "Prince of Humanists."

THE REVOLUTION IN ART

B. Berenson, *The Italian Painters of the Renaissance*, is celebrated; N. Pevsner, *Outline of European Architecture*, and P. J. Murray, *Architecture of the Italian Renaissance*, are also authoritative. J. A. Symonds, *Life of Michelangelo* (1928), is a biography by a famous man of letters; K. M. Clark, *Leonardo da Vinci* (1952), is by an outstanding art historian.

LITERATURE AND DRAMA

H. O. Taylor, *Thought and Expression in the 16th Century* (1959); G. P. Norton, *Montaigne and the Introspective Mind*; and E. Dowden, *Shakespeare: A Critical Study of His Mind and Art* (1963), are all valuable.

9   The Reformation: Division and Reform in the Church

BACKGROUND OF THE REFORMATION

A. G. Dickens, *The Reformation and Society in Sixteenth-Century Europe*, and R. H. Bainton, *The Age of the Reformation*, are brief but excellent; Bainton, *The Reformation of the 16th Century*, and D. L. Jensen, *Reformation Europe*, are fuller accounts.

THE REVOLT OF LUTHER: "JUSTIFICATION BY FAITH"

R. H. Bainton, *Here I Stand*, and J. Maritain, *Three Reformers*, are outstanding biographies by a sympathetic Protestant and a distinguished Catholic, respectively. E. H. Erikson, *Young Man Luther*, is a provocative study by a modern psychiatrist.

CALVIN AND THE ELECT: "PREDESTINATION"

W. Walker, *John Calvin* (1906), is an older but still respected biography. For doctrinal teachings, see also J. T. McNeill, *The History and Character of Calvinism*.

HENRY VIII AND THE CHURCH OF ENGLAND

J. J. Scarisbrick, *Henry VIII*, and A. G. Dickens, *The English Reformation*, are excellent accounts.

THE ROMAN CATHOLIC RESPONSE: REFORM AND REAFFIRMATION

H. Daniel-Rops, *The Catholic Reformation* (1963), is a lengthy Catholic study; A. G. Dickens, *The Counter Reformation*, is a Protestant interpretation. T. Maynard, *St. Ignatius and the Jesuits* (1956), is a sympathetic study of a powerful figure.

HISTORICAL SIGNIFICANCE OF THE REFORMATION

P. Smith, *The Age of the Reformation* (1920), vol. 2, chap. 14, is a masterly critical summing up. Other excellent presentations are O. Chadwick, *The Reformation* (1964), and A. G. Dickens, *The Reformation and Society*, cited above.

ART DURING THE REFORMATION

G. G. Coulton, *Art and the Reformation* (1928), is a good general study; H. Hibbard, *Bernini*, is a valuable specialized account.

10   Science and the New Cosmology

NATIONAL AND INTERNATIONAL DEVELOPMENT

D. Ogg, *Europe in the 17th Century* (1948); R. N. Hatton, *Europe in the Age of Louis XIV;* C. J. Friedrich and C. Blitzer, *The Age of Power;* and H. Kamen, *European Society, 1500–1700* (1984), are excellent general studies. C. V. Wedgewood, *The Thirty Years' War*, and G. Pagès, *The Thirty Years' War, 1618–1648* (1970), are both sound accounts of that terrible struggle. For particular countries: A. Guérard, *France in the Classical Age* (1928), is brilliant; S. B. Fay, *The Rise of Brandenburg-Prussia*, and B. Pares, *Russia* (1953), are more detailed scholarly studies; O. Hoetzsch, *The Evolution of Russia* (1966), is a stimulating popular treatment, as is B. H. Sumner, *Peter the Great*. N. Mitford, *The Sun King* (1966), is a readable, reliable, and sumptuously illustrated account of Louis XIV and his court; J. B. Wolf, *Louis XIV of France* (1968) is also a first-rate biography.

THE SCIENTIFIC REVOLUTION OF THE SEVENTEENTH CENTURY

Among the many first-rate accounts, A. R. Hall, *The Scientific Revolution, 1500–1800*, T. S. Kuhn, *The Copernican Revolution*, and M. Boas, *The Scientific Renaissance*, are of high authority. H. Butterfield, *The Origins of Modern Science*, is popular in the best sense; and A. N. Whitehead, *Science and the Modern World*, is the noted work of a brilliant philosopher. L. Geymonat, *Galileo Galilei* (1963), and F. Manuel, *A Portrait of Isaac Newton* (1978), are stimulating biographies of these scientific giants.

THE IMPACT OF SCIENCE ON PHILOSOPHY: THE ENLIGHTENMENT

F. Copleston, *A History of Philosophy*, vol. 4, is valuable on Descartes; F. E. Manuel, *The Age of Reason*, and part 2 of J. Bronowski and B. Mazlish, *The Western Intellectual Tradition*, are stimulating introductions. Among the longer works, P. Gay, *The Party of Humanity*, and *The Enlightenment*, appears for the defense; while C. Becker, *The Heavenly City of the 18th Century Philosophers*, and P. Hazard, *The European Mind, 1680–1715* (1963), tend to be critical.

THE RATIONAL SPIRIT IN LITERATURE AND ART

P. Smith, *History of Modern Culture* (1962), bk. 2, is excellent for the whole field. B. Willey, *The Seventeenth Century Background* (1953), is valuable on intellectual currents and poetry; H. N. Brailsford, *Voltaire*, and P. Quennell, *Alexander Pope*, are attractive biographies of the two leading writers of the period.

THE CLASSICAL AGE OF MUSIC

A. Einstein, *A Short History of Music* (1987), provides the general background. A. Schweitzer, *J. S. Bach*, and Einstein, *Mozart: His Character, His Work*, are splendid biographies.

11   The Revolutions of Liberalism and Nationalism

THE ENGLISH REVOLUTION: PARLIAMENTARY SUPREMACY AND THE BILL OF RIGHTS

C. Hill, *The Century of Revolution, 1603–1714*, is a stimulating survey; G. M. Trevelyan, *English Revolution, 1688–89*, is an older work of high authority. A. Fraser, *Cromwell*, and M. Cranston, *Locke,* are reliable biographies of two leading figures of the century. For insightful social history, see P. Laslett, *The World We Have Lost*.

The American Revolution and Constitution

L. H. Gipson, *The Coming of the Revolution, 1763–1775* (1954), J. R. Alden, *The American Revolution, 1775–1783*, and E. S. Morgan, *The Birth of the Republic*, are excellent general accounts. On the Constitution, M. Farrand, *Framing of the Constitution of the U.S.*, is standard.

The French Revolution: "Liberty, Equality, and Fraternity"

C. B. A. Behrens, *The Ancien Régime*, is a good study of the background; G. Lefebvre, *The Coming of the French Revolution*, is an outstanding work by a noted French scholar; C. Brinton, *A Decade of Revolution: 1789–1799*, is a readable, scholarly survey. J. M. Roberts, *The French Revolution*, is a good recent work, as is J. F. Bosher, *The French Revolution* (1988). Brinton, *Anatomy of Revolution*, compares the English, French, and American upheavals. For the Napoleonic period, a sound popular account is J. C. Herold, *The Age of Napoleon* (1963); F. Markham, *Napoleon*, and H. Butterfield, *Napoleon* (1962), are excellent studies of the emperor. Brinton, *The Lives of Talleyrand* (1936), is a defensive view of the famous foreign minister.

The Conservative Reaction

H. Nicolson, *The Congress of Vienna*, is an attractive study; H. Kissinger, *A World Restored*, is a sympathetic account of Metternich and his supporters. On Burke, R. Kirk, *The Conservative Mind*, is a well-written, laudatory introduction. On Hegel, H. Marcuse, *Reason and Revolution: Hegel and the Rise of Social Theory*, is an esteemed analysis of a complex subject.

The Romantic Spirit in Literature, Art, and Music

M. Praz, *The Romantic Agony*, and C. M. Bowra, *The Romantic Imagination*, are works of a high order. For an introduction to the vast literature on Rousseau, E. Cassirer, *The Question of Jean-Jacques Rousseau* (1963), is superior. M. Brion, *The Art of the Romantic Era* (1966), is outstanding.

The Spread of Liberal Democracy and Nationalism

L. T. Hobhouse, *Liberalism*, is a short book of distinction. E. J. Hobsbawm offers a Marxist view of the period in *The Age of Revolution, Europe 1789 to 1848*. For nationalism, H. Kohn, *Nationalism: Its Meaning and History*, is a work by a well-known authority; equally valuable is B. C. Shafer, *Faces of Nationalism* (1972). G. Salvemini, *Mazzini* (1957), is a friendly biography of the romantic nationalist; E. Eyck, *Bismarck and the German Empire*, and O. Pflanze, *Bismarck and the Development of Germany*, are penetrating works. A. M. Schlesinger, Jr., *The Age of Jackson*, is a vigorous study of American democracy in this period.

12   The Impact of the Machine

The Industrial Revolution

P. M. Deane, *The First Industrial Revolution*, is a valuable brief study; S. Pollard, *European Economic Integration, 1815–1970*, gives a concise, illustrated account of the spread of industrialization. The classic analysis of the "machine" in Western history is L. Mumford, *Technics and Civilization*. H. J. Habakkuk, *American and British Technology in the 19th Century*, is the work of a highly regarded economist. J. Ellul, *The Technological Society*, presents an original and stimulating analysis by a French sociologist of technology in the West; D. Landes, *Unbound Prometheus*, covers the history of the Industrial Revolution in Europe from 1750 to the present. For a comprehensive study of the social results, see P. N. Stearns, *European Society in Upheaval*; for the formation of a new class, see E. P. Thompson, *The Making of the English Working Class*.

THE BUSINESS CORPORATION AND CAPITALIST EXPANSION

M. Dobb, *Capitalism, Yesterday and Today* (1962), is a short popular sketch; T. C. Cochran and W. Miller, *The Age of Enterprise* (1961), is a view by two historians; and J. K. Galbraith, *American Capitalism*, presents the observations of a perceptive and critical economist. A clear exposition of economic theories from the eighteenth century to the present is R. L. Heilbroner, *The Worldly Philosophers*.

THE REACTION OF LABOR AND GOVERNMENT

C. J. H. Hayes, *A Generation of Materialism, 1871–1900* (1941), puts the whole subject in historical framework; H. M. Pelling, *History of Trade Unionism* (1963), is a reliable account of labor's efforts to organize; E. H. Carr, *The New Society* (1961), is a brilliant and provocative story of the growth of planned economies and mass democracy in the twentieth century.

URBANIZATION AND STANDARDIZATION OF SOCIETY

L. Mumford, *The Culture of Cities*, is a masterly and colorful narration of the influence of the machine on modern urban life; valuable also is A. Briggs, *Victorian Cities*. C. M. Cipolla, *The Economic History of World Population*, tells the demographic consequences of industrialization; S. Giedion, *Mechanization Takes Command*, is a summary of the impact of the machine on industry, agriculture, and the home.

THE DEVELOPMENT OF SOCIALIST THOUGHT AND ACTION

In J. A. Schumpeter, *Capitalism, Socialism and Democracy*, a leading economist examines Europe and America. For an understanding of Marxist theory, see G. D. H. Cole, *The Meaning of Marxism* (1950). I. Berlin, *Karl Marx: His Life and Environment*, is a balanced biography; for the period following Marx's death, see L. Derfler, *Socialism since Marx: A Century of the European Left* (1973).

THE ACCELERATING PROGRESS OF SCIENCE

J. Bronowski, *The Common Sense of Science*, is an explanation of the essential nature of science by a distinguished scientist. For a readable account of the life of Louis Pasteur and his place in the development of medical science, see R. Dubos, *Pasteur and Modern Science* (2d ed., 1988). Einstein's theory of relativity and its influence on the development of physics are briefly and comprehensibly outlined in L. Barnett, *The Universe and Dr. Einstein* (1989).

THE CHALLENGE OF DARWIN'S THEORY OF EVOLUTION

A. D. White, *A History of the Warfare of Science with Theology* (1955), is a modern classic. J. S. Huxley, *Evolution: The Modern Synthesis* (1974), is by a distinguished biologist. L. C. Eisely, *Darwin's Century: Evolution and the Men Who Discovered It*, is by a distinguished anthropologist. R. Hofstadter, *Social Darwinism in American Thought*, is clear and provocative. For a full account of Freud's career and ideas, see E. Jones and others, *The Life and Work of Sigmund Freud*; C. S. Hall, *A Primer of Freudian Psychology*, is a short and reliable summary. An interpretation of his pervasive influence on contemporary culture can be found in P. Rieff, *Freud: The Mind of the Moralist*. The best account of Jungian thought is J. Jacobi, *The Psychology of C. G. Jung*.

LITERATURE AND ART IN THE MACHINE AGE

W. E. Mosse, *Liberal Europe: The Age of Bourgeois Realism*, is a balanced appraisal of European culture for the period 1848–1875; H. R. Hitchcock, *Architecture: 19th and 20th Centuries*, is brief but authoritative; R. Raynal, *The 19th Century* (1951), illustrates the beginnings of modern art.

13   Imperialism, World War, and the Rise of Collectivism

IMPERIALISM AND EUROPE'S WORLD DOMINION

J. A. Hobson, *Imperialism*, is old but still valuable; standard historical accounts are S. L. Easton, *The Rise and Fall of Western Colonialism* (1964), and C. E. Carrington, *The British Overseas* (1950). Recent treatments also are J. Gallagher and others, *Africa and the Victorians: The Climax of Imperialism*, and H. Gollwitzer, *Europe in the Age of Imperialism, 1880–1914*. For a lively and informative biography, read J. Jeal, *Livingstone* (1974).

THE FIRST WORLD WAR AND THE DECLINE OF EUROPE

For the background of the war, read A. J. P. Taylor, *The Struggle for Mastery in Europe, 1848–1918*. Of special interest are L. Lafore, *The Long Fuse*, a fascinating story of the diplomatic step-by-step to war, and F. Fischer, *Germany's Aims in the First World War*. For the early days of the fighting, read B. W. Tuchman, *The Guns of August*; for the horrors of trench warfare, read the classic novel, E. M. Remarque, *All Quiet on the Western Front*. B. H. Liddell Hart, *The Real War, 1914–1918*, and C. B. Falls, *The Great War* (1959), are by military experts.

COMMUNIST COLLECTIVISM: THE RUSSIAN REVOLUTION

M. T. Florinsky, *The End of the Russian Empire* (1973), sets the stage. E. Wilson, *To the Finland Station*, is a spirited survey of the revolutionary tradition from the French Revolution to Lenin's return to Russia in 1917. W. B. Lincoln, *Red Victory* (1990), is a full account of how the Communists triumphed; B. D. Wolfe, *Three Who Made a Revolution*, presents a fascinating study of Lenin, Trotsky, and Stalin; T. H. von Laue, *Why Lenin, Why Stalin?*, raises and answers some crucial questions. J. P. Nettl, *The Soviet Achievement* (1967), is a balanced and insightful interpretation; A. G. Meyer, *Communism*, is a treatment by a political scientist of communist theory and practice.

FASCIST COLLECTIVISM: THE REVOLUTIONS IN ITALY AND GERMANY

H. Arendt, *The Origins of Totalitarianism*, and S. W. Halperin, *Mussolini and Italian Fascism* (1964), deal with the ideological origins of the fascist movements. A more recent analysis for Italy is A. DeGrand, *Italian Fascism*. D. M. Smith, *Mussolini's Roman Empire* (1976), explains the expansionist thrust of the *Duce*; W. L. Shirer, *The Rise and Fall of the Third Reich*, is a lengthy but dramatic presentation on Nazi Germany. A. Bullock, *Hitler: A Study in Tyranny*, is a life of the *Fuehrer*.

DEMOCRATIC COLLECTIVISM: EVOLUTION OF THE WELFARE STATES

A. J. P. Taylor, *English History, 1919–1945*, and D. Thompson, *England in the 20th Century*, deal in part with the welfare state in England. J. K. Galbraith, *The Great Crash, 1929*, describes the economic collapse in America. W. Leuchtenburg, *Franklin D. Roosevelt and the New Deal, 1932–1940* (1963), and T. H. Greer, *What Roosevelt Thought* (1958), treat the nature of the Roosevelt revolution and its central ideas. M. Childs, *Sweden: the Middle Way* (1961), outlines the foundations of the welfare states of Scandinavia.

14   Global Transformation: Dawn of a New Age

THE SECOND WORLD WAR AND ITS CONSEQUENCES

G. Wright, *The Ordeal of Total War, 1939–1945*, and B. H. Liddell Hart, *History of the Second World War*, are excellent; for focus on the Russian front, see A. Werth, *Russia at War*. In C. Wilmot, *The Struggle for Europe* (1952), a critical Australian journalist views the strategy of the war. J. Hersey, *Hiroshima*, gives a moving account of the effects of the first atomic bomb on its victims; the victims of Nazi genocide are the subject of L. Dawidowicz, *The War Against the Jews, 1933–1945*. A compact yet wide-ranging report of the postwar recovery of Europe is given in M. Crouzet, *The European Renaissance since 1945* (1970). More comprehensive studies are W. Laqueur, *Europe since Hitler*, and G. Ambrosius and W. H. Hubbard, *A Social and Economic History of Twentieth-Century Europe*. H. Feis, *From Trust to Terror, 1945–1950* (1970), and D. Yergin, *The Shattered Peace* (1977), explain the coming of the Cold War between the superpowers.

THE SWEEP OF NATIONALISM AND MODERNIZATION

R. L. Heilbroner, *The Great Ascent: The Struggle for Economic Development in Our Time* (1963), is a good general treatment; more specific is R. Emerson, *From Empire to Nation: The Rise to Self-Assertion of Asian and African Peoples* (1960). For Latin America, see S. Clissold, *Latin America: New World, Third World* (1972). B. Ward, *The Rich Nations and the Poor Nations*, deals with four revolutionary ideas at work since the end of the Second World War. E. H. Carr, *The Soviet Impact on the Western World* (1946), is a short book of unusual interest; O. E. Clubb, *Twentieth Century China*, tells the story of change in the world's most populous country; and E. Reischauer, *The Japanese*, is an excellent study of a people on the rise. An incisive analysis of United States policy toward revolutionary struggles is R. J. Barnet, *Intervention and Revolution*; F. Fitzgerald, *Fire in the Lake: The Vietnamese and the Americans in Vietnam*, is a moving account by a gifted writer. For the revolution in Iran, see S. Akhavi, *Religion and Politics in Contemporary Iran*; useful also is R. K. Ramazani, ed., *Iran's Revolution*. For Iraq, see Samir Al-Khalil, *Republic of Fear* (1989). A valuable study of race and racism is M. Leiris, *Race and Culture* (1958); the viewpoint of an African-American militant is articulated in *The Autobiography of Malcolm X*.

ECONOMIC REASSESSMENT AND THE "THREE WORLDS"

G. Borgstrom's *The Hungry Planet* (1965) presents this expert's broad analysis of the world food and population crises; other sound and readable treatments are P. R. Ehrlich, *The Population Bomb*; P. R. and A. H. Ehrlich, *The End of Affluence*; and G. Myrdal, *The Challenge of World Poverty* (1970). The critical issue of birth control is viewed from several perspectives in G. J. Hardin, ed., *Population, Evolution, and Birth Control* (2d ed., 1969). A trailblazing study, based on computer projections, is D. H. Meadows and others, *The Limits to Growth*; M. and R. D. Friedman, *Free to Choose*, is a popular exposition of monetarism and laissez-faire economics. The ferment in portions of the Third World is set forth in R. Emerson and M. Kilson, eds. *The Political Awakening of Africa* (1965), and F. Fanon, *The Wretched of the Earth*. For the rising threat, see W. Laqueur, *The Age of Terrorism*, and Y. Alexander and others, eds. *Terrorism: Theory and Practice*.

END OF THE POSTWAR (COLD WAR) ERA

P. Steinfels, *The Neoconservatives* (1979) gives a clear explanation and evaluation of a powerful force in recent American thought and politics. For detailed assessments of Reagan's "revolution," see J. L. Palmer and J. V. Sawhill, *The Reagan Record*, and K. Phillips, *The Politics of*

Rich and Poor (1990). For the revolutions in eastern Europe, see Z. Brzezinski, *The Grand Failure* (1990); B. Nahaylo and V. Swoboda, *Soviet Disunion* (1990), treats the critical nationalities problem.

15   The Revolution in Western Culture

RECONSTRUCTION IN PHILOSOPHY AND RELIGION

R. N. Stromberg, *European Intellectual History since 1789*, and *After Everything: Western Intellectual History since 1945*, are excellent on the whole range; a useful summation of recent philosophical systems, worldwide, is A. Kaplan, *The New World of Philosophy*. E. Fromm, *Escape from Freedom*, is a highly regarded psychological explanation of twentieth-century mass movements. W. Barrett, *Irrational Man*, gives a clear analysis of existentialism; P. Roubiczek, *Existentialism: For and Against*, presents two opposing viewpoints. J. Robinson, *Honest to God*, explains the religious uncertainties of an Anglican bishop. The widespread revival of religious spirit is discussed in C. Y. Glock and R. N. Bellah, eds., *The New Religious Consciousness*.

THE SHIFTING WAYS OF SOCIETY

Aspects of the new sexuality are examined in D. L. Bender and G. E. McCuen, *The Sexual Revolution: Traditional Mores versus New Values*. For the youth culture, T. Roszak, *The Making of a Counter Culture* (1969), is helpful; J. A. Califano, Jr., *The Student Revolution*, is a concise worldwide review of the campus agitations of the 1960s. C. Lasch, *The Culture of Narcissism*, is a provocative statement on contemporary attitudes and values; currents of dissent in Europe are effectively analyzed in H. S. Hughes, *Sophisticated Rebels* (1988). For the women's movement, J. O'Faolain and L. Martines, eds., *Not in God's Image*, is a valuable presentation of documents on the historical status of women, as background for the contemporary protest and reform; S. de Beauvoir, *The Second Sex*, is the classic modern study. D. G. Wolf, *The Lesbian Community*, brings a scientific explanation of female homosexuality and other sexual variations. The concept of nonviolence is explained in depth in E. H. Erikson, *Gandhi's Truth*; D. Dellinger, *Revolutionary Nonviolence* (1970), is a Left interpretation.

FRESH DIRECTIONS IN LITERATURE AND THE ARTS

On literature, E. Wilson, *Axel's Castle*, is a respected study of imaginative writing, 1870–1930. For the period since 1930, see L. Trilling, *The Liberal Imagination: Essays on Literature and Society* (1979), and I. Howe, *Celebrations and Attacks: Thirty Years of Literary and Cultural Commentary*. On art and architecture, G. Battcock, ed., *The New Art* (1966), is an attractive anthology by professional art critics; E. Kaufman and B. Raeburn, eds., *Frank Lloyd Wright: Writings and Buildings*, and W. Gropius, *New Architecture and the Bauhaus*, are also helpful. For music, S. Bechet, *Treat It Gentle*, illuminates the spirit of jazz; R. J. Gleason, *Celebrating the Duke et al.* (1976), offers readable sketches of the leading jazz heroes. I. Whitcomb, *Rock Odyssey*, is by a musician of the sixties.

THE END OF THE BEGINNING: A NEW AGE OF HUMANITY

K. E. Boulding, *The Meaning of the Twentieth Century*, deals with the transition to a new order growing out of science and technology. R. L. Heilbroner, *An Inquiry into the Human Prospect*, presents a somber view; D. Bell, *Coming of Post-Industrial Society*, is another well-grounded effort of social forecasting. A. Toffler, *Future Shock*, considers the psychological impact of rapid social changes. H. Brown, *The Human Future Revisited* (1978), revises the earlier studies of this insightful scientist on world population, resources, and technology; G. Myrdal, *Beyond the Welfare State* (1960), sets forth the new imperative of transnational planning. R. Barnet, *Roots of War*, explains the dynamics of today's warmaking process. H. York, *Race to Oblivion* (1970), and H. Caldicott, *Missile Envy: the Arms Race and Nuclear War* (1984), warn of the menace of mass-destruction weapons; R. L. Garwin, K. Gottfried, and H. W. Kendall, *The Fallacy of Star Wars* (1984), discusses the controversial plan for defense against ballistic missiles. J. Schell, *The Fate of the Earth*, examines the probable consequences for our planet should nuclear war take place.

Picture Credits

Chapter 1   Page xii © Oscar Savio, Rome   **10** Archives Photographiques, Paris, © SPADEM, Paris   **13** Kestner Museum, Hanover, Germany   **22** Adapted from a drawing at the British Museum   **23** Courtesy of The Oriental Institute of the University of Chicago   **25** Hirmer Fotoarchiv, Munich   **31** © Jack Grover/Rapho, Photo Researchers   **33** © George Holton/Photo Researchers   **34** Trans World Airlines   **36** *Pair Statue of Menkaure and His Queen*, Dynasty IV, 2599–2571 B.C., slate schist. H: 54½ in. Harvard-Boston Expedition. Courtesy, Museum of Fine Arts, Boston   **37** The Metropolitan Museum of Art, Rogers Fund, 1930   **40, 41** Reproduced by courtesy of the Trustees of the British Museum   **46** British Information Service   **Chapter 2   53** © Alison Frantz   **77** © Frederick Ayer, III/Photo Researchers   **80** Alinari/Art Resource   **81** © George Holton/Photo Researchers   **83** (top) Marburg/Art Resource   **83** (bottom) Reproduced by courtesy of the Trustees of the British Museum   **84** (top) Alinari/Art Resource   **84** (bottom) Hirmer Fotoarchiv, Munich   **85, 86** Alinari/Art Resource   **Chapter 3   121** French Government Tourist Office   **124** Hirmer Fotoarchiv, Munich   **125** (top) Alinari/Art Resource   **125** (bottom) National Gallery of Art, Washington, D.C., Samuel H. Kress Collection   **127** Courtesy of the Prints Division, Astor, Lenox, and Tilden Foundations, New York Public Library   **128** © Leonard von Matt/Rapho-Photo Researchers   **129** Alinari/Art Resource   **Chapter 4   169** The Italian State Tourist Office   **Chapter 5   172** © A. F. Kersting   **186** Hirmer Fotoarchiv, Munich   **197** Kaufman-Fabray Photo, Chicago   **205** Dr. Harald Busch   **220** From *An Introduction to English Industrial History* by Henry Allsopp (G. Bell & Sons, Ltd.)   **227** Archives Photographiques, Paris, © SPADEM, Paris   **Chapter 6   233** Alinari/Art Resource   **244, 245** Marburg/Art Resource   **249** Clarence Ward   **250** Archives Photographiques, Paris, © SPADEM, Paris   **251** Aerofilms, Ltd., London   **252** (top) Archives Photographiques, Paris, © SPADEM, Paris   **252** (bottom) Clarence Ward   **253** Fitzwilliam Museum, Cambridge   **Chapter 7   274** Courtesy of the Trustees of the National Gallery, London   **Chapter 8   330** Alinari/Art Resource   **331** © George Holton/Photo Researchers   **332, 333** Alinari/Art Resource   **334** Courtesy of the Trustees of the National Gallery, London   **335, 336** Alinari/Art Resource   **337** Brogi/Art Resource   **338, 339, 340, 341, 343, 344, 345** Alinari/Art Resource   **351** From Watkins, "On Producing Shakespeare," by courtesy of Michael Joseph, Ltd. Drawing by Maurice Percival   **Chapter 9   383** Peter Brueghel the Elder, *The Wedding Dance*, c. 1566, oil on canvas, 47″ × 62″, 30.374. The Detroit Institute of Arts, City of Detroit Purchase   **384** Alte Pinakothek, Munich   **385** © Greater London Council, The Iveigh Bequest, English Heritage, London   **386** Giraudon/Art Resource   **387, 388** Alinari/Art Resource   **389** © 1962 by Charles Rotkin, from *Europe: An Aerial Closeup* (Lippincott)   **390** French Government Tourist Office   **Chapter 10   392** UNESCO/Brent Hannon   **431** A. F. Kersting, London   **432** Courtesy of the General Research and Humanities Division, New York Public Library   **433** © Caisse Nationale des Monuments Historiques, Paris   **433** Virginia Chamber of Commerce, Photo by Phil Flournoy   **434** Art Resource/Wallace Collection, London   **435** © Frick Collection, New York   **436** The Trustees of the Lady Lever Art Gallery, Port Sunlight, Cheshire, England   **Chapter 11   481** Giraudon/Art Resource   **482** Museo del Prado, Madrid   **483** Giraudon/Art Resource   **484, 485** Courtesy of the Trustees of the National Gallery, London   **487** © 1962 by Charles Rotkin, from

INDEX

A page number in *italics* indicates an *illustration*. No separate number is given for related text on the same page.

Years shown in parentheses ( ) following the name of a *ruler* are the years of *reign*. For other individuals, years shown are for *birth* and *death*.

Index entries marked by an asterisk (*) are *important historical terms*. The meaning of each term is explained on the pages of text shown for that entry.